abstracts

Donald W. MacArdle

Information Coordinators, Inc.   Detroit   1973

Copyright 1973 by Mrs. Ruth MacArdle Bechtel
Library of Congress Catalog Card Number 72-96874
ISBN 911772-55-3
Price $20.00

Published by Information Coordinators, Inc.
1435-37 Randolph Street, Detroit, Michigan 48226

Printed and bound in the United States of America

Designed by Vincent Kibildis

Covers, title and part title pages:
Detail of August Borckmann's
Beethoven as Conductor of the Rasumowsky Quartet
Österreichische Nationalbibliothek, Vienna

Table of Contents

Introduction

Donald Wales MacArdle
3 July 1897 - 23 December 1964

One of the most widely experienced specialists in biographic and bibliographic
research on Ludwig van Beethoven, Donald MacArdle first corresponded with us in July
1961 shortly after the announcement of our new series Detroit Studies in Music Bibliography.
He proposed for this series his *Index to Beethoven's Conversation Books* based on
Schünemann's transcription of thirty-seven of the books; this *Index* became the third in the
DSMB series and was published in 1962.

A delightful correspondent, Mr. MacArdle sent us the following autobiographical comments
when we first started to work on his *Index:*

> "As for my life history, I graduated from M.I.T. in Chemistry, then from the
> M.I.T. Evening Division in Mechanical Engineering, then took a Master's degree
> in Chemical Engineering, and now don't know or care whether water is H_2O or
> HO_2. Under the GI Bill in the early 1950's I did doctoral work in Musicology
> at NYU under my good friend Martin Bernstein, dear old Dr. Sachs, and
> admired-at-a-distance Gus Reese. All this fitted me perfectly for my present
> work on paper-shuffling at the Martin-Marietta Corporation plant for the Titan
> missile. How far afield can one get?"

His letter of July 1962, written just after the work on *An Index to Beethoven's Conversation
Books* had been completed and placed in the hands of the printer, contains his first reference
to *Beethoven Abstracts:*

> "Have I mentioned my *Beethoven Abstracts* project to you? This, very simply, is an
> attempt (foredoomed to failure) to read everything that has ever been published
> anywhere about LvB and to summarize it, perhaps in a single word ("Popular,"
> "Unimportant") and in any event in not more than a few hundred words.
>
> "This has been on the stove since the mid-1940's, and to date I have some
> five thousand abstracts from about six hundred journals, newspapers, and books.
> I have placed copies of my typescript in NYPL, L of C, and BM, with the
> thought that anything that furthers Beethoven research helps me.
>
> "This mass of material, as might be expected, contains much in the field of
> the chamber music, and my suggestion to you is that you consider a brochure:
> *The Periodical Literature of Beethoven's Chamber Music.*"

His suggestion was accepted but the monograph was never published. On December 12, 1964,
in his last letter to us, he wrote:

> "My plan was to head for the East Coast about the first of October to do several
> things, including getting my Abstracts up to date. Instead, on 26 September I
> was once again carted off to Fitzsimons General Hospital with another heart
> attack. For ten days or so (they tell me) it was touch and go; I am now back
> home, gaining strength rapidly, and already beginning to struggle with LvB again.
>
> "As soon as we can sell our house here (which will be some time between
> this afternoon and 1969) we plan to move to the Annapolis area so that I can
> avail myself of the major libraries between Washington and Boston. When I do

get to the East, job No. 1 will be to get the chamber-music material in shape for you. I hope it may be soon, but there is no telling. Until our plans jell, I can't recommend that you pick my monograph up in your production schedule."

The work and ensuing correspondence involved in editing and finally publishing *An Index to Beethoven's Conversation Books* were the bases for his expressed desire that we edit and publish his *Beethoven Abstracts*. In January 1964 he commented on its growth each year and prophetically said that it was "one of those projects that will never be completed, just stopped."

Donald MacArdle's widow, Ruth, sent us the manuscript when it was located in September 1965. Her reaction to our announcement that we would publish the *Abstracts* was that "his positive and definite desire to make it available to Beethoven enthusiasts was a driving force and ... will make a fitting memorial to a remarkable man."

For their painstaking work in reorganizing, editing, indexing, proofreading, and preparing the camera copy of this manuscript we wish to express our appreciation to Mary Dorn, Joy Hick, Richard LeSueur, and Sonja Pogodda.

Florence Kretzschmar, Publisher

April 9, 1973

Foreword

The basic format of Mr. MacArdle's manuscript consisted of many central
sections to which miscellanea were appended since the work evolved over decades and
was continually amended as new research came to light. For the convenience of the
user, the material has been consolidated into four sections: primary, secondary
periodicals, newspapers, and catalogs, with general, author, and composition indexes
making the data more accessible. A substantial part of the manuscript which contained
lengthy quoted excerpts from books is given only in abbreviated bibliographic form,
and not indexed since the inclusion of this material would have required the time-
consuming task of requesting copyright permission from the many respective publishers.

In preparing the manuscript for publication, most of the abstracts from over four
hundred periodicals were left intact and their style unaltered. However, minimal
textual editing was done where necessary: periodical title changes and place of
publication were noted if the information was locally available and marginal notes
were inserted if decipherable. Some orthography might appear to be inconsistent but
in most cases, the spelling used in the article has been retained and names should be
traceable through the *Index*. Strikeovers were a consistent puzzlement as sometimes
AmZ and AMZ appeared to be the same while Himmel and Hummel were likewise
indistinguishable. As the burden of numerous similar decisions rested with us, it is
hoped the some unavoidable editorial indiscretions will be tolerated.

Sonja Pogodda, Editor

List of Abbreviations

Alm. d. d. Musikbücherei
Almanach der deutschen Musikbücherei

AMZ
Allgemeine (deutsche) Musik-Zeitung
(Leipzig and Berlin)

AmZ
Allgemeine Musikalische Zeitung (Leipzig)

BForsch
Beethoven Forschung (Vienna)

BJ
Theodor von Frimmel, editor. *Beethoven-jahrbuch,* 2 vols., (Munich and Leipzig, 1908-09); also journal edited by Joseph Schmidt-Görg (Bonn, 1954)

B&H
Breitkopf und Härtel (music publisher, Leipzig)

BusV
Max Unger. *Beethoven und seine Verleger S.A. Steiner und Tobias Haslinger in Wien, Ad. Mart. Schlesinger in Berlin.* (Berlin and Vienna, Schlesingersche Buch und Musikhandlung, 1921)

BusZ
Alfred Chr. Kalischer. *Ludwig van Beethoven und seine Zeitgenossen,* 4 vols. (Berlin and Leipzig, 1909-10)

DM
Die Musik (Berlin and Leipzig, 1901-15); Stuttgart, 1922-43)

EDr
Erstdruck

GA
Beethovens Werke; kritische Gesamtausgabe, 25 vols. (Leipzig, Breitkopf und Härtel, 1866-68, 1888) References are to volume, composition number

GdMf
Gesellschaft der Musikfreunde (Society of the Friends of Music)

H
Willy Hess. *Welche Werke Beethovens fehlen in der Breitkopf und Härtelschen Gesamtausgabe,* NBJ 7 [1937] 104. See also Hess' *Le opere di Beethoven ela loro edizone completa* (Rome, Romano Mezzetti, 1953)

I. M. G. Sammelb.
Internationale Musikgesellschaft. Sammelbände (Leipzig)

JG
Jahrgang

LIST OF ABBREVIATIONS

KA
See KBr

Kal
See KBr

KBr
Alfred Chr. Kalischer, editor. *Beethovens sämtliche Briefe,* 5 vols. (Berlin and Leipzig, 1906-08)

KFr
Alfred Chr. Kalischer. *Beethovens sämtliche Briefe.* Neubearbeitet von Dr. Th. v Frimmel (only vols. II and III published). (Berlin and Leipzig, Schuster und Loeffler, 1910-11)

KHV
Georg Kinsky and Hans Halm. *Das Werk Beethovens; thematisch-bibliographisches Verzeichnis seiner sämtlichen vollendeten Kompositionen.* (Munich, G. Henle, 1955)

KK
Emerich Kastner and Julius Kapp, editors. *Beethovens sämtliche Briefe.* New edition, revised and enlarged by Dr. Julius Kapp. (Leipzig, Hesse und Becker, 1923)

k.k.
kaiserlich und königlich

Köchel
Ludwig Ritten von Köchel. *Drei und achtzig neue aufgefundene original Briefe Ludwig van Beethovens an den Erzherzog Rudolph.* (Vienna, Beck'sche Universitäts Buchhandlung, 1865)

KS
Alfred Chr. Kalischer, editor. *Beethovens Letters,* 2 vols. Translated by J. S. Shedlock (London and New York, 1909)

M&L
Music and Letters (London)

Mf
Die Musikforschung (Kassel and Basel)

MfMg
Monatshefte für Musikgeschichte (Berlin and Leipzig)

MM
Donald W. MacArdle and Ludwig Misch. *New Beethoven Letters.* (Norman, Oklahoma University Press, 1956)

MQ
Musical Quarterly (New York)

NB
Gustav Nottebohm. *Beethoveniana.* (Leipzig and Winterthur, Rieter-Biedermann, 1872) cited as (NB I); and *Zweite Beethoveniana.* (Leipzig, Peters, 1887) cited as (NB II)

NBJ
Adolf Sandberger, editor. *Neues Beethoven-Jahrbuch.* (Augsburg and Braunschweig, 1924-42)

NF
Neue Folge
New series

LIST OF ABBREVIATIONS

TDR, TD
Alexander Wheelock Thayer. *Ludwig van Beethovens Leben,* 5 vols. 3rd ed., revised by Hermann Deiters and enlarged by Hugo Riemann. (Leipzig, Breitkopf und Härtel, 1917-23); vols. I-III (Berlin, 1866, 1872, and 1879); vols. IV and V completed by Riemann (Berlin, 1907-08)

TK
Alexander Wheelock Thayer. *Life of Ludwig van Beethoven,* 3 vols. Revised and enlarged from original English MS and German edition by H. E. Krehbiel. (New York, Beethoven Association, 1921)

NV
Gustav Nottebohm. *Ludwig van Beethoven: Thematisches Verzeichnis.* (Leipzig, 1868); new edition, (Leipzig, Breitkopf und Härtel, 1925)

NZfM
Neue Zeitschrift für Musik (Leipzig, 1834-1920; Mainz, 1951)

TV
Alexander Wheelock Thayer. *Chronologisches Verzeichnis der Werke Ludwig van Beethovens* (Berlin, Schneider, 1865)

Prel
Fritz Prelinger. *Ludwig van Beethovens sämtliche Briefe und Aufzeichnungen,* 5 vols. (Vienna and Leipzig, Stern, 1907-11)

VjfMw
Vierteljahrschrift fürMusikwissenschaft (Leipzig)

SchKH
Georg Schünemann. *Ludwig van Beethovens Konversationshefte,* 3 vols. (Berlin, 1941-43)

WoO
Werk ohne Opuszahl

WTC
Wohltempierte Clavier

Schw MZ
Schweizerische Musik-Zeitung und Sängerblatt (Zurich)

ZfMw
Zeitschrift für Musikwissenschaft (Leipzig)

SIM
S.I.M.; Revue Musicale (Paris)

ZIMG
Zeitschrift der Internationalen Musikgesellschaft (Leipzig)

Primary Periodicals

CHRISTIAN GOTTLOB NEEFES LEBENSLAUF VON IHM SELBST BESCHRIEBEN.   C. G. N e e f e .   (A)
   Neither the first three sections, written by Neefe himself in September 1782, nor the last section, prepared by his
   widow after his death in January 1798, mentions even the name of his most famous pupil.
                                                    1 [1799] 241,257,273,360

DIE BERÜHMTESTEN KLAVIERSPIELERINNEN UND KLAVIERSPIELER WIENS.   (B)
   The pianists mentioned are Mme. Auernhammer, Frl. von Kurzbeck, Beethoven, Wölfl and Hummel. The portion
   of this note referring to Beethoven is quoted in full in TK I 215.   1 [1799] 523

MUSIC IN THE RHINELAND IN 1799.   (C)
   "The war has beaten to the ground the little that had timidly blossomed: except for Neefe, now dead, and the worthy
   pianist Beethoven, who in his thirteenth year had already published sonatas of his own, Bonn is <u>nothing</u>."
                                                    1 [1799] 880

CANON EIN ANDERS IST'S, WHICH TV-80 ERRONEOUSLY ATTRIBUTES TO BEETHOVEN.   (D)
                                                    2 [1800] 251

ANEKDOTE. D. H a g e r .   (E)
   The anecdote of the young Beethoven and the spider, given somewhat more fully (though obviously copied from this
   source) in J. A. Schlösser's 'LvB's Biographie' [1828] 7, and referred to in TK I 59. The spider story was cited as
   having been taken from 'Araneologie' by Quatremere Disjonval.   2 [1800] 653

BEETHOVEN'S AKADEMIE OF APRIL 2nd 1800.   (F)
   Article summarized in TK I 267.   3 [1800] 49

ANNOUNCEMENT OF THE PUBLICATION OF OPUS 18.   (G)
   (August 26th 1801). "Among recent publications are some exquisite works of Beethoven (Mollo). Three quartets
   bear generous witness to his artistry, but they must be played often and extremely well, since they are very difficult
   and far from popular."   3 [1801] 800

NOTICE REGARDING THE ARRANGEMENT OF THE SEPTET OPUS 20 AS A QUINTET.   L u d w i g   v a n   B e e t h o v e n .   (H)
   Notice as given in KS I 64.   5 [1802] Intelligenzblatt p.15

VESTAS FEUER.   (I)
   "Beethoven and Abt Vogler are each composing an opera for the Theater an der Wien."
                                                    5 [March 30th 1803] 458

FIRST PERFORMANCE OF 'CHRISTUS AM OELBERGE' APRIL 5th 1803.   (J)
   "This work bears out my long-held belief that in time Beethoven will work as great a revolution in music as Mozart.
   He is making mighty advances towards this goal."   5 [1803] 489

ADVANCE IN PRICES FOR 'CHRISTUS.'   (K)
   See TK II 5.   5 [1803] 590

FIRST PERFORMANCE OF 'CHRISTUS.'   (L)
   "In the interests of truth I must contradict a statement in the musical press. Beethoven's Cantata was <u>not</u> a success."
                                                    5 [1803] 734

ENGRAVING OF BEETHOVEN BY SCHÖFFNER.   (M)
                                                    6 [1804] facing p.331

[The "warning" against Zulehner's announced "Collected Edition" given in TK II 18]   (A)
6 [1804] Intelligenz-Blatt #3

[Prepublication announcement of Opus 36]   6 [1804] 542   (B)

[Review of the concert of July 1804]   (C)
Included the Second Symphony and the C minor Concerto Op. 37 played by Ries.
6 [1804] 776

[Review of first performance of Opus 21]   7 [1804] 157   (D)

[Review of first performance of Opus 15]   7 [1804] 197   (E)

[Review of the first performance of Opus 55]   (F)
"Your critic has the greatest respect for Herr v. Beethoven, but in this work he must confess that he finds an excess of whimsicalities and novelties, whereby grasp of the work as a whole is made most difficult and unity almost entirely lost."   7 [1805] 321,501;   9 [1807] 497

[Review of the first performance of 'Fidelio']   8 [1806] 237   (G)

FIRST REVISION OF 'FIDELIO.'   (H)
"Beethoven has brought his opera 'Fidelio' back to the stage with many changes and deletions. An entire act was cut out, but the opera is better for it and is now more favorably received."
8 [1806] 460

[Review of the concert at which Symphonies 5 and 6 (here listed as 6 and 5) received   (I)
their first performance]   11 [1809] 267

[Notice]   (J)
Annuity arrangement made by Archduke Rudolph, Prince Lobkowitz and Prince Kinsky to keep Beethoven in Vienna.
11 [1809] 395

[C minor Symphony again called No. 6 and the Pastoral No. 5]   (K)
11 [1809] 433

OFFER FROM CASSEL WAS CONVEYED TO BEETHOVEN BY GRAF TRUCHSESS-WALDBURG, NOT BY REICHARDT.   (L)
11 [1809] 492

[Song 'Als die Geliebte sich trennen wollte' given in full]   (M)
12 [1809] Beilage 2, facing col. 128

[Announcement of forthcoming works]   (N)
"A considerable number of important new works by this master, of various kinds and forms, will appear from the publisher of this journal. These will include the vocal score and the orchestral score of the Overture to Fidelio, Egmont music, Choral Fantasy, a fantasy and various sonatas and variations for pianoforte, a string quartet, various Italian songs, and a collection of original songs of which one is given." Op. 75 No. 4 is given.
12 [1810] 854

[Opus 75 No. 4 ('Gretels Warnung') given in full] 12 [1810] 854   (O)

[Notice of Beethoven's concert in Carlsbad with Polledro]   (P)
14 [1812] 596

[Review of the 'Greater Prometheus' Ballet (performed May 22nd 1813) with music by Beethoven, Haydn, Weigel and Vigano himself]   15 [1813] 435   (A)

[Plea for Beethoven works based on Shakespeare]   15 [1813] 806   (B)

BEETHOVENS MUSIK ZU GOETHES EGMONT.   (C)
    Poems inspired by the Overture and the incidental instrumental music.
                16 [1814] 205

GEDANKEN ÜBER DIE NEUERE TONKUNST, UND VAN BEETHOVENS MUSIK, NAMENTLICH DESSEN FIDELIO.   (D)
    Am. Wendt.
    A not particularly enthusiastic analysis of Beethoven's style.   17 [1815] 345,365,381,391,413,429

AN SIE. K. B. Gumlich.   (E)
    Rhapsodic tributes to Beethoven and to music which Unger (Beethoven und seiner Verleger 100) considered as possibly referred to in a letter of the fall of 1816 (Unger's No. 16) to Steiner.
                17 [1815] 694

PROJECTED OPERA 'ROMULUS.'   (F)
    "We understand that our inspired Beethoven will work on a new opera 'Romulus,' with text by Treitschke."
                17 [1815] 854

HUNGARIAN WINE-MAKING SONG.   Johann Fusz.   (G)
    The melody and the title of this song as it appears in this publication are also used as No. 3 of 24 unpublished National Airs brought to light by Lütge in 'Der Bär' [1927] 164. The name of the contributor of this Beilage is given by Papp 'Beethoven es a magyarok' [1927] 144 as a discovery of Ervin Major.
                18 [1816] Beilage II No. 2

BEETHOVEN AS AN HONORARY CITIZEN OF VIENNA.   (H)
    Vienna note: "Mr. Louis van Beethoven has received a diploma of citizenship from the presiding magistrate in recognition of the many times that he has made his compositions available for charitable purposes." (See Kastner 'Briefe' No. 547a)   18 [1816] 121

DEPARTURE OF SCHUPPANZIGH AND LINKE FROM VIENNA.   (I)
    Schuppanzigh's final concert, like Linke's, was in February 1816, probably earlier than Linke's.
                18 [1816] 197

[Engraving of Beethoven by Riedel, from the crayon portrait by Louis Letronne (1815)]   (J)
                19 [1817] Title page

DIE TEMPOS SÄMTLICHER SÄTZE ALLER SYMPHONIEN DES HRS. L. v. BEETHOVEN, VOM VERF. SELBST NACH MAELZELS METRONOM BESTIMMT.   L. v. Beethoven.   (K)
    Metronome marks for the principal sections of each movement of the Symphonies 1 - 8 incl.
                19 [1817] 873

BEETHOVENS ZWISCHENAKTE ZU GOETHES "EGMONT" MIT DEKLAMATORISCHER BEGLEITUNG.   (L)
    Friedrich Mosengeil.
    Poetic passages summarizing the drama which may be used with a performance of the music as a substitute for stage presentation or a complete reading of Goethe's drama. (See also NF 1 [1863] 451)
                23 [1821] Beilage III, facing col. 392

["B occupies himself, as Father Haydn once did, in the arranging of Scottish songs; for larger undertakings he seems to be completely written out"]   (M)
                23 [1821] 539

[Haslinger's manuscript collection of Beethoven's works]   (N)
                24 [1822] 65; 25 [1823] 129

[Comment on Beethoven's moods]   (O)
    "Our Beethoven has once more renewed his interest in music, from which, as a result of his deafness, he had fled almost as a misogynist. Once again he improvises as he used to for a circle of friends, to the joy of all, and shows that he can still handle his instrument with power, spirit and tenderness."   24 [May 8th 1822] 310

[Review of the concert of May 7th 1824]   (A)
    First performance of the Ninth Symphony and of three parts of the Missa Solemnis were given.
                       26 [1824] 437

[Quotation from "Geschichte der Musik" by Bawr, translated by Lewald]   (B)
    Refers to "Ludwig van Beethoven, born in Bonn in 1772."   27 [1825] 812

BEETHOVEN'S OBITUARY.   Rochlitz.   29 [1827] 227   (C)

BEETHOVEN'S FUNERAL.   29 [1827] 289   (D)

ETWAS ÜBER LUDWIG VAN BEETHOVEN.   W. C. Müller.   29 [1827] 345   (E)

MEMORIAL POEM.   J. G. Seidl.   29 [1827] 365   (F)

DEN FREUNDEN BEETHOVENS.   (G)
    The Heiligenstadt will.   29 [1827] 705

[The public sale of Beethoven's belongings on November 5th 1827]   (H)
                      30 [1828] 27

URTEIL ÜBER BEETHOVEN AUS DER REVUE MUSICALE, VERBUNDEN MIT ANDERN ANSICHTEN.   G. W. Fink.   (I)
    Polemic against article by Fetis.   30 [1828] 165,181

EINIGE WORTE ZU DEN VIELEN ÜBER BEETHOVENS LETZTE WERKE.   (J)
    His striving for originality at any price and the loss of touch with the charm of musical sounds which resulted from
    his deafness explain the fact that Beethoven's last compositions are "eccentric, melancholy, overlong and turgid
    results of an overwrought imagination."   31 [1829] 269

BEETHOVEN.   G. W. Fink.   (K)
    Poem.   31 [1829] 383

SONDERBARLICHER, DOCH AUGENSCHEINLICH BEWEISS DASS EINERLEI TÄNZE VON ZWEIERLEI VERSCHIEDENEN   (L)
    TONSETZERN GLEICHMÄSSING KOMPONIERT ODER GEDRUCKT WERDEN KÖNNEN.
    The "Sehnsuchtwaltz" by Beethoven (listed by NV p. 190 as a work "attributed to Beethoven") bears too close a resem-
    blance for coincidence to the "Trauerwaltz" of Schubert (Op. 9).   31 [1829] 438

ÜBER LUDWIG VAN BEETHOVENS GEBURTSJAHR.   (M)
    The frequent statements that Beethoven was born in 1772 are unfounded.   Search of the registers of St. Remegius
    parish show the baptism of Ludwig van Beethoven on December 17th 1770; no parish in Bonn records the birth of a
    van Beethoven during the years 1771-74.   The birth of Ludwig's elder brother Ludwig Maria on April 2nd 1769 and
    his death six days later are also shown.   36 [1834] 587

THE UNRELIABILITY OF BEETHOVEN ANECDOTES.   A. Schindler.   (N)
    No less a person than Schindler cautions all and sundry against accepting anecdotes referring to Beethoven or sayings
    attributed to him without independent proof of their authenticity.   37 [1835] 13

DAS ÄHNLICHSTE BILDNIS BEETHOVENS.   (O)
    Of eight engravings and lithographs considered, the best likeness is a lithograph by Kriehuber.
                      37 [1835] 17

ÜBER BEETHOVENS ÄHNLICHSTES BILDNIS.   A. Schindler.   (P)
    Contrary to the statement of the author on p. 17 supra, the lithograph by Kriehuber, made five or six years after
    Beethoven's death, is far from being the "best likeness."   "Of all the portraits of himself which he had seen,
    Beethoven quite rightly considered as the best likeness that by Stieler of Munich.   (In it, Beethoven is standing,
    holding a piece of paper bearing the words 'Missa Solemnis.')"   "The most unrepresentative portrait of Beethoven,
    without any question, is that which Waldmüller painted for Herr Härtel."   (See also 'Der Bär' [1927] 35)
                      37 [1835] 117

BEETHOVENS ERSTES GEDRUCKTES WERK.   (Q)
    The three early pianoforte sonatas (pub. 1783) are thus incorrectly described.
                      38 [1836] 148

ÜBER EINE MERKWÜRDIGE TATSACHE BEETHOVENS IN DEN TAGEN SEINER LETZTEN KRANKHEIT. G. W. Fink.   (A)
  The claim of destitution which Beethoven made in his letters of 1827 regarding a benefit concert or other aid from the
  Philharmonic Society of London (KS II 463-64, 470,472) are so far removed from the facts that the letters must be
  looked upon as a result of a failure of mind and spirit brought about by the fatal illness. (See also cols. 435,436)
                                                                39 [1837] 349

A BEETHOVEN LETTER.   (B)
  A very incomplete paraphrase of the letter of February or March 1823 to Peters (probably KS II 236).
                                                                39 [1837] 393

ÜBER LUDWIG VAN BEETHOVENS JAHRESGEHALT, SEINE LAGE UND BITTE IN SEINER LETZTEN KRANKHEIT.   (C)
     A. Schindler.
  Various letters written during Beethoven's last five years show that the letters referred to in col. 349 do not exaggerate
  the difficulties of his finances.   39 [1837] 435

ANTWORT AUF VORSTEHENDES SCHREIBER. G. W. Fink.   (D)
  A collection of Beethoven letters, as complete as possible, is essential for the preparation of any adequate and authentic Beethoven biography. The assistance of Schindler in this project is solicited. All evidence, including that in the
  letter from Schindler here answered, indicates that Beethoven's need was nowhere nearly as desperate as his failing
  faculties believed.   39 [1837] 436

ANFRAGE, BEETHOVEN BETREFFEND. K. B. v. Miltitz.   (E)
  The story (in Seyfried's 'Beethovens Studien': Biographische Skizze p. 4) of Beethoven's improvisation of a double
  fugue when playing for Mozart at the age of 18 is evidence of the falsity of the often repeated statement that
  Beethoven's contrapuntal knowledge was extremely sketchy before his studies with Albrechtsberger.
                                                                40 [1838] 300

HASLINGER'S MANUSCRIPT 'COLLECTED EDITION. '   (F)
  The 62 volumes of this collection, "reviewed and corrected by Beethoven himself" (??), have been presented to the
  Cardinal Archduke Rudolph.   42 [1840] 142

BRIEF SUMMARY OF THE HISTORY OF FIDELIO. G. W. Fink.   42 [1840] 943   (G)

CHARAKTERISTIK DER BEETHOVEN'SCHEN SONATEN UND SYMPHONIEN. C. T. Seiffert.   (H)
  The sonatas (including the violin sonatas) are brought together in three groups, and the symphonies in three groups,
  each from general considerations of style and content. Each group is discussed from a nontechnical and noncritical
  standpoint.   45 [1843] 417,433,449,465

BERICHTIGUNGEN BEETHOVENS FÜNFTE UND SECHSTE SYMPHONIEN BETREFFEND. Breitkopf & Härtel.   (I)
  The facsimile of a part of Beethoven's letter of August 21st 1810 which appears in KS I 203 is given here, as well as
  the discussion quoted in KS I 202. An unidentified letter from Beethoven to the publishers is cited in correction of the
  error in the scores of that time (corrected in the GA) that the following note should appear at the beginning of the
  'Scene at the Brook': "Due Violoncelli soli 1mo e 2do con sordino; i Violoncelli tutti coi Bassi. "
                                                                48 [1846] 461

BEETHOVENS INSTRUMENTE. Alois Fuchs.   (J)
  Description of the four instruments (two vlns, a vla and a vcl) given to Beethoven by Prince Lichnowsky at the suggestion of Schuppanzigh. (This note appears in full in TK I 276)   49 [1847] 30

ÜBER DIE FORM DER SYMPHONIE-KANTATE. AUF ANLASS VON BEETHOVENS NEUNTER SYMPHONIE. A. B. Marx. (K)
  A discussion of the history and form of the Ninth Symphony, with consideration of its resemblance to and difference
  from Mendelssohn's 'Lobgesang. '   49 [1847] 489,505

["Beethoven's brother has died in Vienna"]   50 [1848] 112   (L)

A COMPARISON OF BEETHOVEN AND SCHILLER. Theodor Kriebitzsch.   (M)
                                                                50 [1848] 549

THE BEETHOVEN QUARTET SOCIETY IN LONDON.   50 [1848] 554   (N)

The 'Allgemeine Musikalische Zeitung' ceased publication upon the completion of Volume 50. The Editors explained that the growth of interest in and acceptance of music had made a 'General Musical Journal' an anachronism. In 1848 (unlike 1798) the composition and performance of music was no longer an activity restricted to a few major cities, so that future journalistic record of this activity could better be handled locally. After 14 years, publication was resumed under the same name ('Neue Folge'), but with less emphasis on the record of the current scene.

BEETHOVEN IM MALKASTEN. Otto Jahn.   (A)
   Comments on the artistic impossibility of illustrating a work like the Pastoral Symphony by means of tableaux or living pictures, as was attempted at a recent performance in Düsseldorf. Reprinted in 'Gesammelte Aufsätze' [1866] 260-270.   NF 1 [1863] 293

LEONORE ODER FIDELIO? Otto Jahn.   (B)
   Various matters regarding this opera are discussed as follows: Beethoven's original preference was undoubtedly for the name 'Leonore,' but the management of the Royal Opera insisted on the name 'Fidelio' to avoid confusion with the opera 'Leonore' by Paer, first performed the previous year. By the time of the final revision in 1814, Beethoven had become reconciled to the name by which the opera was generally known. Sketches of the first version are discussed in connection with other works then under way. The changes made in the several revisions of the opera are outlined. Four letters to Fried. Sebast. Meier, the first Pizzaro, are given (KS I 98,99,100,101) Reprinted in 'Gesammelte Aufsätze' [1886] 236-269.   NF 1 [1863] 381,397

VERBINDENDER TEXT FÜR BEETHOVENS MUSIK ZU GOETHES EGMONT. Michael Bernays.   (C)
   Poem suitable for use with a concert performance of the music. (See also 23 [1821] Beilage III following col. 392)
                                                  NF 1 [1863] 451

DAVID STRAUSS UND DIE NEUNTE SYMPHONIE. Joh. Hermann.   (D)
   A discussion of Strauss' aesthetic analysis of the Symphony.   NF 1 [1863] 541,557

ZWEI NOCH UNBEKANNTE BRIEFE BEETHOVENS. M. Fürstenau.   (E)
   Letter of June 26th 1823 from von Könneritz (Director of the Royal Saxon Musical Chapel and of the Court Theater) (KS II 272) and Beethoven's reply of July 17th 1823 (KS II 270) regarding the performance of Fidelio on April 29th 1823 under C. M. v. Weber. Letter of July 25th 1823 to von Könneritz (KS II 272) and fragment of draft of a laudatory letter without date which Weber intended for Beethoven (KS II 271).
                                             NF 1 [1863] 618,631

MEHRERE NOCH UNGEDRUCKTE BRIEFE BEETHOVENS. G. Nottebohm.   (F)
   Letter of June 5th 1822 to Peters (KS II 194), the first of the series continued in 'Neue Zeitschrift für Musik' 6 [1837] 83.   NF 1 [1863] 680

BEETHOVENS THEORETISCHE STUDIEN. G. Nottebohm.   (G)
   A transcription and discussion of the manuscripts contained in Lot 149 of the material sold at auction after Beethoven's death, which Seyfried uncritically transcribed in 'Ludwig van Beethoven's Studien im Generalbass, Kontrapunkte und in der Kompositions-Lehre' (1832), and which was to serve as basis for Nottebohm's book 'Beethovens Studien' (1873). This is the original version of the material which later appeared in 'Beethoveniana' pp. 154-203.
                                   NF 1 [1863] 685,701,717,749,770, 784,810,825,839; NF 2 [1864] 153, 169

MEHRERE NOCH UNGEDRUCKTE BRIEFE BEETHOVENS. G. Nottebohm.   (H)
   Letter of September 10th 1821 to Haslinger (given with very incomplete musical examples in KS II 184).
                                     NF 1 [1863] 727

BEETHOVENS UND SCHUBERTS IRDISCHE RESTE.   (I)
   Account of the exhumation and reinterment of the remains of Beethoven and Schubert in October 1863.
                                     NF 1 [1863] 815

ÜBER ORIGINALHANDSCHRIFTEN VON MOZART, HAYDN ETC. Ferd. C. Pohl.   (J)
   Transcription of the Canon 'Ewig dein' (GA 23/256 No. 14).   NF 1 [1863] 853

BEETHOVENS TRAUERMARSCH AUS DER EROICA IN SEINEM SKIZZENBÜCHERN.   (A)
  Various sketches (mostly of the first theme) which are given in more detail in Nottebohm's 'Ein Skizzenbuch aus dem
  Jahre 1803' pp. 37, 38; also a sketch for the theme of the Rondo of the Violin Sonata Op. 24.
                              NF 2 [1864] 180

AD VOCEM: KONTRABASS-REZITATIV DER 9. SYMPHONIE VON BEETHOVEN. Leop. Sonnleithner.   (B)
  Recollections of the passage as performed during Beethoven's lifetime. Regarding Beethoven's thought of writing a
  new finale for the Ninth Symphony, the author is quoted in NB II 182.
                              NF 2 [1864] 245

BEETHOVEN SITTING FOR A PORTRAIT DURING 1817. A. von Klöber.   (C)
                              NF 2 [1864] 324

BEETHOVENS LIEDER.   (D)
  Review of Series 23 of the GA ('Lieder und Gesänge mit Begleitung des Pianofortes'), and discussion of Beethoven as
  a composer of songs.   NF 3 [1865] 1, 25, 41, 57

ZWEI FAST VERGESSENE CELLO-SONATEN VON BEETHOVEN.   (E)
  Discussion of the two Sonatas Op. 102.   NF 3 [1865] 543

A QUESTIONED READING IN OPUS 102 No. 2.   (F)
  In a review of an edition of the five 'Cello Sonatas for Pf 4 hands, mention is made of a disputed passage which is
  discussed in more detail in NB I 31.   Ser. 3: 1 [1866] 128

DIE MUSIK IN BONN IM VORIGEN JAHRHUNDERT UND BEETHOVENS JUGEND.   (G)
  Discussion of the musical life of Bonn under the last four resident Electors (from 1689 to 1794), and a brief outline of
  Beethoven's youth and early musical studies in Bonn.   Ser. 3: 1 [1866] 375, 383

EIN PORTRÄT BEETHOVENS BETREFFEND. F. Pohl.   (H)
  The portrait by Mähler was made in 1815, not 1817.   Ser. 3: 2 [1867] 19

DIE HANDLUNG DES BALLETS: "DIE GESCHÖPFE DES PROMETHEUS." Grandaur.   (I)
  A monograph on the life and choreo-dramatic work of Salvatore Vigano which recently came to the attention of the
  author contains a detailed summary of the action of the original (1801) "Little Prometheus" ballet.
                              Ser. 3: 2 [1867] 178

EIN NEUER TEXT ZU DEN "RUINEN VON ATHENS."   (J)
  A recently published poem by J. P. Heije may be more suitable for concert performance of Beethoven's music than
  the poem by Kotzebue for which it was originally intended.   Ser. 3: 2 [1867] 282

EINE ALTE PASTORALSYMPHONIE.   (K)
  An account of Knecht's 'Le portrait musical de la nature.'   Ser. 3: 3 [1868] 149

EIN TRIO VON HÄNDEL IN BEETHOVENS ABSCHRIFT. Friedrich Chrysander and G. Nottebohm.   (L)
  The 'Three-Part Fugato in the Broad Inversion' given in Seyfried's 'Studien' (p. 302, 279) was copied by Beethoven
  from the closing portion of the Overture to Handel's Oratorio 'Esther' (Handel-Gesellschaft Vol. 40-41). This composition, in a slightly modified form, was issued by Handel as a movement in the 4th of the 'Trios for 2 Violins,
  Flutes or Hoboys with a Thorough Bass for the Harpsichord or Violincello' Op. 2 (Handel-Gesellschaft Vol. 27 p116).
                              Ser. 3: 4 [1869] 37

ZWEI BRIEFE VON BEETHOVEN. A. W. Thayer.   (M)
  Letter of October 28th 1815 to Birchall (KS I 381). (First of the series continued in 'Jahrbuch für Musikwissenschaft'
  1 [1863] 429. Letter without date to Zmeskall (KS I 54 No. 46). Ser. 3: 4 [1869] 52

BEETHOVENIANA. G. Nottebohm.   (N)
  A series of articles under the general title 'Beethoveniana' appeared in this journal. Abstracts and serial numbers
  are given below for only those articles in this series that were not included in Gustav Nottebohm, Beethoveniana,
  Leipzig and Winterthur, 1872. (NB I)   Ser. 3: 4 [1869], 5 [1870], 6 [1871],
                              8 [1873]

DIE ERSTE AUFFÜHRUNG DES "PROMETHEUS." G. Nottebohm.   (O)
  Transcription is given of a program leaflet (in German and Italian) announcing a performance of the ballet on

21 March 1801, seven days before the date generally accepted as that of the first performance. When this article was written in 1869, the author apparently accepted the date of March 21st 1801 for the first performance, but before his death in 1882 he changed his mind, as evidenced by the statement in NB II 246 that 'the production seems to have met with delays, since the first performance took place only on March 28th 1801.'

Ser. 3: 4 [1869] 289 Beethoveniana II

EINE BERICHTIGUNG. G. Nottebohm. (A)
Schindler I₃ pp. 79-80 refers to a book by Preindl (d. 1826) as having been criticized by Beethoven. Actually, this book appeared as a posthumous publication only after Beethoven's death.

Ser. 3: 4 [1869] 291 Beethoveniana VI

BONNER STUDIEN. G. Nottebohm. (B)
A brief discussion of Beethoven's work with Neefe and of the texts in Generalbass from which he studied.

Ser. 3: 4 [1869] 353,361
Beethoveniana XI

BONNER STUDIEN. G. Nottebohm. (C)
Material which, with slight revision, appears as the first section (pp. 3-18) of 'Beethovens Studien' (1873).

Ser. 3: 4 [1869] 353,361,369,377
Beethoveniana XI

QUESTIONED PASSAGES IN THE BREITKOPF & HÄRTEL SCORE OF 'FIDELIO' GA 20/206. F. Bischoff and (D)
G. Nottebohm.
Presumable errors in dynamics or in vocal lines on pp. 37,58 and 178 of the score are noted and argued about.

Ser. 3: 5 [1870] 18,35,147,172
Beethoveniana XXX

BRIEFE VON DIABELLI. G. Nottebohm. (E)
First publication of letters to Diabelli. EDr of Kal 859,860,1019,1020,1031. Without date (KS II 215); without date (KS II 214,298); August 24th 1824 (KS II 325); September 26th (1824?) (KS II 337. Note that Nottebohm and Kalischer 'Briefe' V 60 have "Quintett" where KS has "Quartet."); without date (KS II 327).

Ser. 3: 5 [1870] 58
Beethoveniana XVII

EIN BRIEF AN TOBIAS HASLINGER. G. Nottebohm. (F)
"The day after the 6th of October 1824" to Haslinger. EDr of Kal 1034. (KS II 339)

Ser. 3: 5 [1870] 68
Beethoveniana XVIII

EIN BRIEF AN KARL HOLZ. G. Nottebohm. (G)
Without date to Holz. EDr of Kal 1106. (KS II 399)

Ser. 3: 5 [1870] 68
Beethoveniana XIX

EIN BRIEF AN ZMESKALL. G. Nottebohm. (H)
Letter dated (not by Beethoven) February 18th 1827. EDr of MM 467. (KK p. 836)

Ser. 3: 5 [1870] 68
Beethoveniana XX

EIN BRIEF AN VINCENZ HAUSCHKA. G. Nottebohm. (I)
Letter without date previously published in an incomplete version. EDr of KBr 738. (KS II 108)

Ser. 3: 5 [1870] 68
Beethoveniana XXI

EIN BRIEF AN DR. BRAUNHOFER. G. Nottebohm. (J)
May 13th 1825. EDr of KBr 1069 (KS II 368)

Ser. 3: 5 [1870] 69
Beethoveniana XXII

EINE ERKLÄRUNG. G. Nottebohm. (K)
A questioned reading in Beethoveniana XII (NB I pp. 60 ff) may have been a variant of another different but equally correct reading.

Ser. 3: 5 [1870] 147
Beethoveniana XXX

LUDWIG VAN BEETHOVEN.   (A)
   Centenary essay copied from the 'Bonn Zeitung.'   Ser. 3: 5 [1870] 409

NOTIZ ZU G. NOTTEBOHMS BEETHOVENIANA. Anton Rée.   (B)
   Nottebohm is asked to explain the reason for the change of fingers on the tied notes in the Pf part of the scherzo of
the Cello Sonata Op. 69 (which he does in Ser. 3: 11 [1876] 356 in connection with a discussion of a comparable
passage in Op. 110). If no explanation is available it is suggested that the fingering (which undoubtedly was assigned
by Beethoven) be omitted in future editions of the Sonata, since it tends to lead to a blurred performance. (See also
Ser. 3: 6 [1871] 25)   Ser. 3: 5 [1870] 414

EIN BRIEF BEETHOVENS AN SEINEN NEFFEN. G. Nottebohm.   (C)
   Letter of August 23rd 1823 (KS II 290).   Ser. 3: 6 [1871] 24

ÜBER EINE STELLE IN DER VIOLONCELLOSONATE OPUS 69 VON BEETHOVEN. W. Oppel.   (D)
   Discussion of possible reasons for the fingering referred to in Ser. 3: 5 [1870] 414.
                                      Ser. 3: 6 [1871] 25

AUF WELCHE ART HERR PROFESSOR HANSLICK SICH ORIGINAL-MANUSKRIPTE BESIEHT. Friedrich Chrysander. (E)
   Polemic against Hanslick in connection with his reference to Wagner's comment on Beethoven's use of the word
"frech" instead of "streng" in the finale of the Ninth Symphony, with supporting data from Nottebohm.
                                      Ser. 3: 6 [1871] 38

BEETHOVEN-PHOTOGRAPHIEN.   (F)
   Description of a series of six photographs by Friedrich Wendling issued in connection with the centenary.
                                      Ser. 3: 6 [1871] 41,106

AUS DEN LETZTEN TAGEN LUDWIG VAN BEETHOVENS. Ferdinand Hiller.   (G)
   Recollections of Beethoven during 1825-27, and of the period immediately following his death.
                                      Ser. 3: 6 [1871] 61

EIN PROGRAMM ZU BEETHOVENS NEUNTE SYMPHONIE. L. Hoffmann.   (H)
                                      Ser. 3: 6 [1871] 72

A BEETHOVEN LETTER. C. F. Pohl.   (I)
   Quotation from Pohl's book 'Die Gesellschaft der Musikfreunde' of Beethoven's letter of January 23rd 1824 to this
Society (KS II 305), with discussion.   Ser. 3: 6 [1871] 134

A BUST OF BEETHOVEN BY F. SCHALLER.   Ser. 3: 6 [1871] 157   (J)

BEETHOVEN ALS PATRIOT. DAS FESTSPIEL VON J. REDENBERG ZU DER DRESDENER BEETHOVEN-FEIER.   (K)
   Description of an allegorical drama on this subject.   Ser. 3: 6 [1871] 170

THE NINTH, TENTH AND ELEVENTH SYMPHONIES. Friedrich Chrysander.   (L)
   After the projected Tenth Symphony (for which sketches are extant) it is quite possible that an Eleventh Symphony
might have been written, based on the 'Faust' story. The relationship between the Choral Fantasy Op. 80 and the
Ninth Symphony is discussed. (See also 'New Music Review' 4 [1905] 184,231)
                                      Ser. 3: 7 [1872] 123

VIOLIN CONCERTO FRAGMENT IN C MAJOR.   (M)
   An incomplete first movement of a Violin Concerto in C major, from Beethoven's earliest period, has been found,
completed and performed by Hellmesberger. (See Schiedermair 'Der junge Beethoven' pp. 383,427)
                                    Ser. 3: 7 [1872] 229

ZUR TEXTESKRITIK DER BEETHOVEN'SCHEN KLAVIERSONATEN. Heinrich Heerwagen.   (N)
   Questioned passages in an edition of the sonatas by Sigmund Lebert.
                                      Ser. 3: 7 [1872] 526

DER LIEBESBRIEF BEETHOVENS.   (O)
   Substantially the material included in Thayer's 'Leben' [1879] III 427-36.
                                    Ser. 3: 7 [1872] 559,575,595,614

EINE VERWANDTE BEETHOVENS.   (A)
   Caroline van Beethoven, widow of nephew Karl, living in poverty in Vienna, applied in vain to the Director of the
   Court Theatre for aid. A fund was presented to her by a musical group in Frankfurt, the Emperor bestowed a pension
   on her, and royalties on performances of Fidelio in Berlin were made payable to her.
                                                                 Ser. 3: 8 [1873] 445,526,540,635

DREI BRIEFE BEETHOVENS. G. Nottebohm.   (B)
   Letter of October 4th 1804 to Simrock (KS I 90). Letter of September 23rd 1810 to Breitkopf & Härtel (KS I 204).
   Letter of February 15th 1823 to Peters (KS II 226).   Ser. 3: 8 [1873] 801; 9 [1874] 17

RICHARD WAGNERS ORCHESTRIERUNG DER NEUNTEN SYMPHONIE VON BEETHOVEN. Charles Gounod.   (C)
   An open letter of protest.   Ser. 3: 9 [1874] 310

EIN BRIEF BEETHOVENS. N. Simrock.   (D)
   Letter of August 2nd 1794 (KS I 10).   Ser. 3: 9 [1874] 805

BEETHOVENS MANUSKRIPT. E. Krüger.   (E)
   The manuscript of the four versions of 'Sehnsucht' (GA 23/250), bearing the date 1808, has been found.
                                                          Ser. 3: 10 [1875] 238

SELTSAME STELLEN IN DEN WERKEN GROSSEN MEISTER. W. Oppel.   (F)
   Possible error in the accompaniment to the tenor interjection "Agnus Dei" in the Dona Nobis of the Missa Solemnis.
   Possible error towards the end of Op. 112.   Ser. 3: 10 [1875] 625,697

A CONVERSATION WITH BEETHOVEN. Friedrich Wieck.   Ser. 3: 11 [1876] 746   (G)

BEETHOVEN'S CONCERT OF MAY 7th 1824. Karl Czerny.   Ser. 3: 11 [1876] 747   (H)

ZUR REINIGUNG DER WERKE BEETHOVENS VON FEHLERN UND FREMDEN ZUTHATEN. G. Nottebohm.   (I)
   The problems of attaining exact accuracy in the publication of Beethoven's works are exhaustively discussed under
   the following headings: Inaccurate notation (a) Accidentals p. 322 (b) Repeated notes p. 353; Slips of the pen p. 356;
   Conflicting readings p. 358; Copyist's errors p. 405; Editors' "improvements" p. 406; Misprints p. 469; Ambiguous
   passages p. 497.

             Textual problems of the following works are discussed

Opus	Page	Opus	Page
1	471	53	417, 418, 484
2	327, 353, 354, 403, 419, 465,	54	418, 470
	468, 481, 497	57	325, 341, 405
5	355	59	404, 498
6	471	60	465, 499
7	420, 470, 498	61	369
9	355, 481	62	370
10	340, 353, 391, 404, 420, 421,	67	465
	481, 482*	69	356
13	419, 421, 470, 483*	72	358, 406
18	403, 498	74	499
22	353, 355, 418, 421	77	370
24	469	78	371, 422, 470, 484
26	404, 406, 419, 422, 470, 483	79	499
27	326, 403, 406, 418, 483	81a	358
28	408, 418	82	499
30	483	85	468
31	390, 483	89	339
34	484	90	337
35	484	92	401
46	484	93	371
51	353, 355, 471	95	342

ZUR REINIGUNG DER WERKE BEETHOVENS, etc., (Continued)

Opus	Page		Opus	Page
101	422, 466, 484*		119	387, 485, 499
102	325, 466, 484		120	338, 339, 340, 486
106	325, 326, 337, 338, 339, 340,		123	467, 469, 513
	341, 401, 404, 422, 465, 466,		125	500, 513
	485*		131	327, 390, 486, 501
109	385, 486		132	501
110	356, 418, 470, 485		133	513

Varns 'Tändeln und scherzen'	486, 513
Varns 'Judas Maccabeus'	423
Three Pf Quartets	353
'Sehnsucht'	487
Canons	487

Ser. 3: 11 [1876] 321,337,353,369,
385,401,417,465,481,497,513

* See also Ser. 3: 13 [1878] 581, 697

PERFORMANCES OF THE THIRD AND NINTH SYMPHONIES IN BEETHOVEN'S PRESENCE. G. Nottebohm.   (A)
   Beethoven conducted the Third Symphony at least four times and was present at its performance at least seven other
   times (dates given). He was present at only two performances of the Ninth Symphony (May 7th and 23rd 1824).
                                        Ser. 3: 11 [1876] 513

L. VAN BEETHOVENS NEUNTE SYMPHONIE. S. Bagge.   (B)
   Analytical essay.   Ser. 3: 12 [1877] 49,65

BEETHOVENS NEUNTE SYMPHONIE UND IHRE BEWUNDERER. D. F. Strauss.   (C)
   Republication of essay which originally appeared in 1853. (See also NF 1 [1863] 541, 557)
                                        Ser. 3: 12 [1877] 129

ZUR BERICHTIGUNG DER LESARTEN EINIGER STELLEN BEETHOVEN'SCHER KLAVIER-SONATEN. C. Klingner.   (D)
                                        Ser. 3: 13 [1878] 581,697

EIN BRIEF BEETHOVENS AN BETTINA BRENTANO. M. Carriere.   (E)
   Carefully annotated version of letter of February 10th 1811 (KS I 208). (See also Ser. 3: 17 [1882] 769, 789, 809)
                                        Ser. 3: 15 [1880] 135

DIE FAMILIE VAN BEETHOVEN IN BONN UND IHRE BEZIEHUNGEN. H. Deiters.   (F)
   The researches of Werner Hesse on the ancestry of Beethoven ('Monatsschrift für die Geschichte Westdeutschlands'
   5 [1879] 200) are reviewed: that the first Beethoven to come to Bonn was not Grandfather Ludwig but Granduncle
   Cornelius; that the Michael van Beethoven (husband of Maria Ludovica v. B. nee Sluykens) was probably the father
   of Cornelius and Ludwig; and that this family came from Malines. Hesse found no record of the birth or baptism of
   Father Johann, but the generally-accepted date 1740 seems more probable to the author than Hesse's conjecture of
   1737-38. The "N. van Beethoven" listed in the Court Calendars of 1785 and 1786 as an assistant organist was actually Ludwig: "N" was either a misprint for "L" or a result of confusing Ludwig with his nine-year-old brother
   Nikolaus Johann.

   Certain minor errors in TD I (First Edition) (corrected in the Second Edition) are noted.
                                        Ser. 3: 15 [1880] 481

BEETHOVEN IN DEN JAHREN 1807-1816. H. Deiters.   (G)
   A review of the third volume of Thayer's 'Leben' in the form of a brief summary of the years covered.
                                        Ser. 3: 16 [1881] 475,491,502

DIE BRIEFE BEETHOVENS AN BETTINA VON ARNIM.   H. Deiters.   (A)
  The three letters to Bettina (KS I 195, 208, 263) are given with variant readings, and reasons are stated in extenso
for lack of confidence in the genuineness of the first and third letters.   (See also Ser. 3: 15 [1880] 135)

                                              Ser. 3: 17 [1882] 769,789,809

DIE ENTSTEHUNGSZEIT DER LEONOREN-OUVERTÜRE Nr. 1, OPUS 138.   Alb. Levinsohn.   (B)
  The date "1805" appearing on the title page of the first edition of this overture (Haslinger, 1832) is more probable
than the date "1807-08" assigned by NV.   Ser. 3: 17 [1882] 785

        Listed below are the reviews of compositions by Beethoven. Reviews marked with an
        asterisk are actually extended analyses, usually with examples in musical notation.

          Composition   Reference

        Twelve Variations on 'Ein Mädchen   1 [1799] 366
        oder Weibchen' and eight Variations
        on 'Mich brennt' ein heisses Fieber'[1]

  Opus 11   1 [1799] 541
  Opus 12   1 [1799] 570

        Ten Variations on 'La stessa, la   1 [1799] 607
        stessissima' [2]

  Opus 10   2 [1799] 25
  Opus 13   2 [1800] 373

        Eight Variations on 'Tandeln und   2 [1800] 425
        scherzen'

  Opus 23, 24[3]   4 [1802] 569

        Variations 'Bei Männern, welche   5 [1802] 188
        Liebe fühlen'

  Opus 28   5 [1802] 188
  Opus 34   5 [1803] 556
  Opus 30   6 [1803] 77
  Opus 35   6 [1804] 338
  Opus 48   6 [1804] 608
  Opus 88   6 [1804] 626

        'Der Wachtelschlag'   6 [1804] 642

  Opus 45   6 [1804] 643

        Variations on 'God Save the King'   6 [1804] 643

  *Opus 37   *7 [1805] 445
  Opus 47   7 [1805] 584,769
  Opus 20   7 [1805] 769
  Opus 52   7 [1805] 769

---

  [1] "That Herr van B. is a very talented pianist is well known . . . but whether he is an equally
talented composer is a question that, from these works, it would be more difficult to answer favorably."
  [2] "Herr v. B. may know how to improvise, but he certainly does not know how to write variations."
  [3] "These works are among the best that Beethoven has written, which means that they are among the
best that have been written by anybody."

Reviews of compositions (Continued)

Composition	Reference
Opus 53	8 [1806] 261
Opus 54	8 [1806] 639
Opus 60	8 [1806] 670
Andante pour le Pianoforte	8 [1806] 671
Opus 32	8 [1806] 815
Opus 36 (Trio version)	9 [1806] 8
*Opus 55	9 [1807] 321
Opus 57	9 [1807] 433
Thirty-two Variations in C minor	10 [1807] 94
Grand Trio pour deux Violons et Violoncelle, ou deux Oboes et Basson, ou deux Clarinettes et Basson	11 [1808] 108
*Opus 68	12 [1810] 241
*Opus 67	12 [1810] 630,652
Opus 76	13 [1811] 152
Opus 74	13 [1811] 349
Opus 77, 78	13 [1811] 548
Opus 75	13 [1811] 593
Opus 85	14 [1812] 3,17
Opus 82	14 [1812] 16
Opus 87	14 [1812] 67
Opus 80	14 [1812] 307
*Opus 62	14 [1812] 519
*Opus 70	15 [1813] 141; Beilage facing col. 164
*Opus 86	15 [1813] 389,409
Opus 84	15 [1813] 473
Opus 90	18 [1816] 60
*Opus 91	18 [1816] 241
*Opus 92	18 [1816] 817; following col. 832
Opus 100	19 [1817] 52
Opus 98	19 [1817] 73
Opus 99	19 [1817] 135
Opus 96	19 [1817] 228
'Das Geheimnis' and 'An die Geliebte'	19 [1817] 435
*Opus 101	19 [1817] 686; following col. 696
*Opus 93	20 [1818] 161
Opus 102	20 [1818] 792
Opus 107	23 [1821] 567
Opus 112	24 [1822] 674
Opus 21 (Simrock edition of the score)	24 [1822] 756
Opus 97	25 [1823] 192
Opus 36, 55 (Simrock edition of the scores)	25 [1823] 408
*Opus 109, 110, 111	26 [1824] 213
Opus 121b, 122	27 [1825] 740
Opus 108	27 [1825] 866; 30 [1828] 283
Opus 126	28 [1826] 47

Composition	Reference
Opus 116	28 [1826] 494
Trauer-Gesang bey Beethovens Leichenbegängnis[1]	29 [1827] 749
Opus 118	29 [1827] 797
Opus 137	29 [1827] 835
Opus 114	30 [1828] 331
*Opus 131	30 [1828] 485,501
L. v. Beethovens sämtliche Werke. Erste Abteilung: Sonaten für das Pianoforte allein. Neue sorgfältige Ausgabe. Wien, bey T. Haslinger	33 [1831] 30
Opus 84 (score of Overture and Entr'actes)	34 [1832] 109
Opus 136	39 [1837] 617; 40 [1838] 84

ALLGEMEINE MUSIKZEITUNG

UNTERHALTUNGEN ÜBER BEETHOVENS SCHAFFEN VON OPUS 81 BIS ZUR VIKTORIA-SYMPHONIE. Louis Köhler. (A)
A discussion of the Pf Sonatas Opp. 81a and 90, and of the 'Battle of Vittoria' Op. 91.
9 [1882] 429,481,494

A SCORE OF 'MEERESSTILLE' OPUS 112 CORRECTED BY BEETHOVEN. Otto Lessmann. (B)
A score of Op. 112 (formerly belonging to Richard Wagner) is described in which Beethoven changed certain passages as written by the copyist and made several marginal notes. 10 [1883] 232

PERSÖNLICHE ERINNERUNGEN AN L. VAN BEETHOVEN. Louis Schlösser. (C)
A visit to Beethoven in November 1822. 12 [1885] 200

FACSIMILE OF THE AUTOGRAPH OF THE CANON 'EDEL SEI DER MENSCH' (GA 23/256 No. 10). (D)
12 [1885] 200

BEETHOVEN AND WAGNER. R. Sternfeld. (E)
Parallels between the personalities and the careers of the two composers.
12 [1885] 271,287,307,319

BEETHOVEN-KONJEKTUREN. Friedrich Spiro. (F)
The setting of the 'Opferlied' for solo, chorus and orchestra (Op. 121b) was certainly written later than that for voice and Pf (NV p. 178); the latter probably dates from 1799-1800 and the former from about a year later. The 'Bundeslied' (Op. 122) is from about the same time as Op. 121b. The Terzet 'Tremate, empi' (Op. 116) may be assumed to have been written not later than 1799. The author of the text is not known, but may well have been Beethoven himself. The Sextet Op. 71 is also attributable to 1797-1800, probably the latter part of this period. In the 'Osanna' of the Missa Solemnis the present capability of valve horns to play the entire melodic line instead of natural notes only should be used. Slight changes in scoring in Opp. 121b and 71 are recommended.
12 [1885] 427,437

ZU BEETHOVENS GEBURTSTAG AM 16 DEZEMBER. Ludwig Nohl. (G)
EDr Kal 510. 12 [1885] 471

---

[1] This was the setting by Seyfried of two of the Equali for 4 trombones for 4-part male choir, as given in NV p. 161.

BEETHOVENS FIDELIO IN ITALIEN.   (A)
  The first performance of the opera in Italy with Italian text was on February 4th 1886 in Rome.
                                        13 [1886] 84,113

EINE LONDONER BEETHOVEN-MYSTIFICATION.   (B)
  The "'Dream of St. Hieronymus' by Beethoven," referred to by Thackeray, was an adaptation of the theme of the
  variations of Op. 26. (But see 'New Music Review' 23 [1924] 374)
                                        13 [1886] 268

ZUR WEIHE DES HAUSES. Siegfried Ochs.   (C)
  The music written by Beethoven for this Festspiel consists of three numbers: The Overture Op. 124; A March and
  Chorus Op. 114 which originally formed a part of the 'Ruins of Athens' music (Op. 113 No. 6), but which in a copy
  revised by Beethoven was changed much more than is given in the GA (20/207 vs 20/207a); A closing Chorus
  (GA 25/266) of which the author gives the themes of the various sections. (But see Hess 'Neues Beethoven-Jahrbuch'
  7 [1937] 115, who lists nine numbers for the complete 'Weihe des Hauses' music)
                                        14 [1887] 161

DIE BILDENDE KUNST IN DER BEETHOVEN-SAMMLUNG.   (D)
  List of portraits and statues in the Town Institute of Heiligenstadt, with comments.
                                        14 [1887] 282

DREI BISHER UNVERÖFFENTLICHE BRIEFE BEETHOVENS. Otto Lessmann.   (E)
  Letter of March 6th 1820 to Winter (KS II 166), and two letters from the summer of 1826 to Czapka (KS II 439).
  (According to B-Jahrbuch 2, these last two letters were first published in the 'Neue Freie Presse' on December
  30th 1887)   15 [1888] 59

KRITISCHE RANDGLOSSEN VON BEETHOVEN. Wilh. Tappert.   (F)
  Two copies of 'Cäcilia' for 1825 which came to the hands of the author contained comments written by Beethoven
  in the margins of articles by Gottfried Weber which are striking examples of Beethoven's irascibility.
                                        15 [1888] 129

EIN BISHER UNGEDRUCKTE BRIEF BEETHOVENS.   (G)
  Letter without date to Treitschke (KS II 26 No. 595).   15 [1888] 140

BEETHOVENS DRITTE BEGRÄBNIS. Otto Lessmann.   (H)
  On June 21st 1888 Beethoven's body was exhumed from its grave in the Währingerfriedhof. Measurements of the
  skull are given, and the statement is made that the cast taken in 1863 was in general accurate, but that it could
  not be trusted in its delineation of details. Other scientific observations are summarized. The body was re-
  interred in the Zentralfriedhof on the afternoon of June 22nd.   15 [1888] 260

BEETHOVENS STREICHINSTRUMENTE.   (I)
  The quartet of instruments presented to Beethoven by Prince Lichnowsky (TK I 276) is now in the Imperial Library
  in Berlin, but their condition has been allowed to deteriorate to the point where they cannot fittingly be used for
  public performance. In 1852 Holz (owner of the set) sold to an English collector an instrument which he falsely
  represented as a Guarnerius violin from this set.   15 [1888] 268

BEETHOVEN UND GRAF OPPERSDORF. Heinrich Reimann.   (J)
  The two letters and a receipt by Beethoven to Count Oppersdorf are given substantially as in 'Signale' 38 [1880] 723
  and Sonneck pp. 104 ff. The author dates the undated letter as earlier than the receipt: probably January 1807 or
  (at the earliest) December 1806. Author says that he first published MM-42 and MM-47 in 'Schlesische Zeitung'
  about nine years before. AMZ article abstracted in MfMg 20 [1888] 191; reprinted in 'Musikalische Rückblicke'
  [1900] 111.   15 [1888] 385

BEETHOVENS SKIZZEN ZUR EROICA. Heinrich Reimann.   (K)
  Description, with many brief examples, of the Sketch Book described by Nottebohm in 'Ein Skizzenbuch von
  Beethoven aus dem Jahre 1803' (1880).   16 [1889] 284,305,323,343

BEETHOVEN'S LAST PIANO.   (L)
  Beethoven's last piano, now in the Beethoven-Haus in Bonn, was strung with four strings instead of the usual three to
  amplify the tone for the deaf composer.   17 [1890] 10

A MEETING WITH BEETHOVEN.   Franz Lachner.   (A)

                                        17 [1890] 61

FRAU KAROLINE VAN BEETHOVEN.   (B)
    The widow of nephew Karl recently died in Vienna (November 15th 1891). A newspaper article by Th. von Frimmel
    is quoted to the effect that the current Viennese pronunciation of the composer's name, with accent on the second
    syllable, was not the pronunciation used by the family.   18 [1891] 614

ZUR GESCHICHTE DER IN LETZTER ZEIT SO VIEL GENANNTEN "KREUTZERSONATE." Ed. Hanslick.   (C)
    Statement that this sonata was written for Bridgetower, not for Kreutzer, with note by the editor that this fact had
    long been known.   19 [1892] 177

ÜBER BEETHOVEN BEI SICH.   (D)
    Translation of excerpts from the Memoires of Baron Tremont published by Michel Brenet in the 'Guide Musical.'
                                        19 [1892] 206

ZU BEETHOVENS FRÜHESTEN BEKANNTSCHAFTEN IN WIEN.   (E)
    Account of Beethoven's informal coaching in counterpoint with Schenk (TK I 153).
                                        19 [1892] 221

BEETHOVENS "WASSERTRÄGER."   Albert Kopfermann.   (F)
    One Siegmund Austerlitz of Vienna states the evidence which convinced him that Beethoven, not Cherubini, wrote
    'Der Wasserträger' and 'Elisa.'   20 [1893] 110

POSSIBLE BORROWINGS BY BEETHOVEN.   Heinrich Reimann.   (G)
    Czech folksongs bear striking resemblance to the first theme of the Pastoral Symphony.
                                        20 [1893] 538

RICHARD WAGNER ALS -- BEETHOVEN-BIOGRAPH.   (H)
    A letter dated May 7th 1841 from Wagner to "Theodor Hell" (Karl Gottfried Winkler) outlines plans for a Beethoven
    biography which he never wrote.   21 [1894] 5

EIN BRIEF BEETHOVENS AN SCHREYVOGEL.   (I)
    Report of a recent publication of a letter to Schreyvogel, dated "Vom Hause am 29ten Novemb." and starting. "Ich
    sende ihnen hier durch Hr. von Bernard die Theater Billete." (See 'Ménestrel' 60 [1894] 61.
                                        21 [1894] 131

ZU BEETHOVENS PROMETHEUS-MUSIK.   (J)
    Report of a performance of the complete 'Prometheus' music, stated to be for the first time since 1802. The history
    of the work is summarized (p. 159). Two readers cite earlier performances of the complete music (p. 187). The
    claim to novelty of the performance referred to is not that it was a complete performance of the music (such per-
    formances have taken place not infrequently) but that the audience was provided with a copy of the original libretto
    to enable them to follow the significance of the music more closely.
                                        21 [1894] 142

BEETHOVENS IX SINFONIE IN ROM.   Hermann Wichmann.   (K)
    Review of the first performance of Op. 125 in Rome, with comments on the effect of Italian temperament on the
    performance and examples of the translations of the Ode.   21 [1894] 252

COMMISSION TO BEETHOVEN FOR AN ORATORIO BY THE HANDEL AND HAYDN SOCIETY OF BOSTON.   (L)
    In 1823 the Handel and Haydn Society of Boston, through the American consul in Vienna as intermediary, com-
    missioned an oratorio from Beethoven. Record of this fact is found in the composer's notebook and in a Vienna
    newspaper, but no indication has been found that work was ever started on the oratorio.
                                        21 [1894] 361

ANTWORT AUF DIE BEETHOVEN'SCHE ENTLEHNUNGSFRAGE. Fr. Xav. Kuhač.   (M)
    The article gives a detailed account of the wanderings of the Croatians, leading to the conclusion that Beethoven
    (and to a greater extent Haydn) had borrowed tunes of Croatian origin. See also 20 [1893] 538.
                                        21 [1894] 396,420,438

EIN BISHER UNGEDRUCKTER BRIEF BEETHOVENS.   (A)
    Long letter dated "Baden am 17 Fbr 1823" to Spohr, starting, "Es war mir sehr angenehm, dass Sie mich auf mein
    Schreiben sogleich mit einer Antwort beehrten." This letter discusses subscriptions to the Missa Solemnis in Cassel,
    improvement of Beethoven's health (especially the condition of his eyes), an opera libretto by Grillparzer, and
    Beethoven's interest in Spohr's Double Quartets. (See also 'Neue Musik-Zeitung' 44 [1923] 248; 45 [1924] 142)
                          21 [1894] 663

NEU AUFGEFUNDENE SKIZZEN VON BEETHOVEN. Wilhelm Kienzl.   (B)
    Facsimile of one of five pages of a sketch book certainly dating from 1809 and probably fitting into the gap referred
    to in NB II 255. Sketches include work on the E Flat Concerto, the Choral Fantasia Op. 80, the song 'Mignon,' and
    extensive sketches for an unknown song 'Oesterreich über Alles.' 22 [1895] 319

BESUCH ROSSINIS BEI BEETHOVEN.   (C)
    Account by one of Rossini's friends of a visit by Rossini to Beethoven in 1822.
                          22 [1895] 374

A VISIT TO BEETHOVEN.   (D)
    Account of a visit to Beethoven in 1808-09 by Joh. Friedr. Reichardt.
                          24 [1897] 560

EIN NEUER ERLKÖNIG! Ludwig Hartmann.   (E)
    Review of an arrangement by Reinhold Becker of Beethoven's sketch of a melody for 'Der Erlkönig.' (But see 'Guide
    Musical' 44 [1898] 74)   24 [1897] 739

EINE SKIZZE BEETHOVENS ZU GOETHES "HEIDENRÖSLEIN."   (F)
    Facsimile of a sketch originally published by H. E. Krehbiel in the New York 'Tribune' of March 6th 1898. The
    transcription of the sketch (with added accompaniment) given by the Tribune is referred to as very faulty, but no
    corrected transcription (except for the first three measures) is given.
                          25 [1898] 217

ERINNERUNGEN AN BEETHOVEN.   (G)
    Account of a visit to Beethoven in 1816 by Johann Peter Pixis.   26 [1899] 288

NEUES UND ALTES ÜBER BEETHOVEN.   (H)
    Extended notes from the journals of Alexander Wheelock Thayer, selected from H. E. Krehbiel's 'Music and Manners
    in the Classical Period' [1898] 196-211.   26 [1899] 313

BEETHOVENS LETZTE WOHNUNGEN IN WIEN. Theodor von Frimmel.   (I)
    A list of the houses in which Beethoven lived from 1822 to his death.
                          26 [1899] 662

WIE SICH BEETHOVEN ZU DER AKADEMISCHEN FRAGE VON DER UNGLEICHEN GRÖSSE DER HALBTÖNE VERHIELT. (J)
    Bernhard Ziehn.
    Examples from most of the quartets later than Op. 18, and from the Ninth Symphony, to show that Beethoven wrote
    for strings in equal temperament, so that (for example) C flat and B natural or E sharp and F natural were considered as
    identical.   26 [1899] 786

EINE BEGEGNUNG MIT EINER ZEITGENOSSIN BEETHOVENS. Felix Weingartner.   (K)
    Frau Grebner (born about 1807) had sung in the chorus at the first performance of the Ninth Symphony. The author
    notes that she consistently used the pronunciation 'BeeTHOven.'   27 [1900] 7

A BEETHOVEN LETTER.   (L)
    Letter of August 24th 1824 to Diabelli (KS II 325).   27 [1900] 10

TWO UNPUBLISHED LETTERS OF BEETHOVEN TO THE ARCHDUKE RUDOLF. Theodor von Frimmel.   (M)
    Letter without date (probably spring 1819) regarding his variations on 'An die Hoffnung' (see KS II 107). Fragment
    of a letter (probably 1818).   27 [1900] 240

BEETHOVEN ODER BEETHÓVEN.   Theodor von Frimmel.   (A)
   There can be no doubt that the composer and his family used the pronunciation with the accent on the first syllable,
   even though the Viennese pronunciation of that day did and still does favor the pronunciation BeeTHOven. (See also
   18 [1891] 614; 27 [1900] 7)   27 [1900] 289

LETTER FROM STEINER TO BEETHOVEN.   (B)
   Letter of December 29th 1820 regarding money due from Beethoven to Steiner (TK III 38).
                                    27 [1900] 493

EINE BEMERKUNG ZUM VORTRAG DER NEUNTEN SYMPHONIE.   Felix Weingartner.   (C)
   The tempo of the trio of the scherzo should be whole note equals 116, not half note equals 116.
                                    28 [1901] 264

BEETHOVEN'S FUNERAL ORATION.   (D)
   A transcription is given of the oration at Beethoven's funeral, written by Grillparzer and delivered by the actor
   Heinrich Anschütz.   28 [1901] 275

FIDELIO UND DIE GROSSE LEONOREN-OUVERTÜRE.   Robert Holtzmann.   (E)
   The author maintains (against the general contemporary opinion in Germany) that the Fidelio Overture is the most
   suitable of the four to precede the rising of the curtain. He considers various alternatives for introduction of the
   Leonora Overture No. 3 -- between the first and second acts, before the closing scene, immediately following the
   Fidelio Overture before the curtain rises, after the close of the opera -- and tentatively favors the last of these. The
   editor states that his recommendation is (1) reserve the "great" Overture for the concert hall, or (2) play it at the beginning, followed by an interval of considerable duration.   28 [1901] 478

RICHARD WAGNERS ANSICHT ÜBER DIE AUFFÜHRUNG DER 3. LEONOREN-OUVERTÜRE VOR EINER "FIDELIO"-   (F)
      VORSTELLUNG.   Peter Raabe.
   Quotations from Wagner's writings show that he believed that the Leonora Overture No. 3 had no place in a performance of the opera: "that he considered it a blunder in the worst of bad taste to anticipate in music what was
   to be portrayed on the stage." In his youth Bülow used this overture in operatic performance, but in his maturity
   he reversed this early judgment.   28 [1901] 494

DIE OUVERTÜRE ZU "FIDELIO." Felix Weingartner.   (G)
   The author believes that the Leonora Overture No. 2 is the most suitable for use in performances of the opera.
                                    28 [1901] 529

BEETHOVEN'S EYESIGHT.   (H)
   There is reason to believe that in his later years Beethoven was nearsighted to the extent that he used spectacles
   while at work and that he carried a double lorgnette or a monocle on the street. Grillparzer relates that in 1805
   Beethoven wore spectacles in company, though in later years he discarded them.
                                    28 [1901] 660

LUDWIG VAN BEETHOVEN.   Rudolf Louis.   (I)
                                    29 [1902] 251

TWELVE MINUETS FOR SMALL ORCHESTRA.   (J)
   Twelve Minuets, written in 1799 but never performed, have been published by Heugel & Cie (Paris) in an edition
   by Chantavoine (H-3).   32 [1905] 112

BEETHOVEN.   Arthur Symons.   (K)
   Translation of an article in the 'Monthly Review' (London).   32 [1905] 473,489

DIE EIGENART DES BEETHOVENSCHEN KUNSTWERKES.   Fritz Volbach.   (L)
   Material appearing in the chapter of the same title in the author's 'Beethoven' [1905] 49-73.
                                    32 [1905] 715,735,757,777,797

BEETHOVENS 'FIDELIO.' Max Puttmann.   (M)
   A history of the opera during the composer's lifetime.   32 [1905] 759

ZWEI KURZE BEMERKUNGEN ZUR FIDELIO-INSZENIERUNG. Peter Raabe.   (N)
   Two changes in stage business are suggested to improve the adjustment between drama and music.
                                    33 [1906] 820

DIE WERKE AUS BEETHOVENS LETZTER SCHAFFENSEPOCHE.   Felix Rosenthal.   (A)
   A discussion of form, harmony and melody as exemplified in Opp. 101, 109, 120, 123 and other works of
   Beethoven's last years, with quotations from other authorities on the characteristics of this period.
                                             34 [1907] 543

A BEETHOVEN LETTER.   (B)
   Letter dated April 10th 1806 to Friedrich Meyer (KS I 101 No. 105). (The postscript is not given, and it is stated
   that the letter had not previously been published, though actually it had appeared in the 'Allgemeine Musikalische
   Zeitung' NF 1 [1863] 397).   34 [1907] 880

BEETHOVEN LETTERS.   (C)
   Extracts from letters to Bernard in the Hajdecki collection.   35 [1908] 17

BEETHOVEN ALS ROMANTIKER.   Johannes Conze.   (D)
   Beethoven is more a romantic composer even than his successors.   35 [1908] 49

BEETHOVEN: ELF WIENER TÄNZE.   Otto Lessmann.   (E)
   The author is not convinced that the dances of this set are by Beethoven.
                                             35 [1908] 403

EINE VERLOREN GEGANGENE EINAKTIGE OPER BEETHOVENS?   Wilhelm Altmann.   (F)
   A letter dated June 22nd 1827 from J. W. Ehlers in the files of Schott & Sons refers to a one act opera 'Simson' with
   text by Ehlers and music by Beethoven. This is presumably the setting of the 'Ruins of Athens' music referred to by
   Beethoven in his letter of August 1st 1826 to Ehlers (KS II 432).   35 [1908] 685,782

BEETHOVEN IN DER SCHWEIZ.   Max Steinitzer.   (G)
   A collection of 'Folk Songs for Boys' and Women's Voices' published in Zürich has lifted Beethoven melodies wholesale
   and deranged them for settings of words "blasphemously chosen." 36 [1909] 913

GRÄFIN THERESE BRUNSVIK -- DIE "UNSTERBLICHE GELIEBTE" BEETHOVENS?   Max Unger.   (H)
   A detailed review of the evidence and of the reasoning of other scholars, leading to the conclusion that the identification of the Immortal Beloved as Therese von Brunswick is highly questionable.
                                             37 [1910] 713,737

MICHAELANGELO AND BEETHOVEN.   Gustav Ernest.   (I)
   While many features of parallelism may be drawn between the two masters, there is this basic difference:
   Michelangelo is the prophet of pessimism and weariness of life; Beethoven is the prophet of optimism and joy.
                                             37 [1910] 801

BEETHOVEN-BRIEFE.   Kurt Singer.   (J)
   In comparison with the letters of other great men, those of Beethoven do not disclose the intimate personality of
   the writer.   37 [1910] 1029

ANTON FRANZ HABENECK, EIN BEETHOVEN-APOSTEL IN PARIS.   M. Murland.   (K)
   Biographical sketch.   37 [1910] 1175

BEETHOVENS "IRISCHE" SINFONIE.   Paul Bekker.   (L)
   The ritornello of the Irish air 'Nora Creina' (GA 24/258 No. 8) is very similar to the theme of the last movement of
   the Seventh Symphony. The author indicates two measures of the Air which furnished the germ for this ritornello.
   (See also Hohenemser, 'Die Musik' 10_2 [1911] 23)   38 [1911] 481

ZUR THAYERS BEETHOVEN-BIOGRAPHIE.   Ludwig Misch.   (M)
   Review of the new edition edited by Deiters and revised by Riemann, with citation of various minor misprints and
   errors.   38 [1911] 785,809,834

DIE NEU ENTDECKTE BEETHOVEN-SINFONIE.   Ludwig Misch.   (N)
   Review of the first Berlin performance of the Jena Symphony.   38 [1911] 1317

BEETHOVEN UND DAS VOLK.   Ludwig Misch.   (O)
   Satirical criticism of a motion picture: 'Beethoven: a Drama.'   39 [1912] 861

NOCH EINMAL "BEETHOVEN UND DAS VOLK."   Richard Fricke.   (A)
  Too large a proportion of the German people are not acquainted with Beethoven either in the movies or in other ways.
                                        39 [1912] 940

EIN NEU ENTDECKTES LIED VON BEETHOVEN.   Georg Kinsky.   (B)
  A recently discovered setting of Matthison's 'An Laura' (H-89) is certainly authentic, since it follows closely the
  sketch quoted in NB I 45 as a source of the Bagatelle Op. 119 No. 12 (see also Schiedermair: 'Der junge Beethoven'
  pp. 342-43). The probable date of the song is 1790-92.   40 [1913] 43

BEETHOVEN AUTOGRAPHS IN THE ROYAL LIBRARY IN BERLIN.   Hermann Springer.   (C)
  A list of the principal items.   40 [1913] 535

BEETHOVEN IN BERLIN.   Adolf Weissmann.   (D)
  An account of Beethoven's only visit to Berlin (in 1796), and of the slow but steady progress which his music made
  towards acceptance in that city.   40 [1913] 536

BEETHOVENS WIEHEKUSS.   La Mara, pseud. (Marie Lipsius).   (E)
  A letter written by Liszt in 1862 indicates the truth of the story that at his concert on April 13th 1823 Beethoven
  kissed him on the forehead.   40 [1913] 544

FRANZ SCHUBERTS PERSÖNLICHE BEZIEHUNGEN ZU BEETHOVEN.   Konrad Huschke.   (F)
  While towards the end of his life Beethoven came to know and admire Schubert's works, statements of two of
  Schubert's closest friends, contradicting Schindler's story, say that the two composers never met.
                                        42 [1915] 555,567,579

AN OPERA 'SIMSON' BASED ON BEETHOVEN'S RUINS OF ATHENS MUSIC.   Wilhelm Altmann.   (G)
  Meyerbeer's library, recently presented to the Königliche Bibliothek in Berlin, includes a manuscript score (without
  title page or overture) of an opera 'Simson,' the music of which is clearly that written by Beethoven for the Ruins
  of Athens. (See Ibid.35 [1908] 685, 782)   43 [1916] 258

DIE BEETHOVEN-OPERETTE.   L. Andro.   (H)
  Unhappy considerations pertaining to the use of Beethoven's life and works on the operetta stage are discussed.
                                        43 [1916] 346

DIE EINAKTIGE OPER "SIMSON."   Wilhelm Altmann.   (I)
  Ehlers, principal stage manager at Mannheim, corresponded with Beethoven regarding the use of the Ruins of Athens
  music for an opera. The opera that was finally made up must have contained long passages of spoken dialogue, but
  a score with words for the musical portions of the opera has been found. This text and its application to the several
  numbers of Beethoven's Ruins of Athens score (plus one number from the Weihe des Hauses) are given herewith.
  (See Ibid.35 [1908] 685, 782; 43 [1916] 258)   43 [1916] 429

ZUM VERSTÄNDNIS VON BEETHOVENS "EROIKA."   Eugen Schmitz.   (J)
  Bearing in mind that this symphony was written during the lifetime of Napoleon (to whom without question, it was
  musically dedicated), it must be considered as a portrayal of the hero in his various aspects rather than as a memorial
  to him. The author thinks of the four movements as representing respectively the hero's struggles, his strength in
  adversity (like 'Zarathustra's Grablied'), his joys and his creativeness. The form of the Funeral March (originating
  in the French operas by Gretry and his successors) was presumably a tribute to the French hero for whom the work was
  written. The suggestion of Bekker (English edition [1925] 163) that the order of the second and third movements be
  reversed is without justification.   44 [1917] 362

DIE GROSSE LEONOREN-OUVERTÜRE IM FIDELIO.   Richard Sternfeld.   (K)
  Various alternatives are discussed, with the recommendation that the Overture be not interjected as a prelude to the
  second act or to the last scene. (See also 46 [1919] 257)   44 [1917] 747

ZUR AUFFÜHRUNG VON BEETHOVENS NEUNTER SYMPHONIE.   Siegmund von Hausegger.   (L)
  Performance of the Ninth Symphony is recommended during wartime as a summons to ever heightening morale of all
  the people.   45 [1918] 3

DIE TRAGIK DES GENIES.   Rud. F. Amplewitz.   (M)
  "An apostrophe to the shade of L. van Beethoven."   45 [1918] 379,393

EINE BEETHOVEN-PROPHETIK VON 1802? Richard Sternfeld.   (A)
   A summons in the 'Allgemeine Musikalische Zeitung' of 1802 to a "successor to Gluck" in the synthesis of opera may
   have referred to Beethoven.   45 [1918] 404

BEETHOVEN UND SCHUBERT BEIM ERFASSEN UND VERARBEITEN IHRER MUSIKALISCHEN IDEEN.   (B)
      Konrad Huschke.
   There is no truth in the concept of Beethoven as a composer who had to struggle for ideas, or of Schubert as one to
   whom they flashed in full perfection. On the contrary, the sketch books and the accounts of intimates show that
   Beethoven poured forth a never ceasing stream of musical ideas (though indeed he labored hard to shape them into
   their most perfect form); while many of Schubert's finest songs were initially written in fair copy, others for which
   three or four versions are extant show his needed effort to attain his ideal.
                                                       45 [1918] 415

JAQUINO AND MARZELLINE. Eugen Kilian.   (C)
   Modifications in action and costuming are suggested to minimize the unreality of the Leonora-Jaquino-Marzelline
   relationship in the last scene of the opera.   46 [1919] 239

DIE LEONOREN-OUVERTÜRE IM FIDELIO. Richard Sternfeld.   (D)
   Omission of the familiar Overture (as recommended in 44 [1917] 747) does not certainly meet with objections from
   the audience.   46 [1919] 257

DER SCHLUSSATZ DER HELDENSYMPHONIE UND BEETHOVENS DARSTELLUNG DES REIN MENSCHLICHEN.   (E)
      Arthur Prüfer.
   Significance is found in the choice of the Prometheus theme for the last movement of the Symphony in Commemoration of a Great Man.   47 [1920] 99

"NON SI FAR UNA CADENZA. . ." Ludwig Misch.   (F)
   Unless a cadenza is available from the pen of the man who composed the concerto, the soloist should make his
   cadenza as brief and simple as possible, or omit it altogether.   47 [1920] 315

AUSBAU ODER EINSCHRÄNKUNG DER BEETHOVENPFLEGE? Peter Raabe.   (G)
   Postwar reparations, however extensive they may be materially, cannot take away from Germany her heritage of
   great music.   47 [1920] 735

BEETHOVEN UND DER "UNTERGANG DES ABENDLANDES." Hans Joachim Moser.   (H)
   The author disagrees with Spengler's contention that, in comparison with Bach, Beethoven's music shows the onset
   of the decline.   47 [1920] 736

BEETHOVEN UND DER FUTURISMUS. Heinz Pringsheim.   (I)
   Beethoven as an innovator did much to determine the future course of music.
                                                       47 [1920] 738

ZU BEETHOVENS STREICHQUINTETT OPUS 104. Wilhelm Altmann.   (J)
   This composition, the 'Duet mit zwei Augengläsern,' and the tenth of the twelve Contradances for Orchestra
   GA 2/17a ("Pour Monsieur Friederich, nommé Liederlich")are the only three examples of humorously titled works
   in Beethoven's output. A facsimile of the title page of the Quintet is given. Like the setting of the Pf Sonata
   Op. 14 No. 1 for string quartet, this transcription of the Pf Trio Op. 1 No. 3 is far from slavish; for purposes of study
   it is desirable that an edition of Op. 104 be issued which gives the trio and quintet versions on parallel staves.
                                                       47 [1920] 743

BEETHOVEN IN UNSERE HOHE SCHULE. Kurt Rosenhauer.   (K)
   It is easier for the school curriculum to provide biographical material on Beethoven than to impart a performing or
   listening knowledge of his music.   47 [1920] 745

MUSIKDRAMATISCHE BEARBEITUNG DER ERSTEN SZENE AUS "FIDELIO." Max Steinitzer.   (L)
   The first scene of 'Fidelio' as Wagner might have written it.   47 [1920] 749

BEETHOVENS EGMONT-MUSIK UND DAS THEATER. Eugen Kilian.   (M)
   A discussion of the music as a component of a stage representation of Goethe's tragedy. (See also 64 [1937] 703)
                                                       48 [1921] 35

"FIDELIO"-AUFFÜHRUNGEN UND DRITTE "LEONOREN"-OUVERTÜRE.   Rudolf Hartmann.   (A)
    There are three possible places for the great Leonora Overture to be inserted into a performance of the opera, but it fits well into no one of the three.   51 [1924] 573

DIE BEDEUTUNG DES RHYTHMISCHEN PHÄNOMENS IN DER MUSIK BACHS UND BEETHOVENS.   Franz Wohlfahrt.   (B)
    "A philosophic discussion."   51 [1924] 627

BOUILLY'S 'LEONORE' AND BEETHOVEN'S 'FIDELIO.'   Eugen Kilian.   (C)
    A comparison of Bouilly's libretto for Gaveaux's opera with the successive versions used by Beethoven.   52 [1925] 687

ANTON SCHINDLERS PERSÖNLICHKEIT IM SPIEGEL SEINES TAGEBUCHES.   Reinhold Zimmermann.   (D)
    52 [1925] 751,771

EINIGE WÜNSCHE FÜR "FIDELIO."   Alfred Weidemann.   (E)
    While the opera of 1805 became dramatically practicable only by the revisions of 1806 and 1813, the excision or modification of some of the numbers in the first version is to be regretted. Of the four Overtures, No. 1 is by far the most suitable for the opera house. Beethoven's title of 'Leonore' is to be preferred to 'Fidelio.'   53 [1926] 159

WIE DACHTE DER JUNGE BEETHOVEN ÜBER POLITIK?   Karl Gerhartz.   (F)
    In Bonn Beethoven was much influenced by the discussions of Rhenish independence and by the liberal ideas of those with whom he came in contact, especially at the University of Bonn, where he matriculated in 1789.   53 [1926] 223

MOZART UND BEETHOVEN ALS KINO-"STIMMUNGSMUSIKER."   Martin Friedland.   (G)
    Ironical.   53 [1926] 274

DER SCHLUSS DER MISSA SOLEMNIS.   Richard Sternfeld.   (H)
    The author thinks of the Missa Solemnis in its perfection as ending with the Credo, with the finale of the Ninth Symphony rounding out Beethoven's statement of his attitude towards life. Comments of other authors on the unity of the Agnus Dei with the rest of the work are given.   53 [1926] 379

BEETHOVENS JOSEPH-KANTATE.   Alfred Wiedemann.   (I)
    This cantata, composed in 1790, presumably received its first performance in 1884. Though the work is not without musical merit, other performances have been rare, largely because of the pompousness and occasional nature of the text. The author has provided new words for the two solo numbers, pointing the cantata to the death of Christ instead of that of Kaiser Joseph.   53 [1926] 1059

BEETHOVEN UND DIESE ZEIT.   Heinz Pringsheim.   (J)
    An imaginative picture of Beethoven as he would have developed had he been born in 1870 instead of 1770.   54 [1927] 291

BEETHOVENS KÜNSTLERISCHES WERDEGANG.   Gustav Ernest.   (K)
    The onset of Beethoven's deafness was the determining event in his development as a composer. Nothing written before 1798 can compare in depth of emotion with the Largo e mesto of the Sonata Op. 10 No. 3 which comes from the time of his realization of approaching deafness. The two cantatas of 1790 display his ability to write with or without inspiration: Kaiser Joseph meant something to Beethoven, whereas his successor Leopold was only a name, and as a result the first of the two cantatas was a work of real merit, whereas the second was of negligible value. After he became aware of his growing deafness his early preoccupation with form and polish lost its importance, and more and more he wrote from within himself. His interest in the Fugue during his last years was in this form not as a conflict but as a resolution of conflict. "The history of his artistic growth is nothing else than the history of his spirit."   54 [1927] 293

BEETHOVENS MISSION FÜR UNSERE ZEIT.   Willi Hille.   (L)
    Beethoven must be taken as an example of the triumph of spirit over material obstacles.   54 [1927] 297

DER UNBEKANNTE BEETHOVEN.   Ludwig Misch.   (M)
    A plea for the performance in the centennial year of some of the less familiar works of Beethoven, with comments on many of them.   54 [1927] 298

BEETHOVEN UND RUSSLAND.   Robert Engel.   (A)
    Errors are pointed out in certain articles in Frimmel's 'Beethoven-Handbuch'; important books on Beethoven by Russian authors are listed; dates of first performance in Russia of various compositions by Beethoven are given.
54 [1927] 301

BEETHOVEN UND DAS KURKÖLNISCHE GEISTESLEBEN.   Jos. Schmidt.   (B)
    The intellectual life in Bonn under Maximilian Friedrich and Maximilian Franz (i.e., after 1761) was such that Beethoven's youth was passed in a cultured and stimulating atmosphere.
54 [1927] 549

DIE WANDLUNGEN IN DER MUSIKALISCHEN BEURTEILUNG BEETHOVENS.   Ernst Bücken.   (C)
    The author traces the attitude of critics and essayists towards Beethoven from his day to our own.
54 [1927] 550

BEETHOVEN-VERUNGLIMPFUNGEN.   Fritz Stege.   (D)
    Protest at certain contemporary publications.   54 [1927] 555

BEETHOVEN AND E. T. A. HOFFMANN.   Hans Kuznitzky.   (E)
    Corrected transcription of KS II 170: for first Herr N. read Herr Neberich; for second our Herr N. read our feeble Herr Starke ("unser schwache Hr. Starke"). (See also 'Die Musik' 13_1 [1913] 147; 'Revue musicale' 8 No. 6 [1927] 110)
54 [1927] 618

ZWEI VERGESSENE KUNSTGENOSSEN BEETHOVENS.   Emil Seling.   (F)
    Brief biographical sketches of Franz Clement and George Polgreen Bridgetower.
55 [1928] 1202

LOUIS SPOHR, GOETHE AND BEETHOVEN.   Leopold Hirschberg.   (G)
    Extracts from Spohr's 'Autobiography.'   56 [1929] 1055

BEETHOVEN IN FRANKREICH.   Robert Greven.   (H)
    Beethoven's name and fame were taken to Paris in the last years of the eighteenth century by his friends Kreutzer, Anton Reicha and Heinrich Simrock. As early as 1806 Beethoven's name is mentioned (unfavorably) in a French treatise on composition. The growth of interest in and acceptance of Beethoven's music in Paris is discussed. (See also 'Revue musicale' 2 No. 3 [1921] 13)   57 [1930] 659,679

DAS ALTE PROBLEM DER 9. SINFONIE VON BEETHOVEN IN NEUER BELEUCHTUNG.   Fritz Brust.   (I)
    Review and summary of Otto Baensch's 'Aufbau und Sinn des Chorfinales in Beethovens neunter Symphonie.'
57 [1930] 881

DIE TEMPI DER "NEUNTEN."   Ernst Zander.   (J)
    The tempi which are almost universally adopted today for the Ninth Symphony are at wide variance from Beethoven's metronome markings. It is generally recognized that two of these metronome markings are erroneous: the trio of the scherzo is half note equals 116, not whole note equals 116, and the opening of the last movement is quarter note equals 66, not quarter note equals 96 (see 'Neues Beethoven-Jahrbuch' 2 [1925] 151 ff). Present day conductors tend to drag the first and third movements at little more than two-thirds of the indicated tempi; the various sections of the last movement (each with its own metronome marking) are dragged or rushed at will. The author's closing statement is that the Ninth should not be used as a vehicle to gain cheap laurels from the public.
58 [1931] 529

DER OBJEKTIVIERTE BEETHOVEN.   Ludwig Misch.   (K)
    Reprint of an article by Edward J. Dent ('Vossische Zeitung' March 26th 1927) in which Dent refers to Beethoven's music as "old music," "a manifestation of the art of a bygone time."
58 [1931] 547

BEETHOVEN ALS "GESCHÄFTSMANN."   Carl Wilh. Marschner.   (L)
    Excerpts from Beethoven's letters to publishers, which show that while he had no flair for business as normally conducted, this very lack of adeptness tended to secure more for him than conventional methods would have done.
58 [1931] 746

WARUM DIE "GROSSE FUGE"? Ludwig Misch.   (A)
    Summary of the history of the Grosse Fuge, and reference to it as a solution of the problem of combining sonata form
with fugal texture.   59 [1932] 55

ZUR NEUNTEN SINFONIE. Otto Baensch.   (B)
    A continuation from 'Neues Beethoven-Jahrbuch' 4 [1930] 133 of the author's study of the text of this work. (See
also 57 [1930] 881)   59 [1932] 134

EINE NOTWENDIGE RETOUCHE IN BEETHOVENS EGMONT-OUVERTÜRE. Felix Weingartner.   (C)
    Changes are recommended in two passages to make use of the chromatic capabilities of the modern horn.
                                                       59 [1932] 376

FRITZ JÖDES BEGEGNUNG MIT BEETHOVEN. Ludwig Misch.   (D)
    Diatribe against article by Jöde in 'Musikantengilde' 5 [1927] 25.   59 [1932] 499

BEETHOVENS PIANISTISCHE WETTKÄMPFE. Konrad Huschke.   (E)
    An account of Beethoven's trials of strength with the other virtuosi in Vienna.
                                                       60 [1933] 518

SUBMISSESTE BITTE AN ALLE FIDELIO-REGISSEURE! Erich Band.   (F)
    It is recommended that the set for the dungeon scene be designed to fit within the set for the closing scene, that
both sets be placed in position during the interval between Act I and Act II, and that the dungeon set be "flied" so
that it can be removed in a minute or so. In this way the present necessity for a 10 or 15 minute wait between the
two scenes will be obviated, thereby avoiding a loss of dramatic momentum, and removing the temptation to in-
ject the Leonora Overture No. 3 at this most inappropriate point.   61 [1934] 464

MUSIKALISCHE GEISTESSCHÖPFUNG UND IHRE DEUTUNG. Edmund Wachten.   (G)
                                                       61 [1934] 493,509

"ALLA DANZA TEDESCA." Ludwig Misch.   (H)
    The kinship in tonality, tempo indication, line and treatment between the theme of the Presto alla tedesca of the
Piano Sonata Op. 79 and the Alla danza tedesca of the String Quartet Op. 130 must be more than coincidence.
                                                       61 [1934] 496

BEETHOVEN IN NEUER DEUTUNG? Friedrich Berghold.   (I)
    Discussion of Schering's contention that many of the works of Beethoven are programmatically based on the writings
of Shakespeare or other poets or dramatists.   61 [1934] 605

BEETHOVEN UND DER SCHÖPFER DES "FREISCHÜTZ." Alfred Weidemann.   (J)
    Although as late as 1809 Weber cast ridicule on Beethoven's symphonies, by November 1814 his admiration for
'Leonora' led him to produce this opera in Prague. In 1823 Weber wrote at least four letters to Beethoven and
received at least three replies, but this correspondence seems to be completely lost except for a draft of a part
of one of Weber's letters (KS II 271). Their slight influence on other music is briefly discussed.
                                                       61 [1934] 668

DIE LOGIK DER "NEUNTEN." Ernst Zander.   (K)
    After looking askance at the many writers (from Wagner to Schenker) who have sought to discover the philosophy or
the program of the Ninth Symphony, the author considers the reasons for the relatively late entry of the voices in the
Finale and for the use of the variations form.   61 [1934] 681

NOCHMALS: SCHERINGS BEETHOVEN-DEUTUNG. Edmund Wachten.   (L)
    (See p. 605)   61 [1934] 729

EIN SCHLUSSWORT ZU SCHERINGS BEETHOVEN-DEUTUNG. Friedrich Berghold.   (M)
                                                       62 [1935] 35

BEETHOVEN ALS SCHLACHTENMALER. Ludwig Misch.   (N)
    A detailed and sympathetic discussion of 'Wellington's Victory' Op. 91 ("The Battle Symphony is not a work unworthy
of Beethoven, but rather a curio which only Beethoven could have written") and a list of Beethoven's various compositions for military music.   62 [1935] 65

BETTINA VON ARNIM UND DIE MUSIK.   Rudolf Werner.   (A)

62 [1935] 229

BEETHOVENS GEISTESGESCHICHTLICHE STELLUNG.   Ernst Heim.   (B)
   Beethoven represents the zenith in musical creation: in him music for the first time became personal and subjective
rather than formalized and objective, and in his successors the doctrines of Romanticism led back again to formalism,
this time a formalism in which the rigid mold was that of poetic content instead of structural and decorative form.

62 [1935] 273

EINE UNBEKANNTE BEARBEITUNG DER 7. SYMPHONIE BEETHOVENS.   Franz Feldens.   (C)
   An arrangement of Op. 92 for nine part military music, almost certainly made during Beethoven's lifetime, has been
found.   62 [1935] 319

BEETHOVENS EWIGE WIRKUNG.   Ernst Wurm.   (D)

62 [1935] 773

BEETHOVEN ALS BEARBEITER EIGENER WERKE.   Richard Petzoldt.   (E)
   The position which transcriptions occupied about 1800 is indicated by the eminence of the musicians whose names
appear as transcribers: e.g., Hummel, Ries, Czerny, Kalkbrenner.   The following transcriptions by Beethoven of
his own works are discussed: Opp. 14 No. 1, 16, 38, 61, 103, 104.   63 [1936] 65, 81

ZUM KAPITEL "BEETHOVEN UND BAYERN."   Max Unger.   (F)
   WRK (p. 215) refers to a letter from Stephan von Breuning to his mother (this letter is given in full in Ley's
'Beethoven als Freund der Familie Wegeler-von Breuning' p. 249) which indicates that in mid December 1795
Beethoven was in Nuremberg, Regensburg and Linz with Stephan and his brother Christoph.   Such an absence from
Vienna necessarily would throw doubts on Beethoven's reported appearance with Haydn at a Redoutensaal concert
on December 18th (TK I 188).   The author gives evidence that the traveling companion of the von Breunings was
not the composer but his brother Johann, so that the tour to Prague, Dresden, Leipzig and Berlin in the spring of
1796 was Beethoven's first venture forth from Vienna.   63 [1936] 260

EINE VERKANNTE "OHNMACHT" BEI BEETHOVEN.   Eugen Schmitz.   (G)
   The first twenty measures of the D Minor Sonata Op. 30 No. 2 are a kind of improvisatory prelude known by
eighteenth century composers as "Ohnmacht," and in performance to be treated with rhythmic freedom.

63 [1936] 415

HAYDN AND GEORGE THOMSON.   Fritz Erckmann.   (H)

63 [1936] 417

BEETHOVEN ALS MUSIKER-POET.   Richard Petzoldt.   (I)
   Discussion of the Schering hypothesis.   63 [1936] 546

FORMPROBLEME BEETHOVENS.   Roderich v. Mojsisovics.   (J)
   Throughout his life Beethoven struggled with two problems of form: the transition to an allegro movement from a
slow introduction, and the writing of a finale in multi-movement works which adequately balanced the opening
movement.   The development of Beethoven's attack upon and solution of these two problems is discussed in detail.
His solution of the latter problem is described as being the use either of the Mozartean form in which the finale is
the culminating movement, or of the two movement (fast movement, adagio) form like Schubert's Unfinished
Symphony, which perhaps was not unfinished.   Failure on the part of Beethoven's successors to solve these problems
(with Liszt's Faust Symphony and the symphonies of Bruckner being among the few exceptions) is given as a primary
reason for the abandonment of the conventional symphonic form in favor of the one movement symphony or the
symphonic poem.   63 [1936] 637

"EIN MISSGRIFF."   Josef Vogler.   (K)
   The author contends that Beethoven's decision to introduce voices into the Ninth Symphony (a decision arrived at
only after a long struggle) was an artistic mistake.   63 [1936] 640

EIN GEDENKBLATT FÜR THERESE VON BRUNSVIK.   Erich Valentin.   (L)
   The author is convinced that only Therese could have been the Immortal Beloved.

63 [1936] 642

DER ANDERE BEETHOVEN.   Wolfgang Schmieder.   (A)
  Facsimiles and excerpts are given from the records of Breitkopf & Härtel with reference to their business relationship
  · with Beethoven.   63 [1936] 642

BEETHOVENS REISE NACH ENGLAND.   Walther Nohl.   (B)
  The conversation books, from the first to the last (1819-27) indicate a continued interest on Beethoven's part in the
  visit to England which never took place. Pertinent passages from the conversation books are quoted in considerable
  number.   63 [1936] 645

DIE STELLUNG DER GROSSEN LEONOREN-OUVERTÜRE IM FIDELIO.   Felix Weingartner.   (C)
  More than thirty years' deep study of Fidelio has led the author to the conclusion that, whatever overture is used to
  open the opera (his preference is for No. 2) and whatever problems of stage mechanics there may be between the
  Dungeon Scene and the Finale, there is no place after the initial curtain for the interjection of an overture.
                                                     63 [1936] 702

RICHARD WAGNER ZUM PROBLEM "BEETHOVEN UND DIE DICHTUNG." Arnold Schering.   (D)
                                                     64 [1937] 17

ÜBER INSTRUMENTATIONSERGÄNZUNGEN IN DEN "FIDELIO-" UND "DON GIOVANNI"-PARTITUREN.   (E)
     Erich Band.
  The author lists more than forty passages in which advantage should be taken of the extended capabilities of today's
  horns, trumpets and timpani as compared with those of Beethoven's time.
                                                     64 [1937] 84

ZUR AUSLEGUNG BEETHOVENS.   Willy Meckbach.   (F)
  The reference by Schindler to Beethoven's association of the Sonata Op. 31 No. 2 with Shakespeare's 'Tempest' is
  attributed to the fact that Schindler, while well meaning, was not very bright. The author points out the substantial
  identity of a passage in the Dungeon Scene of 'Fidelio' with one in the last movement of Op. 57 (and marked
  similarity to a theme in the Funeral March of the Eroica) as bearing on Eleanore von Breuning as the Immortal
  Beloved.   64 [1937] 214

EINE FRAGLICHE STELLE IM FINALE DER EROICA.   Carmen Studer-Weingartner.   (G)
  Evidence is cited, inherent in the music and from old orchestral parts, to indicate that mm. 9-16 should be played
  arco.   ' 64 [1937] 230

JOHANN BAPTISTE ROUSSEAU AND BEETHOVEN.   Eugen Brümmer.   (H)
  · Biographical sketch of J. B. Rousseau, great-grand-nephew of Jean Jacques, founder in his youth of several short-lived
  musical journals in the Rhineland which were enthusiastically outspoken about Beethoven.
                                                     64 [1937] 309

BEETHOVEN AND BRAHMS.   Ernst Wurm.   (I)
                                                     64 [1937] 621

DIE GESAMTAUSGABE VON BEETHOVENS WERKEN.   Walther Nohl.   (J)
  From 1810 until his death Beethoven gave much thought to the project of a complete edition of his works. Extensive
  excerpts (starting in 1820) are given from the conversation books on this subject.
                                                     64 [1937] 656,671

ZUR URAUFFÜHRUNG VON BEETHOVENS EGMONT-MUSIK.   Max Unger.   (K)
  Beethoven's music was first performed as a part of the fourth Vienna performance of the drama on June 15th 1810,
  not having been completed in time for the earlier performances (of which the first was on May 24th). Riemann to
  the contrary, Beethoven's letter to Breitkopf & Härtel regarding this music (KS I 191) is correctly attributed to June,
  not May. (See also 48 [1921] 35)   64 [1937] 703

BEETHOVENS ERSTE LEONORE.   August Pohl.   (L)
  Biographical sketch of Anna Milder-Hauptmann.   · 65 [1938] 370

DIE FAMILIE VAN BEETHOVEN.   Fritz Erckmann.   (M)
  After a review of early unfounded accounts of Beethoven's descent -- that he was the natural son of Kaiser Friedrich
  Wilhelm II; that he was born in a little tavern in Holland in August 1772 while his parents, strolling musicians,

DIE FAMILIE VAN BEETHOVEN (Continued)
   were performing at a fair -- the author traces the composer's ancestry through Ludwig, third son of Henri Adelard
   van Beethoven of Antwerp, referring to the researches of Pols, Schmidt-Görg and others but making no attempt to
   refute their contention that this Ludwig died in infancy or childhood.   The generally known facts about Grandfather
   Ludwig, Father Johann and his three sons are summarized.   The family is further traced through his nephew Karl,
   his son Ludwig, and Ludwig's son Karl Julius Marie (who, dying childless in December 1917 was the last of the
   composer's line).   Some twenty-five alternative spellings of the name Beethoven are given, which led the author
   to associate the name with Betuwe, a province in Holland.   65 [1938] 433,449

BEETHOVEN IN MÖDLING.   Walther Nohl.   (A)
   Beethoven's sojourns in Mödling in the summers of 1818-19-20 are discussed in some detail, with extracts from the
   conversation books.   65 [1938] 652

ZUR 5. SYMPHONIE BEETHOVENS -- EIN NACHTRAG.   Arnold Schering.   (B)
   Amplification of programmatic analysis given in 'Zeitschrift für Musikwissenschaft' 16 [1934] 65.
                                                  65 [1938] 715

BEETHOVEN NANNTE ES: BARBAREI DER MUSIK.   Friedrich Herzfeld.   (C)
   Throughout the eighteenth century the form and content of music so clearly indicated its tempo that the four
   designations: Adagio, Andante, Allegro, and Presto were enough.   Beethoven introduced the use of modifying words
   and phrases, diminutives and intensifiers, which brought the entire system of tempo indications to the point of confusion referred to in his letter (probably from the end of 1817) to Ignaz v. Mosel (KS II 69).   (NOTE by DWM: The
   introduction of modifiers cannot be attributed to Beethoven: Bach ('Bach-Gesellschaft' xxxvi pp. 192-93) used
   Adagissimo and Adagio poco in 1704; Handel ('Handel-Gesellschaft' xlviii pp. 44-45) used Un poco larghetto and
   Largo e affettuoso in 1739; Mozart used similar modifiers almost from the first (e.g., K. 7, 8, 9, 15).
                                                  66 [1939] 17

DAS BEETHOVEN-BILD IM HAUSE WAHNFRIED UND SEINE ENTSTEHUNG.   Ludwig Volkmann.   (D)
   At Wagner's request, Dr. Hermann Härtel sent him in 1869 a far from faithful copy by Robert Krausse of the
   Waldmüller portrait of Beethoven.   66 [1939] 271

NEUES ZUR FAMILIE VAN BEETHOVEN.   Richard Petzoldt.   (E)
   Schmidt-Görg's line of descent for Beethoven is modified to the extent that Arnold (late 16th century) was the grand-
   father (not the father) of Markus; the intermediate generation was Hendrick, who married Catherine van Boevenbeeke.
   Josine (van Vlesselaer), wife of Arnold, was burned as a witch in Brussels in September 1595.
                                                  66 [1939] 621

BEETHOVEN ALS SCHICKSALKÜNDER.   Ernst Wurm.   (F)
   Birthday essay.   66 [1939] 643

EIN ANGEBLICH UNBEKANNTES SKIZZENBUCH BEETHOVENS IN RUSSLAND.   Max Unger.   (G)
   Recent statements that a hitherto unknown sketchbook containing sketches for the Eroica had been found in Russia
   are incorrect in two respects: (1) the sketchbook in question, though lost for about seventy years, had been described
   by Lenz ('Kritische Katalog' III 221) and by Nohl ('Beethoven, Liszt, Wagner' [1874] 95 ff); and (2) there are sketches
   for Opp. 31, 34, 35, 49, 85, 119, and the Duet 'Nei giorni tuoi felici,' but none for the Eroica.   The sketchbook
   may be assigned to the period summer 1802 to March 1803; "in point of time it falls between the Kessler sketchbook
   (autumn 1801 to spring 1802) and the so-called 'Eroica' sketchbook (May 1803 to the beginning of 1804)."   Note
   that Riemann (TD II 421) erroneously dates this book "Spring and Summer 1801," based on Schindler's erroneous
   statement that Op. 85 was written in 1801.   "It is practically certain that not a note of the Eroica was written before
   May 1803;" the period of composition for the Eroica may be assumed as May/June 1803 to November 1803.
                                                  67 [1940] 114

NOCHMALS: ORIGINALHANDSCHRIFT ODER ERSTDRUCK?   Wolfgang Schmerder.   (H)
   The score of the Fifth Symphony was sent to Breitkopf & Härtel at some time between July 16th and September 14th
   1808.   From this, parts were prepared, and the first performance on December 22nd 1808 was from these parts.
   On March 4th 1809 Beethoven advised Breitkopf & Härtel that he was sending some minor corrections which he had
   made during the performance of the symphony (KS I 153), and these corrections had apparently been sent by March
   28th (KS I 158).   Presumably the changes included the addition of the present fourth measure to the 'Fate' motif at
   its various appearances, which did not appear in the first edition of the parts.   This measure was also added to the
   manuscript of the Pf arrangement of the symphony which was published in July, and to the copy from which the score
   was engraved in 1826.   67 [1940] 258

BEETHOVEN UND SEINE VATERSTADT NACH 1792. Eugen Brümmer.   (A)
  The French occupied the Rhineland in 1794, so that Bonn ceased to be the seat of the Electoral Court and the center
  of culture in the area. Restoration of its importance as a musical and cultural center began in the second decade of
  the nineteenth century. The first performance of a Beethoven symphony in Bonn was in March 1824, but by the time
  of Beethoven's death quite a number of his works had been given in his native city.
                                       67 [1940] 409

BEETHOVEN IN WIEN. Ernst Wurm.   (B)
  Apparently an address.   68 [1941] 17

ÜBER AUSGABEN DER BEETHOVENSCHEN KLAVIERSONATEN. Hermann Drews.   (C)
  Comments on changes in the arrangement of the notes on the staves and other changes made in various editions.
                                       68 [1941] 174

ALLGEMEINE MUSIKZEITUNG ZUR BEFÖRDERUNG DER TONKUNST

LUDWIG VAN BEETHOVENS LEICHENBEGÄNGNIS.   (D)
  An article stated to be for the purpose of correcting various erroneous or incomplete accounts published in newspapers
  and journals.   1 [1827] 97

NOCH EIN WORT ÜBER BEETHOVEN.   (E)
  A review in the 'Allgemeine Musikalische Zeitung' expressing the thought that upon repeated hearings the Ninth
  Symphony might prove to be great music causes this correspondent to blow a fuse.
                                       2 [1828] 142

ALMANACH DER DEUTSCHEN MUSIKBÜCHEREI

A PILGRIMAGE TO BEETHOVEN. Richard Wagner.   (F)
  Reprint.   [1922] 202

DIE DEUTSCHE ROMANTISCHE OPER: ROMANTISCHES IN MOZARTS UND BEETHOVENS OPER. Hermann Abert. (G)
  While Fidelio in some of its characteristics foreshadows romanticism, it can in no way be considered a romantic
  opera. The characteristics of romanticism contained in many of the librettos which Beethoven considered and
  abandoned may have been one of the reasons for his ultimate lack of interest in them.
                                       [1924-25] 159

HAYDN, MOZART, BEETHOVEN. Guido Adler.   (H)
  "A triptych at the holy altar of art."   [1926] 53

BEETHOVENIANA. Franz Grillparzer.   (I)
  Poems, addresses and memoirs are republished.   [1927] 49

BEETHOVENS CHARAKTER. Guido Adler.   [1927] 75   (J)

DIE BEIDEN BEETHOVEN. Wilhelm Heinrich Riehl.   [1927] 98   (K)

BEETHOVENS STELLUNG IN DER MUSIKGESCHICHTE. Hans Joachim Moser.   (L)
  "Beethoven's position in the history of music is really his position in the history of mankind."
                                       [1927] 127

BEETHOVEN IN BONN. Ludwig Schiedermair.   (M)
  Chapter 'Die letzten Bonner Jahre' from 'Der junge Beethoven' (pp. 209-227).
                                       [1927] 142

BEETHOVEN UND WIEN. Karl Kobald.   (A)
A popular commentary on the influence of the city on the composer during the first few years of his residence there.
[1927] 167

BEETHOVENS MUSIK ZU GOETHES EGMONT. E. T. A. Hoffmann.   (B)
A reprint from the 'Allgemeine Musikalische Zeitung' 15 [1813] 473 of the fifth and last of Hoffmann's reviews of
Beethoven works.   [1927] 176

BERICHT ÜBER DIE AUFFÜHRUNG DER NEUNTEN SYMPHONIE VON BEETHOVEN IM JAHRE 1846 IN DRESDEN.   (C)
Richard Wagner.
Reprint of article given in 'Gesammelte Schriften' II 50 [1887].   [1927] 187

ZUM VORTRAG DER NEUNTEN SYMPHONIE BEETHOVENS. Richard Wagner.   (D)
Reprint of article given in 'Gesammelte Schriften' IX 231 [1888]. [1927] 206

ÜBER EINIGE NEU AUFGEFUNDENE JUGENDKOMPOSITIONEN BEETHOVENS UND ANDERES. Adolf Sandberger.   (E)
The four manuscripts in the British Museum hitherto attributed to Mozart but stated by Saint-Foix to be by Beethoven
are the Piano Trio Anh. 52a, the Rondo in B flat K. 511a, the Gavotte, Allegro and Funeral March (fragment) Anh.
41a, and the Minuet K. 25a.   This last is identical with one of the twelve Beethoven works published in 1903 by
Chantavoine ('Douze Menuets inédits pour Orchestre -- Ludwig van Beethoven -- Oeuvre posthumous -- Paris, au
Menestrel').   The author dates the first movement of the trio before the piano sonatas of 1783, and the second
movement later; the rondo about 1791; the gavotte about 1790. The author questions the genuineness of the Jena
Symphony for stylistic reasons.   [1927] 235

BEETHOVENS KLAVIERMUSIK. Willibald Nagel.   (F)
A glance at each of the sonatas, with a brief commentary on the piano variations.
[1927] 251

BEETHOVENS KAMMERMUSIK. Fritz Gysi.   (G)
General.   [1927] 270

BEETHOVEN IN SEINEN SYMPHONIEN. Theodor Kroyer.   (H)
A consideration of some of Beethoven's individual mannerisms as they manifest themselves in the symphonies.
[1927] 283

BEETHOVENS CHORMUSIK. Arnold Schering.   (I)
Each of the choral works except the most unimportant is discussed individually.   Though some of the lesser works
(e. g., the Trauerkantate, Meersstille) have their points, "his fame as a choral composer rests solely and entirely
on the two masses."   [1927] 295

FIDELIO. Hermann Abert.   (J)
It is noteworthy that although the first imitators of the original opera on the Leonora story (Bouilly and Gaveaux,
1798) were singspiele (Paer, 1803; Mayr, 1805) Beethoven made of it a tense drama, even though he followed the
opera comique tradition of spoken recitatives.   Beethoven's first act followed the pattern of Gaveaux's opera fairly
closely, but the opening of the second act (original version) with the March and Pizarro's aria changes the mood
completely from the lightness of the predecessor operas, and the opening of the third act with Florestan's aria com-
pletes the change.   "The foundation of the first act, and indeed of the second, are too weak to carry the monu-
mental structure of the third act."   The first revision (to give the 1806 version) was too superficial to have any
appreciable effect in overcoming this weakness.   The further modifications leading to the present (1814) version
were more fundamental and in large measure eliminated the features typical of singspiel (e. g., the opening scene
in Rocco's family circle) but left at least one -- the trumpet call as the dramatic climax.   Fidelio shows a basic
limitation in Beethoven's creative power: inability to write great music when the subject does not strike some responsive
echo in his own emotions.   He is unable to apply to the small and unimportant the same measure of creative power
that he gives to his principal characters or situations, and even his principal characters were subordinated to the underlying idea of the victorious struggle for freedom.   The matter of the overtures illustrates this characteristic: in the
second and the third the subject matter has taken command so that the works were not overtures but Leonora symphonies.

The Fidelio Overture had to be written to provide a suitable introduction for the opera.
[1927] 304

BEETHOVEN UND DIE FLÖTENUHR.   Georg Kinsky.   (A)
    The history of the mechanical organ and of Haydn's and Mozart's writings for this instrument is briefly described.
    Beethoven's hitherto known compositions for mechanical organ (H-70, 71, 72), written for the Countess Josephine
    Deym, are referred to, and an instrument similar to the one which had belonged to the Countess, now in the Heyer
    Museum, is described. Of the eight compositions which were kept in this organ, No. 7 was a 'Grenadier's March
    arranged by Herr Ludwig v. Beethoven.' The last portion of this work (here given in transcription) is virtually iden-
    tical except for key (F instead of B flat) with the March for 2 clarinets, 2 horns and 2 bassoons GA 25/292. The first
    portion of the March and the transition to Part II are believed also to be by Beethoven.   NOTE: In 'Zeitschrift für
    Musikwissenschaft' 14 [1932] 215 it is shown that this first part is a transcription of a March in E flat (for the same six
    wind instruments) by Haydn. It is also shown that the manufacturer of the mechanical organ here referred to died in
    1812, so that a latest date for the instrument is thus fixed.   [1927] 320

BEETHOVENS BRIEFE.   Wilhelm Altmann.   (B)
    Characteristics of Beethoven are illustrated by passages from his letters.
[1927] 333

BEETHOVEN IN DER ZEITGENÖSSISCHEN KRITIK.   Robert Haas.   (C)
    A discussion of the attitude which various journals and individual journalists took towards Beethoven during his lifetime,
    with extended quotations from their writings.   [1927] 347

ANTON SCHINDLER (1795-1864), EIN LEBEN FÜR BEETHOVEN.   Reinhold Zimmermann.   (D)
    Biographical sketch, with special reference to Schindler's efforts to popularize Beethoven's music.
[1927] 374

DIE INSZENIERUNG DES "FIDELIO" UND UNSERE ZEIT.   Josef Turnau.   (E)
    Factors to be considered in the modernistic staging of 'Fidelio.'   [1927] 383

MAX KLINGER'S 'BEETHOVEN.'   Arthur Seidl.   (F)
    Extended commentary on the statue, with 8 plates.   [1927] 395

BEETHOVENMASKE.   Hans Wildermann.   (G)
    Reminder that there was a life mask (Klein, 1812) as well as the better known death mask.
[1927] 418

AMERICAN MUSICOLOGICAL SOCIETY JOURNAL

FIRST PUBLICATION OF MM 281.   Donald W. MacArdle.   (H)
2 [1949] 204

ANBRUCH: ÖSTERREICHISCHE ZEITSCHRIFT FÜR MUSIK

BEETHOVEN IN IMMER NEUER DEUTUNG.   Victor Urbantschitsch.   (I)
    Critical Schering's hypothesis.   16 [1934] 171

UNBEKANNTE KLEINER BRIEF BEETHOVENS.   D. Mosonyi.   (J)
    Letter without date (undoubtedly between 1809 and 1814) to Christian Ludwig Reissig (seven of whose poems Beethoven
    set as songs: see NV pp. 74, 181, 182) reading: Lieber Reisiger Reiszig! ich bitte Sie: heute so früh als moglich zu
    mir zu kommen, da ich notwendig mit ihnen nicht zu singen aber zu reden habe. -- ihr ergebenster L. v. Beethoven.

UNBEKANNTE KLEINER BRIEF BEETHOVENS (Continued)
In the salutation, note the play on words based on the fact that Reissig was a military attaché in Vienna during the five years of Beethoven's acquaintance with him.   18 [1936] 4

BEETHOVENS TEXTDICHTER REISSIG.   Otto Erich Deutsch.   (A)
Detailed biographical sketch of Christian Ludwig Reissig (1784-1847) (see also 'Neues Beethoven-Jahrbuch' 6 [1935] 59.)   18 [1936] 69

EIN VERGESSENES QUARTETT VON BEETHOVEN.   (B)
Brief mention of the string quartet version of Op. 14 No. 1.   19 [1937] 294

ANREGUNG FÜR KUNST, LEBEN UND WISSENSCHAFT

GOETHE, SCHILLER UND DIE 9. SYMPHONIE.   (C)
In spite of Beethoven's admiration for the reserved and impersonal genius Goethe, it was the humanness of Schiller which reflected itself in the ode that became the text of the last movement of the Ninth Symphony.
2 [1857] 212

EINE FRANZÖSISCHE STIMME ÜBER ULIBISCHEFF.   Hans v. Bülow.   (D)
Extended polemic against Ulibischeff by an unnamed Frenchman for whose aesthetic stature the author vouches.
3 [1858] 16

BEETHOVENS MUSIK ZU DEN "RUINEN VON ATHEN" IM CONCERTSAAL.   Franz.   (E)
In a concert performance of Beethoven's Op. 113, the dramatic value of Kotzebue's text suffers materially. Program notes are given which attempt to restore the balance, and minor changes in text are proposed.
4 [1859] 17

BEETHOVENS LETZTE QUARTETTE.   F. F. Weber.   (F)
Brief nonanalytical discussion of the last five quartets, with detailed commentary on Op. 131.
6 [1861] 153,185,306

ARCHIV FÜR MUSIKFORSCHUNG

NEUES ZU BEETHOVENS VOLKSLIEDERARBEITUNG: EIN NACHTRAG.   Willy Hess.   (G)
Corrections and amplifications to 'Zeitschrfit für Musikwissenschaft' 13 [1931] 317.
1 [1936] 123

ZU BEETHOVENS SONATE PATHÉTIQUE.   Arnold Schering.   (H)
This composition is a "Hero and Leander" sonata, but not (as the author had stated earlier) based on Schiller's ballad.   1 [1936] 366

BEMERKUNGEN ZU: WILHELM HAAS, SYSTEMATISCHE ORDNUNG BEETHOVENSCHER MELODIEN.   Paul Mies.   (I)
Detailed and constructive criticism of Haas's book.   1 [1936] 483

DIE SYMBOLIK DES PIZZIKATOS BEI BEETHOVEN.   Arnold Schering.   (J)
Pizzicato may be employed (1) merely as a matter of instrumental technique; (2) in the spirit of a harp or other instrument with plucked strings; or (3) as an integral part of the spirit of the music. Beethoven's uses of pizzicato under headings (2) and (3) are listed exhaustively, with comments on the significance of each instance.
2 [1937] 273

BEETHOVEN'S USE OF THE HARP.   Hans Joachim Zingel.   (K)
In only one case did Beethoven score specifically for the harp: in No. 5 of the 'Prometheus' music and in the Six Easy Variations on a Swiss Song, for Pf or harp (NV p. 156), though in one instance his dramatic music includes a Romanza with harp accompaniment (not identified). His statement in an undated, probably relatively early letter to Streicher

(Sonneck p. 184): "I hope that the time will come when the harp and the pianoforte will be two totally different instruments" throws an interesting light on the tone quality of the instrument he used as a young virtuoso.
2 [1937] 458,464

BEETHOVENS WERKTHEMATIK, DARGESTELLT AN DER "EROICA." Walter Engelsmann.   (A)
   An analysis of the themes and motifs of the Eroica, to show that they are all basically derived from the principal theme of the first movement.   5 [1940] 104,192

ARCHIV FÜR MUSIKWISSENSCHAFT

BEETHOVEN'S ASSOCIATION WITH THE FIRM OF BREITKOPF & HÄRTEL. Georg Schünemann.   (B)
1 [1919] 470

BORROWINGS FROM BEETHOVEN. Heinrich Rietsch.   (C)
   Citations are given of reminiscences of Beethoven which appear in works by Schubert, Schumann, Brahms and Bruckner.   2 [1920] 295

BEITRÄGE ZUR BEETHOVEN-FORSCHUNG. Adolf Sandberger.   (D)
   The music at Mergentheim in the autumn of 1791. Added minutiae are given of the tour discussed in TK I 112. The musicians apparently left Mergentheim on October 22nd.   2 [1920] 394

BEETHOVEN AND BAVARIA.   (E)
   The official documents of the Bavarian court are given which led to the refusal of the court to subscribe to the first issue of the Missa Solemnis (TK III 99). In 1868 the composer's grandnephew and namesake, after difficulties with the law in Vienna, came to Munich. In the next year and a half he cajoled King Ludwig into granting him a total of 1175 florins; thereafter he entered upon a career of out-and-out swindling. On July 30th 1872 he was sentenced to four years imprisonment; his wife Marie received a sentence of six months.
2 [1920] 396

BEETHOVEN AND THE OPERA COMIQUE.   (F)
   Beethoven's service in the opera orchestra at Bonn gave him an intimate acquaintance with the contemporary literature of the Italian opera buffa and (even more) with the opera comique of Piccini and Cimarosa and the singspiele of Mozart, Schuster and others. Saturation with operas of these styles during his formative years left its mark not only on his melodic line and methods of construction, but (as exemplified in 'Fidelio') on his choice and adaptation of a libretto. Generous examples of these influences are given.
2 [1920] 399

EIN UNGEDRUCKTER BRIEF BEETHOVENS. Max Friedlaender.   (G)
   Transcription (with comments) of a letter dated July 12th 1823 to Franz Stockhauser the harpist: "Indem sie mich beehren mit einem Schreiben," discussing subscription to the Missa Solemnis, Beethoven's recent eye trouble, an acquaintance of Beethoven (an unnamed dentist in Paris) who was a musical amateur, and reference to an unidentified 'Sonata in A.' Note that the addressee is mentioned in (KS II 353, 359), where his name is misspelled 'Brockhausen.'
4 [1922] 359

DAS MELODISCHE HAUPTMOTIV IN BEETHOVENS "FIDELIO." Rudolf Steglich.   (H)
   The author presents evidence to support his contention that a single motival germ permeates the entire opera. (Note that Vol. 9 [1952] follows Vol. 8 [1927])   9 [1952] 51

DIE ZEITGENÖSSISCHE ÜBERLIEFERUNG DER B-INTERPRETATION. Hugo Socnik.   (I)
   The detailed commentaries on the performance of B's piano works that are given in Czerny's Op. 500, 'Vollständig theoretischpractischen Pianoforte-Schule,' and especially in the supplementary volume, 'Die Kunst des Vortrags,' have been unjustifiably overlooked, as has the edition of the piano sonatas by Moscheles (Hallberger, 1858). Ries, as well as Schindler and his pupil Franz Wüllner, are further sources for consideration.
11 [1954] 60

ZUR SATZTECHNIK IN BS VIERTE SINFONIE. Arnold Feil.   (J)
   A detailed analysis of the first movement of Op. 60.   16 [1959] 391

BEETHOVENS KONVERSATIONSHEFTE.   (A)
  Prepublication announcement of Nohl's edition of the conversation books.
                                            1 Part 1 [1931] 17

EIN KONVERSATIONSHEFT BEETHOVENS AUS DEM JAHRE 1827 (4. BIS 5. FEBRUAR).   (B)
  A detailed account of two days of Beethoven's last illness, based on an extensive or complete transcription of the
  seven page conversation book No. 133.   2 Part 1 [1933] 16

DER ELFJÄHRIGE FRANZ LISZT UND BEETHOVEN.   Walther Nohl.   (C)
  Entries in the conversation book in use about April 12th 1823 indicate unequivocally that Beethoven took an unfriendly
  attitude towards young Liszt in conversation with Schindler; that he did not accede to Liszt's request for a theme upon
  which to improvise at the concert; and that he did not attend the concert. The story told by Liszt sixty years later
  that he was taken by his teacher Czerny to Beethoven's quarters and played for him there, and that after the concert
  Beethoven kissed him on the brow certainly did not take place in April 1823.
                                            3 Part 1 [1934] 20

DAS TYPISCHE AN BEETHOVENS WERKE.   Ernst Bücken.   (D)
  Excerpt from the author's 'Beethoven.'   4 [1935] 1

BEETHOVENS "KONVERSATIONSHEFTE."   (E)
  Popular explanation by the publishers of Nohl's edition of the conversation books.
                                                     4 [1935] 2

WIE ICH DIE "KONVERSATIONSHEFTE" KENNEN LERNTE.   Walther Nohl.   (F)
  Popular.   4 [1935] 6

GOETHE IM SPIEGEL VON BEETHOVENS "KONVERSATIONSHEFTE."   (G)
  Reference to Goethe of widely varying kinds as they appear in the conversation books.
                                                     4 [1935] 12

BEETHOVENS BEZIEHUNG ZU GEORG FRIEDERICH HANDEL UND JOHANN SEBASTIAN BACH.   (H)
  References to Handel and Bach of widely varying kinds as they appear in the conversation books.
                                                     4 [1935] 20

SCHUBERT AND BEETHOVEN.   Walther Vetter.   (I)
  General.   4 [1935] 26

AUS BEETHOVENS KONVERSATIONSHEFTE.   Walther Nohl.   (J)
  Quotations of Gerhard von Breuning's side of conversations from March or April 1826 to the end.
                                                     4 [1935] 66

                                       AUFTAKT

BEETHOVENS ZWEITE WIENER REISE.   Johannes Heinrich Braach.   (K)
  Fiction.   1 [1921] 92

DAS ETHOS IN DER MUSIK BEETHOVENS.   Robert Lach.   3 [1921] 39   (L)

BEETHOVENIANA.   Max Unger.   (M)
  An unknown letter from Beethoven to Dr. Johann Kanka in Prague (Ein unbekannter Brief Beethovens an Dr. Johann
  Kanka in Prag). Letter of May 1st (1816): "Wenn ich ihnen nicht viel schreibe oder gar nicht . . ." later published
  in 'Neue Musik Zeitung' 44 [1923] 149, concerned chiefly with the annuity due from Prince Kynsky's estate.
                                            3 [1923] 43

EINE GLOSSE ZU BEETHOVENS RECHTSCHREIBUNG.   (N)
  A passage quoted from Stephan von Breuning's 'Aus dem Schwarzspanierhaus' [1874] 98 in which Beethoven
  is described as bursting out in rage at the spelling "Hayden" used by Heller (Stephan's teacher). Note that
  Beethoven himself almost invariably used the spelling "Haidn," and that in writing his own name as late as
  his fiftieth year used the spelling "Beethowen" when using German script. In Latin script, however, his

spelling of his own name was invariably with v, not with w, indicating an idiosyncracy in signature such as
is not unique with Beethoven. He spelled "Klavier" always with a w, and "Wien" almost always with a v.

3 [1923] 45

DIE "LEIPSIGER OCHSEN." (A)

In Beethoven's letter of early 1801 to Hoffmeister & Kühnel (KS I 40) as first published in 'Neue Zeitschrift
für Musik' 6 [1837] 75, reference appears to the "Leipziger O. . ." which Schumann interpreted as meaning
"Leipzig oxen" in reference to the critics who had spoken unfavorably of Beethoven. Study of this manuscript
in the light of present-day familiarity with Beethoven's script leads to the alternative reading "Leipziger R. . ."
which undoubtedly means "Leipzig reviewers (Rezensenten)." KS I 40 suggests "Leipziger Rindfleische"
(blockheads). See also KS I 37, third line from bottom.   3 [1923] 46

DIE FRÜHESTE BEETHOVEN-RELIQUIE. (B)

The earliest of all Beethoven relics, earlier even than his baptismal certificate, is his baptismal cap, still in the
possession of the Wegeler family in Coblenz. In the same collection is the 'Bohemian glass' referred to in Beethoven's letter of September 29th 1816 to Wegeler (KS I 420), which he had acquired in Teplitz in 1811 or 1812.

3 [1923] 47

BEETHOVENS TOD.   Robert Haas. (C)

Factual details about Beethoven's death and funeral are found in letters from Streicher and Stumpff (see also
'Harmonicon' 5 [1827] 84).   3 [1923] 48

ZUM KAPITEL "BEETHOVEN UND PRAG."   Max Unger. (D)

Improved transcription of letter of December 18th 1813 to Dr. (Josef) von Reger (in KS I 302 marked as to a Dr. von
Beyer). Herr von Kraus (not Kranj as in KFr II 159) and Gloschek (not Koschak) are not identified, but were probably
acquaintances in Prague. The "ff" given in Kalischer (II 165) and the "etc." by Frimmel (KFr II 158) after the first
appearance of the word Wolf (KS omits both), is really A (probably for Adlersburg).

5 [1925] 80

DIE RASSE BEETHOVENS.   Fritz Paudler. (E)

An anthropological study. Beethoven's bodily proportions were clearly those typical of the Cro-Magnon race. (This
question is discussed at length by Richard Eichenauer in 'Musik und Rasse' 2nd ed., 1937 pp. 226-32.)

7 [1927] 57

BEETHOVEN UND JOHANN ANDREAS STREICHER (ZWEI UNBEKANNTE BRIEFE).   Max Unger. (F)

Letters given in Sonneck's 'Beethoven Letters in America' pp. 182 ff.

7 [1927] 61

SELTSAME GESCHICHTE EINES BEETHOVENTHEMAS.   Theodor Veidl. (G)

The principal theme of the Finale of the Eighth Symphony apparently had its origin in a canon (now lost) "Kommt zu
Beeneke" written by Beethoven in his Bonn days in honor of a tavern which he frequented.

7 [1927] 64

BEETHOVEN UND DIE BÖHMEN.   Erich Steinhard. (H)

A list of some fifty of Beethoven's friends and acquaintances who were from Bohemia or Moravia.

7 [1927] 65

OBDUKTIONSBERICHT ÜBER DEN LEICHNAM BEETHOVENS.   Joh. Wagner. (I)

Reprint of the original report of autopsy.   7 [1927] 72

BEETHOVEN UND DIE GESTALT.   Adolf Weissmann. (J)

Book review.   7 [1927] 66

AUS BEETHOVENS WIRTSCHAFTSBUCH. (K)

Excerpts showing Beethoven's problems in keeping servants.   7 [1927] 67

UNBEKANNTE BEETHOVEN-BRIEFE.   Max Unger. (L)

Two letters to Zmeskall, without date but certainly in early Vienna years (both published in 'Musikalische
Wochenblatt' 5 [1874] 390): "Wir möchten gerne . . ." and "Wir haben gehört . . ."

First publication of letter to Haslinger or Steiner (probably from 1822): "Nach reiflicher Übelebung übergeben
wir Euch . . ."   8 [1928] 122

DIE FAMILIE RASUMOWSKY.   Erwin Walter.   (A)
  The father Kyrill Grigorjewitsch and the uncle Alexei Grigorjewitsch of Beethoven's patron Andreas Kyrillowitsch
  Rasumovsky bear a significant relationship to music.   10 [1930] 12

EIN PRAGER BEETHOVEN-DRUCK.   Otto Erich Deutsch.   (B)
  The first edition of the Variations for Four Hands on 'Ich denke dein' (published in 1805) refers to them as composed
  in 1800, but in 1896 Max Friedländer described an edition with the following title:

    "Musikalisches Freundschafts-Opfer dargebracht den hochgeborenen Comtessen von Brunswick im Jahre
    1799 von L. van Beethoven.   Andantino canto und Variationen für das Piano-Forte zu vier Händen.
    Zum erstenmal gedruckt.   Herausgegeben von Joh. Stika, Prag, Verlag von P. Bohmann's Erben."

  The book which Friedländer had has since disappeared, and it is not certain that the words "Zum erstenmal gedruckt"
  appeared. Friedländer described the edition as having the Theme and the Variations 5 and 6 identical with the
  generally known version. The publisher Johann Adalbert Stika, known to have been an organist in Prague at the time
  in question, probably issued this edition completely without Beethoven's knowledge.
                                                                          11 [1931] 45

EIN BEETHOVEN-FUND? Wilhelm Mayer.   (C)
  A score of the Choral Fantasy has been found which is largely but not entirely in Beethoven's hand.
                                                                          15 [1935] 28

SPÄTSTIL BEETHOVENS.   Theodor Wiesengrund-Adorno.   (D)
  "In the history of Art, late works are catastrophes."   17 [1937] 65

BEETHOVENS HUMOR IN SEINEN NOTENHANDSCHRIFTEN.   Georg Kinsky.   (E)
  Sundry examples are given of Beethoven's humor as it appeared in notations in scores and elsewhere.
                                                                          18 [1938] 36

                                        DER BÄR

A BEETHOVEN LETTER.   (F)
  Facsimile of letter (date here assigned April 22nd 1801; date assigned in KS I 57 April 22nd 1802) to Breitkopf &
  Härtel.   [1924] 56

GOETHE UND BEETHOVEN.   Theodor von Frimmel.   (G)
  A revision and correction of the author's 'Beethoven und Goethe' (1883) and 'Zwei ungedruckte Briefe' ('Neue
  Beethoveniana' [1890] pp. 335 ff). The attitude of Goethe towards Beethoven the man and towards Beethoven's
  music is discussed, and a brief summary is given of Beethoven's use of Goethe's poems as inspirations for compositions, the earliest instance probably being the aria for bass 'Mit Mädeln sich vertragen' (GA 25/269 No. 2),
  composed about 1790.   [1925] 109

BEETHOVEN UND DAS HAUS BREITKOPF & HÄRTEL.   Wilhelm Hitzig.   (H)
  The advent of Gottfried Christoph Härtel (1763-1827) into the firm (of B. C. Breitkopf und Sohn) in 1795 was of
  the first importance in the history of the firm, of music publishing, and of music as a whole. Two years after his
  entry into the business he founded the 'Allgemeine Musikalische Zeitung' (first issue on October 3rd 1798), and soon
  thereafter brought in Friedrich Rochlitz as editor.

  At the beginning of the nineteenth century the life of a composer and the business of a music publisher alike were
  completely different from what we know now. The composer was a musical artisan -- Court Musician, organist or
  the like -- whose compositions, written as a part of his job, were circulated (if at all) only in manuscript copies
  within a restricted area. The commercial introduction of printing music from type by Johann Gottlob Immanuel
  Breitkopf in 1750 made practicable the publication of musical works for sale by subscription. It was Beethoven,
  however, who completed the revolution: "he was the first great composer to devote his life exclusively to composition, made possible by the sale of his works through commercial channels." In the eighteenth century the
  composer approached the publisher as a supplicant: Beethoven and his successors dealt with him as an equal. The
  greatest further difficulty to be overcome, one which plagued Beethoven and his publishers throughout his lifetime,
  was the lack of effective copyright laws or of the composer's or the publisher's property rights in compositions.

The issuance of the C major Quintet Op. 29 by B&H in December 1801 was the first publication of a work by Beethoven (since his childhood) by other than a Vienna publisher. In the next ten years this house brought out not less than 25 of Beethoven's important works.

As the noteworthy correspondence between the composer and Härtel shows, Beethoven was not easy for a publisher to deal with. Aside from his position as a composer of music much in demand, his irascibility and complete blindness in matters of mathematics made dealings through an intermediary like his brother Karl the simplest procedure, though years of association built up in Beethoven a friendship for and a confidence in Härtel such as he never had again in any other publisher. The correspondence files of the company include 59 letters from Beethoven, 19 from his brother Karl, 19 from the firm to Ludwig and 3 to Karl (note that these 22 letters from the firm are given in 'Monatshefte für Musikgeschichte' 9 [1927] 321). Beethoven and Härtel met only once: on the occasion of Härtel's visit to Vienna on September 14th 1808.

From the spring of 1809, after his brother Karl had dropped out of the picture, until the fall of 1812, Georg August Griesinger, then on the staff of the Saxonian ambassador in Vienna, represented the firm in its dealings with Beethoven. In 1822, after composer and publisher had been estranged for seven years, Griesinger attempted in vain to bring them together again. (Regarding Griesinger's place in the relationship between Beethoven and B&H, see pp. 23 ff infra.)

During Beethoven's lifetime, "complete editions" such as B&H had issued of the works of Haydn, Mozart, Clementi, etc. were actually far from complete, but were little more than a collection of piano works with a few concertos and orchestral scores. No attempt at critical revision was made, and generally speaking the only works included were those already the property of the publisher. For many reasons (not the least, the economic considerations involved) the preparation of a complete edition of Beethoven's works during his lifetime -- a project very close to his heart -- was not practicable. It may well have been that Beethoven's break with B&H after 1815 and his subsequent shifting from publisher to publisher was in no small measure a pursuit of this will-o'-the-wisp. A further reason, no doubt, was the willingness of other publishers to offer more for new works as strengtheners of their catalogs than B&H could afford to pay, for the sake of having the name of the most popular composer of the day on their lists.

A facsimile is given of the last paragraph of Beethoven's letter of November 18th 1806 to Härtel (KS I 108).
[1927] 1

AUS DEN BRIEFEN GRIESINGERS AN BREITKOPF & HÄRTEL ENTNOMMENE NOTIZEN ÜBER BEETHOVEN.   (A)
Wilhelm Hitzig.

Georg August Griesinger was in Vienna during the years following 1799 in various capacities of increasing responsibility in the Saxonian embassy. A friend of Gottfried Christoph Härtel, he was from the first of increasing importance to the publishing firm in its dealings with Haydn. In a letter to Härtel dated December 5th 1802 (given in full in TD II 614), his brother Karl suggests that "Count Schönfeld's steward" be sent to Beethoven to calm him down after a rough letter in connection with the Artaria edition of Op. 29.

Some twenty letters from Griesinger to Härtel are excerpted or summarized as they bear upon Beethoven:

March 26th 1800.   Griesinger speaks highly of Stiebelt's playing, but says that in slow passages Beethoven far surpasses him.

April 3rd 1802.   "Letter writing and figuring are obnoxious to the composer Beethoven. He wants to break with his present publisher: up to now he has not received more than 31 ducats for a piano sonata, yet his piano pieces are better than Haydn's. His brother, who looks after his business affairs, will not let him sign a contract for a period of years, since each year his work will increase in value."

April 7th 1802.   "Haydn has told Beethoven of your fair and adequate prices. In the future Beethoven will write less for piano and more for several voices."

November 27th 1802.   "Beethoven's health is not as good as it is supposed to be. He is at present suffering from a stoppage of the bowels."

December 4th 1802.   Griesinger states that Brother Karl had asked him to soothe Beethoven's wounded sensibilities after a strong letter from Härtel regarding the Artaria-Op. 29 affair.

December 8th 1802.   Griesinger states Beethoven's side of the story regarding the Artaria issue of Op. 29, and says that he has so far mollified Beethoven that the Variations Opp. 34 and 35 will be offered to B&H. (They were received by B&H on December 26th, together with a letter given in KS I 68.)

AUS DEN BRIEFEN GRIESINGERS, etc., (Continued)

December 18th 1802.   Beethoven is still most upset about the trouble over the Quintet; "he solemnly declares that in the future no such difficulty will arise again."

March 16th 1803.   "Beethoven and Abt Vogler are each composing an opera for the Theater an der Wien.   At a benefit performance for Beethoven during Holy Week at the Theater a cantata by him will be given."   This refers to the first performance of Christus am Oelberge Op. 85 on April 5th 1803.

September 17th 1803.   "Beethoven has recently undertaken to make arrangements of Scottish songs, I do not know for whom."   (Note that the first collection of these settings was published by Thomson only in 1814.)

November 12th 1803.   Griesinger suggests that the libretto of 'Polyhymnia' by Christian Schreiber, considered by Haydn but apparently laid aside, be offered to Beethoven, who apparently was not too well satisfied with the Shikaneder libretto ('Vestas Feuer') on which he was then working, or with the book 'Der Weg durchs Leben' which had been submitted to him by Meissner of Prague.

December 7th 1803.   "I asked Beethoven and his brother again why they demanded such exorbitant prices from you. They replied that they asked no more than other publishers were paying them."

January 4th 1804.   "Beethoven's opinion of Polyhymnia is as follows: the book is well written but there is not enough action in it." He went on to say that it was so similar to 'The Creation' that any composer taking it up would put himself in disadvantageous competition with Haydn.   "Dramatic oratorios such as Handel wrote are more suitable for musical composition." Haydn did not agree with Beethoven's criticism that the text was too lacking in action: "An oratorio is in question, not an opera."

November 24th 1804.   This letter deals with the unadjustable cause of friction between the publisher and the composer. The former must safeguard his property rights in any work which he buys and publishes; the latter receives a large share of his income from patrons to whom he gives exclusive rights for a period of months, during which time copies may fall into the hands of pirating publishers. This impasse could be solved only by an equitable copyright law.

December 29th 1804.   "Ludwig van Beethoven is a man without dishonesty or deceit. . . . His brother is however less to be trusted, and I rather believe that he is getting a little something on the side that Ludwig B. probably knows nothing about."

January 26th 1805.   When Griesinger congratulated Beethoven on the success which the Eroica had received, the composer replied: "Herr Härtel will get that one." The Eroica had already been sent to Breitkopf & Härtel on January 16th 1805 (KS I 93) but after failure to agree on honorarium it was returned on June 21st, and was published by the Kunst und Industrie-Comptoir in Vienna.

February 13th 1805.   Performances of the Eroica at Prince Lobkowitz's at the home of "an active musical amateur named Wirth" received "unusual acclaim . . . a work of genius . . . greater than Haydn and Mozart . . . the symphony has been brought to new heights."

April 2nd 1806.   The performance of Fidelio in its second version "caused a furor, and brought the composer the most enthusiastic and well-deserved reception."

June 20th 1810.   Various matters: Beethoven's project of a trip to England; the favorable reception accorded to the Egmont music; Beethoven's lessons in composition to the Archduke Rudolph; favorable reception by Thomson of the Scottish songs.

April 3rd 1819.   "Beethoven's deafness is steadily increasing; it is true that a little while ago he was run over, but was not hurt much."

[1927] 23

(See also 'Neues Beethoven-Jahrbuch' 3 [1927] 49)

WALDMÜLLERS BEETHOVENBILD.   Wilhelm Lütge.   (A)

A letter to Härtel from the eminent portrait painter Ferdinand Georg Waldmüller (1793-1865) dated April 18th 1823 opens: "I shall be delighted to conform to your wish that I prepare a portrait of Herr v. Beethoven." Another letter dated May 3rd states that the painting is half done and that the painter "will complete the portrait in short order, especially since Herr v. Beethoven is going to the country soon." This would seem to disprove the contention in 'Allgemeine Musikalische Zeitung' 37 [1835] 20 that Beethoven had never sat for Waldmüller, though this anonymous writer speaks highly of the fidelity of the portrait. Schindler, on the other hand says that Waldmüller had one sitting with Beethoven (which seems very probable), but he refers to the painting as a "caricature" ('Allgemeine Musikalische Zeitung' 37 [1835] 119). One known copy of this portrait may have been made by Waldmüller himself. At Richard Wagner's request, a copy of this portrait was made for him in the spring of 1869 by Robert Krausse. The author's laudatory review of Waldmüller's accomplishments terms him "one of the creators of modern portrait painting."

[1927] 35

BRIEFE AUS BEETHOVENS FREUNDENKREIS. EIN BRIEF FRIEDRICH AUGUST KANNES. Wilhelm Hitzig.   (A)

Kanne (1778-1833) is described as a man of great talent (or indeed of genius) as a poet, musician and musical journalist who completely squandered his gifts by drunkenness and instability. As editor of the 'Wiener Allgemeine Musikalische Zeitung' from 1820 to 1824 he wrote much about Beethoven, and in at least one instance was asked by the composer to prepare an opera text for him (on the subject of Goethe's 'Claudine') (see TD IV 5 and TK III 117). A letter from Beethoven to Schindler (probably from the first quarter of 1823) (KS II 242 No. 890) comments very favorably on a libretto from Kanne. A lengthy letter from Kanne to Härtel, dated July 15th 1819, is given, containing references to sundry of Beethoven's associates (e.g., Archduke Rudolph, Lobkowitz, Rochlitz) but none to Beethoven.   [1927] 42

BRIEFE AUS BEETHOVENS FREUNDENKREIS. ANDREAS UND NANNETTE STREICHER. Wilhelm Lütge.   (B)

This article is primarily a biographical sketch of Johann Andreas and Anna Maria (Stein) Streicher (the author remarks specifically that her nickname should be spelled Nannette, not Nanette) and a rather extended discussion of the policies which Streicher followed over a period of years in the design and manufacture of his pianos. Beethoven's close association with Streicher dated from 1798, though the two men may have met as early as 1787 at the time of Beethoven's first visit to Vienna (in Augsburg or in Mannheim). Excerpts are given from two letters expressing his praise of Beethoven's sense of honor, written to Härtel by Streicher at the time of the unpleasantness regarding the pirated edition of Op. 29. In April 1803, after the first performance of 'Christus am Oelberge,' Streicher wrote that this work substantiated his "long felt opinion that Beethoven will work as great a revolution in music as did Mozart. He is taking mighty strides towards this goal." As early as 1803 Streicher built pianos for Härtel with range up to six octaves. It was Streicher who prevailed upon Beethoven to allow Franz Klein to make a life mask. For years, especially between 1812 and 1819, Beethoven constantly turned to Nannette on matters of prosaic household detail, as shown in the sixty of his letters to her which are known. It was upon her urging that he bought the bank shares which formed the major part of his bequest to his nephew Karl. Two letters which Streicher wrote in the spring of 1801 to Rochlitz regarding the establishment of a fund for Regina Susanne Bach are quoted.

[1927] 53

BRIEFE AUS BEETHOVENS FREUNDENKREIS. GRÄFIN ERDÖDY UND J. X. BRAUCHLE. Günther Haupt.   (C)

It is not known whether the Count Erdödy referred to in TD I 172 as one of Beethoven's early friends and patrons was Count Peter Erdödy, husband of the Countess Marie, or some other member of the family, possibly the "Count F. d'Erdödy" mentioned in TD II 394. Countess Anna Marie Erdödy (née Countess Niczky) was born in 1779, and married Count Peter Erdödy in 1796. From the time of her first confinement to her death her health was very delicate, and for much of the time she was bedridden. Beethoven's acquaintance with her dates from 1803 (possibly, as Schindler says, from 1801), and by 1808 the friendship was so close that Beethoven had a room in the Erdödy house. The next year a break occurred in their relations, but it was soon healed, as evidenced by the dedication to the Countess in March 1809 of the two Trios Op. 70 (KS I 153) and by the active support which she gave about the same time to the setting up of the annuity whereby Beethoven was prevailed upon to refuse the offer from Cassel (TK II 136).

Letters to Härtel of January 4th 1812 from the Countess and of January 10th from Josef Xaver Brauchle (the Countess' man of business and tutor to her children) commended to the publisher a quartet by the latter which was accepted and published in July of that year. The correspondence of the year 1815 between Beethoven and the Countess indicates that during this year the intimacy reached its height. After a summer at Jedlersee the Countess and her children, with Brauchle, Linke the 'cellist and Sperl (major-domo), left in October for their estate in Croatia. In the following spring the Countess' only son August died suddenly (see Beethoven's letter of May 15th 1816, KS I 408) while the Countess was in Padua. TK II 83 says that about 1820 the Countess was banished for life beyond the limits of the

BRIEFE AUS BEETHOVENS FREUNDENKREIS, etc., (Continued)

Austrian Empire -- "un-happily, for reasons that cannot be impugned. It is a sad and revolting story, over which a veil may be drawn . . . It is very possible that Beethoven's heart was never wrung by a knowledge of the particulars." According to the author, TK was exactly 100 percent wrong in these statements: Neither biographical dictionaries of the period nor official records give any indication that the Countess was banished; charges (the police investigation of which extended from April 1820 to August 1821) that the Countess and Brauchle had brutally mistreated the 19-year-old daughter Marie ("Mimi") and that Brauchle had been responsible for the death of the son August were found to be wholly without foundation: Mimi's love and respect for her mother were displayed in many letters during the period of the investigation, and Brauchle's loyalty and honor were commended in the highest terms; and entries in the conversation books show that Beethoven was aware of the Countess' difficulties. The charges apparently were made out of spite by the Countess' sister-in-law, the widow of Count Sigismund Erdödy, who wanted to secure Mimi for her son and Brauchle for herself. The Countess lived in Munich from 1824 until her death in March 1837. Brauchle continued to attend her, and presumably died in Munich at some unknown time after 1830. The six of Brauchle's ten known published compositions which are still extant are discussed in great detail as being the work of a dilettante much under the influence of Beethoven.

[1927] 70

BRIEFE AUS BEETHOVENS FREUNDENKREIS: IV. ANTON REICHA. Wilhelm Lütge.   (A)

Anton Reicha, born in Klattau, Bohemia in 1770, came to Bonn in 1785 when his uncle Joseph became Kapellmeister of the Electoral Court. Anton entered the orchestra as a flutist and became very intimate with Beethoven, who was then in the orchestra as violist. The two friends both studied with Neefe (to their great benefit) and, together with Carl Kügelgen, matriculated as "studiosi philosophiae" at the University of Bonn on May 14th 1789. How much Beethoven profited by these studies is an open question, but Reicha, who excelled in mathematics, later "used to point out to his students how valuable the philosophical and mathematical studies had been to him, especially in the understanding of the structure and logic of musical forms."

Leaving Bonn in 1794, Reicha went to Hamburg and then to Paris; his ambitions for performance of his first opera 'Oubualdi' were thwarted, but two of his symphonies were well received. Haydn helped him while he was in Vienna in 1802-08, and he gained favor with the Empress Maria Theresa and with Prince Louis Ferdinand of Prussia. He and Beethoven resumed their close friendship, and there can be no doubt that his operatic experience was of help to Beethoven in Fidelio. Between the autumn of 1803 and the spring of 1805, Breitkopf & Härtel issued 18 compositions (mostly chamber works) which however were coolly received. A letter is quoted in which Reicha states in extenso his low opinion of musical taste in Vienna. In 1808 he settled in Paris, where he attained success and position as a teacher of theory and counterpoint (his pupils including Berlioz, Liszt and Franck); his texts in these fields became standard, and were translated into German by no less a musician than Karl Czerny. His letters to Härtel during his years in Paris show an enthusiasm for the state of musical appreciation in that city which is quite in conflict with the low opinions held by his contemporaries. As a composer he was no more successful in Paris than he had been elsewhere, though his quintets for wind instruments aroused transitory interest. "Reicha's compositions are not creations in our sense but musical experiments, bloodless, full spirited without spiritual depth, artistic without artistry." He gave up composing ten years before his death in 1836, and during these last ten years not a single one of his works was heard in the concert halls. Historically, however, his compositions are of interest as an unsuccessful attempt to combine the method and spirit of Bach with the freedom of tone relations and content of the newly burgeoning Romanticism. His '36 Fugues après un nouveau systeme,' in which the answer may be on any step in the scale instead of being limited to the dominant, is a case in point. The author quotes Beethoven in a letter of December (not October) 18th 1802 to Breitkopf & Härtel, that "such a modern fugue is no longer a fugue," though this reference was probably not to Reicha's work.

[1927] 100

BRIEFE AUS BEETHOVENS FREUNDENKREIS: V. ANTON SCHINDLER. Wilhelm Lütge.   (B)

A biographical sketch of Schindler is given, pointing out that while in himself he was a very ordinary person, his entire life was consecreated to serving Beethoven and Beethoven's memory. "No other friend of Beethoven can be thanked for as much authentic information of Beethoven's life as can Anton Schindler." Two letters from Schindler to Breitkopf & Härtel (1841-42) regarding three of the numbers excised in the revision of Fidelio (TK II 54) are given. On December 25th 1841 Schindler wrote that he has manuscripts of 35 settings of National songs which had never been published. The matter was not carried further, and it is not known what the manuscripts contained. A letter of January 2nd 1845 suggests that the unsatisfactory German text of the C

major Mass Op. 86 (by an unknown poet) be replaced in a new edition of the Mass with a much more satisfactory
text by Scholz. This was not done, though Scholz's text was later published separately.

[1927] 110

BRIEFE AUS BEETHOVENS FREUNDENKREIS: VI. JOHANN NEPOMUK MÄLZELS BRIEFE AN BREITKOPF & HÄRTEL.   (A)
    Günther Haupt.

Mälzel's life and his relations with Beethoven are briefly sketched. The archives of Breitkopf & Härtel contain 24
letters from Mälzel from the years 1816-21, most of which are here summarized or given in full. Mäzel's claim
to be the inventor of the metronome is open to grave question: the idea of a movable lead weight on a pendulum
(the basic novelty of the metronome) was conceived by a mechanic by the name of Winkel with whom Mälzel was
associated in 1812. Mälzel's contribution was the graduated scale and his genius for publicity and merchandising.
Schindler was correct in his statement that Mälzel put out two distinct models differing in size, shape and price.
"Schindler's contention that the two metronomes indicated a different time at the same scale setting is false, since
Mälzel's basis was the same regardless of the size of the metronome: the figures on the scale represented the number
of strokes per minute. The principal difference between the two models was that the smaller one beat time but did
not give an audible signal."   [1927] 122

BEETHOVENS LEONOREN OUVERTÜRE Nr. 2. Wilhelm Lütge.   (B)

What is now known as the Leonora Overture No. 2 was used at the first (1805) performance of the opera. The Leonora
Overture No. 3 was written for the second (1806) version; as far as is known, the Leonora Overture No. 2 received during Beethoven's lifetime only one performance except at the premiere of the opera: at a concert in the Augarten in
1806. In 1843 the Leonora Overture No. 2 was published by Breitkopf & Härtel from an incomplete manuscript which
had belonged to Schindler, with restoration of missing material by Mendelssohn in accordance with Beethoven's desires as communicated by Schindler. Ten years later Jahn published a materially different version of this same Overture from a manuscript in the possession of Artaria, the Jahn version being the one adopted in the GA. The differences
between the two versions are stated in detail. The author presents evidence to show with reasonable certainty that
the Mendelssohn version rather than the Jahn-GA version represents Beethoven's final ideas; in particular, the evidence
seems conclusive that the trumpet call should not be repeated (as it is in the Leonora Overture No. 3 and in Jahn's
version of the Second Overture). (See also 'Zeitschrift für Musikwissenschaft' 9 [1927] 235, 349, 368.)

[1927] 146

ZU DER ERSTVERÖFFENTLICHUNG DES BEETHOVENSCHEN HOCHZEITSLIED FÜR GIANNATASIO DEL RIO.   (C)
    Wilhelm Hitzig.

First publication in its original form (notes and text) of epithalamium written by Beethoven on January 14th 1819
to celebrate the wedding of Nanni Giannatasio on February 6th of that year. A modified version with new text had
previously been published in England by Ewer & Co. (See also 'Zeitschrift für Musikwissenschaft' 7 [1924] 164.)

[1927] 157

BERICHT ÜBER EIN NEU AUFGEFUNDENES MANUSKRIPT, ENTHALTEND 24 LIEDER VON BEETHOVEN.   (D)
    Wilhelm Lütge.

GA Ser. 24 includes 132 national airs arranged by Beethoven with accompaniment for violin, 'cello and piano; in
addition, TV pp. 110-13 lists 32 others. A manuscript, originally owned by Thomson, has come to Breitkopf &
Härtel which includes GA 24/259 No. 12, fourteen of the songs listed in TV, and nine hitherto unknown settings.
Thus a total of 155 arrangements of national airs by Beethoven are known in publishable form; it is probable that
Beethoven made not far from 200 such arrangements. (See also 'Neues Beethoven-Jahrbuch' 7 [1937] 119.)

[1927] 159

DER BESUCH DES HOFRATS FRIEDRICH ROCHLITZ BEI LUDWIG VAN BEETHOVEN IN WIEN. Friedrich Rochlitz.   (E)
    Extract from the author's 'Für Freunde der Tonkunst,' most of which is given in TD IV 282-89. Note that the year of
    this visit was 1822, not 1824.   [1927] 166

NEKROLOG. Friedrich Rochlitz.   (F)
    Extract from 'Allgemeine Musikalische Zeitung' 29 [1827] 227. Note statement: "He had attained his fifty-fifth
    year," based on the assumption then accepted that Beethoven was born in 1772.

[1927] 174

GOTTFRIED VAN SWIETEN.   Reinhold Bernhardt.   (A)
   Beethoven's close acquaintance with van Swieten in his first Vienna years led to his deep appreciation of the works
of Handel (for which van Swieten had an insatiable interest) and of the writings of Homer and Shakespeare that
Beethoven found in van Swieten's library.   The friendship became progressively less intimate after 1795 as Beethoven's
more personal style developed.   [1929/30] 153

DAS SCHICKSAL DEN FAMILIE JOHANN SEBASTIAN BACHS.   Reinhold Bernhardt.   (B)
   This article includes a summary of the good intentions expressed by Beethoven at the time that Bach's youngest
daughter Regina Susanna was found by Rochlitz to be destitute.   [1929/30] 167

BAYREUTHER BLÄTTER

AUCH EINE STIMME AUS DER VERGANGENHEIT.   Kretzer.   (C)
   Opinions about Beethoven and remarks attributed to him by Bettina Brentano should be given great weight.
2 [1879] 149

ÜBER BEETHOVENS X. SYMPHONIE.   Ludwig Nohl.   (D)
   The belief that a Tenth Symphony exists or ought to exist was given foundation by the statement in Beethoven's
letter of March 18th 1827 to Moscheles (KS II 472): "A whole sketched symphony lies in my desk," and pairing of
the first eight symphonies indicates that a companion to the Ninth would in the normal course of events probably
have been written.   Sketches marked in one way or another to indicate that they were for a new symphony exist in
the sketch books in considerable number, and various remarks in Beethoven's sketch books, letters and conversations
with friends are cited to indicate that a Tenth Symphony was planned.   There is however no evidence that work on
it had progressed to the point where we can do more than guess at its form or content.
7 [1884] 220

EIN UNGEDRUCKTER SCHLUSS DES "BEETHOVEN" VON RICHARD WAGNER.   H. v. Wolzogen.   (E)
   A new closing section of some 700 words is given from documents in the Wagner estate.
29 [1906] 1

BISMARCK - BEETHOVEN.   Richard Sternfeld.   (F)
   An obscure passage in a letter by Bismarck explains itself as a reference to two Beethoven piano sonatas.
42 [1919] 306

ZUM 150. GEBURTSTAGE LUDWIG VAN BEETHOVEN.   Hermann Seeliger.   (G)
   Essay.   43 [1920] 160

BEETHOVEN.   Karl Grunsky.   (H)
   Centennial essay.   50 [1927] 45

BEETHOVENS 9. SYMPHONIE ALS GEISTESERLEBNIS.   Robert Bosshart.   (I)
   An extended metaphysical interpretation.   51 [1928] 73

ELISABETH AND LEONORA.   Walter Taube.   (J)
   In these two operas based on redeeming love, the happy ending of Fidelio is dramatically the sharpest point of
differentiation.   57 [1934] 182

BEETHOVEN UND GOETHE ALS TROSTSPENDER -- EINE VERGLEICHENDE BETRACHTUNG.   Ernst Kroeger.   (K)
60 [1937] 17

All articles are by the Editor, Dr. Theodor von Frimmel, unless otherwise stated.   (A)

Volume	Number	Date	Pages
1	1	Jan 1911	1- 32
	2	July 1911	33- 68
	3	Mar 1912	69-100
	4	Feb 1913	101-132
2	5	Mar 1915	1- 38
	6-7	Aug 1916	39-114
	8	Oct 1918	115-166
3	9	Aug 1923	1- 36
	10	Jan 1925	37- 60

DREI BRIEFE BEETHOVENS AN JOSEF VON SONNLEITHNER. Rudolf Kotula.   (B)
   Contents include: Letter without date (probably from spring or summer 1804) requesting that Sonnleithner expedite
   work on the book of 'Fidelio,' and commenting on Beethoven's troubles in his lodgings; brief note without date
   (probably from late autumn 1805) requesting certain verses and saying that it was Beethoven's definite plan to write
   the overture only during the rehearsal period; and letter without date (probably from early March 1806) regarding the
   publication of the libretto of 'Fidelio.' (See also 1 [1913] 116)   1 [1911] 3

EIN BRIEF BEETHOVENS AN KOTZEBUE. Albert Leitzmann.   (C)
   The complete version of the letter of January 28th 1812 to Augustus von Kotzebue, of which a portion is given in
   KS I 239. The second paragraph (hitherto missing) assures the poet that Prince Lobkowitz will pay a suitable hono-
   rarium for the desired libretto.   1 [1911] 11

A HITHERTO UNKNOWN NOTE OF BEETHOVEN. P. Dehne.   (D)
   A note, without date or name of addressee but presumably from about 1817, suggesting the time of a meeting.
                                   1 [1911] 12

[General comments on Beethoven's correspondence with Karl Bernard]   (E)
                                   1 [1911] 12

[Letter of July 19th 1819 to Franz Xaver Piuk regarding Nephew Karl]   (F)
                                   1 [1911] 14

[Note to Zmeskall]   (G)
   Received October 25th 1804 requesting the correct spelling of the names Brunswick and Deym presumably in connection with the dedication of the song and variations 'Ich denke dein' (NV p. 146).
                                   1 [1911] 18

[Various receipts and other Beethoven autographs]   (H)
                                   1 [1911] 21

[Letter presumably from Beethoven to Theresa von Brunswick]   (I)
   Theresa copied it in a letter of February 2nd 1811 to her sister.   1 [1911] 24

BEMERKUNGEN ZUR SONATE PATHÉTIQUE.   (J)
   The repeat in the first movement. The original text and other editions of this sonata do not give any clear indication
   of whether or not the reprise at the end of the allegro exposition goes back to include the grave in the repetition. The
   autograph of this sonata is lost, but the earliest editions (first edition by Hoffmeister (in spite of statement in NV),
   edition by Peters from the Hoffmeister plates) show repeat marks at the double bar following the grave. The fact
   that the grave does not appear at the beginning of the recapitulation is further evidence that in accordance with the
   almost invariable tradition of the period the grave is to be considered a separate section and not repeated.

   Count Leo N. Tolstoi and the Pathétique (p. 36). Quotations are given from Tolstoi's autobiography showing that in
   his boyhood the Pathétique had a strong effect on him. Its relationship to Mozart (p. 39). In the Pathétique the
   author finds reminiscences of K.475 and K.457, as well as of sonatas by Haydn and by F. W. Rust.
                                   1 [1911] 33

ZUR BIOGRAPHIE BEETHOVENS IN DEN JAHREN 1796, 1797 UND 1801.   (A)
    In April 1796 Baron Karl Friedrich Kübeck (1780-1855) met Beethoven and was asked by him to supervise the practice of one of Beethoven's pupils, Julie M. . .n (Manin?, Molin?), the daughter of a marquis. This assignment continued for about a year. Kübeck met Beethoven again briefly in 1801.   1 [1911] 42

DER GEIGER JOSEF MAYSEDER UND BEETHOVEN.   (B)
    A note to Mayseder (1789-1863) without date but apparently written between November 29th and December 2nd 1814, such as a famous composer might write to a brilliant young musician to solicit his best efforts in a forthcoming performance of one of his compositions.   1 [1911] 49

EIN VERGESSENES BRIEFCHEN AN DEN GEIGER JOSEF BÖHM.   (C)
    A note to Böhm, first published in 1861, without date but apparently written about the time (spring of 1825) of the first performances of Op. 127.   1 [1911] 58

TITLE ERRONEOUSLY GIVEN AS: DER BRIEF LUDWIG FREIHERRN VON TÜRCKHEIMS AN BEETHOVEN.   (D)
    A rather ironical letter of introduction of his brother Johann to Türckheim. The letter probably dates from the summer of 1815. Note that the addressee was not the Baron von Türckheim concerned in the performance of the Missa Solemnis (TK III 97).   1 [1911] 62

ZUR JUGENDSYMPHONIE BEETHOVENS.   (E)
    This work, much less mature than Opp. 1 or 2, undoubtedly was written in Bonn rather than in Vienna. Resemblances to Haydn's D major London Symphony set the earliest possible date of completion (this work was first performed in London on March 11th 1791 and was probably known in Bonn not long thereafter) though portions of the symphony are undoubtedly earlier. Similarity to the Bagatelle Op. 33 No. 4 establishes a dating for this latter composition. The author points out passages reminiscent of Mozart and Bach. See also 'Sammelbände den Internationalen Musikgesellschaft' 13 [1911] 127 and 'Die Musik' 11$_2$ [1912] 3.   1 [1912] 69

BEETHOVEN IN WIENER-NEUDORF.   (F)
    On his journeys to and from Baden, Mödling, and other nearby places, Beethoven passed through Wiener-Neudorf more than forty times, to say nothing of holiday outings to this spot.
        1 [1912] 73

BEETHOVENS TAUBHEIT.   (G)
    A popular, nonmedical summary of the known facts, with quotations from Beethoven's letters and from accounts of contemporaries.   1 [1912] 82

DIE METRONOMIZIERUNG DER IX. SYMPHONIE.   (H)
    A brief discussion of the validity of Beethoven's tempo indications in general, with special reference to the tempo of the scherzo of the Ninth Symphony.   1 [1913] No. 4: Notizen

BEMERKUNGEN ZU NEU AUFGEFUNDENEN BEETHOVEN-BRIEFE.   (I)
    A note without date (probably from early February 1823) to Herr von Meissel (sic) of the Gebrüder Meisl (a wholesale house in Vienna) asking that he promptly send to Peters in Leipzig a package of music which Beethoven had given him. This package is probably one of those referred to in Beethoven's letter of February 15-18 1823 to Peters (KS II 226). New transcription of the letter originally published in 'Die Musik' 9$_1$ [1909] 42 to Bernard regarding a letter of his to Frau Johanna van Beethoven. The probable date of this letter is mid 1819 to 1824, most likely near the beginning of this time. (See also 'Die Musik' 13$_1$ [1913] 148). The letter of July 19th 1819 to Piuk and the fragment of a letter without date to Bernard, given in 1 [1911] 12-18 and the letter given in 'Der Merker' 1 [1909] 177 are from about this same time. In 'Die Musik' 12$_1$ [1912] 220 Unger published a letter dated October 10th 1824 to Tobias Haslinger from which he drew the conclusion that Nephew Karl's running away took place not in 1824 but in 1825. The author points out that the letter to Haslinger dated "evening of the 6th October" (without year) (KS II 338) and the letter to Philip Haslinger dated "the day after the 6th of October 1824" (sic) (KS II 339) are obviously consecutive, indicating without doubt that Karl had been missing during these few days of 1824. The present letter,

following these by a few days, does not in any way contradict this assumption. The letter of October 5th 1825 to Karl (KS II 407) refers to a second and quite distinct absence. Note that the present letter closes with the phrase "Es muss sein," indicating that the 'motto phrase' of the last quartet was in Beethoven's mind as early as 1824 (see also TV-262). A letter dated October 15th 1819 to the Archduke Rudolf in which Beethoven makes an appointment to see the Archduke, asks his help in connection with his difficulties regarding Karl, comments on a set of variations which the Archduke had written, and mentions his work on the Missa Solemnis. The author states that this letter had been previously published, but with many errors.   1 [1913] 101

JOSEPH, IGNATZ AND LEOPOLD SONNLEITHNER.   (A)
A biographical sketch of Joseph Sonnleithner (1766-1835), adviser to Beethoven during his legal difficulties regarding Op. 29 and translator into German of the original French text of 'Fidelio' (see TK II 34), and briefer mention of his brother Ignatz (1770-1831) and his nephew Leopold. The latter wrote a notable article in 1864 to the effect that in Beethoven's day the contrabass recitative in the last movement of the Ninth Symphony was played at a good speed: "not presto (to be sure) but not andante." An article written by Leopold in 1860 is reprinted in full, in which he discusses the anecdote by Hiller (TK I 291) regarding Beethoven's plagiarism of a theme from an opera by Paer.
1 [1913] 116

ANECDOTES.   (B)
Reminiscences of Beethoven from about the year 1800, as given to her great-grandson by a woman who had presumably been Beethoven's landlady.   1 [1913] 128

BEETHOVEN AND THE MÖDLINGER BRÜHL.   (C)
An attempt to picture the open country around Mödling as Beethoven saw it in 1799 and in the summers (1818-20) when in that area he did so much of his work on the Hammerklavier Sonata, the Missa Solemnis, and other works. The "Mödlinger Tänze" were probably written for the musicians of the tavern "zu den zwei Raben" in the Brühl.
2 [1915] 1

BEETHOVENS CIS-MOLL-SONATE.   (D)
"The C sharp minor Sonata is one of the most played but also one of the most misunderstood works of the great master." The sonata may indeed be an expression of Beethoven's love for Giulietta Guicciardi to whom it is dedicated, but equally probably it may have arisen from the emotional turmoil of Beethoven's realization of his oncoming deafness. Its programmatic association with Seume's poem 'Die Beterin' ('The Praying Maiden'-- see TD II 256 and TK I 292) is most improbable. There is little reason to believe that the name "Moonlight Sonata" arose from any remark by Beethoven; the use of this name cannot certainly be fixed at earlier than 1840. In its form, the first movement may best be thought of as a prelude or fantasia, though in a rudimentary way the five sections of a sonata-allegro movement are present. The second movement corresponds reasonably well in form to the classical minuet, though in content it is neither minuet nor scherzo. The presto is clearly in sonata-allegro form. As regards performance, it is to be wished that a pianoforte might be available which could give the necessary brilliance without the overpowering volume of tone of the modern concert grand. Suggestions regarding tempi, etc., and the traditions of performance as exemplified by the great virtuosi from Beethoven's day to present are given in great detail. An extensive bibliography regarding this sonata is appended.
2 [1916] 39

AUSFÜHRUNGEN.   (E)
Baroness Dorothea Ertmann (born Dorothea Graumann) on May 3rd 1781 in Offenbach. Married Stephan Freiherr von Ertmann, k. k. Hauptmann, who died in 1835 in Milan, having attained to the rank of Feldmarschalleutnant. The Baroness died in Vienna on March 16th 1849. A bibliography regarding her is given.
2 [1916] 95

[Brief biographical sketch and bibliography]   2 [1916] 98   (F)

MOZARTS TAUFNAMEN. Alexander Hajdecki.   (G)
At his baptism on January 27th 1756 Mozart received the names Johannes Chrysostomus Wolfgangus Theophilus (in German, Johann Chrysostom Wolfgang Gottlieb). The first two of these names were soon dropped. After his visit to Italy in 1770 he regularly signed himself "Wolfg. Amade" or simply "Wolfgang." Little known is the fact that in 1782 he signed the various ecclesiastical and legal documents connected with his marriage with the name "Wolfgang Adam Mozart."   2 [1916] 103

EIN STAMMBUCH VON BEETHOVEN AUS DEM JAHR 1794.   (A)
    A biographical sketch of Franz Clement (1780-1842) and a copy of a laudatory little note from Beethoven in a
'memory book. '   2 [1916] 106

UNBEACHTETE BRIEFE BEETHOVENS.   (B)
    Letter without date (probably from February 1814) to Hartmann inviting him to a concert on February 27th 1814.
Original German version of the letter of February 5th 1816 to the Philharmonic Society of London (KS I 396), first
published in the 'Zeitschrift den Internationalen Musikgesellschaft' 15 [1913] 78. The German versions which had
previously appeared were translations of an English translation which had been published. Listing of titles of the
Songs Op. 108 (though not in their final order) and reference to a lost letter from Beethoven to Schlesinger dated
July 3rd 1821.   2 [1916] 108

BEETHOVEN IN MÖDLING.   (C)
    Remarks on Beethoven's three summers in Mödling (1818-20): the houses in which he lived and a discursive account
of his activities and living conditions. (See also 2 [1915] 1)   2 [1918] 115

EINE ÜBERSEHENE AUFFÜHRUNG DER PASTORAL SYMPHONIE.   (D)
    The Pastoral Symphony was performed at a concert in the Altwiener Augarten on May 1st 1811, with many of the
listeners sitting in the gardens outside the concert hall.   2 [1918] 164

BEETHOVENS SPAZIERGANG NACH WIENER-NEUSTADT.   (E)
    Höfel's story (TK III 42) of Beethoven's arrest as a tramp in Wiener-Neustadt in the summer of 1821 or 1822 or
1823 may be accepted as substantially true.   3 [1923] 2

BEETHOVENSPUREN BEI ROBERT SCHUMANN.   (F)
    Citations are given of many passages in Schumann's music which bear strikingly close resemblances to fragments
of Beethoven's.   3 [1923] 13

BEETHOVENS AUFENTHALTE IN DEN BÖHMISCHEN BÄDERN.   (G)
    Although Beethoven went to the Bohemian baths (Teplitz, Karlsbad, Franzenbad) in 1811 and 1812 to take the cure,
of equal importance on the occasion of his first visit were his interest in Bettina von Arnim and in the possibility of
meeting Goethe. From the standpoint of his health, this first visit (Teplitz, August-September 1811) was favorable,
though he did not meet Goethe, who was in Karlsbad. The next year he returned to Teplitz on July 5th 1812,
and his first meeting with Goethe was on July 19th. A few days prior to July 27th Beethoven left Teplitz for Karlsbad.
He had already arrived there by July 31st, and on August 6th gave a concert with the violinist Polledro for the benefit
of the fire victims in Baden-bei-Wien. By August 12th he had arrived in Franzenbad. Retracing his route, he met
Goethe in Karlsbad on September 8th, and was again in Teplitz not later than September 17th. The effect of this
summer on his health had not been beneficial: he was bedridden when he wrote to Breitkopf & Härtel on September
17th (KS I 269). His return journey to Vienna was broken by a visit to Dr. Kanka in Prague and (at the beginning
of October) to his brother Johann in Linz. He never returned to the Bohemian spas.
                                                                 3 [1925] 37

BEETHOVENSTELLEN AUS ZEITGENÖSSISCHEN BRIEFEN.   (H)
    A letter dated November 10th (1825) from Tobias Haslinger to J. N. Hummel includes the statement: "Beethoven
is well again, but has aged greatly. At a concert for his own benefit last Sunday, Linke gave a performance of
Beethoven's recently completed thirteenth Quartet in A minor, with great success. " A letter dated "London, December 10th 1814" (sic; this is undoubtedly a misprint for 1824) from J. E. Schultz to Haslinger, requesting a copy of
the 'Dedication of the House' Overture Op. 124, and saying: "Since I have had such bad luck with the Beethoven Trio,
I have not wanted to take the risk of publishing the sonatas which you gave me. " What the trio and the sonatas are to
which he referred is not known.   3 [1925] 48

BEETHOVEN UND DIE GRAZEN MUSIKALISCHEN KREISE. F. Bischoff.   (A)
   Beethoven's friends Prof. Julius Schneller and Councillor Josef von Varena lived in Graz. At a concert on July 25th
   1811 the Pastoral Symphony was the featured work, repeated on October 8th 1811 for the benefit of the Ursulines;
   on December 22nd 1811 the Choral Phantasy with Marie Koschak; on March 29th 1812 several Beethoven works at
   a concert for the Ursulines; on April 11th 1813 the Christus. The last of these Beethoven concerts was on June 6th
   1813. "Almost all the great works of Beethoven were produced in Graz during the composer's lifetime." Bischoff
   quotes and refers to much correspondence between Beethoven and his associates at Graz. Two previously unpublished
   letters are given: one to Rettich of March 22nd or 23rd 1812, the other (without date) to Varena. Neither of these
   letters is listed in the Index of First Words in BJ 2. (See also 2 [1909] 155)
                                              1 [1908] 6

FÜNF-UND- ACHTZIG VARIATIONEN ÜBER DIABELLIS WALZER. Heinrich Rietsch.   (B)
   On June 9th 1824 two sets of variations were announced simultaneously by Diabelli: (1) Beethoven's Op. 120, and
   (2) variations on the same theme by fifty other composers. The project had been under way for at least three years;
   Schubert's variation is dated 'March 1821.' The first edition of the 50 Variations "by the most notable composers
   and virtuosi" is carefully described as regards format and content. Two contributors (W. A. Mozart the son and
   G. Rieger) each submitted two variations, of which only one was published by Diabelli. The two which were omitted
   are given in this article.   1 [1908] 28

EIN UNAUSGEFÜHRT GEBLIEBENER PLAN BEETHOVENS.   Hans Volkmann.   (C)
   In 1825 Beethoven gave consideration to the composition of a Festival Cantata for the dedication of a synagogue
   in Vienna.   1 [1908] 51

ZUR KLAVIERSONATE OPUS 111. Theodor von Frimmel.   (D)
   The opening notes of the principal theme of the first movement allegro resemble a brief passage in Sacchini's
   'Dardanus,' which Beethoven quite possibly heard during his youth in Bonn.
                                              1 [1908] 58

EINE ÜBERLIEFERUNG AUS DEM JAHRE 1806. Theodor von Frimmel.   (E)
   The incident in which Beethoven stormed out from Prince Lichnowsky's (TK II 68) probably took place towards the
   end of October (certainly before November 18th 1806). The story that by thus rushing into the rain without his hat
   his deafness was aggravated does not seem to be well-founded.   1 [1908] 63

EINE BEMERKUNG ZU LYSERS BEETHOVEN-BILDNIS. Theodor von Frimmel.   (F)
   Lyser's lithograph of Beethoven (full-length walking profile) was almost certainly not from a life portrait or life
   sketch by Lyser.   1 [1908] 68

BRIEFE. Theodor von Frimmel.   (G)
   April 18th 1825 to Dr. Braunhofer. A note, hitherto unpublished, in which Beethoven says he does not feel well
   and requests a professional visit.   1 [1908] 74

   May 13th 1825 to Ferdinand Piringer. A letter, hitherto unpublished, thanking Piringer for a copy of the 'Missa   (H)
   Solemnis' which he had corrected, and making reference to Boehm the violinist and to Beethoven's continued
   intestinal trouble.   1 [1908] 77

   June 16th (1819?) to Josef Karl Bernard. A letter mentioning Beethoven's difficulty in finding the right school for (I)
   his nephew Karl, and referring to Beethoven's thought of writing an oratorio on a text by Bernard.
                                              1 [1908] 83

   Minor variant of KS I 57 (letter No. 52).   1 [1908] 87   (J)

   Minor variant of KS I 63 (letter No. 57).   1 [1908] 90   (K)

   Minor variant of KS I 65, with postscript not in KS.   1 [1908] 92   (L)

   March 28th 1809 to Zmeskall. This note refers to Baroness E. to a basset-horn player, and says that Beethoven   (M)
   will come when the new Vcl Sonata is played.   1 [1908] 99

   Note of period 1817-20 to Dr. Bihler.   1 [1908] 100   (N)

BRIEFE (Continued)
    Note (probably 1817) to Dr. Bihler.   1 [1908] 101   (A)

VERZEICHNISSE.   (B)
    Lists of Beethoven items in the Vienna Municipal Collection and in the collections of private holders include the
following letters not in Kalischer: M-647, M-661, M-606, M-801, M-544, M-607, M-508, M-648.
                                               1 [1908] 105

EINE WALLFAHRT DURCH ALTE KIRCHHÖFE.   Robert Müller.   (C)
    The burial places of many of Beethoven's friends are identified.   1 [1908] 121

ZU JOH. NEPOMUCK HUMMEL.   Theodor von Frimmel.   (D)
    Brief biographical sketch and anecdotes. Regarding the credibility of Schindler, the author says, "In matters having
to do with Beethoven, Schindler is to be believed without hesitation when he speaks of things of which he has actual
memory," but in matters outside his personal knowledge he is not to be trusted.
                                             1 [1908] 125

NOTIZEN.   (E)
    Anecdote of visit of a Dr. Podracky to Beethoven.

    A lock of Beethoven's hair is preserved in Péces (Hungary). (See Papp: Beethoven es a magyarok, p. 123)
                                             1 [1908] 133

BIBLIOGRAPHIE.   Emerich Kastner.   (F)
    Partial review of the Beethoven literature for the period 1900-1906.
                                           1 [1908] 139

FACSIMILES.   (G)
    (1), (2) Sketches for Op. 29; (3) Kal 93; (4) Kal 1114.   1 [1908] 185

ZUM TITELBILDE.   (H)
    Discussion of bust by Dietrick, with letter to Dietrick (M-606).   1 [1908] 191

BEETHOVEN UND FÜRST KINSKY.   V. Kratochvil.   (I)
    Except for greater detail and continuity of narrative, this paper adds little to the account given in TK II: that Prince
Kinsky did not know Beethoven prior to entering into the contract of endowment in 1810, but that he undertook this
obligation as a part of the responsibility of his social position; that the Prince during his lifetime strictly lived up to
the provisions of the contract (limited only by his military duties in the field); and that his widow continued payments until Beethoven's death on a basis more generous than the contract as a legal document required. More than
forty exhibits from Kinsky's books of account and files of receipts are quoted in full.
                                             2 [1909] 3

DIE C-MOLL SYMPHONIE ALS AUSGANG DER MODERNER MOTIVTECHNIK.   Max Chop.   (J)
    A parallel is drawn between the thematic modifications in the four movements of the Fifth Symphony and Liszt's
'Les Preludes,' in which the former is considered as expressing "a self-realizing power of will in the successive
phases of struggle, misfortune, recovery from misfortune, and final victory."
                                           2 [1909] 48

BEETHOVENS SONATE OPUS 110. EINE ERLÄUTERUNG IHRES BAUES.   Herman Wetzel.   (K)
    An analysis in great detail.   2 [1909] 75, 403

BEETHOVENS BRIEFWECHSEL MIT VARENA.   Ferdinand Bischoff.   (L)
    Beethoven's published correspondence with Varena has been based almost entirely on copies made by Otto Jahn of
letters which were later sold by Varena's executors. From other material available to the author, the paper in
1 [1908] 6 was prepared. In this paper many corrections are given to the Varena letters as they appear in Kalischer's
'Briefe.'   2 [1909] 155

EIN KONVERSATIONSHEFT BEETHOVENS AUS DEM JAHRE 1825.   Theodor von Frimmel.   (M)
    Complete and annotated transcription of a conversation book in the Musical History Museum at Cologne. This book,
used while Beethoven was in Vienna and in Baden, covers the early days of September 1825.
                                         2 [1909] 161

EIN BRIEF AN FERDINAND RIES. Alfred Einstein.   (A)
  A letter fitting into the series KS II 130-35, of date March 8th 1819, giving 33 corrections in the parts of Op. 104.
  Note that the chronological order of these letters is apparently: 766A, this letter, 766 (March 30th, not April 30th),
  764, 765 (complete version of which is given in 'Musical Times' 37 [1896] 305).
                                        2 [1909] 180

A BEETHOVEN LETTER. Edward Speyer.   (B)
  A letter dated February 3rd 1823, apparently to Schlesinger, giving corrections to Op. 111.
                                        2 [1909] 185

BRIEFE AUS DEN JAHREN 1809 BIS 1824. Theodor von Frimmel.   (C)
  First publication of a note received on August 11th 1809 by Breitkopf & Härtel regarding corrections to Op. 69.
                                        2 [1909] 187

  First publication of a note dating probably from about 1809 to Fries & Co. asking if any letters for Beethoven from   (D)
  George Thomson had been received.   2 [1909] 188

  Letter not dated but almost certainly of February 28th 1811 to J. Mähler which appears in TD III 260 and is referred (E)
  to in TK II 198.   2 [1909] 189

  First publication of the draft of a letter dictated in June 1815 by Beethoven to Neate, with salutation: "E.   (F)
  Durchlaucht." ("Your Highness!") perhaps referring to Viscount Castlereagh, perhaps to Prince Esterhazy. The draft
  deals with the reception which the 'Battle of Victoria' (Op. 91) had received in England and with the suggestion of an
  issue there of a piano transcription of the work.   2 [1909] 191

  Attempt at a definitive transcription of the letter of March 6th 1820 to Winter (KS II 166).   (G)
                                        2 [1909] 196

  Newly made transcription of KS II 197.   2 [1909] 202   (H)

  Newly made transcription of KS II 203.   2 [1909] 205   (I)

  Newly made transcription of KS II 287.   2 [1909] 206   (J)

  Newly made transcription of Kastner-Kapp No. 1181.   2 [1909] 209   (K)

BRIEFE UND ANDERE SCHRIFTSTÜCKE L. VAN BEETHOVENS, NACH DEN TEXTANFÄNGEN GEORDNET.   (L)
     Emerich Kastner.
  1433 letters, etc. arranged in the order of the opening words of the text. For each entry there is also given the date
  (as far as known), the name of the addressee, and the book or journal in which the writing in question was first
  published or referred to.   2 [1909] 213,397

A BEETHOVEN LETTER. Edw. Speyer.   (M)
  First publication of letter without date (probably 1816-17) to Steiner & Co.: "Das Poenale wird vermehrt und
  zwar . . ." (KFr III 112 No. 593).   2 [1909] 310

AUS BEETHOVENS KREISE. Theodor von Frimmel.   (N)
  Notes on Archduke Rudolf, his secretary Baumeister, Franz Hölzl, and Paul and Peter Maschek.
                                        2 [1909] 321

                        BEETHOVEN-JAHRBUCH 1953/54

BEETHOVEN BRIEFE AUS DER SAMMLUNG H. C. BODMER-ZÜRICH. Dagmar Weise.   (O)
  Journal references are given for the publication of about 30 letters referred to in SBSK as "missing from volumes of
  collected letters." Complete texts are given of 43 other letters which were hitherto unpublished, incompletely
  published, or published only in translation.   [1953/54] 9

ZUR GESCHICHTE DES BONNER BEETHOVENDENKMAL.   Willi Kahl.   (A)
    A letter of 22 November 1844 from Schindler to Peter Joseph Simrock (previously published in VjfMw 4 [1888] 516)
is given in which Schindler bitterly criticizes the Beethoven statues of Hähnel and of Bläser. The author points out
that Schindler's praise of the Schimon painting and the Letronne-Höfel engraving, and his criticisms of other like-
nesses, must be viewed in the light of the fact that he was apparently acquainted with only a few of the portraits of
Beethoven. Schindler's hostility towards the conduct of the 1845 festival is discussed.
[1953/54] 63

LUDWIG VAN BEETHOVENS WERKE ÜBER SEINEN KONTRATANZ IN ES-DUR.   Paul Mies.   (B)
    A detailed study of the development of Op. 35 as it appears in the Kessler sketch book and of the Eroica finale from
the sketch book referred to by Nottebohm in 'Zwei Skizzenbücher aus den Jahren 1801-03.' Mies disagrees with the
contention of Riemann (DM 9_3 [1910] 19, 107) that 'Prometheus' is a gigantic set of variations, and with the contention of Fischer (Schw MZ 89 [1949] 282) that Op. 35 has the underlying characteristics of a three movement sonata
and that the Eroica finale is based on sonata-allegro form.
[1953/54] 80

BEETHOVENS ZAPFENSTREICHE IN F-DUR.   Willy Hess.   (C)
    Corrected versions and brief notes on revisions of GA 24/287 Nos. 1 and 2 (WoO 18 and 19), in each case including
the trio omitted in the GA.   [1953/54] 103,251

BEETHOVEN-SCHRIFTTUM VON 1939 BIS 1952.   Ernst August Ballin.   (D)
    A bibliography of 2011 titles.   [1953/54] 109

BEETHOVEN-JAHRBUCH 1955/56

IN MEMORIAM DR. MED DR. PHIL h. c. H. C. BODMER.   Joseph Schmidt-Görg.   (E)
    Obituary of Dr. Hans Conrad Bodmer (1891-1956).   [1955/56] 7

NEUE BRIEFE UND SCHRIFTSTÜCKE AUS DER FAMILIE BRUNSVIK.   Joseph Schmidt-Görg.   (F)
    First publication of 4 letters that passed between the sisters in 1801-03, a letter of 1805 from Franz to Josephine,
and 5 business documents, all giving fragments of information about the members of the family and their interest
in Beethoven.   [1955/56] 11

BEMERKUNGEN ZU BEETHOVENS TEMPI.   Hermann Beck.   (G)
    The author tabulates the underlying rhythmic patterns and the tempo designations for the movements for which
Beethoven gave metronome marks, as a guide to the most appropriate tempi for other Beethoven works.
[1955/56] 24

BEETHOVEN-ZENTENARFEIER

BEETHOVEN UND DAS RHEINLAND.   Ludwig Schiedermair.   (H)
    Beethoven's formative years in the Rhineland were of profound effect on his personality and on the nature of his
artistry throughout his life.   [1927] 7

AUS DER BONNER GESELLSCHAFT IN BEETHOVENS JUGENDZEIT.   Paul Kaufmann.   (I)
    The musical life of Bonn during Beethoven's boyhood, as handed down in the tradition of the author's forebears,
long residents of Bonn.   [1927] 11

LES PARTICULARITÉS FLAMANDES DE BEETHOVEN.   Ernest Closson.   (J)
    Although Beethoven's descent was Flemish, he never visited Flanders nor indicated any desire to do so. His early
teacher Van den Eeden and two of his acquaintances (the violinist Van Blumenthal and Victor Coremans) were Flemish.
In personality and character, however, Beethoven was the direct heir of his grandfather the Kapellmeister, a true
Fleming. It is these traits that appear most strongly in Beethoven's music and life.
[1927] 16

BEETHOVENS VERHÄLTNIS ZUR RELIGION. Karl Weinmann.   (A)
Haydn's contention that Beethoven was an atheist are wholly disproved by the few statements on religion which have
come down to us from the composer. Of the other alternatives -- deist, pantheist, Christian -- the last seems most
probable on the basis of Beethoven's own remarks and on the nature of his religious music. It is possible but not
probable that Beethoven was a Freemason.   [1927] 19

LES AUTOGRAPHES DE BEETHOVEN A LA BIBLIOTHEQUE DU CONSERVATOIRE DE PARIS. Julien Tiersot.   (B)
A brief list of the dozen or so musical manuscripts of Beethoven in the library.
[1927] 25

ÜBER EINIGE AMERIKANISCHE BEETHOVEN-AUSGABEN. Alicia Simon.   (C)
Works by Beethoven had been published in the United States before 1816; collections of compositions by Beethoven,
Haydn and Mozart were issued in 1818; a review of a Beethoven composition (an adaptation of one of the Bagatelles
Op. 33 as a song: 'The Bird Let Loose') appeared in 1820 ('Euterpiad,' 9 September 1820). In 1823 the Handel and
Haydn Society of Boston commissioned "a biblical oratorio in the English language" from Beethoven (see KS II 213
No. 856). In 1821 or earlier a Beethoven Society was formed in Portland, Maine ('Euterpiad,' 21 May 1821). The
First Symphony was performed (probably incomplete) in Philadelphia in 1821; in 1828 the Eroica was performed in
arrangement for septet; in 1846 the Ninth Symphony was performed in New York. In 1846 a military quickstep used
in the Mexican War was based on themes from Beethoven's Op. 11 and from Meyerbeer. In the period 1830-70 some
sixty waltzes and ten marches attributed to Beethoven were issued by American publishing houses. (NOTE by DWM.
There seems to be little in this article that is not given better and more fully in 'Musical Quarterly' 13 [1927] 217.)
[1927] 26

ZUM BEGRIFF DER WIENER KLASSIK. Alfred Orel.   (D)
The three great men grouped together as the Vienna classicists differ not only because of their individual personalities, but even more fundamentally because they stem from three distinct streams of artistic development within
the classical tradition: Haydn from Vienna rationalism, Mozart from the baroque tradition and from the tradition
of episcopal domination, Beethoven from the atmosphere of Sturm und Drang.
[1927] 29

BEETHOVEN UND DIE MUSIKKRITIK. Hermann Springer.   (E)
Beethoven's first real contact with the critics came about the turn of the century (see AmZ 1 [1799] 366, 541, 570,
607); his famous reference to the "Leipziger Ochsen" (KS I 40) dates from this period. At first the tone of criticism
was patronizing or unfavorable, but after the First Symphony was performed in 1800 (see AmZ 3 [1800] 49) his
ability was recognized in the AmZ, though not in every other influential journal. The advent of E. T. A. Hoffmann as a critic (or, more properly, as an essayist) on Beethoven, AmZ 12 [1810] 630 (Op. 67); 14 [1812] 519
(Op. 62); 15 [1813] 141, 163 (Op. 70); Ibid. 389, 409 (Op. 86); Ibid. 473 (Op. 84) was "the most significant fact in
contemporary Beethoven criticism and a milestone in the history of music criticism." A series of articles by
Amadeus Wendt (AmZ 17 [1815] 345, 365, 381, 391, 413, 429) pointed out that Beethoven's unmistakable mannerisms stemmed from strength, not from weakness. Adolph Bernhard Marx (in the 'Berliner Allgemeine Musikalische
Zeitung' from 1824 to 1830) and the reviews by Seyfried in 'Cäcilia' (e. g., of Opp. 123, 125, 131) were of importance. The critics of some other journals, it is true, continued to oppose Beethoven, but their acceptance was
not great.   [1927] 32

ART UND WESEN DER TONSPRACHE BEETHOVENS. Karl Hasse.   (F)
A discussion of the effect on Beethoven's style of the Mannheim tradition in which he was raised, and the various
ways (e. g., chord distribution, use of devices like broken chords and tremolos in middle voices, careful consideration
of instrumental color) in which his individual style developed.   [1927] 35

BEETHOVEN ROMANTIKER? Willibald Nagel.   (G)
Only a superficial consideration of Beethoven's style would class him among the romantics; the man himself was
even further removed from romanticism.   [1927] 40

DIE INNERE EINHEIT DER KLASSISCHEN SYMPHONIE. Arthur Willner.   (H)
A brief discussion of Beethoven's symphonies from the standpoint of the classical criterion of economy of materials.
[1927] 43

BEETHOVEN ET LES RYTHMES COSMIQUES. Alexander Denéréaz.   (A)
  A parallel is found between the dynamic profile of the 'Storm' movement of the Pastoral Symphony and the perio-
  dicity of various natural phenomena, astronomical and meteorological.
                                                      [1927] 45

DIE DRAMATURGISCHE BEDEUTUNG DES FIDELIO. Egon Wellesz.   (B)
  Fidelio had no successors during the nineteenth century; it may be that only in the operas of our time will its
  influence be truly felt.   [1927] 48

BEETHOVENS ZYKLISCHES FORMPRINZIP. Hans Mersmann.   (C)
  In his early compositions Beethoven attained unity by his choice of material; in the period culminating in the Fifth
  Symphony and the Appassionata Sonata the unifying influence was content. From the Sixth Symphony and the Sonata
  Op. 78 the bond between the movements continued equally strong but became more and more intangible and of the
  spirit, culminating in the Missa Solemnis and the last Quartets. The replacement of the closing fugue of Op. 130
  by the present dance finale does no violence to this concept of unity.
                                                      [1927] 52

BEETHOVEN UND DIE VARIATION. Josef Müller-Blattau.   (D)
  General   [1927] 55

DIE FORM DES ERSTEN SATZES DER MONDSCHEINSONATE. Ilmari Krohn.   (E)
  The author analyzes this movement as being in Sonata Form: measures 1-4 constitute the Introduction; 5-22 the
  Exposition with 5-8 being First Theme, 9-14 the Transition, 15-18 Second Theme and 19-22 Concluding Theme;
  23-41 the Development; 42-59 the Recapitulation; and 60-69 the Coda. (See ZIMG 3 [1902] 256)
                                                      [1927] 58

NEUE BEITRÄGE ZUR ENTWICKLUNG DER POLONAISE BIS BEETHOVEN. Lucian Kamienski.   (F)
  Comments on two collections with 85 polonaises from the eighteenth century (of which 9 are here given in extenso).
  Beethoven's Polonaise Op. 89 is said to be stylistically authentic.   [1927] 66

EINE STUDIE ZUR DYNAMISCHE SCHICHTUNG IN BEETHOVENSCHEN SONATENTHEMEN. Wilhelm Heinitz.   (G)
  A statistical study of the placement of accents in the themes of 18 Beethoven sonatas.
                                                      [1927] 75

BEETHOVEN UND DIE POLYPHONIE. Alfred Einstein.   (H)
  "Beethoven, like Haydn and Mozart, lived in a homophonic, an anti-polyphonic, era, but also in an era in which
  the innocence of homophony, the 'galant' style, was long forgotten." Like Haydn and Mozart (aside from such
  examples of formal counterpoint as the finale of the Jupiter Symphony) Beethoven's principal use of polyphony was
  in the development of his musical thought by imitation; a passage from the first movement of Op. 18 No. 1 (GA
  6/37: 4, 2, 7-10) is cited as an excellent example. The slow movements of the Seventh Symphony and of the
  F major Quartet Op. 59 No. 1 (mm. 9-16) are examples of a polyphonic treatment of melody completely foreign
  to the polyphony of Bach. It is in these ways, far more than in such formal fugues as that of Op. 125, that
  Beethoven made of polyphony a new language. (See also 'Studien zur Musikwissenschaft' 14 [1927] 75)
                                                      [1927] 79

ENHARMONIK ("POLARE HARMONIK") BEI BEETHOVEN. Hermann Stephani.   (I)
  The author cites many instances of the use for emotional purposes of chords which by enharmonic changes may lead
  to remote keys.   [1927] 83

EIN MOSKAUER SKIZZENBUCH VON BEETHOVEN. M. Iwanow-Boretzky.   (J)
  Summary of article of the same title on pp. 7-91 of 'Musikalische Bildung' (Moscow) for January-March 1927. The
  sketch book in question includes sketches for the Quartets Opp. 132 and 130, and was apparently used at the same
  time as the book described by Roda in 'Rivista Musicale Italiana' 12 [1905] 63, 592, 734.
                                                      [1927] 88

ROBERT SCHUMANN IN SEINEN SKIZZEN GEGENÜBER BEETHOVEN. Wilibald Gurlitt.   (K)
                                                      [1927] 91

SKIZZEN ZUR III. UND V. SYMPHONIE UND ÜBER DIE NOTWENDIGKEIT EINER GESAMTAUSGABE DER SKIZZE (L)
    BEETHOVENS (AUSZUG). Karl Lothar Mikulicz.
  Emphatic statement is made of the importance to Beethoven scholarship of complete publication of all known sketches.

The ideal order of publication of such material would be: (1) facsimiles, (2) complete transcriptions, and (3) assembled sketches for each composition.   [1927] 95

AUFTAKT UND ABTAKT IN DER THEMATIK BEETHOVENS. Felix Rosenthal.   (A)
    Support of Wiehmayer's contention that "heavy-light," rather than Riemann's "light-heavy," seems most typical of the dynamic structure of Beethoven's themes.   [1927] 97

ZÄHLZEIT, TEMPO UND AUSDRUCK BEI BEETHOVEN. Franz Marschner.   (B)
    In a large number of cases the time signature and the unit of counting in the metronome marking do not correspond with the actual rhythmic pulse of the movement.   [1927] 100

ÜBER DUALISMUS DER TAKTQUALITÄT IM BEETHOVENS SONATENSATZ. Rudolf Steglich.   (C)
    [1927] 104

DAS KONFESSIONELLE ELEMENT BEI BEETHOVEN. Alfred Schnerich.   (D)
    Addenda to an article published a year before on the sacred music of the Vienna composers.
    [1927] 107

HAYDN UND BEETHOVEN UND IHRE STELLUNG ZUR KROATISCHEN VOLKSMUSIK. Božidar Širola.   (E)
    The contention of Kuhač ('Allgemeine Musik Zeitung' 21 [1894] 396, 420, 438) that Haydn and Beethoven drew heavily on Croatian folk music does not seem to be adequately substantiated.
    [1927] 111

LES DEBUTS DE BEETHOVEN EN FRANCE. J. G. Prod'homme.   (F)
    It is probable that as late as 1800 the name of Beethoven had never been printed in Paris, either on a concert program or in a review. As late as 1815 his music was known only very sketchily, but in the years to come Heinrich Simrock the publisher, Baillot the violinist and Habeneck the conductor made great strides in bringing Beethoven's music to general knowledge.   [1927] 116

BEETHOVEN KIRCHENMUSIKER? Johannes Wolf.   (G)
    Whether from a liturgical or a musical point of view, there is nothing unsuitable in the use of Beethoven's Masses as part of a church service. Beethoven himself unquestionably planned the Missa Solemnis for use in a religious ceremony (see KS II 333), and his sketch books show that he contemplated other sacred compositions.
    [1927] 123

E. T. A. HOFFMANN AND BEETHOVEN. Erwin Kroll.   (H)
    The effect of Beethoven on Hoffmann's music is noticeable but not controlling; in no specific way can the influence of Hoffmann on Beethoven be detected. "With his reviews of works by Beethoven, Hoffmann brought to full stature the romantic spirit in German music criticism." (See also NBJ 3 [1927] 125)
    [1927] 128

BEETHOVEN IN PORTUGAL. José Vianna da Motta.   (I)
    In 1822 an orchestra was founded by Domingos Bomtempo "which had the honor of giving the first performances in Portugal of orchestral works by Haydn, Mozart and Beethoven." No further information is given. Liszt in his concerts of 1845 played no works by Beethoven. A series of chamber music concerts founded in 1863 by the pianist Daddi performed Op. 16. Only when a permanent orchestra was formed in 1879, under visiting conductors, were the Fifth, Sixth and Seventh Symphonies heard. Nikisch in 1902 gave the first complete performance of the Eighth Symphony. In Porto in 1900 a series of Beethoven string quartets were given for the first time; the last piano sonatas were first played there in 1898. Opp. 127 and 131 were heard in Lisbon only after 1918. Fidelio and the Masses have never been performed in Portugal. Of Portuguese artists, Beethoven knew the singer Luisa Todi, who visited Bonn in 1790. Beethoven may have heard operas by Marcos Portugal which were performed in Vienna in 1794-95-99. The first symphony written in Portugal was in 1896; there had been no chamber music since Bomtempo (1775-1840). Currently (1927) Luis de Freitas Branco, alone among Portuguese composers, is writing in classical forms.
    [1927] 132

ZUM KANON IM FIDELIO. Robert Haas.   (J)
    Other examples of canon in serious music of the period are cited. [1927] 136

CHOPIN SONATEN UND IHR VERHÄLTNIS ZUM BEETHOVENSCHEN STIL.   Henry K. Opienski.   (A)
    An attempt to show (1) that Chopin, after his student days, gained considerable familiarity with Beethoven's music;
    and (2) that the form of Chopin's Sonatas in B flat minor Op. 35 and B minor Op. 58 are not foreign to the spirit of
    Beethoven.   [1927] 138

BEETHOVENS MISSA SOLEMNIS UND DAS MOTU PROPRIO DES PABSTES PIUS X. ÜBER KIRCHENMUSIK.   (B)
    Hermann Müller.
    The author contends that in all respects the Missa Solemnis falls within the limits stated by the Motu proprio as
    permissible for music used for liturgical purposes, except that in some cases modifications need to be made in the
    use of the text.   [1927] 229

ÜBER THEMATISCHE KATALOGE. Wilhelm Altmann.   (C)
    This paper includes a critique of Nottebohm's Beethoven Verzeichnis, and a thoughtful list of the desirable features
    of a thematic catalog.   [1927] 283

STILKUNDLICHE PROBLEME BEI BEETHOVEN.   Paul Mies.   (D)
    Various stylistic problems of Beethoven's compositions are suggested for further research.
                                                   [1927] 304

BERLINER ALLGEMEINE MUSIKALISCHE ZEITUNG

MISSA SOLEMNIS.   (E)
    Notice that the Missa Solemnis scores have been sent to the royal subscribers.
                                         1 [1824] 34

ETWAS ÜBER DIE SYMPHONIE UND BEETHOVENS LEISTUNGEN IN DIESEM FACHE.   (F)
    The growth of the symphony before Beethoven is summarized, and Beethoven's Third, Fifth and Seventh Symphonies
    are discussed in detail.   1 [1824] 165,173,181

KLAVIERSTÜCK.   (G)
    First publication of the Klavierstück in B flat GA 25/301.   1 [1824] following p. 424

BEETHOVENS SINFONIEN.   (H)
    Poetry   2 [1825] 24

ÜBER BEETHOVENS NEUESTES QUARTETT.   (I)
    Meditation on genius.   2 [1825] 165

BITTE AN BEETHOVEN.   (J)
    A plea to Beethoven that he write cadenzas for his piano concertos.
                                         3 [1826] 220

"BEETHOVEN IST GESTORBEN."   4 [11 April 1827] 113   (K)

ENDLICH NOCH PERSÖNLICHES! (GOTTFRIED WEBERS ÜBELTAT AN BEETHOVEN). A. B. Marx.   (L)
    Weber's attack on Beethoven ('Cäcilia' 8 No. 29 [1828] 60) is reprinted verbatim; the facsimile letters are tran-
    scribed as far as the author was able. Weber's charges against Beethoven are vigorously contradicted, and Weber
    is scathingly rebuked for his unmannerly diatribe against the dead Beethoven.
                                         5 [1828] 121

Reviews published during Beethoven's lifetime   (A)

Opus 109	1 [1824]	37
110		87
111		95
119*		128
108		159
112		391
102		409
126	2 [1825]	417
128**	3 [1826]	1
124		2
122		34
? ***		118
121		253
125		373
127	4 [1827]	25

*Published as 'Opus 112' by Schlesinger (Paris) (NV p. 115)
**Published as 'Opus 121' by Schott (NV p. 123)
***'Musique de Ballet en forme d'une Marche, arrangée pour le Pianoforte à 4 mains, par Louis van Beethoven.
       Leipzig, Hofmeister. '

BLÄTTER FÜR HAUS- UND KIRCHENMUSIK

LUDWIG VAN BEETHOVENS EROIKA-SINFONIE. Albert Tottmann.   (B)
   An analysis (most detailed for the first two movements) which attempts to write in psychological connotations.
                    1 [1897] 57,77

LUDWIG VAN BEETHOVEN UND DIE VARIATIONENFORM. Otto Klauwell.   (C)
   Discussion of Beethoven's works for piano solo in this form, not overlooking the earlier sets of variations.
                    5 [1901] 83,100

IN QUESTA TOMBA OSCURA.   (D)
   Brief comments on the entire group of settings of this text by eighteen composers (only fifteen are named on the
   title page), published probably in the first quarter of the nineteenth century by Lipsia presso A. Kühnel.
                    5 [1901] 158

DIE ARIETTA "IN QUESTA TOMBA," EIN KOMPONISTEN-WETTKAMPF. B. Widmann.   (E)
   A volume of 205 pages, published by Mollo some time after mid-1808 and dedicated to Prince Lobkowitz, contains
   no fewer than sixty-three settings of this text. According to the account given, the project started as a joke among
   a small group of musicians in Vienna, and grew spontaneously to the proportions of the volume referred to.
                    5 [1901] 171

GOETHE AND BEETHOVEN. Willibald Nagel.   (F)
   An address which includes a detailed consideration of the Egmont music.
                    6 [1902] 102

BEETHOVEN UND SEINE KLAVIER-SONATEN. Willibald Nagel.   (G)
   Material later given in the introduction to the author's book of the same title.
                    6 [1902] 161

BEETHOVENS SONATE OPUS 2 Nr. 1. Willibald Nagel.   (H)
   Material later given in the author's book on the piano sonatas.   7 [1903] 4

BEETHOVENS SONATE OPUS 10 Nr. 3 I SATZ. Willibald Nagel.   (I)
   Material later given in the author's book on the piano sonatas.   7 [1903] 21

BEETHOVENS SONATE OPUS 13 IN C MOLL. Willibald Nagel.   (A)
Material later given in the author's book on the piano sonatas.   7 [1903] 69

WER KENNT DER KOMPONISTEN? Hugo Riemann.   (B)
Detailed discussion of the works now known as Beethoven's "Mödlinger Tänze," with generous musical quotations.
8 [1904] 113,131

BEETHOVENS KLAVIERSONATE OPUS 54. Wilh. Caspari.   (C)
Extended but completely nonanalytical discussion of the content of this sonata.
8 [1904] 167

BEETHOVENS FIDELIO IN DER URGESTALT. Rudolf Friege.   (D)
The 1805 version of Fidelio as reconstructed by Prieger is discussed in detail as regards its divergencies from the
1814 version.   10 [1906] 71

BEETHOVENS FIDELIO IN DER URGESTALT. Erich Prieger.   (E)
The editor of the reconstructed 1805 version amplifies some points made by Friege and makes a few minor corrections
in his commentary.   10 [1906] 89

WIEDERGEFUNDENE TÄNZE VON BEETHOVEN.   (F)
Before Riemann identified WoO 17 as the "Mödlinger Tänze" by Beethoven, he stated that they were undoubtedly by
a "most distinguished composer" from the time 1800-10.   12 [1907] 45

WIEDERGEFUNDENE KOMPOSITIONS BEETHOVENS.   (G)
Brief discussion of WoO 17.   12 [1907] 76

EINEN BRIEF BEETHOVENS.   (H)
Reprint of MM 126 (see BForsch 1 No. 2 [1911] 63).   15 [1911] 160

HAYDN, MOZART UND BEETHOVEN IN DEN GEWANDHAUSKONZERTEN BIS 1845. Friedrich Schmidt.   (I)
Dates of first performances at these concerts and initial reviews of a few of the works.
16 [1912] 167

BULLETIN DE LA SOCIÉTÉ 'UNION MUSICOLOGIQUE'

BEETHOVENS STELLUNG ZU DEN FÜHRENDEN GEISTERN SEINER ZEIT IN PHILOSOPHIE UND DICHTUNG.   (J)
Adolf Sandberger.
It is known that Beethoven matriculated at the University of Bonn on May 14th 1789 and that during the summer
of 1790 lectures on Kant were given, though it may be doubted that Beethoven attended these lectures. Nevertheless,
Beethoven's personal philosophy was in many ways Kantian. He also had enough in common with Goethe so that his
admiration for the poet was foreordained (though personal cordiality between the two men could never have been
possible), and his general approach to life brought him in close kinship with Herder.
2_2 [1922] 1

ZU DEN GESCHICHTLICHEN VORAUSSETZUNGEN DER BEETHOVEN'SCHEN PASTORALSINFONIE.   (K)
Adolf Sandberger.
An exhaustive study of the efforts and methods of Beethoven's predecessors since the seventeenth century in the
portrayal of the various aspects of nature which occur in the Pastoral Symphony.
3 [1923] 133

EINIGE BEMERKUNGEN ÜBER DIE AUFNAHME DER ACHTEN SINFONIE VON BEETHOVEN. Karl Nef.   (L)
Although Rochlitz and some other critics praised it highly, and although it was one of the first of the symphonies
to be published in score, the Eighth Symphony gained general acceptance very slowly. A possible reason for this
is that musical humor is a closed book to many (or most) listeners.
6 [1926] 61

NOUVELLES BAGATELLES OEUVRE 112 (sic). A. B. Marx.   (A)
   Review of Op. 119.   1 No. 2 [June 1824] 140

BRIEF REVIEW OF CONCERT OF MAY 7th 1824.   1 No. 2 [June 1824] 200   (B)

'AUTOGRAPHON' VON L. BEETHOVEN.   (C)
   A few lines of the letter of May 20th 1824 to Schott (KS II 312) in facsimile.
                                                  1 No. 3 [July 1824] 274

ANNOUNCEMENT OF THE PUBLICATION OF THE FOURTH SYMPHONY IN SCORE.   (D)
                                                  1 No. 4 [October 1824] 364

ANNOUNCEMENT THAT THE MISSA SOLEMNIS WOULD BE PUBLISHED BY SCHOTT.   (E)
                                                  1 No. 4 [October 1824] 372

REVIEW OF THE FIRST PERFORMANCE OF THE NINTH SYMPHONY.   (F)
                                                    1 No. 4 [October 1824] 373

KANONS NEBST ERWÄHNUNG IHRER VERANLASSUNG. Ludwig van Beethoven.   (G)
   Satirical "life history" of Tobias Haslinger substantially as given in Beethoven's letter of January 22nd 1825 to Schott
   (KS II 354) and exactly as reprinted in Unger's 'Beethoven und seine Verleger' (1921) p. 18, and Canons 'Schwenke'
   GA 23/256 No. 11 and 'Hofmann und kein Hofmann' GA 23/256 No. 8. (NOTE by DWM. In connection with the
   uncertainty referred to in KS II 171 regarding this Canon, note that neither KS nor the GA follow the spelling as it
   appears in this first publication of the Canon, the title being: 'Auf einen welcher Hoffmann geheissen,' and the text
   being: "Hoffmann! Sei ja kein Hofmann, ja kein Hofmann! Nein, nein, nein, nein, ich heisse Hoffman und bin
   kein Hofmann.")   2 No. 7 [April 1825] 205

INVITATION TO SUBSCRIBE TO OPP. 123-125.   (H)
   Published in 'Intelligenzblatt' No. 9 [20 April 1825] p. 12; No. 10, p. 19; No. 11, p. 29; No. 12 (?), p. 43; No. 11,
   p. 30 gives warning dated 30 July 1825 against 4-hand arrangement by Henning of Op. 123 (see TDR IV 308). No.
   12 (?), p. 46 announces copyright for Schott in the Prussian States of Opp. 121-128 incl.).

F. S. KANDLERS TÄTIGKEIT ZUR VERBREITUNG DEUTSCHER MUSIK IN ITALIEN.   (I)
   Ricordi in Milan has brought out an edition of 'Christus am Oelberge' Op. 85, with Italian text by Franz Salomon
   Kandler.   3 No. 10 [August 1825] 124

'WELLINGTON'S VICTORY' OPUS 91. Gottfried Weber.   (J)
   Analysis in intimate detail. "To think that Beethoven could have such tawdry thoughts about so great an event!"
                                                   3 No. 10 [August 1825] 155

OPFERLIED OPUS 121, BUNDESLIED OPUS 122, NAMENSFEIER OVERTURE OPUS 115, DEDICATION OF THE HOUSE   (K)
   OVERTURE OPUS 124. Grosheim et al.
   Reviews. The reviewer remarks that Op. 115 is the first work (to his knowledge) in which the composer describes
   his function with the word "gedichtet" rather than "Componirt." (See also 5 No. 20 [November 1826] 250)
                                                5 No. 17 [June 1826] 30

QUARTET IN E FLAT OPUS 127 (parts). J. A. L. de La Fage.   (L)
   Review.   5 No. 18 [August 1826] 145

QUARTET IN E FLAT OPUS 127 (score).   (M)
   Review.   5 No. 20 [November 1826] 239

OPFERLIED OPUS 121. Ignaz v. Seyfried.   (N)
   Review.   5 No. 20 [November 1826] 247

DER KUSS OPUS 128. Ignaz v. Seyfried.   (O)
   Review.   5 No. 20 [November 1826] 250

METRONOMISCHE BEZEICHNUNG DER TEMPI DER NEUESTEN BEETHOVENSCHEN SYMPHONIE, OPUS 125 (MITGETHEILT (A)
    VOM COMPONISTEN). Ludwig van Beethoven.
    Markings as given in Nohl's 'Neue Briefe Beethovens' p. 291, except for incorrect count of 96 for the Finale Presto
    (see 'London Sunday Times' 17 October 1948).   6 No. 21-22 [December 1826] 158

CORRECTIONS.   (B)
    Corrections to Schott edition of Opp. 125 and 127 substantially as given in NB J 3 [1927] 59, of which Kal 1198 is
    a faulty copy.   6 No. 23 [1827] fol. p. 26

LUDW. V. BEETHOVEN (necrology).   (C)
    Material given in KS II 474, to which is appended facsimile and transcription of letter of September 17th 1824 to
    Schott (KS II 335), the first paragraph being omitted.   6 No. 24 [May 1827] 309

ANNOUNCEMENT.   (D)
    Announcement of the publication of the Missa Solemnis (sic) Op. 123 in score, parts and piano arrangement, and of
    the forthcoming publication of "Beethoven's last Quartet, in C sharp minor, Op. 129 (sic)."
                         6 Intelligenzblatt No. 24 [May 1827] 27

KLEINE BEITRÄGE ZU L. VAN BEETHOVENS CHARAKTERISTIK UND ZUR GESCHICHTE SEINE WERKE.   (E)
    Anton Schindler.
    A letter from Schindler to Schott, dated September 29th 1827, in which Schindler mentions incidents in connection
    with the composition of the Missa Solemnis, refers to an opera book submitted to Beethoven the previous year, and
    continues: "A little while ago I received a song which a court singer in Karlsruhe (I think his name was Schütze)
    brought out, and which is attributed to Hr. C. van Beethoven. Hr. C. van Beethoven is the nephew of the revered
    master L. Beethoven, and during the latter's lifetime it never occurred to him to write a note of music. Now, what
    do we have: two waltzes with text printed below; the first one is by F. Schubert and the second by Himmel, copied
    note for note. Should not the public be openly warned against so atrocious an act?"
                         7 No. 26 [1828] 90

LIBERA AND MISERERE. G. v. Weiler.   (F)
    Review. (See Seyfried 'Studien' (1853) Appendix pp. 56, 63)   7 No. 26 [1828] 123

AUFFORDERUNG. Ernst Woldemar.   (G)
    Uncomplimentary reference to Beethoven's later works.   8 No. 29 [1828] 36

PASQUILL AUF GFR. WEBER VON DEN HERREN L. VAN BEETHOVEN UND ABBÉ STADLER. Gottfried Weber.   (H)
    An attack on Beethoven as a result of the publication of his letter of February 6th 1826 to Abbé Stadler (KS II 420),
    facsimile of which is given. A facsimile is also given of the first part of Beethoven's letter of May 7th 1825 to
    Schott (KS II 365) and (to show how rough Beethoven's tongue could be) of that part of the letter of February 5th 1825
    to Schott (KS II 358) in which Beethoven pays his respects to Steiner and Haslinger. The author attributes the first
    of these letters to Beethoven's anger at the author's unfavorable comments on 'The Battle of Vittoria' (3 No. 10
    [August 1825] 155). See also 8 No. 30 [1828] 135 and 'Berliner allgemeine musikalische Zeitung' 5 [1828] 121.
                         8 No. 29 [1828] 60

KLEINE ENTGEGNUNG. C. F. Becker.   (I)
    Defense of Beethoven against the criticisms of Woldemar (p. 36).   8 No. 30 [1828] 135

'GALERIE DES MUSICIENS CÉLÈBRES' F. J. Fétis.   (J)
    Review of book in which the entry appears: "Beethoven, Ludw. Van, born in Bonn in 1772."
                         13 No. 50 [1831] 134

REVIEW OF THE 'EASY SONATA' IN C MAJOR GA 16/159.   (K)
    "The publisher (Dunst, Frankfurt) received the original manuscript from Hr. geheimen medicinalrathe Dr. Wegeler
    in Coblenz, whose wife, the former Frl. von Breuning received it in 1796 from the master whom her family had
    greatly befriended, and who had retained it until now."   13 No. 52 [1831] 285

L. VON BEETHOVEN IN SEINER GUTEN LAUNE.   (L)
    Title page of Op. 104.   21 [1842] 59

DEUTSCHE TEXT ZU L. VAN BEETHOVENS MESSE OPUS 86.   (A)
  Text to the "Three Hymns" by Musikdirektor Scholz of Warmbrunn referred to by Schindler (1840) p. 136 as most
  moving to Beethoven.   23 [1844] 54

UNPUBLISHED LETTERS. F. M. Gredy.   (B)
  EDr (incomplete) of Kal 1017, Kal 1041, Kal 1045.   25 [1846] 26

EINIGE GEDANKEN ÜBER DIE AUFFASSUNG VON INSTRUMENTALKOMPOSITIONEN IN HINSICHT DES ZEITMASSES, (C)
  NAMENTLICH BEI BEETHOVEN'SCHEN WERKE. Joseph Fischhof.
  There is no one and only correct tempo.   26 [1847] 84

CHESTERIAN

SOME NOTES ON BEETHOVEN'S STRING QUARTETS. Felix White.   (D)
  Alone among Beethoven's works, the quartets do not in the present day appear dated because of later advances in
  instrumental writing. Various books on the quartets are discussed; for that by de Marliave, Beethoven's motto for
  Op. 131 is suggested: "Zusammengestohlen aus Verschiedenem diesem und jenem." The use in the Cavatina of
  Op. 130 of the echoes so effectively used in the Adagio of Op. 125 is mentioned.
                                                 8 [1927] 122

BEETHOVEN IN PARIS. J. G. Prod'homme.   (E)
  Abridgement of article appearing in 'Die Musik' 19$_1$ [1927] 400.   8 [1927] 150

SOME INDICATIONS REGARDING THE NINTH SYMPHONY. J. G. Prod'homme.   (F)
  Summary of the article by Otto Baensch in 'Neues Beethoven-Jahrbuch' 2 [1925] 137.
                                                 9 [1928] 218

'WACHTELSCHLAG' AND OPUS 31 No. 3. J. G. Prod'homme.   (G)
  Translation of article appearing in 'Revue de Musicologie' 11 [1930] 36.
                                                12 [1930] 70

LAST PERIODS. R. W. S. Mendl.   (H)
  "The essence of a 'third period' is that the works comprised in it should possess a quality of which we should have
  no inkling if the composer had died before producing them."   13 [1931] 11

BEETHOVEN'S SECOND THOUGHTS. R. W. S. Mendl.   (I)
  Beethoven's decision not to use the D minor theme for a Finale Istrumentale for Op. 125 but instead for Op. 132
  was advantageous for the Symphony. The second thought by which a new finale was written for Op. 130, with the
  original published as Op. 133, was not a good one.   31 [1957] 88

COCK'S MUSICAL MISCELLANY

INSTRUMENTAL COMPOSITIONS OF LUDWIG VAN BEETHOVEN. Charles Theodore Seiffert.   (J)
                                                 1 [1852] 6, 18

THE GENIUS OF BEETHOVEN, WITH RECOLLECTIONS OF BEETHOVEN. Carl Czerny.   (K)
  Of value only as reminiscences of a musician of importance who knew Beethoven intimately.
                                                 1 [1852] 53, 65

THE DOCTRINE OF MELODY ILLUSTRATED FROM BEETHOVEN. A. B. Marx and W. G. F. Beale et al   (L)
  Marx cites a passage toward the end of Op. 81a to show that a clash of tonic and dominant may be justified for
  dramatic reasons. His critic attempts to justify the chord progression by the rules of harmony, and Marx and others
  point out his error.   1 [1852] 79, 92, 101

CARL CZERNY AND THE RECOLLECTIONS OF BEETHOVEN. Carl Czerny.   (A)
   A letter from Czerny includes the statement that in the year 1809 "Beethoven's hearing was perfect -- he played in
   public, conducted with the greatest precision, and one could converse with him in a low voice (although he frequently
   suffered from pain in the ear)."   1 [1853] 124

THE PERIODS OF BEETHOVEN'S COMPOSITIONS. Carl Czerny.   (B)
   A letter from Czerny includes the statement: "Up to the year 1812 he heard perfectly well; but from that period his
   hearing became continually weaker. Complete deafness supervened only in 1816 or 1817." Czerny divides the
   works from Op. 100 to Op. 137 into three groups according to whether they were completed prior to the onset of total
   deafness, started before this critical time and completed thereafter, or conceived and worked out while completely
   deaf.   1 [1853] 137

OBSERVATIONS ON THE PERFORMANCE OF CERTAIN DOUBTFUL PASSAGES IN BEETHOVEN'S SYMPHONIES.   (C)
     Carl Czerny.
   Mention of errors already brought to notice by Schumann ('Neue Zeitschrift für Musik' 15 [1841] 149) and by Czerny
   himself (Ibid. p. 168) in the Fourth, Fifth and Sixth Symphonies, and statement that the alla breve in the scherzo
   of the Eroica must be taken fully up to tempo.   2 [1853] 29

                                        CORONA

EINIGE BRIEFE BEETHOVENS ERSTMALS MITGETEILT. Max Unger.   (D)
   (1) Letter of February 28th 1812 to G. C. Härtel: "Also im sachsen Lande sagt man . . . " speaks pessimistically of
   his health and happiness, and inquires about several works (Opp. 83, 86, Overture to Egmont) and about copies of the
   Mozart Requiem and Don Giovanni which Härtel was to send. (2) Letter without date (probably about 1812) to the
   Gebrüder Offenheimer: "Hr. Stoll hat mich ersucht, Bürge . . . " in which Beethoven offers to guarantee a loan of
   four louis d'or to Joseph Ludwig Stoll. (3) Letter without date (probably February 1814) to von Hartmann: "Unser
   Beethoven bittet Unsern Hartmann Seine Akademie . . . " inviting Hartmann to the concert of February 27th 1814
   and requesting that an announcement of the concert be inserted in the Oesterreichische Beobachter. (4) Letter without date (about December 1814) to Friedrich Treitschke: "Hier lieber Freund der Brief von Prag . . . " asking
   Treitschke's help in bringing about a few performances of Fidelio. (5) Letter without date probably May 1823) to
   Diabelli: "Stechen Sie mir nach dem E (xemplar) von Paris . . . " regarding Op. 111, Beethoven's eye trouble, a
   possible loan of 300 florins if needed, and various other compositions. (6) Letter without date (about September
   25th 1826) to Tobias Haslinger: "Wenn Sie wöllten die Gefälligkeit haben, die Hier . . . " requesting a fine binding for the copy of the Missa Solemnis to be sent to Friedrich Wilhelm III. (NOTE. See this same material in
   'Music & Letters' 15 [1934] 1)   3 [1933] 512

                                   COURRIER MUSICAL

LA SUCCESSION DE BEETHOVEN.   (E)
   A list of the items constituting Beethoven's estate, with appraised value and sale price, as given in Frimmel's
   'Beethoven-Studien' II 171ff. The net yield of the estate was approximately 8948 florins, bequeathed entirely to
   Nephew Karl, who received the income but was not authorized to touch the principal. The principal reverted to
   Karl's widow Caroline, who gradually drew upon it, the last withdrawal being in 1874. The quartet of instruments
   in the Nachlass (presumably those presented by Lichnowsky, TK I 276) were valued only at 78 florins for the four
   and sold for a total of 96 florins. "As one can see by this price, these were not genuine instruments.
                                              7 [1904] 153

UNE VISITE À LA MAISON DE BEETHOVEN.   A. de Marsy.   8 [1905] 593   (A)

SUR LES TRENTE-DEUX SONATES DE BEETHOVEN.   Paul Locard.   (B)
   General.   8 [1905] 669,703;   9 [1906] 52

LA RELIGION DE BEETHOVEN ET LA "MISSA SOLEMNIS."   Fritz Volbach.   (C)
   Translation of pp. 93-101 of the author's book 'Beethoven' (1905).   8 [1905] 689;   9 [1906] 6 = 726

NOTES SUR LE QUINZIÈME QUATUOR, OPUS 132, DE BEETHOVEN.   Guillaume Lekeu.   (D)
   Rhapsodic.   9 [1906] 733

M. WEINGARTNER ET LES SYMPHONIES DE BEETHOVEN.   (E)
   Translation of the first part of the preface to Weingartner's 'Ratschläge für Aufführung der Symphonien Beethovens'
   (1906).   10 [1907] 133

LE POÈTE AUTRICHIEN CASTELLI ET BEETHOVEN.   H. Kling.   (F)
   Remarks by Castelli (1781-1862) on his acquaintance with Beethoven, and comments by the author.   A prose translation is given of the poem which Castelli read at Beethoven's funeral.
                                 11 [1908] 488

"L'IMORTELLE BIENAIMÉE" DE BEETHOVEN.   Michel Brenet.   (G)
   Summary of the controversy.   12 [1909] 2

L'EXAMPLE DE BEETHOVEN.   Edouard Schneider.   13 [1910] 748   (H)

UN CHEF-D'OEUVRE DIGNE D'ÊTRE SIGNÉ PAR BEETHOVEN.   Vulius.   (I)
   Comments on Brahms' 'Alto Rhapsody' Op. 53.   14 [1911] 426

RÉFLEXIONS SUR LA MESSE EN RÉ MAJEUR.   Camille Mauclair.   (J)
   Emotional description of the music in its parallelism to Michelangelo's 'Last Judgment.'
                                 15 [1912] 2

NOTRE ÉPOQUE ET BEETHOVEN.   Emile Bourge.   (K)
   Essay stimulated by d'Indy's 'Beethoven.'   15 [1912] 296

EN ÉCOUTANT LA "NEUVIÈME."   Camille Mauclair.   (L)
   General.   16 [1913] 2

BEETHOVEN ET LES PEINTRES DE L'ÉCOLE FLAMANDE.   Elie Poirée.   (M)
   Beethoven's Flemish ancestry is stressed to support the conclusion that there are "numerous affinities between
   Beethoven's conceptions and those of the Flemish and Dutch masters."
                                 16 [1913] 62

BEETHOVEN MALGRÉ LUI.   Camille Mauclair.   (N)
   Essay.   22 [1920] 1

COURRIER MUSICAL ET THÉÂTRAL*

BEETHOVEN.   Adolphe Boschot.   26 [1924] 191   (O)

CONSEILS SUR L'INTERPRÉTATION (SONATA "L'AURORE" DE BEETHOVEN).   Georges Sporck.   (P)
   Detailed suggestions for the performer.   27 [1925] 511,571

LES DÉDICACES BEETHOVENIENNES.   Vincent d'Indy.   (Q)
   Beethoven rarely used his dedications to curry favor.   Most of those named were either friends or patrons (e. g. ,
   Waldstein, Lichnowsky, Lobkowitz, Rasumovsky, Galitsin and (above all) the Archduke Rudolph) or else pupils or
   interpreters (e. g. , Eleanore von Breuning, Babette Keglewicz, Zmeskall, Therese von Brunswick).
                                 29 [1927] 53

---

* Before 1923 Courrier Musical.

BEETHOVEN À LA SOCIÉTÉ DES CONCERTS DU CONSERVATOIRE.   Philippe Gaubert.   (A)
Vague but laudatory account.   29 [1927] 55

LES NEUF SYMPHONIES.   J. G. Prod'homme.   (B)
Brief and general discussion of each Symphony.   29 [1927] 56

LES QUATUORS À CORDES.   Lucien Capet.   (C)
Rhapsody.   29 [1927] 57

L'INTERPRÉTATION DE LA "SONATE APPASSIONATA."   Edouard Risler.   (D)
A few hints on fingering, dynamics, timbre, etc.   29 [1927] 58

LES TRENTE-DEUX SONATES POUR PIANO.   Goutran Arcouet.   (E)
Brief comments on each sonata.   29 [1927] 59

QUELQUES CONSIDÉRATIONS SUR LE MYSTICISME DE BEETHOVEN ET LE SYMBOLISME DE SA LANGUE MUSICALE.   (F)
     Paul Loyonnet.   29 [1927] 62

LES MESSES DE BEETHOVEN.   Félix Raugel.   (G)
Brief and popular discussion.   29 [1927] 64

LES ORIGINES FLAMANDES DE BEETHOVEN.   Adolphe Boschot.   (H)
Without significance.   29 [1927] 64

BEETHOVEN ET L'AUVERGNE.   J. Canteloube.   (I)
Several traditional melodies of Auvergne bear marked similarity to themes of the Pastoral Symphony.
                                          29 [1927] 65

LE FINALE DE LA IXe SYMPHONIE.   Albert Bertelon.   (J)
Discussion after the style of a lecture on music appreciation.   29 [1927] 477

L'ATAVISME DE BEETHOVEN.   Julien Tiersot.   (K)
Review and summary of book by van Aerde 'Les ancêtres flamands de Beethoven' (1928).
                                    30 [1928] 141,171

LES DIX-SEPT QUATUORS DE BEETHOVEN.   Lucien Capet.   (L)
Interpretation in great detail of Op. 135, which bears not the slightest relationship to Beethoven's music.
                                    30 [1928] 213

Volumes 7 - 30 checked complete except for the following:

Vol.	16	Nos. 11, 14-24 inc.
	17	all
	18	all
	21	No. 5
	22	No. 10
	23	No. 11

Absence of an index and the superficial nature of the few articles on Beethoven appearing since World War I made it seem not worth while to check subsequent volumes.

DENKMÄLER DER TONKUNST IN OESTERREICH

DIE STILEIGENTÜMLICHKEITEN DES JUNGEN BEETHOVEN.   Hans Gal.   (M)
"Absolute melody" is diatonic melody without suspensions or appoggiaturas. This style characterizes the mature Beethoven; it is the goal which the young master steadily approaches. The Mozartean style (epitomized in the Andante of the G minor Symphony K.550) is the complete antithesis of this type of melody.

The Mannheim-Mozart-contemporary Italian opera style (characterized by suspensions, ornamentation and chromaticism) is the most conspicuous characteristic of the Bonn compositions, and is the style from which Beethoven's own development took place. Commenting on Riemann's discussion of Beethoven's relationship to the Mannheim school ('Die Musik' 7₃ [1908] 3, 85), the author says that it was Mozart who sublimated this style but Beethoven who escaped from it. In Thayer's careful list of the considerable amount of contemporary music performed in Bonn, there is no mention of a single composition by Haydn. The tremendous advance in Beethoven's work from the Cantatas of 1790 to the Op. 1 Trios of 1793-94 may well have been due in large measure to the familiarity which he had gained with Haydn's music, a style based directly on the folk song.

The young Beethoven, unlike Mozart and Haydn, made much use of the turn (e. g. , first theme of Op. 1 No. 3; andante of Op. 10 No. 1) and of the pralltrill (e. g. , finale of the F minor Bonn Pf Sonata, second theme of the first movement of Op. 13). Suspensions and appoggiaturas, very typical of Mozart, are also typical of early Beethoven (e. g. , finale of the Sonata Op. 7) and (in vocal works or in instrumental melodies of a vocal character) of Beethoven in all periods (e. g. , Benedictus of the Missa Solemnis, Arioso of Op. 110). The use of sequences in this connection is especially typical (e. g. , second theme of the finale of Op. 27 No. 2, first theme of the Horn Sonata Op. 17). A similar detailed discussion is given of the influences of Haydn on Beethoven (notably the importance of melodies built on triads). The characteristics of the mature Beethoven are also discussed in great detail: harmony, rhythm, period construction (Beethoven's frequent use of sequences in his melodies, whereas Mozart continues with new invention. a perfect example of this difference being found in two very similar melodies: the second theme of the finale of Op. 1 No. 3 vs. the theme of the andante of K. 311), major structural form (Beethoven's practice of using all his thematic material in development sections). Consideration is also given to Beethoven's typical figurations, his characteristic harmonic progressions and cadences, his rhythmic tendencies, his marked tendency towards threefold repetition. Comparison of Op. 4 with Op. 103 shows his great advance in the technique of composition between 1792-93 and 1796. From stylistic considerations, the author has the greatest doubt of the geniuneness of the Jena Symphony.

4 [1916] 58

BEETHOVEN'S IMPORTANCE IN THE HISTORY OF SONG WRITING. Editha Alberti-Radanowicz.   (A)
In an exhaustive study of the song in Vienna from 1778 to 1815, the author says, "I have not been able to detect any influence of Beethoven's songs on his contemporaries, aside from the inevitable fact that many contemporaries in their musical development were completely under his spell. "   10 [1923] 74

DIE FUGENARBEIT IN DEN WERKEN BEETHOVENS. Friedrich Deutsch.   (B)
Drawing examples from the 25 or so fugues or fugal passages dating from all periods of Beethoven's life, the author gives detailed discussion of (a) Beethoven's technique of fugal composition, and (b) the influence on Beethoven's writing of the baroque and the Vienna fugal schools, the growth of Beethoven's own fugal style, and the effect of his work on the further development of the fugue.   14 [1927] 75

DIE OBOE BEI BEETHOVEN. Hans Wlach.   (C)
A consideration of the instrument and its technique, in Beethoven's time and today; remarks on Beethoven's familiarity with the instrument, its capabilities and its limitations (which must have been considerable); his use of the oboe in chamber music and in orchestral music; his delineative use of the oboe.   14 [1927] 107

DAS HAUPTTHEMA IN DEN SONATENSÄTZEN BEETHOVENS. Walter Senn.   (D)
A detailed analysis of the structure of the principal themes in Beethoven's 180 movements in sonata form, with a consideration of the practices of his predecessors in this connection.   16 [1929] 86

DEUTSCHE GESELLSCHAFT FÜR MUSIKWISSENSCHAFT

BEETHOVENS RELIGIOSITÄT. Arnold Schmitz.   (E)
Passages in Schindler's 'Biography' gave rise to the idea of Beethoven as a deist or a pantheist rather than as an adherent of any formal religious belief. While he was much influenced by the writings of a Protestant author (Sturm's 'Betrachtungen über die Werke Gottes im Reich der Natur und der Versehung') and while his freedom of thought and

BEETHOVENS RELIGIOSITÄT (Continued)
   practice was considerable by twentieth century standards (it is quite possible that he was a Freemason) there can be
   no doubt that he considered himself a Catholic.   [1925] 274

DEUTSCHE MUSIK-ZEITUNG (Bagge)

BEETHOVENS VARIATIONEN IN C-MOLL Nr. 36.   (A)
   Substantially the material given by Wilhelm von Lenz in 'Beethoven -- eine Kunst-Studie' (1860) V 324-32.
                                                1 [1860] 36,43

EIN BRIEF VON BEETHOVEN.   (B)
   First publication of letter of June 18th 1818 to Nanette Streicher (KS II 114).
                                                2 [1861] 123

BEETHOVENS E-MOLL-QUARTETT, OPUS 59.   S. Bagge.   (C)
   Penetrating analysis.   2 [1861] 289

IN SACHEN BEETHOVENS.   (D)
   Critical comments on a preface by Franz Espagne to an edition of the National Airs which Beethoven arranged for
   Thomson.   2 [1861] 372

IN SACHEN BEETHOVENS.   Franz Espagne.   (E)
   Polemic (see p. 372 supra).   2 [1861] 394

IN SACHEN BEETHOVENS.   (F)
   Conclusion of the exchange of comments with Espagne.   2 [1861] 413

ÜBER WÜNSCHENSWERTHE ÄNDERUNGEN IN VIELEN CLAVIERCOMPOSITIONEN MOZARTS UND BEETHOVENS.   (G)
   A recommendation that editors revise the piano works of Mozart and Beethoven to take advantage of the more extended range of the present-day piano.   3 [1862] 4

BEETHOVEN IN GNEIXENDORF.   (H)
   Anecdotes from an unnamed man who lived in Gneixendorf during the 1820's.
                                                3 [1862] 77

SIND "ÄNDERUNGEN IN VIELEN CLAVIERCOMPOSITIONEN MOZARTS UND BEETHOVENS" DER ERWEITERTEN   (I)
       CLAVIATUR WEGEN WIRKLICH UNBEDINGT "WÜNSCHENSWERTH"?
   A few passages are cited in which Beethoven's musical expression undoubtedly suffered as a result of the five octave
   limitation of his piano. It seems inevitable, however, that when an editor starts to change Beethoven's original he
   feels that he must improve on Beethoven's ideas.   3 [1862] 153,161

ZUR VERSTÄNDIGUNG.   (J)
   The author of the note on page 4 agrees with the opinions expressed on pp. 153 and 161. He suggests that where
   changes in Beethoven's text seem advisable the changes be shown as suggested variants, with the original text given
   as Beethoven wrote it.   3 [1862] 208

VON BEETHOVENS HAND CORRIGIRTE ORCHESTERSTIMMEN, IN BESITZ DER GES. D. MUSIKFREUNDE.   (K)
   Some orchestra parts from each of the last five symphonies (from the Seventh Symphony, almost complete) and of
   the Overture 'Die Weihe des Hauses' Op. 124, corrected in Beethoven's own hand, have been found in the library of
   the Gesellschaft der Musikfreunde in Vienna.   3 [1862] 215

BEETHOVENS LETZTE QUARTETTE.   (L)
   Detailed analyses of the last five Quartets (with, however, no mention of the Grosse Fuge), and survey of all sixteen
   quartets to show that the last five are formally akin to the earlier ones and differ from them only as Beethoven had
   grown technically and spiritually.   3 [1862] 281,289,297,305,313

THE GUARNERIUS VIOLIN OWNED BY BEETHOVEN.   (M)
   The general understanding that the Guarnerius violin from the set of instruments presented to Beethoven by Prince

Lichnowsky had come into the possession of Karl Holz and had been sold by his widow to an English collector is apparently without foundation. The four instruments in the Imperial Library in Berlin are undoubtedly genuine.

3 [1862] 328,360

(A)

EINE JUGENDARBEIT BEETHOVENS.
Brief analyses of the three youthful piano quartets.   3 [1862] 350

After 1862 the 'Deutsche Musik-Zeitung' made way for the Neue Folge of the 'Allgemeine Musikalische Zeitung. '

DEUTSCHE MUSIKER-ZEITUNG

(B)

EINIGE BRIEFE BEETHOVENS.
Republication of letters given in KS I 59, II 420 (abridged), I 263 (here dated January 15th 1812), II 447 (No. 1189), II 472.   1 [1870] 273,281

(C)

ZUM HUNDERTJÄHRIGEN GEBURTSTAG L. V. BEETHOVENS.   Hermann Mendel.
Poem.   1 [1870] 289

(D)

ZUR CHARAKTERISTIK BEETHOVENS.
Popular biographical sketch.   1 [1870] 297

(E)

DIE AN BEETHOVENS GRABE GEHALTENE LEICHENREDE.
The funeral oration written by Grillparzer and delivered by Anschütz.
1 [1870] 299

(F)

EIN BRIEF BEETHOVENS.
Letter given in KS I 33.   2 [1871] 31

(G)

EIN BRIEF BEETHOVENS.
Letter given in KS I 360.   2 [1871] 55

(H)

HEKTOR BERLIOZ ÜBER DIE C-MOLL-SYMPHONIE VON BEETHOVEN. 2 [1871] 89

(I)

HEKTOR BERLIOZ ÜBER DIE SINFONIE EROICA VON BEETHOVEN.   2 [1871] 97,105

(J)

EINE ERINNERUNG AN BEETHOVEN.
Summary of an account by Ferdinand Hiller of Beethoven's death and funeral.
2 [1871] 119

(K)

PRAG ZU ANFANGE DES 19. JAHRHUNDERTS UND BEETHOVENS BESUCH DA SELBST.   Alfred Meissner.
The domicile in Prague of the Abbé Vogler and the concerts which Stiebelt gave there in 1799 set the musical tone for the city at the beginning of the century. Beethoven first visited Prague in February 1796, and was then introduced by the painter (Alexander) Macco to (August Gottlieb) Meissner the poet (grandfather of the author of this article). At that time Beethoven already had the libretto of Fidelio (!), and planned to follow this work with other operas. Meissner suggested an oratorio to be based on the conflict between St. Paul and Nero in A.D. 64 (see Beethoven's letter of November 2nd 1803 to Macco (KS I 80) but nothing came of it.
2 [1871] 145

(L)

BEITRAG ZUR LEBENSGESCHICHTE LUDWIG V. BEETHOVENS.   Alois Fuchs.
Letter given in KS I 110.   2 [1871] 260

(M)

ZUR GESCHICHTE VON BEETHOVENS FIDELIO.
General.   2 [1871] 354

(N)

AUFRUF.   Josef Scheu.
Appeal for aid for Caroline van Beethoven, widow of Nephew Karl.
4 [1873] 332

AUS BEETHOVENS LEBEN.   F. X. Boch.   (A)
  The story of Beethoven's refusal to play for French officers at Prince Lichnowsky's palace (as summarized in TK II 68).
  (This article was presumably reprinted from the 'Wiener Deutsche Zeitung' of August 31st 1873.)
                                      5 [1874] 10

EINE PASTORALSINFONIE VOM JAHRE 1784.   (B)
  A symphony 'Le Portrait Musical de la Nature' by Justin Heinrich Knecht, with program paralleling Beethoven's
  Sixth Symphony, was published in 1784 by the same firm (Bossler) which had issued Beethoven's three early Pf sonatas
  the previous year. (See also 'Niederrheinische Musik-Zeitung' 14 [1866] 379)
                                      6 [1875] 414

BEETHOVENS LETZTE WOHNUNG IN WIEN.   (C)
  Description of the 'Schwarzspanierhaus' as given by Gerhard von Breuning.
                                      6 [1875] 463

FIDELIO.   (D)
  Popular account of the history of the opera.   8 [1877] 137

EIN BEITRAG ZU BEETHOVENS LEBEN.   (E)
  Reminiscences of Ludwig Spohr.   8 [1877] 223

FIDELIO.   Rudolph Bunge.   (F)
  Reminiscences of 1805-06 by Joseph Röckel, the Florestan of the 1806 performances.
                                      10 [1879] 19,29,40

BEETHOVEN UND DIE FREIHEITSIDEEN.   Ludwig Nohl.   (G)
  An extended discussion of the importance which Beethoven gave throughout his life to the idea of freedom, and of
  the effect upon him of the political events of his period.   10 [1879] 499,511

BEETHOVENS ERSTES DEBUT.   Gustav Mey.   (H)
  Tale that in 1785 Franz Wegeler, then only slightly acquainted with Beethoven, heard him 'conducting' a violent
  summer thunder storm, then went with him to an abbey where he heard Beethoven play on the organ, and thereby set
  in motion the chain of events which led to Beethoven's appointment as Court Organist.
                                      11 [1880] 33

BEETHOVENS LETZTE LEBENSTAGE.   Ludwig Nohl.   (I)
  Biographical sketch with no especial reference to Beethoven's last days.
                                      11 [1880] 121,132,141

BEETHOVENS VIOLINE.   (J)
  Description of the violin sold by Karl Holz's widow to an English collector on the claim that it was Beethoven's
  favorite instrument given by him shortly before his death to Holz.
                                      11 [1880] 198

BEETHOVENS BEGRÄBNIS.   (K)
  Account of the funeral as given in the Appendix to Seyfried's 'Studien.'
                                      12 [1881] 496

BEETHOVEN AND GOETHE.   (L)
  General.   14 [1883] 557

ZWEI VERSCHOLLENE KANTATEN VON BEETHOVEN.   (M)
  Summary of article by Eduard Hanslick in the Vienna 'Neue Freie Presse' (May 13th 1884) describing and commenting
  upon the Trauerkantate GA 25/264 and the Erhebungskantate GA 25/265, the manuscripts of which had been recently
  found after having been lost for more than ninety years.   15 [1884] 229

BEETHOVENS BEZIEHUNGEN ZU BERLIN.   Alfr. Chr. Kalischer.   (N)
  Preliminary study of a small portion of the material later covered in the author's book 'Beethoven und Berlin' (1908).
                                      15 [1884] 517,528,539,564,576;
                                      16 [1885] 11

EINE BÜSTE VON BEETHOVEN.   (A)
   Brief account of the preparation of the death mask.   16 [1885] 372

BEETHOVENS 'TRAUERKANTATE.' W. Lackowitz.   (B)
   General.   17 [1886] 171

BEETHOVEN VON HOHER ABSTAMMUNG.   (C)
   The tradition, current since 1810 (Alexander Choron and Francois Fayolle: 'Dictionnaire historique des musiciens
artistes et amateurs morts et vivants') that Beethoven was the natural son of the Emperor Friedrich Wilhelm II of
Prussia took color of authenticity from the facts (1) that the Emperor himself possessed musical talent and enthusiasm;
(2) that he manifested much interest in Beethoven while in Bonn; and (3) that he paid Beethoven signal recognition as
musician and composer when in 1796 Beethoven, at that time known chiefly as a brilliant improvisor, came to Berlin.
                                    18 [1887] 469

BEETHOVENS ZWEITE TOTENFAHRT.   (D)
   Detailed account of Beethoven's exhumation and his reinterment in the Zentalfriedhof.
                        19_2 [1888] 2

DER BEETHOVEN-SCHÄDEL UND DIE WISSENSCHAFT.   (E)
   Anthropological and phrenological judgments based upon measurements and study of Beethoven's skull.
                        19_2 [1888] 78

"DIE NEUNTE."   (F)
   Fiction.   20 [1889] 35,47

DAKES BEETHOVENBILD.   (G)
   Favorable comment on a portrait of Beethoven recently made by Carel L. Dake of Holland.
                   21 [1890] 242

LACHNER AND BEETHOVEN.   (H)
   An account by Lachner (first published in the Munich 'Zeitung') of his close acquaintance with Schubert and of his
recollections of Beethoven, whom he saw several times.   21 [1890] 363

BEETHOVENS C-MOLL-SYMPHONIE.   (I)
   Address by Richard Wagner at the ceremonies in 1872 when the cornerstone of the Bayreuth Festspielhaus was laid.
                   22 [1891] 178

ZUR GESCHICHTE DER KREUTZERSONATE.   (J)
   Article by Eduard Hanslick, with no new data, which appeared in an undated issue of the 'Neue Freie Presse' and
in the 'Allgemeine Musik-Zeitung' 19 [1892] 177.   23 [1892] 172

ÄLTESTE BERICHTE ÜBER BEETHOVENS "FIDELIO."   (K)
   Reviews of the performances of 1805 and 1806, and a blistering account by Clemens Brentano of his impressions of
the opera at the time of its first Berlin performance on October 11th 1815 (first published in the 'Spener'sche Zeitung'
of October 16th 1815, and reprinted in 'Music & Letters' 27 [1946] 248).
                   24 [1893] 52

GOUNOD ÜBER BEETHOVEN.   (L)
   Excerpts from a letter written in 1842 by Gounod (b. 1818), expressing extravagant admiration for Beethoven.
                26 [1895] 319

EIN KURIOSUM.   (M)
   Account of a performance supposed to have been given in London on April 30th 1884 of a 'Tenth Symphony' by
Beethoven, dictated by his shade to a medium named Helen Edith Green.
                26 [1895] 319

BEETHOVEN VOR NEUNZIG JAHREN IN BADEN.   (N)
   Fiction.   26 [1895] 564

EIN BESUCH IM GEBURTSHAUS BEETHOVENS.   H. Mund.   (A)

  27 [1896] 293

ANMERKUNGEN ZU BEETHOVENS INSTRUMENTALMUSIK.   Gunther Baum.   (B)
  Unimportant.   53 [1922] 100

BEETHOVENS GROBHEIT.   Max Unger.   (C)
  While Beethoven had reason enough to be rude, that characteristic represented only one side of his nature. Familiar
  examples of this type of conduct are given. A letter without date to Blöchlinger: "Ohnerachtet ihrer Aufkündigung
  . . ." ('Neue Musik-Zeitung' 45 [1924] 9) is "one of the most furious that Beethoven ever put to paper." Another
  letter from this same time (KK 957), probably to Bernard, was published in 'Die Musik' 9_1 [1909] 42 with many
  errors and unhelpful comments. A corrected version is given. Various instances of Beethoven's roughness with his
  publishers are cited, and his letter of July 17th (7th?) to Peters (KS II 267) is given with sundry corrections, as well
  as Peters' reply which broke off further dealings between Beethoven and this publisher.

  55 [1924] 149,164

EIN BEETHOVEN-GEDENKTAG.   Max Unger.   (D)
  The date in question, May 7th 1824, is that of the first performances of Opp. 123 and 125. A circumstantial account
  of the events leading to this concert, of the concert itself, and of the confusion in plans for publication is given.
  Two letters to Spohr are printed, those given in 'Neue Musik Zeitung' 44 [1923] 248 and 45 [1924] 142. (NOTE by
  DWM. The author says, "Both had appeared in newspapers, the first only recently, the second in the 1890's." No
  publication of the first prior to that in 'Neue Musik Zeitung' has been noted; the second appeared in 'Allgemeine
  Musik Zeitung' 21 [1894] 663.)   55 [1924] 204

UNBEKANNTE MEISTERBRIEFE.   (E)
  Account of a sale in May 1924 by Henrici includes reference to a letter without date to Brother Karl's widow Johanna,
  of which the following passages are given: "In Zukunft haben sie die gefälligkeit, wenn sie sich hier in Wien befinden,
  immer der Quittung ihre Wohnung bejzuzufügen, sind sie nicht hier, so haben sie vom Ortspfarrer . . . Zeugnis
  einzusenden, die 6# für den Stempel werde ich ersezen . . ." (Not in the KK letters)

  55 [1924] 285

BEETHOVEN IM KÄMPFE MIT DEM SCHICKSAL.   (F)
  Review of book of this title by Max Reinitz.   55 [1924] 345

DIE FRAUEN UM BEETHOVEN.   Felix von Lepel.   (G)
  Account of a meeting by the violinist Eduard Rappoldi with Giulietta Guicciardi and Therese von Brunswick about
  1850.   55 [1924] 440

BEETHOVEN ALS "KAPITALIST."   Max Unger.   (H)
  Beethoven's letter of July 16th 1816 to Steiner and Steiner's letter of December 29th 1820 to Beethoven ('Beethoven
  und seine Verleger' p. 79) show that for the four years before Beethoven bought the eight bank shares on July 13th
  1819 Beethoven had had 10,000 fl. WW invested in Steiner's business. The shares became a part of Nephew Karl's
  estate (by Beethoven's will he was entitled only to the income from them), and the proceeds from them went in part
  for the marriage bond which Karl's daughter Gabriele had to post for her fiancé and in part for vocal lessons for
  daughter Hermione.   55 [1924] 640

EIN MUSIKALISCHES KURIOSUM.   Anna Schwabacher-Bleichröder.   (I)
  Account of a concert in the 1880's when von Bülow performed the Ninth Symphony twice in one evening.
  56 [1925] 300

AUS BEETHOVENS LETZTEN LEBENSTAGEN.   Max Unger.   (J)
  Beethoven's letter of March 18th 1827 to Moscheles, previously published from the autograph and here given again,
  differs in some details from the version made public by Schindler and others in KS II 472.
  56 [1925] 330

VERSCHLEPPTE STICHFEHLER IN BEETHOVENSCHEN SINFONIEN.   Max Unger.   (A)
   A correction in the exposition section of the Eroica first movement, pointed out by Czerny in the 'Neue Wiener
   Musik-Zeitung' 2 [1853] 59 and by the author in 'Max Hesses Musikerkalender' for 1914 (p. 138) -- two omitted
   measures -- seems to have been overlooked by editors and conductors. Reference is also made to an article by
   Heuss on a superfluous measure in the Pastoral Symphony.   56 [1925] 620

BEETHOVENS SINFONIEN.   P. Martell.   (B)
   Popular.   56 [1925] 992,1012

BEETHOVEN.   Georg Gräner.   (C)
   "Phantasiestück."   56 [1925] 1160

BEETHOVEN AND WILHELMINE SCHROEDER-DEVRIENT.   (D)
   Schindler's story of the first appearance of Schroeder-Devrient in Fidelio, accepted in general by Thayer-Deiters-
   Riemann, is challenged in an article in 'Die Musik' 18$_1$ [1926] 438 from which excerpts are given.
                                                       57 [1926] 358

BEETHOVENS WORTSPIELE.   Theodor von Frimmel.   (E)
   Various examples of Beethoven's puns and his sportive use of words are quoted from the letters.
                                                       57 [1926] 584

BEETHOVEN AND WEBER.   Theodor von Frimmel.   (F)
   Summary of generally known facts.   57 [1926] 679

BEETHOVENS WURFGESCHOSSE.   Theodor von Frimmel.   (G)
   Instances are given of Beethoven's ire.   57 [1926] 700

BEETHOVEN AND GOETHE.   (H)
   The familiar anecdote regarding the encounter at Teplitz with nobility.
                                                       57 [1926] 865

DIE UNSTERBLICHE GELIEBTE BEETHOVENS.   Elsa Bienenfeld.   (I)
   Popular outline of Beethoven's relationship with Therese von Brunswick, Josephine Deym and Giulietta Guicciardi.
                                                       57 [1926] 888

BEETHOVENS KLAVIERSONATE OPUS 27 Nr. II.   Fritz Müller.   (J)
   Fanciful analysis.   57 [1926] 960

EIN BESUCH BEI BEETHOVEN.   Max Unger.   (K)
   An account of a visit to Beethoven in 1825 by the musician Gottlieb Wiedebein of Braunschweig, first published in
   an obscure journal of the time, is reprinted and commented on.   57 [1926] 1028

DIE LETZTE TAGE BEETHOVENS.   Ferdinand Hiller.   (L)
   The author, then fifteen years old, made several visits to Beethoven's sick room with Hummel. (Reprinted from
   'Insel-Almanach' for 1927)   57 [1926] 1144

BEETHOVEN AND JOHANN ANDREAS STREICHER.   (M)
   Comment on the two letters to Streicher given in Sonneck pp. 181ff. (Reprinted in 'Deutsche Allgemeine Zeitung,'
   March 25th 1927)   58 [1927] 228

BEETHOVEN AND THE HOHENZOLLERNS.   (N)
   Brief account of Beethoven's relations with the Prussian court.   58 [1927] 253

DEM ANDENKEN BEETHOVENS.   (O)
   Centennial essay.   58 [1927] 273

BEETHOVEN.   Max Unger.   (P)
   Centennial essay.   58 [1927] 274

NEUE KUNDE VOM TOTENBETTE BEETHOVENS.   Max Unger.   (A

Two recently discovered letters from Johann Baptist Streicher (son of Andreas) to Johann Andreas Stumpff were published a year or so ago by Elsa Bienefeld in the 'Neue Wiener Journal.' The letter of March 28th 1827 brought out the points: Beethoven's pleasure at the gift from the London Philharmonic Society, communicated to him on March 17th, caused a spontaneous flow of fluid which made additional tapping unnecessary. Thereafter he weakened steadily, and by Sunday evening March 25th had lost consciousness. Johann Schickh, editor of the 'Wiener Zeitschrift,' came to see Beethoven a few hours before his death. Beethoven died at 5:45 p.m. in the arms of his brother, in the presence of Anselm Hüttenbrenner, the painter Telscher, and J. B. Streicher (note that this disagrees with Hüttenbrenner's account, as told by him to A. W. Thayer TK III 307).

Some of Beethoven's old friends were hurt that he turned to London for financial help instead of to them or to the city where he had lived for so many years, and that meanwhile he had refused even the smallest gifts from them. Reference to a Dr. Landesheimer who offered to attend Beethoven without fee is probably meant for the Dr. Staudenheimer (or Staudenheim) mentioned by Schindler as one who often said he would come but who never appeared. In this connection the author says, "In my Beethoven studies I have over the years come to the firm conclusion that whenever Schindler makes a statement which is in conflict with that of a trustworthy witness, his opinion or comment is to be disregarded, and that he is least trustworthy when he disparages others."

In the letter of June 16th 1827 Streicher pointed out, regarding the disparity between Beethoven's pleas of poverty and his true financial condition, that it is the opinion of many physicians that a patient in Beethoven's condition may be expected to be highly anxious and parsimonious without real cause. As for the willingness of the Viennese to come to Beethoven's assistance, he mentioned that the proceeds of a concert to establish a Beethoven memorial amounted to barely 200 gulden and that the concerts of March 1824, requested to elaborately by an "Address" from many notables, did not even meet expenses, so that his request to London for a loan (not a gift) was not unjust to his associates.

Beethoven could with reason refer to "Wiener ohne Herz" (KS II 359), whereas from the days of Handel and Haydn, England had been known as a country generous to musicians, and was the home of Beethoven's friends Salomon, Moscheles, Stumpff, Neate, and others.   58 [1927] 276

DER HEITERE BEETHOVEN.   Anna Schwabacher-Bleichröder.   (B)

Apposite quotations from the letters.   58 [1927] 278

BEETHOVEN UND JOHANN STRAUSS IM KAMPF MIT DEN MUSIKVERLEGERN HASLINGER.   Fritz Lange.   (C

Beethoven had his troubles and quarrels with Tobias, Strauss with the son Carl (1816-68).
                    58 [1927] 304

BEETHOVENS ALLTAG.   (D

General remarks on Beethoven's eating habits and on his frequenting of taverns.
                    58 [1927] 305

BEETHOVEN ALS MILITÄRMARSCH-KOMPONIST.   (E)

Brief discussion of the 'Yorkscher Marsch' ('Marsch für die böhmische Landwehr' H-6), the 'Grenadiermarsch' in F ('Almanach der deutschen Musikbücherei' [1927] 320), and the lost march "1810 in Baden componiert für Erzherzog Anton 3 Sommermonath" (H-8).   58 [1927] 329

NEUE BRIEFE AN BEETHOVEN.   (F)

Reference to the letters from Härtel published in 'Zeitschrift für Musikwissenschaft' 9 [1927] 321.
                    58 [1927] 353

VON BEETHOVENS GEBURTSSTÄTTE.   Anna Schwabacher-Bleichröder.   (G)

Popular.   58 [1927] 376

BEETHOVEN ALS KULTURFAKTOR.   (A)
   Considering the large proportion of Germans who neither know nor care about Beethoven's music, his cultural
   importance is at best only coming to be.   58 [1927] 395

BEETHOVEN IN LIEBESBANDEN.   Max Unger.   (B)
   General discussion, unequivocally accepting 1812 as the year of the Immortal Beloved letters.
                                          58 [1927] 396,420,445

BURGER BEETHOVEN.   Eugen Braudo.   (C)
   Extracts from an article in the Russian journal 'Musik und Revolution,' pointing out the revolutionary tendencies
   shown in all periods of Beethoven's life.   58 [1927] 442

GOETHE AND BEETHOVEN.   (D)
   Reference to Beethoven's letter of 24 July 1812 to Breitkopf & Härtel, published in 'Die Musik' 19_2 [1927] 465.
                                          58 [1927] 474

BEETHOVENS PISTOLE.   (E)
   Summary of an article in 'Revue de musicologie' (?) regarding the pistols used in the 1822 Vienna performance of
   Fidelio, now in the museum of the Paris Opera.   58 [1927] 521

EINE ZEITGENÖSSISCHE HUMORISTISCHE KRITIK ÜBER BEETHOVEN.   (F)
   Quotation of a review of the concert of 2 January 1815 (Wellington's Victory and numbers from the Ruins of Athens)
   as observed by a countryman, quoted from 'Almanach der deutschen Musikbücherei' [1927] 347.
                                          58 [1927] 624

BEETHOVENS KLAVIERDRAMEN ALS SPIEGEL SEINER SEELE.   Konrad Zech.   (G)
                                          58 [1927] 630,649

EINE UNBEKANNTE KLEINE FREUNDIN BEETHOVENS.   Max Unger.   (H)
   Discussion of the letter of 17 July 1812 to Emilie (KS I 259) (Frimmel says EDr in 'Bothe für Tirol und Vorarlberg'
   1832; then Thayer III_1 205). The mood of this letter is especially notable for the fact that it was written only
   eleven days after the letter to the Immortal Beloved, and parallels between the two letters are cited. Emilie's
   surname is not known, but the "H" in the address stands for Hamburg: vide recently discovered letter to Breitkopf
   & Härtel: "Beiliegenden Brief bitte ich . . ." ('Zeitschrift für Musikwissenschaft' 7 [1924] 191). The date of the
   latter letter must be October 1812, since it refers to the letter to Emilie as having been written three months before.
   The letter regarding music for Amalie (KS I 258) was written the same day as the letter to Emilie. (NOTE by DWM.
   In the article including "Beiliegenden Brief . . ." referred to above, this letter is spoken of as the letter of trans-
   mittal of the Emilie letter, and probably written the following day.)
                                          58 [1927] 664

BEETHOVENS KONZERTREISE NACH DEUTSCHLAND.   Max Unger.   (I)
   The statement of Dlabacz that Beethoven had appeared in Prague in 1795 has not been verified, though Beethoven's
   letter of 19 February 1796 to Brother Johann (KS I 12) shows that he was in Prague early in 1796. It was probably on
   this trip that he finished 'Ah perfido' for Frau Duschek, and made the acquaintance of Dr. Kanka. A letter quoted
   in Schiedermair, written from Dresden on 24 April 1796, says: "Young Beethoven arrived here yesterday," and (from
   6 May): "Beethoven stopped here for about a week . . . . He is going from here to Leipzig and Berlin." No contemporary records showing his presence in Leipzig are known, but in 1822 Rochlitz referred to Beethoven's visit there
   "as a young man when he was traveling from Vienna." Schindler refers to the impression that Beethoven made in
   Leipzig by his playing and his improvising, a comment which Thayer questions. It seems certain that in Dresden
   and Leipzig his playing was in private concerts only, with no public appearances. Much is known about Beethoven's
   time in Berlin from WR and other sources. Thayer says that Beethoven left Berlin early in July. He probably returned
   by way of Dresden and Prague, possibly also visiting Dresden. During this return trip he met Kapellmeister Christian
   Kalkbrenner and his son Friedrich, then eight years old. In his autobiography (1842) Kalkbrenner said that the meeting took place in Dresden. In 1801 a formal invitation was drawn up inviting Beethoven to visit Dresden again, but
   nothing came of it.   58 [1927] 752,778,800

BEETHOVEN IN BUDAPEST. S. Eichner.   (A)
  Records of the 'Ofener und Pester Theatertaschenbuch' show that on 7 May 1800 a concert was given by "Herr
  Bethover" and Herr Punto. The report includes the following: "Who is this Bethover? The history of music in
  Germany does not know this name. Punto indeed is well-known." The records of a well-to-do music loving
  family named Vegh living in Vereb near Budapest at this time state that "in May 1800 Punto and Beethoven gave
  a concert in Pest, and both planned to stay at Vereb, but only Punto arrived, since a quarrel had arisen between
  him and Beethoven in Pest, as a result of which Beethoven remained there." A Budapest newspaper of the time
  referred to a concert to be given on 7 May by "a famous musician named Beethoven." On this visit Beethoven remained in Hungary for at least two months, but it is not known how he spent most of his time.
                                                            58 [1927] 840

BEETHOVENS HAUSHALTUNGSSORGEN.   (B)
  Beethoven's troubles with his household servants are illustrated by excerpts from letters to Nanette Streicher: Kal 577,
  Kal 658, and a presumably unpublished letter (just auctioned for 700 schillings): Schon diesen Morgen wollte ich zu
  Ihnen schicken, denn das . . ." (only fragments of the letter are given.) Letters to Zmeskall include Kal 212, Kal
  238, and Kal 275. A letter of 28 October 1810 to Zmeskall was just sold at auction for 500 schillings: "Ich bitte
  um das Stiefelwichsrezept . . ." (This letter appeared in 'Musical Courier' 24 March 1927 p. 16)
                                                            58 [1927] 976

BEETHOVENS TOLLHEITEN IN WORT UND TON. Leopold Hirschberg.   (C)
  Examples of whimsical canons, letters with musical additions, and the like, especially to Zmeskall, Haslinger and
  Schuppanzigh.   58 [1927] 996

EIN INTERESSANTES URTEIL ÜBER BEETHOVENS "NEUNTE."   (D)
  Uncomplimentary comments from Spohr's 'Autobiography.'   58 [1927] 1026

EIN UNBEKANNTER BEETHOVENBRIEF. Max Unger.   (E)
  Letter to Zmeskall from the summer of 1810: "Es wird wohl in Ihrem Bureau Abschreiber geben, ich wünsche die
  Recension . . ." asking for a copy of a poem written on the death of Princess Schwarzenberg. (See also
  'Schweizerische Musikzeitung' 80 [1940] 138)   58 [1927] 1146

BEETHOVEN UND DER "TAUBE MALER." Leopold Hirschberg.   (F)
  Johann Peter Lyser, though nearly deaf, was nevertheless a great lover of music. Some of his Beethoven sketches
  are well known, but it has been proved that he never saw Beethoven in the flesh.
                                                            59 [1928] 71

WAR LUDWIG VAN BEETHOVEN RELIGIÖS? Richard Hagel.   (G)
  Festival address. The speaker's thought was apparently that Beethoven was spiritually rather than formally religious.
                                                            59 [1928] 256

ZUM KAPITEL VON BEETHOVENS KRANKHEITEN.   (H)
  A prescription (not given) was prepared for Beethoven which might have been contemplated as treatment of syphilis,
  though it might also have been used as a remedy for other ailments.
                                                            59 [1928] 413

BEETHOVEN IN FROHLAUNE. Max Unger.   (I)
  The two letters "Wir möchten gerne . . ." and "Wir haben gehört . . ." from 'Musikalische Wochenblatt' 5 [1870]
  390 are given, and assigned to the early Vienna years. The letter 'Nach reiflicher . . .' published in 'Auftakt'
  8 [1928] 122 to Haslinger, addressed "Grosskanzlertum," is in the hand of Nephew Karl and signed by Beethoven.
  It cannot be dated closer than "not before 1822."   59 [1928] 920

BEETHOVEN GRATULIERT ZUM NEUJAHR.   (J)
  Beethoven's New Year's greetings include those sent to the Baroness Ertmann in 1804 (KS I 82), to Nanette Streicher
  (KS I 433), a card to Nanette Streicher at the end of December 1817, many to the Archduke Rudolph, including an
  entire composition sent on 1 January 1820 (KS II 166), and the letter of 8 January 1824 to Johanna van Beethoven
  (KS II 304).   60 [1929] 4

BEETHOVEN SORGT FÜR SEBASTIAN BACHS KIND. Leopold Hirschberg.   (A)
    Regina Susanna Bach (1742-1809), youngest daughter of the composer, was the subject of a plea in the Intelligenzblatt
    XIII of the 'Allgemeine Musikalische Zeitung' in May 1800. A note of thanks for gifts from various donors appeared
    in the Intelligenzblatt IV of 1801. Beethoven's letter of 22 April 1801 to Breitkopf & Härtel (KS I 43) showed his in-
    terest and good intentions. The Intelligenzblatt IX of June 1801 tells of further progress of the fund and states: "The
    eminent Viennese composer and virtuoso, Herr v. Beethoven, will publish one of his newest works in the Breitkopf &
    Härtel edition for the sole benefit of Bach's daughter, so that the worthy old lady may from time to time receive in-
    come therefrom."   60 [1929] 24

HERRIOT AUF SPUREN VON BEETHOVENS "UNSTERBLICHE GELIEBTE."   (B)
    If Herriot is seeking more information of the Brunsvig family to show that Therese was the Immortal Beloved, he
    might well save himself trouble, since her name has been out of consideration ever since it was determined that the
    letter was written in Teplitz in 1812.   60 [1929] 44

DER GRÜNE BEETHOVEN.   (C)
    Fantasy.   60 [1929] 89

BEETHOVEN AND CLEMENS BRENTANO.   (D)
    The two men met in Teplitz in the summer of 1811. Beethoven planned to write a cantata on the death of Queen
    Luise to a text by Brentano, but nothing came of it. Brentano was in Vienna in 1813 and 1814. An undated letter
    from the poet to Beethoven (given here) dates from this period, as does a poem on Milder-Hauptmann's performance
    as Fidelio on 26 May 1814.   60 [1929] 352

BETTINA ALS TONDICHTERIN.   (E)
    An auction catalog of Bettina material lists a notebook with settings by her of sixteen poems by Goethe, eleven by
    Achim von Arnim, and others.   60 [1929] 352

ROMAIN ROLLAND ALS BEETHOVEN-FORSCHER. Max Unger.   (F)
    Favorable comment on Rolland's researches on the Immortal Beloved, Beethoven and Goethe, Bettina, and other
    subjects. The disputed Wedding Sonnet (attributed to Beethoven) is given.
                    60 [1929] 416,440

DER LETZTE NACHFAHR BEETHOVENS.   (G)
    Summary of that part of an article in 'Velhagen und Klasings Monatschrift' 43_2 [1929] 153 dealing with great-grand-
    nephew Karl Julius Maria.   60 [1929] 678

REISE DURCH DIE BEETHOVENWELT. Heinrich Mandt.   (H)
    Description of the archives at the Beethovenhaus in Bonn.   60 [1929] 716

EIN WICHTIGER BEETHOVENFUND.   (I)
    Summary of an article by Fuchs in the 'Kölnische Zeitung' of 29 June 1929 describing the discovery of the journals,
    lost for fifty years, which Beethoven used during his last days in Bonn and his first days in Vienna.
                    [n.d.]

EIN NEUER BEETHOVENBRIEF A. D. VERLEGER S. A. STEINER. Max Unger.   (J)
    A letter to Steiner, received 13 July 1824: "Geld aufzunehmen . . ." was published by Lorenz in the 'Süddeutsche
    Monatshefte' 27 [1929] 47. This letter shows that in 1823 Beethoven gave a pledge (possibly one of the bank shares)
    and interest for a loan of 600 fl. from Steiner. Beethoven's relations with the house of Steiner, especially in con-
    nection with this loan, are summarized. An article by Klages, also in 'Süddeutsche Monatshefte' 27 [1929] 49, on
    Beethoven's handwriting from the standpoint of graphology is discussed. (See also 'Die Musik' 22 [1930] 398)
                    61 [1930] 64,84,108,128

BEETHOVEN UND DER ÖSTERREICHISCHE STAATSBANKEROTT IM JAHRE 1811. Max Unger.   (K)
    The effect of the currency depreciation on Beethoven's circumstances and especially on the annuity from the three
    princes is discussed. A letter of 4 January 1814 to Prince Lobkowitz: "Jene Schritte . . .," first published in the
    'Generalanzeiger für Bonn' 14 December 1929, is given. This letter was written by an amanuensis (Franz Oliva?)
    and only signed by Beethoven. (See also 'Die Musik' 22 [1930] 398)
                    61 [1930] 252,274

AUS DER GESCHICHTE DER OPER "FIDELIO." Alfred Mello.   (L)
    Brief summary of the history of the opera.   61 [1930] 876

UNBEKANNTE SCHATTENRISSE MOZARTS UND BEETHOVENS?   (A)
    An article in 'Velhagen und Klasings Monatschrift' 44 [1930] 581,584 tells of the discovery in the archives of a
noble family in Budapest of cut out silhouettes of W. A. Mozart, L. Mozart, and Beethoven. The Beethoven silhouette bore the inscription, "Ludwig van Beethoven. I received this little picture as a gift from Stephanie von
Breuning. Mozart." Aside from the fact that there was a Stephan von Breuning but no Stephanie, known facts of
chronology leave little doubt that this relic is spurious.   62 [1931] 198

FEHLERHAFTE UND FRAGLICHE STELLEN IN BEETHOVENSCHEN WERKEN. Max Unger.   (B)
    Reprint of letter from Carl Czerny regarding errors in the Third, Fourth, Fifth and Sixth Symphonies, first published
in the 'Neue Wiener Musikzeitung' 2 [1853] 59. Most of these errors had already been brought to light, but the corrections had not been made by publishers. The same is true today. The differences between the exposition and the
recapitulation in Op. 14 No. 1 are cited as passages which must be considered questionable. (See also 56 [1925] 620)
                                            62 [1931] 347,362,379

RODOLPHE KREUTZER, DER PATE DER KREUTZERSONATE.   (C)
    Biographical sketch.   62 [1931] 428

NEUES ÜBER DEN BEETHOVEN- UND SCHUBERT-KREIS UND DIE WALZERFÜRSTEN LANNER UND STRAUSS.   (D)
    Fritz Lange.
    Excerpts from a recently published book by Leo Grünstein, 'Das Alt-Wien Antlitz,' including a biographical sketch
of the Archduke Rudolph.   62 [1931] 564,575,588

200 METER BEETHOVEN. Heinz Warschauer.   (E)
    Review of a sound film which includes some works by Beethoven. 62 [1931] 622

EIN BEITRAG ZUM HUMOR BEI BEETHOVEN. Georg Kinsky.   (F)
    Examples of Beethoven's sense of humor and his fondness for puns, taken from his letters and manuscripts.
                                        63 [1932] 29,40

DIE FREIHEITSIDEE IN DER BEETHOVENSCHEN MUSIK. Karl Steinman.   (G)
    Summary of an address.   63 [1932] 595

EINE BEETHOVEN-ERINNERUNG.   (H)
    Poem written in 1820 by a young maiden who had just met Beethoven.
                                  64 [1933] 140

DEUTSCHE MUSIKKULTUR

BEETHOVEN-HAUS UND BEETHOVEN-ARCHIV ZU BONN. Joseph Schmidt-Görg.   (I)
    An account of the development of the Beethovenhaus, its library and its memorabilia, from the day (in April 1888)
when a house which proved to have been Beethoven's birthplace was put up for sale.
                                  1 [1936] 266

EINE NEUE BEETHOVENDEUTUNG. Ludwig Schiedermair.   (J)
    A discussion of Schering's association of poetic writings with Beethoven's music.
                                  1 [1937] 347

BEETHOVEN? -- JA, BEETHOVEN! Erich Wintermeier.   (K)
    "This is the word of the younger generation."   2 [1937] 73

DIE BEETHOVEN-DEUTUNG ARNOLD SCHERINGS.   (L)
    Polemic letters or articles by Schering, Ludwig Schiedermair, Hans Pfitzner, Kurt Schubert and Walter Abendroth.
                                  2 [1937] 77

BEETHOVEN ALS DIONYSIKER. Frank Wohlfahrt.   (M)
    "The essence of Greek Tragedy, which (as Friedrich Nietzsche so aptly said) finds its culmination in the summoning
up of spirits, was brought into being again by Beethoven in the field of music." Examples are quoted from the Third
and Fourth Symphonies.   2 [1937] 99

BEETHOVEN OR BEETHOWEN? Joseph Schmidt-Görg.   (A)
    Beethoven's use of a w instead of a v when writing his name in German script was presumably an attempt at phonetic spelling to avoid the pronunciation and spelling 'Beethofen' which was not infrequently used. This same type of misspelling occurred often in other words (e.g., 'Klawier'). It must be borne in mind that in the late eighteenth century our present-day concern for accuracy in the spelling of proper names had not come into existence, as indicated by the many variants in the spelling of the name of Beethoven's father as written by himself and by others. The paper also gives many changes in brief phrases or individual words in the transcriptions of letters or conversation books which materially change the sense of entire passages. (See also 5 [1940] 106; 'Die Musik' 17$_1$ [1925] 432)

2 [1937] 108

BEETHOVEN IM KONZERTSAAL. Willy Seibert.   (B)
    "Without Beethoven, concerts today are unthinkable."   2 [1937] 114

DER RUNDFUNK: "BEETHOVEN FÜR ALLE?" Johann Georg Bachmann.   (C)
    Since broadcasting was taken over by the State in 1934, the amount of Beethoven's music broadcast has increased tremendously.   2 [1937] 115

BEETHOVEN IM FILM. Walter Gronostay.   (D)
    The tying of a piece of music to some romantic story, true or false, is a method of approach which film directors must get away from if motion pictures are ever to serve as a vehicle of artistic validity in the presentation of Beethoven's music.   2 [1937] 119

EIN UNBEKANNTE BEETHOVEN-BILD. Karl Lütge.   (E)
    The author describes and reproduces two hitherto unknown portraits of Beethoven: (1) a charcoal drawing of questionable authenticity by an unidentified artist, and (2) a crayon copy by A. von Kloeber of this artist's well-known drawing made in 1818. (See also 5 [1940] 45)   2 [1938] 345; 3 [1938] 130

BEETHOVENS WOHNUNGEN IN WIEN. Georg Schünemann.   (F)
    During the years 1822-23 Beethoven had no fewer than six successive addresses in Vienna, as well as three others in the country.   3 [1938] 144

URAUFFÜHRUNG EINES ORCHESTERDUETTES VON BEETHOVEN IN WINTERTHUR. Max Unger.   (G)
    World premiere of the duet 'Nei giorni tuoi felici' (1802-03) for soprano, tenor and orchestra.

4 [1939] 46

DIE BEZIEHUNGEN BEETHOVENS ZUM INSTRUMENTBAU. Albrecht Ganse.   (H)
    Because of his musical stature and as a friend of Stein the piano manufacturer through his sister Nannette Streicher, Beethoven exercised a tremendous influence on the transition of the piano within a few years in the early 1800's from the Mozartean cembalo to the 'hammer-piano' which we now know. Reference is also made to Beethoven's work with Maelzel on the Panharmonicon. (See also 'Zeitschrift für Instrumentenbau' 56 [1936] 364)

4 [1939] 85

EIN SCHULDNER BEETHOVENS. Gottfried Schweizer.   (I)
    Two unpublished letters from Schindler to the editor of the 'Neue Zeitschrift für Musik' regarding his attack on Prince Galitsin ('Neue Zeitschrift für Musik' 37 [1852] 58, 155, 166) in connection with payment to Beethoven for the last quartets.   4 [1939] 132

VON ECHTEN UND UNECHTEN BEETHOVENBILDERN. Max Unger.   (J)
    Of more than a dozen new Beethoven pictures discovered during the past twenty years, only two were probably painted during his life.   5 [1940] 44

ZU BEETHOVENS HANDSCHRIFT UND BRIEFEN. Max Unger.   (K)
    Those examples of Beethoven's writing which were intended for other eyes are relatively easy to read, but those for his private use (notebook entries, drafts of letters, etc.) are often completely undecipherable. The same is true of musical sketches, which for him were merely reminders: in many cases no real attempt was apparently made to place the notes on the right lines, so that any attempt to transcribe the sketch books with exact accuracy must

ZU BEETHOVENS HANDSCHRIFT UND BRIEFEN (Continued)
necessarily fail. Similarly, the transcription of marginal notes, reminders, etc. , is at best a guess; it is better to characterize a word or a line as "illegible" than to transcribe a meaningless string of letters. The author discusses the editorial technique of various transcribers of Beethoven letters, and points out the importance (at least in the first published transcription of a piece of writing) of the strictest adherence to Beethoven's orthography and spelling. Several of the corrections suggested by Schmidt-Görg 2 [1937] 108 are accepted. The letter to Hammer-Purgstall Kal 146 probably dates much later than 1809; the suggestion by Kinsky (NBJ 5 [1933] 61) of "March 1823" is reasonable. Kal 199 must be much later than 1809-10; the author agrees with Kinsky's estimate: "end of April 1823," and suggests Grillparzer as the recipient. The datings of some other letters are questioned. Revised transcriptions and discussions of the following letters are given: Kal 91. Kal 497 given complete at about twice the length of the KS version. Kal 93 giving evidence that the letter could not have been written earlier than December 1822, and that the Ries referred to was certainly not Ferdinand Ries, but probably the Riess (not Friesz) referred to in Kal 1085, who according to TD V 531 was a piano maker in Vienna. Kal 838 letter from Peters of 18 May 1822, with comments on Beethoven's reply. Kal 855. Kal 882.   5 [1940] 104;   8 [1943] 14

DREIKLANG (Dresden)

BEETHOVEN IN BERLIN.   Siegfried Bergengruen.   (A)
A popular and superficial account of Beethoven's visit to Berlin in June 1796.
[1928] 10 (No. 7)

DREIKLANG (Vienna)

DAS "FREUDENTHEMA" AUS BEETHOVENS IX. SINFONIE.   Paul Berl.   (B)
An analysis according to Schenker principles.   [1937] 33

MISCELLEN: EINE SKIZZE BEETHOVENS ZUR VIOLINSONATE OPUS 23.   Oswald Jonas.   (C)
Brief comment on an unpublished sketch.   [1937] 114

BEETHOVEN IN DER INTERPRETATION.   Oswald Jonas.   (D)
Sketches for the Piano Sonata in D minor Op. 31 No. 2 show even more clearly than the perfected work the improvisatory nature of the first movement. The ideal to be sought in any performance of any piece of music is that the work seems to be growing spontaneously from itself.   [1937] 154

EIN KOMMENTAR ZU SCHINDLER, BEETHOVENS SPIEL BETREFFEND.   Heinrich Schenker.   (E)
A discussion in exhaustive detail of the passages in Schindler's 'Biographie von Ludwig van Beethoven' (lst ed. , 1840, pp. 232-35 and 229-31) which describe Beethoven's own playing of his two Piano Sonatas Op. 14.
[1937] 190

NACHTRAG ZU SCHENKERS AUFSATZ ÜBER SCHINDLER.   Oswald Jonas.   (F)
Further commentaries on Beethoven's general method of piano playing.
[1937] 200

DER DRITTEN SYMPHONIE ERSTES STÜCK. Fritz Cassirer.   (A)
  Excerpt from the author's book 'Beethoven und die Gestalt.'   4 [1922] 192

LE GUIDE MUSICAL

LA NEUVIÈME SYMPHONIE DE BEETHOVEN ET L'ART MODERNE. Erasme Raway.   (B)
  A discussion of the aesthetic and metaphysical principles by which all music earlier than the Ninth Symphony differentiates itself from that work and its successors ("decorative" music, affecting primarily the sensory organs, vs.
  "real" music, the objective of which is primarily the influencing of the psychological (sic) status of the auditor).
  The comments of Berlioz and of Victor Wilder on the Ninth Symphony are discussed from this standpoint, denying
  utterly that this composition is programmatic.   31 [1885] 159,170,181,193,201,
                                                                    219,237,249,257,277

CE QUE BEETHOVEN A FAIT DE LA VARIATION. Léonce Mesnard.   (C)
  Beethoven's later variations are discussed as the transition between the true variations technique and the self-develop-
  ment of the leit-motif as used by Berlioz and his successors.   35 [1889] 259,267

L'EXPOSITION BEETHOVEN À BONN. M. Kufferath.   (D)
  A description of the exhibition, with many extracts from the letters, conversation books, etc. which were on display.
                                                           36 [1890] 164,172,180,186,195

BEETHOVEN IN 1809, D'APRÈS UNE RÉLATION INÉDITE. Michel Brenet.   (E)
  EDr of the memoirs of Baron Trémont.   38 [1892] 101,111

ANCIENS JUGEMENTS SUR BEETHOVEN. Michel Brenet.   (F)
  Excerpts from contemporary reviews of Opp. 30, 47, 57, and a movement from one of the symphonies.
                                                           38 [1892] 223

UNCERTAINTIES OF TEMPO. R. Prieur and H. Alvin.   (G)
  As part of an extensive study of the tempi actually used by various artists or groups and by the same performers at
  different times, a detailed analysis (by metronome indications) is given for movements of Opp. 95, 130 and 131.
                                                           40 [1894] 875,899

HENRI TAIRE AND BEETHOVEN. Hugues Imbert.   (H)
  A comparison of the natures of the metaphysician and the composer.
                                                           41 [1895] 299

ROSSINI AND BEETHOVEN AT VIENNA. Hugues Imbert.   (I)
  While Schindler may have been correct in saying that Beethoven twice refused to see Rossini, a visit did take place
  in 1822. An account of this visit by Rossini is given.   41 [1895] 395

LES LIVRES D'ESQUISSES DE BEETHOVEN. J. S. Shedlock.   (J)
  Resume of articles in 'Musical Times' for 1893-95.   41 [1895] 559

BACH AND BEETHOVEN. J. S. Shedlock.   (K)
  General.   43 [1897] 675

LE ROI DES AULNES DE BEETHOVEN.   (L)
  The ballad "'Erlkönig' by Beethoven" recently issued by Reinhold Becker as editor is merely the melodic line given
  in NB I 100 plus an accompaniment added by Becker. The ballad certainly cannot properly be called "an un -
  published work of Beethoven."   44 [1898] 74

BEETHOVEN-WAGNER-BACH. Coralie Castellin.   (M)
  Rhapsodic.   45 [1899] 727

HANS DE BULOW ET LES SONATES DE BEETHOVEN.   Ernest Closson.   (A)
   Review.   48 [1902] 435,459

TROIS LETTRES INÉDITES DE BEETHOVEN.   (B)
   French translation of KS II 221 No. 868 and of KS II 285 No. 952, and excerpts from KS II 239 No. 884. (See 'Die
   Musik' 3_2 [1904] 412)   50 [1904] 406

LES NEUF SYMPHONIES.   Michel Brenet.   (C)
   Essay in honor of a series of four concerts in which Weingartner conducted all nine symphonies.
                            51 [1905] 311

LES LIEDER ET AIRS DÉTACHÉS DE BEETHOVEN.   Henri de Curzon.   (D)
   Detailed discussion, in chronological order, of the eighty-odd songs by Beethoven, as well as of certain of the other
   vocal works.   51 [1905] 575,591

LE CENTENAIRE DE "FIDELIO."   Henri de Curzon.   (E)
   History of the opera and of its acceptance in France.   51 [1905] 743

BERLIOZ "FOUDROYÉ" PAR BEETHOVEN.   Adolphe Boschot.   (F)
   The impact of Beethoven's works (especially the symphonies) on the young Berlioz was tremendous and of lasting effect.
                            52 [1906] 23

LE SCHERZO DE LA IXe SYMPHONIE.   (G)
   Summary of a part of the article by Stanford (ZIMG 7 [1906] 271) regarding the metronome markings of the trio of
   the scherzo of the Ninth Symphony.   52 [1906] 334

LES MOUVEMENTS DE LA IXme SYMPHONIE DE BEETHOVEN.   (H)
   French translation of letter of March 18th 1827 to Moscheles (KS II 472) with metronome marks as given in 'Musical
   Times' 47 [1906] 387, and statement by Stanford (ZIMG 7 [1906] 271) regarding the Bsn II part in the finale of the
   Ninth Symphony. (See also p. 334 supra and 'Ménestrel' 72 [1906] 145)
                            52 [1906] 499

BEETHOVEN ET L'ECOSSAIS THOMSON.   Gaston Knosp.   (I)
   Discussion of Thomson's work and of his dealings with Beethoven.   53 [1907] 459

LES COLÈRES DE BEETHOVEN.   (J)
   Beethoven's notation on the letter from Wolanek (KS II 357).   53 [1907] 482

UNE VISITE À BEETHOVEN.   (K)
   Account of a visit in 1826 by the tenor Ludwig Cramolini.   53 [1907] 658

UNE PAGE ÉGARÉE DE LA NEUVIÈME SYMPHONIE DE BEETHOVEN.   (L)
   Four pages of the autograph of the Ninth Symphony, including the last 29 measures of the scherzo, were recently
   sold. (See also 'London Times,' November 28th [1907] 6)   54 [1908] 183

UNE LETTRE INÉDITE DE BEETHOVEN.   Frank Choisy.   (M)
   First publication of Pr 1284, giving changes in dynamics in the Missa Solemnis which do not appear in the GA.
                            54 [1908] 611

UNE SYMPHONIE DE JEUNESSE DE BEETHOVEN.   Paul Magnette.   (N)
   The premiere of the Jena Symphony satisfies this author that the work is genuine. Unlike others of the early works,
   it shows the influence of Haydn rather than of Mozart.   56 [1910] 103

LETTRES INÉDITES DE BEETHOVEN.   Gaston Knosp.   (O)
   French translation and summary of discussion given in 'Die Musik' 9_3 [1910] 35 by Anton Schlosser regarding six
   letters probably of the period 1811-15 to Dietrichstein, Duport and Clement and three probably of 1822-23 to
   Dietrichstein.   56 [1910] 607

LES "SFORZANDES" DE BEETHOVEN.   Frank Choisy.   (P)
   The sudden erratic flashes of anger and the broad practical joking which characterized Beethoven were expressions of
   the same temperamental characteristics that made the unexpected sforzando so typical a feature of his music.
                            56 [1910] 696

UNE VISITE À LA MAISON NATALE DE BEETHOVEN.   Paul Cazabonne.   (A)
56 [1910] 731

UN PRÉTENDU TRIO DE MOZART.   G. de Saint Foix and T. de Wyzewa.   (B)
The incomplete 'Trio for Piano, Violin and Violoncello' K. Anh. 284h, apparently dating from 1765-66, cannot
be a Trio or an original work of Mozart, but apparently is a transcription for two pianos of a concerto by an unknown composer (possibly Johann Christian Bach). For reasons pointed out by Charles Malherbe, however, the
authors change their minds and agree that the manuscript, even as a transcription, cannot be from the hand of
Mozart. (For identification of this Trio as a composition of Beethoven, see 'Musical Quarterly' 6 [1920] 276)
56 [1910] 851; 57 [1911] 3,123

L'IMMORTELLE BIEN-AIMÉE.   Maurice Kufferath.   (C)
Discussion of what was represented to be a newly discovered letter to the Immortal Beloved ('Die Musik' 10_4 [1911]
131) and later statement that this letter had been shown to be almost certainly spurious.
57 [1911] 567,594

FIDELIO.   Maurice Kufferath.   (D)
The libretto which Sonnleithner prepared for Beethoven followed very closely Bouilly's book for Gaveaux (1798) except for division into three acts instead of two. A summary of Bouilly's libretto is given. The history of the opera
and the differences between the versions of 1805, 1806 and 1814 are discussed in detail (see also 'Die Musik'
5_1 [1905] 227).

The first Paris performance of the opera in French was in 1860 in a completely distorted version which, nevertheless,
was the only one used for many years. The Gevaert edition (1889) with sung recitatives followed the Fidelio libretto
more closely, but introduced many "corrections" in the musical text and action, examples of which are given.
58 [1912] 3,23,43,63

A PROPOS DE LA NEUVIÈME SYMPHONIE.   (E)
Rehash of 52 [1906] 499 above, with the statement that Weingartner did not agree with Stanford's correction of the
Bsn II part. (NOTE by DWM. In the first edition of 'Ratschläge für Aufführungen der Symphonien Beethovens' (1906)
p. 185 Weingartner reserves judgment, but in the third (1928) edition p. 195 he agrees that the change is authentic
and a great improvement.)   58 [1912] 9

LÉONORE OU FIDELIO.   Maurice Kufferath.   (F)
Beethoven's choice of name for the opera was unequivocally Leonora, as shown by the name given to the three
overtures and by the title as printed on the second (1806) version of the libretto. Only by 1814 had Beethoven apparently resigned himself to the title which the theater directors had insisted on from the first. The statement by
Stefan von Breuning in his letter of June 2nd 1806 to his sister and her husband (quoted in Ley: 'Beethoven als Freund'
[1927] 137) that the title of the original French version of the story was 'Fidelio' is in error.
58 [1912] 290

LES MOUVEMENTS DE LA NEUVIÈME SYMPHONIE.   Edward Speyer.   (G)
The author questions the soundness of the reason (and, to some extent, of the facts) which Stanford brought forth in
his letter to the London Times of October 30th 1911 (see also ZIMG 7 [1906] 271, 'Ménestrel' 72 [1906] 145, and
p. 9 supra). He points out that in several cases the metronome markings for the Ninth Symphony as given by
Beethoven in his letter of October 13th 1826 to Schott (KS II 454) differ completely from those in his letter of
March 18th 1827 to Moscheles (KS II 472). He throws doubt on the validity of other metronome markings certainly attributable to Beethoven for parts of the Fourth and Eighth Symphonies and for the Piano Sonata Op. 106,
and concludes that for the Ninth Symphony and all other compositions by Beethoven the musicianship of the
conductor or performer must be the guide to the fixing of the tempi.
58 [1912] 649

A PROPOS DES MOUVEMENTS DE LA NEUVIÈME SYMPHONIE.   Hugo Riemann.   (H)
The author disagrees with Beethoven's choice of a rhythmic basis, and suggests metronome markings which he
considers suitable.   58 [1912] 671

A PROPOS DU MANUSCRIT DE LA NEUVIÈME SYMPHONIE.   Maurice Kufferath.   (I)
In an interview with the author, St. Saens points out various passages in the manuscript of the Ninth Symphony and
of the Emperor Concerto which differ from the presently accepted versions.
59 [1913] 743

DEUX PIANISTES VIRTUOSES DU TEMPS PASSÉ.   Henri Kling.   (A)
   Anecdote of the first performance of the Concerto in E flat Op. 73.

                                                    60 [1914] 396

GRILLPARZER AND BEETHOVEN.   May de Rudder.   (B)
   Excerpts from Grillparzer's 'Souvenirs.'   60 [1914] 444

                              LE GUIDE MUSICAL (New Series)

LE TESTAMENT D'HEILIGENSTADT.   (C)
   French translation.   10 [1936] 12

PIERRE GAVEAUX, L'AUTEUR DE "FIDELIO." Auguste Convers.   (D)
   A recent performance of Gaveaux's opera discloses many points of marked similarity to Beethoven's Fidelio.
                                                    11 [1938] 105

                                    HARMONICON

MEMOIR OF LUDWIG VAN BEETHOVEN.   (E)
   A biographical summary which tells more about the current attitude of English musicians towards Beethoven than
   it does about the composer himself.   1 [1823] 155

A DAY WITH BEETHOVEN.   (F)
   "Extract from a letter from Vienna to a friend in London."   2 [1824] 10

MEMOIR OF FERDINAND RIES.   (G)
   Biographical sketch.   2 [1824] 33

BEETHOVEN'S PUBLIC REAPPEARANCE IN VIENNA.   (H)
   Address tendered to Beethoven by a group of musical patrons and amateurs; review of the first performance of the
   Ninth Symphony and of parts of the Missa Solemnis.   2 [1824] 178

A VISIT TO BEETHOVEN.   (I)
   Extract from a letter written by an English lady; dated 'Vienna, October 1825.'
                                                    3 [1825] 222

HOPELESS STATE OF BEETHOVEN.   (J)
   Letter describing a visit in January 5th 1827.   5 [1827] 23

BEETHOVEN'S LAST ILLNESS AND DEATH.   (K)
   Letter of March 18th 1827 from Beethoven to Moscheles (KS II 472); letter of March 24th and April 4th 1827 from
   Schindler to Moscheles describing the last days and the funeral services; letter of March 28th 1827 from F. B.
   Streicher to Stumpff expressing embarrassment at Beethoven's request for funds from the Philharmonic Society.
                                                    5 [1827] 84

FUNERAL HONOURS FOR BEETHOVEN.   5 [1827] 154   (L)

BEETHOVEN'S WILL.   (M)
   The Heiligenstadt will.   6 [1828] 6

SALE OF BEETHOVEN'S MANUSCRIPTS AND MUSICAL LIBRARY.   6 [1828] 72   (N)

CORRECTION OF A MISPRINT IN CURRENT EDITIONS OF OPUS 29 AT M. 78 OF THE FIRST MOVEMENT.   (O)
                                                    8 [1830] 242

BEETHOVEN.   (A)
  Biographical and critical essay.   9 [1831] 291

PROGRAM OF BEETHOVEN'S OPERA OF 'FIDELIO.'   (B)
  Synopsis. (See p. 145 for an unenthusiastic review of the first performance of 'Fidelio' in England, May 18th 1832)
                                                              10 [1832] 160

CHARACTERISTIC TRAITS AND ANECDOTES OF BEETHOVEN.   (C)
  Excerpts from appendix to Seyfried's 'Studien.' (See also p. 46)   11 [1833] 25

ON CANON. L. van Beethoven.   (D)
  Chapter 12 of the third section of Seyfried's 'Studien.'   11 [1833] 47

HARVARD MUSICAL REVIEW

NOTES ON BEETHOVEN'S OPUS 132. Leo Rich Lewis.   (E)
  A patronizing article in which the author alternates comments on effective passages with suggestions which Beethoven
  might have used for self-improvement.   1 No. 7 [1913] 8

BEETHOVEN'S RELATION TO HIS TIME. Cuthbert Wright.   (F)
  A contention that Beethoven's music was completely independent of the political and social tendencies of his day.
                                                              2 No. 4 [1914] 10

IM NEUEN REICH

BEETHOVENS "MUSIKGRÄFERL." L. Nohl.   (G)
  A popular account of the relationship between Beethoven and Zmeskall, with many quotations from Beethoven's
  letters. 8_2 [1878] 821

DIE FISCHOFSCHE HANDSCHRIFT. L. Nohl.   (H)
  The origin of this chronicle is given as follows: After the appearance of Schlosser's incredibly faulty biography in
  1828, the guardian of Nephew Karl made a public appeal for documents of all kinds which might be used to prepare
  a biography more worthy of the composer. A considerable amount of material was assembled, copies of which
  came into the hands of J. Fischof, a piano teacher in Vienna, who took extensive notes from them. The originals
  were ultimately lost. The eleven pages of notes by Fischof are now in the Berlin Library. Extensive quotations
  given from the manuscript probably represent substantially its entire contents. It covers Beethoven's ancestry and
  most of the high spots of his entire life, quoting a number of letters and documents and giving various anecdotes.
  Considering its many limitations of space and available material, the manuscript appears to be biographical
  work of considerable merit. 9_1 [1879] 313

DIE MITTLEREN DREI SYMPHONIEN BEETHOVENS. L. Nohl.   (I)
  A biographical summary of the years 1806-1811. 9_2 [1879] 90

DIE ZERSTÖRUNG DER BEETHOVEN-LEGENDE. G. Doempke.   (J)
  A great service to Beethoven and to Beethoven lovers was rendered by the writings of Alexander Wheelock Thayer
  in clearing up false information and unfounded anecdotes. 10_2 [1880] 769

BEETHOVENS RONDO IN B FÜR PIANOFORTE UND ORCHESTRA.   Eusebius Mandyczewski.   (A)
  The manuscript of this work was found in an unfinished condition in Beethoven's Nachlass; it was completed by
  Czerny and published in 1829. Discovery of the manuscript and comparison of it with the published version (NV p.
  141; GA Ser. 9 No. 72) show that the orchestral accompaniment required little change by Czerny, but that the solo
  part in many passages was a mere indication, to be filled out by the performer. Czerny's contribution was merely
  that of a faithful and intelligent editor: "he altered not a note of the orchestral part, and to the Pf part he merely
  added the necessary glitter." The manuscript bears no date, but may with confidence be attributed to the period
  before 1800; various points of similarity to the Rondo of the B flat Concerto Op. 19 (1795) indicate that the work
  under discussion may well be considered a preliminary study for the Finale of the Concerto.
                                        1 [1900] 295

LÉONORE OU L'AMOUR CONJUGAL, DE BOUILLY ET GAVEAUX.   J. G. Prod'homme.   (B)
  An opera of this title, with argument very similar to that of the libretto which Sonnleithner prepared for Beethoven,
  was given in Paris on February 19th 1798. A summary is given of the various numbers which made up this work. From
  this was drawn the Italian libretto 'Eleanora ossia l'Amore conjugale' which Paer set (Dresden, October 4th 1804) and
  in turn Sonnleithner's libretto for Beethoven.   7 [1906] 636

A LETTER FROM BEETHOVEN TO SIR GEORGE SMART.   Charles Maclean.   (C)
  In a chatty article about Sir George Smart, quoting extensively from his diary, there is first publication of a letter to
  him in English, signed by Beethoven, from the spring of 1816: "Mr. Haring told me often . . ." in which Beethoven
  complained about Neate and authorized Sir George to take over from Neate seven works, which presumably are Opp.
  92, 72, 95, 102 No. 1, 112, 136 and probably 102 No. 2. (This letter is given in KFr III 50)
                                        10 [1909] 301

BEETHOVEN'S ACQUAINTANCE WITH THE WELL-TEMPERED CLAVIER.   Wilhelm Altmann.   (D)
  In a letter of 23 March 1828 to Gottfried Weber, Nikolaus Simrock says: "For more than fifty years I have revered
  Sebastian Bach as the greatest German. I owned his Preludes and Fugues as long ago as 1776, as well as his Studies
  for Violin (probably the Sonatas and Partitas), which Salmon (J. P. Salamon?) played brilliantly . . . I presented
  the Preludes and Fugues to young Beethoven in the ninth year of his age on the condition that he be able to play
  some of them for me soon. I did not have long to wait; he worked on them every day with all his might."
                                        10 [1910] 494

BEETHOVENS JUGENDWERKE IN IHREN MELODISCHEN BEZIEHUNGEN ZU MOZART, HAYDN UND PH. E. BACH.   (E)
      Heinrich Jalowetz.
  The melodic styles of Beethoven's early works and of K. P. E. Bach are analyzed in detail, and many features of
  similarity are pointed out. (See 13 [1911] 139; 13 [1912] 336; TK I 70)
                                        12 [1911] 417

KLEINE BEETHOVENIANA.   Willibald Nagel.   (F)
  The principal subject of the Rondo of Beethoven's Sonata Op. 22 bears a marked resemblance to a theme from a
  sonata by Ernst Wilhelm Wolf which Beethoven quite possibly knew.

  The author believes that the first paragraph of the letter of April 8th 1802 to Hoffmeister (KS I 56) refers to two
  separate works: (a) Beethoven refuses the request for a sonata made by the publishers, but (b) accedes to the request of an unidentified lady that he write a sonata to her specifications. The sonata in question is probably that
  in G major Op. 31 No. 1. The fact that this sonata does not bear the dedication which Beethoven referred to in
  the letter may be explained by a letter a few months later than Beethoven's in the files of Hoffmeister & Kühnel
  from a Countess von Kielmansegge refusing an offer by Beethoven (presumably though not certainly the offer in
  the letter of April 8th). The writer of this letter was probably Countess Auguste Charlotte Kielmansegg (nee von
  Schönberg).   12 [1911] 586

EINE UNBEKANNTE JUGENDSYMPHONIE BEETHOVENS?   Fritz Stein.   (G)
  There is every reason to believe that in his youth Beethoven wrote much material for orchestra that now is not
  known, and that he made a number of essays in symphonic writing. Orchestra parts of a Symphony in C major
  recently found in Jena bore the notation "Par Louis van Beethoven" or "Symphonie von Bethoven (sic)." The
  evidence bearing on the authenticity of this work is examined in great detail, and the author concludes that the
  newly found symphony may with complete confidence be attributed to Beethoven, with 1792 or a year or so later
  as the probable date of composition.   13 [1911] 127

HAYDN-REMINISZENZEN BEI BEETHOVEN.   Karl Nef.   (H)
  Many instances are given of thematic similarity between Beethoven and Haydn. (See also 12 [1911] 417)
                                        13 [1912] 336

DIE CIS-MOLL-SONATE VON BEETHOVEN. I. Krohn.   (A)
    The first movement is in sonata form, with the observations that: (1) all themes are very concise; (2) the exposition
closes at m. 23 with the third subject in the subdominant; (3) the second theme remains on the dominant chord of
the relative major, without cadence to the tonic; and (4) in the recapitulation the appearance of the second theme in
the relative major takes on the coloring of the dominant of the subdominant. In the second movement the first full
measure and the upbeat before it are really a giant upbeat, with the primary accent on the E flat. (See also 'Beethoven-
Zentenarfeier' [1927] 58)   3 [1902] 256

"KLINGER'S BEETHOVEN" VOM MUSIKALISCHEN STANDPUNKTE AUS BETRACHTET. G. Münzer.   (B)
    Max Klinger's statue of Beethoven (1899) is avowedly an attempt to represent in marble the idea of Beethoven rather
than merely to make a portrait. The statue does not in any glaring way deviate from the known facts of Beethoven's
appearance, but the man who is portrayed could not conceivably have possessed the titanic humor which must be so
integral a part of any faithful representation of the composer. (See also Joseph Mantuani's 'Beethoven und Max
Klinger's Beethovenstatue' Vienna, 1902)   4 [1902] 112

EIN KOPIERBUCH DER SIMROCK'SCHEN MUSIKHANDLUNG IN BONN VOM JAHRE 1797. Alfr. Chr. Kalischer.   (C)
    Copies of correspondence written by the Simrock firm during the last half of 1797 include letters to Grossheim, Neefe,
Reicha, and others of Beethoven's associates, as well as a letter stating that a pianoforte of range from F (below 'cello
C) to a''' (above high C) (not the usual F - f''') was available.   4 [1903] 531

BEETHOVEN'S SONATAS AND THE THREE STYLES. Fr. Niecks.   (D)
    There can be no accurate assignment of boundaries, either of opus number or of time, between the three style periods.
                                                           6 [1905] 421

BEETHOVEN. Amedee Boutarel.   (E)
An appreciation of the nine symphonies.   6 [1905] 457

A COMPARISON OF THE MOOD OF CERTAIN PASSAGES IN MOZART AND BEETHOVEN WHICH ARE OUTWARDLY   (F)
      SIMILAR. Alfred Heuss.
    A discussion which refers to passages from Opp. 10, 13, 23, 37, 47, and 67.
                                                           7 [1906] 179

DAS FALSCH GEDRUCKTE METRONOMZEICHEN IN BEETHOVENS NEUNTEN SYMPHONIE. Charles V. Stanford.   (G)
    In the first edition of the Ninth Symphony the metronome mark half note = 116 was given for the trio of the scherzo,
but in the engraving this indication was placed so near the top of the copper plate that the stem of the note was almost
indistinguishable. In the next edition, therefore, the metronome mark was copied whole note = 116, and this error
was carried into the Gesamtausgabe. The manuscript editions of the Symphony did not carry this error, and accordingly the traditional tempo until the last years of the century was the correct one, but more recently the doubled speed
has been used, to the great detriment of the music. (Note that Beethoven's letter of October 13th 1826 to Schott (KS
II 454; K 'Briefe' V 279; Prelinger III 273), giving the metronome marks for the Symphony, shows for the trio half
note = 116 as stated above; the same indication is used for the scherzo, with a half note instead of a dotted half.) The
author points out a variation in the manuscript score in the possession of the Philharmonic Society of London which apparently does not appear elsewhere. In the last movement, when the theme is taken by Vla and Vcl with counter
melodies in Bsn I and Cb (GA pp. 183-87) there is the notation "Bsn II coi Bassi." The autograph in the Royal Library
in Berlin indicates that this may have been Beethoven's original plan, but manuscript dedication copy sent to Emperor
Friedrich Wilhelm III shows clearly that Bsn II was silent through the measures under discussion, as in standard editions
of the score.   7 [1906] 271

ÜBER BEETHOVENS 'LEONORE.' Ludwig Schiedermair.   (H)
    The first opera on the Leonora story was apparently that by J. N. Bouilly (who wrote countless opera texts, including
that of 'Les deux Journees') and Pierre Gaveaux (1761-1825). This opera was first produced in Paris on February 19th
1798 (see also 'I. M. G. Sammelb.' 7 [1906] 636). An unknown librettist adapted the plot for Ferdinando Paer,
whose Italian opera was first produced in Dresden on October 3rd 1804. An adaptation by Gaetano Rossi with music
by Johann Simon Mayr appeared in Padua in the spring of 1805, though with the names of the characters changed. In
working up the libretto for Beethoven, Sonnleithner followed Bouilly's libretto very closely (in many passages verbatim),
the principal change being the splitting of Bouilly's first act into two acts. The argument and the music of each of
these four operas is discussed in detail.

Beethoven's opera as first performed on November 20th 1805 was coolly received. At the suggestion of Prince
Lichnowsky and Stephan von Breuning, various changes were made; the revised work was presented on March 29th 1806.

ÜBER BEETHOVENS 'LEONORE.' (Continued)

This second version was published (Op. 72a) in a piano arrangement by the composer. The first version never attained publication until Erich Prieger compiled a vocal score from the scattered fragments. This version (under Beethoven's original title of 'Leonore') was published by Breitkopf & Härtel, and was performed on the hundredth anniversary of its premiere, November 20th 1905. In 1814 the Viennese librettist Friedrich Treitschke was commissioned by Beethoven to revise the entire libretto. Beethoven carried out the necessary musical revision and new composition, and the opera in its present form (Op. 72b) was first performed on May 23rd 1814. The differences between the three versions are discussed, not always to the advantage of the second version as compared with the first.

8 [1907] 115

BEETHOVENS MÖDLINGER TÄNZE VOM JAHRE 1819. Hugo Riemann.   (A)

Schindler ('Biographie von Ludwig van Beethoven' (1840) p.116) states that while Beethoven was at work on the Credo of the Missa Solemnis in Mödling in the summer of 1819 he composed a series of dances for the players in an inn near by, and continues: "but Beethoven lost the score of these waltzes." The anonymous orchestral parts of eleven dances found in the archives of the Thomasschule in Leipzig are from internal and other evidence the missing compositions of 1819. The evidence leading to this conclusion is given in detail. (See also 11 [1910] 103; TD IV p. V)

9 [1907] 53

DAS "RICHTIGE" DATUM DES BRIEFS L. VON BEETHOVENS "AN DIE UNSTERBLICHE GELIEBTE."   (B)
Zdzislaw Jackimecki.

On the assumption that Therese von Brunswick was the Immortal Beloved, the letters must have been written in 1807, one of the years (1795, 1801, 1807, 1812) in which July 6th fell on a Monday. The same assumption indicates that in dating his letter of May 11th 1806 to Franz von Brunswick (KS I 102) Beethoven was in error regarding the year, which was actually 1807. In support of this contention, attention is called to the fact that the letter to Franz refers to a bargain just completed with Clementi, which is almost certainly that of April 1807 (KS I 120). Regarding the author's assumption that the letter to the Immortal Beloved was written in 1807 to Therese von Brunswick, the editor points out the improbability that in this same summer Beethoven would also write so warmly to and about Therese von Malfatti (KS I 125, 126).   9 [1908] 349

ÜBER EINIGE STELLEN DER CORIOLANOUVERTÜRE NACH BEETHOVENS MANUSKRIPT. Hugo Grüters.   (C)

Many differences are cited between the autograph score of the Coriolanus Overture recently added to the library at Bonn and the score as it appears in the GA.   11 [1909] 79

BEETHOVENS MÖDLINGER TÄNZE. Hermann Wetzel.   (D)

Stylistic considerations and details of technique convince the author that these dances are authentic Beethoven. (See also 9 [1907] 53)   11 [1910] 103

EINE BEKANNTE TATSACHE? H. Hammer.   (E)

The melodic line of a part of the scherzo of the Ninth Symphony is identical with an old Russian peasant dance.

11 [1910] 258

DIE BERLINER BEETHOVENBRIEFE. Curt Sachs.   (F)

Corrections are given to about fifty of the letters in the first edition of Kalischer's 'Beethoven-Briefe.'

12 [1910] 20

BEETHOVENS ZWEITE BRIEF AN DIE UNSTERBLICHE GELIEBTE EINE FÄLSCHUNG? Albert Leitzmann.   (G)

Considerations of orthography and content throw great doubt on the authenticity of the letter recently described in 'Die Musik'(10_4 [1911] 131). (See also 'Die Musik' 11_2 [1912] 40)

12 [1911] 350

EIN WEITERER NEUER BEETHOVENFUND? Hermann Abert.   (H)

In a collection of old music there were found the orchestral and vocal parts for a "Good Friday Cantata (or Motet) for 4 voices with accompaniment of 3 Cl, 3 Hrn and 3 Trb, by L. Beethofen (sic)," to a German text. The author believes, subject to further investigation, that the work (published with the article) may be "a composition which Beethoven prepared while he was studying under Neefe -- perhaps his first important experiment in choral writing."

13 [1912] 218

ZUR "CHARFREITAGSKANTATE" BEETHOVENS. Hermann Abert.   (I)

The 'Good Friday Cantata' referred to above proves to be an arrangement for mixed chorus and wind instruments of the 'Miserere' and 'Amplius' for male chorus which Seyfried arranged ('Beethovens Studien' -- Anhang) from two of Beethoven's three Equali for Four Trombones (1812).   13 [1912] 311

AN AUTOGRAPH AGREEMENT OF BEETHOVEN'S. Richard Aldrich.   (A)
   Beethoven's agreement of February 5th 1816 with the Philharmonic Society of London regarding the sale to them of
   the Overtures to the Ruins of Athens (Op. 113), Namensfeier (Op. 115), and King Stefan (Op. 117) (KS I 396) had
   previously appeared (e.g., Kalischer 'Briefe' III 18) as though it had been written in English: TD III 542 gives a
   translation of the English version into German. Actually, it was written in German in Beethoven's own hand, and
   this original version is here published for the first time.   15 [1913] 78

JAHRBUCH DER MUSIKBIBLIOTHEK PETERS

EIN UNBEKANNTES JUGENDWERK BEETHOVENS. Max Friedlaender.   (B)
   The Rondo in C major (H-39, printed herewith), originally published in 1783 in the 'Blumenlese für Klavierliebhaber,'
   bears no name of composer. It immediately follows the song 'Schilderung eines Mädchen' (sic) which is described as
   being by "Hrn Ludw. van Beethoven alt eilf Jahr." Internal and external evidence point definitely to Beethoven as
   composer of the Rondo.   6 [1899] 68

DER ORIGINALTEXT VON BEETHOVENS 'ICH LIEBE DICH.' Max Friedlaender.   (C)
   The poem by Herrosee from which Beethoven took the text of his song (NV p. 178) consisted of five stanzas, of which
   Beethoven used only the second and the third. All five are given herewith. At least two settings of the verses by
   eighteenth century composers are known.   6 [1899] 76

BEETHOVEN UND SEINE GÖNNER. Guido Adler.   (D)
   The creative artist is economically dependent either on sidelines of his art (teaching, performing, etc.), on payments from publishers (in 1800 even more than now a meager income), or on the patronage of those who admire his
   work and are willing and able to contribute to his maintenance. Beethoven was loath to teach for pay, so that after
   his deafness precluded public performance he was in appreciable measure dependent upon patrons, whom he nevertheless dealt with as an equal; the nobleman of art meeting the nobleman of the realm. The 76 persons to whom he
   dedicated a total of 119 works pretty completely summarize his list of patrons and friends, though the names of two
   of his oldest and closest friends (Amenda and Wegeler) do not appear. "The dedication of a work was to Beethoven
   an act either of friendship or of gratitude; in but few cases was a dedication in the hope of a quid pro quo extended."
                                     7 [1900] 69

DEUTSCHE DICHTUNG IN BEETHOVENS MUSIK. Max Friedlaender.   (E)
   "Beethoven was the first composer for a century and a half upon whom the mighty influence of the literary creations
   of the great poets could have its influence." Beethoven drew on at least 65 German poets and 8 poets writing in
   other languages, to say nothing of 25 others whose verses were used in the National Songs for Thomson. For each
   poet a list is given of the Beethoven works to which he contributed.
                                  19 [1912] 25

ANTONIE BRENTANO AN JOHANN MICHAEL SAILER WEGEN BEETHOVENS NEFFEN. Adolf Sandberger.   (F)
   When the project of sending Nephew Karl to Landshut to be under the care of Sailer was being considered (TK III 4-7),
   Antonie Brentano wrote to her friend Sailer on February 22nd 1819, describing Karl as a boy who needed the help and
   guidance that Sailer could give.   21-22 [1914-15] 43

ZUR TONSYMBOLIK IN DEN MESSEN BEETHOVENS. Gerhard von Keussler.   (G)
   A discussion of Beethoven's use of line, harmony, rhythm, color, etc. in the two Masses to extend the significance
   of the text by his music.   27 [1920] 31

ZU BEETHOVENS PERSÖNLICHKEIT UND KUNST. Hermann Abert.   (H)
   To answer the question, "Who was Beethoven and what does he say to us moderns?" the conventional and obvious
   sources of information must be used with caution. His day differed from ours in thought and in understanding; the
   comments of his contemporaries describe not Beethoven but only the effect that Beethoven had on them. His correspondence was of a day when letters were little more than a means for conveying information. The notebooks,
   conversation books and sketch books must from their very unplanned nature be more revealing and more significant
   of the man himself. Beethoven's temperament shows that he was by birth a mixture of Fleming and Rhinelander.
   His character (and accordingly his art) was further influenced by the town of Bonn in which he grew up, and by his
   deafness. From these causes, and from his interest in Rousseau and Schiller which stimulated his passionate love of
   freedom, Beethoven was the first of the great creators of music to give any thought to politics. His most important

ZU BEETHOVENS PERSÖNLICHKEIT UND KUNST (Continued)
characteristic was "the almost superhuman energy of his will, coupled with a no less powerful self-discipline. "
With features of character other than these he could not have created the scherzo and recreated the adagio, "two
new musical types which stem from the same root and cannot be understood each without the other. In the adagio
and the scherzo, Beethoven discovered his own method earlier than in the first or the last movements; the contem-
plative Beethoven has matured earlier than the active Beethoven, the striver. " His great changes in the welding together of the thematic material of the exposition section, his art in variations are two further examples of the effect
of his character on his musical method and content. "It is impossible to dissociate Beethoven's ethics and his art. "
                                    32 [1925] 9

EINE UNBEKANNTE LEIPZIGER ERLEBNISSCHRIFT NEEFES.   Ludwig Schiedermair.   (A)
A love affair of Beethoven's first teacher, Christopher Gottlob Neefe, in 1775-76, as set forth in an autobiographical
sketch and in letters.   40 [1933] 38

JAHRBUCH DER SAMMLUNG KIPPENBERG

GOETHE AND BEETHOVEN.   Romain Rolland.   (B)
Translation of the French original. Facing p. 32 is given a reproduction of Lyser's lithograph of the walking Beethoven
(usually only a part of this lithograph is reproduced); on p. 67 is a reproduction of the title page of the first edition of
'Meeres Stille und Glückliche Fahrt' Op. 112 (Haslinger plate 3838).
                                    7 [1928] 9

BEETHOVENS GOETHE-KOMPOSITIONEN.   Otto Erich Deutsch.   (C
A very careful bibliographic description of the compositions by Beethoven based on writings of Goethe: 14 solo songs
and 3 works for chorus, Variations on a Song (for Pf 4 hands), 8 numbers as incidental music to 'Egmont,' and sketches
for 8 other songs. Of all of this, "admittedly only the Overture to Egmont and the song 'Mignon' are of importance. "
A reproduction is given of the title page of the first edition of the 'Lied mit Veränderung' (K&lC plate 198).   (See
also 'Jahrbuch Peters' 19 [1912] 33)   8 [1930] 102; 10 [1935] 319

BEETHOVEN AND CARL FRIEDRICH ZELTER.   Johann-Wolfgang Schottländer.   (D
The relationship between Beethoven and Zelter is discussed in detail, with special reference to the judgment of the
composer which Zelter formed as a result of review of his works (many of which are quoted). Zelter's influence on
Goethe's attitude towards Beethoven is discussed. Three letters from Beethoven to Zelter and their replies are given,
with comments: letter of September 18th 1819 (KS II 142), of February 8th 1823 (KS II 223) and of March 25th 1823
(KS II 238).   8 [1930] 175

JAHRBÜCHER FÜR MUSIKALISCHE WISSENSCHAFT

BEETHOVENS VERBINDUNGEN MIT BIRCHALL UND STUMPFF IN LONDON.   Friedrich Chrysander.   (E
Copies are given (substantially without comment) of the correspondence of 1815-16 between Beethoven and Robert
Birchall (and Birchall's associate C. Lonsdale), and of letters and journal articles by J. A. Stumpff, whose contact
with Beethoven was on a social rather than a business basis. (For the first letter in the series to Birchall (KS I 381) see
'Allgemeine Musikalische Zeitung' Ser. 3: 4 [1869] 52.)   1 [1863] 429

JOURNAL OF MUSICOLOGY

BEETHOVEN: A WORLD FORCE AND VISION COSMIC.   Paul C. Squires.   (F
Mystic and rhapsodic.   4 [1944 as of 1942] 20

AN UNKNOWN LETTER BY BEETHOVEN.   Nathan Broder.   (A)
　　Facsimile, transcription and translation of letter of February 1824 to the pianist Kalkbrenner: Ein unvorhergesehner
　　Zufall nöthigt mich . . .   4 No. 1 [1957] 16

BEETHOVEN'S BROADWOOD: A PRESENT-DAY MEMOIR.   Bennet Ludden.   (B)
　　An 1817 Broadwood owned by the author is described, and its peculiar suitability for certain passages in the piano
　　sonatas is discussed.   8 No. 2 [1961] 9

KASTNER'S WIENER MUSIKALISCHE ZEITUNG

NEUE BEETHOVEN-BRIEFE.   Theodor von Frimmel.   (C)
　　First publication and exhaustive annotation of the following letters:

7	KS	992	170	KS	54
7	KK	1179	203	KS	479
30	KS	1129	204	KFr	433
52	KS	480	357	KS	713
85	KS	481			

1 [1885-86] pages as shown

BEETHOVEN-BÜSTEN.   Theodor von Frimmel.   (D)
　　The bust of Beethoven in the possession of Frau Pauline Neumann of Vienna, supposedly an original work based on
　　the death mask, instead is without doubt a later version of Dietrich's bust of 1821.
                              1 [1886] 118

BEETHOVEN-BILDNISSE.   (E)
　　Summary of a talk on this subject given by Frimmel. The only representations of Beethoven which the speaker
　　considered to have any value were Hornemann's miniature (1802), the bust by Klein (1812), the engraving by
　　Höfel from Letronne's drawing, and the portraits by Stieler and Schimon.
                              1 [1886] 341

BEETHOVEN AM STERNENHIMMEL.   Jos Böck.   (F)
　　With great regret the author finds that astronomical nomenclature has no suitable place for the name of Ludwig
　　van Beethoven.   1 [1886] 377

DREI SELTEN AUFGEFÜHRTE CHORWERKE BEETHOVENS.   (G)
　　Detailed program notes for a Berlin performance of the Trauerkantate, the Opferlied Op. 121b, and Meeresstille
　　Op. 112.   1 [1886] 425

ZUR GESCHICHTE DER NEUNTEN SYMPHONIE.   (H)
　　The statement that the first performance of the Ninth Symphony in Dresden (August 27th, 1838 under Reissiger)
　　was with only a single rehearsal is wholly without foundation.   2 [1886] 98

NEUE BEETHOVEN-BRIEFE.   Theodor von Frimmel.   (I)
　　First publication in the original of KS 114; a French translation had previously appeared in Oscar Comettant's
　　'Un nid d'autographes.' KS 115 in Comettant's French translation is also given. First publication of KFr 609.
                              2 [1886] 196,245

MEINE ERINNERUNG AN BEETHOVEN.   Hermann Rollett.   (J)
　　Through a friend of the family, Nannette Streicher, the author as a child met Beethoven in 1825.
                              2 [1886] 318

EIN BEETHOVEN-MUSEUM.   Theodor von Frimmel.   (K)
　　Call for the establishment of a Beethoven Museum in Vienna.   3 [1886] 72

BEETHOVEN IN HEILIGENSTADT -- DIE BEETHOVENSAMMLUNG.   Theodor von Frimmel.   (A)
                                                      4 [1887] 426,444

EIN UNGEDRUCKTE BILLET VON BEETHOVEN.   Theodor von Frimmel.   (B)
    First publication of KK 223.   4 [1887] 592

KEYNOTE

BEETHOVEN AND MONEY.   Albert Lancaster.   (C)
    By 1809 Beethoven was well established financially, but the fall of Vienna and the devaluation of the currency
    completely destroyed this security. "By now (1812-15) financial success had come to mean much to Beethoven.
    Money poisoned his life, his conversation." "He constantly voiced the idée fixe that he was a poor man. The
    fact is that he was very comfortably off indeed."   1 [1945] No. 1, p. 6

BEETHOVEN AS FOSTER PARENT.   R. C. James.   (D)
    An account of Nephew Karl's life under the guardianship, indicating that his admitted faults of character stemmed
    in large measure from his impossible relationship with the composer. "After Beethoven's death he turned out well."
                                                           1 [1945] No. 2, p. 12

KUNST

EEN EN ANDER OVER BEETHOVENS LAATSTE KWARTETTEN. H. A. Viotta.   (E)
    Popular analysis of the last five quartets.   1 [1920] 145,169,269

1770 -- 16 DECEMBER -- 1920.   H. A. Viotta   (F)
    Centenary essay.   1 [1920] 265

BEETHOVEN EN DE KRITIEK.   H. A. Viotta.   (G)
    Quotations from adverse contemporary criticisms.   1 [1920] 282

ANDREAS STREICHER EN ZIJN VERHOUDING TOT SCHILLER EN BEETHOVEN.   H. A. Viotta.   (H)
                                                           3 [1922] 49

BEETHOVENS VOKALE MUZIEK.   H. A. Viotta.   (I)
    General comments on the Missa Solemnis and the Ninth Symphony.
                                                           4 [1923] 29

EEN WEINIG BEKEND WERK VAN BEETHOVEN.   H. A. Viotta.   (J)
    A comparison of various passages in the piano version and the string quartet version of Op. 14 No. 1.
                                                           4 [1923] 112

UIT BEETHOVENS LAATSTE LEVENSJAREN.   H. A. Viotta.   (K)
    Popular discussion of the principal events of the composer's last fifteen years.
                                                           4 [1923] 221

FIDELIO-HERINNERINGEN. H. A. Viotta.   (L)
    A popular account of the opera's inception and early history.   4 [1923] 252

HONDERD JAAR GELEDEN. H. A. Viotta.   (M)
    Account of the completion and first performance of the Ninth Symphony, in commemoration of the centenary of
    its completion.   5 [1924] 1

'LA MALINCONIA.' H. A. Viotta.   (N)
    Brief commentary on the passage of that designation in Op. 18 No. 6.
                                                           5 [1924] 61

BEETHOVEN-SCHENNIS.   (A)
    A list of the vocal arrangements from compositions by Beethoven, as given by von Lenz.
5 [1924] 151

MEISTERWERK IN DER MUSIK

NOCH EINMAL ZU BEETHOVENS OPUS 110.   (B)
    Supplement to the discussion in the author's 'Die letzten fünf Sonaten von Beethoven' (U. E. 3977), as polemic
against Engelsmann ('Neue Musik-Zeitung'46 [1925] 203, 222).   1 [1925] 117

RAMEAU ODER BEETHOVEN? ERSTARRUNG ODER GEISTIGES LEBEN IN DER MUSIK?   (C)
    The supremacy of the vertical (harmony according to rules) was brought about by the laying down of laws of harmony
which Rameau initiated in his 'Traite de l'Harmonie.' The only hope for music as an art is that it break away from
the dominance of the tonic chord and instead be written horizontally, with voice leading the ruling structural factor.
3 [1930] 11

BEETHOVENS DRITTE SINFONIE ZUM ERSTENMAL IN IHREM WAHREN INHALT DARGESTELLT.   (D)
3 [1930] 29

    DARSTELLUNG DES INHALTES.   (E)
        An exhaustive analysis according to Schemker's established methodology.

    EINE VON BEETHOVEN REVIDIERTE ABSCHRIFT UND DIE ORIGINALSTIMMEN VOM JAHRE 1806.   (F)
        With reference to the projected dedication to Napoleon, the symphony was first of all a Heroic Symphony,
not a symphony written for any stated hero. Beethoven, who all his life had lived close to the nobility, knew
'heroes' too well for that. The autograph of the symphony has disappeared, but a copy revised by Beethoven
is at hand. A detailed comparison is made between this revised score and the first edition of the orchestra
parts, disclosing many minor variations in phrasing, dynamics, bowing, etc.
3 [1930] 85

    VORTRAG.   (G)
        Suggestions for the conductor.   3 [1930] 93

    Literature. The only writings on this Symphony worth referring to are Nottebohm's 'Ein Skizzenbuch von
Beethoven aus dem Jahre 1803' (1880) and August Halm's 'Der Fremdkörper im ersten Satz der Eroica' ('Die
Musik' 21$_2$ [1929] 481).   3 [1930] 100

MELOS

BEETHOVEN. Hans Mersmann.   (H)
    Centenary essay.   6 [1927] 125

BEETHOVEN UND DER GENIALISMUS. Karl August Meissinger.   (I)
    Both novels and portraits give a false and superficial representation of Beethoven, much as they do of Mozart. The
personal characteristics and life history of Beethoven are discussed as they bear upon the manifestations of his genius
and upon the accepted concept of the man.   7 [1928] 390

ZUR INTERPRETATION VON BEETHOVENS STREICHQUARTETTEN. Willi Schmid.   (J)
    A thoughtful and penetrating analysis of the problems of understanding and performance which face the ensemble
whose ideal is a truly faithful rendering of Beethoven's thoughts.   7 [1928] 396

ZUM BEETHOVENBILD DER GEGENWART. Wolfgang Engelhardt.   (K)
    The tendency of recent biographers is to interpret Beethoven to the extent that the man himself is lost to sight.
7 [1928] 405

EIN MOSKAUER SKIZZENBUCH VON BEETHOVEN.   M. Iwanow-Boretzky.   (A)
   Condensation of the material presented in 'Musikalische Bildung' (Moscow) January 1927 p. 75 as a discussion of
   a sketch book falling between those discussed in NB II 540 and NB II 1, and paralleling the one described in Roda's
   'Un quaderno di autografi di Beethoven (1825)' as containing sketches of Opp. 132 and 130.
                                    7 [1928] 407

EIN UNBEKANNTES SKIZZENBLATT BEETHOVENS.   Alfred Rosenzweig.   (B)
   First publication of a facsimile of a sketch book page in which themes later appearing in the String Quartet Op. 18
   No. 2 and the Kreutzer Sonata Op. 47 are treated together.   7 [1928] 414

                                    MÉNESTREL

LES LETTRES DE BEETHOVEN.   J. B. Weckerlin.   (C)
   Review of a French translation of the Wegeler & Ries 'Notizen' by A. F. Legentil.
                                    29 [1862] 309

LES LETTRES DE BEETHOVEN.   A. F. Legentil.   (D)
   French translation of letters given in KS I 29, II 449, and I 87 (No. 88).
                                    29 [1862] 313

NOTICES BIOGRAPHIQUES SUR BEETHOVEN.   A. F. Legentil.   (E)
   Excerpts from the author's French translation of the Wegeler & Ries 'Notizen.'
                                    29 [1862] 329,337

DEUX LETTRES INÉDITES DE BEETHOVEN.   J. B. Weckerlin.   (F)
   Letters of April 26th 1807 to Camille and to Ignaz Pleyel (KS I 112).
                                    33 [1866] 210

BEETHOVEN (PENSÉES DÉTACHÉES SUR LES ARTS).   H. Barbedette.   (G)
   This series of articles is described as "extracts from the author's 'Notice on Beethoven,' which has been completely
   rewritten."   37 [1870] 167,175,183,193,201,
                                             217,225

LA JEUNESSE DE BEETHOVEN.   Victor Wilder.   43 [1877] pp. 185ff (26 parts)   (H)

BEETHOVEN -- LES JOURS DE GLOIRE ET DE SOUFFRANCE.   Victor Wilder.   (I)
                                    45 [1879] pp. 33ff (22 parts)

LES DERNIÈRES ANNÉES DE BEETHOVEN.   Victor Wilder.   (J)
   These three sets of articles are in effect the first draft of the author's 'Beethoven: sa Vie et son Oeuvre' (1883).
                                    46 [1880] pp. 313ff;
                                    47 [1880-81] pp. 1ff (24 parts)

LES COMPOSITEURS-VIRTUOSES.   A. Marmontel.   (K)
   A superficial sketch of Beethoven's life and works.   46 [1880] 153,161

UN MANUSCRIT DE BEETHOVEN.   (L)
   Description of the manuscript of Op. 57, and its history as told by M. Bigot, to whose wife Marie it was given
   by Beethoven.   46 [1880] 261

LA SYMPHONIE AVEC CHOEURS DE BEETHOVEN.   Victor Wilder.   (M)
   Introduction to a new translation of the 'Ode to Joy' which the author made on the assumption that Schiller's
   poem is actually an 'Ode to Liberty.'   48 [1882] 61

SEVERAL BEETHOVEN LETTERS.   Oscar Comettant.   (N)
   Letter of April 26th 1807 to Camille Pleyel (KS I 112) in facsimile and French translation (see also 33 [1866] 210),
   with comments by Pleyel on Beethoven's appearance and Pf playing.   Notes without date to Hummel, in French
   translation (KS I 23 Nos. 27,28).   51 [1885] 86

AN IMPROVISATION BY BEETHOVEN. Ernest Legouvé. (A)
Rhapsodic account by Pleyel.   52 [1886] 85

UNE LETTRE INÉDITE DE BEETHOVEN. J. B. Weckerlin. (B)
French translation of letter without date to Marie Bigot and her husband (note that KS I 137 states that this letter
had been published as early as 1867).   52 [1886] 165

LA MESSE EN RÉ DE BEETHOVEN. Julien Tiersot. (C)
History and popular analysis of the Missa Solemnis in connection with the first complete performance of this work
by the Société des Concerts du Conservatoire. 54 [1888] 17,25

LES CONDOLÉANCES DE BEETHOVEN. Eugène Manuel. (D)
Poem.   58 [1892] 99

A BEETHOVEN. Charles Grandmougin. (E)
Poem.   59 [1893] 107

FIDELIO. Julien Tiersot. (F)
In spite of opinions to the contrary, this opera by the great symphonist is music admirably written for the stage.
                                               60 [1894] 49

UNE LETTRE INÉDITE DE BEETHOVEN. (G)
French translation of a letter of November 29th (year not stated) to Joseph Schreyvogel, returning theater tickets
which Beethoven had not been able to use because of his deafness, and expressing interest in writing for the theater.
(This letter does not appear in KS, K 'Briefe,' or KK, but is presumably the one referred to in Kastner's 'Briefe'
(1910) as No. 77 (dated 1803) with the notation: "A note which by its friendly tone stands as quite distinct from
many of the known letters of the Master. Unpublished. ")   60 [1894] 61

UN PORTRAIT INÉDIT DE BEETHOVEN. (H)
Dr. Alfred Nagl recently published in the Leipzig 'Illustrierte Zeitung' a reproduction of an oil painting of
Beethoven by an unknown artist, dating from 1805, reputed to have been given by Beethoven to Count Franz
von Brunswick. (This is probably the portrait referred to in TK I 341.)
                                               60 [1894] 68

SOUVENIRS DE SCHUBERT ET BEETHOVEN. Franz Lachner. (I)
Lachner met Beethoven several times during the last year of his life.
                                               61 [1895] 292

BEETHOVEN ET SON ÉDITEUR STEINER. (J)
French translation of a letter of December 29,1820 from Steiner to Beethoven, transmitting scores of three Overtures
(Steiner published Op. 113 in 1823 and Op. 115 in 1825. Questions by DWM: (1) What was the third overture referred
to? (2) Why the delay of three and five years before publication?), referring to a loan of 10 000 fl. WW which
Beethoven had made to Steiner and which had been repaid, and dunning Beethoven for certain monies owed by him
to Steiner. Pencil figures by Beethoven on this letter indicate an indebtedness of 2420 fl. which he proposed to clear
up by semiannual payments of 600 fl.   66 [1900] 269

LE SECRET DE BEETHOVEN. Raymond Bouyer. (K)
A series of articles republished in a book of that title (1905). The secret of Beethoven "is a living heart in an urn
which endlessly pours forth sounds; the art of music is the beating of that great heart. "
                                               71 [1905] 97,105,113,129,137,
                                                      153,169 185,193,201

SCHILLER. Amédée Boutarel. (L)
A list is given of a dozen or more composers who made musical settings on the 'Ode to Joy. ' The development of
Beethoven's setting is discussed, with excerpts from the sketch books, and a 16th century Hungarian battle song is
quoted ('Joyeusement je change') which bears much resemblance, in line and in rhythm, to the 'Ode' as it appears
in the Ninth Symphony.   71 [1905] 329,337

UNE "SOCIÉTÉ BEETHOVEN" ET L'ART D'APPLAUDIR. Raymond Bouyer.   (A)
   Comments on an early appearance of the present-day practice of withholding applause until the close of a work.
                                             71 [1905] 356

LES "LIEDER" DE BEETHOVEN. Raymond Bouyer.   (B)
   "Beethoven the composer of songs is still Beethoven."   72 [1906] 10

THE SCHERZO OF THE NINTH SYMPHONY.   (C)
   Review of article by Stanford in 'Zeitschrift der Internationalen Musikgesellschaft' 7 [1906] 271. (See 73 [1907] 172)
                                             72 [1906] 145

LES CONCERTOS DE BEETHOVEN À LA BIBLIOTHEQUE ROYALE DE BERLIN. C. Saint-Saens.   (D)
   Several divergencies are listed between the manuscripts of the C minor and the E flat concertos and the accepted
   versions.   73 [1907] 130

LE SCHERZO DE LA SYMPHONIE AVEC CHOEUR. Julien Tiersot.   (E)
   In support of the contention of Stanford (see 72 [1906] 145) that the metronome marking of the Trio was given by
   Beethoven as half note = 116, not whole note = 116, the author gives a French translation of Beethoven's letter of
   March 18th 1827 to Moscheles (KS II 472) with the metronome markings which accompanied this letter (these are
   copied from 'Musical Times' 47 [1906] 37, and are identical with those given by (KS II 454) in the letter of October
   13th 1826 to Schott except (a) for dots after the 2nd, 6th, 9th and 12th notes, and (b) for the 'Finale Presto,' which
   is half note = 96, not half note = 66). He also points out that the generally accepted first edition of the score is
   probably a reprint of the true first edition, since copies are known without metronome markings which were presumably added to the plates before printing the "so-called" first edition.
                                             73 [1907] 172

UNE COLLABORATION MANQUÉE: SPORSCHIL ET BEETHOVEN. Amédée Boutarel.   (F)
   Extended summary of material on this subject contained in Volkmann's 'Neues über Beethoven' (1905). (See TK
   III 118)   74 [1908] 19

'BEETHOVEN.' Amédée Boutarel.   (G)
   Review of a play of this name by René Fauchois.   75 [1909] 84

DU VIRTUOSE À L'INTERPRÈTE -- ET BEETHOVEN INCONNU. Raymond Bouyer.   (H)
   General.   75 [1909] 115

LE SENTIMENT RELIGIEUX CHEZ BEETHOVEN. Raymond Bouyer.   (I)
   A discussion of Rubinstein's statement: "I do not look upon the Missa Solemnis as one of Beethoven's major works."
                                             76 [1910] 90,107

L'IMMORTELLE BIEN-AIMÉE DE BEETHOVEN. Amédée Boutarel.   (J)
   Discussion based on the fourth letter to the Immortal Beloved ('Die Musik' 10_4 [1911] 131) which was later ('Die
   Musik' 11_2 [1912] 40) admitted to be spurious.   77 [1911] 267

L'IMMORTELLE BIEN-AIMÉE DE BEETHOVEN. Amédée Boutarel.   *   (K)
   Admission that the fourth letter (see p. 267) had been proved to be a forgery; biographical sketch of Therese von
   Brunswick.   77 [1911] 307

LES MALADES DE BEETHOVEN. Jean Chantavoine.   (L)
   Review and summary of Schweisheimer's book 'Beethovens Leiden' (1922) in which the author discusses the deafness
   (probably attributable to neuritis acoustica rather than to otosclerosis) and the digestive disorders (an unverified but
   suspected youthful attack of typhoid fever might be the explanation of this), and denies the existence of heart
   trouble or syphilis.   85 [1923] 245

DEUX LETTRES DE BEETHOVEN. Jean Chantavoine.   (M)
   Transcription and French translation of letter without date or name of addressee (marked "this letter was addressed
   to me and received March 23rd. Rettich.") saying that the two overtures would almost certainly be sent the next
   day. This letter probably forms a part of the series regarding the proposed concert in Graz, as follows: KS I 241;
   KS I 243 (assigned by KS to February 8th 1812 but almost certainly a month or more later than this); this letter,
   immediately preceding or immediately following KS I 248; KS I 249,250,253. Transcription and French translation of letter of April 22nd 1826 to Maurice Schlesinger, saying that a new quartet (Op. 135) would be completed

in two or three weeks at the latest, promising to send the score of Op. 132 at once, and requesting a remittance of
80 ducats. This letter obviously follows KS Nos. 1145 and 1149 (II 426, 427), which accordingly should be dated
"Spring, 1826" instead of "Summer, 1826."   A verbatim translation of this paper appears in 'Musical Times'
66 [1925] 329.   86 [1924] 137

POUR LE CENTENAIRE DE LA "BEUVIÈME."   Raymond Bouyer.   (A)
                                                          86 [1924] 253,265

Y A-T-IL UNE MESURE DE TROP DANS LA "SYMPHONIE PASTORALE"? Jean Chantavoine.   (B)
    The author disagrees with Tetzel ('Zeitschrift für Musikwissenschaft' 3 [1921] 613) and Heuss ('Zeitschrift für Musik'
    JG 92 [1925] 288, 460) that in the passage mm. 9-29 of the first movement of the Sixth Symphony there is a re-
    dundant measure. It is possible that an extra measure was inadvertently put in between m. 20 and m. 28, or that
    a measure was unwittingly dropped in the corresponding passage in the recapitulation (mm. 304-11), but the author
    does not feel that an apparent unevenness of scansion or a lack of identity in exposition and recapitulation is reason
    enough to change the accepted text.   88 [1926] 473

SOURCES THÉMATIQUES DE LA SYMPHONIE PASTORALE. Julien Tiersot.   (C)
    The author cites various French folk songs which bear marked resemblance to themes of the Pastoral Symphony, and
    refers to a collection of Czech folk songs in which similar likenesses are evident. He cautions against the tendency
    of the collector of folk songs to make unconscious adaptation of the melodies in the shape of themes from the classics,
    and points out that Beethoven took, not folk songs themselves, but phrases and cadences which contained the essence
    of the folk song style, and from them built themes with the atmosphere which he sought.
                                                          89 [1927] 153,166,177

LE VRAI BEETHOVEN.   Maurice Cauchie.   (D)
    The real Beethoven was not the titan wrestling with fate which has become the conventional conception, but a man,
    far from stern or forbidding, who appears in the many contemporary portraits given by Frimmel ('Beethovens äussere
    Erscheinung' 1905), the frequenter of taverns ('Neues Beethoven-Jahrbuch' 1 [1924] 128), the punster and practical
    joker, and -- most of all -- the writer of some of the happiest and most lighthearted music ever put on paper.
                                                          89 [1927] 189

RELIQUES BEETHOVENIENNES.   Charles Bouvet.   (E)
    French translation of the postscript to a letter without date, presumably to Reisser (Reissig?), referring to problems
    connected with Nephew Karl and expressing the wish that the score of the Missa Solemnis be returned. (This may
    have been written in early 1825 or 1826.) Other relics: a pistol belonging to Beethoven which had been used in
    various performances of Fidelio, and given by Beethoven in 1822 to Mlle. Schroeder; a satin lined copper box
    which had contained the Heiligenstadt will; a peg from a violin which had belonged to Beethoven, etc.
                                                          89 [1927] 216

BEETHOVEN ET NOUS.   Paul Landormy.   (F)
    Centenary essay.   89 [1927] 221

QUELQUES PRÉCISIONS SUR LA NEUVIÈME SYMPHONIE. J. G. Prod'homme.   (G)
    Summary of article by Baensch ('Neues Beethoven-Jahrbuch' 2 [1924] 137). (This article is translated verbatim in
    the 'New Music Review' 27 [1928] 49.)   89 [1927] 297

BARON DE TRÉMONT (SOUVENIRS ENÉDITS). J. G. Prod'homme.   (H)
    Material given in 'Musical Quarterly' 6 [1920] 374.   89 [1927] 362

A PROPOS DE LA "SIXIÈME SYMPHONIE" DE BEETHOVEN. Paul Gilson.   (I)
    The author contends that in the eighth measure of the Finale the horn should remain in dominant harmony (G, C, C)
    against the tonic of the strings, as shown in the first edition, instead of playing A, C, C.
                                                          89 [1927] 493

LA SURDITÉ DE BEETHOVEN.   Raoul Blondel.   (J)
    Summary of the known facts, and mention of the hypothesis that Beethoven had formed the practice of inducing
    cataleptic trances in himself to stimulate the act of composition, and that the cerebral congestion thus brought
    about may have aggravated an otitis.   90 [1928] 173,181

SCHUBERT AND BEETHOVEN. Paul Landormy.   (A)
    Contrasts in the natures of the two great composers.   90 [1928] 193

LE "TRIO À L'ARCHIDUC." Paul Landormy.   (B)
    Critical discussion of the recorded performance of Cortot, Thibaud and Casals.
                                                                  92 [1930] 57

LES FORMULES MÉLODIQUES CHEZ BEETHOVEN. Jean Chantavoine.   (C)
    Essay inspired by Haas's "Systematische Ordnung Beethovenscher Melodien."
                                                                  94 [1932] 333

A TRAVERS UNE COLLECTION D'AUTOGRAPHES. Jean Chantavoine.   (D)
    Note without date to "Hr. Riedel, Bürgerl. Orgelmach." reading: "Have the kindness to come to my apartments
    so that I can talk with you about the organ which you have submitted to me, which I cannot use." The author
    suggests that the description "Bürgerl. Orgelmach." might mean a manufacturer of organs for secular use (as
    opposed to "Kirchlich Orgelmach."), so that this note might have to do with the "Battle of Vittoria." In any
    event, this is the only letter of Beethoven referring to the organ.   94 [1932] 356

LETTRE OUVERTE À M. ANDRE SAURÈS. Maurice Dauge.   (E)
    Reply to Saurès ('La Revue Musical' 16 [1935] No. 160 p. 266).   97 [1935] 385

BEETHOVEN MOMIFIÉ. Maurice Dauge.   (F)
    Reply to Saures ('La Revue Musical' 17 [1936] No. 169 p. 336).   99 [1937] 9

LE "CAS" BEETHOVEN. Armand Machabey.   (G)
    "What is the importance, I ask, of the naively heroic rhythms of the worthy Ludwig in comparison with 'La Mer'?
    of the rural painting of the Sixth Symphony in comparison with 'Fetes'? of the Apotheosis of the Dance in com-
    parison with 'Daphnis et Chloe'?"   99 [1937] 185,193,205,213

REMARQUES SUR LE "CAS" BEETHOVEN. Maurice Dauge.   99 [1937] 229   (H)

COMPLÉMENTS AU "CAS" BEETHOVEN. Armand Machabey. 99 [1937] 265   (I)

                                        MERKER

BEETHOVEN ALS BRIEFSCHREIBER. Theodor von Frimmel.   (J)
    Note without date (presumably from the spring of 1811) to the Archduke Rudolph, sending a copy of the sonata
    'Les Adieux' Op. 81a.   Note without date (almost certainly within a few days from June 22nd 1819) to an un-
    named addressee (almost certainly Karl Bernard) mentioning the possibility of withdrawing Nephew Karl from
    Blöchlinger's school after the first half year. Fragment of a letter (presumably from March-April 1820) regard-
    ing the appointment of Karl Peters as joint guardian for Nephew Karl.
                                                                  1_1 [1909] 173

BEETHOVEN AND BERLIN. Ignaz Schwarz.   (K)
    Letter dated April 8th 1815 from Bernard Anselm Weber (Musical Director at the National Theatre) presumably
    to Treitschke (reviser of the Fidelio libretto for the first Berlin performance on October 11th 1815) regarding
    preparations for this performance and the possibility of presenting other Beethoven works in the coming winter.
                                                                  3 [1912] 88

FIDELIO. Oscar Bie.   (L)
    An account of the early history of this opera by "the most untheatrical of composers" through its three successive
    forms, and discussion of the individual numbers.   3 [1912] 362,402,486

BEETHOVENS KOMPOSITIONEN FÜR MANDOLINE, MIT EINEM UNVERÖFFENTLICHTEN SONATINEN-SATZ BEETHOVENS. (A)
   Arthur Chitz.
   In the library of Count Franz Clam-Gallas are several compositions by Beethoven for Mandoline and Cembalo, presumably written for the Countess Josefine Clary (to whom the scena and aria 'Ah! perfido' Op. 65 is dedicated) before her marriage to the then Count on November 30th 1797. One of these, a Sonatina in C major, presumably
   dating from 1796, is here published for the first time.   3 [1912] 446

BEETHOVENS TAUBHEIT. Theodor von Frimmel.   (B)
   Republication with unimportant additions of the popular, nonmedical account which had appeared in 'Beethoven-
   Forschung' 1 [1912] 82.   3 [1912] 522,571

DIE "JENAER" SYMPHONIE VON BEETHOVEN. Egon Wellesz.   (C)
   A popular account of the discovery and characteristics of the recently discovered youthful work.
                                    3 [1912] 605

KOSTBARKEITEN AUS DEM ARCHIV DER K. K. GESELLSCHAFT DER MUSIKFREUNDE IN WIEN.   (D)
   Eusebius Mandyczewski.
   A detailed description (with facsimiles) of the sketch for the first of the projected 'Leichte Lieder' mentioned in
   NB II 574.   4 [1913] 123

BEETHOVENS ENDE. Emil Lucka.   (E)
   "From the sum of the last works we gain the impression that Beethoven had come to positively hate his art, that it
   could no longer say for him what he was compelled to say, that he must transform it or annihilate it to attain the
   means of expression which his spirit demanded." Michelangelo, faced with this same problem, was able to take
   refuge in his religious faith, but this was not for Beethoven, who believed that the problems of man must be worked
   out on earth. The Ninth Symphony, the Missa Solemnis, and the last piano works and quartets are discussed from
   this viewpoint. His struggle manifests itself (among other ways) in the importance which the fugue takes in his last
   period; of all art forms the one which most completely can express the conflict of variety in unity, and which with
   Beethoven becomes the absolute antithesis of the Bach fugue. "Muss es sein? Es muss sein!" is prophetically the
   last movement of his last great work.   5 [1914] 11

THE 'BEBUNG' MEASURE OF THE ADAGIO OF OPUS 110. Heinrich Schenker.   (F)
   An attempt to clarify questions of notation to show precisely what Beethoven wished for this passage. This same
   discussion appears on pp. 51-54 of 'Die letzte fünf Sonaten von Beethoven' (UE 3977).
                                    6 [1915] 13

VERGESSENES UND NEUES VON BEETHOVEN. Max Unger.   (G)
   Complete and carefully transcribed version of the letter of August 2nd 1825 to Schott (appearing as No. 1323 in KK),
   giving corrections for the Missa Solemnis, referring to the dedication of this work and of the Ninth Symphony, and
   mentioning an attempt to steal the score of the 'Dedication of the House' Overture. Letter without date (probably
   late August or early September 1826) without name of addressee but obviously to Karl Holz (appearing as No. 1406
   in KK) regarding the appointment of Stephan von Breuning as co-guardian for Nephew Karl. Letter without date
   (probably early June 1823) to Anton Diabelli (appearing as No. 1115 in KK) regarding corrections and publication
   of Opp. 110 and 123. Transcription of a page from Beethoven's journal of early 1826.
                                    6 [1915] 91

DAS HELDENTUM VON BEETHOVENS "EROICA." Otto Kleinpeter.   (H)
   An essay written in the spirit of the first year of World War I.   6 [1915] 612

VON ERTMANN. Eugen Meller.   (I)
   A summary of Beethoven's relations with "the first truly great woman performer of his pianoforte works," with
   quotations from Schindler and other contemporaries regarding her playing. In 1831 in Milan she played unforgettably
   for the 20-year old Mendelssohn. (See also 'Beethoven-Forschung' 2 [1916] 95)
                                    7 [1916] 17

THE PERFORMANCE OF OPUS 111.   Heinrich Schenker.   (A)
    Material also appearing on pp. 27-31 of 'Die letzte fünf Sonaten von Beethoven' (UE 3978).
                                      7 [1916] 81

BEETHOVENS AUFENTHALT 1812 IN KARLSBAD.   M. Kaufmann.   (B)
    Beethoven arrived in Karlsbad on July 27th or a little before, gave a concert with the violinist Polledro on August 6th,
and left for Franzenbad shortly thereafter.   His departure from Teplitz had been so hasty that he forgot to bring his
traveling papers.   Returning to Teplitz, he passed through Karlsbad, probably arriving on September 8th and depart-
ing that day or the next.   It may safely be assumed that Beethoven's visit to this town was to see friends and not to
take the baths.   (See also 'Neue Zeitschrift für Musik' JG 79 [1912] 85; 'Beethoven-Forschung' 3 [1925] 37)
                                      7 [1916] 231

BEETHOVENS KLAVIER -- EINE ÄSTHETISCHE BEARBEITERFRAGE.   Max Arend.   (C)
    The Pf for which Beethoven wrote his earlier sonatas extended upwards only to the F above high C -- the F in m. 58
of Op. 13 represents the extreme compass of the instrument for which this sonata was written.   This limitation explains passages such as that in the first movement of Op. 31 No. 2 where octaves (to the top F) are used in the exposition, but a dominant soprano pedal on D in the recapitulation which otherwise would go to the B flat above this
F.   The composer was of necessity restricted within the limitations of the instrument for which he was writing.   It
may be noted that towards the end of his life he had available a piano of somewhat greater range, but that he did
not revise his early works to take advantage of this increased scope.   The modern editor must weigh all facts before
making such a revision.   7 [1916] 291

EIN UNBEACHTETES KLAVIERSTÜCK VON BEETHOVEN AUS STARKES PIANOFORTESCHULE.   (D)
      Theodor von Frimmel.
    TK III 48 is correct in saying that the Bagatelles Op. 119 Nos. 7-11 incl. appeared in the third part of Starke's
'Wiener Pianoforteschule' of January 1821, not the second part.   To Part II (1820) Beethoven contributed a revision
of the Andante and Rondo of the D major Sonata Op. 28, with his own fingering and with expression marks carefully noted.   In No. 24 of Part III is a "Concerto Finale by L. van Beethoven" which is a slight modification of the
coda (C major) of the finale of the Piano Concerto Op. 37 (a total of 12 measures being omitted), with fingering
freely indicated.   This version is given herewith.   8 [1917] 24

AN UNPUBLISHED BEETHOVEN LETTER.   Adolph Kohut.   (E)
    Letter without date or name of addressee, reading: "Hier lieber falscher Dichter die Rechnung wegen dem Lied; ich
habe selbst die 15 Kreutzer per Bogen bezahlt, da aber das Theater ein blutarmer Narr ist (i bina kein knicker) so
bin ich mit 13 Kreutzern zufrieden.   Leben Sie wohl, Dichter und Trachter!   Um Verzeihung!   In Eile Ihr Beethoven. "
                                      8 [1917] 331

BEETHOVENS "LIEBQUARTETT."   H. von Perger.   (F)
    In one of the conversation books, Beethoven referred to Count Rasumovsky's private quartet (Schuppanzigh, Sina,
Weiss, Linke) as his "Liebquartett."   From 1808 to 1816 these four brought him youth, undoubted talent, and de-
votion to the art of quartet playing; with them available Beethoven could immediately put his ideas to the test of
performance.   After seven years of dispersal the group joined together again, with Holz as Vln II in place of Sina.
The reformation of the quartet was hailed in Vienna with great enthusiasm.   For various reasons Schuppanzigh fell
into disfavor for some months after the first performance of the E flat Quartet Op. 127, but he returned with brilliant
success to bring the later quartets to life and to repeated hearings until his death in 1830.
                                      8 [1917] 381

ALEXANDER WHEELOCK THAYER -- ZUR HUNDERTSTEN WIEDERKEHR SEINES GEBURTSTAGES (22 OKTOBER).   (G)
      Theodor Bolte.   8 [1917] 734

BEETHOVEN ALS DIRIGENT DER ERSTEN AUFFÜHRUNG SEINER NEUNTER SYMPHONIE 1826 (AUS EINEM ALTEN   (H)
      BERICHT DARÜBER.
    Neither the year nor the program mentioned in this account correspond with the actual first performance on May 7th
1824 (see TK III 164).   9 [1918] 732

BEETHOVENS CIS-MOL-QUARTETT, EIN FORMSTUDIE.   Carl Prohaska.   (I)
    A brief and very general discussion, without examples in music notation.
                                  11 [1920] 269

BEETHOVEN. Franz Theodor Csokor.   (A)
Festival address on the occasion of a performance of the Missa Solemnis.
11 [1920] 338

BEETHOVENS SENDUNG. Hermann Csillag.   (B)
Brief metaphysical essay.   12 [1921] 2

BEETHOVENS WOHNUNG IM PASQUALATIHAUSE ZU WIEN. Wolfgang Madjera.   (C)
Description of the house in which Beethoven lived from 1804 to 1815.
12 [1921] 33

DER UNFUG DER BEETHOVEN-MASKE. Theodor Haas.   (D)
In 1812 the sculptor Franz Klein made a life mask of Beethoven. The author believes that the method used for molding such a mask makes it important that the facial muscles of the subject remain in their normal tone. This mask
reproduces not the true appearance of the subject but an involuntary grimace. It is to be regretted that this mask
has become the principle source from which the public visualizes Beethoven's appearance.
13 [1922] 8

MONATSHEFTE FÜR MUSIK-GESCHICHTE

A LETTER ABOUT BEETHOVEN. Wilhelm Rust.   (E)
A letter from Rust to his sister, dated July 9th 1808, telling her that he had played for Beethoven.
1 [1869] 68

EIN BRIEF BEETHOVENS.   (F)
Letter of March 11th 1818 to George Thomson, dickering about prices for Scottish Songs and the Overture that
Thomson had requested. This letter is not in KS; B-Jahrbuch II lists its first publication as in TD IV 572 (1907).
3 [1871] 195

THE VIOLIN SONATAS OPUS 12.   (G)
A devastating review of the Violin Sonatas Op. 12 which appeared in the 'Allgemeine Musikalische Zeitung' 1 [1799] 570
at the time of their first publication.   12 [1880] 199

BEETHOVEN'S SUPPOSED QUINTET ARRANGEMENT OF OPUS 20.   (H)
Refutation of Ries' statement that Beethoven himself arranged the Septet Op. 20 as a quintet by quoting Beethoven's
notice which appeared in the 'Allgemeine Musikalische Zeitung' 5 [1802] Intelligenzblatt p. 15 (given in KS I 64).
13 [1881] 18

BEETHOVEN AS A PIANIST IN 1822.   (I)
Quotation from the 'Allgemeine Musikalische Zeitung' 24 [1822] 310: "From time to time he still gives masterful
improvisations when with his friends, to their great enjoyment, and shows that he still knows how to handle his instrument with power, freedom and facility."   13 [1881] 181

URTEILE ÜBER BEETHOVEN AUS DEN JAHREN 1805 U. F.   (J)
Contemporary reviews of Opp. 47, 55, and 57.   14 [1882] 8

A LETTER AND A RECEIPT TO COUNT OPPERSDORF. H. Riemann.   (K)
Digest of an article in the 'Allgemeine Musik-Zeitung' 15 [1888] 385 to the effect that Count Oppersdorf had commissioned a symphony from Beethoven and had paid 200 gulden in advance. An undated letter from Beethoven, saying
that the symphony was ready, described it as having 3 trombones and piccolo in the last movement (obviously referring
to the C minor Symphony), and saying that the total price would be 550 gulden, which the Count paid. (See Sonneck
p. 104 for an extensive discussion of the series of letters of which these form a part)
20 [1888] 191

GRILLPARZER AND BEETHOVEN. Alfr. Chr. Kalischer.   (L)
Digest of an article dealing with Grillparzer's relations with Beethoven.
23 [1891] 35

WANN IST BEETHOVEN GEBOREN? Alfr. Chr. Kalischer.   (A)
  Digest of an article to the effect that it was by no means an invariable custom in the Rhineland for baptism to be
  exactly two days after birth, so that December 15th can be taken only as a conjectured date of the birth of
  Beethoven.   23 [1891] 35

DIE BEETHOVEN-AUTOGRAPHE DER KÖNIGL. BIBLIOTHEK ZU BERLIN. Alfr. Chr. Kalischer.   (B)
  Complete tabulation of the manuscripts, sketches, conversation books, letters and memorabilia of Beethoven in the
  Royal Library. In 27 [1895] 154 are transcribed for the first time the last sketches which Beethoven put on paper,
  shortly before his death.

EDrs of Kal	200	27 [1895] 159
	405	28 [1896] 31
	598	27 [1895] 159
	987	28 [1896] 47
	1177	28 [1896] 32
	1178	28 [1896] 33
	M-569	28 [1896] 33

                                            27 [1895] 145,153,165;
                                            28 [1896] 1,9,17,25,41,57,73

SETTING OF GOETHE'S 'HEIDENRÖSLEIN.' H. E. Krehbiel.   (C)
  Almost illegible sketches have been found, and were published in the New York Tribune for March 6th 1898.
                                            30 [1898] 79

ZWEI BEETHOVENBRIEFE DER DONAUESCHINGER BIBLIOTHEK. Caroline Valentin.   (D)
  Letter of August 2nd 1825 to Schott regarding corrections and other matters having to do with the Missa Solemnis.
  Letter without date (probably August 1826) to Karl Holz regarding the guardianship over Nephew Karl.
                                            31 [1899] 133

A CONTEMPORARY OF BEETHOVEN.   (E)
  Digest of an account by Weingartner of a talk with a 91-year old woman who had sung in the first performance of
  the Ninth Symphony.   32 [1900] 57

AUSZUG DER LEITARTIKEL BEETHOVEN BETREFFEND AUS DER NEUEN ZEITSCHRIFT FÜR MUSIK.   (F)
  A. Wohlgeboren.   33 [1901] 7

LEITARTIKEL UND KLEINERE AUFSÄTZE BEETHOVEN BETREFFEND, AUS DER NIEDERRHEINISCHEN MUSIKZEITUNG.   (G)
  A. Wohlgeboren.   33 [1901] 13,29

AUSZUG DER LEITARTIKEL UND KLEINEREN AUFSÄTZE BEETHOVEN BETREFFEND AUS DEM 'KLAVIERLEHRER.'   (H)
  A. Wohlgeboren.   33 [1901] 33

AUSZÜGE DER LEITARTIKEL UND KLEINEREN AUFSÄTZE BEETHOVEN BETREFFEND, AUS DER 'NEUEN BERLINER   (I)
  MUSIKZEITUNG' (BOCK). A. Wohlgeboren.   33 [1901] 48,73,95

AUSZÜGE DER LEITARTIKEL BEETHOVEN BETREFFEND. ALLGEMEINE LEIPZIGER MUSIKALISCHE ZEITUNG   (J)
  REDIGIERT VON SELMAR BAGGE (NEUE FOLGE). A. Wohlgeboren.
                                            33 [1901] 151,173

AUSZUG DER LEITARTIKEL BEETHOVEN BETREFFEND. DEUTSCHE WIENER MUSIKZEITUNG (BAGGE).   (K)
  A. Wohlgeboren.   33 [1901] 176

GRANDFATHER LUDWIG AS A SINGER.   (L)
  Digest of an article in a Dutch musical journal: "According to the program of a church concert (in Amsterdam) in
  1747, Beethoven sang a bass aria, and was referred to as 'a musician of the Elector of Cologne.'"
                                            34 [1902] 54

RECOLLECTIONS OF BEETHOVEN IN 1817. August von Klöber.   (M)
  A reprinting of the article which Klöber (the artist for whom Beethoven sat in 1817) which appeared in the 'Allgemeine
  Musikalische Zeitung' NF 2 [1864] 324.   35 [1903] 8

BEETHOVEN AND EQUAL TEMPERAMENT.   (A)
    Several enharmonic changes in the transition before the recapitulation of the first movement of the Fourth Symphony
    are cited as proof that in Beethoven's conception the pitch of (say) A sharp and B flat written for an orchestral in-
    strument were identical.   35 [1903] 147

MONATSSCHRIFT FÜR DIE GESCHICHTE WESTDEUTSCHLANDS

DIE FAMILIE VAN BEETHOVEN IN BONN UND IHRE BEZIEHUNGEN. Werner Hesse.   (B)
    This paper gives a considerable number of facts about the composer, his siblings, parents, grandparents and grand-
    uncle which are now generally accepted but which were presumably provocative additions to Beethoveniana in 1879.
    This paper was reprinted in 'Allgemeine (Deutsche) Musik-Zeitung' 6 [1879] 257, 265, and was summarized and
    discussed in 'Allgemeine Musikalische Zeitung' Ser. 3: 15 [1880] 481.
                                                            5 [1879] 200

MONDE MUSICAL

ESSAI D'INTERPRÉTATION D'UNE SONATE DE BEETHOVEN. E. Marchand.   (C)
    From an analysis of the Sonata in C sharp minor Op. 27 No. 2 in particular and of numerous other works (of
    Beethoven, his predecessors and contemporaries) in general, the conclusion is drawn that "for the same ideas we
    find the same melodic fragments, the same harmonies, the same usage. "
                                                            34 [1923] 123,163

ESSAIS D'INTERPRÉTATION: LA SONATE EN UT DIÈZE MINEUR DE BEETHOVEN. Jeanne Thieffry.   (D)
    Syrupy.   35 [1924] 268

VISAGES DANS LA PÉNOMBRE: BEETHOVEN. Jeanne Thieffry.   (E)
    Rhapsodic sketch.   35 [1924] 399

LES QUATUORS DE BEETHOVEN. Marc Pincherle.   (F)
    Review of de Marliave's book.   36 [1925] 347

LES SONATES POUR PIANO ET VIOLON DE BEETHOVEN. Marcel Herwegh.   (G)
    A portion of the introduction to the author's 'Technique d'interprétation.'
                                                            38 [1927] 13

LA MORT DE BEETHOVEN. A. Wawruch.   (H)
    First publication in French of the account of Beethoven's death written by his attending physician, originally
    published in the 'Wiener Zeitschrift' of April 30th 1842 and republished in Nohl's 'Beethoven nach den Schilderungen
    seiner Zeitgenossen' [1877] 247.   38 [1927] 87

LE 26 MARS 1927. A. Mangeot.   (I)
    Centenary tribute and translation into French of the Heiligenstadt will.
                                                            38 [1927] 133

LA SONATE OP. 111 DE BEETHOVEN. Hélène Kaz.   (J)
    Prize winning essay on the history and analysis of this work.   38 [1927] 403

THÉRÈSE DE BRUNSWICK ET BEETHOVEN: LA SONATE OPUS 78 EN FA DIÈZE MAJEUR ET LE LIED MIGNON. (K)
    E. Marchand.
    Parallelism between the song 'Mignon' (Op. 75 No. 1) and the Sonata Op. 78 (dedicated to Thérèse von Brunswick)
    is taken as an indication that Thérèse was the Immortal Beloved.   39 [1928] 168

BEETHOVEN: LES GRANDES ÉPOQUES CRÉATRICES. Romain Rolland.   (L)
    Introduction to the book 'From the Eroica to the Appassionata. '   39 [1928] 399

LES 32 SONATES DE BEETHOVEN.   Alfred Cortot.   (A)
   Introduction to Cortot's edition of the pianoforte sonates.   43 [1932] 231

COURS D'INTERPRÉTATION DE A. CORTOT: LES 32 SONATES DE BEETHOVEN.   Jeanne Thieffry.   (B)
   A digest of Cortot's lectures at the Ecole normale.   43 [1932] 265,309,339,379;
                                                             44 [1933] 10,45

FIDELIO ET LA SONATE OPUS 110 DE BEETHOVEN.   E. Marchand.   (C)
   The author finds a parallelism between the chief themes of the Sonata and passages of Fidelio.   (See also 45 [1934] 43)
                                                             44 [1933] 220

BEETHOVEN: LA DERNIÈRE SONATA POUR PIANO (1822), L'OPUS 111, DÉDIÉE À L'ARCHIDUC RODOLPHE.   (D)
     E. Marchand.
   As with Op. 110 (see 44 [1933] 220), the author believes that this Sonata shows close kinship to Fidelio.
                                                             45 [1934] 43

DISCUSSION À PROPOS DE LA SONATE OPUS 26, EN LA BÉMOL, DE BEETHOVEN (1800).   E. Marchand.   (E)
   Thematic analysis.   46 [1935] 8

BEETHOVEN: LE BALLET DES CRÉATURES DE PROMÉTHÉE.   E. Marchand.   (F)
   An attempt to show a motival kinship between the Prometheus Overture, the Sonata in A flat Op. 26, the Second
   Symphony, and a Bohemian folk song.   46 [1935] 75

BEETHOVEN ET LA MUSIQUE "TRADUCTRICE."   Serge Petitgirard.   (G)
   "It cannot be denied that the aspirations and the efforts of Beethoven were steadily turned towards the creation of
   works always more precise, more intelligible -- in a word, more programmatic. This fact is evident in his
   symphonies."   46 [1935] 155

LE SENTIMENT ET L'AMITIÉ DANS LA MUSIQUE DE BEETHOVEN.   E. Marchand.   (H)
   Analyses of the Pf sonata in A major Op. 101 and of the two sonatas for Pf and Vcl Op. 102.
                                                             47 [1936] 8

LE CLASSICISME ET LE ROMANTISME DE BEETHOVEN.   Alfred Cortot.   (I)
                                                             47 [1936] 83,118

COURS D'INTERPRÉTATION D'ALFREDO CASELLA.   (J)
   Notes on the interpretations of the Sonatas Opp. 53, 109, 110.   47 [1936] 215

MONTHLY MUSICAL RECORD

BEETHOVEN'S TRIO, OPUS 97.   H. W. L. Hine.   (K)
   A fanciful description of the music.   1 [1871] 76

THE SYMPHONIES OF BEETHOVEN.   Hector Berlioz.   (L)
   General analyses.   1 [1871] 97,126,141; 2 [1872] 2,15

NOTES ON THE TEXT OF BEETHOVEN.   Edward Dannreuther.   (M)
   Careful discussion of disputed passages in Opp. 109, 110, 111.   2 [1872] 167; 3 [1873] 2,42

BEETHOVEN'S 'EROICA SYMPHONY.'   Richard Wagner.   (N)
   Translation from the "Programmatische Erläuterungen."   3 [1873] 57

BEETHOVEN'S OVERTURE TO 'CORIOLANUS.'   Richard Wagner.   (O)
   Translation from the "Programmatische Erläuterungen."   3 [1873] 87

BEETHOVEN'S VARIATIONS IN A FLAT, FROM THE SONATA OPUS 26.   (P)
   Highly rhapsodic interpretation.   3 [1873] 86

WAGNER ON BEETHOVEN'S INSTRUMENTATION.   (A)
    Extensive paraphrasing of Wagner's comments and suggested changes.
                                                    4 [1874] 51

BEETHOVEN'S LAST DAYS.   Ferdinand Hiller.   4 [1874] 82   (B)

WHAT THE PARIS CONSERVATORY THOUGHT OF BEETHOVEN.   (C)
    Translation from the 'Memories de Berlioz.'   4 [1874] 150

A PILGRIMAGE TO BEETHOVEN.   Richard Wagner.   (D)
    What Wagner called an "art-novel," to express his disgust with conditions of musical art in Paris when he was
    there as a young man.   5 [1875] 65,81,97

THE TEMPO DI MINUETTO IN BEETHOVEN'S EIGHTH SYMPHONY.   (E)
    Wagner's comments (from 'Über das Dirigieren') and reply by August Manns. The latter claims that all Beethoven
    metronome marks should be reduced by 1/6 to 1/5 to meet present conditions.
                                                    8 [1878] 5

BEETHOVEN'S DEATH.   Ludwig Nohl.   8 [1878] 145   (F)

A NEW COMPOSITION OF BEETHOVEN.   F. Nohl.   (G)
    The Lobkowitz Cantata (TV 208; GA Ser. 25 No. 274) with an account of the circumstances leading to its
    composition.   12 [1882] 34

GUSTAV NOTTEBOHM AND THE BEETHOVEN SKETCH BOOKS.   J. S. Shedlock.   (H)
    An obituary notice, with discussion of some of Nottebohm's findings from the sketch books: Beethoven's molding
    of themes, use of the sketch books for establishment of chronology, etc. Comments are based chiefly on the
    symphonies and the last quartets; about thirty excerpts in musical notation are given.
                                                    13 [1883] 59,81

BEETHOVEN'S INTENTION TO WRITE AN OVERTURE ON 'MACBETH.'   J. B. Krall.   (I)
                                                    13 [1883] 115,134

BEETHOVEN AS A HUMORIST.   Joseph Verey.   (J)
    Humor is found in his compositions and his letters, and in accounts of him by friends.
                                                    17 [1887] 28

BEETHOVEN'S PIANOFORTE VARIATIONS.   Fr. Niecks.   (K)
    History of and comments on each work.   19 [1889] 27,51,75,97

BEETHOVEN'S SONATAS FOR PIANOFORTE AND VIOLIN.   Fr. Niecks.   (L)
    Analyses and comments on the style of each sonata.   20 [1890] 145,169,193

BEETHOVEN AND CRAMER.   (M)
    Beethoven admired Cramer's Etudes, and toyed with the thought of writing a Pianoforte School which would better
    express his own ideas.   23 [1893] 150

BEETHOVEN'S PIANOFORTE SONATAS.   (N)
    Questioned readings in Opp. 2 No. 2, 7, 22, 27 No. 1, 53, 81a, 106, and 109 from the Mandyczewski Edition.
                                                    23 [1893] 52

MOZART AND BEETHOVEN CRITICIZED.   (O)
    Extracts from the writings of de Momigny, a contemporary, who felt that Beethoven should be "more careful in
    his choice of subject matter and in the ordering of his material," with specific examples from Op. 81a.
                                                    24 [1894] 217

WAGNER ON BEETHOVEN'S SYMPHONIES.   (P)
    Two articles in the 'Neue Zeitschrift für Musik' (1850), signed by Theodor Uhlig, are paraphrases or verbatim
    copies of opinions expressed by Wagner in letters to his follower Uhlig.
                                                    24 [1894] 25

THE GOETHE OF MUSIC: A MUSICIAN'S ESTIMATE OF BEETHOVEN'S GENIUS AND WORKS.   Ernst Perabo.   (A)
    Laudatory newspaper article.   24 [1894] 76

A CRITIQUE OF SEVENTY YEARS AGO.   (B)
    A review of the newly issued Op. 111 from 'The Harmonicon' of 1823.
                                     24 [1894] 3

THE TWO REDUNDANT BARS IN THE SCHERZO OF THE C MINOR SYMPHONY.   (C)
    According to Breitkopf & Härtel, these measures were a prima volta for a repeat which was later stricken out but
    without elimination of the two measures (see NB I 17). Schindler, Marx and Berlioz favored retaining these two
    measures, the first of these on the strength of Beethoven's failure to object to their presence in the engraved score.
    See also Shedlock 13 [1883] 59.   24 [1894] 50

BEETHOVEN AND MARIE BIGOT.   (D)
    Beethoven presented the autograph of Op. 57 to Marie. The letter given in KS I 136 (there dated "summer 1808";
    referred to in letter (KS I 137) attributed by TK II 84 to "before 1809" since in that year the Bigots moved to Paris)
    is more probably 1804-05. (Regarding this earlier dating, note that Bigot came from Berlin to become librarian to
    Prince Rasumovsky only in 1808.)   26 [1896] 76

THE BEETHOVEN PIANOFORTE SONATAS.   Carl Reinecke.   (E)
    Detailed discussion of the performance and interpretation of each of the sonatas. These articles were subsequently
    issued in book form and reviewed in 28 [1898] 271.   26 [1896] - 28 [1898] passim

SOME REMARKS BY BEETHOVEN WITH REGARD TO THE PERFORMANCE OF HIS WORKS.   E. van der Straeten.   (F)
    Quotations from Schindler and Ries, with comments.   27 [1897] 79

ALEXANDER WHEELOCK THAYER.   (G)
    Translation of obituary notice by Dr. Erich Prieger.   27 [1897] 195

SHAKESPEARE AND BEETHOVEN.   (H)
    "Close examination of their works will show how thoroughly they were akin -- how like each other in their aims
    and method of working."   29 [1899] 49

CLEMENTI CORRESPONDENCE.   (I)
    Excerpts from letters over the period 1803-09 which include various references to Beethoven.
                                    32 [1902] 141

PERFORMANCE OF BEETHOVEN'S "LEONORE" AT BERLIN.   (J)
    Reconstruction of the original (1805) version performed November 20th 1905, probably for the first time anywhere
    since 1805.   35 [1905] 222

BONN.   Herbert Antcliffe.   (K)
    Brief description of the town.   37 [1907] 51

BEETHOVEN'S PIANOFORTE SONATAS.   C. Edgerton Lowe.   (L)
    A statistical summary of form and tonality.   39 [1909] 102

BEETHOVEN'S LETTERS.   Ebenezer Prout.   (M)
    A review of KS, with many comments on Beethoven as a letter writer and a brief list of errata in KS.
                                   39 [1909] 123,147

BEETHOVEN'S "LEONORE."   Ed. by Erich Prieger.   (N)
    An attempted restoration of the original (1805) version.   40 [1910] 265

SOME CONTEMPORARY ENGLISH CRITICISM OF BEETHOVEN.   (O)
    Excerpts from 'The Harmonicon' of 1823-31.   42 [1912] 89

BEETHOVEN AND BRAHMS.   (P)
    Mention of a letter bearing on early Berlin performances of "Fidelio."
                                  42 [1912] 150

BEETHOVEN'S STRING QUARTETS. Arthur Eaglefield Hull.   (A)
    Brief comments as a part of a historical survey of chamber music. 42 [1912] 118

BEETHOVEN'S 32 VARIATIONS IN C MINOR. Francesco Berger.   (B)
    Suggestions for study and performance.   44 [1914] 300

BEETHOVEN AND HIS COPYISTS.   (C)
    Remarks on Schlemmer, Rampel, Peter Gläser, and Ferdinand Wolanek.
                                                                  45 [1915] 220

BEETHOVEN'S BAGATELLES. Francesco Berger.   (D)
    Suggestions for study and performance.   46 [1916] 7,39

ANDREAS RASOUMOWSKY.   (E)
    Brief biographical sketch.   47 [1917] 196

JOSEPH WOELFL AND DANIEL STEIBELT.   (F)
    Brief biographical sketches.   47 [1917] 147

BEETHOVEN'S CHAMBER MUSIC. Frederick Niecks.   (G)
    General.   50 [1920] 193

BEETHOVEN, SPOHR AND HUMMEL. Francesco Berger.   (H)
    If Beethoven had not lived, these other two "would each have worn his own crown of immortal laurel. Our just
    and proper appreciation of Beethoven should not blind us to the merits of his contemporaries Spohr and Hummel. "
                                                     51 [1921] 248

BEETHOVEN'S RELIGION. Fr. Erckmann.   (I)
    Excerpts from letters, conversation books, etc. to show "that Beethoven was not only a thoroughly religious man,
    but that he believed firmly in a personal, living God, and that he found strength and consolation in this faith. "
                                                     53 [1923] 206,262

BEETHOVEN'S DEAFNESS. Fr. Erckmann.   (J)
    Nontechnical discussion of the first symptoms and early progress of the deafness.
                                                     53 [1923] 297

BEETHOVEN AND HIS VISITORS: THE FIRST PUBLICATION OF HIS NOTEBOOKS. Rudolf Friedman.   (K)
    Excerpts from the 137 conversation books.   54 [1924] 70

A LONG LOST LETTER BY BEETHOVEN. A. M. Henderson.   (L)
    Facsimile and transliteration of KS I 256, with the KS translation. 55 [1925] 266

THE EFFECT OF BEETHOVEN IN 1927. Cyril Scott.   (M)
    Lack of appreciation of Beethoven by many good musicians (e. g. , Debussy) may be due to too great familiarity
    with it: to the fact that now his music "may give his listeners sensations but cannot give those new sensations which
    it gave while Beethoven was alive. The time has now arrived which Beethoven is beginning to be understood by
    nonmusical people. "   57 [1927] 65

AN INTRODUCTION TO BEETHOVEN'S MUSIC. Arthur Eaglefield Hull.   (N)
    Brief and superficial.   57 [1927] 67,98,130,162

BEETHOVEN AS A READING MAN. A. M. Henderson.   (O)
    Beethoven owned a relatively small number of books (Shakespeare, Homer, Goethe, Schiller, Latin and Greek
    classics) but those volumes were well thumbed and in many cases much marked and annotated.
                                                     58 [1928] 355

A CURIOUS PARALLEL. C. H. Kitson.   (P)
    Similarity between the adagio of Beethoven's Sonata Op. 31 No. 1 and Hummel's Op. 55.
                                                     61 [1931] 99

THE RONDO OF BEETHOVEN'S OPUS 10 No. 3.   C. H. Kitson.   (A)
    Detailed analysis leading to the conclusion that the movement is in modified sonata-rondo form.
                                             61 [1931] 268

THE VARIATIONS OF BEETHOVEN'S OPUS 109.   Moriz Rosenthal.   (B)
    An analysis to show that in these variations "there glows a microcosm of musical architectural art, the audacity
    and creative originality of which are probably without a parallel." 63 [1933] 3

BEETHOVEN AND THE VIOLINIST.   Jeffrey Pulver.   (C)
    General and superficial.   63 [1933] 145

BEETHOVEN'S PIANO SONATAS: THEIR PLACE IN HISTORY.   Eric Blom.   (D)
    Virtually identical with the "Prelude" of his "Beethoven's Pianoforte Sonatas Discussed."
                                             63 [1933] 175

BEETHOVEN'S KEYBOARD MANNER.   Eric Blom.   (E)
    Virtually identical with "Interlude III" of his "Beethoven's Pianoforte Sonatas Discussed."
                                           63 [1933] 223

BEETHOVEN'S MUSIC IN THE RHINELAND.   Willi Reich.   (F)
    Review of a volume of excerpts from the contemporary press of the Rhineland. "Beethoven's masterpieces found
    a comparatively quick and intelligent reception in the Rhineland in contrast to other musical centers of Germany."
                                           64 [1934] 33

BEETHOVEN'S THREE STYLES.   Eric Blom.   (G)
    Virtually identical with "Interlude VIII" of his "Beethoven's Pianoforte Sonatas Discussed."
                                           65 [1935] 169

BEETHOVEN'S PROGRAM SONATA.   Eric Blom.   (H)
    Virtually identical with "Interlude IX" of his "Beethoven's Pianoforte Sonatas Discussed," with historical additions.
                                         65 [1935] 193

BEETHOVEN'S REPEATS.   Eric Blom.   (I)
    Virtually identical with "Interlude II" of his "Beethoven's Pianoforte Sonatas Discussed."
                                           65 [1935] 226

DIALOGUES IN ELYSIUM: BEETHOVEN AND NAPOLEON.   F. Bonavia.   (J)
    Fantasy.   66 [1936] 103

LISZT AND BEETHOVEN.   Gerth Baruch.   (K)
    Beethoven's reception of Liszt at their first meeting was apparently chilly and unfriendly. The incident of the much
    discussed kiss on the brow, if it ever took place, must have been after the farewell concert.
                                         66 [1936] 176

THE MILITARY ELEMENT IN BEETHOVEN.   Alfred Einstein.   (L)
    The "military" type of movement -- "brisk four-in-a-bar, with decisive beginning, pushing boldly on, often
    brusque in manner; dotted quavers on the upbeats and a constantly pulsing rhythm" -- is a style of composition
    probably borrowed from Viotti, and is typical only of the first movements of Beethoven's concertos.
                                         69 [1939] 270

BEETHOVEN AND THE VARIATION.   Eric Blom.   (M)
    A discussion of the importance of the variation form in Beethoven. The Diabelli Variations are "the only work
    by Beethoven in the form that is to be taken quite seriously which has a theme not his own for its foundation. It
    is a transfiguration into fantasy and poetry and into what is beyond historical exposition and technical analysis
    to illuminate."   70 [1940] 222

A POINT IN BEETHOVEN'S VIOLIN CONCERTO.   F. Bonavia.   (N)
    "Is it pedantry to suggest that the great violinists who adopt a slow tempo (for the second theme as it appears
    immediately following the cadenza of the first movement) do violence both to the letter and to the spirit?"
                                         71 [1941] 14

DIALOGUES IN ELYSIUM: BEETHOVEN AND A CRITIC. F. Bonavia.   (A)
   Fantasy.   72 [1942] 123

ARTICLES ABOUT BEETHOVEN. Donald W. MacArdle.   (B)
   Abstracts of articles which had appeared in this journal, as given herein.
                                             77 [1947] 262

THE COMPOSER OF THE SPURIOUS KONZERTSATZ IN D MAJOR GA 25/311.   (C)
   " . . . F. A. Růžička, a contemporary of Beethoven who wrote a piano concerto which that astute scholar Guido
   Adler actually took to be the work of Beethoven, called himself alternately Rössler and Rosetti. "
                                           79 [1949] 114

THE PARTICIPATION OF THE SOLO INSTRUMENT IN THE TUTTIS OF THE C MAJOR CONCERTO OPUS 15.   (D)
   The standard editions of Mozart's piano concertos "all conceal the composer's intention that the piano should be
   played not only as a solo instrument but as a continuo instrument in the tuttis. We recently had occasion to consult
   the first edition (in parts) of Beethoven's C major Piano Concerto and found that the original piano part shows that
   this was Beethoven's intention, too: the part is continuous, though printed only as bass with figuration in the tuttis.
   Beethoven's figured bass has been suppressed in every edition we have been able to consult, with the exception of
   the most recent edition of the Eulenberg miniature score in which the figuration has been -- quite preposterously --
   transferred to the string bass part, where indeed (as the editor naively remarks) it 'may be regarded as superfluous. '"
   (See also Ibid. p. 142)   79 [1949] 115

CONTINUO IN THE NINTH SYMPHONY.   (E)
   "A piano was certainly used in the first performance of the Ninth Symphony but Beethoven wrote no part for it. "
                                           79 [1949] 143

BEETHOVEN'S THIRD PERIOD BAGATELLES. Philip T. Barford.   (F)
   Discussion of certain puzzling points of aesthetics in Opp. 119 and 126.
                                 81 [1951] 256; 82 [1952] 13

BEETHOVEN'S 'DREAM OF ST. JEROME. '   (G)
   Brief account of this spurious composition.   82 [1952] 87

BEETHOVEN'S SKETCHBOOKS.   (H)
   An appraisal of major publications to date, and a review of the first issue of the new Beethovenhaus series.
                                       83 [1953] 57

EDITORIAL COMMENT ON THE RECENT DETERMINATION THAT THE JENA SYMPHONY WAS THE WORK OF   (I)
   FRIEDRICH WITT.   87 [1957] 122

BEETHOVEN'S FOURTH PIANO CONCERTO. Harold Truscott.   (J)
   "The piano at the beginning of this concerto is Beethoven's only solution to the <u>orchestral</u> problem which faced
   him in his material; it is an orchestral instrument, and does not assume its solo character until 69 bars later. "
                                    88 [1958] 91

BEETHOVEN AND THE CZERNYS. Donald W. MacArdle.   (K)
   A discussion of the relations of Beethoven with the little-known Joseph Czerny and the well-known Karl Czerny.
                                     88 [1958] 124

THE NINTH IN PERSPECTIVE. Harold Truscott.   (L)
   The Ninth Symphony is a great work, but nothing is to be gained by seeing it as other than it is: possibly the greatest,
   and certainly the largest, eighteenth-century symphony in existence. The most profound influence on nineteenth
   century symphonies (those of Bruckner, especially his ninth, are discussed in detail) was not Beethoven's Ninth but
   some of Schubert's music, notably the D minor quartet.   88 [1958] 223

PROBLEMS OF BEETHOVEN'S 'DIABELLI' VARIATIONS. William Yeomans.   (M)
   Inconclusive discussion of some of the "many puzzling features to the scholar, performer, and listener. "
                                   89 [1959] 8

BEETHOVEN AND HAYDN. Donald W. MacArdle.   (A)
  A discussion of Beethoven's relations, personal and musical, with Haydn.
                                        89 [1959] 203

FIRST EDITIONS OF BEETHOVEN PUBLISHED IN ENGLAND. Donald W. MacArdle.   (B)
  Records of Stationer's Hall in London indicate that Clementi anticipated B&H in the publication of Opp. 73, 74, 75
  (except perhaps No. 6), 77, 78, 79, 80, 81a, and 82.   90 [1960] 228

MUSIC

IMPRESSIONS OF BEETHOVEN'S SONATAS. Frederic Horace Clark.   (C)
  Detailed analyses of Opp. 27 No. 1, 27 No. 2, 31 No. 2 and 54.   1 [1892] 243,368

BEETHOVEN AT HOME -- AN EYEWITNESS.   (D)
  Extracts from the memoirs of Baron de Tremont.   2 [1892] 215

BEETHOVEN'S 'IMMORTAL BELOVED.'   Mariam Tenger (Marie von Hrussoczy).   (E)
  A translation by Caroline T. Goodloe of the book of the same title, maintaining the position of Therese von Breuning
  as the person to whom the famous letters were addressed.   4 [1893] 1

BEETHOVEN PLAYING. William Mason.   (F)
  General.   5 [1894] 434

THE PIANOFORTE SONATAS OF BEETHOVEN. W. S. B. Mathews.   (G)
  General.   6 [1894] 200

BEETHOVEN'S NOTEBOOK OF 1803. Gustav Nottebohm.   (H)
  A translation by Benjamin Cutter of the first 33 pages of 'Ein Skizzenbuch von Beethoven aus dem Jahre 1803.'
                                        7 [1895] 371,473; 8 [1895] 149

TEN EVENINGS WITH GREAT COMPOSERS: III. CHARACTERISTIC MOODS OF BEETHOVEN; IV. BACH, MOZART AND (I)
    BEETHOVEN COMPARED; VIII. BACH, BEETHOVEN, SCHUMANN, CHOPIN; X. BACH, BEETHOVEN, CHOPIN,
    SCHUMANN, LISZT. W. S. B. Mathews.
  Suggested programs of piano music, with popular notes.   11 [1896] 214; 11 [1897] 337;
                                        12 [1897] 97,365

BEETHOVEN'S RANK AS A COMPOSER.   (J)
  Dicta of certain American musicians.   11 [1897] 342

THE PERSONAL APPEARANCE OF BEETHOVEN. Egbert Swayne.   (K)
  Reproductions of 18 portraits or statues of Beethoven, with comments.
                                        13 [1897] 139

JOSEPH WOELFL, RIVAL OF BEETHOVEN. E. A. Richardson.   (L)
  Biographical and critical essay.   14 [1898] 557

BEETHOVEN'S SONATA PASTORALE OPUS 28. Frederic Horace Clark.   (M)
  Fanciful interpretation.   15 [1899] 304

CONCERNING THE SLOW MOVEMENTS OF BEETHOVEN. Egbert Swayne.   (N)
  Superficial discussion of the slow movements of certain of the piano sonatas.
                                        18 [1900] 429

THE BIOGRAPHER OF BEETHOVEN. Amy M. M. Graham.   (O)
  Brief biographical sketch of Alexander Wheelock Thayer and popular review of the 'Leben.'
                                        20 [1901] 143

BEETHOVEN AS RELATED TO MOZART, HAYDN AND BACH. W. S. B. Mathews.   (P)
  Popular and noncritical.   21 [1902] 301

RECOLLECTIONS OF BEETHOVEN. Franz Grillparzer. (A)
Grillparzer maintained contact with Beethoven from 1804 to the time of his death.
4 [1923] 54

THE ORCHESTRAL TREATMENT OF THE TIMPANI. P. A. Browne. (B)
Beethoven was the first to tune the drums other than in fourths or fifths (almost invariably tonic and dominant) -- he used tuning in sixths in the Seventh Symphony and octaves in the Eighth and Ninth Symphonies -- "but throughout he never used more than two drums and never changed their tuning during the course of a movement." He was apparently the first to use "the drum in soft passages, especially for long soft rolls."
4 [1923] 334

BEETHOVEN'S FLUTE DUET AND FLUTE SONATA. L. Fleury. 6 [1925] 117 (C)

A CENTURY OF BEETHOVEN. H. C. Colles. (D)
"If he dictated a form to the art which it was destined to follow for at least a hundred years, he also imposed on the creative artist a spirit of unflinching sincerity which must live for all time."
8 [1927] 104

A SPEECH FOR THE OPPOSITION. John Ireland. (E)
"One might say that as the outstanding musical figure of the century he influenced the course of music towards an unduly logical classicism of form and expression which is the very reverse of all modern ideals of art."
8 [1927] 109

THE CHORAL FANTASIA. Edward J. Dent. (F)
A discussion of the spiritual influence of Mozart on Beethoven, and a consideration of the Choral Fantasia as "an improvisation and a vision." 8 [1927] 111

BEETHOVEN'S APPEARANCE. W. Barclay Squire. (G)
Summary from Frimmel's 'Beethovens äussere Erscheinung.' 8 [1927] 122

VARIATION FORM. W. H. Hadow. (H)
"In no kind of music is he so unequal; in none is it more interesting to study the development of his genius."
8 [1927] 126

SOME ASPECTS OF BEETHOVEN'S ART FORMS. Donald Francis Tovey. (I)
A demonstration that the term 'sonata form' is not, upon close examination, subject to any simple exemplification that conforms to any considerable proportion of sonata movements. This fact is illustrated by a detailed analysis of the first movement of the Pf Sonata Op. 22, "the closest approach, by Beethoven or any composer, to 'normal' sonata form," and a similar analysis of the String Quartet Op. 131, "outwardly the most abnormal of all his larger works." 8 [1927] 131,366

THE SIGNIFICANCE OF BEETHOVEN'S "THIRD PERIOD." John B. McEwen. (J)
The composers who in the eighteenth century first solved the problem of composing for instruments based their aesthetics chiefly on the sensuous and intellectual effects of structure and design. Beethoven's tendency, more and more as he matured and as deafness eliminated the sensuous appeal from his outlook on art, was to accentuate expressiveness and significance. "To the idiom which he inherited from the eighteenth century he added the expressive methods of the older polyphony." 8 [1927] 156

BEETHOVEN AND GOETHE. Scott Goddard. (K)
Beethoven was much influenced by Goethe's writings, especially the earlier ones, but "Goethe had little knowledge of Beethoven's work, and what he did know failed to move him." At their meeting in 1812 Goethe was impressed not by Beethoven's spiritual grandeur but by his roughness of temperament and by the social handicap of his deafness.
8 [1927] 165

BEETHOVEN'S ORCHESTRA - CONDUCTOR'S REFLECTIONS. Sir Hamilton Harty. (L)
"We are often forced to the conclusion that he could not have possessed great natural aptitude or gift for the happy use of orchestral instruments. Without some radical change, either by a reduction of the strings or by an increase of wind instruments, it is impossible to give performances (of the Third, Fifth, Seventh or Ninth Symphonies) which are really satisfactory." 8 [1927] 172

THE BEETHOVEN QUARTETS AS A PLAYER SEES THEM. Rebecca Clarke.   (A)
"In Beethoven the player must himself illumine the hidden obscurities, and unless he well understands them he
cannot hope to make others do so. " The characteristics of each of the quartets are discussed 'from the inside. '
                                              8 [1927] 178

THE VIOLIN SONATAS. Jelly d'Aranyi.   (B)
Comments on each of the sonatas by an experienced concert artist. 8 [1927] 191

THE VIOLIN CONCERTO. F. Bonavia.   (C)
This concerto differs from the many others of the era not by intent of the composer but by the unwitting accomplishment of his genius.   8 [1927] 198

HIS "INFINITE VARIETY." A. E. Brent Smith.   (D)
No other composer is a serious rival of Beethoven in the importance of his writing for every medium, his thematic
and melodic fertility and the aptness of his pairing of subjects, in his sure command of form and proportion, and
in the vitality of his rhythm and harmony. "The great popularity of Beethoven and the reverence felt by the multi-
tude for his personality and music are due, in a great measure, to his capacity for expressing with the utmost intensity and vividness the common emotional experiences of mankind. "
                                              8 [1927] 202

BEETHOVEN AND THE PIANOFORTE. George Dyson.   (E)
Beethoven's works for the piano "do in fact portray the most striking features of his temperament with remarkable
fidelity. There is little that he said elsewhere which cannot be found in essence in the volume of his piano sonatas. "
                                              8 [1927] 206

THE PIANOFORTE SONATAS: SOME TEXTUAL PROBLEMS. Ernest Walker.   (F)
Questioned readings in Opp. 10 No. 1, 10 No. 3, 14 No. 1, 26, 31 No. 2, 90, 106 and 109.
                                              8 [1927] 211

RANDOM NOTES ON THE PIANOFORTE SONATAS AND THEIR INTERPRETERS. J. A. Fuller-Maitland.   (G)
"Memories of remarkable performances ranging over a period of sixty years. "
                                              8 [1927] 218

THE PIANOFORTE CONCERTOS. Fanny Davies.   8 [1927] 224   (H)

THE SONGS. Walter Ford.   (I)
Beethoven wrote, "I do not like composing songs," and "when he turned to song he could not leave his instruments
behind: he continued to think instrumentally. " At the same time, however, by setting serious poetry to music "he
was inaugurating the movement which raised the art of song to its true status and dignity," and for the first time the
accompaniment "begins to take its proper place as joint interpreter along with the voice. " Many of the sixty songs
are discussed in some detail.   8 [1927] 228

BEETHOVEN AND GEORGE THOMSON. Richard Aldrich.   (J)
Starting in 1790 Thomson engaged Pleyel and Kozeluch to write sonatas on Scottish airs. Later he secured the
collaboration of Haydn for settings of songs. In 1803 he approached Beethoven for compositions like those of Pleyel
and Kozeluch, and in 1806 suggested six string trios, six string quintets and some songs, but neither time did anything come of it. In 1809 they came to terms for 43 songs (published in 1814), and relations continued for some
years thereafter (to a total of 132 song settings) with constant bickering over fees, text, and difficulty of the accompaniment. "It seems today mostly hack work. This Scottish episode in his life seems to have made only a
transitory effect upon anything except his bank account. "   8 [1927] 234

BEETHOVEN AS A COMPOSER OF OPERA. Dyneley Hussey.   (K)
"Though Beethoven pestered every literary man of his acquaintance with requests for libretti," his one completed
opera shows the unsuitableness of his genius for this medium. "Beethoven's acceptance of this libretto is the first
proof of his inherent lack of sense of the theatre. " His tremendous dramatic power was hampered by the necessity
of expressing the drama through stage personages, and he did not possess the power of dramatic characterization to
individualize them or to make them grow with the progress of the drama. The history of 'Fidelio' in its various
stages is given: the unsuccessful performances in 1805, the curtailed version (after textual revisions by Stefan von
Breuning) in 1806, and the more complete rewriting by Friedrich Treitschke leading to its final form in 1814.
                                              8 [1927] 243

SOME UNCERTAIN READINGS IN THE NINTH SYMPHONY. Donald Francis Tovey.   (A)
                                    8 [1927] 254

A SKETCH FOR THE PIANOFORTE SONATA OPUS 27 No. 2. Donald Francis Tovey.   (B)
                                    8 [1927] 258

BEETHOVEN AND HIS TIME. Richard Capell.   (C)
    "Beethoven fixed the spirit of his sanguine generation, and made of its ephemeral dreams a perpetual monument."
                                    8 [1927] 262

WILHELM VON LENZ. Ernest Newman.   (D)
    An account of 'Beethoven et ses trois styles' and its author.   8 [1927] 268

A BEETHOVEN BIBLIOGRAPHY. C. B. Oldman.   8 [1927] 276   (E)

THE CHORAL WRITING IN THE MISSA SOLEMNIS. W. G. Whittaker.   (F)
    "In the 148 pages of the vocal score only a total of about two pages come in the third class (not very serious assaults
    on the endurance of the singers), four into the second class (not commendable but not wholly condemnable), and two
    into the first class (crimes of the worst malignity). Of miscalculations there are not a few." Rehearsal methods and
    minor readjustments for the troublesome passages are suggested, and some of the most effective choral passages are
    discussed.   8 [1927] 295

THE MINOR COMPOSERS. Eric Blom.   (G)
    Discussion of many of the composers and performers with whose work Beethoven was familiar, leading to the con-
    clusion "that for all that can be traced of immediate indebtedness to him in the composers of the nineteenth
    century who still count, he might never have existed, any more than his great precursors need have lived and
    worked so far as his music is concerned."   8 [1927] 306

CHAMBER MUSIC WITH PIANOFORTE. Richard Walthew.   (H)
    Discussion of the trios and of some of the duo-sonatas.   8 [1927] 317

SCHUBERT AND BEETHOVEN: A CONTRAST IN METHODS. A. E. F. Dickinson.   (I)
    "While Beethoven enriched and supplemented his purely musical conceptions with constructive thinking, Schubert
    similarly drew upon another side of the new century, its poetic ideas."
                                    9 [1928] 44

BEETHOVEN AND SHELLEY. R. V. Dawson.   10 [1929] 35   (J)

STRING CHAMBER MUSIC -- THE LESSER FORMS. J. Arthur Watson.   (K)
    A brief survey of the literature for two or three stringed instruments, including mention of various Beethoven
    compositions.   10 [1929] 292

BEETHOVEN AND CESAR FRANCK. R. V. Dawson.   11 [1930] 110   (L)

THE 'GROSSE FUGE': A HUNDRED YEARS OF ITS HISTORY. Sidney Grew.   (M)
                                    12 [1931] 140

THE 'GROSSE FUGE': AN ANALYSIS. Sidney Grew.   12 [1931] 253   (N)

THE ASSOCIATED BOARD'S EDITION OF BEETHOVEN'S PIANOFORTE SONATAS. Ernest Walker.   (O)
    A review of Tovey's 'A Companion to Beethoven's Pianoforte Sonatas' and of the Associated Board's edition of the
    sonatas (Tovey-Craxton).   13 [1932] 11

SIX NEW LETTERS OF BEETHOVEN.   (P)
    First publication of translations of six letters from the Bodmer collection in Zurich, with annotations.
    28 February 1812 to Breitkopf & Härtel, requesting copies of the songs Op. 83 and inquiring about the Egmont
    music and the C major Mass. 1812 to Messrs. Offenheimer, going security for an advance of four louis d'or to
    Joseph Ludwig Stoll, poet of 'An die Geliebte' (NV p. 183). February 1814 to von Hartmann (editor) requesting

SIX NEW LETTERS OF BEETHOVEN (Continued)
  publication of an announcement of the Academy held 27 February 1814 at which the Eighth Symphony and
  'Tremati, empi' were first performed.   August 1814 to Friedrich Treitschke (reviser of 'Fidelio' libretto) sending letter regarding Prague performance of 'Fidelio.'   May 1823 to A. Diabelli, requesting proofs of Op. 111
  and a loan of 300 florins.   25 September 1826 to Tobias Haslinger requesting presentation binding for a copy
  of Op. 125 for Friedrich Wilhelm III.   15 [1934] 1

AUSTRIAN CURRENCY VALUES IN PERIOD 1811-57.   (A)
  There were two kinds of currency in use: (1) Viennese currency (Wiener Während, W. W. Redemption Bonds,
  Discount Bonds) ordinarily used for small purchases, and (2) Imperial currency (Conventionsmünze C. M.), same
  as Dutch currency.   100 fl W. W. were worth 40 fl C. M.

Fl	Kr			₤	s	d	1933
-	27.5	=	1 schilling	-	-	11	$ 0.67
-	60	=	1 florin or gulden	-	2	0	1.46
2	0	=	1 thaler	-	4	0	2.92
4	30	=	1 ducat	-	9	0	6.58
7	26	=	1 libre	-	14	10.5	10.86
9	45	=	1 guinée	-	19	6	14.25
13	20	=	1 louis d'or	1	6	8	19.50

  Above values are for Vienna in 1825.   For London in 1933, values may be tripled.   Otto Erich Deutsch (M&L
  15 [1934] 236) says that values before 1811 were about double those after 1825.
                                                            15 [1934] 5

BEETHOVEN'S VIOLIN CONCERTO. L. Sommers.   (B)
  Anecdotes and reviews of the composition and of early performances.
                                                            15 [1934] 46

THE MEANING OF BEETHOVEN. R. W. Wood.   (C)
  "The great, the unique quality in Beethoven's essential genius is a matter of form, of unified grip and urgent
  continuity of feeling. It is possible, taking a work piecemeal, to find nothing particularly attractive and much
  that is positively distasteful, whereas once the all through attitude is adopted everything falls into place   and a
  moving and overwhelming musical experience attends each hearing of the work. "
                                                            15 [1934] 209

THREE EDITIONS OF BEETHOVEN'S VIOLIN CONCERTO. Albert Jarosy.   (D)
  Phrasing, dynamics, etc. of the David, Joachim and Marteau editions are compared and discussed. "In their
  printed pages we can find neither Joachim's austere grandeur nor Marteau's modern spirit, for their editions are
  in no wise different from the ordinary. "   15 [1934] 329

THE TRAGIC BEETHOVEN. C. R. McLaughlin.   15 [1934] 336   (E)

BEETHOVEN AND THE GOETHE-ZELTER CORRESPONDENCE. Jeffrey Pulver.   (F)
  Carl Friedrich Zelter (Goethe's Boswell and a well-accepted conductor and composer) "was quite unable to assess
  Beethoven at his proper value," and thus his letters display "to some extent the effect that Beethoven's work had
  upon the average musician of the period. " Extensive quotations regarding Beethoven from Zelter's letters to
  Goethe are given.   17 [1936] 124

A BEETHOVEN FRIENDSHIP - LOST DOCUMENTS RECOVERED. C. B. Oldman.   (G)
  What is presumably the first version (key of A, for 4-part mixed chorus) of the Wedding Song for the marriage
  of Nanni Giannatasio del Rio on 6 February 1819 (see TD IV 155, 518; TV #219).   Seventeen letters to
  Giannatasio, all but one appearing in KS, but inaccurately; e.g., KS II 75, for: "I wish to put the mother

into better odour in the neighborhood," read: "The mother is anxious to put herself in better odour with her neighbors." Undated note (hitherto unpublished), to Giannatasio in 1816, referring to song by addresse which Beethoven proposed to set. Leaf from a conversation book giving the answer to the question regarding painting vs. music quoted in KS II 10. For "ladies" (Damen) possibly read "the poor" (Armen).

17 [1936] 328

BEETHOVEN'S DEBT TO MOZART. J. Arthur Watson.   (A)
    Many examples (especially from the early chamber music), to show that Beethoven followed Mozart in election of instrumental combinations, in overall form, in choice of thematic material, and in technical methods.

18 [1937] 248

(No Title) A. Hyatt King.   (B)
    MS in the British Museum attributed to Mozart include K. Anh 293 (unfinished trio), K. Anh 284g (3 pieces for piano duet), and K. 25a (Minuet for Orchestra), all most probably by Beethoven. Note by DWM. Should the second reference be to K. Anh 284h, and should not the list include K. Anh 284i (Rondo for Piano)?

18 [1937] 345

LENAU AND BEETHOVEN. R. H. Thomas.   (C)
    "It is not generally realized that one of the first people to accept Beethoven's works with enthusiasm was Nikolaus Lenau (1802-50)."   18 [1937] 374

A DISCREPANCY IN BEETHOVEN. Paul Hirsch.   (D)
    The autograph score (see Schünemann, 'Musiker Handschriften' pl. 59) and the first engraved edition of the parts (about April 1809, 100 copies) of the C minor Symphony show that the second fermata of the opening measures, like the first, is on one minim only. The same difference is found in the four other appearances of this passage in the movement. The MS from which the parts were engraved shows one minim only, with correction in red ink to two.   19 [1938] 265

BEETHOVEN. Richard Capell.   (E)
    Biographical and character study.   19 [1938] 375

THE AUTOGRAPH OF BEETHOVEN'S EIGHTH SYMPHONY. Oswald Jonas.   (F)
    Discussion of corrections by Beethoven in the completed score, presumably to secure greater clarity and effectiveness.
20 [1939] 177

SOME NEW BEETHOVEN LETTERS. B. Schofield and A. D. Wilson.   (G)
    Transcription but not translation of MM 147, MM 320, MM 321, MM 325, and a fragment of Kal 575, translations of which had appeared in the 'Daily Telegraph and Morning Post' of 18 February, 4 March and 25 March 1939.
20 [1939] 235

A BEETHOVEN MOVEMENT AND ITS SUCCESSORS. Mosco Carner.   (H)
    Comparative analyses to show that the allegretto of the Seventh Symphony was in many ways progenitor of the corresponding movements of Schubert's C major Symphony, 'Harold in Italy,' and Mendelssohn's A major Symphony
20 [1939] 281

AN ERROR IN THE TIME SIGNATURE IN SEVERAL EDITIONS OF BEETHOVEN'S VIOLIN SONATA OPUS 30 No. 2.   (I)
        Paul Hirsch.
    In the second movement, the pianoforte part as well as the violin part should be alla breve, not common time.
21 [1940] 204

FOUR UNKNOWN EARLY WORKS BY BEETHOVEN. Jack Werner.   (J)
    MSS in the British Museum (Rondo for Pf solo, Gavotte and Allegro for Pf duet, Trio for Pf, Vln and Vcl) previously attributed to Mozart, are surely by Beethoven.   22 [1941] 36

RELEVANCE OF THE LAST BEETHOVEN QUARTETS TO MOZART'S. Martin Johnson.   (K)
25 [1944] 80

KOZELUCH RITROVATO. Otto Erich Deutsch.   (A)
Of the works listed by Werner (supra) as "unknown early works by Beethoven," the two Pf duets are shown to be
transcriptions from a ballet by Leopold Kozeluch.   26 [1945] 47

ABOUT A BALLET BY LEOPOLD KOZELUCH. Georges de Saint-Foix.   (B)
Saint-Foix maintains Beethoven's authorship of the MSS discussed by Werner and Deutsch supra.
                                             27 [1946] 24

A CHECK-LIST OF BEETHOVEN'S CHAMBER MUSIC. Donald W. MacArdle.   (C)
An attempt to tabulate all the chamber works of Beethoven (94 are listed), with the best available data (carefully
documented) as to dates of composition, of first performance, and of publication. A bibliography of books and
periodical articles on Beethoven's chamber music is appended.   27 [1946] 44,83,156,251

A FORGOTTEN BEETHOVEN DOCUMENT. Willi Reich.   (D)
Review by Clemens Brentano of the first Berlin performance of 'Fidelio' (11 October 1815).
                                             27 [1946] 248

THE SOURCES OF BEETHOVEN'S FIFTH SYMPHONY. Adam Carse.   (E)
A detailed examination of the various source manuscripts and first engraved editions, with listing of some of the
many discrepancies, leading to the conclusion that it is "difficult or even impossible to achieve a pure and authoritative text in the case of Beethoven's orchestral works," and showing why the services of an editor are absolutely
indispensible in preparing score and parts for orchestral performance.
                                             29 [1948] 249

BEETHOVEN'S CHORAL FANTASIA, OPUS 80 -- A NEW ENGLISH VERSION. Robert Elkin.   (F)
Translation.   30 [1949] 108

BEETHOVEN'S "ALLEGRO ASSAI." Stewart Deas.   (G)
Evidence is presented to show that Beethoven's "allegro assai" is not as rapid as his "allegro."
                                             31 [1950] 333

A NOTE ON OPUS 27 No. 2. Irwin Fischer.   (H)
Remarks on the uncertainty of the second note in the second triplet of m. 12 of the first movement of the C sharp
minor Sonata (B natural or C natural?).   32 [1951] 45

THE 'CHORAL SYMPHONY' IN LONDON. Adam Carse.   (I)
Comments on the 20 performances of Op. 125 in London between 21 March 1825 and 1855.
                                             32 [1951] 47

BEETHOVEN'S MASS IN D. Thomas B. Crow.   (J)
It is suggested that for the sake of the chorus the work be transposed down to C for performance.
                                             32 [1951] 203

KOZELUCH PERDUTO ANCORA UNA VOLTA. O. E. Deutsch.   (K)
Kozeluch's authorship of several works hitherto attributed to Mozart or Beethoven (cf. 26 [1945] 46) has not yet become
public knowledge.   33 [1952] 99

BEETHOVEN AND KOZELUCH. Jack Werner.   (L)
The author contends that the gavotte and allegro arrangement for piano duet of a number from a Kozeluch ballet of
1794 was pilfered by Kozeluch from an unpublished work of Beethoven.
                                             33 [1952] 189

BEETHOVEN'S LAST COMPOSITION. Willy Hess.   (M)
The canon 'Da ist das Werk' is Beethoven's last composition.   33 [1952] 223

BEETHOVEN'S OPUS 96. Geraldine de Courcy.   (N)
The omission of the flat before the A in m. 160 of the first movement (as compared with the written A flat in m. 19)
may have been inadvertent.   33 [1952] 276

BEETHOVEN'S OPUS 96. Geraldine de Courcy.   (O)
Invitation for comments on the questioned A flat / A natural in the first movement of this sonata.
                                             33 [1952] 276

(No Title) O. E. Deutsch and C. L. Cudworth.   (A)
  Polemic against Werner (p. 189). Neither correspondent accepts the contention that Kozeluch was a proven
  plagiarist.   33 [1952] 277,279

THE HORN IN BEETHOVEN'S SYMPHONIES. Robin Gregory.   (B)
  "Beethoven's writing for the horn as a member of the orchestra was undoubtedly an advance over anything that had
  previously been attempted . . . He enlarged the horizon of the orchestral horn practically to the greatest extent
  possible before the invention of the valve." The crooking and stopping called for in the symphonies are discussed
  in detail.   33 [1952] 303

BEETHOVEN AND KOZELUCH. Donald R. Wakeling.   (C)
  Intimation that the debate regarding the questioned works in the British Museum is not capable of incontrovertible
  solution, and is not very important.   33 [1952] 374

BEETHOVEN'S NOTTURNO OPUS 42. Willy Hess.   (D)
  This arrangement and Op. 41 (from the Trio Op. 25) were probably by Ferdinand Ries and were numbered without
  Beethoven's knowledge.   33 [1952] 375

THE TEXT OF BEETHOVEN'S LETTERS. Emily Anderson.   (E)
  The general inaccuracy of available transcriptions of Beethoven letters is discussed. A corrected transcription is
  given of Kal 668; corrections are given to Kal 35, 178, 294, 660, 765, 928, and 1120 and to MM 181 and MM 253.
  It is pointed out that KK 167 and KK 1050 are the same (MM 52), that KK 166 is the postscript of KK 154 (see Kal
  159, 262), that KK 911 is a complete version of KK 941 (see MM 275), that KK 942 is a fragment of KK 905 (see
  MM 259, 260). Kal 221 and 222 form a single letter; the same is true with KK 1291 and KK 1288 (Kal 1069). The
  only known letters to P. J. Simrock are MM 190 and MM 212; the others are to Nikolaus. The order of the letters
  from Hetzendorf (summer of 1823) is all wrong; the same is true of the last letters to Smart and Moscheles. Facsimile, transcription, and translation are given of the letters of 11 July 1825 to Braunhofer or Bach.
                                                34 [1953] 212

BEETHOVEN'S LAST COMPOSITION. Otto E. Albrecht.   (F)
  Claim of priority over Hess (33 [1952] 223) in discovery and publication of 'Da ist das Werk.'
                                                34 [1953] 275

BEETHOVEN'S LETTERS. Ludwig Misch.   (G)
  Questioned reading in a letter published by Anderson (p. 212).   34 [1953] 363

BEETHOVEN'S LETTERS. Emily Anderson.   (H)
  Polemic against Misch.   35 [1954] 184

BEETHOVEN'S LAST SONATA. Philip T. Barford.   (I)
  Aesthetic discussion of Op. 111.   35 [1954] 320

FOUR UNFAMILIAR BEETHOVEN DOCUMENTS. Donald W. MacArdle.   (J)
  Transcriptions, translations, and commentaries on MM 74, MM 153, MM 335, and MM 388.
                                                36 [1955] 331

BEETHOVEN AND GEORGE THOMSON. Donald W. MacArdle.   (K)
  Abstracts are given of all of the 65 known letters and other documents exchanged by the two men, with a list of
  other letters known to have been written but that are now lost. Transcriptions of Kal 111 and MM 213 are published
  for the first time.   37 [1956] 27

BEETHOVEN'S GRANDNEPHEW IN AMERICA. Paul Nettl.   (L)
  After frauds committed for several years on King Ludwig of Bavaria, Nephew Karl's only son Ludwig, with his wife
  and baby son Karl Julius Maria, emigrated to the United States on 30 August 1871. He changed his name to
  Louis von Hoven, and prospered greatly in business. By 1890 he was back in Paris with his family, destitute and
  gravely ill. It is probable that he died in either Paris or Brussels. 38 [1957] 260

BEETHOVEN AND THE BACH FAMILY. Donald W. MacArdle.   (M)
  Discussion of the influence of the music of J. S. Bach on Beethoven, of the music by Bach that Beethoven owned,
  and of Beethoven as a player and arranger of Bach's music; of the influence on Beethoven of K. P. E. Bach; and of
  Beethoven's proposals for financial aid to Susanna Bach.   38 [1957] 353

BEETHOVEN AND GRILLPARZER. Donald W. MacArdle.   (A)
   A brief biographical sketch of Grillparzer, and a detailed discussion of his relationship with Beethoven.
                                            40 [1959] 44

BEETHOVEN AND HANDEL. Donald W. MacArdle.   (B)
   A discussion of the influence of Handel on Beethoven.   41 [1960] 33

BEETHOVEN AND KANT. Robert L. Jacobs.   (C)
   "This brief study . . . of Beethoven's moral idealism in the light of the influence of Kant's moral philosophy . . .
   is designed to offset the unpleasantly clinical picture of Beethoven drawn recently by Richard and Editha Sterba in
   their psychoanalytical monograph, 'Beethoven and His Nephew.'" 42 [1961] 242

THE TEXT OF BEETHOVEN'S OPUS 61. Alan Tyson.   (D)
   The earliest editions of the concerto (for violin and for piano) are examined with relation to the manuscripts from
   which they presumably were engraved, and several textual errors of long standing are discussed.
                                            43 [1962] 104

MUSIC REVIEW

ON PERFORMING BEETHOVEN'S THIRD AND FIFTH SYMPHONIES. Robert Sondheimer.   (E)
   It is desirable that there be great flexibility in tempo and dynamics, in accordance with the conventions established
   in the performances of the preclassical symphonies. These characteristics are illustrated in excerpts from several
   symphonies written ca. 1760.   2 [1941] 36,263

MUSICAL INTERPRETATION. Herbert Lichtenthal.   (F)
   The proper phrasing of many of Beethoven's works (e.g., the Third, Fourth, Fifth and Seventh Symphonies, the
   Sonata Pathetiquè, the Sonata Op. 10 No. 3) may be quite different from that indicated by Beethoven's slurs or binds.
                                            4 [1943] 163

THE PROBLEM OF EVIL AND SUFFERING IN BEETHOVEN'S PIANOFORTE SONATAS. E. H. W. Meyerstein.   (G)
   An essay on the interpretation "of four pianoforte sonatas (Opp. 13, 31 No. 2, 57, 110) as reflections of the composer's personal burdens."   5 [1944] 96

A BEETHOVEN RELIC. Rudolf F. Kallir.   (H)
   Six measures of manuscript, with the notation "L. van Beethoven's own handwriting, written on his death bed for me.
   J. A. Stumpff" have been found. It is stated that the edition of Handel which Stumpff sent was Arnold's edition in
   forty volumes; Beethoven's receipt was dated December 14th 1826. Beethoven wrote in thanks on February 8th 1827;
   in Stumpff's reply (received in Vienna on March 14th) he requested "a few notes written by your dear hand . . ."
   TD V 481 says that nothing is definitely known about a line of music which Beethoven is said to have written on his
   death bed. This presumably is that line. Note that Schindler ('Jahrbücher für musikalische Wissenschaft' 1 [1863]
   no page given) is correct in saying that Beethoven did not write an autograph for Stumpff.
                                            9 [1948] 173

A BEETHOVEN RELIC. E. H. W. Meyerstein.   (I)
   Speculation on the musical idea behind the sketch for Stumpff (p. 173 supra).
                                            9 [1948] 327

FURTWÄNGLER 'ON CONDUCTING BEETHOVEN.'   (J)
   Abstract of a BBC 'Third Program' talk.   10 [1949] 37

BEETHOVEN'S 'VARIATIONS ON NATIONAL THEMES': THEIR COMPOSITION AND FIRST PUBLICATION.   (K)
     C. B. Oldman.
   Detailed study of the early history of Opp. 105 and 107.   12 [1951] 45

BEETHOVEN IN 1950. Philip F. Radcliffe.   (L)
   The variety which is Beethoven's music has not been completely grasped even in 1950.
                                            12 [1951] 52

CONTEMPORARY ENGLISH EDITIONS OF BEETHOVEN. Paul Hirsch and C. B. Oldman.   (A)
   Discussion of contemporary British publishers, and list of 130 works by Beethoven that appeared in one or more
   British editions during Beethoven's lifetime.   14 [1953] 1

HARMONIC RHYTHM IN THE BEETHOVEN SYMPHONIES. Jan LaRue.   (B)
   "The close integration of (rhythm and harmony) with the form produces a unity of effect which in part explains
   the sense of inevitability and the deep emotional impact of Beethoven's music." Extensive quotations from the
   symphonies are given to support this thesis.   18 [1957] 8

THE JENA SYMPHONY. H. C. Robbins Landon.   (C)
   The monastery at Göttweig owns a contemporary set of parts of a symphony by (Jeremias) Friedrich Witt (1770-1837)
   that is the work more recently known as the 'Jena Symphony.' "No Jena Symphony by Ludwig van Beethoven ever
   existed."   18 [1957] 109

THE BRENTANO FAMILY IN ITS RELATIONS WITH BEETHOVEN. Donald W. MacArdle.   (D)
   A discussion of Beethoven's associations with Franz von Brentano, his wife Antonia, and their daughter Maximiliane;
   with Franz's half sisters Sophie and Bettina; and with his half brother Clemens.
                                                                    19 [1958] 6

BEETHOVEN AND THE PHILHARMONIC SOCIETY OF LONDON. Donald W. MacArdle.   (E)
   A discussion of Beethoven's sale of three overtures to the Society, of negotiations regarding possible visits to London,
   of the writing of the Ninth Symphony for the Society, and of the Society's contribution to Beethoven during his last
   weeks.   21 [1960] 1

BEETHOVEN AND LONDON CONCERT LIFE, 1800-1850. Nicholas Temperley.   (F)
   An analysis of concert programs shows the early and continuing popularity of Beethoven's works in London.
                                                                    21 [1960] 207

MUSIC SURVEY

SOME NOTES ON A BEETHOVEN CONCERT. E. H. W. Meyerstein.   (G)
   Program notes for a concert consisting of Wellington's Victory, Op. 61 as a piano concerto, and the complete Egmont
   Music. Regarding Op. 91, "The person who hears in this odd piece of program music nothing but drum thumps and
   rattles is missing a great deal of the essential Beethoven, especially in the matter of tonality . . . No, Maelzel
   or no Maelzel, the Battle Symphony is not to be laughed at."   1 [1948] 89

A PENCILLED NOTE OF BEETHOVEN. E. H. W. Meyerstein.   (H)
   If the note was written shortly after Karl's shooting, the "Doctor" would probably have been Smetana or the surgeon
   Dögl; if later, Gassner or Sang. EDr of M-383.   1 [1948] 132

OBSERVATIONS ON THE 'JENA' SYMPHONY. Robert Simpson.   (I)
   Parallelisms of melody and treatment in the first two movements of the Jena Symphony and Haydn No. 97 indicate
   that the former could not have been written before the latter, which was composed about 1792 and published on the
   Continent in 1795-96. Beethoven of 1792 might have written the Jena; Beethoven of 1795 was far past it. Two
   possibilities are suggested: (1) that Beethoven, while studying with Haydn, came to know No. 97, and patterned
   this student work after it; and (2) that in view of the fact that the finale of the Jena is "a marked advance over the
   rest" with more than a trace of Beethoven's characteristic blend of Mozart's symmetry with Haydn's rough unpre-
   dictability, it seems not impossible that Beethoven added a finale to an unfinished work of some other composer.
                                                                    2 [1950] 155

MUSICA (Kassel)

VARIOUS MANUSCRIPTS: SKETCHES FOR OPUS 106, 'RAGE OVER A LOST PENNY' OPUS 129, CANON 'DA IST DAS   (J)
    WERK WoO 197. Otto E. Albrecht.
   Reprint of article in MQ 31 [1945] 495.   2 [1948] 129

BEETHOVENS BEGRABNIS. Georg Poensgen.   (A)
   Description of the ceremonies, with two contemporary pictures of the funeral procession by the artist Stöber, probably
   Franz Xaver Stöber (1795-1858); possibly his father Joseph (1768-1852).
                                                                6 [1952] 96

DER ZERSTÜCKELTE EROICA. Rudolf Steglich.   (B)
   Discussion of various details of performance in which conductors almost invariably depart from Beethoven's expressed
   intentions.   6 [1952] 228

BEETHOVEN AND AMERICA. Paul Nettl.   (C)
   In SchKH I 323 Blöchlinger said, "It seems to me that we Europeans are going backwards and that America is increasing its culture." In 1820 or 1821 Beethoven contemplated an opera 'The Founding of Pennsylvany (sic)' to a
   book to be written by Johann Baptist Rupprecht. About 1815 the Handel and Haydn Society of Boston requested an
   oratorio, and there is evidence that a similar request was made by a Boston banker in 1823. Note that Kal 856 of
   20 December 1822 refers to offers "even from North America." Theodore Molt of Quebec visited Beethoven in
   December 1825, and for him Beethoven wrote the canon 'Freu dich des Lebens' WoO 195. Publication in the United
   States of works by Beethoven began as early as 1812; the first performance of a Beethoven symphony in the United
   States took place in 1821, and in that same year a Beethoven Society was formed in Portland, Maine.
                                                                6 [1952] 297

BEETHOVENS AUGENGLÄSERNDUETT -- EIN TORSO. Willy Hess.   (D)
   To the first movement of this work (WoO 32) as published in 1912 and to the minuet published in 1952 by Karl Haas
   may be added the first 21 measures of an uncompleted movement (possibly an andante, possibly a closing allegro).
   Facsimile and transcription are given.   7 [1953] 535

DAS ÜBERGANGENE WIEDERHOLUNGSZEICHEN. Ludwig Misch.   (E)
   Repetition of the exposition in sonata-allegro movements, while customary in pre-Beethoven works, was not invariable; examples from Bach's sons and Mozart are given. Beethoven omitted repeat marks in a substantial number of
   his compositions, apparently based on the character of the individual work. In classical and romantic movements
   where repeat marks are used, decision on omitting the repeat must carefully consider the harmonic and thematic
   content of the closing portion of the exposition and the general character of the movement. The same principle
   may (and should) lead to occasional deviations from the now established practice of omission of repeats in the da
   capo section of minuets and scherzos (e.g., Opp. 21,29).   8 [1954] 185

URTEXTPROBLEME BEI BEETHOVEN. Max Unger.   (F)
   The objective of the editor of musical works must be to reflect on the printed page the true intention of the composer
   so far as it can be determined. The author questions the correctness of the universally accepted dominant-tonic
   passage in the first movement of the Eroica. The methods and sources which must be used are indicated. It is
   pointed out that the accuracy of the text of vocal works is often disregarded by composer in his proofreading and
   equally by the editor.   9 [1955] 111

BEETHOVEN UND DER KAMM. Annalise Wiener.   (G)
   Fantasy.   9 [1955] 160

ZWEI RÄTZELKANONS VON BEETHOVEN. Carl Dahlhaus.   (H)
   'Si non per portas' WoO 194 may be solved as a canon in retrograde inversion. An artifical but technically correct
   solution of 'Ich küsse Sie' WoO 169 is given.   9 [1955] 500

ZU BEETHOVENS RÄTZELKANONS. Ludwig Misch.   (I)
   Comments on article by Dahlhaus.   10 [1956] 66,295

BEETHOVENS BEZIEHUNGEN ZU UNGARN. Zoltan Falvy.   (J)
   Facsimiles and transcriptions of two letters (MM 12, MM 355) which previously had been published only in a Hungarian journal(see 'Uj zenei szemle' 5 [1954] No. 10, p. 38).   10 [1956] 125

EIN UNBEKANNTER BEETHOVEN. Willy Hess.   (K)
   Review of 'Allegretto in E flat for Piano, Violin and Cello' recently published in transcription by Jack Werner.
                                                                10 [1956] 166

DIE BEETHOVEN-SILHOUETTE. Stephan Ley. (A)
   The generally accepted dating "1786" for the silhouette by von Neesen seems sound.
10 [1956] 363

'DER FREIE MANN.' Willy Hess. (B)
   EDr of an early version of WoO 117 differing only in details of the accompaniment from that given in GA 23/232.
   The vocal line is also given of a third sketched version.   10 [1956] 382

EIN ZWEITÖNE MOTIV BEI BEETHOVEN. Gustav Gärtner. (C)
   In Op. 12 No. 2, the first two notes of the violin part are of structural importance throughout the composition.
11 [1957] 294

IM PARK VON MARTONVASSAR. Stephan Ley. (D)
   The "Beethoven tree" referred to by Therese von Brunsvik is still standing.
11 [1957] 762

AUF DEN SPUREN VON BEETHOVENS 'UNSTERBLICHE GELIEBTE.' Paul Nettl. (E)
   Kazne lson marshals much evidence in support of his contention that Josephine von Deym was the Immortal Beloved.
12 [1958] 14

BEETHOVEN -- "EIN MANN VON NUR MITTELMÄSSIG INTELLIGENZ." Rudolf Steglich. (F)
   Based on the presumed breadth of Beethoven's reading and his presumed facility in languages, the author takes issue
   with the statement of Ernest Newman (13 [1959] 132) that in matters not connected with music, "Beethoven was a
   man of only moderate intelligence."   13 [1959] 269

MOZART AND BEETHOVEN. Hans Joachim Moser. (G)
   Mozart was of the eighteenth century, Beethoven of the nineteenth.
13 [1959] 530

BEETHOVENS "BRIEFTAUBE." Stephan Ley. (H)
   A portrait is reproduced of Sophie Streicher, Nannette's daughter, who sometimes acted as Beethoven's "carrier
   pigeon."   13 [1959] 733

BEETHOVEN AUS DER SICHT ROMAIN ROLLAND. Hermann Fähnrich. (I)
   Summary of the scope of the last three volumes of Rolland's great study of Beethoven.
13 [1959] 773

BEETHOVENS GEBURTSHAUS. Otto von Fisenne. (J)
   A review of the controversy: Bonngasse vs. Rheingasse.   14 [1960] 466

MUSICA DIVIANA

BEETHOVENS BEDEUTUNG FÜR UNSERE ZEIT. Max Springer. (K)
   Sesquicentennial essay of the theme that if "sacred music" (Kirchenmusik) is defined as music which conforms to
   the rubrics and spirit of Catholicism, whereas "religious music" means music of a highly spiritual nature, Beethoven cannot be put in the class of composers of "sacred music" but is by his Missa Solemnis in the forefront of
   religious composers.   8 [1920] 105

DREI NOCH UNVERÖFFENTLICHTE BRIEFE ALBRECHTSBERGERS AN BEETHOVEN. Andreas Weissenbäck. (L)
   These letters were written nearly two years after Beethoven's lessons with Albrechtsberger had ceased, showing
   that the friendship remained strong. Letter dated 15 December 1796 beginning, "Zu Ihrem morgigen Namensfeste wünsche ich Ihnen das Allerbeste." If "Namensfeste" is taken to mean birthday instead of name day
   (there is no St. Ludwig or St. Louis in the calendar with a name day in December) this letter is almost conclusive proof that within the Beethoven family circle the composer's birthday was celebrated on 16 December.

DREI NOCH UNVERÖFFENTLICHTE BRIEFE, etc., (Continued)
(See NBJ 7 [1937] 29) Letter dated 20 February 1797 states that Albrechtsberger had recommended Beethoven to Baron Joseph Gleichenstein as a teacher for his son Ignaz. Acknowledgement of an unknown letter from Beethoven.   9 [1921] 10

BEETHOVENS RELIGIOSITÄT. Andreas Weissenbäck.   (A)
Quotations from Beethoven's letters and journals, from statements of his friends and from known facts to show that he was a good Christian and a good Catholic.   15 [1927] 73

ZUR LITURGISCHEN AUFFÜHRUNG DER MISSA SOLEMNIS VON L. VAN BEETHOVEN. Karl Vetterl.   (B)
Score and parts of the Missa Solemnis recently discovered in the library of St. Jacob's Church in Brünn (Czechoslovakia) give strong indication that this work received its original liturgical performance in that church during the first half of 1824, Leopold Streit (Director of Music of the church) leading an orchestra of about 40 players and a chorus of more than this number of singers. It is very probable that Beethoven never knew of this performance.
17 [1929] 6

MUSICAL QUARTERLY

IRISH AIRS IN BEETHOVEN'S SEVENTH SYMPHONY. Charles Villiers Stanford.   (C)
See also Dr. Gratton Flood in 'Musical Times' (56 [1915] 474).   1 [1915] 244

A POST-IMPRESSIONISTIC VIEW OF BEETHOVEN. T. Carl Whitmer.   (D)
Content indicated by its title.   2 [1916] 13

THE EQUALI AS FUNERAL MUSIC. Orlando A. Mansfield. 2 [1916] 208   (E)

BEETHOVEN'S DEVELOPMENT OF THE SONATA FORM. Philip Greeley Clapp.   (F)
2 [1916] 305

FRANZ GRILLPARZER: CRITIC OF MUSIC. Philip Gordon.   (G)
Discussion of an important contemporary and friend of Beethoven. 2 [1916] 552

BEETHOVEN'S INSTRUMENTAL MUSIC. Arthur Ware Locke.   (H)
Translated from E. T. A. Hoffmann's 'Kreisleriana,' with an introductory note.
3 [1917] 123

AN UNPUBLISHED LETTER OF BEETHOVEN. J. G. Prod'homme.   (I)
Facsimile, translation and annotation of a letter apparently written to Holz towards the end of 1825.
3 [1917] 620

ALEXANDER THAYER AND HIS LIFE OF BEETHOVEN. Henry Edward Krehbiel.   (J)
Substantially identical to the greater part of the introduction to the Thayer-Krehbiel 'Life.'
3 [1917] 629

THE THREE BEETHOVENS. James Frederick Rogers.   (K
An attempt to assign physiological and psychological reasons for the differing characteristics of Schindler's "three periods."   5 [1919] 505

MOZART AND THE YOUNG BEETHOVEN. Georges de Saint-Foix.   (L
Discussion of many of Beethoven's early compositions with particular reference to their derivation from Mozart in style, content and form; attribution to Beethoven of certain MSS hitherto attributed to Mozart.
6 [1920] 276

THE BARON DE TREMONT (SOUVENIRS OF BEETHOVEN AND OTHER CONTEMPORARIES). J. G. Prod'homme.   (N
Detailed accounts of visits to Beethoven in 1809.   6 [1920] 366

BEETHOVEN'S 'LEONORE' AND 'FIDELIO.' Edgar Istel.   (A)
   History of the composition and performances of the opera; detailed discussion of the separate musical numbers.
                              7 [1921] 226

THE MAN BEETHOVEN: AN ESTIMATE OF HIS CHARACTER. Alexander Wheelock Thayer.   (B)
   Substantially identical to TK I 245-54.   7 [1921] 483

IF BEETHOVEN HAD WRITTEN FAUST. Oscar Thompson.   (C)
   Beethoven's interest in the subject; guesses as to certain aspects of the treatment he might have given it.
                              10 [1924] 13

BEETHOVEN AND THERESE VON MALFATTI. Max Unger.   (D)
   (a) In 1810 Beethoven seriously considered marriage with Therese von Malfatti. (b) Letter to Gleichenstein
   (KS I 114) and presumably others to him and to Therese (KS I 126) date from 1810, not from 1807. (c) Letter of
   2 May 1810 to Wegeler (KS I 188) requesting baptismal certificate was in connection with the project of marriage
   to Therese. (d) Albumblatt 'Für Elise' was actually 'Für Therese.'
                              11 [1925] 63

BEETHOVEN AFTER A HUNDRED YEARS. W. J. Henderson.   (E)
   "He remains, not a man of historic yesterdays, but a man of all time."
                              13 [1927] 161

BEETHOVEN'S INTELLECTUAL EDUCATION. J. G. Prod'homme.   (F)
   Beethoven's formal schooling ended at the age of 12 or 13, with "barely the primary instruction of our own day."
   He had little Latin and no Greek, but read the classics in translation. He had a working knowledge of Italian and
   French, with some English, and read those languages over a broad field. He was influenced greatly by German
   authors and poets, especially Goethe and Schiller. "Nowhere in his letters, his notes or his conversations does he
   mention painters or sculptors of any period: he was interested exclusively in music, literature, history and philosophy. He had acquired a sum total of knowledge very superior to that possessed by many musicians of his day."
                              13 [1927] 169

SAYINGS OF BEETHOVEN.   (G)
   Excerpts from the letters and the conversation books.   13 [1927] 183

BEETHOVEN'S "ADELAIDE." Martial Douël.   (H)
   This song, written with care and inspiration quite out of proportion to the merits of the poem, was a result of
   Beethoven's attraction in 1795-96 to Magdalena Willmann (who in 1799 married a certain Galvani). The same
   influence appears in parts of Opp. 2, 7, 15 and 37, and perhaps even in Opp. 30, 59 and 61.
                              13 [1927] 208

BEGINNINGS OF BEETHOVEN IN AMERICA. Otto Kinkeldey.   (I)
   Beethoven was almost certainly completely unknown in America as late as 1800, but (with almost equal certainty)
   was known before 1815. An edition of Op. 6 was published in Philadelphia about 1815. The first known public
   performance of a work by Beethoven was that of a chorus from 'The Mount of Olives' in December 1820. One
   movement from the C major Symphony was performed the following spring, but the first performance of a complete symphony apparently did not take place until February 1841. "The appearance of genuine Beethoven solo
   or chamber music on a public concert program will have to be dated about the late thirties or early forties."
                              13 [1927] 217

THE "IMMORTAL BELOVED." Max Unger.   (J)
   The often printed letters certainly date from July 1812, but the identity of the addressee is still a complete mystery,
   almost certainly not being any one of the ladies usually named in this connection.
                              13 [1927] 249

BEETHOVEN'S OPUS 3 -- AN "ENVOI DE VIENNE"? Carl Engel.   (K)
   The key date for the chronology of this work is the date of Dobbeler's departure from Bonn with the MS which
   Gardiner secured. Thayer accepted Gardiner's statement of "1792" for this departure, though in various writings
   Gardiner gave 1793, 1794, 1795 and 1796 as the year of his first performance of the Trio. Detailed evidence is
   given to show that Dobbeler's departure was actually no earlier than the latter part of 1794. "The conjecture is
   fairly safe that the whole work was written in Vienna, in 1793 or the first part of 1794," and presented "as an example of the progress he had made since his arrival in Vienna" by Beethoven to the Elector Max Frank, who had
   continued financial aid to Beethoven as late as March 1794.   13 [1927] 261

HANS VON BÜLOW AND THE NINTH SYMPHONY. Walter Damrosch.   (A)
  Examples of markings from Bülow's conductor's score.   13 [1927] 280

BEETHOVEN TO DIABELLI: A LETTER AND A PROTEST. Oscar Sonneck.   (B)
  Substantially identical with 'Beethoven Letters in America' pp. 16-38.
                                                                    13 [1927] 294

BEETHOVEN AND THE YOUNGER GENERATION. Edward J. Dent.   (C)
  "I see no reason to be shocked when the younger musicians say they will have no more to do with Beethoven."
                                                                    13 [1927] 317

BACH, BEETHOVEN, BRAHMS. Hermann Abert.   (D)
  "What is greatest and most characteristic about Bach, Beethoven and Brahms is not that which unites them, but
  rather that which differentiates them, one from the other."   13 [1927] 329

REVIEW OF 'THE UNCONSCIOUS BEETHOVEN' BY ERNEST NEWMAN. Carl Engel.   (E)
  Discussion in particular of (1) Newman's comments regarding the luetic origin of Beethoven's deafness, and (2) the
  melodic fragment referred to by Newman as Beethoven's "fingerprint."
                                                                    13 [1927] 646

BEETHOVEN AS A WRITER OF PROGRAMME MUSIC. R. W. S. Mendl.   (F)
  While capable of writing what is normally thought of as "program music" (e. g., parts of the Pastoral Symphony
  or the Leonora overtures), "with Beethoven the expression of feeling, of character, of motives and thoughts, was
  of supreme importance."   14 [1928] 172

INFLUENCE OF GOETHE ON BEETHOVEN. Edgar Istel.   14 [1928] 231   (G)

BEETHOVEN'S AND SCHUBERT'S PERSONAL RELATIONS. Walther Nohl.   (H)
  Each knew and respected the other, but each went his own way "without any exchange of thought in connection
  with the lofty art common to them both."   14 [1928] 553

THE SIGNIFICANCE OF THE "TRILL" AS FOUND IN BEETHOVEN'S MOST MATURE WORKS.   Edwin Hall Pierce. (I)
  "The trill, as used by Beethoven in his mature style, is structural rather than ornamental, and denotes intensification
  of any sentiment or mood into a conscious thrill of vital emotion."
                                                                    15 [1929] 233

THAT "FINGERPRINT" OF BEETHOVEN. Hugh Arthur Scott.   (J)
  The "fingerprint" is a figure of three consecutive ascending notes used at a climactic point of the melodic design
  with a certain emotional significance, as discussed by Newman in 'The Unconscious Beethoven.' Scott points out
  that the figure itself is perhaps the most frequently employed of all three-note sequences, that its use at a climactic
  point of the design is standard practice in melody writing from plain song to Strauss, and that the emotional uplift
  is inherent in the figure itself.   16 [1930] 276

BEETHOVEN'S "GROSSE FUGE." Sidney Grew.   (K)
  General.   17 [1931] 497

MINNIE VAN BEETHOVEN. Maria Komorn.   (L)
  The author's personal recollections of one of the three daughters of Nephew Karl.
                                                                    18 [1932] 628

GRANDFATHER BEETHOVEN. Ernest Closson.   (M)
  Louis van Beethoven (son of Michael) was born in Malines (between Brussels and Antwerp) in 1712. He was a church
  singer in Louvain and Liege in 1731-32. In 1733 he joined his brother Cornelius in Bonn, where the latter was a
  chandler and purveyor to the court. That same year he married Maria Josepha Poll in Bonn. He became a chorister
  and later director of the chapel, the concerts, the theatre, and the court balls. His side activity of wine merchant
  developed excessive drinking in his wife and son Johann (father of LvB). The various ways in which he spelled his
  name indicate surely that "ee" was pronounced long (as in "beet"). He died in 1774.
                                                                    19 [1933] 367

BEETHOVEN AND MECHANICAL MUSIC. Hugo Leichtentritt. (A)
Mention is made of Beethoven's interest in and compositions for the "musical clock" (on the principle of the present-day music box), the "flute clock," and Maelzel's "Panharmonikon."
20 [1934] 25

BEETHOVEN'S COMPOSITIONS FOR THE FLUTE. H. Macaulay Fitzgibbon. (B)
20 [1934] 226

BEETHOVEN'S OPUS 1. Alfred Einstein. (C)
Upon the playing of this work, "a new era had begun." 20 [1934] 374

CELTIC ELEMENTS IN BEETHOVEN'S SEVENTH SYMPHONY. James Travis. (D)
Kinship in spirit is pointed out between some of the "Irish Songs" arranged by Beethoven for Thomson in 1810
(TK II 194) and certain passages in the Seventh Symphony composed in 1809-12 (TK II 166, 237).
21 [1935] 255

BEETHOVEN AND THE CREATIVE LAW IN SYMPHONIC ART. Walter Engelsmann. (E)
Application in detail to a specific composition (the First Symphony) of the "ruling principle" laid down by the
author in previous writings ('Die Musik'17 [1925] 424; 'Die Neue Musikzeitung'1927, Nos. 19 and 20; 'Beethovens
Kompositionspläne' 1931) that in every sonata or symphony of Beethoven a single chief theme or germ motif is the
reservoir for the melodic stream of the entire composition. 23 [1937] 56

THE LAST FIVE STRING QUARTETS. Alfred Einstein. (F)
These, as together forming Beethoven's "opus ultimum," are considered briefly in comparison with the last works
of other composers. 23 [1937] 186

FROM BEETHOVEN'S WORKSHOP. Max Unger. (G)
An attempt is made to trace the psychological and spiritual factors involved in Beethoven's work of creation.
24 [1938] 323

AN UNKNOWN SKETCH BY BEETHOVEN. Oswald Jonas. (H)
A single sheet at the New York Public Library (dating from the end of 1809 or the beginning of 1810) with early
studies for two of the "Clärchenlieder" from the Egmont music. 26 [1940] 186

AN UNKNOWN BEETHOVEN LETTER WITH COMMENT. Artur Holde. (I)
A letter of February or March 1808 to Heinrich von Collin (author of 'Coriolanus') regarding difficulties with
Regierungsrat Hartl in connection with a proposed concert of Beethoven's works. This letter probably immediately
preceded the letter to Collin given in KS I 133 as written "to an unknown poet."
28 [1942] 463

TEMPO AND CHARACTER IN BEETHOVEN'S MUSIC. Rudolf Kolisch. (J)
Traditions of performance have grown away from Beethoven's metronome marks by constant disregard on the part
of performers and conductors. Beethoven himself gave metronome indications for the various movements of the
nine symphonies, the string quartets through Op. 95, the Pf Sonata Op. 106, Meersstille Op. 112, and the Opferlied
Op. 121b. Letters from Beethoven showing the importance in his mind of authentic tempi are found in KS II 69,
458. These show that he recognized the indefiniteness of conventional (Italian) tempo designations, which Kolisch
further proves by comparative tabulations and by 164 illustrations in musical notation with metronome marks assigned by Beethoven or by Kolisch. 29 [1943] 169,291

BEETHOVEN'S TRIBUTE TO MOZART IN FIDELIO. Mark Brunswick. (K)
Discussion of what is apparently an intentional and appropriate "lifting" of a brief motif from 'Zauberflöte' for
use in 'Fidelio.' 31 [1945] 29

BEETHOVEN'S PHYSICIANS. Waldemar Schweisheimer. (L)
Discussion of the various ailments that Beethoven experienced and of the physicians who treated him. "Beethoven's
tragic deafness was the consequence of a disease of the inner ear, a neuritis acoustica. The most probable cause of
this neuritis was a severe early attack of typhoid fever. There is not the faintest medical proof that Beethoven ever
had syphilis. The autopsy demonstrated an incurable disease of the liver." Wawruch, who attended him in his last
illness, "was a careful and sympathetic physician who made no mistake either in the diagnosis or the treatment of
Beethoven's disease." 31 [1945] 289

VARIOUS MSS: SKETCHES FOR OPUS 106. Otto E. Albrecht.   (A)
    'Rage over a lost penny' (this title Schindler's, not Beethoven's) and Beethoven's last completed work (a canon for
    Holz, inaccurately described in TD V 408).   31 [1945] 495-500

THE NEWLY DISCOVERED AUTOGRAPH OF BEETHOVEN'S 'RONDO À CAPRICCIO,' OPUS 129. Erich Hertzmann. (B)
    "The Rondo à Capriccio was written between 1795 and 1798"; it was left unfinished quite possibly because the draft
    was merely "a provisional notation on which he based improvisations." The printed version "is an arrangement pre-
    pared after the composer's death by someone not painstaking enough to preserve Beethoven's intentions." The iden-
    tity of this editor is not ascertainable, but Carl Czerny seems "most likely." Beethoven originally titled the work
    "Alla ingharese quasi un capriccio"; later added the designation "Leichter Kaprice." A detailed formal analysis
    is given.   32 [1946] 171

MEMOIRS. J. W. Tomaschek.   (C)
    Excerpts from these memoirs by a musician and composer referred to as historically important in the transition from
    classicism to romanticism include references to Beethoven as an opera composer and a conversation with Beethoven
    (pp. 251ff), and Tomaschek's low opinion of Wellington's Victory TK II 256 (p. 260), as well as many remarks on
    the contemporary musical scene.   32 [1946] (no page given)

UNPUBLISHED LETTERS OF BEETHOVEN, LISZT AND BRAHMS. Artur Holde.   (D)
    A previously unpublished note to Zmeskall, dated by the latter 28 October 1810, requesting "the recipe for shoe
    polish."   32 [1946] 278

THE VIENNESE VIOLINIST, FRANZ CLEMENT. Robert Haas.   (E)
    Biographical study.   34 [1948] 15

BEETHOVEN, ARTARIA AND THE C MAJOR QUINTET. Donald W. MacArdle.   (F)
    An account of the suit brought by Artaria against Beethoven as a result of Beethoven's accusations in connection
    with the unauthorized Artaria edition of the C major Quintet Op. 29.
                                                                 34 [1948] 567

THE FAMILY VAN BEETHOVEN. Donald W. MacArdle.   (G)
    The composer's family is traced from the earliest identified ancestor (mid-fifteenth century, nine generations re-
    moved from the composer) to the death of the childless grandson of Nephew Karl in 1917. A copious bibliog-
    raphy is appended.   35 [1949] 528

FIVE UNFAMILIAR BEETHOVEN LETTERS. Donald W. MacArdle and Katherine Schultze.   (H)
    EDr in a scholarly journal of M-142, M-350, M-299 and M-180; complete publication of M-648.
                                                                 37 [1951] 490

A LESSON WITH BEETHOVEN BY CORRESPONDENCE. Oswald Jonas.   (I)
    Facsimile, translation and critical discussion of Kal 1094. The passage referred to in the letter is Op. 127, 2nd
    movement, 2nd variation, 10th measure, 3rd beat.   38 [1952] 215

LUDWIG SPOHR. Paul Henry Lang.   (J)
    Brief but unconventional and refreshing pen picture.   39 [1953] 234,238

MINOR BEETHOVENIANA. Donald W. MacArdle and Ludwig Misch.   (K)
    EDr of MM 31 and MM 280 (H-229); first publication in generally accessible journals of MM 222, MM 258, and
    MM 364 (note that 9 words were accidentally omitted from the German text of MM 258); discussion of the 9 con-
    certs which Beethoven gave for his own account, including first English translation of 8 newspaper announcements
    of these concerts, for 3 of which the German original is given for the first time since the contemporary publication.
                                                                 41 [1955] 446

FUGUE AND FUGATO IN BEETHOVEN'S VARIATION FORM. Ludwig Misch.   (L)
    A discussion of fugal writing in WoO 76 and Opp. 35, 55, 96, 105, 107, 120, 121a, 125, and 132.
                                                                 42 [1956] 14

THE EDUCATION OF A. W. THAYER. Christopher Hatch.   (M)
    Thayer's cultural background is discussed in connection with its effect on his approach to his biography of
    Beethoven.   42 [1956] 355

BEETHOVEN AND THE FRENCH VIOLIN SCHOOL. Boris Schwarz.   (A)
   The author discusses the effect upon Beethoven's writing for the violin of the concertos of Viotti, Kreutzer, and Rode.
                                   44 [1958] 431

BEETHOVEN'S IRISCHE LIEDER: SOURCES AND PROBLEMS. Alice Anderson Hufstader.   (B)
   "Of the 62 tunes that became Irische Lieder, only about 8 or 9 had words, and Thomson was therefore commissioning
   verses from a group of poets just as he was commissioning arrangements from (Beethoven) . . .   The texts of the
   Irische Lieder were produced piecemeal by mediocre poets." Kal 319 is quoted to show Beethoven's approval of
   Thomson's practice of setting the words to the music.   45 [1959] 343

THE WEATHER AT MOZART'S FUNERAL. Nicholas Slonimsky.   (C)
   Meteorological records in Vienna show that, "mirabile dictu, the famous thunder storm at the time of Beethoven's
   death, reported by all Beethoven biographers, actually did occur ! . . . At 3 o'clock in the afternoon stormy weather
   began, and at 4 o'clock lightning and thunder struck, with strong winds."
                                   46 [1960] 21

MINOR BEETHOVENIANA II. Donald W. MacArdle.   (D)
   The following are discussed: the quartet of stringed instruments from Prince Lichnowsky; Gottfried Christoph Härtel
   and the Eroica Symphony; the date of Giulietta Guicciardi's emotional visit to Beethoven; a Brodmann piano owned
   by Beethoven; identity of a song offered by Beethoven to B&H on 4 February 1810 (WoO 139); annuity payments from
   Prince Lobkowitz to Beethoven (apparently carried out as agreed until Beethoven's death); evidence that the first performance of Op. 123 in St. Petersburg was on 6 April 1824 NS (25 March OS).
                                   46 [1960] 41

BEETHOVENIANA IN SOVIET RUSSIA. Boris Schwarz.   (E)
   The histories of the "Wielhorsky" sketch book (1802-03) and the "Moskauer" sketch book (1825) are discussed and
   the contents of the two books listed. Descriptions are given of 13 sketches and autograph copies of various compositions and of the following letters: And 92, MM 104, MM 221, KK 241, MM 244, And 1072, *And 1186, *And
   1457, *And 1536, MM 467. Facsimiles (complete or partial) are given of the letters marked with an asterisk and
   of a hitherto unknown vocal score of 'Freudvoll und leidvoll' (Op. 84 No. 4).
                                   47 [1961] 4

CLEMENTI AND THE EROICA. Alexander L. Ringer.   (F)
   The strong formal and motival resemblance between Op. 55 and Clementi's sonata in G minor Op. 7 No. 3 is ex-
   plored and discussed at length.   47 [1961] 454

                             MUSICAL TIMES

RECOLLECTIONS OF BEETHOVEN, WITH REMARKS ON HIS STYLE. Cipriani Potter.   (G)
   Impressions of a close acquaintance and student of Beethoven's music.
                                   10 [1861] 150

INCIDENTS IN THE LIFE OF BEETHOVEN. R. M. Hayley.   (H)
   Anecdotal biographical sketch.   13 [1868] 439,471,505,538;
                                   14 [1869] 41,138

BEETHOVEN AND THE MODERN SCHOOL. H. H. Statham.   (I)
   "No theory of the art which excludes symmetrical form and finish and subordination of detail can really claim to be
   based upon the art of Beethoven, except in the sense of being an amplification and systematic reproduction of his
   few comparative failures."   19 [1878] 65

ON BEETHOVEN AND HIS MISSA SOLEMNIS. Fr. Niecks.   (J)
   "The most extraordinary work of so extraordinary a man as Beethoven."
                                   20 [1879] 193

AN ANALYSIS OF BEETHOVEN'S MISSA SOLEMNIS. Fr. Niecks.   (K)
   Detailed analysis of the music and its setting of the text.   20 [1879] 472,515,572,638

BEETHOVEN'S TENTH SYMPHONY.   L u d w i g   N o h l.   (A)
    Evidence that Beethoven had planned and sketched a Tenth Symphony as a companion to the Choral Symphony.
                                                         20 [1879] 9,66

BEETHOVEN'S GRANDFATHER: A BIOGRAPHICAL SKETCH.   L u d w i g   N o h l.   (B)
    Extensive discussion, based largely on the Fischer MS.   21 [1880] 443

BEETHOVEN, THE MAN.   J o s e p h   B e n n e t t.   (C)
    Biographical lecture of a popular nature.   28 [1887] 201,272

MISPRINTS IN BEETHOVEN'S SONATAS.   (D)
    Citation of note by Bussler in 'Neue Berliner Musik Zeitung' 41 [1887] 250 regarding passages in Opp. 106 and 101.
    The editor questions the first of these corrections but agrees with the second.
                                                         29 [1888] 303

BEETHOVEN'S SKETCH BOOKS.   J. S.   S h e d l o c k.   (E)
    Studies after the general style of Nottebohm, covering various sketch books in the British Museum and "a sketch
    book apparently unknown to G. Nottebohm.   33 [1892] 331,394,461,523,589,
                                                             649,717;   34 [1893] 14,530;
                                                             35 [1894] 13,449,596

Works covered in the Shedlock articles

Opus		Opus	
1	33 394ff, 525	60	33 717
2	33 333; 35 16, 596	65	33 333, 462
3	33 397	67	33 717; 35 598
4	33 462	68	33 717; 34 14ff
5	33 649ff	69	34 14
7	33 462	70	34 14
10	33 462ff	71	33 333, 462, 651
13	33 461, 650; 35 450	72a	35 598
14	33 332, 464, 522	86	33 717
15	33 333, 523ff, 592	109	35 596
16	33 333, 651	111	35 597
18	33 333, 650; 34 531	120	35 596
19	33 333, 464, 523ff	121b	33 333, 395
20	33 650	123	35 449, 599
21	33 591	125	35 449ff, 597
22	33 397; 35 596	130	34 530, 532
26	35 596	131	34 530ff; 35 599
27	33 464, 589	133	34 530
36	35 597	135	34 530ff
37	33 332, 333, 525	"140"	33 525
46	33 333	"152"	33 333
49	33 332, 461	"153"	33 395
52	33 333, 591	"174"	34 532
53	33 650	"180"	33 589
58	35 597	"188"	33 397
59	33 650		

Ecossaise (Pf) E flat 34 530	Rondo (Pf, Orch) B flat (posth) 33 333
Various Pf Variations 33 333	Romance cantabile (cembalo, Fl, Bsn + acc) 33 333
'La ci darem' Variations 33 396	Sonata movement in G (unfin) 33 464
Symphony in C (unfin) 33 332, 591	Miscellaneous sketches 33 589ff, 651
"Sinfonia" 33 333	Canons 34 530, 532
Pf Concerto in A (unfin) 33 333ff, 523	Bach, Handel, Mozart, Haydn in the sketch books 35 13ff

SOME THOUGHTS ON THE MAN AND HIS GENIUS. (A)

Beethoven's feeling of resentment against the world and his wrath against established institutions, as well as the manifest destiny of his artistic career, were shaped by his proud and passionate nature, by recognition of his genius inadequate to place him above the more vulgar trials and troubles of life, and by the peculiarly distressing calamity of his deafness. 33 [1892 sup] 7

THE BIRDS IN THE PASTORAL SYMPHONY. George Grove. (B)

Beethoven's story to Schindler (Schindler-Kalischer 'Beethoven-Biographie' (1909) p. 198) that the flute arpeggios in mm. 58ff were intended to represent the yellow hammer must have been one of Beethoven's jokes, since the song of this bird is completely different. 33 [1892 sup] 14

LETTER FROM FERD. WOLANEK, WITH REMARKS ADDRESSED TO THE WRITER BY BEETHOVEN. (C)

Facsimile, transliteration and translation of letter attributed by KS II 357 to "January 1825(?)" 33 [1892 sup] 18

A TALK WITH BEETHOVEN. (D)

Tomaschek's account (somewhat abridged) of visits to Beethoven on 10 October and 24 November 1814 (see TK II 297). 33 [1892 sup] 20

BEETHOVEN IN LOVE. (E)

German and English versions of the letters given in KS I 47-49. 33 [1892 sup] 21

WORD PICTURES OF BEETHOVEN. (F)

Physical appearance as described by contemporaries. 33 [1892 sup] 25

FOLK TUNES IN BEETHOVEN'S ORCHESTRAL WORKS. (G)

A seventeenth century dance tune was used in the E flat Piano Concerto and in the Seventh Symphony, as well as by Schumann in 'Papillons' and 'Carnaval.' 33 [1892 sup] 28

SALE OF BEETHOVEN'S EFFECTS. (H)

Account of the auction of 5 November 1827 (the date of this report is obviously 1828 instead of 1827 -- see 'Harmonicon' 6 [1828] 72). 33 [1892 sup] 29

BEETHOVEN'S PORTRAITS AND MASK. Gustave Droz. (I)

Effect of the passage of time (1801-27) on Beethoven's facial appearance as shown by portraits. 33 [1892 sup] 30

BEETHOVEN: MOODS AND MANNERS. (J)

Anecdotes from Potter, Schindler, Seyfried et al. 33 [1892 sup] 34

THE DRUM PARTS OF BEETHOVEN'S SYMPHONIES. (K)

"Beethoven was the first who elevated the drum from a mere noise producing machine into an orchestral instrument having definite and accurate sounds." 35 [1894] 81

WAS THE LEONORE OVERTURE No. 1 (OPUS 138) WRITTEN BEFORE THE OTHER TWO? Albert Levinson. (L)

Probable answer: Yes. 35 [1894] 311

PERSONAL REMINISCENCES OF BEETHOVEN. Louis Schloesser. (M)

Account of several visits to Beethoven in 1822-23, with letter quoted in KS II 250. 35 [1894] 225,305

A BEETHOVEN AUTOGRAPH. (N)

Report of facsimile publication of Pf Sonata Op. 26, pointing out differences between autograph and published editions. 36 [1895] 368

EIGHT SHEETS OF SKETCHES FOR OPUS 130. (O)

Some allusions to Opp. 93 and 131. 36 [1895] 375

BEETHOVEN AND THE SORDINO. (P)

What pedal indications were used in the autographs of the Pf compositions, and exactly what (mechancially) did Beethoven mean by them? 36 [1895] 516

FIVE SHEETS OF SKETCHES FROM 1809.   Wilhelm Kienzl.   (A)
    Sketches for Opp. 73, 75 No. 1, 80 and an unpublished patriotic song 'Wenn es nur will.'
                                36 [1895] 451

A NEGLECTED MASTERPIECE OF BEETHOVEN'S.   (B)
    General discussion of the 'Diabelli Variations,' with a list of the fifty composers who contributed one variation each
    to Diabelli's publication.   36 [1895] 593

A LETTER OF BEETHOVEN'S.   (C)
    Complete version of the letter grossly abbreviated in KS II 130, with list of some fifty corrections to the first English
    edition of Op. 106.   37 [1896] 305

THE TWO SUPERFLUOUS MEASURES IN THE SCHERZO OF THE C MINOR SYMPHONY.   (D)
    Contention that there are stylistic reasons for the two disputed measures, in spite of Beethoven's letter to Breitkopf
    and Härtel requesting their deletion (KS I 202). Furthermore, the work was often performed in Beethoven's presence
    with these measures and without remark from him, indicating that "in this matter Beethoven changed his opinion."
                                37 [1896] 310

IS BEETHOVEN PLAYED OUT?   G. V. Bouncingham.   (E)
    Ironic.   37 [1896] 800

BEETHOVEN AND THE BARONESS ORTMANN.   38 [1897] 741   (F)

HISTORY OF BEETHOVEN'S EQUALI.   39 [1898] 454   (G)

BEETHOVEN AND HIS "TERMS."   (H)
    Review of a biography of George Thomson by Hadden, with extensive quotation of Beethoven's letters to him, showing
    that "in regard to business matters, Beethoven proved quite a match for the Scotchman, which is saying a great deal."
                                39 [1898] 457

BEETHOVEN AND DUSSEK.   (I)
    Letter from a leading music critic in 1835, saying that he was familiar with Beethoven's Pf sonatas "but can find
    nothing in them at all comparable to the masterpieces of Dussek." 40 [1899] 386

CENTENARY OF BEETHOVEN'S FIRST SYMPHONY.   (J)
    First performed in Vienna 2 April 1800; first English performance 18 May 1803.
                                41 [1900] 235

A BEETHOVEN AUTOGRAPH.   (K)
    Confirms earlier belief that the Rondo in E flat for Pf and Orchestra was intended to form part of the E flat Pf Concerto.
                                41 [1900] 236

BEETHOVEN: HIS PORTRAIT AND -- ITS BLOT!   (L)
    Autographed portrait presented by Beethoven to Charles Neate.   42 [1901] 15

BEETHOVEN AND OUR NATIONAL ANTHEM.   (M)
    Appearance of 'God Save the King' in one of the sketch books.   42 [1901] 163

NOTES ON THE WORDS OF BEETHOVEN'S CHORAL SYMPHONY.   (N)
    Beethoven contemplated setting the Ode to Joy as early as 1793. In the verses as he incorporated them into the Choral
    Symphony he changed one word (apparently intentionally) to give the poem greater force.
                                42 [1901] 590

FIRST PERFORMANCE IN ENGLAND OF BEETHOVEN'S MASS IN D.   (O)
    24 December 1832.   43 [1902] 236

VISIT TO BEETHOVEN BY AN UNNAMED ENGLISH LADY.   (P)
    Account of a visit in October 1825.   43 [1902] 533

BEETHOVEN AND CLEMENTI.   (A)
    Letter from Clementi to his partner (22 April 1807) saying in part: "I have at last made a complete conquest of
    that haughty beauty Beethoven!"   43 [1902] 600

THE HOUSE IN WHICH BEETHOVEN DIED.   (B)
    Photograph and description.   44 [1903] 236,791

FACSIMILE OF A BEETHOVEN SKETCH.   (C)
    Part of the last movement of Op. 27 No. 2.   44 [1903 sup] No page given

BEETHOVEN IN BADEN.   (D)
    Review of a monograph by Hermann Rollet on Beethoven's many visits to Baden.
                                                         44 [1903] 102

BEETHOVEN'S LEONORE OVERTURE NO. 3.   George Grove.   (E)
    Detailed comparison with No. 2.   44 [1903] 535

BEETHOVEN'S USE OF TROMBONES.   (F)
    The doubling of voices is harmful in passages with chorus, like the opening measures of the "In gloria Dei patris"
    fugue of the Missa Solemnis.   45 [1904] 444

BEETHOVEN'S CONCERTO FOR PIANOFORTE AND ORCHESTRA NO. 5 IN E FLAT OPUS 73.   George Grove.   (G)
    Detailed analysis.   46 [1905] 172

BEETHOVEN'S VIOLIN CONCERTO.   George Grove.   (H)
    Detailed analysis.   46 [1905] 459

BEETHOVEN'S E FLAT PIANOFORTE CONCERTO: FIRST PERFORMANCE IN ENGLAND.   (I)
    8 May 1820.   47 [1906] 241

BEETHOVEN'S CHORAL SYMPHONY.   (J)
    Dates are given of the sixteen performances in London between 21 March 1825 and 17 May 1906. The metronome
    marks are given which are omitted in KS II 472 from Beethoven's letter of 18 March 1827 to Moscheles.
                                                         47 [1906] 387

GEORGE P. BRIDGETOWER AND THE KREUTZER SONATA.   F. G. Edwards.   (K)
    Biographical sketch of Bridgetower and copy of death certificate (29 February 1860).
                                                         49 [1908] 302

BEETHOVEN SKETCHES HITHERTO UNPUBLISHED.   J. S. Shedlock.   (L)
    Sketches showing that Opp. 73, 77, 79 and 80 were under way at the same time.
                                                         50 [1909] 712

TEMPI OF THE SCHERZO OF THE NINTH SYMPHONY.   52 [1911] 783;   53 [1912] 18,33,784 (M)

WHO WAS BEETHOVEN'S 'UNSTERBLICHE GELIEBTE'?   Ernest Newman.   (N)
    The letters may be definitely assigned to the year 1812. They were probably addressed to Therese von Brunsvik
    and definitely not to Giulietta Guicciardi.   52 [1911] 370

A BEETHOVEN HOAX?   Ernest Newman.   (O)
    Newman agrees with Leitzmann ('Zeitschrift der Internationalen Musikgesellschaft' 12 [1911] 350) that the letter
    newly published by Bekker ('Die Musik' 10 [1911] No. 21, p. 131) as belonging to the series to the 'Unsterbliche
    Geliebte' is a forgery.   52 [1911] 714

THE NEWLY FOUND BEETHOVEN SYMPHONY.   Charles Maclean.   (P)
    Evidence supporting the authenticity of the Jena Symphony.   53 [1912] 28

A BEETHOVEN FIND.   (Q)
    Composition described in 'Der Merker,' resembling the finale of the C minor Pf Concerto.
                                                         58 [1917] 157

BEETHOVEN AFTER A HUNDRED YEARS. George Gardner.   (A)
    Mention of movements or passages which the author considers by present standards to be less than inspired.
                                61 [1920] 172

SOME CONTEMPORARY CRITICISMS OF BEETHOVEN. Muriel Silburn.   (B)
    Excerpts from writings of English reviewers of early nineteenth century.
                                63 [1922] 732

THE 'EROICA' SYMPHONY. R. W. S. Mendl.   (C)
    "The Symphony in fact does not tell a story: it unfolds a character." Regarding the appropriateness of the scherzo,
    "the Hero could not always be heroic"; in the Finale Beethoven "shows us how even the greatest of mankind begins
    by being quite undistinguished, and yet may become a mighty leader of men."
                                65 [1924] 125

LUDWIG VAN BEETHOVEN. Alexander Brent-Smith.   65 [1924] 214   (D)

STUDIES ON THE HORN: III. THE FOURTH HORN IN THE 'CHORAL SYMPHONY.' W. F. H. Blandford.   (E)
    The problem offered by the fourth horn part in the adagio of the Ninth Symphony is in essence based on two fea-
    tures in mm. 83-98: (1) the writing of the G between the first and second harmonics, and (2) the writing of
    extended and completely exposed solo passages containing notes not natural to the hand horn. To these may be
    added: (3) why was the part written for the fourth horn (and marked in the Philharmonic manuscript of the Sym-
    phony: "Sempre Corn: 2do")? By an extended discussion of the horn playing methods and practices of Beet-
    hoven's day the author shows that (1) this passage was completely within the scope of a skillful performer (being
    much easier than certain passages in the Sextet Op. 81b of thirty years earlier), so that there is no reason to pos-
    tulate the existence in the early 1820's of a valve horn or the equivalent; (2) for reasons stated at length, the
    passage (under conditions of the day) was appropriate for the 2nd or 4th horn and not for the 1st or 3rd horn, and
    that the player assigned to the lower of a pair of horn parts was usually the more competent performer; (3) there
    is no reason to believe that Beethoven wrote this passage with a particular horn player in mind, though the tradi-
    tion exists that the 4th horn of the premiere performance was Eduard C. Lewy, "a first-rate soloist." The author
    agrees with Weingartner's contention that the lower G's in mm. 89-90 should be tied.
                               66 [1925] 29,124,221

TWO UNPUBLISHED LETTERS OF BEETHOVEN. Jean Chantavoine.   (F)
    1. Late March 1812 to Rettich regarding concert by the Ursulines of Graz. 2. Letter dated 22 April 1826 to
    Maurice Schlesinger stating that the Quartet (probably Op. 135) would be ready in a few weeks. This is prob-
    ably the letter referred to in KS II 427, No. MCXLIX.   66 [1925] 329

WAGNER AND THE NINTH SYMPHONY. Edith A. H. Crawshaw.   (G)
    An account of the powerful influence which the Ninth Symphony had on Wagner during his young manhood, and of
    the objectives which he laid out for himself in his first performance of the Symphony in 1846.
                                66 [1925] 1090

THROUGH THE 'IMMORTAL NINE' ON THE GRAMOPHONE. D. Batigan Verne.   (H)
    Not every note of the symphonies is inspired, and this fact shows more clearly on performances from records than
    in the concert hall.   67 [1926] 896

WILLIAM GARDINER, OF LEICESTER. Orlando Mansfield.   (I)
    Biographical sketch of an enthusiastic musical amateur and proponent of Beethoven, important in the chronology
    of Op. 3.   67 [1926] 900

THE MUSIC OF FRIENDS: SOME THOUGHTS ON THE STRING QUARTETS.   (J)
    A brief and general discussion of the quartets.   68 [1927] 113

REFLECTIONS ON BEETHOVEN'S SONGS. Erik Brewerton.   (K)
    Beethoven's song writing lacked the "rapid, spontaneous, and often spasmodic outburst" of Schubert, Schumann and
    Wolf. "Beethoven was too great to write songs."   68 [1927] 114

BEETHOVEN'S MENTAL POWERS. "Feste."   (L)
    "The purely musical faculty so far outweighed all others as to prevent their development." Shortcomings in speech
    and writing attributed to this fact and to his limited education and the unhappy circumstances of his youth.
                                  68 [1927] 123

WEBER AND BEETHOVEN. John W. Klein. (A)
Scathing criticisms by Weber of Beethoven's works; Beethoven's unfulfilled predictions for Weber's growth and accomplishment. 68 [1927] 129

LUDWIG VAN BEETHOVEN. (B)
Centenary memorial. 68 [1927] 209

THE MIND OF BEETHOVEN. Walford Davies. (C)
"One of the great clearinghouses of musical thought." 68 [1927] 212

CONCERNING BEETHOVEN'S SYMPHONIES: A TALK WITH SIR HENRY WOOD. (D)
Interview. 68 [1927] 216

BEETHOVEN: PORTRAITS AND PERVERSIONS. "Feste." (E)
Beethoven's personal appearance as indicated by portraits and descriptions. 68 [1927] 223

BEETHOVEN'S IRISH MELODIES. W. H. Grattan Flood. (F)
Genesis of the songs for Thomson. 68 [1927] 254

THE STRENGTH OF BEETHOVEN'S MUSIC. Julius Harrison. (G)
"Its compelling force is due in largest measure to its tonic dominant foundation and its sparing use of dissonant auxiliary notes in the molding of his big themes." 68 [1927] 305

SOME TRIBUTES TO BEETHOVEN IN ENGLISH VERSE. Felix White. (H)
68 [1927] 308

BEETHOVEN AS A LETTER WRITER. "Feste." (I)
Quotation from and comments on certain of the letters. 68 [1927] 318

BEETHOVEN'S DEAFNESS. William Wallace. (J)
In a photograph of Beethoven's skull, the author finds convincing evidence of luetic involvement. 68 [1927] 538

WHO WAS BEETHOVEN'S FIRST MAECENAS? (K)
Count Philip George Browne (1727-1803), "a brilliant Irish soldier whose father and grandfather were also brilliant soldiers of the Austrian service." 69 [1928] 512

BEETHOVEN AND DAVY. Reginald Silver and E. Benjamin Britten. (L)
Correspondence based on the fact that a motif in the Cello Sonata Op. 102 No. 1 bears a "great similarity" to a song by John Davy (1763-1824). 70 [1929] 448,541

BEETHOVEN'S BELGIAN ANCESTRY. (M)
Grandfather Louis was born in Malines. 70 [1929] 751

SKETCHES BY BEETHOVEN IDENTIFIED. (N)
Discussion of "two pieces for an opera on a Schikaneder libretto" mentioned in Nottebohm's 'Ein Skizzenbuch aus dem Jahre 1803' (pub. 1880). 71 [1930] 510

BEETHOVEN'S TENTH SYMPHONY. Tom Sargant. (O)
Traditional story that the completed score of such a symphony once existed in the library of a Czechoslovakian nobleman. 72 [1931] 270

THE GRAVE OF BEETHOVEN'S MOTHER FOUND AT BONN. 73 [1932] 558 (P)

TOSCANINI AND BEETHOVEN. Roger Fiske. (Q)
Toscanini is more consistent than other conductors in his tempi for certain movements of Beethoven symphonies. 76 [1935] 703

MENDELSSOHN AND BEETHOVEN. Ralph W. Wood. (R)
"Is it not one of the enigmas of music" that hardly a trace of Beethoven appears in Mendelssohn the composer? 76 [1935] 886

THE 'VAN' IN BEETHOVEN.   Herbert Antcliffe.   (A)
    Tracing ancestry back to the first half of the seventeenth century, it is indicated that the family then belonged to
the landed gentry if not to the nobility, so that the 'van' is properly used.
                               77 [1936] 254

BEETHOVEN AND THE ORGAN.   Cecil Austin.   (B)
    Beethoven's early training as an organist; the organs on which he played.
                               80 [1939] 525

A BEETHOVEN MS.   Jack Werner.   (C)
    Sketch book sheet (probably before 1800) with brief passage for wind instruments and voices resembling the 'Ode
to Joy.'   80 [1939] 725

BEETHOVEN'S QUARTET IN C SHARP MINOR OPUS 131.   Ivor James.   (D)
    A detailed analysis.   81 [1940] 176

BEETHOVEN'S OPUS 14 No. 1.   Watson Forbes.   (E)
    A comparison of the two versions -- Pf solo and string quartet.   86 [1945] 108

A MUSICAL CENTENARY.   (F)
    The Beethoven Quartett Society (London) started its first cycle of the quartets on 28 April 1845; Rousselot's edition
of the quartets was published 1 August 1846.   87 [1946] 331

FACSIMILE OF A PAGE FROM A BEETHOVEN SKETCH BOOK.   (G)
    "If you wish to keep your love and reverence for the Master unimpaired, don't go near his sketch books."
                             92 [1951]108

'LEONORE' AND 'FIDELIO.'   Mosco Carner.   (H)
    An analytical comparison of 'Leonore' (1805) and 'Fidelio' (1814), prompted by a broadcast of the 1805 version.
The original Sonnleithner libretto was vastly inferior to Treitschke's revision for the 1814 version. Of the 16
numbers in the 1814 version, five were taken unchanged from the first version, six others were only slightly changed,
and in the remaining five only sections were completely altered; the only entirely new material was the overture,
and two numbers from 'Leonore' were dropped entirely. In the second (1806) version, Beethoven ruthlessly cut whole
chunks out of certain numbers without attempting to smooth over the cuts. The differences between the individual
numbers in the two versions are discussed in detail.   92 [1951] 113

TEMPI IN BEETHOVEN'S SEVENTH.   Alfred W. Bulley.   (I)
    A comparison of the tempi adopted by various conductors in the several sections of the allegretto.
                             92 [1951] 278

BEETHOVEN'S TRUMPET PARTS.   Adam Carse.   (J)
    In the coda of the Eroica first movement, "Beethoven broke (the trumpet part) off because his rule was not to write
the high G (twelfth of the harmonic series) for a trumpet crooked in any key higher than D." GA 1/6 p. 61 (climax
of the storm in the Pastoral Symphony) is cited as the only instance known to the writer of a high G by Beethoven for
a trumpet in E flat.   94 [1953] 32

THE TRILL IN BEETHOVEN'S LATER MUSIC.   John Harley.   (K)
    "I . . . receive the impression that when one of these trills appears, 'reality,' which Beethoven has until now been
examining, dissolves under his touch."   95 [1954] 69

BEETHOVEN'S EARLY FUGAL STYLE.   A. E. F. Dickinson.   (L)
    EDr of a 3-voice fugue in C major for keyboard, dating probably from 1794.
                             96 [1955] 76

BEETHOVEN'S BACH.   John Harley.   (M)
    The Czerny edition of the WTC (1837) may well reflect the essence of Beethoven's style in Bach playing.
                             96 [1955] 248

BEETHOVEN'S EARLY FUGAL STYLE.   Jack Werner.   (N)
    Suggested alternative readings at five points in the recently published C major Fugue (p. 76).
                             96 [1955] 319

BEETHOVEN'S EARLY FUGAL STYLE. Jack Werner.   (A)
    The same sketch book in the British Museum that contains the C major Fugue also contains a virtually complete
    movement in E flat for piano trio, which will be published shortly.
                                             96 [1955] 377

GOETHE AND MUSIC. Mosco Carner.   (B)
    "Goethe's interest in music and its problems was both sincere and profound, yet there is nothing in all these writings
    (conversations with Eckermann, correspondence with Zelter) to show that his interest . . . was prompted by more
    than a purely intellectual curiosity . . . To put it more bluntly, Goethe was intrinsically unmusical."
                                             97 [1956] 72

BEETHOVEN'S AUTOGRAPHS. Adolf Aber.   (C)
    A discussion of the situs of the autographs, based on KHV App. VII.
                                             97 [1956] 249

KARL VAN BEETHOVEN'S "SUICIDE." R. Gruneberg.   (D)
    The attempted suicide is considered as "a dramatic attempt at communication," not as a serious attempt by Karl
    to take his own life.   97 [1956] 269

"BEETHOVEN AUTOGRAPHS." Donald W. MacArdle.   (E)
    The autographs listed in KHV as being in the Deutsche Staatsbibliothek are actually in unknown hands.
                                           97 [1956] 428

SCHUBERT AND BEETHOVEN. John Reed.   (F)
    Evidence is presented that Beethoven and Schubert met.   100 [1959] 24

THE 'DIABELLI' VARIATIONS. Harold Truscott.   (G)
    A discussion of the set by fifty Austrian composers, with comments on many of the individual variations, and a
    consideration of what led Beethoven to write his set.   100 [1959] 139

THE 'DIABELLI' VARIATIONS. Maurice J. E. Brown and Donald W. MacArdle.   (H)
                    100 [1959] 271-72

IN DEFENSE OF FUNCTIONAL ANALYSIS. Deryck Cooke.   (I)
    The thematic elements of Op. 92 and (in less detail) of Op. 55 are analyzed to show how "functional analysis" may
    be used to isolate and identify a few germinal motifs from which an entire composition is built.
                                    100 [1959] 456

LÉONORE AND FIDELIO. Michael Levey.   (J)
    A popular but penetrating analysis of the differences between the libretto by Bouilly that Gaveaux used and the
    Sonnleithner book, with its reworking by Treitschke, that Beethoven set. "Bouilly had written in Léonore the sort
    of sentimental romantic play which Greuse might have illustrated, but Beethoven's Fidelio is something between
    Shakespeare and Schiller in its common sense and its liberal sentiments . . . It is no wonder that the men of
    Napoleon's army did not care much for Fidelio."   102 [1961] 87

THE HAMMERKLAVIER SONATA AND ITS ENGLISH EDITIONS. Alan Tyson.   (K)
    A critical bibliographical discussion.   103 [1962] 235

MUSIK

NEUE BEETHOVEN-STUDIEN. Theodor von Frimmel.   (L)
    Beethoven's seal and signature. The seal which Beethoven used on the contract with Artaria for the publication of
    Op. 1 (TD I 505) bears the monogram LvB and a crown. On no other known seal of Beethoven does a crown appear,
    but its use in this case may have furthered the belief current during his first few years in Vienna that he was Ludwig
    von Beethoven, of noble birth. His signature in 1795 was in legible German script, unlike his signatures of the last
    years in almost illegible Latin characters.

    Certain examples in Beethoven of melodic middle voices, and previous use of this device. Neefe and Haydn, in

NEUE BEETHOVEN-STUDIEN (Continued)
  works undoubtedly known to Beethoven, had used the "singing middle voice" found (among other examples) in the
  fourth variation of Op. 12 No. 1 and the fifth variation of Op. 26.   The idea was not original with Beethoven.
  1_1 [1901] 13

BEETHOVENS FRAUENKREIS.   Alfr. Chr. Kalischer.   (A)
  Discussion of Anna Milder-Hauptmann which later appeared in pp. 261-321 of book of the same title (Vol II of
  'Beethoven und seine Zeitgenossen'). 1_1,2 [1901-02] 481,595,680,872
                                                                             969,1091

'DER SIEG DES KREUZES.'   (B)
  The original manuscript of Bernard's oratorio, with many corrections by Beethoven, was sold at auction in the
  spring of 1902. 1_2 [1902] 1012

BEETHOVENS HEILIGENSTÄDTER TESTAMENT.   Wilibald Nagel.   (C)
  Beethoven's first reference to his deafness was in a letter of June 29th 1801 (assigned by KS I 29 to 1800), in which
  he says: "For the past three years my hearing has been becoming weaker."   Dr. Frank, then Dr. Vering did not help.
  In the letter of December (November?) 16th 1801 to Wegeler (KS I 35) Beethoven mentions his dissatisfaction with
  Vering and inquires about the professional competence of Schmidt.   Note that the "Will" dates the deafness back to
  1796 (six years before 1802), whereas the first of these letters indicates 1797 or 1798 (three years before the date of
  the letter).   The latter dating (from correspondence with his physician friend regarding his malady) seems probably
  more authentic.   Beethoven first went to Schmidt in the winter of 1801-02.   His trip to Heiligenstadt was upon
  Schmidt's advice to take advantage of the therapeutic possibilities of the town.   Lack of manifest improvement and
  absence of any physician to encourage him might well have led to the state of depression which gave rise to the "Will."
  The successive owners of the document are listed, and certain minor variants from the reading of TD II 333 are noted.

                                     1_2 [1902] 1050

EIN UNBEKANNTES ADAGIO VON BEETHOVEN.   A. Kopfermann.   (D)
  An adagio included in the manuscripts forming Lot 184 of the auctioned material (TV p. 179) is apparently for
  mechanical organ, and is listed as H-70. 1_2 [1902] 1059; 1_3 [1902] 1193

BEETHOVENS AUGEN UND AUGENLEIDEN.   Alfr. Chr. Kalischer.   (E)
  For about four months in the summer of 1823 (KS II 248 (April 25th) to Ries: "I am not well; even my eyes are
  bad"; KS II 289 (August 22nd) to the Archduke Rudolph: "Thank God my eyes have been so much better that I can
  use them pretty well again during day time.") Beethoven had trouble with his eyes.   "There is no indication that
  before or after this period Beethoven had any concern regarding the use of his eyes."   "No one of the many acquaintances of the master throughout all periods of his life commented on any affliction of his eyes (with the above mentioned exception), on his myopia, or on his wearing spectacles in his chambers, though it is known that he used a
  lorgnette on the street and that he wore spectacles at the piano.   Almost all commented on the spiritual beauty which
  shone from his eyes." 1_2 [1902] 1062; 1_3 [1902] 1155

BEETHOVENBRIEFE.   Theodor von Frimmel.   (F)
  Publication or republication without comments of the following:
       KS I 126
       KS I 114
       KS II 194 (No. 838)
       Letter without date to Josef or Karl Czerny: "Sagen sie mir gefälligst, wann sie abends" (not in KS)
           regarding an appointment for a piano lesson for Nephew Karl.   Presumably first publication of
           KK 550.
       Letter of January 28th 1821 to Artaria: "Ich bezeuge mit Dank" (not in KS) acknowledging receipt
           of 150 fl. for compositions promised.   Presumably first publication of KK 992.
       KS II 415 (No. 1129)
       KS II 325
       KS II 215 (postscript appearing in KS not given)

Letter without date, presumably to Zmeskall: "Ich danke ihnen lieber Z" (not in KS). Presumably
  first publication of KK 112.
Note without date to Carl Holz: "Noch ist die neue Haushälterin nicht da" (not in KS), apparently
  one of the many letters of 1825-26 to Holz regarding Beethoven's domestic cares. Presumably
  first publication of KK 1372. 1_2 [1902] 1072

ZWEI FRANZÖSISCHE LIEDER BEETHOVENS. Jean Chantavoine.   (A)
  Discussion of sketch of a song to the words of Rousseau: "Que le temps me dure" (H-90), probably dating from 1793,
  and a sketch from 1799 to the words: "Plaisir d'aimer" (H-92). 1_2 [1902] 1078

NACHTRÄGLICHES ZU BIOGRAPHIE KARLS VAN BEETHOVEN. Max Vancsa.   (B)
  Ludwig (son of Karl), after the birth of Karl Julius on May 8th 1870, left Munich, presumably as a commercial traveler.
  The last record of his was an application made in London in 1889 for a passport for various European countries. When
  Karl Julius was called to military service in 1890 he could not be found, and the family thought that he had died in
  childhood. Nephew Karl was born on September 4th 1806 (not November 4th 1807) -- did Brother Kaspar marry
  Johanna Reiss in 1806 (May 25th) or in 1805? 1_2 [1902] 1083

DIE INSTRUMENTAL-REZITATIV IM SCHLUSSSATZ DER "NEUNTEN." Georg Göhler.   (C)
  Words are set to this recitative on the assumption that the orchestra is addressing the singers. (See also 1_3 [1902] 1442)
                                                      1_2 [1902] 1086

BEETHOVENS STREICHQUINTETT OPUS 4. Wilhelm Altmann.   (D)
  Op. 4 is definitely not a mere arrangement of Op. 103, but rather a new work drawing upon the Octet for much
  material. 1_2 [1902] 1097

TEXTUNTERLEGUNGEN ZU BEETHOVENSCHEN INSTRUMENTALWEISEN. Arthur Smolian.   (E)
  Like the suggestion of Göhler (1_2 [1902] 1086), words supposedly suitable to the instrumental recitatives of the last
  movement of the Ninth Symphony. 1_3 [1902] 1442

LENAU UND BEETHOVEN. Julius Blaschke.   (F)
  Lenau was very fond of Beethoven's music and was much influenced by it.
                                                      1_4 [1902] 1983

EIN UNGEDRUCKTER BRIEF BEETHOVENS. Alfr. Chr. Kalischer.   (G)
  First publication of the letter of February 1st 1819 to the Vienna Magistrate given in KS II 124, with notes.
                                                      2_1 [1902] 403

BEETHOVEN NACH DER SCHILDERUNG DES BARON DE TRÉMONT. Jean Chantavoine.   (H)
  Practically the same as material in 'Musical Quarterly' 6 [1920] 374-78, plus a copy of a sketch dating from 1809
  which bears some resemblance to the principal theme of the first movement of the Ninth Symphony.
                                                      2_1 [1902] 412

RICHARD WAGNER UND DIE NEUNTE SYMPHONIE. Edgar Istel.   (I)
  Wagner's first contact with Schott & Sons was his suggestion (not adopted) that he be engaged to prepare for them a
  piano transcription of the Ninth Symphony, a work which fired his imagination beyond description. A performance
  of the Ninth in Paris under Habeneck in 1839 turned Wagner's thoughts away from grand opera like Rienzi to the
  type of music in which his fame rests. His performances of the Ninth Symphony in Dresden in 1846-49 raised enthusiasm in the minds of critics and public alike. The foundation of the Festspielhaus in Bayreuth in 1872 was celebrated by a performance of the Ninth Symphony, "the mystic work which at every significant turning point in his life
  had shaped his course like a spiritual hand." 2_1 [1902] 419

BEETHOVEN UND MENZEL. Franz Hermann Meissner.   (J)
  Though influenced less than most contemporary artists by the current progress of musical development, (Adolph
  Friedrich Erdmann von) Menzel (1815-1905) did one piece of work connected with Beethoven: a crayon drawing of
  the Beethoven Memorial at Bonn. 2_1 [1902] 428

EIN UNBEKANNTER BOLERO A SOLO VON BEETHOVEN. Alfr. Chr. Kalischer.   (K)
  A hitherto unpublished Bolero for Vln, Vcl, Pf and wordless voice (but see 30_2 [1938] 820).
                                                      2_1 [1902] 431

WO WOHNTE BEETHOVEN IN WIENS UMGEBUNG? Josef Böck-[Gnadenau].   (A
    An attempt is made to locate the houses in various suburbs of Vienna (Döbling, Heiligenstadt, etc.) in which
    Beethoven lived or spent holidays. 2_1 [1902] 433

EIN UNBEKANNTER KANON BEETHOVENS AUF DEN GEIGER IGNATZ SCHUPPANZIGH. Alfr. Chr. Kalischer.   (B
    A five-voice canon (hitherto unpublished) dated April 26th 1823 to the words: "Falstafferel, Falstaff lass dich sehen."
    (Listed as H-194) 2_3 [1903] 24

NACHTRAG UND BERICHTIGUNG. Max Vancsa.   (C
    Minutiae regarding Nephew Karl's descendants (see 1_2 [1902] 1083).
                                                 2_3 [1903] 54

VON BEETHOVENS KLAVIEREN. Theodor von Frimmel.   (D
    Descriptions, histories and (in the supplement) photographs of three pianos (Broadwood, Graf, Erard) which Beethoven
    had owned. 2_3 [1903] 83

LUDWIG VAN BEETHOVENS LEBEN, VON ALEXANDER WHEELOCK THAYER. Alfr. Chr. Kalischer.   (E
    A review of the second edition (1901) of Vol. I. 2_4 [1903] 214

ZUM BEETHOVEN-MEDAILLON VON JACQUES ÉDOUARD GATTEAUX. Theodor von Frimmel.   (F
                                                 3_1 [1903] 434

EINE BEETHOVENSTUDIE. Max Graf.   (G
    "Beethoven is the outstanding example of an artist whose works cannot be separated from his life."
                                                 3_2 [1904] 395

EINE SKIZZE ZUM ES-DUR KONZERT VON BEETHOVEN. Julius Levin.   (H
    Detailed discussion of the sketch book (formerly owned by M. Charles Malherbe) used in working out the first two
    movements of the E flat Concerto Op. 73. The author postulates that the finale, of much slighter musical content,
    was written with little or no sketch book study. 3_2 [1904] 401

NEUE BEETHOVEN-BRIEFE. Adolf Schmidt.   (I
    KS II 221, 239, 285 (the latter two published for the first time), with comments on the project of issuing the Missa
    Solemnis first in MS. 3_2 [1904] 412

BEETHOVENS F DUR STREICHQUARTETT OPUS 18 No. 1 IN SEINER URSPRÜNGLICHEN FASSUNG. Carl Waack.   (J
    The development section of the first movement is given in the early version and the final version in parallel staves,
    and the differences are discussed. 3_2 [1904] 418

BEETHOVENS WIDMUNGEN. Carl Leeder.   (K
    Biographical sketches of the various persons to whom Beethoven dedicated his works, with remarks on the circumstances
    which led to the dedications. 3_2 [1904] 421; 3_3 [1904] 26;
                                      3_4 [1904] 39,367; 4_4 [1905] 177,247

ZU BEETHOVENS "FIDELIO" UND "MELUSINE." Wilhelm Altmann.   (L
    Letter given in KS I 331 and letter from Treitschke to Iffland (Director of the Imperial National Theatre in Berlin)
    leading to the first performance of 'Fidelio' in Berlin on October 11th 1815. In the spring of 1826 Schlesinger offered
    to Count Brühl, Iffland's successor as director of the Imperial National Theatre, an opera by Beethoven on Grillparzer's
    'Die schöne Melusine.' In a letter of April 6th 1826 given here, Brühl rejects the suggestion because of the similarity
    of the book of the proposed opera to others then in favor. 3_2 [1904] 433

[Facsimile in color of New Year's card from Beethoven to the Baroness Dorothea von   (M
    Ertmann, 1804, KS I 82 No. 81] Alfr. Chr. Kalischer.
                                       3_2 [1904] Beilage to No. 12

BEETHOVENS BEZIEHUNGEN ZU MOZART. Alfr. Chr. Kalischer.   (N
    Discussion of (a) Beethoven's appearance before Mozart in the spring of 1787; (b) Whether Beethoven heard Mozart play
    (Ries says no, Czerny says yes, Kalischer says probably.); (c) effect of Mozart on Beethoven's style in 'Christus' and
    'Leonore'; (d) Beethoven's familiarity with Mozart's vocal music; (e) remarks by Beethoven regarding Mozart to friends
    and in conversation books, with facsimile of letter given in KS II 420.
                                       4_1 [1904] 41,113

BEETHOVEN, GOETHE UND VARNHAGEN VON ENSE. Emil Jacobs. (A)
   Letters exchanged by Varnhagen with Beethoven, Goethe, Oliva and others bearing on Beethoven's acquaintance with
   Varnhagen and with Goethe. 4_1 [1904] 387

BEETHOVEN IN EIGENEN WORT. Friedrich Kerst. (B)
   Several chapters from book of the same title. 4_1 [1904] 423; 4_3 [1905] 14

"LEONORE": DIE ERSTE FASSUNG DES "FIDELIO." Max Hehemann. (C)
   After three performances (November 20th, 21st, 22nd, 1805) 'Leonore' in its original form disappeared from the stage.
   A piano transcription remained, but the full score was lost or stolen. The original version has been reconstructed by
   Dr. Erich Prieger; the differences between this version and the generally-known 'Fidelio' are discussed in detail.
   5_1 [1905] 227

EIN KONVERSATIONSHEFT VON LUDWIG VAN BEETHOVEN. Alfr. Chr. Kalischer. (D)
   Complete transcription of a conversation book from 1820. 5_1 [1905] 238,307,404; 5_2 [1906] 100

EIN VERGESSENES STREICHQUARTETT BEETHOVENS. Wilhelm Altmann. (E)
   The differences between the Pianoforte Sonata Op. 14 No. 1 and its version for string quartet are discussed in detail.
   5_1 [1905] 250

BEETHOVENDRAMEN. Hans Volkmann. (F)
   Outlines and discussions are given of various plays based on some aspect of Beethoven's life.
   5_1 [1905] 258

BEETHOVEN UND DIE PROGRAMMUSIK. Fritz Volbach. (G)
   Pages 82-87 from book 'Beethoven.' 5_1 [1905] 269

VORSCHLÄGE ZUR AUFFÜHRUNG DES "FIDELIO." Hugo Conrat. (H)
   The title 'Fidelio' was used for the present version against the expressed wish of the composer, who repeatedly indicated preference for the name 'Leonore.' For the 2nd Act Finale, the dramatic situation would be much better
   served if Leonore should appear in women's clothes. 5_1 [1905] 275

VIERZEHN (BEZW. FÜNFZEHN) UNGEDRUCKTE BRIEFE BEETHOVENS. Alfr. Chr. Kalischer. (I)
   Fourteen letters (later published in KS) here published for the first time. In addition, letter 818 (KS II 179) published
   with notations similar to conversation book material. 5_3 [1906] 355

EIN AUS DEM BESITZE VON BRAHMS STAMMENDES BEETHOVEN-SCHUBERT AUTOGRAPH. (J)
   Facsimile of the autograph of Beethoven's 'Ich liebe dich,' on the back of which Schubert had written an andantino
   for Pf. The autograph is authenticated by Brahms. (See 'Neues Beethoven-Jahrbuch' 2 [1925] 46)
   6_2 [1907] Beilage following p. 136

EIN FRANZÖSISCHES BEETHOVENDRAMA. Eduard Platzhoff-Lajeune. (K)
   Drama by Walther Schinz. 6_2 [1907] 358

EIN DRUCKFEHLERVERZEICHNIS VON BEETHOVEN ZU SEINER SONATE IN AS-DUR (sic) OPUS 69. (L)
      Alfr. Chr. Kalischer.
   Material given in KS I 354, with notation of several of the corrections as not having been made in the GA.
   6_4 [1907] 285

BEETHOVENS TRAUERKANTATE. Albert Mayer-Reinach. (M)
   History of the 'Cantata for the Death of Kaiser Joseph II' (GA Ser. 25 No. 264), with detailed analysis and corrections.
   Suggestions are given for changes in the text to make the cantata of general applicability as funeral music.
   6_4 [1907] 330

TÄNZE BEETHOVENS AUS DEM JAHRE 1819. Hugo Riemann. (N)
   A collection of eleven dances (all in triple time) of which parts were found a few years before the date of this paper
   is doubtless the "set of waltzes" composed for a group of players at an inn near Mödling, about which TK III 23 says,
   "These waltzes have disappeared." Their authenticity seems beyond question.
   6_4 [1907] 365

DIE PROPORTIONEN DER BEETHOVENSCHEN INSTRUMENTALSÄTZE. Gustav Ernest.   (A)
    A count of measures in the several sections of 64 movements in sonata form shows that in almost all cases the relative
    proportions of the sections follows some simple mathematical rule.
$$7_1 \; [1907] \; 223$$

BEETHOVEN UND DIE MANNHEIMER. Hugo Riemann.   (B)
    "The demonstrable presence of a strong Mannheim influence explains in many cases what hitherto has been defined
    as the influence of Mozart. Thayer and Deiters had no realization of the immense popularity of Mannheim orchestral
    music in the time of Beethoven's youth, and thus it did not occur to them that Beethoven's early compositions could
    have had other patterns than P. E. Bach, Mozart and Haydn." Examples of Mannheim influence are given in great
    detail for many of the early works; traces of this same effect are pointed out in important compositions of Beethoven's
    second and third period. $7_3 \; [1908] \; 3,85$

HERZSCHLAG UND RHYTHMUS -- EIN VERSUCH, DEM VERSTANDNIS VON BEETHOVENS WERKEN DURCH DAS   (C)
    STUDIUM SEINER OHREN- UND HERZKRANKHEIT NÄHER ZU KOMMEN.   J. Niemack.
    Beethoven's deafness and his arteriosclerosis resulted in a ringing and a pounding in his ears which may have been
    reflected in certain characteristics of his style. References from his correspondence are cited over the entire period
    of his deafness to indicate the existence of this aural parasthesia and its influence on his thoughts.
$$7_3 \; [1908] \; 20$$

BEETHOVEN ALS EPIGRAMMATIKER.   Hans Volkmann.   (D)
    The title of this paper is based on Beethoven's remark: "I make them (canons) just the way a poet makes epigrams."
    The forty-odd canons by Beethoven, most of them dating from his last decade, are considered as regards their text
    and their music. $7_3 \; [1908] \; 26$

BEETHOVENS BRIEFE AN BERHARD.   Alfr. Chr. Kalischer.   (E)
    Polemic against a recent article by Alexander Hajdecki regarding Beethoven letters, and contention that a letter
    given by Hajdecki as from Beethoven to Bernard (October 10th 1818 (?); No. 489 in 'Beethoven-Jahrbuch' 2 [1909] 246)
    is spurious. $7_3 \; [1908] \; 32$

EINE HÄNDEL-BEETHOVEN-BRAHMS PARALLELE.   Alfred Heuss.   (F)
    Comment on the melodic similarity of the opening notes of 'Behold and see,' a passage a few measures before the
    recapitulation of the adagio of Op. 106, and the opening measures of the E minor Symphony.
$$7_4 \; [1908] \; 147$$

BEETHOVEN ALS KULTURMACHT -- EINE STUDIE.   Paul Bekker.   (G
    Study for the author's 'Beethoven.' $9_1 \; [1909] \; 3$

EIN UNBEKANNTE BRIEF BEETHOVENS AN DEN FÜRSTEN N. VON GALITZIN.   Georges Humbert.   (H
    A recently published letter of December 13th 1823 to Prince Galitsin, written in French by an amanuensis and signed
    by Beethoven, is undoubtedly genuine. The letter refers to possible inadvertent omissions from the copy of the Missa
    Solemnis sent to Galitsin. A facsimile of this letter is given, as well as the first publication of the full text of a letter
    from Galitsin to Beethoven dated November 29th 1823 (TD V 556). See also 9_1 [1909] 233.
$$9_1 \; [1909] \; 16$$

BEETHOVENS SKIZZEN ZUR KANTATE "DER GLORREICHE AUGENBLICK" ZUM ERSTEN MAL MITGETEILT.   (I)
    Georg Schünemann.
    Brief history of the cantata and virtually complete transcription of the sketches referred to in NB II 307.
$$9_1 \; [1909] \; 22,93$$

BEETHOVENS "CORIOLAN" OUVERTURE.   Ernst Zander.   (J)
    A brief outline of the drama and its musical portrayal; detailed suggestions to the conductor regarding doubling of
    wind instruments and amplifying the horn and trumpet parts to take advantage of present-day valve instruments.
$$9_1 \; [1909] \; 36$$

EIN UNGEDRUCKTER, UNBEKANNTER BRIEF VON BEETHOVEN.   Alfr. Chr. Kalischer.   (K
    "An extremely sharp protest by Beethoven to a letter from Bernhard to Frau Johanna von Beethoven," undated and
    addressed only to "W." $9_1 \; [1909] \; 42$

DAS AUTOGRAPH DER GELLERT-LEIDER OPUS 48 No. 5 UND 6 VON BEETHOVEN. Alfred Ebert. (A)
  The autograph of the last two songs of Op. 48 is compared in detail with the first edition (Artaria, 1803) and with
  the GA (Ser. 23 No. 217). As for the date of composition of the cycle, "one of the Gellert-Lieder dates back in its
  conception to the Bonn period; for a second, sketches are at hand from 1798. No definite date can be assigned to
  the other four, though their style gives no compelling indication of a later period. When the six songs were being
  written in fair copy (probably about 1800 or 1801), Beethoven made many changes, especially in the pianoforte
  part (the 'Busslied' being most changed) which gave a more mature character to the style. The songs were engraved
  in 1803." 9_1 [1909] 44

DIE WIEDERGEFUNDENEN BILDNISSE DES STERBENDEN BEETHOVEN. Otto Erich Deutsch. (B)
  Circumstances leading to the making of the recently discovered sketches by Josef Teltscher (1802-37) of Beethoven
  on his deathbed, and a biographical sketch of the artist. 9_1 [1909] 64

EINIGE BEMERKUNGEN ZU DEM BRIEFE BEETHOVENS AN DEN FÜRSTEN GALITZIN VOM 13 DEZEMBER 1823. (C)
  Alfred Ebert.
  The letter in question (see 9_1 [1909] 16) is in the handwriting of Nephew Karl; from the style it is probable that
  Beethoven himself only gave an outline of what Karl was to say. Galitsin replied to Beethoven's letter under date
  of December 30th 1823 (TD V 557). 9_1 [1909] 233

BEETHOVEN IN SEINEN BRIEFEN. Fritz Cassirer. (D)
  The true Beethoven, in his complexity and his simplicity, may be brought most clearly in focus by a rapid reading
  of a large number of his letters. 9_3 [1910] 3,75

BEETHOVENS PROMETHEUS-MUSIK EIN VARIATIONENWERK. Hugo Riemann. (E)
  It may be not without significance that Beethoven used the same theme (or pair of themes) in several works dating
  from the period 1800-04: No. 7 of the Twelve Contredanses for Orchestra (NV p. 137), the finale of the 'Prometheus'
  music Op. 43, the Theme and Variations in E flat for Pianoforte Op. 35, and the ostinato of the finale of the Eroica
  Symphony Op. 55. During this period Beethoven had apparently given renewed thought to the variations form, as
  evidenced by Opp. 34 and 35, the Eroica finale, and the 32 Variations in C minor (sketched in 1804). A detailed
  analysis is given of the eighteen numbers of the 'Prometheus' music to show that the entire work is unified by extremely free but quite definite variations on relatively few thematic, harmonic and stylistic units. The Variations
  in E flat for Trio Op. 44 and the song 'Andenken' (NV p. 180), presumably composed about this time, also show the
  influence of the technique and the material used in 'Prometheus.' 9_3 [1910] 19,107

UNGEDRUCKTE BRIEFE BEETHOVENS. Anton Schlossar. (F)
  Six letters, all without date but probably from the period 1811-15 (apparently written: four to Count Dietrichstein,
  one to Duport of the Royal Theatre, and one to Franz Clement) and three to Count Dietrichstein, also without date
  but apparently from 1822-23, with a letter dated March 30th 1836 from von Schleger to Count Dietrichstein regarding the projected Beethoven monument in Bonn. The originals of these letters are lost; this text is from copies made
  by Faust Pachler of originals possessed by his mother Marie Pachler (nee Koschak), a friend and worshiper of Beethoven.
                                                             9_3 [1910] 35

DIE ERSTEN AUFFÜHRUNGEN VON BEETHOVENS ES-DUR QUARTETT (OPUS 127) IM FRÜHLING 1825. Alfred Ebert. (G)
  Extensive quotations from the conversation books and other sources bring out the following information. Beethoven
  had promised a new quartet to Schuppanzigh for performance during the winter of 1824-25. A hitherto unpublished
  letter to him, from the end of 1824, states that the new quartet will not be ready for some time. To hold Beethoven
  to his promise, Schuppanzigh announced a performance of the new work for January 23rd 1825. However, Beethoven
  had also promised it to Linke for a benefit concert, but he finally decided to stick to his commitment to Schuppanzigh
  and to give Linke the A minor Quartet, then well advanced. The E flat Quartet was not ready for the January 23rd
  concert, so Schuppanzigh played Op. 95. Meanwhile Schuppanzigh was making arrangements for a benefit concert
  for Beethoven at which, among other works, the Ninth Symphony and the Missa Solemnis would be performed. A
  fair copy of the E flat Quartet (probably the parts) was made in the few days following February 15th, so that Schuppanzigh had barely two weeks to prepare the Quartet for its performance on March 6th -- far too short a time for a work
  of such great and novel technical and interpretive difficulties. Rehearsals were probably held in Beethoven's presence,
  so that by watching the bows he could check on tempi, phrasing, etc. (see TD V 181). It was presumably at one of
  these rehearsals that the agreement of the four members of the quartet given in KS II 361 was signed.

The first performance took place on March 6th 1825. Schuppanzigh's poor playing contributed notably to the work's
lack of success. Upon urging by Karl and Brother Johann, who were hostile towards Schuppanzigh, a repeat performance
was arranged in which Joseph Boehm was to take Schuppanzigh's place at the first desk, though Schuppanzigh wished to

DIE ERSTEN AUFFÜHRUNGEN VON BEETHOVENS ES-DUR QUARTETT, etc., (Continued)
give the work again after more rehearsals. The coolness set up between Beethoven and Schuppanzigh by this withdrawal lasted until the summer. Boehm hesitated to undertake the assignment, but finally consented. A public
rehearsal with Boehm took place on March 20th or 22nd, with a successful public performance on March 23rd.
Joseph Mayseder, a brilliant technician but not capable of understanding the work, asked permission through Karl
to play it with his quartet. Boehm apparently played the Quartet again at a benefit concert during the first half
of April; Mayseder played it during this same period, and again during the last week of the month. The repeated
performances -- six times in less than two months -- began to win the approval of the work from the music lovers
of the city (see KS II 384). The author throws doubt on the entire Rellstab story regarding this Quartet (see
TK II 201). His reference to the "elderly and famous performers" and to their "seventeen or more rehearsals"
can hardly apply to any of the known performances. No performance after Rellstab's arrival in Vienna on 30-
31 March was before a "small intimate audience." Rellstab's purported statements to Beethoven do not appear
in any of the conversation books. 9_3 [1910] 42,90

DIE TAKTART IM ERSTEN SATZE VON BEETHOVENS C-MOLL SYMPHONIE. Martin Frey.   (A)
Based on recommendations by Reger, the author extends and makes more flexible Weingartner's device of beating
(or thinking) pairs of measures to secure the true rhythmic pulse of the movement, in favor or 2/4, 4/4, or 6/4 as
the music itself demands. 9_3 [1910] 64

SECHS BRIEFE BEETHOVENS AN DIE GRÄFIN MARIE VON ERDÖDY UND EINER AN THERESE VON MALFATTI (?) NACH   (B)
DEN ORIGINALEN MITGETEILT. Alfred Ebert.
Six letters to the Countess Erdödy are given, of which one (without date) is apparently published for the first time.
The other five had been published previously in transcriptions made in the 1850's by Dr. Otto Jahn from originals
supposed to have been since destroyed. The originals were brought to light by the author, and the transcriptions
given here differ in some respects from Jahn's versions. Another letter (without date), presumably to Therese von
Malfatti, is published for the first time. 9_3 [1910] 126

BEETHOVEN ALS BEARBEITER SCHOTTISCHER UND ANDERER VOLKSWEISEN. Richard Hohenemser.   (C)
The songs for Thomson are discussed from several standpoints. The harmonizations are considered as regards their
suitability to the folk song style, especially with penta-tonic melodies. The accompaniments are for the most part
monotonous and without imagination: the Pf figuration is routine, and the Vln and Vcl usually double melody and
bass. Only in the ritornellos does the composer manifest any notable degree of invention. Ten of the sixteen
melodies in Opp. 105 and 107 are taken from Thomson songs, as a rule without change in harmonization. Each set
of variations is on a pretty well standardized plan; the result is "lively and not mannered." The folk melodies which
Beethoven used in independent compositions are handled with far more imagination and effectiveness. The only two
cases definitely identified as such are in Op. 59, but citation is given of two Russian melodies which may have provided the ideas for important themes in the Seventh and Ninth Symphonies.
                                10_1 [1910] 323; 10_2 [1911] 23

BEETHOVEN IN DER DICHTUNG. Leopold Hirschberg.   (D)
Unlike various other great German creative artists (e.g., Goethe, Mozart), Beethoven was the subject of very few
poems written during his lifetime. After his death, starting with the material in Seyfried's 'Studien,' there has been
a steady output of such poetry. A few quotations and many citations are given.
                                10_1 [1910] 339

DER QUARTSEXTAKKORD ALS VORHALTSBILDUNG DES BASSES VOR DER TONIKA BEI BEETHOVEN.   (E)
Lorenz Matossi.
The cadence in which the harmony passes from V_7 to I while the bass remains suspended on the dominant before a
final resolution to the root position, thus giving rise to a $\frac{6}{4}$ chord, first came into use by Beethoven, is a typical feature of his style, and has been used only sparingly by his successors. Many examples are given of this device in its
various possible modifications. 10_1 [1910] 356

BEETHOVEN-STUDIEN. Gustav Ernst.   (F)
Beethoven and Bettina. Of the three letters published by Bettina von Arnim (nee Brentano) as from Beethoven, the
third, dated August 1812 (KS I 263), is generally regarded as spurious, and the second, dated February 10th 1811
(KS I 208) is equally accepted as genuine. Ernst contends that the first letter in this series, dated August 11th 1810
(KS I 195), is spurious: the reference to Bettina's written words to Beethoven does not correspond with the develop-
ment of his deafness at that time, and the orthography is far too correct for it to resemble Beethoven's own writing.

Beethoven's instrumental fugues (p. 97). The use of the fugue in Beethoven's last period was particularly appropriate
for the reason that this form involves the struggle of a single idea. "Never is the flight of his inspiration so free,
never does his music show such a spiritual outpouring, as in this form."

10_3 [1911] 95

BEETHOVEN AN DIE UNSTERBLICHE GELIEBTE -- EIN UNBEKANNTE BRIEF DES MEISTERS. Paul Bekker.   (A)
The question of the identity of the Immortal Beloved is briefly reviewed, with a quotation from a conversation book
of February 1823 indicating that Giulietta Guicciardi had loved Beethoven greatly. Facsimiles are given of the pertinent pages from the conversation book, of the three letters accepted as genuine (KS I 47-53), and also of a fourth
letter, presumably in Beethoven's hand, dated "July 8th in the afternoon" (the present ownership and past history of
which were not revealed to Bekker), in which a theme from the finale of Op. 29 is quoted as one which had just occurred to the writer. If this meant that the theme had just been conceived, the letter may be definitely dated as
having been written in 1801 (the year of composition of Op. 29). From this new evidence and all the known facts,
the conclusion is drawn that Giulietta Guicciardi was the Unknown Beloved. (See p. 354)

10_4 [1911] 131

1801 ODER -- 1812? ZUM PROBLEM DER BRIEFE AN BEETHOVENS UNSTERBLICHE GELIEBTE. Max Unger.   (B)
Regarding the letter discussed by Bekker (p. 131), Unger contends that the theme from Op. 29 was remembered at
the time of the writing, not conceived then, so that the year from which the letter dates is not determined. He
states various reasons which incline him to 1812 as the year of its origin. (But see 11_2 [1912] 40)

10_4 [1911] 354

EINE JUGENDSYMPHONIE BEETHOVENS. Fritz Stein.   (C)
In the library of the Akademischen Konzertes at Jena there were recently discovered parts of a symphony which bore
Beethoven's name (not in autograph) as composer. Though no trace of this work can be found in the sketch books,
external and internal evidence (which is discussed in detail) point to its authenticity. It was probably composed in
1793. 11_2 [1912] 3

"LEONOREN" - FRAGEN. Arthur Seidl.   (D)
Comments on the suggestions by Conrat (5_1 [1905] 275): Though Beethoven unquestionably preferred the name
'Leonore,' there were reasons considered adequate during his lifetime for the use of the name 'Fidelio.' To go back
to the other name now would be flying in the face of a hundred years of usage; moreover, confusion would be avoided
by reserving the name 'Leonore' or the original version reconstructed by Erich Prager (5_1 [1905] 227) and performed in
1905. The change of costume so that Leonore could appear in feminine clothing in the finale is not practicable from
the standpoint of time, would be incongruous dramatically, and is not required as a part of Beethoven's aesthetic plan.
"From the standpoint alike of dramatic technique and musical aesthetics, the 'Leonore No. 3' Overture has no place in
a performance of the opera." 11_2 [1912] 21

BEETHOVEN-STUDIEN. Gustav Ernst.   (E)
The sound of birds in the 'Scene at the Brook.' The greater artistic effect of the violin trills (m. 34ff) as compared
with the flute arpeggios (m. 58ff) as bringing into the 'Scene at the Brook' the concept of birds is in accordance with
the rule: "Music which attempts to portray an idea (Die malende Musik) should only indicate, not imitate, since the
closer it approaches fidelity to Nature, the more it departs from fidelity to Art."

The high points of Beethoven's creative achievement (p. 38). In most forms, Beethoven's last works are generally
accepted as his greatest (e. g. , the last Piano Concerto, the last Piano Trio, the last Songs (the cycle 'An die ferne
Geliebte'), etc. Beethoven's taste almost unerringly told him when he had attained a climactic point, so that he
then turned his attention to another form rather than trying to duplicate the unique.

10_3 [1911] 95

BEETHOVENS ZWEITER LIEBESBRIEF -- SCHLUSSWORT. Paul Bekker.   (F)
Supplementing the report in 10_4 [1911] 131, certain characteristics of the letter itself, together with the opinion of
an expert on questioned documents, have convinced Bekker that this letter is spurious. (See also 'Zeitschrift der
Internationalen Musikgesellschaft' 12 [1911] 350 and 'Musical Times' 52 [1911] 714)

11_2 [1912] 40

EINIGE BEMERKUNGEN ZUR ZWEITEN AUFLAGE VON BEETHOVENS SÄMTLICHEN BRIEFEN. Alfred Ebert.   (G)
Review of the third volume of Kalischer-Frimmel. The reviewer points out that the letter to the Philharmonic
Society of February 5th 1816 (KS I 396) and the letter to Neate of February 25th 1823 (KS II 229) were written in
German, not in English. A transcription of the letter of May 18th 1816 to Neate (KS I 410) is given from the original,
differing in many details from the version previously published. 11_2 [1912] 356

EIN FEHLER IN BEETHOVENS ERSTER VIOLINSONATE. Gustav Altmann.   (A)
   In the second movement, the upbeat before measure 17 should certainly be an eighth note, not a sixteenth note;
   the binds in this and the following measure contradict the natural phrasing. (See p. 290)
                                    11_3 [1912] 28

BEETHOVEN-RETOUCHEN -- UND KEIN ENDE! Felix Gotthelf.   (B)
   Since, in the trio of the scherzo of the Seventh Symphony, the violin dominant pedal point is twice broken by a
   drop to the neighboring note, and since the natural trumpets could not do this but the modern valve trumpets can,
   the author contends that in the similar passage later in the trio the trumpet pedal should break in the same way.
   (This article is presumably not ironical) 11_3 [1912] 161

ÜBER FEHLER, NACHLÄSSIGKEITEN, UNGENAUIGKEITEN UND ZWEIDEUTIGKEITEN IM MUSIKALISCHEN TEXT.   (C)
      G. H. Witte.
   Witte is not certain that Altmann's correction (p. 28) is well founded, and cites various other readings (from Opp. 2,
   7, 49, 68, and 125 of Beethoven and from other composers) in which the orthography results in uncertainties.
                                    11_3 [1912] 290

NOVA BEETHOVENIANA. Max Unger.   (D)
   Remarks on Neefe's difficult situation in the years 1784-85. The mental and financial distress caused to Neefe by
   the intrigues against him in favor of Beethoven (TK I 83) and by the great reduction in his salary are made clear in
   a letter to his friend and supporter Grossmann of July 23rd 1784. A letter of January 19th 1785, by which time Neefe
   had decided that nothing would be gained by further waiting, indicates that in his mind Beethoven had had no part in
   the demonstration. 12_1 [1912] 149,214

   Two new acquaintances of Beethoven: Friedrich Kalkbrenner and Philipp Carl Hoffmann. Reference is made to an   (E)
   article in 'The Quarterly Musical Magazine and Review' 6 [1824] 500 where the statement is made that in 1796, when
   Kalkbrenner Sr. was taking his talented son (age 8) to Italy: "In the journey from Prague to Vienna, he unexpectedly
   met Beethoven, whom he took in his carriage to Vienna." Reference is also made to an article in 'Neue Zeitschrift
   für Musik' (18 [1843] 19), discussing a recently published biography of Kalkbrenner, in the accuracy of which the
   author has less confidence. Beethoven may have known Hoffmann in Vienna during the period 1800-10.
                                    12_1 [1912] 153

   The 'Pathetique' and Clementi's D minor Sonata. The similarity between the opening measures of these two works   (F)
   is noteworthy, but the Clementi sonata was almost certainly several years later than the 'Pathétique.'
                                    12_1 [1912] 158

   Friedrich Rochlitz's published request for assistance for Susanna Bach. The files of Breitkopf & Härtel contain a copy   (G)
   of their reply to Beethoven's letter of April 22nd 1801 (KS I 43) in which he expressed a wish to contribute a composition to alleviate the poverty of Bach's aged daughter. In this reply (May 19th 1801) the publishers favor the idea,
   and they bring the project up again in a letter of June 30th 1803 (dealing with the subject matter of letters KS I 68,
   70 and 74). Beethoven mentions it still again in his letters of September 1803 (KS I 75) and April 18th 1805 (KS I 96),
   but his good intentions apparently came to naught. 12_1 [1912] 160

   A letter from Friedrich Rochlitz regarding a proposed performance of Egmont. This letter, written to an unidentified   (H)
   person some time after Beethoven's death, indicates the regard for Beethoven's music which was held by the writer,
   one of the first journalists to support him. 12_1 [1912] 214

   Some performances of Beethoven's works in Vienna in 1812. Quotations from contemporary journals regarding the   (I)
   first performance in Vienna of the E flat Piano Concerto and regarding other concerts in the spring of 1812.
                                    12_1 [1912] 215

   An explanation of the attack (on Beethoven's behalf) on the 'Allgemeine Musikalische Zeitung.' This polemic,   (J)
   accusing the Breitkopf & Härtel journal of neglecting those works of Beethoven which that house did not publish, may
   have been advance publicity for the appearance of the 'Berliner allgemeine musikalische Zeitung,' published by
   Schlesinger, which Beethoven praised in his letter of July 15th 1825 (KS II 390).
                                    12_1 [1912] 218

   An unknown letter from Beethoven to Tobias Haslinger. This letter, dated October 10th 1824 from Baden, requests   (K)
   parts of the terzet "Tremate, empi" and states that Nephew Karl would probably be with him the coming week. Note
   that this is further proof that Karl's running away (see KS II 338) was in 1825, not in 1824.
                                    12_1 [1912] 220

Beethoven and Baron Carl August von Klein. A biographical sketch of the man to whom Beethoven wrote on May 10th (A)
1826 (KS II 423). 12_1 [1912] 221

Beethoven's death. Extracts from contemporary accounts of Beethoven's funeral and memorial ceremonies.   (B)
                                                              12_1 [1912] 223

BEETHOVEN UND ANTON REICHA. Ernst Bücken.   (C)
Anton Reicha came to Bonn in 1785 when his uncle Joseph was called there to assume the leadership of the Electoral
Chapel (TK I 84). Beethoven's intimacy with Reicha dates from this time. They matriculated together at the University of Bonn on May 14th 1789; the author believes that Beethoven actually attended some lectures at the University. Beethoven retained a warm recollection of his old friend throughout his life; the influence of Beethoven appears
in Reicha's compositions. 12_2 [1913] 341

DER STIMMUNGSGEHALT DER SIEBENTEN SYMPHONIE VON BEETHOVEN. Alfred Ebert.   (D)
Fanciful interpretations by various authors and poets are given, and the conclusion is drawn: "Certainly music and
the appreciation of music are not served, but rather are harmed, by such poetical explanations. Musical aesthetics
would have advanced further had not so much valuable time been wasted in such useless spinning of phantasy."
                                                              $12_{[?]}$ [1913] 30

BEETHOVENS "MISSA SOLEMNIS" UND DIE KATHOLISCHE LITURGIE. Alfred Schnerich.   (E)
In his musical setting, Beethoven considered not only the text itself but the liturgical situation. The not infrequent
liturgical performances of the work indicate its suitability for that purpose.
                                                              12_4 [1913] 150

BRIEFE BEETHOVENS AN CARL BERNARD, E. T. A. HOFFMANN, S. A. STEINER & CO., UND ANTON SCHINDLER --   (F)
    VERBESSERTE ABDRUCKE. Max Unger.
New transcription of the letter to "W" first given by Kalischer in 'Die Musik' 9 [1909] 42 and later by Frimmel in
'Beethoven-Forschung' 1 No. 4 [1913] 106. Unger agrees with Frimmel in assigning the letter to the period mid-
1819 to latter part of 1823. The addressee was probably Carl Bernard.   New transcription of letter of March
23rd 1820 to E. T. A. Hoffmann (KS II 170). New transcription of letters of December 1816 to Steiner & Co.
(KS II 1 (No. 552), 2). New transcription of a letter to Schindler, KS II 241 (No. 888), with the addition of
material omitted from previous versions. 13_1 [1913] 147

ÜBER KRITISCHE NEU-AUSGABEN VON MUSIKWERKEN. Maurice Moszkowski.   (G)
Questioned passages in various editions of piano works, including Beethoven's Opp. 2, 7, 10, 27, 31, 35, 78, 96,
111 and 129. 13_1 [1913] 259

BEETHOVEN UND BREMEN. Friedrich Wellmann.   (H)
A group of admirers, led by Wilhelm Christian Müller, brought about performances of Beethoven's symphonies in
Bremen as early as 1809, and stimulated a general appreciation of his works throughout the city.
                                                              13_1 [1913] 279

BEETHOVENIANA. Theodor Müller-Reuter. 13_2 [1914] 3, 86   (I)

The Eroica. In the first edition of the score (1805) and of the parts (1806) the two measures immediately before the
first ending of the first movement are duplicated, but on the reissue of the parts from these plates the two duplicated
measures were erased, and no future edition (score or parts) has included them. It is not known whether this change
was requested by Beethoven, approved by him, or (indeed) known to him.
                                                              13_2 [1914] 4

The First Symphony. Various facts indicate the possibility that this symphony was originally scored without clarinets, (J)
and that the present clarinet parts were added later. A sketch (NB II 228) which foreshadows the first theme of the
last movement of this symphony comes in all probability from mid-1796, not from 1794-95 as postulated by
Nottebohm. 13_2 [1914] 6

The First and Second Pianoforte Concertos. An ingenious commentary is given on the story of the first rehearsal of (K)

BEETHOVENIANA (Continued)
the C major Concerto (TK I 184) in which Beethoven was obliged to transpose his solo part because of a low-ptiched piano. The author contends that the work concerned was the B flat Concerto (known as the Second, but the first in order of composition). A note is given on the first edition of the scores of the concertos Opp. 15, 19, 37, 56. (See also pp. 281, 283 and 13_3 [1914] 39)

13_2 [1914] 9

The Sixth Symphony. The horn call at the beginning of the last movement is correct as it appears in the GA.   (A
13_2 [1914] 12

The Seventh Symphony. In the first edition of the parts, the opening was marked ala breve, not common time,   (B
though the change to the present designation was apparently at Beethoven's direction. It is noted that the title page of the first edition of the parts of the Fifth, Sixth, Seventh and Eighth symphonies states the instrumentation as "2 violins, 2 (sic) violas," etc. The importance is stressed of the differentiation between staccato marked with dots and staccato marked with strokes. 13_2 [1914] 14

The Fifth Symphony. Study of the autograph leads the author to believe that in the passage of repeated chords on   (C
pp. 17-18 of the GA one measure is superfluous. The contention of Weingartner that the present empty measure should be considered as a short fermata is wholly without justification. (See also pp. 275, 277)
13_2 [1914] 86

DER KLAVIERSTIL DES LETZTEN BEETHOVEN. Walter Georgii.   (D
A discussion of many aspects of the style which characterizes the last five piano sonatas.
13_2 [1914] 16

DER GEWALTIGE PAUSENTAKT IN BEETHOVENS FÜNFTEN. Felix Weingartner.   (E
Weingartner considers the evidence of the autograph as brought out by Müller-Reuter (p. 86) and arrives at precisely the opposite conclusion: that the version generally accepted is what Beethoven wrote very clearly, is what he heard in performances, and must be accepted as what he wanted. 13_2 [1914] 275

DER PAUSENTAKT IN BEETHOVENS FÜNFTEN. Emil Liepe.   (F
Liepe's conclusion is identical with that of Weingartner (p. 275), with the additional point that the "Fate" motif is never on an upbeat as it would be if a measure were dropped in accordance with Müller-Reuter's suggestion.
13_2 [1914] 277

EIN KLEINER IRRTUM. Fritz F. Steffin.   (C
Müller-Reuter's comment on the first rehearsal of one of the early piano concertos (p. 9) is not sound. Wegeler's story (Wegeler: 'Notizen' (ed. Kalischer, 1905) p. 47) is correct: the composition concerned must have been the C major Concerto (No. 1). 13_2 [1914] 281

ZUR ERSTEN PROBE DES BEETHOVENSCHEN C-DUR KONZERTES. Arthur Rydin.   (H
Same conclusions as Steffin (p. 281). 13_2 [1914] 283

EIN KLEINER ODER EIN GROSSER IRRTUM? Theodor Müller-Reuter.   (I
The author defends his position against the criticism of Steffin (13_2 [1914] 281) and Rydin (13_2 [1914] 283). (See also 13_4 [1914] 144). 13_3 [1914] 39

ZUM 29. MÄRZ 1795: BEETHOVENS C-DUR ODER B-DUR KONZERT? Fritz F. Steffin.   (J
Weighing the accounts of contemporaries, the sketch book data from Nottebohm, and the contentions of Müller-Reuter (13_2 [1914] 9; 13_3 [1914] 39), the author concludes that the concerto played at Beethoven's first public appearance in Vienna (TK I 184) was that in C major (Op. 15), not that in B flat (Op. 19).
13_4 [1914] 144

SINFONIA EROICA: BETRACHTUNGEN ÜBER BEETHOVENS ETHIK. Walther Vetter.   (K
An elaborate analysis, devoted principally to the first movement, in which the author finds much extra musical symbolism. 14_1 [1914] 107

BEETHOVENS NEUNTE SYMPHONIE UND JOHANN SEBASTIAN BACH. Robert Handke.   (L
The author sees Beethoven's entire creative life as an effort to combine "the intellectual clarity of Bach with the expressive genius of Mozart." The thematic development and thematic unity of the Ninth Symphony is considered in great detail, and the conclusion is reached that from the standpoint of thematic and harmonic development alike,

the work is a spiritual successor to the great compositions of Bach.   14$_3$ [1915] 51,99

WAS GAB UNS BEETHOVEN?   Ferruccio Busoni. (A)
An essential in the creation of works of art is the sincerity which limits the creator to the expression of his own thoughts in his own way. In this respect, Beethoven was completely true to himself and his art. We have him to thank for the trend away from virtuosity as an end in itself. While we may refer to the "divine" Mozart, Beethoven is above everything else human. (See also p. 203)   15$_1$ [1922] 19

BEETHOVEN UND DIE ERSTE AUFFÜHRUNG DES FIDELIO IN DRESDEN.   Hans Volkmann. (B)
Excerpts from the conversation books regarding the first performance of 'Fidelio' in Dresden (April 29th 1823) under the direction of Carl Maria von Weber.   15$_1$ [1922] 177

BEMERKUNGEN ZU BUSONIS FRAGE: WAS GAB UNS BEETHOVEN?   Willy Bardas. (C)
The author takes issue with the statement of Busoni that "Mozart, when his style resembles that of Beethoven, appears significant and original, but when Beethoven reminds one of Mozart, the result seems unimportant and derivative."
                    15$_1$ [1922] 203

BEETHOVENS KLAVIERSTÜCK "FÜR ELISE."   Max Unger. (D)
Though definite proof cannot be secured in the absence of the autograph, the author is convinced that the work was not "for Elise" but "for Therese" Malfatti, and that it should be designated as a bagatelle, not as an albumblatt. (See also 'Musical Quarterly' 11 [1925] 68)   15$_1$ [1923] 334

ZUR BEETHOVENS "SONATE PATHETIQUE."   Richard Hohenemser. (E)
Although Cherubini's 'Medea' did not receive its first performance in Vienna until 1802 (three years after the publication of the 'Sonata Pathétique'), the score had been available since 1797. A copy of this score was in Beethoven's 'Nachlass,' and his admiration of the composer was well known. The similarity of important material (especially in the first movement) to passages in 'Medea' lead the author to believe that the sonata was a quite subconscious result of the composer's study of the opera.   15$_2$ [1923] 655

ZWEI NEUE BEETHOVEN-BRIEFE.   Max Unger. (F)
First transcription in German of letter of February 25th 1824 to Heinrich Albert Probst (first published in French in 'Revue de Musicologie' 3 [1922] 13), offering songs (probably Opp. 121b, 122, and 128), bagatelles (Op. 126) and the 'Dedication of the House' Overture (Op. 124) for publication. This is probably Beethoven's first letter to Probst. These works were finally published by Schott. The circumstances leading to the composition of the Overture are stated in detail.   Transcription of a letter (probably from about November 10th 1825) to Holz (first published in 'Musical Quarterly' 3 [1917] 620) referring to (a) matters concerning Karl, (b) difficulties with a housekeeper, (c) request for tickets to a concert, and (d) delivery of a copy of the Missa Solemnis to Reisser of the Polytechnic Institute.   16$_1$ [1923] 11

DIE GEBURT DER MUSIKALISCHEN IDEE BEI BEETHOVEN.   Hermann Hans Wetzler. (G)
The characteristic manner in which a basic idea (melodic, rhythmic, etc.) emerges and (so to speak) creates itself in a Beethoven introduction is discussed and exemplified by quotations from Opp. 70, 73, 92, 106, and 124. A hitherto unpublished sketch book sheet showing the formulation of the variations theme of Op. 97 is transcribed and discussed.   16$_1$ [1923] 157

STATUE OF BEETHOVEN AT NÜRNBERG, BY KONRAD ROTH.   16$_{[?]}$ [1924] facing p. 341 (H)

BEETHOVEN UND SCHUBERT.   Theodor von Frimmel. (I)
"It may be stated as a definite fact that the two masters were personally acquainted, but that they had no active intercourse." Schubert was broadly and intimately familiar with Beethoven's works; the influence of specific Beethoven compositions on compositions of Schubert is discussed.   17$_1$ [1925] 401

BEETHOVEN AUS RÖMISCHEN HORIZONT.   Wilhelm Peterson-Berger. (J)
"Beethoven is the last great manifestation of the spirit of Roman antiquity, and at the same time is its first appearance in music," though Handel and Bach foretold this characteristic which culminated in Beethoven.
                    17$_1$ [1925] 416

DIE SONATENFORM BEETHOVENS -- DAS GESETZ.   Walter Engelsmann. (K)
"Every sonata of Beethoven is developed in all its movements, parts and themes from a single Principal Theme or

DIE SONATENFORM BEETHOVENS -- DAS GESETZ (Continued)
Principal Motif." The application of this law is shown in Opp. 2, 13, 22, 27, 30, 36, 53, 57, 59, 69, 70, 95, 97, 106, 110, 111 and 125. 17_1 [1925] 424

BEETHOVENS HANDSCHRIFT. Max Unger.   (A
Examples are given of each letter of the German script alphabet (upper and lower case) and of many Roman letters to indicate Beethoven's typical method of forming letters. Certain thoughts in his letter of December 15, 1800 to Hoffmeister (KS I 37) were continued in the letter of January 15th 1801 (KS I 39), so that "Leipziger O (or R)" in the latter undoubtedly refers to the similar phrase "Leipziger Rezensenten" ("Leipzig critics") in the earlier letter. As late as his fiftieth year he spelled his name "Beethowen" when writing in German script though he used the correct spelling when using Roman characters. Idiosyncrasies of his orthography are discussed in great detail.
17_1 [1925] 432

DIE BEZIEHUNGEN ANTON SCHINDLERS ZU BEETHOVEN. Walther Nohl.   (B
Schindler (1795-1864) met Beethoven in 1814, and during the period 1819-1825 was with him almost every day. The relationship between the two men is indicated by extensive quotations from the conversation books.
17_1 [1925] 441; 17_2 [1925] 497

BEETHOVEN ALS MUSIKER DES UNBEGRENZTEN. Adolf Weissmann.   (C
The author disagrees with the contentions of Fritz Cassirer in his book "Beethoven und die Gestalt."
18_1 [1925] 1

BEETHOVEN'S LETTER OF MARCH 15th 1823 TO CHERUBINI.   (D
Facsimile and transcription of letter given in KS II 234, almost identical with version in KBr IV 207.
18_1 [1925] facing p. 16; p. 81

PORTRAIT OF BEETHOVEN BY AN UNKNOWN ARTIST.   (E
First publication of an unsigned oil painting of skillful workmanship, presumably dating from the first decade of the nineteenth century. 18_1 [1925] facing p. 420; p. 457

BEETHOVENS GEISTIGE WELTBOTSCHAFT. Richard Benz.   (F
Beethoven "sings not the domination of the individual over all the earth nor the communistic destruction of the world's civilization -- he heralds the new era, he summons all to the world domination of the spirit."
18_1 [1926] 405

BEETHOVEN IM URTEIL DER ZEITEN. Karl Grunsky.   (G
Contemporary reviews of the symphonies and the Missa Solemnis are quoted which now seem characterized either by naivete or malice, and an attempt is made to explain the reasons for such judgments.
18_1 [1926] 409

STATUE OF BEETHOVEN BY FRANCESCO JERACE IN NAPLES. 18_1 [1926] facing p. 421; p. 457   (I

BEETHOVEN-PROBLEMATIK. Hans Joachim Moser.   (I
"There are two chief causes that bring our generation into a changed relationship with Beethoven: the difference in the picture which we have of the man himself, and the place which his compositions have in our concert programs." The tendency to romanticize the man out of all relationship to real life has in large measure passed; his music is heard almost to the point of satiety. 18_1 [1926] 425

BEETHOVENS JUGENDKOMPOSITIONEN. Karl Gerhartz.   (J
A discussion of the 44 compositions which Schiedermair ('Der junge Beethoven') lists as dating from the Bonn period.
18_1 [1926] 430

STATUE OF BEETHOVEN BY PETER BREUER. 18_1 [1926] 436,458   (K

A BEETHOVEN LETTER.   (L
Facsimile and transcription of letter of March 14th 1827 to Pasqualati (KS II 469).
18_1 [1926] facing p. 437; p. 458

BEETHOVEN UND WILHELMINE SCHROEDER-DEVRIENT. Max Unger.   (M
An account has been found of the rehearsal of 'Fidelio' for its performance in November 1822 (TK III 83) written about 1845 by Schroeder-Devrient herself. Her account differs from the familiar one of Schindler principally in

the statements that Beethoven himself conducted the entire dress rehearsal, that he was present at the performance of November 3rd, and that at the end of the performance (or, at the latest, the next day) he extended his thanks to the young soprano.   18$_1$ [1926] 438

DAS BILD DES IRDISCHEN BEETHOVEN. Walther Nohl.   (A)
  The composer's appearance, dress and customs as described by contemporaries.
                                           18$_1$ [1926] 444

ENGELBERT HUMPERDINCK ALS BEETHOVEN-FORSCHER. Max Friedlaender.   (B)
  Goethe's poem 'Bundeslied,' which was used as the text for Op. 122, was also set by Beethoven to the melody of the fourth (variations) movement of the Septet Op. 20. This setting, which Humperdinck found in the Beethoven-Haus in Bonn, is given.   18$_1$ [1926] 450

LICHT- UND BEWEGUNGSREGIE IN DER OPER (STUDIEN AM GEFANGENENCHOR IM "FIDELIO").   (C)
    Friedrich Stichtenoth.
  With the thought that the effectiveness of any stage presentation is enhanced by lack of realism and imitation of the everyday, the author recommends that the Prisoner's Chorus be mimed by draped and masked dancers in a highly stylized gesture dance.   18$_2$ [1926] 817

BEETHOVEN (ZUM 26. MÄRZ 1827). Hermann Abert.   (D)
  Centenary tribute.   19$_1$ [1927] 385

BEETHOVEN, DER METAPHYSIKER. Willi Hille.   (E)
  The deafness which so completely drove Beethoven's consciousness into itself resulted in a metaphysical conception of music exemplified in the works beyond Op. 100, notably in such cases as the introduction to the last movement of Op. 106 and the arietta of Op. 111.   19$_1$ [1927] 389

DER UNBEKANNTE BEETHOVEN. Walther Krug.   (F)
  The relatively small proportion of Beethoven's output which makes up the overwhelming bulk of his performances is characterized by intense emotionalism.   19$_1$ [1927] 393

DIE ENTDECKER BEETHOVENS IN FRANKREICH. J. G. Prod'homme.   (G)
  Prior to 1800, Beethoven's name had not appeared in Paris, either in a journal or on a concert program. In that year Heinrich Simrock opened a Paris branch of the publishing firm which his brother Nicholas had founded in Bonn in 1792. As late as 1826, only the First and Second Symphonies and single movements of some of the others had been performed, chiefly by Habeneck. The overtures to Prometheus and Fidelio were heard in 1814 and 1824 respectively. Schindler states that by 1832 all of the symphonies, as well as the overtures, concertos and some of the vocal works, had for some time been in the repertoire of the Societe des Concerts. A French edition of Op. 109 in 1822 was followed shortly by Opp. 110 and 111 and by other piano compositions. From 1827 on the chamber music began to be heard. Fidelio was first performed in 1829.   19$_1$ [1927] 400

BEETHOVEN: DER "ROMANTISCHE" ERFÜLLER "KLASSISCHE" RATIONALISTIK. Frank Wohlfahrt.   (H)
  In its form, Beethoven's music is the necessary result of the classical concept foreshadowed by Haydn and Mozart. In Beethoven, however, music reached a development in form, in harmonic freedom, and in its use of materials, to the point which, in its further use, is known as romanticism.   19$_1$ [1927] 412

BEETHOVENS KRANKHEIT UND ENDE (EINE MEDIZINISCHE STUDIE). Richard Loewe.   (I)
  During Beethoven's youth his health was good (but see TD I 218). In his 28th year early otiosclerosis manifested itself, and about the same time Beethoven suffered a dysenteric or typhous illness resulting in ulceration and subsequent cicatrization of the intestine. Though these conditions resulted in definite hypochondria, Beethoven's health was, in general, robust until his last two years. As regards liquor, Beethoven was by no means abstemious (see TK III 204), but there is no convincing evidence that the liver ailment can be attributed to the family vice of excessive drinking. The symptoms described in Beethoven's letter of May 13th 1825 to Dr. Braunhofer (KS II 368) mark the approximate time of the onset of the ultimately fatal liver cirrhosis. As is typical of the disease, symptoms did not become grave for more than a year -- until his sojourn in Gneixendorf in the fall of 1826. The judgment and competence of Dr. Wawruch, who attended him in this illness, cannot fairly be impugned. The findings of the autopsy point definitely to cirrhosis of the liver, not to cancer and not to syphilis, either congenital or acquired.
                                           19$_1$ [1927] 418

EIN NEUENTDECKTER BEETHOVEN-BRIEF. Karl Joseph Friedrich-Grünhain.   (A)
    A letter from Teplitz dated July 24th 1812 to Breitkopf & Härtel, requesting a presentation copy of the Six Songs
    Op. 75 for Beethoven to give to Goethe, whom he had first met a few days before. This letter supplements a similar
    request of April 4th 1812 (KS I 250) for the Three Songs Op. 83. 19_2 [1927] 465

WAS UNS DURCH BEETHOVENS VORZEITIGEN TOD VERLORENGING. Konrad Huschke.   (B)
    Beethoven's death at the age of 56, when his creative powers were at their height, probably deprived us of the following
    works (which had been sketched, planned or discussed): a Tenth Symphony (wholly instrumental) and an Eleventh Sym-
    phony (probably with chorus in the last two movements); music to Faust; an oratorio 'The Triumph of the Cross' ('Der
    Sieg des Kreuzes') and probably other oratorios; a Mass and a Requiem; an opera 'Melusine' on a text by Grillparzer,
    and possibly others on Macbeth and King Lear; an Overture on the name 'Bach.' After the last sonatas and the Diabelli
    Variations, there is little indication of more piano music planned, except for a Sonata for Four Hands which had been
    sketched. One movement of a Quintet had been completed, and he might have taken up the sketches for a Vcl sonata
    ('Pastorale') which he made in 1815. 19_2 [1927] 470

BEETHOVENS HOMER-STUDIEN. Hans Boettcher.   (C)
    Beethoven's interest in Homer is shown by his heavily-annotated copy of the Odyssey, by references in the conversation
    books and in correspondence, by fragments of Homer's verse copied in Beethoven's journal, by studies of his prosody,
    and by at least two sketches in which words of Homer were set to music.
                                    19_2 [1927] 478

ZUR STRITTIGEN TEXTSTELLE IN DER IX. SINFONIE. Max Unger.   (D)
    The passage in question appears on pp. 260-63 of the GA. It was originally engraved in 1826 from an inserted sheet
    (in the hand of a copyist) which quite possibly had not been carefully checked by Beethoven. In the previous appear-
    ances of this text (GA pp. 199-200; 231-32) the word "streng" is used as in Schiller's poem, but at this third appear-
    ance the word "frech" was used instead in the first edition (though not in the GA). The author is of the opinion that
    this change of word was a copyist's error which Beethoven overlooked. (See also 'Neues Beethoven-Jahrbuch' 2 [1925]
    162; 3 [1927] 103; 4 [1930] 133; 5 [1933] 7) 19_2 [1927] 486

BEETHOVEN, BADEN, BIEDERMEIER. Alfred von Ehrmann.   (E)
    A brief comment on the uninspired architecture of the city in which Beethoven spent many of his summers.
                                    19_2 [1927] 494

BEETHOVEN IM ROMAN UND IN DER NOVELLE. Paul Bülow.   (F)
    A listing and brief summary of some twenty novels and stories in which Beethoven is a principal figure. (See also
    5_1 [1905] 258; 10_1 [1910] 339) 19_2 [1927] 497

BEETHOVENS GROSSE FUGE OPUS 133. Hermann Scherchen.   (G)
    Replacement of the fugue finale of Op. 130 by the present last movement changed the work from a dual form (with
    the last movement contrasting with and balancing the first five) to a form of relatively unified style and content. The
    Grosse Fuge itself is analyzed in detail from the standpoint of its comparability with the standard sonata form of five
    sections. 20_1 [1928] 401

DER FREMDKÖRPER IM ERSTEN SATZ DER EROICA. August Halm.   (H)
    The 'new theme' which is introduced in the development section of the first movement of the Eroica (mm. 284ff,
    322ff) is in fact a countermelody to the disguised version of the principal theme which each time occurs as its bass
    and which immediately after the second appearance of the 'new theme' (mm. 330ff) receives a brief independent
    development. 21_2 [1929] 481

ZWEI UNBEKANNTE BRIEFE BEETHOVENS. Alfred Lorenz.   (I)
    Reprint from the 'Süddeutsche Monatshefte' 27 No. 1 of letter without date (certainly from the last few years of
    Beethoven's life) to Steiner: "Geld aufzunehmen ist nicht, voriges Jahr musste ich . . ." in which Beethoven pro-
    tests at Steiner's demands on all his compositions in connection with money which Beethoven owed. Reprint from
    the 'Generalanzeiger für Bonn' of December 14th 1929 of a letter of January 4th 1814 to Prince Lobkowitz:
    "Jene Schritte, wozu ein dringendes Bedürfnis, welches . . ." in which Beethoven expresses lack of confidence in
    the basis on which the Prince proposes to carry out his responsibilities under the annuity agreement.
                                    $22_{[?]}$ [1930] 398

"VESTAS FEUER" -- BEETHOVENS ERSTER OPERNPLAN. Raoul Biberhofer.   (J
    The sketches which Nottebohm (NB I 82) gives for an uncompleted opera represent Beethoven's draft of the opening

scene (not the closing scene as stated by Nottebohm) of an opera 'Vesta's Fire' to a book furnished by Schikaneder and presumably written by him. When Beethoven dropped this project in favor of 'Fidelio,' the libretto was set by Joseph Weigl; the opera received 17 performances between August and November 1805.

$$22_1 \; [1930] \; 409$$

EIN VERGESSENES GOETHELIED VON BEETHOVEN. Otto Erich Deutsch.   (A)
    An early version of 'Neue Liebe neues Leben' (Op. 75 No. 2) was published about 1807 by Simrock, together with two other songs, in an edition apparently overlooked by Nottebohm (NV, top of p. 178). Since these other songs were written in 1791-95, this first version of the Goethe song (a sketch of which is referred to in NB II 481) may well date from earlier than 1800.

$$23_1 \; [1930] \; 19$$

AN ANCESTRAL BEETHOVEN HOUSE.   (B)
    The house at Steenstrasse 11 in Malines in which Grandfather Ludwig and his father and grandfather lived has been demolished.

$$23_{[?]} [1930] \; 238$$

WAR GOETHE MUSIKALISCH? Emil Voigt.   (C)
    "He had at least reached the point of recognizing the greatness and sublimity of music, but he observed the flowering gardens of Polyhymnia from afar."

$$23_1 \; [1931] \; 321$$

EIN NEUER BEETHOVENFUND IN ANTON SCHINDLERS NACHLASS. Reinhold Zimmermann.   (D)
    Fifty-six pages from conversation books are transcribed for the first time.

$$23_1 \; [1931] \; 401$$

NEUE BEETHOVEN-FUNDE. Marie Mirska.   (E)
    A letter (in French) of January 25th 1823 to Prince Galitsin, acknowledging his letter of November 9th 1822, offering to write the quartets which the Prince requested for 50 ducats each, and stating that the first quartet would be ready by the end of February or, at the latest, by mid-March. (See TD V 552) A letter of May 26th 1824 to Prince Galitsin, referring to academies held for Beethoven (May 7th and 23rd 1824), promising all three of the quartets, and mentioning his plan of sending several of his newest works (Missa Solemnis, Ninth Symphony, etc.) to St. Petersburg. (See TD V 560) Leaf from a 'Stammbuch' for Marja Szymanowska, written by Beethoven about 1818.

$$24_2 \; [1932] \; 481$$

BEETHOVEN IN FRANKREICH. Friedrich Baser.   (F)
    Beethoven's youthful training in the court of the son of Marie Antoinette brought him at a formative age under the influence of French musical culture: Gossec, Gretry, Cherubini, Mehul, etc. This influence was continued by his contact with Rode, Kreutzer, Baron de Tremont, etc. Habeneck did what he could to further the acceptance of Beethoven's music in Paris, and he himself played first violin in performances of the chamber music. Potpourris and single symphonic movements preceded the more general acceptance of the orchestral and stage works, which followed the first complete performance of the Seventh Symphony in 1826 and of 'Fidelio' by a company from Vienna in 1828. Liszt and his group became a powerfully favorable influence; the writings and concerts of Berlioz and Wagner completed the acceptance of Beethoven as a supremely great composer. The chauvinism which followed the Franco-Prussian War brought resistance to Beethoven as a German musican, but Colonne, Lamoreux, Cortot and Rolland fought this trend with vigor. (See also 19_1 [1927] 400)

$$25_1 \; [1932] \; 166$$

BEARBEITUNGEN EIGENER WERKE SEITENS DER KOMPONISTEN. Wilhelm Altmann.   (G)
    The work of many composers in arranging their own compositions for groups other than those originally written for is discussed. Beethoven's arrangements include:

Certain: E major Pf Sonata Op. 14 No. 1 as String Quartet in F major
           Quintet for Pf and Wind Instruments Op. 16 as Pf Quartet (the author makes the questionable statement
               that Mozart did the same with K. 452).
           Septet Op. 20 as Clarinet Trio Op. 38
           Op. 4 used as a basis for String Quintet Op. 103
           Pf Trio Op. 1 No. 3 as String Quintet Op. 104
           Grosse Fuge for String Quartet Op. 133 as Fugue for Pf Four Hands Op. 134
           The author does not mention the certainly genuine arrangement of the Violin Concerto Op. 61 as a Pf Concerto

BEARBEITUNGEN EIGENER WERKE, etc., (Continued)
    Doubtful: The arrangement of the Second Symphony Op. 36 as a Pf Trio was at least made under Beethoven's
               supervision.
          ꞌ   The arrangement of the String Trio Op. 8 for Pf and Viola Op. 42 is probably genuine.

    Spurious: Beethoven stated publicly (TK I 228) that the arrangements for String Quartet of the Septet Op. 20 and
               the First Symphony Op. 21 were not by him.
               The arrangements of the Trio Serenade Op. 25 for Pf and Flute Op. 42 and of the String Trio Op. 3 for
               Pf and Vcl Op. 63 are certainly spurious. 26_1 [1934] 348

BEETHOVEN, DER REVOLUTIONÄR. Gustav Ernest.   (A
    Radio broadcast. 26_1 [1934] 354

FREUDE, SCHÖNER GÖTTERFUNKEN . . . Joseph Müller-Blattau.   (B
    Schiller's poem, published in 1786, immediately took the fancy of musicians. The first composition based on it
    appeared the same year, and in 1792 a four-part setting of considerable merit was made by K. F. Zelters. There
    is reason to believe that in 1792 Beethoven had told friends that he planned to set the verses. In 1812 he sketched
    a theme for an overture on this poem (NB I 41). The author gives the melodic line of settings of the hymn by sev-
    eral other composers, including Schubert. 27_1 [1934] 16

EIN BEETHOVEN-FUND? Wilhelm Mayer.   (C
    Quoted from 'Frankfurter Zeitung' of June 16th 1934. A score of the Choral Fantasy Op. 80 recently discovered in
    Munich is probably partly in Beethoven's hand. $26_{[?]}$[1934] 867

BEETHOVENS KONVERSATIONSHEFTE. Ernst Jerosch.   (D
    The transcription and annotation of the conversation books by Walther Nohl opens to the world what is perhaps the
    most important single source of information on many aspects of the composer's life and character.
                                           27_2 [1935] 881

DIE WAHRHEIT ÜBER DEN VATER LUDWIG VAN BEETHOVENS. Heinz-Ernst Pfeiffer.   (E
    As an argument against the measures to insure racial purity has been used the generally accepted belief that the
    great Beethoven was the son of a mere "whiskey-tenor." Archives of the Director of the Court Theatre in Bonn for
    the years 1778-84 which have recently become available disclose instead that Johann von Beethoven was an inspired
    artist who labored for decades to build up a German national theatre in the important cultural city of Bonn. During
    his boyhood he must have taken part in the theatrical activities of the Jesuit Gymnasium which he attended (though
    his name does not appear in any of the records of their theatrical performances). In his twentieth year (1760) he
    formed his own theatrical troupe, small in numbers but mighty in ambition, playing in competition with the foreign
    groups brought to Bonn by the Elector. As years went on, the training and leadership which Johann gave these players
    increased their ability, scope and prestige, but in 1774 Chancellor Belderbusch, under the influence of the Freemasons,
    abolished Johann's troupe entirely. The personal hostility of Belderbusch followed Johann for the rest of his life to sti-
    fle all further manifestations of his talent and his zeal for the advancement of things German. "Every outstanding char-
    acteristic which later raised his son Ludwig to lofty heights had already shown itself in the father."
                                       28_1 [1935] 13

VOM KUHLAU-BACH-KANON BEETHOVENS. Walther Nohl.   (F
    The author transcribes the pages still extant from the conversation books which were used during the dinner party of
    September 2nd 1825 (TK III 204) to show that these pages give no indication of a Bach canon by Kuhlau, and to show
    that the canon by Beethoven (KS II 400) might well have been born under the conditions referred to by Beethoven in
    his letter of September 3rd. 28_1 [1935] 166

MARCHESI BESUCHT BEETHOVEN? Walther Nohl.   (G
    A visitor to Beethoven towards the end of September, whose remarks appear briefly in the conversation books but who
    has not been identified with certainty, might have been the famous male soprano Luigi Marchesi.
                                        28_1 [1936] 356

SCHERING CONTRA BEETHOVEN. Friedrich W. Herzog.   (H
    Polemic against Schering. 29_1 [1936] 187

STIELERS BEETHOVEN-BILDNIS. Walther Nohl.   (I
    The painting of Beethoven by Karl Joseph Stieler (1781-1858) is perhaps the most effective of all portraits in showing

the composer as inspired from another world. Contemporaries referred to it as a very faithful likeness. Excerpts
from the conversation books are given which mention incidents concerned with the making of this portrait.

29_1 [1937] 327

ANTON SCHINDLER ALS BEETHOVENS SCHÜLER. Walther Nohl.   (A)
Quotations from the conversation books to show that Schindler studied a considerable number of Beethoven's works
(Pf Sonatas, Trio Op. 97, Vcl Sonatas Op. 102) with him. (See 30_1 [1937] 44)

29_2 [1937] 685

LUDWIG VAN BEETHOVEN WIDMET DIE "NEUNTE" DEM PREUSSISCHEN KÖNIG. Walther Nohl.   (B)
Beethoven's letters of December 20th 1822 to Ries (KS II 213) and of July 1st to the Archduke Rudolph (KS II 263)
state specifically that the Ninth Symphony was being written for the London Philharmonic Society, to whom the
dedication would naturally fall. A notation in a conversation book of April 1824 indicates that instead Beethoven
was undecided between Ries and the King of Prussia as the recipient of the dedication. A letter of January 28th
1826 to Schott (KS II 418) states: "With regard to the dedication of the Symphony, I will let you know my decision before long. It was settled to dedicate it to the Czar Alexander, but circumstances have occurred which cause
this delay." The decision not to offer the dedication to the Czar may have been due to Beethoven's unwillingness to
follow protocol in clearing the matter through the Foreign Office. The ultimate decision to dedicate the Symphony
to the relatively unmusical King Friedrich Wilhelm III (TK III 233; KS II 448) was apparently made because of Beethoven's desire to receive a royal decoration. In his anger and disappointment at receiving instead only a ring with a
semi-precious stone (valued at 300 fl. paper, corresponding to a 1933 value of approx. $450) Beethoven presented the
autograph to Schindler. Quotations from the conversation books, letters, etc. are given bearing on various aspects of
this dedication. 30_1 [1937] 38

WERK 29 ODER 31? Carl Heinzen.   (C)
Schindler's reference to "three Pf sonatas Op. 29" (cited in 29_2 [1937] 689) is not without foundation: the sonatas
now known as Op. 31 Nos. 1 and 2 were originally published as Op. 29, and Op. 31 No. 3 first appeared as Op. 33.

30_1 [1937] 44

WAS FESSELTE BEETHOVEN AN SEINER FIDELIO-DICHTUNG? Friedrich Baser.   (D)
Beethoven's enthusiasm about the 'Fidelio' story, with all the difficulties of the libretto upon which he had to work,
was due to its combination of the story of conjugal fidelity with the atmosphere of terror which had become of artistic importance as the result of the French Revolution. 30_1 [1937] 45

BEETHOVEN IN DER MILITÄRMUSIK. Erich Schenk.   (E)
The period in which Beethoven lived and the nature of his temperament led quite naturally to the writing of many
works and movements of a martial nature (e.g., his early compositions for wind band, the Funeral Marches of the
Pf Sonata Op. 26 and the Eroica, parts of 'Fidelio,' etc.). A list is given of the arrangements of Beethoven compositions for wind band which have been made during the past half century or so.

30_1 [1937] 159

ANTON HALMS BEZIEHUNGEN ZU BEETHOVEN. Walther Nohl.   (F)
Excerpts from the conversation books and from accounts of members of Beethoven's circle regarding his relations
with Anton Halm (1789-1872), pianist and composer. 30_1 [1938] 230

BEETHOVEN UND DAS WIENER AUFGEBOT. Alfred Orel.   (G)
The circumstances leading to the composition of the 'Abschiedsgesang' and the 'Kriegslied' of 1796-97 (NV p. 177)
are given in much detail. Beethoven had been appointed Capellmeister of the Vienna Corps of Volunteers in 1796,
though his duties were apparently of an honorary nature which did not require his absence from Vienna nor his appearance in uniform. 30_2 [1938] 458

WIE VIELE FASSUNGEN VON BEETHOVENS MARZELLINEN-ARIE GIBT ES? Willy Hess.   (H)
No less than six versions of this aria (No. 2 in 'Fidelio') are known: two written and discarded before the first performance in 1805, the version then used, the slight modification of this version for the 1814 revision, and a still
further change apparently made after the revival. An abbreviated version of the 'Leonora No. 2' Overture, presumably made by Beethoven for the 1806 revival before he wrote the 'Fidelio' Overture, has been discovered. Two
numbers from the opera were taken from earlier compositions: one from the Trauerkantate, the other from the studies
for the opera 'Vestas Feuer' which Beethoven abandoned to start work on Fidelio. (See also 'Neues Beethoven-Jahrbuch'
7 [1937] 116) 30_2 [1938] 515

BEETHOVEN'S "LEONORE."   Friedrich M. Herzog.   (A)
   Comments on the difference between the 1805 version (as restored by Prager) and the familiar 'Fidelio' of 1814.
                                 $30_{[?]}$ [1938] 626

FERDINAND RIES: ZUM HUNDERTSTEN TODESTAGE VON BEETHOVENS MEISTERSCHÜLER.   Gustav Funcke.   (B)
   Biographical sketch. 30_2 [1938] 664

DIE BADENEN AUFENTHALTE BEETHOVENS.   Alfred von Ehrmann.   (C)
   Beethoven stayed in Baden at various times from 1803 or 1804 (or possibly even earlier) until 1825. This paper is
   an attempt to clear up certain points left unsettled by Frimmel ('Neues Beethoven Jahrbuch'4 [1930] 39).
                                 30_2 [1938] 748

BEETHOVEN'S 'BOLERO A SOLO.'   Willy Hess.   (D)
   The 'Bolero a solo' described by Kalischer (2_1 [1902] 431) was in fact the early version of a song setting for Thomson
   from 1810 or 1816? (see 'Der Bär' (1927): facsimile facing page 160.) The difference between the Kalischer version
   and this revised version are given in detail. 30_2 [1938] 820

BEETHOVEN UND SEIN ARTZ ANTON BRAUNHOFER.   Walther Nohl.   (E)
   After a long succession of physicians, Beethoven put himself in the hands of Dr. Braunhofer, who proved more successful than the others in securing Beethoven's obedience to his instructions, and who attended him until the onset of his
   illness at the end of 1826. Schindler says that Dr. Braunhofer first attended Beethoven in 1824, but from the conversation books it appears probable that he was the physician who cared for Beethoven in April 1823.
                                 30_2 [1938] 823

BEETHOVENS MUTTER.   Josef Pohé.   (F)
   The grave of Beethoven's mother, unidentified for more than a century, was finally located, and in 1932 the body
   was given a more fitting burial. (See also 'Zeitschrift für Musik' JG 102 [1935] 1216)
                                 30_2 [1938] 829

UNBEKANNTE KLAVIERBAGATELLEN BEETHOVENS.   Willy Hess.   (G)
   A discussion of the works for pianoforte listed as Nos. 39-51 incl. and 245-46 in 'Neues Beethoven Jahrbuch' 7 [1937] 111,
   128, and of the 17 transcriptions which Beethoven made for pianoforte of orchestral and chamber works.
                                 31_1 [1939] 312

BEETHOVEN-WOHNUNGEN.   Willy Brix.   (H)
   An account of the author's difficulty in locating the various houses in Baden where Beethoven had lived, and an expression of joy that the Gauleiter of the Lower Danube is "setting to work vigorously to drive Jews and other godless
   people from our temples." 31_1 [1939] 382

BEETHOVENS OPERNPLÄNE.   Walther Nohl.   (I)
   An outline is given of the pursuit of a satisfactory opera book which Beethoven continued from the completion of
   'Fidelio' (or even before) to within a few months of his death. A dozen or more poets and subjects were vainly
   considered. 31_2 [1939] 741

EIN TAG AM KRANKENBETT BEETHOVENS.   Walther Nohl.   (J)
   A somewhat fictionalized narrative, based on the conversation books for February 4th-5th, 1827.
                                 32_1 [1940] 188

BEETHOVENS TANZKOMPOSITIONEN.   Willy Hess.   (K)
   A tabulation is given of the 13 sets of dance pieces and the 16 separate compositions in dance form (8 of the former
   and 10 of the latter being in the GA). The author attempts to show a cyclic relationship of tonalities within each of
   the six sets of 12 dances for orchestra (2 sets of deutsche Tänze, 2 of Minuets, a set of Contradances and a set of
   Ecossaises). 32_1 [1940] 191

BEETHOVEN AND GRILLPARZER.   Egon v. Komorzynski.   (L)
   Beethoven was strongly attracted to the poet as an artist, not merely as a possible source of the long sought opera
   book. His name had appeared frequently in the conversation books for several years before the two men met in 1823.
                                 32_2 [1940] 265

GERHARD VON BREUNING ALS KNABE. Walther Nohl. (A)
    An amplification of 'Aus dem Schwarzspanierhause' from Beethoven's conversation books.
$$32_2 \; [1940] \; 374$$

BEETHOVENS "KANONE." Georg Schünemann. (B)
    The Military March (GA Ser. 2 No. 15) was written in 1815 (not 1816) as the result of a request which Franz Xaver Embel, magistrate and an officer of the artillery corps, sent to the composer on a drawing of a field artillery cannon which is reproduced herewith.
$$32_2 \; [1940] \; 377$$

GRUNDSÄTZLICHES ÜBER REVISIONSAUSGABEN VON BEETHOVENS WERKEN. Max Unger. (C)
    The author points out the problems which face the editor of an 'Urtext-Gesamtausgabe' of Beethoven's works, with instances of specific puzzling passages.
$$33_1 \; [1940] \; 52$$

IST DIE GESAMTAUSGABE VON BEETHOVENS WERKEN VOLLSTÄNDIG? Willy Hess. (D)
    A list is given of the more important works which do not appear in the GA. This list is based closely on the author's article in 'Neues Beethoven Jahrbuch' 7 [1937] 104. A brief allegretto (previously published in journals not readily accessible) written on February 18th 1821 for F. Piringer is appended.
$$33_1 \; [1940] \; 81$$

24 UNBEKANNTE ITALIENISCHE A-CAPELLA-GESÄNGE BEETHOVENS. Willy Hess. (E)
    Of the 32 songs listed by Thayer (TV-264), Nos. 1-6, 16-22 and 26-31 are apparently genuine. No. 32 (GA Ser. 25 No. 271) is also genuine but is not a capella; in addition, five others are given by Nottebohm ('Beethoven Studien') and by Nohl are to be included with the Italian a capella songs. No. 28 of TV-264 is here published for the first time.
$$33_2 \; [1941] \; 240$$

FIDELIO-AUFFÜHRUNGEN UND GROSSE LEONOREN-OUVERTÜRE. Rudolf Hartmann. (F)
    There is no place in a performance of the opera in which the Leonore Overture No. 3 can be fitted with artistic verity. The only proper place for the performance of this overture is in the concert hall.
$$33_2 \; [1941] \; 342$$

BEETHOVENS LETZTE BRIEFE UND UNTERSCHRIFTEN. Max Unger. (G)
    The difficulties of writing an accurate and complete Beethoven biography are many: a large proportion of the composer's letters are undated, and many of these do not show the name of the addressee; his handwriting is extraordinarily difficult to decipher (resulting in some cases in ludicrous misreadings); the biographical writings of his younger contemporaries (e. g., Schindler, Ries, and to a lesser extent Wegeler and Gerhard von Breuning) are to a considerable extent misleading or definitely incorrect, both as to chronology and in statements of fact.

    Specifically, there are various errors and ambiguities in Schindler's account of Beethoven's last days, in his letter to Schott of April 12th 1827 (KS II 474) and elsewhere: The statement that after receiving the Sacrament on March 24th, Beethoven said: "Plaudit, amici; comoedia finita est" is contradicted not only by Gerhard von Breuning (who was present) and by Hüttenbrenner on the authority of J. B. Jenger and Therese van Beethoven (who also were present) (Ley: 'Beethoven als Freund' p. 199; see also TK III 304ff), but is further contradicted by Schindler himself in his letter of March 24th 1827 to Moscheles (Ley, p. 236): "He realized that his end was near, for yesterday he said to me and Herr von Breuning: 'Plaudite etc.'" The assignment of the C sharp minor Quartet which Schindler sent to Schott with his letter (KS II 476) was not Beethoven's last bit of writing, as repeated from Schindler by TD V 489 and by TK III 307. The correctness of the date which this assignment bears (March 20th 1827) may safely be assumed from the fact that it was witnessed by Imperial Court Councillor Stephan von Breuning, whose legal mind would certainly not countenance the incorrect dating of a deathbed document. The statement attributed to J. N. Hummel that Beethoven's last written words were a note to Schott three days before his death in thanks for wine must also be ruled out.

    It is probable that Beethoven signed at least four documents after the assignment to Schott: (a) A letter dated March 21st to the banking house of Stieglitz & Co. in St. Petersburg regarding payments due from Count Galitsin (TD V 570). This was Beethoven's last letter. Note that, disregarding this letter, TD V 472 refers to Beethoven's letter of March 18th to Moscheles as his last. (b) The codicil to the Will, dated March 23rd (KS II 474). (c) The transfer of the guardianship of Nephew Karl to Stephan von Breuning (TK III 304), a document which is now lost. (d) According to Gerhard von Breuning's recollection (though after fifty years he was uncertain of many details of this most nerve-wracking experience of a 13-year-old boy) the letter of January 3rd 1827 to Dr. J. B. Bach (KS II 461), presented as Beethoven's last will, was signed at this time. The original of this letter has been lost, so that the accuracy of this statement cannot be checked from the letter itself. Some one of these last three documents (very likely the letter to Bach) bore Beethoven's last signature.
$$34 \; [1942] \; 153$$

ZU BEETHOVENS VOLKSLIEDERBEARBEITUNGEN.   Max Unger.   (A)
   A review of Schünemann's 'Neues Volksliederheft,' containing 22 hitherto unpublished arrangements by Beethoven
   of National Songs with accompaniment for Pf, Vln and Vcl. Beethoven's interest in national songs was shown by
   the fact that, between the arrangements for Thomson and his independent writing, he made more than two hundred
   arrangements of this kind.   34 [1942] 210

BEETHOVEN AND B. SCHOTT'S SÖHNE.   Max Unger.   (B)
   The firm of B. Schott's Söhne was founded in 1770, and from 1809 the two active partners were Bernhard Schott's
   sons Andreas and Johann Joseph. The first letter from Beethoven to this firm was dated March 10th 1824. It was
   first published in TD V 102, and here is given with minor corrections. In this letter Beethoven offers Opp. 123,
   125, and 127. Letters from Schott dated March 14th, April 10th and April 27th are referred to (for these letters
   and others see TD V 106ff). Then followed Beethoven's letter of May 20th 1824 (KS II 312) enclosing "a letter
   written by a businessman" (KS II 313) suggesting price and terms for the sale of Opp. 123 and 125. Schott's reply
   of May 27th (now probably lost) accepted Beethoven's offer. Beethoven's next letter of July 3rd 1824 (KS II 322)
   was answered on July 19th (TD V 110). The further correspondence of the next two and a half years is summarized.

                     Following dates of publication from records of the firm

                     Opp. 126, 128   beginning of 1825
                          121b, 122   23 July 1825
                          124   7 December 1825
                          127 (parts)   March 1826
                          125   28 August 1826
                          123, 131   April 1827

   Letters of November 28th 1826 (referred to in TD V 395) and December 18th 1826 (given in abbreviated form in
   TD V 396) are given in full, and the correspondence of this period is summarized and discussed. A letter written
   by Schott on March 29th 1827 (of course, in ignorance of Beethoven's death) is given. The relationship between
   Beethoven and the firm of Schott was on a most friendly basis of mutual high esteem, as indicated by excerpts
   given from Beethoven's letters. This cordial relationship lasted until Beethoven's death, the only rift (a temporary one) being referred to in Beethoven's letter of August 10th 1825 to Holz (KS II 395).
                                                          34 [1942] 285

DER "FIDELIO-MARSCH" UND SEIN ZEITMASS.   Eugen Schmitz.   (C)
   Although the March (No. 6) is marked 'Vivace,' dramaturgic and historic reasons alike indicate a tempo not to
   exceed quarter note = 72 - 76.   34 [1942] 298

VERDI UND WAGNER ÜBER DEN SCHLUSSCHOR VON BEETHOVENS NEUNTER.   Alfred Weidemann.   (D)
   "Beethoven's Ninth Symphony: a masterful work in the first three movements, a very poor job in the last" (Verdi
   in a letter to Ricordi). "Considering the Ninth Symphony as a work of art, the last movement with chorus is definitely the weakest part" (Wagner in a letter to Liszt).   34 [1942] 361

BEETHOVENS KONVERSATIONSHEFTE ALS BIOGRAPHISCHE QUELLE.   Max Unger.   (E)
   A lengthy study inspired by the publication of the first volume of Schünemann's edition of the conversation books
   which includes all the books now extant from the period February 1818 - March 1820. The point is made that the
   conversation books represent for the most part conversations held away from Beethoven's lodging, since at home he
   usually used a slate. The chief matters recorded in the books considered in this volume are Beethoven's guardianship of Nephew Karl, Beethoven's financial matters (leading to the purchase of the bank shares in July 1819), his
   relations with Joseph Carl Bernard, and his health. These and various other matters referred to in the conversation
   books are discussed by the author in great detail, partly to give background for the study of the books and partly to
   correct current knowledge of incidents of Beethoven's life through new evidence available from the books. This
   article is a very rich contribution to Beethoven biography for the period 1818-20.
                                                          34 [1942] 377; 35 [1942] 37

DIE FERMATE IN BEETHOVENS SINFONIEN.   Eugen Schmitz.   (F)
   In baroque music the fermata was often used in the following places: At the close of a cadential ornament (the only
   instance of this in the Beethoven Symphonies is the oboe cadenza in the Fifth Symphony); and at the end of a composition in place of the word "Fine" (thus used at the end of the 2nd, 3rd, 6th, 8th and 9th Symphonies). All other
   uses of the fermata by Beethoven are for its normal purpose: to extend to an indefinite degree a rhythmic value
   (note or pause), though the author observes that sometimes in baroque music the fermata is an instruction to shorten

a rhythmic value, especially in the case of a general pause, and that in the Classical period a more or less exact doubling of duration was usually intended. The discussion here given leads to results such as the following:

(close of the first movement of the Second Symphony)

(opening of the Fifth Symphony)

The author points out that this last gives an eight-measure phrase which therefore is in symmetry with the next phrases, and cites this fact as explaining Beethoven's addition of the extra half note after the first edition of the parts had been engraved. (NOTE by DWM. Actually the addition of this note introduces an extra measure which throws the passage out of symmetry.) In the last measures of the Fourth Symphony a similar interpretation has a similar result.

(last movement of First Symphony)

(opening of Second Symphony)

Of the Beethoven Symphonies, fermatas are most common in the Fifth, then the Ninth; next (though not nearly as many) the Third -- all works of great emotion. They are relatively uncommon in the First (last movement only), Second, Sixth, Seventh and Eighth. The First, Fourth and Eighth show the use of the fermata in works of a humorous nature.

34 [1942] 386

MUSIK IM KRIEGE

100 JAHRE PARISER BEETHOVENKULT. Reinhold Zimmermann.   (A)
   Habeneck, son of a German born bandmaster in the French service, was induced to undertake the performance of Beethoven's music by Sina, formerly second violin in the Schuppanzigh Quartet. The first concert (9 March 1828) opened with the Eroica; at the next concert the Eroica was repeated, and the Violin Concerto Op. 61 was performed with Baillot as soloist. The third concert included the Egmont Overture and the C minor Symphony.
1 [1943] 86

BEETHOVENS KONVERSATIONSHEFTE ALS BIOGRAPHISCHE QUELLE. Max Unger.   (B)
   Extensive commentaries on the second and third volumes of Schünemann's edition of the conversation books (see 'Die Musik' 34 [1942] 377; 35 [1942] 37).
1 [1943] 87,209; 2 [1944] 144

BEETHOVENS MILITÄRMÄRSCHE. Max Unger.   (C)
   Among the compositions which could properly be classed as "military marches by Beethoven" are the following:
      Kriegslied, the fifth of the eight numbers of the Ritterballet of 1791 (GA 25/286).
      Abschiedsgesang (15 November 1796) (GA 23/230).
      Kriegslied der Oesterreicher (14 April 1798) (GA 23/231).
      Yorcksche Marsch in F, at its first publication in 1809 called 'Marsch für S. K. Hoheit den Erzherzog Anton and 'Marsch für die böhmische Landwehr,' and ultimately grouped with several similar works as 'Zapfenstreich.' (GA 25/287 No. 1).
      Militärmarsch in F "zum Karrussel" (ca. 1809-10) (GA 25/287 No. 2).
      Marsch zur grossen Wachparade in D major (1815?). A certain Franz Xaver Embel, an official of the city and of the volunteer artillery, sent as a gift to Beethoven a large drawing of a cannon, and requested a march for "Turkish music." In early 1816 this March was the result. Beethoven considered it his best work of military music. It is very fully scored (33 instruments). A piano arrangement appeared in 1827; the score was first published in GA 2/15.

BEETHOVENS MILITÄRMÄRSCHE (Continued)
>Two Ecossaises (1810) (GA 25/290).
>Polonaise (1810) (GA 25/289).
>Third versions of the two marches in F, with trios (unpublished; H-7, 9). Possibly referred to in Beethoven's letter of 13 September 1822 to Peters (KS II 208).
>Turkish March from the 'Ruins of Athens' music Op. 113 No. 4 (1811). Based on the Variations Op. 76 (1809 or earlier). First published in 1846.
>Militärmarsch in C major (Zapfenstreich No. 2) (GA 25/288).

Excerpts are given from Peters' letter of 1823 rejecting various marches as well as three songs and a collection of bagatelles. The marches were later offered to Schott (KS II 366 No. 1066) and finally to Schlesinger (BusV p. 97). The Yorckscher Marsch was published in 1827. (Hess, NBJ 7 [1927] 106 says rescored by an unknown editor.) A facsimilie of Beethoven's arrangement of this march for piano is given.

1 [1943] 121

MEYERBEER CONTRA BEETHOVEN. Hans Joachim Moser.   (A)
>Marginal notes in Meyerbeer's copy of Op. 127, criticizing Beethoven's harmony, voice-leading, etc., are transcribed.   1 [1943] 131

BEETHOVENS VATERLÄNDISCHE MUSIK. Max Unger.   (B)
>Beethoven into his forties, if indeed not into his fifties, was very much a man of the world as well as an artist. This is shown by the subjects of various of his compositions. The Trauerkantate and the Erhebungskantate of the 19-year-old Beethoven, works in praise of two emperors, were his first two definitely patriotic compositions. His opposition to Napoleon's ambition, shown by his change in the dedication of the Eroica, is well known, but in 1796 and 1797 his two patriotic songs Abschiedsgesang and Kriegslied were directed against Napoleon. In the first (Artaria) edition of the Abschiedsgesang (and in no other edition) at the words "Lasst uns folgen . . ." at the beginning of the last stanza, "in the margin appear the words in the hand of the Empress herself: 'Für meine biedern Mitbürger.'" Anecdotes attribute to Beethoven various remarks in opposition to Napoleon. The impression which Napoleon made on him is indicated by a remark in a journal of October 1810, presumably regarding the Mass in C major Op. 86: "Die Messe könnte vielleicht noch dem Napoleon dedizirt werden."

>At the height of his production, Beethoven wrote a few works far from the tone of his symphonies: Wellington's Victory, the Yorcksche Marsch and the March for the Ruins of Athens, and he made extensive sketches for a cantata 'Europas Befreiungsstunde.' At this time he also wrote numbers for two patriotic singspiele, 'Germanias Wiedergeburt' and 'Kriegslied für die zum heiligen Kriege verbündeten deutschen Heere' (see KS I 315 No. 380). He also made a setting (now lost) of a text by Zacharias Werner beginning, "Gott mit uns, wir zieh'n in den heiligen Krieg!" That same summer and fall Beethoven worked on a number for a Huldigungskantate to greet the delegates of the Council of Vienna (see NB II 300; TK II 288), and also on the cantata 'Der glorreiche Augenblick' Op. 136, published in 1836 by Haslinger with a new text by Rochlitz: 'Preis der Tonkunst' (see NV p. 130). The cantata, with Wellington's Victory and the Seventh Symphony, was performed for the delegates on 29 November 1814. Finally, a bass solo with chorus and orchestra, 'Es ist vollbracht' GA 20/207c was written for a stage work, 'Die Ehrenpforten,' to celebrate the fall of Paris in 1815. An extended synopsis of the work is given from its review in the 'Allgemeine Musikalische Zeitung' 17 [1815] 34.

>Various solo songs from Beethoven's youth are of a patriotic nature: Der freie Mann (1795), Der Bardengeist (1813), Des Kriegers Abschied (1814), Der Mann vom Wort (1816). Of these, the second is of the greatest musical merit, though simple and brief. It was written to a text by C. R. Herrmann in November 1813 at the request of one of Beethoven's admirers, Dr. Johann Erichson, and published in the 'Musenalmanach für das Jahr 1814' issued by the lyricist. Des Kriegers Abschied was written in January 1814 at the request of Christian L. Reissig. The last of these songs was presumably planned as a supplement to the Wiener 'Allgemeine Musikalische Zeitung,' but Steiner instead issued it as Op. 99. Note that Merkenstein Op. 100 was also intended as a supplement. The music to King Stephan and to the Ruins of Athens (1811) may also be considered as of a patriotic nature. The same is of course true of the various military marches, of which the fifth (TV 284) "Marsch in geschwindem Tempo" is still unpublished.   1 [1943] 170

BEETHOVENS FRÜHE KLAVIERSONATEN. Johannes Haller.   (A)
   In the early sonatas the author hears much of string quartet and orchestral style.

                   1 [1944] 217

MUSIK-WOCHE

DIE FÜNF STILE BEETHOVENS. Roderich von Mojsisovics.   (B)
   The five styles which the author finds are: Classical, Naturalistic (Naturempfinden), Bourgeois (Biedermeierstil),
Romantic, and Transcendental (Hohenstil). These do not succeed one another in any fixed chronological succession,
but appear according to the subject matter or the conditions under which a given work was written.

                   3 [1935] No. 10, p. 1

WIE STAND BEETHOVEN ZU BACH UND HÄNDEL? Konrad Huschke.   (C)
   While Beethoven was acquainted with relatively little of Bach's music (he did not know the Cantatas, the Passions,
the B minor Mass, the organ works or the Brandenburg Concertos), the influence of Bach's music on him was very
great. Beethoven's regard for Händel (whose work he knew to a greater extent) was equally deep and perhaps more
noticeable in his music, especially in his late variations technique and choral writing.

                   3 [1935] No. 11, p. 17

DIE ENTZIFFERUNG DER "KONVERSATIONSHEFTE" BEETHOVENS. Walther Nohl.   (D)
   The difficulties of transcribing the conversation books include: identifying the writers; deciphering the pencilled
words which in many cases after the handling which they have received are almost effaced; following the line of
thought which leaps erratically from one subject to another, with only one side of the conversation to depend on.
The fact that pages have been torn out complicates this problem, and still further difficulty is encountered when
in a group conversation the book had apparently passed rapidly from hand to hand. The expression of thoughts as
written in the conversation books is so compressed that it is not safe to count on a few deciphered words as giving
the key to a passage: virtually every word must be worked out with a minimum of help from the context. If a
single word is misread, the sense of an entire conversation may be completely and perhaps ludicrously garbled.

                   3 [1935] No. 41, p. 2

BEETHOVEN AND BERLIN. Walther Nohl.   (E)
   An account of Beethoven's visit to Berlin in 1795, with discussion of the various people whom he met there.

                   3 [1935] No. 42, p. 3; No. 43, p. 4

HAT ROSSINI BEETHOVEN BESUCHT? Walther Nohl.   (F)
   In spite of the statements of Schindler and of Rossini himself, the author, from the testimony of the conversation
books, finds no reason to believe that Rossini and Beethoven ever met.

                   4 [1936] No. 1, p. 2

BEETHOVENS AHNEN IN FLÄMISCH-BRABANT. Ph. van Boxmeer.   (G)
   Summary of article in 'De Brabantsche Folklore' which is also summarized in 'Zeitschrift für Musik' JG 103 [1936] 7.

                   4 [1936] No. 5, p. 14

KEINE ZWISCHENAKTS MUSIK MEHR NACH DER "FIDELIO"-KERKERSZENE. Ernst Stolz.   (H)
   In a presentation of Fidelio at Karlsruhe, the Leonore Overture No. 3 was played at the beginning of the performance,
and the change of scenery after the Dungeon Scene was carried out in not more than five minutes.

                   5 [1937] No. 2, p. 4

BEETHOVEN'S TESTAMENT. Walther Nohl.   (A)
Schindler's account of Beethoven's last days as it bears upon Beethoven's will is quoted, with comments from
Frimmel's 'Handbuch.' Frimmel's entire account is quoted or summarized. In addition to the Heiligenstadt will
of 1802 there were: Letter of March 6th 1823 to Dr. Bach (KS II 232), with a letter regarding this from Stephan von
Breuning to Beethoven; letter of January 3rd 1827 to Bach (KS II 461); and codicil of March 23rd 1827 (KS II 474),
with Gerhard von Breuning's account of the signing of the codicil. Passages are quoted from conversation books of
January and February 1827 (chiefly remarks by Schindler) regarding the signing of the will.
                                                        5 [1937] No. 13-14, p. 1

DER "ENTLARVTE" BEETHOVEN. Ernst Höpfner.   (B)
Adverse comment on the Schering hypothesis.   5 [1937] No. 18, p. 1

UNGEDRUCKTE ZAPFENSTREICHE BEETHOVENS. Willy Hess.   (C)
Beethoven's compositions for military band include:

   Published

      (1)   March in D "zur grossen Wachtparade" (1816). (Note that this is scored in 33 parts) GA   2/15
      (2)   Ecossaise für Militärmusik (1810).   GA 25/290
      (3)   Polonaise für Militärmusik (1810).   GA 25/289
      (4, 5) Zwei Märsche für Militärmusik, verfasst zum Carrousell (1810). (Note that these
                 are arrangements of Nos. 9 and 11 below, simplified and with Trios)   GA 25/287
      (6)   Zapfenstreich Nr. 2 (1809).   GA 25/288

   Unpublished

      (7)   Marsch in geschwindem tempo. (Listed in the Artaria Catalog but now lost)   H-263
      (8)   Marsch für die böhmische Landwehr (1809). (First version of (4) above)   H- 6
      (9)   Zapfenstreich Nr. 2 (1809). (Second version of (4) above, with trio)   H- 7
      (10)   Marsch für Erzherzog Anton (1809-10). (First version of (5) above)   H- 8
      (11)   Zapfenstreich Nr. 3 (1809-10). (Second version of (5) above, with trio. The
                 main portion of this version is lost, but the trio is still extant)   H- 9

The trios of Nos. 9 and 11 represent "Beethoven's writing for military band at its best, and manifest almost the deli-
cacy of chamber music." In particular, the trio of No. 11 is "a miniature scherzo that should be numbered among
Beethoven's masterpieces." (The above abstract was prepared jointly from this article and from an earlier version of
the same material in the 'Schweizerische Musik Zeitung' 77 [1937] 525. See also 'Neues Beethoven-Jahrbuch'
7 [1937] 106; 9 [1939] 75)   7 [1939] 292

BEETHOVENS MUSIK ZUM SCHAUSPIEL "TARPEJA." Georg Schünemann.   (D)
Beethoven's first collaboration with the poet Chr. Kuffner (1777-1846) was in 1808 in the Choral Fantasy Op. 80. In
1813 Kuffner completed his drama Tarpeja, for which Beethoven wrote incidental music. Thereafter a number of
other works were planned for joint preparation, but none came to actual composition. A detailed synopsis of Tarpeja
is given. (See also 'Neues Musikblatt' 18 [1939] No. 44 p. 1)   7 [1939] 322

                    MUSIKALISCHE BILDUNG (Moscow)

EIN MOSKAUER SKIZZENBUCH VON BEETHOVEN. A. Iwonow-Boretzky.   (E)
A 50-page sketch book, privately owned in Moscow and presumably dating from April-August 1825, contains sketches
of the last four movements of Op. 132 and the first movement of Op. 130. Facsimiles of each page are given and
discussed.   April [1927] 75

ZUM METRO-TEKTONISCHEN PLAN DES ADAGIO SOSTENUTO VON BEETHOVEN (Sonate Op. 27 Nr. 2).   (A)
    Georg Conûs.
    A detailed analysis according to the techniques of metrotectonics.
                                        April [1927] 104

BEETHOVEN AND ODOJEWSKY. Z. Ssawelowa.   (B)
    Commentary on the thought underlying Odojewsky's novel, 'Beethoven's letztes Quartett.'
                                        April [1927] 118

AUS DER BEETHOVEN-LITERATUR IN RUSSLAND. A. Chochlowkina.   (C)
    Excerpts from reviews of early performances of Beethoven's works in Russia.
                                        April [1927] 131

MUSIKALISCHES WOCHENBLATT

BEETHOVEN. A. Ziegert.   (D)
    Centenary essay.   1 [1870] 801

LIEBLINGSTONARTEN DER MEISTER. Theodor Helm.   (E)
    A listing of Beethoven's principal compositions according to their tonalities.
                                        2 [1871] 35, 49

RICHARD WAGNER ÜBER BEETHOVEN. Hans von Wolzogen.   (F)
    A review and summary of Wagner's essay. (See also 37 [1906] 1, 115)
                                        2 [1871] 145

BEETHOVENS CLAVIERSONATEN. Wilhelm Tappert.   (G)
    This series of articles is primarily a discussion of the changes which can properly be made in the sonatas as a result
    of the increase in the range of the keyboard from about 61 notes to the present 88 notes.
                                        2 [1871] 209,225,257,289,305,337,
                                                 420

THE MEANING OF BEETHOVEN'S PEDAL NOTATIONS. Wilhelm Tappert.   (H)
    The author points out that in the sonatas before Op. 53 the notation "senza sordino" or "con sordino" refers to the
    damper pedal, not to the una corda or the practice pedal. At times (e.g., Op. 26) Beethoven differentiates be-
    tween "senza sordino" and "senza sordini," a shading which was possible on the piano of his time for the reason
    that the damper pedal mechanism was such that the dampers could be raised over either half of the range without
    affecting the other half.   2 [1871] 259

THE "BEBUNG" IN OPP. 69 AND 110. Wilhelm Tappert.   2 [1871] 338   (I)

BETRACHTUNGEN IM JAHRE NACH DER HUNDERTJAHRIGEN GEBURTSTAGFEIER LUDWIG V. BEETHOVENS.   (J)
    Carl Billert.
    Centenary essay.   2 [1871] 625

BRIEFE LUDWIG VAN BEETHOVENS AN LEIPZIGER VERLEGER.   (K)
    Letter of April 22nd 1801 to Hoffmeister (KS I 41).   Letter of April 22nd 1801 to Breitkopf & Härtel (KS I 43).
    Letter of June 1801 to Hoffmeister (KS I 45).   2 [1871] 645

DER ERSTER SATZ DER NEUNTEN SYMPHONIE BEETHOVENS. F. Stade.   (L)
    A philosophical and metaphysical analysis.   3 [1872] 545,561,593,657,689
                                                           703,751,783,815

ZUM VORTRAG DER NEUNTEN SYMPHONIE BEETHOVENS. Richard Wagner.   (M)
    Detailed discussion of certain passages from the conductor's standpoint.
                                        4 [1873] 209,225

AUS BEETHOVENS LEBEN. Franz Xav. Boch.   (A)
   An account of Beethoven's irate departure from a party at Prince Lichnowsky's in 1807-08, as referred to in TK II 68.
4 [1873] 540

BEETHOVENS STREICHQUARTETTE. Theodor Helm.   (B)
   Material which later (1885) appeared as a book of the same title. 4 [1873] - 6 [1875]; 12 [1881] -
13 [1882] passim

ZWEI SCHRIEBEN VON BEETHOVEN.   (C)
   Note dated October 20th without year (here postulated 1796-97), probably to Prince Lichnowsky: "Wir haben gehört,"
with eight measures of a German dance in minor key (not in KS or in BJ II list). Note without date, presumably to
Zmeskall (here described as probably to Prince Lichnowsky): "Vortrefflichster Musikgraf! wir möchten gern eine
Flasche eures Tokaierweins besitzen" (not in KS or in BJ II list).
5 [1874] 390

NEUE BEETHOVENIANA. G. Nottebohm.   (D)
   Material which later appeared in revised form as a book of the same title.
6 [1875] - 10 [1879] passim

DIE PHANTASIE OPUS 80. G. Nottebohm.   (E)
   The introduction to the Choral Fantasy was sketched only in the latter half of 1809, though the work received its
first public performance on December 22nd 1808. Ideas regarding this introduction which appeared among earlier
sketches may have been used to write out an introduction for use at this first performance, or (also quite possible)
have been used merely as reminders in an improvised performance. The text of the Choral Fantasy was probably
not by Kuffner, but may have been by Treitschke.   6 [1875] 222

BEETHOVEN ALS EHEFEIND. Richard Falckenberg.   (F)
   A pro-Wagnerian polemic having virtually nothing to do with Beethoven.
6 [1875] 358

EINE FRAGLICHE STELLE IN DEN VARIATIONEN OPUS 120. G. Nottebohm.   (G)
   Recent editions of the Diabelli Variations (including the GA) have dropped the equivalent of a measure which appeared in the first edition in Variation No. 12. NB I 47 refers to letters from Beethoven (KS II 215; KK No. 1115)
which indicate conclusively that Beethoven himself corrected the first edition of this work, so any deviation from
that version must be a falsification of the music as Beethoven wrote it. A number of other errors in modern editions
of Op. 120 are pointed out: "We have no completely accurate edition of the Variations Op. 120."
6 [1875] 393

EINIGE UNGEDRUCKTE BRIEFE BEETHOVENS. Richard Falckenberg.   (H)
   Letter without date to Treitschke (KS I 313). Letter of February 10th 1820 to Simrock: "Sehr beschäftigt kann
ich jetzt" regarding Opp. 107, 108, 120 and 123, and referring to Karl's schooling (not in KS). "Sendet Karl
die Ouverture Stimmen . . ." (KK 1333) M-296. Letter without date (postulated January 2nd 1825) to
Schuppanzigh: "Von heute an den 2ten Sonntag" regarding a rehearsal or performance of Op. 127 (not in KS or
BJ II list). KK 1261.   9 [1878] 268,280

VON BEETHOVEN BIS BRAHMS.   (I)
   Nontechnical discussion of a few disputed passages in the symphonies and of Beethoven's writing for orchestra
and for Pf.   9 [1878] 301,321

DIE BONNER STADTMUSIKANTEN. Werner Hesse.   (J)
   An account of the town musicians of Bonn throughout the eighteenth century.
10 [1879] 166,181

WIE WILL BEETHOVEN SEINE CLAVIERSONATE IN CISMOLL (Opus 27 No. 2) VORGETRAGEN HABEN?   (K)
   Rudolf Westphal.
   In the opening measures of the finale, the phrasing is to be broken (definitely though in varying degrees) at each
measure.   14 [1883] 397

KLANGFUSS, KLANGVERS, MIT BESONDERER BEZIEHUNG AUF BEETHOVENS CLAVIERSONATEN.   (A)
    B. Sokolowsky and R. Westphal.
    Applications of considerations of prosody to musical phrasing and dynamics.
                        16 [1885] 325,341,353,365,377

ZUM VORTRAG VON BEETHOVENS NEUNTER SYMPHONIE.   G. H. Witte.   (B)
    In the performance of this work, as of any classical composition, the conductor must consider the advisability of
    changing the orchestration to take advantage of today's extended instrumental capabilities, and to compensate for
    the composer's miscalculations. Similarly, the phrasing must be reviewed to avoid unwise dependence on editors'
    or engravers' errors. (See also p. 531)   19 [1888] 197

BEETHOVENS FISDUR-SONATE OPUS 78.   Hugo Riemann.   (C)
    An analysis in the usual Riemann style, quite distinct from the one which appeared thirty years later in his 'L. van
    Beethovens sämtliche Klavier-Solosonaten.'   19 [1888] 465,481,493

NOCHMALS BEETHOVENS 'NEUNTE.' Hugo Grüters.   (D)
    Polemic against Witte (p. 197). (See also p. 571)   19 [1888] 531

NOCH EINIGE BEMERKUNGEN ÜBER DEN VORTRAG VON BEETHOVENS NEUNTER SYMPHONIE UND ANDEREN   (E)
    CLASSISCHEN ORCHESTERCOMPOSITIONEN.   G. H. Witte.
    Defense against Grüters (p. 531). (See also 20 [1889] 306)   19 [1888] 571,586,599

DAS TEMPO DI MENUETTO IN BEETHOVENS ACHTER SYMPHONIE.   Richard Pohl.   (F)
    Taking the third movement of the Eighth Symphony in a rapid scherzo tempo rather than more slowly ('Tempo di
    Menuetto') is a false and distorting reading stemming from Mendelssohn, whose nervous temperament led him to
    drive all tempi. The concert-master of the Hamburg orchestra, who had played this Symphony under Spohr (who,
    in turn, had played it under Beethoven) states that the Wagner-von Bülow tradition of a more leisurely pace is the
    true one.   20 [1889] 289

HR. WITTE UND DIE AENDERUNGEN DER WERKE BEETHOVENS UND ANDERER MEISTER.   Hugo Grüters.   (G)
    Continuation of polemic (see 19 [1888] 571 and 20 [1889] 363).   20 [1889] 306

NOCH EINIGES ÜBER DIE ZULÄSSIGKEIT EINZELNER ABWEICHUNGEN VON DER VORSCHRIFTEN DER COMPONISTEN.   (H)
    G. H. Witte.
    Conclusion of polemic with Grüters (see p. 306).   20 [1889] 363,375

BEETHOVENS ALLEGRETTO SCHERZANDO UND SEINE SYMPHONIE.   Moritz Wirth.   (I)
    The question of the tempo of the third movement of the Eighth Symphony which Pohl (p. 289) discussed is only a
    part of the entire tempo-rhythmic-dynamic problem of the symphony. The author discusses the first three move-
    ments from this standpoint in much detail.   20 [1889] 529,541,557,573,589,
                                        601,614,630

BEETHOVENS "NEUNTE": VERSUCH EINER DEUTUNG.   Willy Pastor.   (J)
                        21 [1890] 313

BEETHOVENS 'UNSTERBLICHE GELIEBTE.' Theodor Helm.   (K)
    Summary of book of this title by "M. T."   21 [1890] 459

DIE OUVERTURE ZU "FIDELIO" (in E).   Moritz Wirth.   (L)
    Quotation of comments by many musicians on this work, and a detailed analysis to support the author's contention that
    "the Overture delineates Leonora's emotions from the first moment of the thought of deliverance to its completed ac-
    complishment."   22 [1891] 289,309,324,337

BEETHOVEN ALS CLAVIERPÄDAGOG.   Hugo Riemann.   (M)
    An extended review of Shedlock's edition of 'Selection of Studies by J. B. Cramer with Comments by L. van
    Beethoven' (Augener, 1893), in which the author groups together studies and Beethoven's comments on them which
    are designed to inculcate specific features of Beethoven's pianism. As Shedlock points out in his Preface, Cramer
    and Schindler were doubtless correct in considering these etudes, annotated by Beethoven for Nephew Karl, as a not
    completely inadequate substitute for the 'Pianoforte Method' which Beethoven spoke of writing (WRK p. 220) but
    which he never got to.   24 [1893] 541,553,569,581

DAS ALLEGRETTO VON BEETHOVENS ADUR-SYMPHONIE UND EIN BISCHEN DIESE SELBST.   Moritz Wirth.   (A)
    Partly a discussion of what Wagner and others said about the Seventh Symphony and partly a consideration of the
    psychology underlying the allegretto, and the other movements in relationship to the allegretto.

25 [1894] 53,65,77,93,105,117,
129,145

EIN BESUCH IM GEBURTSHAUS BEETHOVENS.   H. Mund.   27 [1896] 293   (B)

ÜBER DEN VORTRAG DES ANFANGSMOTIVS IN BEETHOVENS C-MOLL-SYMPHONIE.   Otto Taubmann.   (C)
    There is no justification, either artistically or in Beethoven's tempo indications, for the often encountered practice
    of taking the first five measures of the C minor Symphony at a 'largo ad lib.'

27 [1896] 429,441,453

NEUE BEETHOVEN-STUDIEN: I. ÜBER DIE SPIELWEISE EINIGER STELLEN IN BEETHOVENS CLAVIERCOMPOSITIONEN.   (D)
    Theodor von Frimmel.
    The problem here considered is the case in which a sustained note in one voice occurs shortly thereafter in another
    voice, so that decision must be made as to whether or not to release the note for the purpose of striking it again. The
    author agrees in general with the rule of K. P. E. Bach (quite possibly passed through his pupil Neefe to Beethoven)
    that the sustained note should not be released for the purpose of restriking immediately after the first sounding (e.g.,
    the E in m. 20 of the first movement of Op. 10 No. 2), but that the release and restriking should be adopted if the
    interval is greater (e.g., the E flat in the second measure of the Funeral March of Op. 26). Numerous examples
    from the Pf works are cited.   28 [1897] 105,121,137,153,169

ÜBER DIE RHYTHMISCHE BEDEUTUNG DES HAUPTMOTIVS IM ERSTEN SATZE DER C-MOLL-SYMPHONIE VON   (E)
    BEETHOVEN.   Theodor Müller-Reuter.
    A detailed study of the 'Fate Motif' in its several occurrences, from the standpoint of the dynamics within the motif,
    the significance of the fermati, and the duration of the fermati.

    The author builds his thesis on the necessary distinction between ♪♪♪| 𝄽   ♪♪♪|♩|𝄽 ' In evaluating this
    discussion, due weight should be given to the fact that the extra half note in the second phrase was an afterthought
    added by Beethoven after the first edition of the symphony had been published (see 'Music & Letters' 19 [1938] 265).

29 [1898] 381,397,413

BEETHOVENS ERSTES AUFTRETEN IN KÖLN.   (F)
    The advertisement given in TK I 59.   30 [1899] 386

DIE ZEITMASSE DES ERSTEN SATZES VON BEETHOVENS VIERTER SYMPHONIE.   Moritz Wirth.   (G
    The movement in question is analyzed in the most minute detail, with metronome marks given for dozens of passages,
    ranging from whole note = 100 to half note = 64.   34 [1903] 701,721,737

DAS SCHERZANDO VIVACE IN BEETHOVENS ES DUR-QUARTETT OPUS 127.   Eva Siegfried.   (H
    A detailed analysis of this movement.   36 [1905] 33,59

EINIGES ÜBER BEETHOVEN'SCHE SYMPHONIEN UND IHRE INSTRUMENTATION.   W. Kes.   (I)
    A plea that horn and trumpet parts should be rewritten to take advantage of the notes now available by the use of
    valves. As an example, suggested changes in the Seventh Symphony are given. (See also p. 151)

36 [1905] 57

BEETHOVEN IM "ERGÄNZTEN" GEWANDE?   H. Hammer.   (J
    Polemic against Kes (p. 57).   36 [1905] 151

"DAS WORT SIE SOLLEN LASSEN STAHN."   S. de Lange.   (K
    Polemic against Kes (p. 57).   36 [1905] 151

EIN NEUER, BISHER UNVERÖFFENTLICHTER SCHLUSS ZU R. WAGNER'S "BEETHOVEN."   Hans von Wolzogen.   (L

37 [1906] 1,115

DIE RHYTHMISCHEN VERHÄLTNISSE DES I. AND III. SÄTZES IN BEETHOVENS V. SYMPHONIE C MOLL.   (N
    Carl Schroeder.
    An article which points out rather than solves the rhythmic problems in the movements discussed.

39 [1908] 136,196

DER BRIEF BEETHOVENS AN FREIHERRN VON NEFFZERN IM BESITZ EMERICH KASTNERS.   Theodor von Frimmel. (A)
    Facsimile and transcription of the letter to "von Neftzer" given in KS I 389, written most probably in 1813 or 1815.
    A brief biographical sketch is given of Baron Alexander von Neffzern 1780 (?) - 1864. (See also Kalischer 'Briefe'
    V 41)   39 [1908] 307

HAYDN AND BEETHOVEN. Max Burkhardt.   (B)
    A summary of Beethoven's relationship to Haydn as given in certain recently issued books.
                                        40 [1909] 133

ZUM PROBLEM BEETHOVENS "UNSTERBLICHER GELIEBTEN." Max Unger.   (C)
    A review of various studies of the 'Immortal Beloved' problem, indicating that the letter was intended for Bettina
    von Arnim. (See however 'Neue Zeitschrift für Musik' 108 [1911] 505, where the author withdraws this opinion)
                                        40 [1909] 356

MUSIKANTEN GILDE

AUS BEETHOVENS STUDIEN. Max Schlensog.   (D)
    An edited version of Beethoven's 'Nachahmung a tre' (Seyfried [1832] 167 and 'Fuga a due Violini e Violoncello'
    (Ibid. p. 197) with analysis.   6 [1923] 56

DIE HARMONIK DER ERSTEN BEETHOVEN-SYMPHONIE. Arthur Willner.   (E)
    Harmonic analysis.   1 [1925] 2,22

BEETHOVEN ALS SCHLUSSSTEIN DER ABSOLUTEN MUSIK. Richard Wagner.   (F)
    Extract from 'Kunstwerk der Zukunft.'   3 [1925] 72

BEETHOVEN UND WIR. Fritz Jöde.   (G)
    Centennial essay. (See also 'Allgemeine Musik Zeitung' 59 [1932] 499)
                                        5 [1927] 25

MUSIKBLÄTTER DES ANBRUCH

BEETHOVEN UND DIE MODERNE MUSIK. Wilhelm Fischer.   (H)
    Beethoven led the way and in his music foreshadowed the fundamental changes in musical methods and thought which,
    starting with the Romantics, have continued to our day.   2 [1920] 624

BEETHOVEN. Hugo von Hofmansthal.   (I)
    Excerpt from a centenary essay.   9 [1927] 114

DAS GEDANKLICHE PRINZIP IN BEETHOVENS MUSIK UND SEINE AUSWIRKUNG BEI SCHÖNBERG. Erwin Stein.   (J)
    A parallelism is seen between the motival development used by Beethoven in constructing his melodic lines and that
    used by Schönberg.   9 [1927] 117

BEETHOVEN UND UNSERE ZEIT. Paul A. Pisk.   (K)
    Specific ways are cited in which music of today shows the accomplishment of ideas first laid out by Beethoven.
                                        9 [1927] 121

MUSIKFORSCHUNG

PSEUDOKANONS UND RÄTSELKANONS. Ludwig Misch.   (L)
    Material appearing in 'Beethoven Sketches' [1953] 106. (See also Mf 7 [1954] 511)
                                        3 [1950] 253

EIN UNBEMERKTER THEMATISCHER ZUSAMMENHANG IN BEETHOVENS IV. SYMPHONIE. Ludwig Misch.   (A)
    The melody in violin and violoncello and later in clarinet in the development section of the first movement of the
    Fourth Symphony (GA 1/4 pp. 16, 17) has some similarity to the E minor episode of the Eroica first movement and is
    an amplification of the countermelody in GA 1/4 8-1-5ff.   5 [1952] 375

EIN FEHLER IN BEETHOVENS LETZTEN VIOLIN-SONATE? Gunter Henle.   (B)
    In the recapitulation of the first movement of Op. 96, GA 12/101, at 6-1-5, should the fifth note be A natural as in
    the GA or A flat to correspond with the similar passage in the exposition at 1-3-5? Justifications are proposed for each
    of the conflicting readings.   5 [1952] 53

ZUR FRAGE "EIN FEHLER IN BEETHOVENS LETZTER VIOLINSONATE?" Ludwig Misch.   (C)
    The questioned note is probably A flat.   5 [1952] 367

BEETHOVENS INDISCHE AUFZEICHNUNGEN. Walther Schubring.   (D)
    A new and more accurate transcription (with commentary) from the Fischoff manuscript of the material appearing in
    Leitzmann's 'Berichte der Zeitgenossen' II pp. 252ff as entries 74-77 incl. and 106.
                                    6 [1953] 207

UNBEKANNTE WERKE BEETHOVENS FÜR BLASINSTRUMENTE. Willy Hess.   (E)
    A listing, with brief comments of Beethoven's compositions in this category, both those in the GA and those not
    therein included.   7 [1954] 207

CANON: BESTER HERR GRAF. Ludwig Misch.   (F)
    In this canon (WoO 183) as published in Mf 3 [1950] 264, the last note in the fourth measure should be C, not A.
                                    7 [1954] 511

DIE WIENER HANDSCHRIFTEN ZUR ERSTEN UND ZWEITEN FASSUNG VON BEETHOVENS "FIDELIO." Willy Hess.   (G
    Material in the library of the Gesellschaft der Musikfreunde is listed.
                                    8 [1955] 208

NOCH EIN VERSTÜMMELTER KANON VON BEETHOVEN. Ludwig Misch.   (H
    All versions thus far proposed of the canon 'Es muss sein' WoO 196 are in conflict either with the autograph or with
    the rules of canon writing. A revised and presumably correct version is given.
                                    8 [1955] 325

EIN UNBEMERKTES STÜCK BEETHOVENSCHER FUGENKUNST. Ludwig Misch.   (I
    Fugal writing in the finale of Op. 29 is analyzed and discussed.   10 [1957] 517

RÄTSEL UM EINEN BEETHOVEN-BRIEF. Ludwig Misch.   (J
    Corrected transcription of a letter to B. Schotts Söhne of 8 (?) March 1826 (the date "1820" was a typographical error
    corrected later) with reference to the dedication of the Ninth Symphony and the sale of a new quartet (probably Op.
    131).   12 [1959] 81

ACHT WIEDERHOLUNGSTAKTE ZU VIEL IN DEN DRUCKEN VON BEETHOVENS OPUS 5 No. 2? Rudolf Steglich.   (K
    The author suggests that a prima volta indication was inadvertently omitted at the end of the exposition of the first
    movement.   12 [1959] 473

ZUR ENTSTEHUNGSGESCHICHTE VON MOZARTS UND BEETHOVENS KOMPOSITIONEN FÜR DIE SPIELUHR.   (L
      Ludwig Misch.
    The author is not convinced that WoO 33 Nos. 4 and 5 were written for mechanical organ.
                                    13 [1960] 317

ZUR BEETHOVENS HOCHZEITSLIED VOM JAHRE 1819. Willy Hess.   (M
    The version of WoO 105 in C major (soprano solo, unison chorus) was probably transposed by Beethoven to the key of A,
    with tenor solo and chorus for mixed quartet, and later rewritten (before its performance at Nanni Giannatasio's
    wedding) for male chorus.   13 [1960] 323

PAGANINI AND BEETHOVEN. Zdenek Vyborny.   (N
    There is no record of any public performance by Paganini of a composition by Beethoven, but he is known to have
    played Beethoven's chamber music and his Op. 61 in private with appreciation of their greatness.
                                    13 [1960] 325

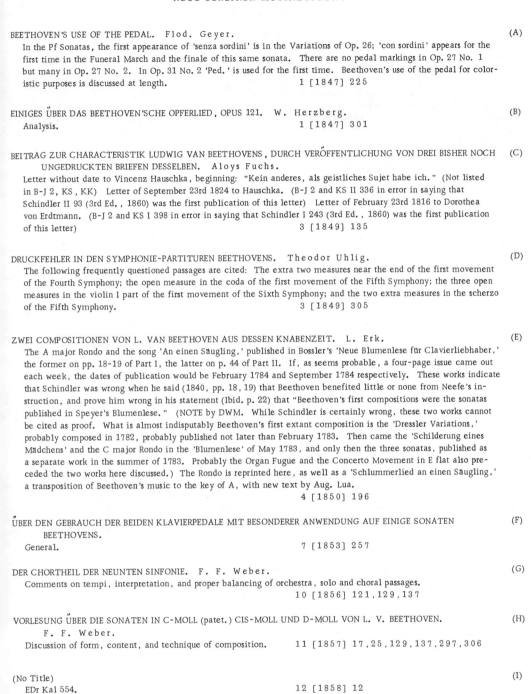

BEETHOVEN'S USE OF THE PEDAL. Flod. Geyer.   (A)
   In the Pf Sonatas, the first appearance of 'senza sordini' is in the Variations of Op. 26; 'con sordini' appears for the
first time in the Funeral March and the finale of this same sonata. There are no pedal markings in Op. 27 No. 1
but many in Op. 27 No. 2. In Op. 31 No. 2 'Ped.' is used for the first time. Beethoven's use of the pedal for color-
istic purposes is discussed at length.   1 [1847] 225

EINIGES ÜBER DAS BEETHOVEN'SCHE OPFERLIED, OPUS 121. W. Herzberg.   (B)
   Analysis.   1 [1847] 301

BEITRAG ZUR CHARACTERISTIK LUDWIG VAN BEETHOVENS, DURCH VERÖFFENTLICHUNG VON DREI BISHER NOCH   (C)
   UNGEDRUCKTEN BRIEFEN DESSELBEN. Aloys Fuchs.
   Letter without date to Vincenz Hauschka, beginning: "Kein anderes, als geistliches Sujet habe ich." (Not listed
in B-J 2, KS, KK) Letter of September 23rd 1824 to Hauschka. (B-J 2 and KS II 336 in error in saying that
Schindler II 93 (3rd Ed., 1860) was the first publication of this letter) Letter of February 23rd 1816 to Dorothea
von Erdtmann. (B-J 2 and KS I 398 in error in saying that Schindler I 243 (3rd Ed., 1860) was the first publication
of this letter)   3 [1849] 135

DRUCKFEHLER IN DEN SYMPHONIE-PARTITUREN BEETHOVENS. Theodor Uhlig.   (D)
   The following frequently questioned passages are cited: The extra two measures near the end of the first movement
of the Fourth Symphony; the open measure in the coda of the first movement of the Fifth Symphony; the three open
measures in the violin I part of the first movement of the Sixth Symphony; and the two extra measures in the scherzo
of the Fifth Symphony.   3 [1849] 305

ZWEI COMPOSITIONEN VON L. VAN BEETHOVEN AUS DESSEN KNABENZEIT. L. Erk.   (E)
   The A major Rondo and the song 'An einen Säugling,' published in Bossler's 'Neue Blumenlese für Clavierliebhaber,'
the former on pp. 18-19 of Part I, the latter on p. 44 of Part II. If, as seems probable, a four-page issue came out
each week, the dates of publication would be February 1784 and September 1784 respectively. These works indicate
that Schindler was wrong when he said (1840, pp. 18,19) that Beethoven benefited little or none from Neefe's instruction, and prove him wrong in his statement (Ibid. p. 22) that "Beethoven's first compositions were the sonatas
published in Speyer's Blumenlese." (NOTE by DWM. While Schindler is certainly wrong, these two works cannot
be cited as proof. What is almost indisputably Beethoven's first extant composition is the 'Dressler Variations,'
probably composed in 1782, probably published not later than February 1783. Then came the 'Schilderung eines
Mädchens' and the C major Rondo in the 'Blumenlese' of May 1783, and only then the three sonatas, published as
a separate work in the summer of 1783. Probably the Organ Fugue and the Concerto Movement in E flat also preceded the two works here discussed.) The Rondo is reprinted here, as well as a 'Schlummerlied an einen Säugling,'
a transposition of Beethoven's music to the key of A, with new text by Aug. Lua.
                                                   4 [1850] 196

ÜBER DEN GEBRAUCH DER BEIDEN KLAVIERPEDALE MIT BESONDERER ANWENDUNG AUF EINIGE SONATEN   (F)
   BEETHOVENS.
   General.   7 [1853] 257

DER CHORTHEIL DER NEUNTEN SINFONIE. F. F. Weber.   (G)
   Comments on tempi, interpretation, and proper balancing of orchestra, solo and choral passages.
                                            10 [1856] 121,129,137

VORLESUNG ÜBER DIE SONATEN IN C-MOLL (patet.) CIS-MOLL UND D-MOLL VON L. V. BEETHOVEN.   (H)
   F. F. Weber.
   Discussion of form, content, and technique of composition.   11 [1857] 17,25,129,137,297,306

(No Title)   (I)
   EDr Kal 554.   12 [1858] 12

ÜBER DIE REINHEIT DER AUSGABEN BEETHOVEN'SCHER KLAVIERWERKE. Flod. Geyer.   (J)
   With few exceptions, all the passages in the Pf Sonatas for which Beethoven himself proposed fingerings are given
and commented upon.   12 [1858] 233

MENDELSSOHN'S SYMPHONY-CANTATA 'LOBGESANG' AND BEETHOVEN'S NINTH SYMPHONY.   Wilhelm Wauer. (A)
A discussion of the considerations which led each of the two composers to adopt the choral-orchestral form, and
statement of reasons for believing that the later work was in no sense an imitation of the earlier one. (See also
'Allgemeine Musikalische Zeitung'49 [1847] 489,503)   12 [1858] 361,369

L. V. BEETHOVENS 'STUDIEN.'   F. M. Böhme.   (B)
The book by Seyfried contains more than 80 pages taken verbatim from Fux's 'Gradus ad Parnassum' and some 20
pages from Albrechtsberger's classic textbook. Since this material was falsely claimed as being Beethoven's own
work, doubt must be thrown upon the genuineness of what are claimed to be exercises worked out by Beethoven.
(See also 'Rheinische Musikzeitung' 2 [1851] 572)   13 [1859] 353

BEETHOVEN AND MARIE PACHLER-KOSCHAK.   Faust Pachler.   (C)
Extensive biographical notes on Marie Leopoldine Koschak (born February 2nd 1794) who on May 12th 1816 married
Dr. Carl Pachler. Facsimile and transcription are given of a hitherto unpublished letter without date from Beethoven
to Frau Pachler-Koschak (KS II 84), and transcription of a letter without date to her husband, a physician (KS II 86).
The author, son of Frau Pachler-Koschak, denies unqualifiedly that Beethoven was in love with his mother, as claimed
by Schindler, and gives evidence to controvert various of Schindler's supposed proofs. (See also TK II 382, III 140)
                                                            19 [1865] 381,389,397,405,413;
                                                            20 [1866] 1

LUDWIG VAN BEETHOVEN ALS BAHNBRECHENDER GENIUS AUF DEM GEBIETE DER SYMPHONIE.   (D)
     C.E.R. Alberti.
General discussion of the symphonies.   23 [1869] 201,209,217,225,281,
                                                                      289,301,309,317

BEETHOVEN, GOETHE AND MICHEL ANGELO.   A. W. Ambros.   (E)
                                                            24 [1870] 273,281

ZUM SECHZEHNTEN DEZEMBER, BEETHOVENS GEBURTSTAG.   H. Ehrlich.   (F)
Centenary essay.   24 [1870] 395

BEDENKLICHKEITEN.   Heinrich Dorn.   (G)
The rescoring of passages to take advantage of the greater capabilities of modern instruments (e.g., use of the
chromatic horn in place of the bassoon at mm. 303ff. of the first movement of the Fifth Symphony) violates the rule
that "every work of art reflects not merely the characteristics of the artist but the characteristics of the age in which
it was created."   25 [1871] 281

DIE LIEBESBRIEFE BEETHOVENS. A. C. Kalischer and A. W. Thayer.   (H)
Early draft of Appendix I to Volume III of Thayer's 'Beethovens Leben' (1879), with extensive comments by Kalischer.
Commenting on Thayer's conclusion (see TK I 332) that there is an error of one day in Beethoven's date, Kalischer
makes the logical suggestion that just as easily Beethoven might have made a mistake in the month -- the difference
between 'Juli' and 'Juni' is only a single letter.   26 [1872] 193,201,209

AUFRUF.   (I)
Announcement that the widow of Nephew Karl is in destitute circumstances, and call for assistance to her. Repeated
in two subsequent issues with contributions received (pp. 230ff.) also listed.
                                                            27 [1873] 201

BEETHOVEN'S 33 VARIATIONEN ÜBER EINEN WALZER ETC. OPUS 120.   Carl Kossmaly.   (J)
The opinion is stated that even the most accurate available edition is not free from errors.
                                                            27 [1873] 321

BEETHOVENS A-DUR-SYMPHONIE.   Alfred Kalischer.   (K)
To justify the statement: "The A major Symphony portrays the training of Mankind," the author gives a detailed
and flowery analysis of the symphony.   27 [1873] 401,409

MUSIKALISCHE ÜBERMALUNGEN UND RETOUCHEN.   A. W. Ambros.   (L)
A plea that Beethoven be spared the improvements and corrections suggested by his admirers, with examples drawn
from the 3rd, 4th, 5th and 6th Symphonies.   28 [1874] 33

EINE BEETHOVEN'SCHE PAUSE.   Louis Köhler.   (A)
   Comments on the open measure before the second subject in the recapitulation of the first movement of the Pf Sonata
   Op. 10 No. 1 and on the modulation to which it leads.   28 [1874] 49

EINE BEETHOVEN'SCHE PAUSE.   W. von Lenz.   (B)
   The modulation referred to by Köhler (p. 49) is based on the harmonic system of the ecclesiastical modes.
                                                         28 [1874] 81

EINE BEETHOVEN'SCHE PAUSE.   Louis Köhler.   (C)
   Reply to Lenz (p. 81).   28 [1874] 121

ÜBER DIE VORSCHLÄGE ZU AENDERUNG IN BEETHOVENS COMPOSITIONEN.   Alexis Hollaender.   (D)
   Various passages are quoted from the Pf Sonatas which editors have changed without sufficient justification.   Analogy
   with a similar passage in another part of a movement is never by itself justification for a change in Beethoven's text.
                                                         29 [1875] 1,9

LÄSST SICH DIE RÜCKKEHR DES SCHERZOMOTIFS DER BEETHOVEN'SCHEN C-MOLL-SYMPHONIE, IM FINALE   (E)
   DERSELBEN, ORGANISCH VERSTEHEN?   W. von Lenz.
   The reappearance of this motif is of a part with Beethoven's use of the rhythmic motif throughout the symphony.
                                                         31 [1877] 258

BEETHOVEN-BILDNISSE.   Robert Springer.   (F)
   A description of portraits and busts of Beethoven, those taken from life and those made after his death.
                                                         34 [1880] 66,74,83

EIN NEUER BRIEF VON BEETHOVEN.   Theodor von Frimmel.   (G)
   First publication of letter without date to Steiner (KS II 23).   34 [1880] 268

BEETHOVEN ALS CLAVIER-VIRTUOSE.   (H)
   Quotation from 'Allgemeine Musikalische Zeitung' given in TK I 215.
                                                         35 [1881] 114

BEETHOVENS LEHRJAHRE.   Louis Köhler.   (I)
   Biographical sketch covering the first 26 years of Beethoven's life.   Regarding the Bonn sonatas the statement is made
   that they are definitely more mature than were the compositions of Mozart at the same age (approx. K. 46).
                                                         35 [1881] 122,130,138

BEETHOVEN IN DER WENDE DES JAHRHUNDERTS.   Louis Köhler.   (J)
   Continuation of the previous article, covering events and compositions of the period 1795-98.
                                                         35 [1881] 218,226,234,242,250

BEETHOVEN'S SONATAS OPP. 53 and 54.   Louis Köhler.   (K)
   Brief analyses.   35 [1881] 314

BEETHOVENS DRITTE PERIODE IM BEGINN.   Louis Köhler.   (L)
   Comments on Opp. 101, 102, 106.   35 [1881] 394,402,410

BEETHOVEN'S USE OF GERMANIC TERMINOLOGY.   A. W. Thayer.   (M)
   Beethoven's decision to replace the word 'Pianoforte' by 'Hammerklavier' was made in 1817, long before he met
   Holz.   There is no truth in the story of Schindler's Paris visiting card reading "Anton Schindler avec (sic) de
   Beethoven."   35 [1881] 411

BEETHOVEN'S SONATA OPUS 110.   Louis Köhler.   (N)
   A discussion of the melodic style of Beethoven's last period as exemplified in this sonata.
                                                         36 [1882] 2,10

BEETHOVEN'S VARIATIONS.   Carl Kossmaly.   (O)
   Brief analysis of the 32 Variations in C minor.   36 [1882] 233,241

FRANZ LISZT ALS ELFJÄHRIGER PIANIST UND CONCERTGEBER.   Th. Rode.   (P)
   Brief account of Liszt's first appearance before Beethoven.   37 [1883] 226

BEETHOVENS ABSTAMMUNG.   Carl Kossmaly.   (A)
   Brief biographical sketch of the Antwerp (Henry Adelard) branch of the family and of Grandfather Ludwig.
                             38 [1884] 82,90

BEETHOVENS MISSA SOLEMNIS.   Robert Hirschfeld.   (B)
   An aesthetic study.   38 [1884] 105

BEETHOVENS OPFERLIED OPUS 121b.   Carl Kossmaly.   (C)
   Review, with critical comments on the Breitkopf & Härtel edition.
                             38 [1884] 177

EIN UNGEDRUCKTE BRIEF BEETHOVENS.   (D)
   The letter to Marie Bigot and her husband (KS I 137), referred to in 'Le Menestrel' 52 [1886] 165 as not previously
   published, had been published by Otto Jahn in 'Der Grenzbote' in 1867. M. Bigot's story is recounted of his wife
   playing the Appassionata Sonata at sight from rough manuscript, as a result of which Beethoven presented the autograph to her.   40 [1886] 146

EINE LONDONER BEETHOVEN-MYSTIFICATION.   (E)
   Same as 'Allgemeine Deutsche Musik Zeitung' 13 [1886] 268.   40 [1886] 211

BEETHOVEN IM HAUSE.   (F)
   Anecdotes.   40 [1886] 362,370

BERECHTIGUNG ZWEIER FEHLER IN BEETHOVEN'SCHEN SONATEN.   Ludwig Bussler.   (G)
   Changes are suggested in m. 171 of the first movement of Op. 106 and in m. 109 of the last movement of Op. 109
   which (the author believes) are corrections of errors in the versions generally accepted.
                             41 [1887] 250

ÜBER BEETHOVENS MISSA SOLEMNIS.   William Wolf.   (H)
   The general characteristics of the work and of Beethoven's approach to it are discussed, and the music is analyzed
   in great detail.   41 [1887] 314,323,333,343,353,
                                  364

DRUCKFEHLER IN BEETHOVEN'SCHEN SONATEN.   (I)
   Citation of a note by F. J. S. in 'Musical Times' 29 [1888] 303 giving corrections listed in 41 [1887] 250 and stating
   that these corrections had been made in some editions of the sonatas.
                            42 [1888] 177

DIE BEISETZUNG BEETHOVENS.   (J)
   Account of the reinterment ceremonies at the Vienna Central Cemetery on June 22nd 1888.
                            42 [1888] 260

ÜBER BEETHOVENS "WALDMÄDCHEN" VARIATIONEN.   William Wolf.   (K)
   Detailed analysis of Beethoven's variations technique as exemplified in this composition.
                           42 [1888] 359,369,379

DESCRIPTION OF THE PRESENT STATE OF BEETHOVEN'S BIRTHPLACE.   (L)
                            43 [1889] 114

AUSDEUTUNG VON BEETHOVENS A-DUR-SYMPHONIE.   Karl Friedrich Ebers.   (M)
   Imaginative explanation appearing in Volume 2 of 'Cäcilia,' with comments by Otto Schmid.
                            43 [1889] 234

EBERS'SCHE DEUTUNG VON BEETHOVENS A-DUR-SYMPHONIE.   H. Simon.   (N)
   Remarks on the foregoing.   43 [1889] 250

BEETHOVEN ALS CONCERTGEBER. Eduard Hanslick.   (A)
  Beethoven's first public appearance in Vienna was on March 29th 1795, giving the first performance of his Concerto
  in C major Op. 15. On April 2nd 1798 he played the piano part of his Quintet Op. 16. In ensemble he appeared
  with Punto, April 18th 1800 in Op. 17 and with Bridgetower, May 17th 1803 in Op. 47. On April 2nd 1800 the Septet Op. 20 and the Symphony in C major Op. 21 received their first performances: (the program of this concert TK I
  266 states that Beethoven also appeared as soloist in one of his concertos and in improvisations). He also appeared
  as soloist and conductor with Clement and with Sebastian Meyer. At his own concert on April 2nd 1803 there were
  three first performances: the Concerto in C minor Op. 37, the Symphony in D major Op. 36, and 'Christus' Op. 85.
  At a similar concert on December 22nd 1808 the Choral Fantasy Op. 80 was performed for the first time. On April
  11th 1814 he took part in the premiere of the Trio Op. 97; his repetition of this next month was his last public
  appearance as a pianist. In concerts "for his own advantage" Beethoven gave more importance to his compositions
  than to his repute as a virtuoso. "Beethoven never performed a work of another composer in public, nor (in all probability) even before private gatherings." His playing was especially notable in his improvising; critics and other virtuosi looked upon his pianism with distinct reservations. His great influence was as a composer for the piano, not as
  a pianist. Like Mozart, he was above all a tone-poet in the great tradition who composed for the piano, and who incidentally sometimes acted as pianist in performances of his works.

  Beethoven usually conducted the first performances of his larger works, e.g., on April 7th 1805 he conducted the
  first performance of the 'Eroica' (then and later referred to on the program as "Symphonie in Dis"). On December
  8th 1813 he conducted first performances of the A major Symphony Op. 92 and the 'Battle of Vittoria' Op. 91; on
  February 27th 1814 the first performances of the F major Symphony Op. 93 and 'Tremate, empi' Op. 116, etc.
  Because of growing deafness and the inability, because of his violence, to secure best results from the orchestra,
  he appeared seldom as conductor during his last 12-14 years. Some of his appearances brought brilliant displays
  of public enthusiasm, notably three: the concert of December 8th 1813 (first performances of Opp. 92 and 91),
  that of November 29th 1814 (Opp. 92 and 91, and first performance of 'Der glorreiche Augenblick' Op. 136), and
  that of May 7th 1824 (the author says "1827"), his last public appearance as a conductor (first performances of the
  Ninth Symphony Op. 125 and of parts of the Missa Solemnis Op. 123). At this concert "he only appeared to conduct, since the participants had secretly agreed to follow only the directions of the concert master and the chorus
  master and not Beethoven's conducting, since the Master's deafness had advanced to the point where he could no
  more hear the orchestra than he could the tumultuous storm of applause from the audience." Some concerts, on
  the other hand, were coldly received: e.g., that of December 22nd 1808 (the author says "December 17th"), at
  which, among other works, the Fifth and Sixth Symphonies received their first performances, and at which the
  first performance of the Choral Fantasy Op. 80 caused confusion described in TK II 130. At one concert, in February 1807, Beethoven performed the first four symphonies, the Fourth for the first time. (TD III 8 refers to two
  concerts in March 1807 at which the first four symphonies, among other works, were performed.) During the first
  decade of the century, Mme. Bigot had given "all-Beethoven" concerts, and during 1817-19 Karl Czerny did the
  same. Except for these, in the years following Beethoven's withdrawal as a public performer his piano compositions (solo and with orchestra) and his songs were almost never performed in public. In 1815 the Gesellschaft der
  Österreichischen Musikfreunde offered Beethoven 300 ducats for the first year's rights to a new oratorio (see KS II
  306). Beethoven considered books by Seyfried and by Bernard, but nothing came of it.
                                                August 11 [1868] no page given

ZWEI NEU AUFGEFUNDENE CANTATEN VON BEETHOVEN. Eduard Hanslick.   (B)
  Beethoven's two long-lost Bonn cantatas (GA 25/264-5) have been discovered in autograph. The two works are
  described in detail, and the author says (as all later critics have agreed) that the Trauerkantate is a far better
  and more significant work than the Erhebungskantate. (See also 'Deutsche Musiker Zeitung' 15 [1884] 229)
                                                May 13 [1884] no page given

DIE SCHÄDEL BEETHOVENS UND SCHUBERTS. Gerhard von Breuning.   (C)
  An account of Beethoven's death, burial and reinterment, and an expression of regret that his skull was not held
  out for museum display.   September 17 [1886] no page given

DREI BISHER UNVERÖFFENTLICHTE BRIEFE BEETHOVENS. Gerhard von Breuning.   (D)
  EDr of Kal 803, 1171, 1172.   December 30 [1887] 1

BEETHOVENS ÄUSSERE ERSCHEINUNG.   (E)
  Review of Frimmel's book of the same title.   January 6 [1888] no page given

---

  * Unless otherwise stated all references are to the Morgenblatt.

AUTOGRAPH OF 'DA IST DAS WERK.'   (A)
The Heiligenstadt Library has received the autograph of this canon from Karl Holz's son. The lines and notes are
in Beethoven's hand, the text in Holz's hand.   April 18 [1889] 6

EIN ANGEBLICHER CANON VON BEETHOVEN.   Theodor von Frimmel.   (B)
No part of the autograph in question is in Beethoven's hand, and the authenticity of the canon is very doubtful.
April 19 [1889] 4

EIN CANON VON BEETHOVEN.   Karl Holz, (d.j.)   (C)
Karl Holz's son says that the manuscript in question was dictated to his father a few days before Beethoven's death,
at the time the revised finale of Op. 130 was sent off.   April 24 [1889] 4

EIN CANON VON BEETHOVEN.   Theodor von Frimmel.   (D)
The author still questions the authenticity of this canon, and points out that in a letter of 16 July 1857 to Lenz, Holz
said that Beethoven sent him the canon, which of course conflicts with the statement by his son that Beethoven had
dictated it to him.   April 26 [1889] 4

DIE LETZTE BEETHOVEN.   (E)
Obituary of Caroline, widow of Nephew Karl, who died at the age of 84. "Karl van Beethoven vanished in America
many years ago." Caroline is referred to as "the last bearer of the name Beethoven."
November 18 [1891] 7

CORRECTION.   Gabriele Heimler and Caroline Weidinger.   (F)
The daughters of Karl and Caroline van Beethoven say, "Our father never left Austria"; the location of his grave in
Vienna is given exactly.   November 19 [1891] 5

BEETHOVEN.   Adolph Wilbrandt.   (G)
Long poem.
December 17 [1893] no page given

EIN BRIEF BEETHOVENS AN SCHREYVOGEL.   Theodor von Frimmel.   (H)
First publication of letter given in KFr III No. 798. (See also 'Allgemeine Musik-Zeitung' 21 [1894] 131;
'Menestrel' 60 [1894] 61)   February 17 [1894] 1
Abendblatt

NEUE MITTHEILUNGEN ÜBER BEETHOVEN.   Theodor von Frimmel.   (I)
Comment on Beethoven's relations with Joseph Blöchlinger van Bannholz. Blöchlinger rendered many services to
Beethoven; in Karl's first years with Blöchlinger his instruction was of value much more than Beethoven paid.
Blöchlinger was definitely on Beethoven's side in the dispute with Karl's mother. An account is given of a dispute
between Blöchlinger and one of his instructors, in which the latter tried to bring a charge of blasphemy against Beethoven, but was bought off by Blöchlinger at a cost of 300 fl. "At that time Blöchlinger's Institute was one of the
best in Vienna, if not indeed the best." The discipline was strict, and a list of eminent graduates is given. Personal
recollections are given from Blöchlinger's son, who was six or seven years old when Karl was at the school. He mentions that Beethoven often improvised at the piano which was in Mme. Blöchlinger's room. It is known that Blöchlinger burned many letters (doubtless including letters from Beethoven) in 1848. The author will in due time publish
a hitherto unknown letter to Blöchlinger now in the possession of Hr. Moriz Brichta, and another letter from the same
time bearing on the Blöchlinger period.   November 4 [1894] 6

BEETHOVENS TRAUERKANTATE.   (J)
Long letter written by Brahms in May 1884 to Hanslick regarding the two Bonn cantatas. Hanslick states that the
first performance of the Trauerkantate was in November 1884.
June 27 [1897] no page given

BEETHOVEN UND DIE SCHOTTEN.   G. A. Crüwell.   (A)
   Extensive quotation (with comments) from the correspondence between Beethoven and George Thomson as given in
   the book by J. Cuthbert Hadden: 'George Thomson, the Friend of Burns; his Life and Correspondence.'
                                     March 17-18 [1898] no page given

BEETHOVEN AND A. W. THAYER.   (B)
   Extracts from Krehbiel's 'Music and Manners from Pergolesi to Beethoven.'
                                     April 14 [1899] 1

BEETHOVENS WOHNUNGEN IN WIEN.   Theodor von Frimmel.   (C)
   A listing, with brief description, of some of the principal lodgings which Beethoven occupied in Vienna.
                                     August 11 [1899] 6

EIN UNGEDRUCKTER BRIEF BEETHOVENS.   Theodor von Frimmel.   (D)
   A newly discovered letter is described as being one of the most interesting of all the letters from Beethoven to the
   Archduke Rudolph. It is without date but may certainly be ascribed to the spring of 1819. The letter, opening
   with a few notes on 'O Hoffnung,' contains Beethoven's comments on the variations which the Archduke wrote on
   this theme. The close of the letter is missing. (See also 'Allgemeine Musik-Zeitung' 27 [1900] 240)
                                     February 28 [1900] 6

BEETHOVEN'S NAME AND AN UNPUBLISHED LETTER. Theodor von Frimmel.   (E)
   Though the composer undoubtedly pronounced his name Bee͟thoven, the customary pronunciation in Vienna at the
   time of this article is certainly Beet͟hoven, and a musical tribute to the composer by the Archduke Rudolph opened:
   "Lieber Beet͟hoven, ich danke . . ." The accent on the first syllable by the composer himself was authenticated by
   Gerhard von Breuning and by Caroline van Beethoven (widow of Nephew Karl). The customary pronunciation in Bonn
   and the Netherlands today is on the first syllable.

   The letter given in KK 549 is here published for the first time.   April 23 [1900] no page given

DER BEETHOVENSTEIN IM HELENENTHAL.   (F)
   Account of dedication ceremonies of a memorial in Helenenthal (near Baden).
                                     July 1 [1900] no page given

EIN BISHER UNBEKANNTES BEETHOVEN-AUTOGRAPH.   (G)
   A letter from Steiner to Beethoven (Unger: 'Beethoven und seine Verleger' No. 102) bears various notations in pencil
   by Beethoven (as given in Prel. 1275).   August 17 [1900] 6

DER VERKEHRTE BEETHOVEN.   (H)
   Rhapsodic.   October 16 [1901] 1

KLINGER'S 'BEETHOVEN.'   Franz Servaes.   (I)
   "One may hope that Klinger's 'Beethoven' will be for our time what Phidias's 'Zeus' and Michelangelo's 'Moses'
   were (and still are) for theirs."   April 16 [1902] 1

DIE BEETHOVEN-WOCHE.   (J)
   Essay on the spirit behind the week of celebration at which Klinger's statue was dedicated.
                                     April 20 [1902] 3

WIE KLINGERS "BEETHOVEN" ENTSTAND.   (K)
   Review of Elsa Asenijew's 'Max Klinger's Beethoven' (Seeman, Leipzig).
                                     September 12 [1902] 1

BEETHOVEN IN BADEN.   Theodor von Frimmel.   (L)
   Summary and review of Hermann Rollett's book of the same title.
                                     November 3 [1902] 1
                                     Abendblatt

BEETHOVEN IN HEILIGENSTADT. Ludwig Speidel.   (M)
   Popular.   May 31 [1903] 1

BEETHOVENS LETZTE WOHNUNG.   Th. Thomas.   (A)
   The Schwarzspanierhaus as a Beethoven shrine.   September 20 [1903] 10

BEETHOVENS C-DUR-QUINTETT.   Theodor von Frimmel.   (B)
   Summary of articles in 'The Musical World' 69 [1889] 487, 509, 526 regarding the lawsuit with Artaria. (See also
   'Musical Quarterly' 34 [1948] 567)   November 15 [1903] 11

NEUES ZU BEETHOVEN.   Theodor von Frimmel.   (C)
   (1) Letter without date, name of addressee or salutation (but doubtless written to Gleichenstein in the first half
   of 1809): "Ist es wirklich wahr? bist du hier?" mentioning Beethoven's advice to Gleichenstein of the dedication
   to him of Op. 69, and mentioning that Beethoven had taken a residence at Walfischgasse 1087.   (2) Letter without
   date, name of addressee or salutation (but marked, presumably in the writing of Ferdinand Piringer, "Received November 6th 1821"): "Hier erhalten Sie das Verlangte, ich bitte mir . . ." in Beethoven's facetious mood, mentioning the 'O Tobias' Canon.   (3) Note written before the concert of April 22nd 1824: "Unterzeichneter ladet hiemet
   Höfflichst sämtliche Hr. Dilettenten ein" and giving list of friends concerned.   (4) Letter to Nephew Karl, probably
   1825 (Prelinger gives date August 22nd 1825): "Hier lieber Sohn w(enn) du glaubst, könnte man auch dem
   Peters für ein quartett 80 und das andere 70 Dukate (abverlangen)."   (5) Letter to Karl dated October 12th 1825
   starting: "Ich erhielt deinen Brief gestern ohne Datum und Tag."   (6) Letter to Karl dated February 24th 1826 starting: "Diese Quittung muss Morgen Vormittag am 25ten Februar bej Hofe erhoben werden."   (7) Note without address
   or date (probably about 1820): "Ich ersuche höfflichst um einen Karpfen von 3 pfund und einen kleinen hechten oder
   Schill oder sonst was d. g. Ergebenster Beethoven."   (8) Similar note starting: "Ich ersuche höfflichst um einen Karpfen
   von 3, auch 4 pfund oder noch lieber um einen hechsten von wenigstens 3 pfund . . ." Of these letters, No. 1 is
   correctly shown in BJ 2; Nos. 4, 5, and 6 are listed there, but first publication is credited to Prelinger (1907); Nos.
   2, 3, 7, and 8 are not listed.   None of these letters is included in KS.
                                                         December 20 [1903] 35

DIE WIENER PREMIERE VON "FIDELIO."   (D)
   An account of the circumstances leading to the composition of Fidelio, written in commemoration of the centenary
   of the first performance on November 20th 1805.   Beethoven's knowledge of Paer's 'Leonore' is denied for the reason
   that Paer's opera, while performed in Leipzig in 1804, received its first Vienna performance only in 1809.   The interesting coincidence is noted that in both operas the first duet between Marcelline and Jaquino starts in A major and
   modulates to C major.   November 19 [1905] 9

GRILLPARZERS GESPRÄCHE.   Robert Hirschfeld.   (E)
   Neither 'Melusine,' the opera book which Grillparzer wrote for Beethoven, nor the lyrics used or considered by
   Schubert and Mendelssohn are suitable for musical setting.   "Grillparzer had no sense of music."
                                                         November 26 [1905] 31

BEETHOVEN'S METRONOME.   Theodor von Frimmel.   (F)
   Papers in the Nachlass of Faust Pachler include correspondence from Johann Baptist Jenger which refers to Beethoven's
   last days, and states (letter of May 5th 1827) that Jenger had procured Beethoven's metronome from Beethoven's Nachlass as a memento for Frau Pachler-Koschak.   The metronome is still in the possession of the Pachler family; it was
   made in London, stands 31 cm. high, and is graduated from 50 to 160, giving the stated number of beats per minute.
                                                         March 26 [1906] 10

NOCH EINIGES ÜBER DIE DENKMALMISERE.   (G)
   "Instead of another statue of Beethoven, preserve the Beethoven houses!"
                                                         December 28 [1906] 7

BEETHOVEN-ERINNERUNGEN.   Wilhelm Ruland.   (H)
   Review of the memoirs of Friedrich Wähner, friend of Beethoven, written in 1827 but only recently published.
                                                         February 13 [1907] 1

ANGEBLICHE AUFFINDUNG NEUER BEETHOVEN-BRIEFE.   Theodor von Frimmel.   (A)
  A considerable number of letters from the Nachlass of Karl Bernard are to be released for publication.
                                                December 19 [1907] 11

KAISER FRANZ UND BEETHOVENS NEFFE.   (B)
  A memorandum dated June 20th 1820 is given regarding Nephew Karl and his mother, requested by Kaiser Franz
  from Count Sedlnitzky.   December 25 [1907] 13

EIN ECHTER BRIEF VON BEETHOVENS HAND IN WIENER BESITZ.   Theodor von Frimmel.   (C)
  Summary of the article in 'Musikalische Wochenblatt' 39 [1908] 307 regarding the letter given in KS I 389.
                                                April 7 [1908] 7

BEETHOVENS KREUTZERSONATE UND DER VIOLINVIRTUOSE BRIDGETOWER.   Theodor von Frimmel.   (D)
  Resume of article by Edwards in 'Musical Times' 49 [1908] 302.   May 31 [1908] 11

DIE UNSTERBLICHE GELIEBTE BEETHOVENS.   W. A. Thomas-San Galli.   (E)
  Contention that the famous letter was written in 1812 to Amalie Sebald.
                                                August 23 [1908] 31

BEETHOVEN ALS ERZIEHER IN FRANKREICH.   Gaston Deschamps.   (F)
  Fine writing on Beethoven's influence.   August 13 [1909] 1

NEU AUFGEFUNDENE TÄNZE VON BEETHOVEN.   Julius Korngold.   (G)
  General comments on the Mödlinger Dances; general remarks on Schindler's relations with Beethoven in connection
  with a newly published biography of Schindler by Hüffer.   October 22 [1909] 1

MONDSCHEINSONATE.   M. E. delle Grazie.   (H)
  Fiction   October 31 [1909] 14

ANDREAS AND NANNETTE STREICHER.   (I)
  Biographical sketch.   November 10 [1909] 9

BEETHOVENHÄUSER.   A. F. Seligman.   (J)
  Review of book of the same title (by A. Roessler?).   April 18 [1910] 1

GOETHE AND BEETHOVEN IN TEPLITZ.   Stephan Hock.   (K)
  General, with extensive quotations from Bettina Brentano.   July 21 [1912] 31

MANUSKRIPTE VON BEETHOVEN UND HAYDN IM BRITISCHEN MUSEUM.   (L)
  In 1911 the King of England presented to the British Museum a collection of music manuscripts which included the
  autographs (with corrections in Beethoven's hand) of the Ninth Symphony and the Overtures Opp. 113, 115, 117 and
  124. The manuscripts of other composers in this collection are listed.
                                                August 4 [1914] 10

NEU AUFSTELLUNG DER SAMMLUNGEN DER GESELLSCHAFT DER MUSIKFREUNDE.   (M)
  The exhibits of the Society include various Beethoven memorabilia.
                                                December 17 [1914] 11

BEETHOVENS GANG ZUM GLÜCK.   Rudolf Hans Bartsch.   (N)
  Fiction.   April 23 [1916] 36

BEETHOVEN ALS BANKAKTIONÄR.   Max Reinitz.   (O)
  No one but Schindler knew that on July 13th 1819 Beethoven had bought eight shares of bank stock. This article
  gives a circumstantial discussion of Beethoven's thinking and acting before he bought the shares Nos. 28623-30 at
  the advice of the bank director Baron von Eskeles (husband of the former Countess Wimpffen, for whom the Albumblatt 'Der edle Mensch' was written).   May 28 [1916] 16

ABENDSPAZIERGANG IM XIX BEZIRK.   Raoul Auernheimer.   (P)
  Reminiscences of Dobling in the Beethoven-Grillparzer period.   July 28 [1916] 1

TOD EINES NACHKOMMEN BEETHOVENS IN WIEN. (A)
"Today an infantryman of the Deutschmeisterregiment by the name of Beethoven died in Garrison Hospital No. 1. His full name was Karl Julius Maria Ludwig van Beethoven; he was born in Munich and was believed to be a relative of the great Beethoven, probably a grandnephew. Before the war he lived abroad in Paris and London as a journalist, and in 1916 he enlisted in Vienna as a 46-year-old infantry militiaman. He was last stationed as an Ordnance corpsman in the Ministry of War. He suffered from a foot ailment which through neglect had become malignant, so that he could not be saved."
December 11 [1917] 7

GRILLPARZER IM GESPRÄCH MIT BEETHOVEN. (B)
Much material in biographies of Grillparzer that is taken from the conversation books is distorted by erroneous readings, and Grillparzer's 'Reminiscences' are faulty in details. Detailed accounts are given of Grillparzer's visits to Beethoven in May 1823 (two visits), January 1824, and April 10th 1826.
January 3 [1918] 1

HENRIETTE SONNTAG. (C)
Memoirs of Sonntag give an account of her relations with Beethoven, and include a presumably unpublished letter: "Meine schöne werthe Sontag! Es war immer mein Vorsatz sie derweil einmal zu besuchen . . ." The letter is dated May 12th (probably 1824), but is damaged so that it cannot be quoted completely. It was presumably written a few days after the first performance of the Ninth Symphony.
January 27 [1918] 1

EIN UNBEKANNTE AKTENSTÜCK ÜBER BEETHOVEN. (D)
Letter from Paul Taussig. The concert of November 29th 1814 had been announced successively for the 20th, 22nd and 27th. The program included 'Der glorreiche Augenblick' and the 'Battle of Vittoria.' The reason for the postponement from Sunday November 27th was that the British ambassador had scruples against concerts on Sunday. A contemporary review of the concert was not enthusiastic. April 17 [1918] 8

EIN UNBEKANNTE AKTENSTÜCK ÜBER BEETHOVEN. (E)
The material given under this title in the previous day's issue was not new, but had been published in 1913.
April 18 [1918] 8

EIN UNVERÖFFENTLICHTER BRIEF BEETHOVENS. Theodor von Frimmel. (F)
Publication of the extant fragment of a letter to one of Blöchlinger's teachers named Köferle regarding bank shares. The extant portion starts: "Ich lege hier (einen Brief bej) an den Oberbuchhalter der (Oesterreicheschen) National Bank, woraus sie sehen . . ." Köferle's name appears in the conversation books. The conclusion of the letter is extant, together with a note to Köferle from Karl. May 4 [1918] 9

SALE AT AUCTION OF AN UNPUBLISHED BEETHOVEN LETTER. Adolf Donath. (G)
Summary is given of a letter of April 20th 1820 to the firm of Schlesinger (written by Nephew Karl as amanuensis, signed by Beethoven), beginning: "Meine Zeit ist sehr kurz," discussing the Scottish Songs Op. 108 at length, and saying that new sonatas, and perhaps trios or quartets, would be available, for which he must receive 40 ducats. (This letter was later published in full as No. 105 in Unger's 'Beethoven und seine Verleger.')
February 4 [1919] 1
Abendblatt

DIE BEETHOVEN-GEDENKTAFEL AM PASQUALATI-HAUS. (H)
Brief account of the relationship between Beethoven and Baron Joseph Pasqualati.
July 25 [1920] 10

ARTARIA & CO. Ernst Gross. (I)
Brief history of the firm, in honor of its sesquicentennial. November 16 [1920] 1

BEETHOVEN. Hugo v. Hofmannsthal. (J)
Sesquicentennial essay. (Reprinted in 'Inselschiff' 2 [1921] 97; published in translation in 'The Nation' 111 [1920] 776.)
December 12 [1920] 1

BEETHOVEN UND SEINE ZEIT. (K)
Sesquicentennial essay stressing Beethoven's German nationalism.
December 12 [1920] 1

DOKUMENTE ÜBER BEETHOVEN.   (A)
    Heiligenstadt will, an excerpt from 'Aus den Schwarzspanierhaus' ("Beethovens letzte Stunden"), and Grillparzer's
    funeral oration.   December 12 [1920] 2

GOETHES "KIND" BEI BEETHOVEN.   Alice Schmutzer.   (B)
    Romantic account of Bettina's meeting with Beethoven.   December 12 [1920] 8

BEETHOVEN-HÄUSER IN DER UMGEBUNG WIENS.   (C)
    Lengthy but probably incomplete list.   December 15 [1920] 7

BEETHOVEN UND DIE MODERNE.   Julius Korngold.   (D)
    Beethoven was himself a Modernist.   December 16 [1920] 1

BEETHOVEN ALS KAMMERMUSIKER.   Rudolf Seiller.   (E)
    Popular historical account of the early chamber music and the string quartets.
                                                  December 20 [1920] 2

SCHUTZ DEN BEETHOVEN-HÄUSERN.   (F)
    Account of a visit to the house at Hetzendorferstrasse 75 in which Beethoven lived in 1823.
                                                  December 23 [1920] 8

DER TAUBE BEETHOVEN.   Richard Smekal.   (G)
    Brief excerpts from the conversation books.   December 28 [1920] 1

BEETHOVEN UND SEIN MÄZEN FÜRST KINSKY.   Max Reinitz.   (H)
    Polemic against Josef Erwin Folkmann, who in 1860 published a monograph in which it was contended that the
    Kinsky estate had been overgenerous in its payments to Beethoven in consideration of the currency depreciation.
                                                  December 30 [1920] no page given
                                                  Abendblatt

BEETHOVEN IN VIENNA.   Heinrich Steger.   (I)
    Extracts from Beethoven's journal of 1819 to show his constant preoccupation with petty domestic matters. The
    letters given in KK 1372, KS 1163 and KS 1129 are published, as well as apparent first publication of a letter
    written in 1822 to Rochlitz: "Was wollen Sie in Wien hören?" pointing out that at that time Beethoven's works
    were out of fashion and little played.   January 21 [1921] 1

EINE VERWANDTE BEETHOVENS GESTORBEN.   (J)
    Death at the age of 90 of Juliana Schachner, whose mother's sister had been the wife of Nephew Karl.
                                                  November 27 [1921] 9

DER UR-FIDELIO.   (K)
    Announcement of a forthcoming performance of excerpts from Prieger's restoration of the original (1805) version
    of Fidelio, with brief comments on this version.   February 22 [1922] 5

EINE VERGESSENE BEETHOVEN-STÄTTE IN WIEN.   Theodor von Frimmel.   (L)
    The building in which Nephew Karl attended Blöchlinger's Institute, now known as Josefstädterstrasse 39, is de-
    scribed in detail.   April 6 [1923] 1
                                                  Abendblatt

DAS LEBEN BEETHOVENS AUS SEINER HANDSCHRIFT.   Max Hayek.   (M)
    A few lines from a facsimile of the Heiligenstadt will enabled a graphologist to read Beethoven's past, present
    and future.   April 8 [1923] 24

EIN GEZEICHNETES BEETHOVEN-BILDNISS.   (N)
    The Böhm sketch of the striding Beethoven is about to be offered at auction in Berlin.
                                                  June 23 [1923] 5

BEETHOVENS KONVERSATIONSHEFTE.   Josef Reitler.   (O)
    General.   November 14 [1923] 12

176

NEUE FREIE PRESSE (Continued)

THERESE MALFATTI -- EPISODE AUS BEETHOVENS LEBEN. Rudolf Hans Bartsch. (A
    Fiction.   February 2 [1924] 31

BEETHOVENS BRATSCHE. (B
    See 'Signale' 82 [1914] 721.   April 17 [1924] 7

BEETHOVEN IN DER UNGARGASSE. Theodor von Frimmel.   May 6 [1924] 1 (C
                                               Abendblatt

RICHARD WAGNER ÜBER BEETHOVENS NEUNTE SYMPHONIE.   May 8 [1924] 9 (D

BEETHOVEN RELIQUIEN IN WIEN. Siegfried Loewy. (E
    Transcription of the following letters: KS 1129, KK 1372, KFr 572, KS 954.
                                       August 4 [1924] 1
                                       Abendblatt

BEETHOVEN AUF WASHINGTON HEIGHTS. Ann Tizia Leitich. (F
    Essay based on a performance of the Ninth Symphony at the Stadium Concerts in New York.
                                     August 24 [1924] 23

DIE GESCHICHTE EINES BEETHOVEN-KLAVIERS. (G
    Description of a piano made by S. A. Vogel in Budapest, presented to Beethoven by Prince Lichnowsky (presumably in the 1790's) and given by Beethoven to Bernhard Feiler. It is noted that the piano had a range of six octaves.
                                     December 6 [1924] 1
                                     Abendblatt

DIE BEETHOVEN-ZENTENARFEIER. (H
    Tributes from many musicians.   March 26 [1927] 3
                                       Abendblatt

BEETHOVEN. Julius Korngold. (I
    Centenary essay.   March 27 [1927] 1

VÖLKERVERSÖHNUNG ALS GEDENKFEIER FÜR BEETHOVEN. Louis Barthou. (J
    Centenary essay by the French Minister of Justice.   March 27 [1927] 2

BEETHOVEN AND BISMARCK. Maximilian Harden. (K
    Imaginitive essay based on Bismarck's admiration for Beethoven.   March 27 [1927] 3

AUFFÜHRUNG DER "KANTATE AUF DEN TOD KAISER JOSEFS II." (L
    Program notes and review. The author of the text may have been either Eulogius Schneider, Greek Professor in Bonn, or Severin Anton Averdouc, Canon of Ehrenbreitstein; this text and that of the Erhebungskantate are probably by the same man.   March 27 [1927] 12

BLICK AUF BEETHOVEN. André Suarès. (M
    Centenary essay.   March 27 [1927] 31

BEETHOVENS TOD. Rudolf Hans Bartsch. (N
    Fantasy on Beethoven's deism.   March 27 [1927] 31

DIE FRAUEN UM BEETHOVEN. Paul Wiegler. (O
    Beethoven's many friendships with women represent his pursuit of the ideal.
                                     March 27 [1927] 32

DIE ZWEITE "LEONOREN"-OUVERTÜRE. Felix Weingartner. (P
    The version of this Overture described by Lütge ('Der Bär' [1927] 146) is of much historical importance.
                               March 27 [1927] 33

BEETHOVEN ALS REVOLUTIONÄR. Bernard Shaw. (Q
    Beethoven introduced into music the spirit of the people.   March 27 [1927] 34

N UNBEKANNTER BRIEF BEETHOVENS. Viktor Papp.   (A)
   Facsimile and transliteration of letter of 22 September 1807 to Hofrat Karner of Prince Esterhazy's staff in Eisenstadt
   (M-213). The author comments on the friendly tone of the letter.
                                             March 27 [1927] 36

UF DEN SPUREN DER "UNSTERBLICHEN GELIEBTEN." Jeno Mohacsi.   (B)
   Therese von Brunsvik's diaries from 1810 to 1855-56 are still extant, although the volumes for 1826-27, which
   might have contained references to Beethoven, are missing. The author appears to have found no significant information in these diaries.   April 3 [1927] 35

UF DEN SPUREN BEETHOVENS. Hermine Cloeter.   (C)
   Popular account of Beethoven's last visit to Gneixendorf.   November 8 [1927] 1;
                                                                  November 10 [1927] 1

                         NEUE MUSIK-ZEITUNG

JDWIG VAN BEETHOVEN.   (D)
   Biographical sketch.   1 [1880] No. 6

UR BEETHOVENSKIZZE IN Nr. 6 DER 'NEUES MUSIK-ZEITUNG.' Ludwig Nohl.   (E)
   Corrections   1 [1880] No. 8

DETISCHE ERKLÄRUNG VON BEETHOVENS SONATE E MOLL OPUS 90. Franziska Lomtano.   (F)
   Verses inspired by the sonata.   1 [1880] No. 17

ETHOVEN AND GOETHE. Otto Keller.   (G)
   Parallels in the characteristics and histories of the two men.   1 [1880] No. 17

HALT UND VORTRAG DER HERVORRAGENDSTEN SONATEN VON BEETHOVEN. Aug. Reiser.   (H)
   Pupils' guide to Opp. 13, 26, 27 No. 2, and 31 No. 1.   2 [1881] Nos. 14, 15, 16, 17, 18

DELIO: DATEN UND DEUTUNGEN. Louis Köhler.   (I)
   An outline of the history of the opera and its overtures, and a brief discussion of the importance of 'Fidelio' in the
   growth of operatic form and content.   3 [1882] No. 1

ETHOVEN AND WILHELMINE SCHRÖDER-DEVRIENT.   (J)
   A dramatic account of Schröder-Devrient's first appearance as Leonora.
                                                3 [1882] No. 5

J BEETHOVENS STERBETAG. E. Felix.   (K)
   Allegory.   3 [1882] No. 7

ETHOVENS TOD.   (L)
   Summary from the memoirs of one Heinrich Börnstein, giving no new information regarding Beethoven's death and
   funeral.   3 [1882] No. 8

ETHOVENS NEUNTE UND DIE TRADITION. Aug. Guckeisen.   (M)
   For the performance of the Ninth Symphony (and, to a large extent, for all other works of Beethoven) there can be
   no such thing as a truly founded Beethoven tradition. Beethoven himself conducted the symphony only once, and
   then after only two rehearsals of an orchestra which had of course never seen the music before. Furthermore, Beethoven was almost completely deaf at the time. Metronome markings, even those which he himself had assigned,
   meant nothing to Beethoven. In performance he would disregard them, and if he had occasion to re-metronomize
   a work (as he did the Ninth Symphony) his second markings would be quite different from his first ones. Marks of
   expression and dynamics, at best only a sketchy indication for the performer, were disregarded by Beethoven in
   his performances of his own works. Schindler pointed out that Beethoven's performance of the Sonata Op. 13 made
   of it a completely different work from what was written on paper. "No one has the right to criticize the performance

BEETHOVENS NEUNTE UND DIE TRADITION (Continued)
    of a musician by saying that it is not in accord with Beethoven's intentions, for no one knows what those intentions
    were. There can be only one interpretation balanced against another, one opinion against another."
                                                        3 [1882] No. 18

LUDWIG VAN BEETHOVEN, DER HEROS DER KLASSISCHEN MUSIK.   C. Plato.   (A
    General.   4 [1883] No. 4

BEETHOVEN'S A MAJOR SYMPHONY.   (B
    An ecstatic account.   4 [1883] No. 6

BEETHOVEN'S NINTH SYMPHONY.   (C
    An ecstatic account.   4 [1883] No. 11

EIN JUGENDTAG AUS DEM LEBEN LUDWIG VAN BEETHOVEN.   Mathieu Schwann.   (D
    Fictionalized account of improvising a storm on the organ to match a real storm in 1785.
                                                        4 [1883] No. 18

GIULIETTA AND LEONORA.   Carl Zastrow.   (E
    Fiction.   5 [1884] 114,126,139,150

BEETHOVENS EINZIGER SCHÜLER.   Ludwig Nohl.   (F
    Anecdotes of Ries's relations with Beethoven.   5 [1884] 253,265

KLEINE MUSIKALISCHE HUMORESKEN AUS BEETHOVENS LEBEN.   Anna Morsch.   (C
    A discussion of some of the canons.   6 [1885] 9

DIE "NEUNTE SINFONIE" VON BEETHOVEN.   (I
    Fiction.   6 [1885] 105

SONNIGE TAGE AUS DEM LEBEN EINES EINSAMEN.   Clare Gerhard.   (I
    Romantic account of Beethoven's days in Teplitz in 1811 and 1812 with (Christoph August) Tiedge, Elise von der
    Reckem and Amalie Sebald, and with Goethe.   7 [1886] 62

DIE SONATEN VON LUDWIG VAN BEETHOVEN.   Aug. Reissmann.   (J
    Description for pupils.   7 [1886] 89

BEETHOVEN'S PASTORAL SYMPHONY.   Th. Erasmus.   (k
    Poem.   7 [1886] 137

DISCOVERY OF THE COMPLETE SCORE OF THE MUSIC TO 'THE DEDICATION OF THE HOUSE.'   (
    See NBJ 7 [1937] 115.   7 [1886] 178

DIE GEBEINE BEETHOVENS AND SCHUBERTS.   Aug. Lesimple.   (
    Neither composer was allowed to lie quiet in his grave.   8 [1887] 66

BEETHOVEN UND SEIN NOTENSCHREIBER.   (
    Letter to Wolanek (KS II 357).   8 [1887] 230

ZWEI BISHER UNGEDRUCKTE BRIEFE L. VAN BEETHOVENS.   Emil Jonas.   (
    Letters dated March 1st 1823 to the Royal Academy at Stockholm and to the King of Sweden (KS II 230,231).
                                                        9 [1888] 55

GOETHE AND BEETHOVEN.   (
    One who claimed to have been present says that Goethe attended the concert given by Beethoven and Polledro in
    Teplitz in August 1812.   10 [1889] 191

DIE VIER OUVERTÜREN ZU FIDELIO.   H. Simon.   (
    Brief historical account.   10 [1889] 219

GOETHE AND BEETHOVEN.   (A)
   Summary of Beethoven's letter to Goethe of April 17th 1811 ("Nur einen Augenblick Zeit gewährt mir" -- not in KS;
   first published in Frimmel's 'Neue Beethoveniana' p. 349 [?]) and February 8th 1823 (KS II 224).
                                                    11 [1890] 7

DIE 9. SYMPHONIE BEETHOVENS.   (B)
   Interpretation.   11 [1890] 79

LUDWIG VAN BEETHOVEN UND GRÄFIN GIULIETTA.   J. Barber.   (C)
   Fiction.   11 [1890] 261,277,293

BEETHOVENS E-MOLL SONATE.   Alfred Schütz.   (D)
   Analysis of form and content.   12 [1891] 115,126,140

EIN BEETHOVENBILD.   Ad. Gründler.   (E)
   Description of an unidentified picture of Beethoven.   12 [1891] 154

EIN BEETHOVEN-BILDNIS.   Oskar Linke.   (F)
   Comments on the paper by Gründler (p. 154). The "heaven-storming" type of portrait does not represent the real
   Beethoven.   12 [1891] 211

GOETHE, MOZART AND BEETHOVEN.   H. v. Winterfeld.   (G)
   An account of Goethe's relationship and attitude towards Beethoven.
                                                    13 [1892] 28

ÜBER DAS FINALE DER NEUNTEN.   Oskar Linke.   13 [1892] 158   (H)

BEETHOVENS HÄNDE.   Oskar Linke.   (I)
   Accounts of contemporaries.   13 [1892] 173

EINE FREUNDIN BEETHOVENS.   L. Erbach.   (J)
   Brief account of Baroness Dorothea von Ertmann. 13 [1892] 210

DIE BEETHOVEN-SAMMLUNG ZU HEILIGENSTADT.   Armin Friedmann.   (K)
                                                    15 [1894] 279,296

BEETHOVEN STUDIES.   Theodor von Frimmel.   (L)
   A note without date (not in KS; KK No. 947; BJ 2 says "1819?"), regarding a portrait of Beethoven, was not written
   to Stöber (the engraver) but most likely to Zmeskall. This note accordingly gives no positive evidence of contact
   between Beethoven and Stöber or his associate, the painter Denhauser.
                                                    16 [1895] 33

FRANZ SCHUBERT AND BEETHOVEN.   R. Batka.   (M)
   A comparison of the personalities and works of the two men.   16 [1895] 44,56

ÜBER BEETHOVENS STREICHQUARTETTEN.   Wilhelm Mauke.   (N)
   A discussion of the quartets at some length, with musical examples.
                                                    16 [1895] 79,91,103,115,126

HAYDN, MOZART, BEETHOVEN.   Rudolph Prochazka.   17 [1896] 79   (O)

BEETHOVEN ALS HARMONIKER.   Cyrill Kistler.   (P)
   Many passages from compositions by Beethoven are cited in which the harmonies (in the opinion of the author)
   foreshadow Wagner.   17 [1896] 81

BEETHOVENS KLAVIERVARIATIONEN.   (Q)
   A discussion of various sets of variations (both independent compositions and movements from sonatas) from the
   standpoint of their advance beyond the routine and the mechanical.
                                                    17 [1896] 82,98

DIE NATURSCHILDERUNG IN BEETHOVENS PASTORALSYMPHONIE. Wilhelm Mauke. (A
 "Between the tone painting of Beethoven and of one of our young German contemporaries is the difference between
 Nature and Naturalism." 17 [1896] 83

ZADOW'S BEETHOVEN BUST. 17 [1896] 220 (B

BEETHOVENS 'UNSTERBLICHE GELIEBTE.' (C
 Discussion of some of the conjectures as to her identity. 18 [1897] 161

DIE SAMMLUNG ARTARIA. (D
 A list of the Beethoven manuscripts in the collection which is about to be broken up.
  18 [1897] 275

SKIZZEN BEETHOVENS ZUR 10. SYMPHONIE UND ZUR BACHOUVERTÜRE. (E
 The sketches described (and quoted in part) in NB II 11, 12. 19 [1898] 154

BEETHOVENS FIDELIO IN FRANKREICH. (F
 The first Paris performances, in 1829 by a German company, were coldly received. In 1852 six performances were
 given by an Italian company, but only in 1860 with Pauline Viardot as Leonore did the opera really take hold.
  20 [1899] 89

NEUE ANEKDOTEN AUS DEM LEBEN BEETHOVENS. H. E. Krehbiel. (G
  20 [1899] 135

ERINNERUNGEN AN BEETHOVEN. (H
 The horn virtuoso Joseph Rudolf Lewy tells of having played Opp. 16 and 17 in 1822 with Beethoven at the Pf, and of
 having heard him improvise for Prince Lobkowitz about the same time, though later the advance of his deafness precluded this activity. 21 [1900] 42

BEETHOVEN'S RONDO IN C MAJOR (1783). (I
 Reprint of the music (see also 'Peters-Jahrbuch' 6 [1899] 68). 21 [1900] following p. 154

BEETHOVENS CHARAKTER. K. Grunsky. 21 [1900] 182,195 (J

DIE BEETHOVEN-HÄUSER IN WIEN. Hugo Klein. (K
 During Beethoven's 35 years in Vienna he lived in some thirty different dwellings. Many of these are identified and
 commented upon, and the history of his last dwelling, the Schwarzspanierhaus, is given.
  24 [1903] 273

EINE BEETHOVENSCHE SONATE. Willibald Nagel. (L
 Causes leading to the development of the sonata form; detailed analysis of Op. 10 No. 3.
  25 [1903] 12,35

ALLERLEI VON BEETHOVEN. Hugo Klein. (M
 Description of the Schwarzspanierhaus; a reminiscence of Beethoven by the poet Hermann Rollett; the relationship of
 Giulietta to Beethoven. 25 [1903] 104

DREI BEETHOVEN-BRIEFE. (N
 KS II 221 and 285 are transcribed and KS II 239 summarized (see 'Die Musik' 3$_2$ [1904] 412).
  25 [1904] 301

BEETHOVEN LANDSCHAFTEN. Egon v. Komorzynski. (O
 A description of the countryside what was so important to Beethoven.
  26 [1904] 3

BEETHOVENS 'UNSTERBLICHE GELIEBTE.' (P
 Biographical sketch of Therese von Brunswick. 26 [1904] 34

GLOSSEN ZUR BEETHOVEN-KENTNISS. Friedrich Kerst. (Q
 A portrait claimed to be that of the youthful Beethoven is actually a portrait of the poet Max von Schenkendorf (see

also Frimmel's 'Beethovens äussere Erscheinung' (1905) p. 164). A report is mentioned of a conversation book recently acquired by the Beethoven-Haus at Bonn, described as having been owned by Beethoven's great-grandson! La Mara, in a collection of Beethoven letters, said that Nephew Karl had contemplated suicide, but had been dissuaded by Ferdinand Holz. Actually, the suicide was attempted, and it was Holz (Karl, not Ferdinand) who told Beethoven of the attempt. The statement in a recent book that Goethe made only a single specific comment about Beethoven is false. The original of the letter of February 10th 1811 to Bettina (KS I 208) has long been known. Beethoven's unanswered letter of February 8th 1823 to Goethe (KS II 224) has long been known and was most admirably written.

26 [1905] 263

ZUM JUBILÄUM DER EROICA-SYMPHONIE.   (A)
  A historical account of the composition and early performances of the symphony.
26 [1905] 285

IM ZEICHEN FRIEDRICH SCHILLERS. Wilhelm Weber.   (B)
  Verses from Schiller as commentaries on the Seventh Symphony.
26 [1905] 292

KOMPOSITIONEN SCHILLERSCHER GEDICHTE. Julius Blatchke.   (C)
  Beethoven once remarked that Schiller's poetry was most difficult to set to music. Settings by various composers are listed, and a setting of the 'Ode to Joy' by Zelter is given in full.
26 [1905] 343

BEETHOVENS LIEBESLEBEN UND FIDELIO. Fritz Volbach.   (D)
  The opera, a painting in tones of the perfect wife, reflects Beethoven's association with and deep interest in many noble and lovely ladies.   27 [1905] 73

DIE ERSTE AUFFÜHRUNG DES "FIDELIO." Egon v. Komorzynski.   (E)
  Circumstances leading to the composition of the opera and to its disappointing first performance.
27 [1905] 76

BEETHOVENS FIS DUR-SONATE. P. Goos.   (F)
  Appreciation.   27 [1906] 230

DAS ORIGINAL-MANUSKRIPT DER WALDSTEIN SONATE VON BEETHOVEN.   (G)
  Description.   28 [1906] 18

NEUAUFGEFUNDENE TANZ-KOMPOSITIONEN BEETHOVENS. Hugo Riemann.   (H)
  Publisher's announcement of the discovery and publication of the eleven Vienna dances ('Mödlinger-Tänze').
28 [1907] 111

BEETHOVEN AND GEORGE THOMSON. Fritz Erckmann.   (I)
  Summary based on the book by Cuthbert Hadden.   28 [1907] 161

EIN ARMENKONZERT BEETHOVENS. M. Kaufmann.   (J)
  Account of the concert with Polledro at Karlsbad on August 6th 1812 for the benefit of the fire sufferers at Baden-bei-Wien.   28 [1907] 269

DEATH OF A PERSON WHO HAD SEEN BEETHOVEN.   (K)
  Michael Kleppel, who recently died at the age of 88, had often seen Beethoven in Heiligenstadt and Nussbaum.
28 [1907] 355

C MOLL-SYMPHONIE UND PASTORALE. Egon v. Komorzynski.   (L)
  Centennial essay.   28 [1907] 408

EIN URTEIL ÜBER BEETHOVEN. Egon v. Komorzynski.   (M)
  A writer in 1803 compares Beethoven and Anton Eberl as instrumental composers, to the advantage of the latter.
28 [1907] 425

BEETHOVEN'S CHORAL FANTASY. Victor Lederer.   (A)
  Description.   29 [1908] 228

NEUE BEETHOVEN-LITERATUR. Ernst Rychnovsky.   (B)
  Extensive reviews of the two volumes of Frimmel's 'Beethoven-Studien,' of the collections of letters by Kalischer
  and by Prelinger, and of other writings on Beethoveniana.   29 [1908] 317

BEETHOVEN-ERRINERUNGEN VON FRIEDRICH WÄHNER, EINEM ZEITGENOSSEN. Wilhelm Ruland.   (C)
  Description, anecdotes and personal comments, written in 1827 by a member of Beethoven's circle of friends in
  Vienna. (Reprinted in toto in Frimmel's 'Beethoven-Handbuch' II 393)
                                                  29 [1908] 457

EIN BESUCH BEI BEETHOVEN.   (D)
  Account of a visit in 1825 by Karl Gottlieb Freudenberg.   30 [1908] 22

FÜR DEN KLAVIERUNTERRICHT: LUDWIG VAN BEETHOVEN: SONATE OPUS 2 No. 3. Heinrich Schwartz.   (E)
                                                  30 [1909] 318,431

BEETHOVENS MARSCH FÜR DIE BÖHMISCHE LANDWEHR. Otto Schmid.   (F)
  Detailed account of the history of the March in F (NV p. 140; GA 25/287 No. 1).
                                                  30 [1909] 434

SKETCHES BY JOSEF TELTSCHER OF BEETHOVEN ON HIS DEATH BED.   (G)
                                                  30 [1909] 440

FÜR DEN KLAVIERUNTERRICHT: LUDWIG VAN BEETHOVEN: SECHS VARIATIONEN OPUS 34. Heinrich Schwartz. (H)
                                                  31 [1910] 270

BEETHOVENS "EGMONT"-MUSIK. Egon v. Komorzynski.   (I)
  Centenary essay, stressing the intimate suitability of the music for the drama.
                                                  31 [1910] 394

ZUM VERSTÄNDNIS UND RICHTIGE VORTRAG VON BEETHOVENS F MOLL-SONATE OPUS 2. A. Schütz.   (J)
  A detailed analysis from the performer's standpoint.   31 [1910] 449

A NOTE TO ZMESKALL.   (K)
  The sale is reported of a letter without date to Zmeskall, apparently starting: "Wir sind ihnen ganz kuriose zugethan."
  The statement is made that this note is not in the Kalischer 'Briefe'; it is not #1319 in BJ II.
                                                  31 [1910] 458

EIN BESUCH WIECKS BEI BEETHOVEN.   (L)
  Account of a visit in May 1826. "He improvised for me for half an hour or more, having put on his ear trumpet and
  applied it to the sounding board of the pianoforte."   32 [1911] 25

BEETHOVEN AND GOETHE. Leopold Hirschberg.   (M)
  Beethoven's attitude towards Goethe and vice versa; Goethe's influence on Beethoven; Bettina's part in the relationship; the meeting of the two men in 1812 and their subsequent attitudes regarding one another. A list is given of 18
  settings by Beethoven of writings by Goethe.   32 [1911] 121,152

EINE VERSCHOLLENE BEETHOVEN-ANEKDOTE. Leopold Hirschberg.   (N)
  An unknown and unconventional traveler who shared a room at a country inn which Count Franz Pocci proved to be
  Beethoven.   32 [1911] 128

DER GEMISSHANDELTE BEETHOVEN. Karl Fuchs.   (O)
  Vigorous criticism of Frederic Lamond as an interpreter of Beethoven, with many examples drawn from his readings
  of Op. 110 and of the C minor Variations.   32 [1911] 289,362

NEUE BEETHOVEN-STUDIEN. I. BEETHOVENS BEZIEHUNGEN ZU MUZIO CLEMENTI. Max Unger.   (P)
  Beethoven held Clementi in very high regard as a pianist, pedagogue, composer, and musician. The first meeting
  of the two men was in late 1803, while Clementi was in Vienna on a tour (artistic and business) which traversed much
  of the continent. A letter of June 10th 1804 from Clementi to his partner Collard in London states that he had entered

into an agreement with Härtel whereby Clementi would pay half of the purchase price of any new works by Beethoven, receiving therefore the rights for the British Dominions. A letter of September 1804 from Härtel to Clementi states that Beethoven had offered an Oratorio (Op. 85), a Symphony (Op. 36), the Triple Concerto (Op. 56), and three Piano Sonatas (Op. 31), and suggests that the two firms refuse the Oratorio (which, as time proved, was the only one of these works eventually to be published by Breitkopf & Härtel) and make an offer for the others. The contract between Beethoven and Clementi (in German translation) and the letter of April 22nd 1807 from Clementi to Collard are given as in TK II 102-04. A letter of December 28th 1808 is given from Clementi in Vienna to Collard in London asking why the contract with Beethoven had not been carried out. A letter of September 1809 is given from Clementi in Vienna to Collard in London, berating him for not having paid Beethoven. (Note that more than two years had passed since the inception of the contract, presumably with no payment at all.) Business dealings between Beethoven and Clementi seem to have ceased on the publication in London in 1809 of the last of the works covered by the 1807 contract. After Clementi returned to London in the summer of 1810 he did not revisit Vienna until after Beethoven's death.   32 [1911] 389

BEETHOVENS HEIRATSPROJEKT.   Max Unger.   (A)
 Beethoven's first acquaintance with Therese von Malfatti may safely be assigned to the spring of 1807 (KS I 128) when Therese was 14 years old. (The author here gives 1793 (1 January) as the birth date of Therese, but elsewhere ('Musical Quarterly' 11 [1925] 72) he cites reasons for assuming a birth year of 1791.) Gleichenstein had become welcome in the Malfatti household because of his skill as a 'cellist. The letter of March 1809 to Gleichenstein (KS I 155) may indicate Beethoven's continued interest in Gleichenstein's future sister-in-law. The dedication of Op. 69 about this time to Gleichenstein is compatible with this interest. The following letters to Gleichenstein, assigned by Kalischer to 1807 or 1808, were probably written in late 1809 or 1810; KS Nos. 122, 124, 126, 127, 132, 143, and 149; the letter to Zmeskall given in KA as No. 23 is also probably from this period. The series of letters to Gleichenstein from April and perhaps the first few days of May 1810 (KS Nos. 116, 117, 119, 120, 125, 133, 134, 135) portrays this growing interest. Beethoven's offer to purchase a piano for the Malfattis at his preferential price (letters Nos. 133, 135) is otherwise quite out of character. (For perhaps the only other case of this kind see KS I 371) Beethoven's requests to Zmeskall for a looking-glass (KS I 187-88) also explain themselves quite easily.

The letter to Therese (KS No. 136), which in spirit is certainly a love letter, certainly dates from 1810, probably in April or the first day or two of May. From its text it is evidently a week or somewhat more before the eighth of some month; the month could not have been June or later, since about the middle of May Beethoven met Bettina Brentano, who promptly swept every other woman out of his mind. As stated specifically by Wegeler (WRK p. 211), Beethoven's request for a copy of his birth certificate (KS I 188) was in connection with his hopes for a marriage, which shortly thereafter were blasted. Two very low-spirited letters to Gleichenstein (KS Nos. 147, 148) undoubtedly date from the days of May immediately following the rejection of the proposal of marriage which Beethoven may have made to Therese (quite possibly in the "half hour" referred to in KS No. 136). Melancholy passages in Beethoven's notebooks over the period 1810-20 may well refer to Therese. Bettina Brentano's letter of May 28th 1810 to Goethe (TK II 187) proves conclusively that she first met Beethoven only during this month (probably later than the 15th -- see TK II 178), so the assumption of Kalischer (see KS I 190) that Beethoven's marriage plans of April and early May 1810 (leading to the request for the birth certificate) were based on a proposal made to Bettina in 1809, is quite untenable.   32 [1911] 429, 453

MUSIKALISCHE ORNAMENTIK: L. VAN BEETHOVEN.   Edward Dannreuther.   (B)
 Translation of material in the author's 'Musical Ornamentation' (Novello) II pp. 111-20.
                               33 [1912] 108, 373;   34 [1913] 191

ERLÄUTERUNGEN ZU KLAVIERABENDEN: BEETHOVEN-ABEND.   C. Fuchs.   (C)
 Nontechnical program notes for the 'La stessa, la stessissima' Variations and the Sonatas Opp. 7, 57, 109.
                               33 [1912] 173

ZUR JUGEND-SYMPHONIE BEETHOVENS.   Bruno Schrader.   (D)
 In the late 1880's the author, while cataloguing the music collections in Jena, came across the parts of what is now known as the Jena Symphony. Two more experienced and eminent musical scholars agreed with him that the work was not by Beethoven, so no further attention was paid to it.   33 [1912] 226

PREVIOUSLY UNKNOWN NUMBERS IN THE PROMETHEUS MUSIC.   (A)
    The original score of the Prometheus music in the Vienna Royal Library contains three numbers which are to be
found in no other score.   34 [1913] 261

BEETHOVEN ALS KLAVIERSPIELER.   Konrad Volker.   (B)
    A detailed account of Beethoven's training and career as a pianist, with many quotations from contemporaries.
                                                               36 [1915] 17,41,65

GEMEINSAME ZÜGE DER "ANTIPODEN" BEETHOVEN UND SCHUBERT.   Konrad Huschke.   (C)
    The two men, different in so many ways, possessed in common a love of nature, an independence of spirit, and
idealistic approach to their art, vigor of their support of German music against Italian, and their reverence for Goethe
and Handel.   36 [1915] 253

BEETHOVEN UND SEINE ANKLÄGER.   Gustav Ernest.   (D)
    A condensation by the author of his articles of the same title in 'Deutsche Rundschau' 162 [1915] 27, 450, defending
Beethoven's good name in connection with his action against Brother Karl's widow for the recovery of 1500 fl. and
for the guardianship of Nephew Karl, his suit against the Kinsky estate, his relations with publishers (especially in
the matter of the Missa Solemnis), his failure to compose the cantata for which the Gesellschaft der Musikfreunde
had paid him, his suit against Maelzel, and his pleas of destitution during his last years.
                                                               36 [1915] 282

LUDWIG UND JOHANN VAN BEETHOVENS BEZIEHUNGEN ZU LINZ.   Franz Gräflinger.   (E)
    For the most part, a resume of material from Thayer, with the further information that in 1813 Johann bought a
pharmacy in Urfahr (a suburb of Linz), and that from 1834 to 1843 he owned a dwelling in this town.
                                                               37 [1916] 28,41

VON ALTEN UND NEUEN BEETHOVEN-BRIEFEN.   Max Unger.   (F)
    A transcription of some 75 Beethoven letters (of many of which the originals have been lost) by Aloys Fuchs has
been found.   A corrected version of a letter to C. F. Peters (KS II 330) is given; the author attributes this letter
to shortly before the break with Peters in December 1825.   Facsimile and transcription of a hitherto unpublished
letter without date or name of addressee, but presumably to Steiner in the spring of 1826, regarding change of
title of a transcription which they were publishing.   Note without date or name of addressee, but possibly to
Holz in connection with the note given in TD V 585.   Note without date or name of addressee (probably from
Beethoven's last years), reading: "Kann man sich heute nicht barberen lassen? Btvn. "
                                                               37 [1916] 378

DIE MUSIKERFAMILIEN STEIN-STREICHER.   Theodor Bolte.   (G
                                                               38 [1917] 322,333,352,383

NATIONAL-GUARDSMAN BEETHOVEN.   (H
    An emotional word-picture of Karl Julius van Beethoven (Nephew Karl's grandson), an unsuccessful journalist become
an unsuccessful soldier.   38 [1917] 375

BEETHOVENS TEPLITZER BADEREISEN VON 1811 UND 1812.   Max Unger.   (I
    Analysis of the guest registers of this spa for the years in question.
                                                               39 [1918] 86

EIN DOKUMENT JOHANN VAN BEETHOVENS.   Theodor Haas.   (J
    A petition dated February 19th 1803 (which was refused) to the Magistrate of Vienna that Johann be accepted as
lessee of the pharmacy "Zum guten Hirten. " In this petition Johann signs his name Johann von Beethowen, and
states his age as 30 years instead of 27.   40 [1919] 6

HUGO RIEMANN: ANALYSE VON BEETHOVENS KLAVIERSONATEN.   Hugo Holle.   (K
    A detailed and critical review.   40 [1919] 198

BEETHOVENS KLAVIERSONATE IN AS DUR. Theodor von Frimmel. (A)
Suggestions for performance. 41 [1920] 136

ZUR BEETHOVENS TONSPRACHE. Armin Knab. (B)
Similarities are pointed out between certain Beethoven themes and those of Mozart and other predecessors.
41 [1920] 294,311

EIN WORT ZUR AUSGABE DER BEETHOVEN-BRIEFE BEI SCHUSTER & LÖFFLER. Theodor Haas. (C)
Kalischer's 'Beethoven-Briefe' is criticized as being most carelessly transcribed from the originals. Eleven unequiv-
ocal errors in the Heiligenstadt will are listed. 42 [1921] 4

BEETHOVENS REZITATIV-SONATE. Theodor von Frimmel. (D)
Suggestions for performance. 42 [1921] 18

DIE ZWEITE DEUTSCHE AUFFÜHRUNG VON BEETHOVENS NEUNTER SYMPHONIE ZU AACHEN AM 23. MAY 1825. (E)
Reinhold Zimmermann.
Details are given of the circumstances leading to the performance described in TK III 188. A corrected transcription
is given of Beethoven's letter of April 9th 1825 to Ries (KS II 362). 42 [1921] 71

BEETHOVEN UND WIR. Hermann Abert. (F)
Essay commemorating the sesquicentennial of Beethoven's birth. 42 [1921] 81

ZUR PSYCHOLOGIE DES BEETHOVENSCHEN SCHAFFENS. Arnold Schering. (G)
Beethoven's method of working up inspired music from trivial initial ideas is exemplified in the development of the
first song of the 'An die ferne Geliebte' cycle (Op. 98), written at the time (1815-16) when Beethoven was at the
height of his creative powers. The steps in this refining process are given from NB II 334, and the successive changes
are discussed. 42 [1921] 85

BEETHOVEN UND DIE VORCLASSISCHE ÜBERGANGSZEIT. Wilhelm Fischer. (H)
Beethoven is considered as the culmination of his predecessors of the previous hundred years.
42 [1921] 87

BEETHOVEN UND DIE ZEITSTILE. Hans Joachim Moser. (I)
Beethoven is certainly not a representative of the Rococo, nor can he properly be pigeonholed as either 'Classical'
or 'Romantic.' Rather he is "a true German representative of the 'Directoire,' a 'Noble Jacobin.'" Many features
of his style stem from the psychology of the French Revolution, not the least the use of quasi-military music (e.g.,
the episode in the Agnus Dei of the Missa Solemnis). 42 [1921] 89

BEETHOVEN IN MÖDLING. Theodor von Frimmel. (J)
Introductory words before a quartet concert in Mödling (see also Frimmel's 'Beethoven-Forschung' 2 [1918] 115).
42 [1921] 91

BEETHOVENS GEISTIGE PERSÖNLICHKEIT. Ernst Ludwig Schellenberg. (K)
42 [1921] 94

DER BEETHOVEN-KULT DER ZUKUNFT. W. Nagel. 42 [1921] 96 (L)

BEETHOVEN AND GOETHE. G. v. Graevenitz. 42 [1921] 102 (M)

A SCHÜSSERL UND A REINDL." Theodor Haas. (N)
Words and music are given to the song which Beethoven requested in his letter of December 1st 1816 to Steiner & Co.
(KS II 1) and which (slightly modified) appears as an 'Air autrichien' in Op. 105 No. 3.
42 [1921] 103

BEETHOVEN-SPIELER. Walter Niemann. (O)
Brief comments on Eugen d'Albert, Frederic Lamond, Conrad Ansorge and Max Pauer.
42 [1921] 104

SCHINDLER ÜBER BEETHOVENS 8. SYMPHONIE. Reinhold Zimmermann. (P)
Fanciful program notes written by Schindler for a performance of this symphony in 1835.
42 [1921] 124

BEETHOVENS OPUS 31 II.   Wilhelm Dauffenbach.   *   (A)
    Discussion of similarities between the first movement of this sonata and the first movement of the Fifth Symphony.
                                    42 [1921] 153

BEETHOVEN IM KURORT BADEN BEI WIEN.   Theodor von Frimmel.   (B)
    Beethoven's first known visit to Baden was to see Count Browne in 1802 or 1803 (WRK p. 108). Letters from Beethoven,
    and other information, show that he was in Baden in the summers of 1804, 1807, 1810, probably 1812 (in this year he
    gave a benefit concert with the violinist Polledro in Karlsbad for the benefit of the inhabitants of Baden who had suf-
    fered from the fire of July 26th), 1813, probably 1814, 1815, 1816, possibly 1817 and the three following summers,
    certainly during the summers of 1821-25. For many of these years his place of residence is known.
                                    43 [1922] 97

JOSEPH WÖLFL, DER RIVALE BEETHOVENS.   Fritz Erckmann.   (C)
    Biographical sketch.   43 [1922] 119

DER LETZTE SATZ DER EROICA.   Theodor Veidl.   (D)
    This movement proves that "even up to today, Beethoven is the greatest musical humorist."
                                    43 [1922] 178

BEARBEITUNG DER STREICHQUARTETTEN BEETHOVENS FÜR KLAVIER ZU ZWEI HÄNDEN, EIN KLAVIERSATZPROBLEM.   (E)
        August Stradal.
    In the last quartets the importance of the lower register falls off, and the emphasis is on the upper tones. Accordingly
    these works are easier to transcribe faithfully for Pf 2 hands than the works of Beethoven's first or second period, in
    which the distribution of the parts is too wide for two hands to cover (see also p. 349). It was presumably regarding
    the Op. 18 quartets that Liszt made the statement that they defied transcription. In the opinion of the author, Op.
    133 is no more unplayable in transcription for Pf 2 hands than the fugue of Op. 106. The orchestral works prove more
    amenable to transcription than the quartets, if only that the technique of writing for the orchestra is separated from
    the piano by a less unbridgeable gap.   43 [1922] 220

DER LANDSKNECHTMARSCH IN BEETHOVENS 5. SYMPHONIE.   W. Hisgen.   (F)
    The opening measures of the finale of the Fifth Symphony are foreshadowed by a Landsknechtmarsch which Beethoven
    doubtless heard during his boyhood in Bonn.   43 [1922] 348

ZUR BEETHOVENS GEHÖRLEIDEN.   Willi Möllendorff.   (G)
    Beethoven was no exception to the general rule that loss of hearing affects the upper range of sounds first, and the
    bass last of all. Therefore the tendency in his last years to give greater importance to the treble register (see p. 220)
    cannot soundly be attributed to his deafness. It should be noted that although he was increasingly hard of hearing, he
    never became completely deaf.   43 [1922] 349

GEDANKEN BEI BETRACHTUNG DER BEETHOVEN-MASKE.   Theodor Haas.   (H
    The technique of preparation of a life mask, at least in Beethoven's day, made it impossible to secure a faithful like-
    ness of the subject.   43 [1922] 391

AUF BEETHOVEN-SPUREN. I. EIN UNBEKANNTER BEETHOVEN-BRIEF.   Max Unger.   (I)
    A letter without date (but from its contents certainly written in 1816) to Kanka regarding collection of the annuity
    from the Kinsky estate. A receipt for the semiannual payment of 600 gulden for the period April 1st to September
    30th 1825 (see also 'Beethoven Jahrbuch' 2 [1909] 42) has also been found.
                                    44 [1923] 149

AUF BEETHOVEN-SPUREN. II. BEETHOVEN UND KASSEL.   Max Unger.   (J
    This article is described as an amplification of the material assembled by Thayer (TK II 135ff) and by Heinrichs in
    'Beethovens Beziehungen zu Cassel' (1920). Beethoven's invitation to Kassel (Beethovens Berufung nach Kassel). The
    known facts are given at some length. (NOTE by DWM. In discussing the annuity contract, the author says that some
    years before 1809 an annuity of 600 florins had been settled upon Beethoven by Prince Lobkowitz. In a private com-
    munication to DWM through Dr. Georg Kinsky, Dr. Unger states that this was a slip of the pen, the annuity referred
    to being that mentioned in two of Beethoven's letters of 1800 (KS I 27, 29) as having been bestowed by Prince
    Lichnowsky.)   44 [1923] 245

BEETHOVEN AND DR. G. CHR. GROSHEIM.   (K
    A summary of the material given by Heinrichs, with evidence that Beethoven received a letter from Grosheim in
    1823 (hitherto unsuspected). (See also 45 [1924] 141)   44 [1923] 247

BEETHOVEN AND LUDWIG SPOHR.   (A)
    The relationship between Beethoven and Spohr is described much as in TK II 236. To a canon which Beethoven wrote
    in Spohr's album on March 3rd 1815 (KS I 353) he added the words: "Mögten Sie doch lieber Spohr, überall, wo Sie
    wahre Kunst und Künstler finden, gerne meiner gedenken/ ihres Freundes/ Ludwig von Beethoven." Reference is made
    to two unpublished letters to Spohr, dated July 27th 1823 and September 17th 1823 (see 45 [1924] 141). For letter of
    Sept (Feb ?), see 'Allgemeine Musik-Zeitung' 21 [1894] 663.)   44 [1923] 248

AUF BEETHOVEN-SPUREN. III. Max Unger.   (B)
    First publication of facsimile and transcription of an abusive letter without date (probably from the first half of
    August 1819, thus preceding KK # 906 August 27th and KS II 141 September 14th and perhaps KK # 932 without
    date) to Blöchlinger. The author mentions the possibility that this letter was never sent. Transcription of letter
    without date or name of addressee (probably to Carl Bernard) previously discussed in 'Die Musik' 9_1 [1909] 42,
    'Der Merker' 1_1 [1909] 177, Frimmel's 'Beethoven-Forschung' 1 No. 4 [1913] 106, and 'Die Musik' 13_1 [1913] 148.
    Letter(previously published only in the 'Wiener Zeitung') dated January 24th (almost certainly 1823) to Dr. Johann
    Baptist Bach, making an appointment to meet him with Karl. This letter without doubt goes with one to Schindler
    (KS II 244 No. 895) on the same subject, so that the latter may accordingly be dated January 24th 1823. Many
    corrections to previous transcriptions of the letter of March 6th 1827 to Sir George Smart (KS II 468).
                                                        45 [1924] 8,10,13

AUF BEETHOVEN-SPUREN. IV. Max Unger.   (C)
    In celebration of the centenary of the Missa Solemnis and the Ninth Symphony, the circumstances leading to the
    performance of May 7th 1824 are summarized (along the general lines of TK III 153ff), stressing the temporary loss
    of interest in Beethoven and his works which had resulted from the intense and shallow rooted enthusiasm for Rossini
    in Vienna at that time. First publication of a letter of July 27th 1823 to Louis Spohr, soliciting his help in securing
    a subscription to the manuscript edition of the Missa Solemnis from the ruler of Hesse-Kassel. Letter of September
    17th 1823 to Spohr (previously published but generally overlooked by scholars) referring to subscriptions to the Missa
    Solemnis, to an attack of conjunctivitis, and to an opera libretto submitted by Grillparzer, and expressing interest
    in Spohr's double quartets.   45 [1924] 139

DIE "UNSTERBLICHE GELIEBTE." Franz Rabich.   (D)
    A resemblance between a passage in the Sonata in F sharp Op. 78 (dedicated to Therese von Breuning) and one in
    one of the songs of the 'Ferne Geliebte' cycle (Op. 98) leads the author to ask whether this is a cryptic indication
    that Therese von Breuning was the 'Unsterbliche Geliebte.'   45 [1924] 303

EINE STELLUNG AUS BEETHOVENS KLAVIERSONATE OPUS 14 I. Paul Mies.   (E)
    The several appearances of the second subject of the first movement of this sonata, in the exposition and in the
    recapitulation, are compared as to deviation from identity of the melodic line. Slight but very important differ-
    ences (at m. 30 vs. m. 121), shown by sketches not to be copist's errors, prove that Beethoven definitely did not
    look upon the recapitulation as a simple transposition. In the string quartet version, mm. 30ff are similar to mm.
    121ff, but (unlike the Pf original) differ from mm. 22ff.   46 [1925] 64

KARL HOLZ IN SEINEM VERHÄLTNIS ZU LUDWIG VAN BEETHOVEN. Walther Nohl.   (F)
    Brief biographical sketch of Holz, and extensive quotations from the conversation books to indicate Holz's relations
    with Beethoven, his character and personality, and the (predominantly unfavorable) opinion of Holz expressed by
    others who were close to Beethoven.   46 [1925] 180,206

DIE SONATENFORM BEETHOVENS: PROBLEME IN DER KLAVIERSONATE AS DUR OPUS 110. Walter Engelsmann. (G)
    A solution is proposed for an apparent obscurity in the voice leading at the meno allegro of the fugue. Alternative
    explanations are given of the melodic content of the D flat section of the second movement. Correction is re-
    commended of what is believed to be an erroneous reading in the 20th measure from the end of the last movement.
    A difference of opinion with Schenker as to the significance of a passage in the first movement is stated.

DIE SONATENFORM BEETHOVENS, etc., (Continued)
The author gives his answer to the question: What is (formally) the theme of the first movement? The thematic material of the entire sonata is shown to be in accord with the author's "Law" (see 'Die Musik' 17_1 [1925] 424).

46 [1925] 203,222

ZUR AUFFÜHRUNG DER III. LEONOREN-OUVERTÜRE. Rudolf Hartmann.   (A)
This overture is for the concert hall, not for the opera house.   46 [1925] 333

BEETHOVENS FIDELIO UND SEINE LITERARISCHE VORLAGE. Eugen Kilian.   (B)
A general comparison of the several versions of the 'Fidelio' libretto with the libretto by Bouilly which was used in 1798 by Gaveaux (see 'Zeitschrift der Internationalen Musikgesellschaft' 8 [1907] 115).

46 [1925] 510

BEETHOVEN ALS HUMORIST. Theodor Veidl.   (C)
"There are relatively few works by Beethoven which are serious throughout." The author discusses briefly the principal works in which Beethoven's humor is displayed most openly (see also 43 [1922] 178).

47 [1925] 115

KRITISCHE BEMERKUNGEN ZUR AUFFÜHRUNG VON BEETHOVENS DRITTE SYMPHONIE. Friedrich Berger.   (D)
The interpreter of the Eroica Symphony must give great weight to the firey days of 1801-03 in which it was written.   47 [1925] 117

BEETHOVENS WIRTSCHAFTLICHE PERSÖNLICHKEIT. Paul Nettl.   (E)
Review and summary of Reinitz's 'Beethoven im Kampfe mit dem Schicksal' (1924).

47 [1925] 121

BÜCHER-NOTIZEN BEETHOVENS AUS ZEITUNGEN UND ZEITSCHRIFTEN. Walther Nohl.   (F)
The extraordinarily broad scope of Beethoven's interests in his last years is shown by a list of the books regarding which he made notations in the conversation books from advertisements or reviews which had come to his attention.

47 [1925] 122,143

THE EFFECT OF BEETHOVEN'S PREDECESSORS ON HIS STYLE. Karl Hasse.   (G)
47 [1926] 54

FRANZ OLIVA AND LUDWIG VAN BEETHOVEN. Walther Nohl.   (H)
An account of the relationship between Beethoven and Oliva (the close friend of Varnhagen) from their meeting in 1810 to Oliva's departure for Russia, with extensive quotations from Oliva's entries in the conversation books.

47 [1926] 377

EINIGE BEETHOVEN-ANEKDOTEN.   47 [1926] 413   (I)

ZUR 100. WIEDERKEHR VON LUDWIG VAN BEETHOVENS TODESTAG. Hermann Ensslin.   (J)
Centenary essay.   48 [1927] 221

BEETHOVEN UND DIE GEGENWART. Karl Grunsky.   (K
Centenary essay.   48 [1927] 224

WENIG BEACHTETE BEETHOVEN-STÄTTEN. Theodor von Frimmel.   (L)
Data regarding sundry buildings connected with Beethoven's life history.

48 [1927] 226

BEETHOVENS MENSCHENTUM. Otto zur Nedden.   48 [1927] 230   (M

BEETHOVENS ZWEI PRINZIPE UND DIE SONATEN OPUS 14. Hermann Keller.   (N
Schindler ('Leben' [1840, 1845] 195 but apparently not in the third edition 1860), stated that in 1816 Beethoven contemplated a complete edition of his Pf sonatas for the purpose of adapting all his previously published Pf compositions to the extended (6 1/2) octave scale of the Pf of that time, and further of indicating the poetic ideas which form the ground work of these sonatas and of defining the nature of musical declamation. Schindler quotes Beethoven as stating, in connection with the second of these objectives, that a basic consideration in the

two sonatas Op. 14 was the concept of a conflict between two principles or a dialogue between two persons, and (Ibid. p. 224ff) analyzes in great detail the two sonatas and Beethoven's manner of performing them to illustrate the "two principles," which he designated as the "entreating" and the "resisting." It may be noted that this is perhaps the only detailed account which we have of Beethoven's interpretation of his own Pf works.   Marx and (following him) Thayer disregard Schindler's explanation of Beethoven's thoughts in this connection.   In the past 50 years Schindler has become recognized as an intelligent and competent musician, so that his firsthand accounts of Beethoven's words and interpretations should not be lightly discarded.   As for explanations of the "poetic ideas" which Beethoven associated with various works, "it is not true that 'the work speaks for itself'; rather, Beethoven speaks to us through his works, and we must do everything we can to understand him aright."
48 [1927] 233

"FIDELIO" ODER "LEONORE"? Rudolf Hartmann.   (A)
   The historical reason for the use of the name 'Fidelio' instead of Beethoven's originally requested title 'Leonora' (possible confusion with the opera of that name by Paer which had appeared a year before Beethoven's work) has long since ceased to be valid. While it is known that Beethoven made strenuous objection to the change of title, no logical reason for this objection has been suggested. Little weight should be given to the hypothesis that Beethoven urged the name 'Leonora' as a reminder of his youthful friend Eleanor von Breuning: his selection of Bouilly's material was for its spiritually elevated content, not for the name of the heroine. The title 'Fidelio' should be retained: it connotes the underlying spirit of the drama as 'Leonora' does not (Leonora was the wife of Florestan during their days of happiness), and by a hundred years of usage the title 'Fidelio' has become one with the inspired music drama for which any other name would now be foreign.   48 [1927] 239

BEETHOVENS HANDSCHRIFT. Theodor Haas.   (B)
   Many specimens of Beethoven's handwriting (notably in the conversation books) should not be taken as representative because of the conditions of haste or inconvenience in which they were written. Because of their importance and of the emotional stress under which they were written, perhaps the two most revealing specimens of Beethoven's hand writing are the Heiligenstadt will and the letter to the Immortal Beloved. The characteristics of these two documents are considered from the standpoint of the accepted laws of graphology, and the conclusion is reached that from the application of these laws "a not too incomplete picture of his character could be developed."
48 [1927] 242

WELTANSCHAUUNG IN BEETHOVEN MUSIK? Otto Schilling Trygophorus.   (C)
   A discussion of the philosophical and metaphysical content of Beethoven's music.

FACSIMILE OF THE CANON "ALLES GUTE, ALLES SCHÖNE!"   (D)
   GA 23/256 No. 7 (KS II 166).   48 [1927] 255

ZEITFRAGEN IN BEETHOVEN-FORSCHUNG. Ernst Bücken.   (E)
   General.   48 [1927] 256

LUDWIG VAN BEETHOVEN UND GNEIXENDORF. Walther Nohl.   (F)
   Extensive excerpts from the conversation books.   48 [1927] 258

. VAN BEETHOVEN UND UNSERE ZEIT. Karl Hasse.   (G)
   Centenary essay.   48 [1927] 281

DER ELFJÄHRIGE LISZT UND BEETHOVEN. Walther Nohl.   (H)
   In spite of Liszt's earnest and circumstantial account in 1885 of his visit to Beethoven in 1823, and the statements by various writers (La Mara, Ludwig Nohl) that Beethoven attended Liszt's concert on April 13th 1823 and honored the lad with a kiss, the conversation books show convincingly that Beethoven did not attend this concert, nor in discussion of Liszt with Schindler show any friendliness of feeling towards him. Errors of fact in Liszt's account of his visit to Beethoven's apartments and lack of any evidence of such a visit in the conversation books throw doubt on the truth of Liszt's story.   48 [1927] 307

BEETHOVEN AND GOETHE. Bertha Witt.   (I)
   An account of the relationship between the two men.   48 [1927] 334,354

ÜBER DAS BEETHOVENSCHE SCHERZO UND ÜBER DEN DRITTEN SATZ DER EROICA. F. X. Pauer.   (A)
    Beethoven's use and modification of the scherzo is discussed, and the scherzo of the Eroica is analyzed in great detail.
                48 [1927] 393

DIE SONATENFORM BEETHOVENS, SEIN KOMPOSITIONSPRINZIP. Walter Engelsmann.   (B)
    A detailed analysis to prove that the C minor Symphony follows Englesmann's law: "In all its movements, sections
and themes it is developed from a single basic theme or basic motif."
                48 [1927] 417,444

STILKUNDLICHE BEMERKUNGEN ZU BEETHOVENS OPUS 91. Paul Mies.   (C)
    This much maligned work "manifests the true touch of the master in almost every measure." (See also 'Allgemeine
Musik-Zeitung' 62 [1935] 65)   48 [1927] 509

NEUZEITLICHE "FIDELIO"-INSZENIERUNG. Felix v. Lepel.   (D)
    Summary of article by Turnau ('Almanach der deutschen Musikbücherei' [1927] 383).
                49 [1928] 295

GEDANKEN ZU BEETHOVENS 33 VARIATIONEN ÜBER EINEN WALZER VON DIABELLI. Richard Gress.   (E)
    Op. 120 is considered as an exhaustive and definitive exemplification of the types of variation technique developed
during two hundred years of composing in this form.   49 [1928] 775

NEUE WIENER MUSIK-ZEITUNG (Glöggl)

BEMERKUNGEN ZUM RICHTIGEN VORTRAGE BEETHOVENSCHER SINFONIEN. Carl Czerny.   (F)
    The sixth measure from the end of the first movement of the Fourth Symphony is redundant and should be eliminated.
(This measure is retained in the GA)   Measures 2 and 3 on p. 108 of the B&H score of the Fifth Symphony should be
eliminated. (This change has been made in the GA)   In the last half of the eighth measure of the finale of the
Sixth Symphony the horn notes, instead of being DGG (as in the B&H score) should be EGE. (In the GA this half-
measure is given EGG)   In the last section of the scherzo of the Eroica the four measures in double time should be
played alla breve.   Each measure of alla breve is of precisely the same duration as a measure of the 3/4 passage
preceding and following it.   The alla breve measures are frequently played much too slowly.   In the orchestra
parts of the first edition of the Eroica (Kunst- und Industrie-Comptoir, 1805) the two measures immediately preceding the prima volte of the first movement (GA p. 10, 2nd system, mm. 3 and 4) are in all parts marked for repetition.
                2 [1853] 59

EIN BESUCH RELLSTABS BEI BEETHOVEN 1825.   (G
    Excerpt from 'Novellen und vermischte Schriften' (1854).   4 [1855] 43,46a,49a,53,57

BEETHOVEN AS A COMPOSER OF SONGS.   4 [1855] 153   (H

EINE WAHRE ANEKDOTE AUS LUDWIG VAN BEETHOVENS LEBEN.   (I
    First publication of letter without date or name of addressee, given in KS II 414.
                7 [1858] 110

BEETHOVEN. Pierre Marque.   (J
    Biographical sketch.   8 [1859] 111

BEETHOVEN AND PAER.   (K
    Reprint from 'Niederrheinische Musikzeitung' 8 [1860] 190.   8 [1860] 102

SPOHR ÜBER BEETHOVEN.   (A)
   Excerpt from Spohr's autobiography.   9 [1860] 121

NEUE ZEITSCHRIFT FÜR MUSIK

ÜBER DIE SYMPHONIE, ÜBER DIE SYMPHONIEN BEETHOVENS, UND ÜBER IHRE AUSFÜHRUNG IN PARIS.   (B)
   General comments on "the three rivals" (Gossec, Haydn and Mozart) and on the Eroica and the Pastoral symphonies.
                                                    1 [1834] 101,105,109

GEDANKEN UNTER DIE NEUNTE SYMPHONIE VON BEETHOVEN.   J. Feski.   (C)
                                                    4 [1836] 125

MONUMENT FÜR BEETHOVEN.   Robert Schumann.   (D)
   Suggestions from Florestan, Jonathan, Eusebius and Raro.   4 [1836] 211

BRIEFE VON BEETHOVEN.   C. G. S. Böhme.   (E)
   Contention that the exclusive rights to Opp. 19-22 and 39-44 lie in the publishing firm of C. F. Peters is based on
   letters from Beethoven to the founder of the firm Hofmeister, which are published herewith but with omission of
   certain names and passages. The letters given are those found in KS I 37, 39, 41, 45, 56, and 77.   Also are given
   letters to Herr Peters of this firm which are found in KS II 200, 202, 211, 212, and 236.
                                                    6 [1837] 75,83

BEETHOVEN AN MATTHISSON.   (F)
   Letter of August 4th 1800 to Dr. Friedrich von Matthisson (KS I 33). 7 [1837] 201

DER BESUCH BEIM MEISTER.   G. Wedel.   (G)
   Reminiscences.   8 [1838] 1,9,13

ÜBER BEETHOVEN ALS CONTRAPUNCTIST.   Herrmann Hirschbach.   (H)
   The lack of importance of contrapuntal writing in Beethoven's compositions in comparison with Haydn and Mozart
   was not due to any lack of contrapuntal skill but rather to the different content of his works.
                                                    8 [1838] 189

BEETHOVENS NEUNTE SYMPHONIE.   Herrmann Hirschbach.   (I)
   Analysis.   9 [1838] 19,27,31,80

BEETHOVEN'S NINTH SYMPHONY.   (J)
   Comments on Hirschbach's analysis (9 [1838] 19, 27, 31, 80).   9 [1838] 59,63,163,167

DREI BRIEFE VON MOZART, BEETHOVEN UND HUMMEL.   (K)
   EDr Kal 1216.   9 [1838] 164

MUSIKALISCHE BEILAGE Nr. 6.   (L)
   EDr WoO 104   10 [1839] no page given

ÜBER BEETHOVENS LETZTE STREICHQUARTETTE.   Herrmann Hirschbach.   (M)
   Analysis   11 [1839] 5,9,13,49

NOCH EINE STIMME ÜBER BEETHOVENS MONUMENT.   11 [1839] 25   (N)

FIRST COMPLETE PERFORMANCE OF OPUS 123 IN GERMANY.   (O)
   The first performance of the complete work took place in Warnsdorf in Saxony under the leadership of the local
   schoolmaster Johann Vincenz Richter.   11 [1839] 36,56

AN ERROR IN THE SCORE OF THE FOURTH SYMPHONY.   (P)
   In the review of a concert which included Beethoven's Fourth Symphony, the critic (undoubtedly Schumann) pointed
   out the presence of a superfluous measure shortly before the close of the first movement (see also 15 [1841] 149).
                                                    13 [1840] 144

ÜBER EINIGE MUTHMASSLICH KORRUMPIRTE STELLEN IN BACH'SCHEN , MOZART'SCHEN UND BEETHOVEN'SCHEN   (A)
    WERKEN.   Robert Schumann.
    Of the three fortissimo measures eight measures before the close of the first movement of the Fourth Symphony,
    one is clearly superfluous. In the fifth measure from the end of the adagio of the Fourth Symphony, second beat,
    instead of playing an octave C (written), the horns should play G or be silent (!). On page 35 of the Breitkopf &
    Härtel score of the Sixth Symphony (1826) the three empty measures in Violin I should instead repeat the figure
    of the previous measure. (This correction has been made in the GA -- last four measures on page 16)
                                     15 [1841] 149

ERRORS IN THE SCORE OF THE SIXTH SYMPHONY.   Karl Holz.   (B)
    From his intimate knowledge of the autograph of the Sixth Symphony, Karl Czerny confirms the correction suggested
    on page 149 supra. The author points out another error in the Breitkopf & Härtel score , in the horn part at the last
    half of the eighth measure of the closing movement. According to the autograph, the notes d',g, g' should read
    e', g, e'. An appended comment by the editor (Schumann) suggests that if indeed that passage as it appears in the
    score is in error, the correct version must be e', g, g'. (This last suggestion is adopted in the GA, on p. 66)
                                     15 [1841] 168

DAS BEETHOVENDENKMAL IN BONN.   16 [1842] 7   (C)

DIE LEONORENOUVERTUREN VON BEETHOVEN.   (D)
    The accepted numbering of the overtures correctly represents their order of composition. A missing passage in the
    autograph of No. 2 was provided in the Breitkopf & Härtel score by inserting the similar passage from No. 3.
                                 16 [1842] 167

DIE BEETHOVEN'SCHEN OUVERTUREN.   Herrmann Hirschbach.   (E)
    General.   17 [1842] 159

EIN BRIEF VON BEETHOVEN.   (F)
    Letter of June 1st 1815 to Johann Peter Salomon (KS I 361), with identification of the works therein referred to:
    "grand Terzett" Op. 97; "Sonata for Pianoforte with a Violin" Op. 96; "Grand Symphony in A major" Op. 92;
    "small Symphony in F" Op. 93; "Quartet" Op. 95; "grand Opera in score, 30 ducats" could refer only to the revised
    version of 'Fidelio'; regarding the low price of 30 ducats the comment is made: "probably a slip of the pen";
    "Cantata" Op. 136; "Battle of Vittoria" Op. 91.   18 [1843] 17

CHARACTERISTIK DER BEETHOVEN'SCHEN SONATEN UND SYMPHONIEN.   C. T. Seiffert.   (G`
                                     18 [1843] 111

DIE BEETHOVEN'SCHE GROSSE MESSE.   (H
    Brief analysis.   18 [1843] 123

AERTZLICHER RÜCKBLICK AUF L. VAN BEETHOVENS LETZTE LEBENSEPOCHE.   Andreas Wawruch.   (I)
    Account of Beethoven's last days by his attending physician in a memorandum dated May 20th 1827. (See also 'Le
    Monde Musical' 38 [1927] 87)   18 [1843] 188

BEETHOVENS SYMPHONIEWERKE IN BETREFF DER TONARTEN.   R. Stoeckhardt.   (J
                                  21 [1844] 25,29

HAYDN, MOZART UND BEETHOVEN: EINE VERGLEICHENDE CHARACTERISTIK.   Franz Brendel.   (K
    A comparison of the three composers in their attitudes towards established authority, love, religion, and their creative
    art.   28 [1848] 1,13,25,37,49

ÜBER DEN CONTRABASS UND DESSEN BEHANDLUNG , MIT HINBLICK AUF DIE SYMPHONIEN VON BEETHOVEN.   (L
        August Müller.
    Reasons for the lack of acceptance of the double-bass as a virtuoso instrument; problems of its technique; a detailed
    discussion of passages of difficulty or importance in each of the symphonies of Beethoven.
                         28 [1848] 265; 29 [1848] 161,172,224;
                         30 [1849] 9,15,28,65,82,109

DER STATUS QUO DER BEETHOVEN-LITERATUR UND DIE BETHEILIGUNG RUSSLANDS AN DERSELBEN.   (A)
    Alexander Sferòf.
    Almost exclusively a discussion of the writings of Lenz and Ulibischeff, to the great advantage of the former.
                        58 [1863] 4,11,20,27,37

REFLEXIONEN AM CLAVIER: BEETHOVENS SONATA APPASSIONATA. L. Köhler.   (B)
                        63 [1867] 421

ZUR BEGRÜNDUNG EINER LOGISCHEN IDEENFOLGE IN BEETHOVENS 33 VERÄNDERUNGEN ÜBER EINEN DIABELLI'SCHEN   (C)
    WALZER.
    Stimulated by a performance of this work by Bülow, "who, as far as the writer knows, is the only artist who has brought
    Op. 120 to a public performance," the author assigns descriptive titles to each of the variations.
                        65 [1869] 229

BEETHOVENS HUNDERTJÄHRIGER GEBURTSTAG. Ludwig Nohl.   (D)
    Centenary essay.   66 [1870] 1

BEETHOVENS MISSA SOLEMNIS. Richard Pohl.   (E)
    Brief account of its history and discussion of its content.   66 [1870] 129

UNGEDRUCKTE MUSIKERBRIEFE. Ludwig Nohl.   (F)
    Letters given in KS I 85, 233; II 142 (No. 776), 181, 333, 409 (No. 1120), 429 (No. 1152). Here and in Frimmel's
    B-Jahrbuch 2 [1909] 289 these are listed as written to Zmeskall, but by KS as to 'Holz (?).'
                        66 [1870] 374

BEETHOVENS MISSION IN DER GESCHICHTE UND ENTWICKLUNG DER DEUTSCHEN MUSIK. Wilhelm Christern. (G)
    Centenary essay.   66 [1870] 445,457

GRILLPARZER ÜBER BEETHOVEN.   (H)
    Funeral oration.   66 [1870] 466

ZUR BIOGRAPHIE BEETHOVENS. Ludwig Nohl.   (I)

    Amenda und Op. 18 No. 1. Letters to Amenda (KS I 25, 26 No. 32); inscription on the first page of Op. 18 No. 1
    (KS I 26); letters to Amenda from Constance Mozart and W. A. Mozart; biographical information about Amenda
    from his grandson.   68 [1872] 46,55,66

    Ein Skizzenbuch von 1802-3. The sketch book dates from somewhere between the early winter of 1801-2 and
    February 1803 (probably from the latter part of this period). It contains sketches relating to Opp. 30, 33, 34, 35, 47,
    85, and 'Nei giorni tuoi felici.'   68 [1872] 117

    Noch einmal Amenda. Letter of April 12th 1815 from Beethoven (KS I 360); transcript of and comments on an
    obituary notice of Amenda.   68 [1872] 163

DIE AUFFÜHRUNG DER NEUNTEN SYMPHONIE UNTER RICHARD WAGNER IN BAYREUTH. Heinrich Porges.   (J)
    Detailed analysis of Wagner's interpretation.   68 [1872] 257,278,297,308,316

LUDWIG VAN BEETHOVENS NEUNTE SYMPHONIE UND DAS STYLPRINCIP DER MUSIK DES NEUNZEHNTEN   (K
    JAHRHUNDERTS. Heinrich Porges.   73 [1877] 351,363,369

BEETHOVENS JUGENDBILDUNG. Ludwig Nohl.   (L)
    Popular biographical sketch.   75 [1879] 357,370

BEETHOVEN UND DIE BILDENDEN KÜNSTE. Theodor von Frimmel.   (M
    Beethoven as a subject for portraits, statues, poems, and other manifestations of creative art; the Beethoven monument
    in Vienna.   76 [1880] 204

BRIEFWECHSEL BEETHOVENS UND SCHUMANNS MIT CPLM. G. WIEDEBEIN. E. Gustav Jansen.   (N
    Brief biographical sketch of Gottlob Wiedebein (1779-1854). Letter of July 6th 1804 to him, given in KS I 85. (See
    also Nohl's 'Beethoven nach den Schilderung seiner Zeitgenossen' [1877] 225)
                        76 [1880] 269,279,308

NEUE BEITRÄGE ZU BEETHOVENS BIOGRAPHIE AUS DEM JAHRE 1817.   Theodor von Frimmel.   (A)
   The author interviewed Carl Friedrich Hirsch (b. 1802), grandson of Albrechtsberger, who saw much of Beethoven
   during the period November 1816 to April 1817, and who studied harmony with him for a part of this time.   Although
   letters from the end of 1816 (e. g. , KS I 426, 428) show 1055 Sailerstette as Beethoven's address, Hirsch said that
   when he first met the composer he was living at the in "zum römischen Kaiser." Of the various portraits of Beethoven,
   the little relief medallion by Jos. Dan. Böhm (from about 1820) was the best likeness; the portrait by Schimon was
   also good.   Various minor comments on Beethoven's appearance and customs are given.
                                                    76 [1880] 361

EIN NEUER BRIEF VON BEETHOVEN.   Theodor von Frimmel.   (B)
   EDr Kal 850.   76 [1880] 553

MEDITATIONEN ÜBER BEETHOVEN'SCHE WERKE.   Louis Köhler.   (C)
   General thoughts on a considerable number of Beethoven's works.   77 [1881] 337,345,449,458

BEETHOVEN'S SONATA OPUS 111 AND THE 33 VARIATIONS OPUS 120.   Louis Köhler.   (D)
   General.   78 [1882] 333,371

ANSICHTEN UND MITTHEILUNGEN ÜBER EINE STELLE IN BEETHOVENS CISMOLL-SONATE OPUS 27 Nr. 2.   (E)
      Carl Richter.
   According to the author, the twelfth measure of the first movement of the C sharp minor Sonata is incorrectly given
   in practically all editions, since the fifth note in the right-hand triplets should remain at C natural, not follow the
   bass from C natural to B.   A parallelism is drawn with the first two measures of the movement.
                                                    79 [1883] 395

ÜBER EINIGE GRÖSSERE UND KLEINERE COMPOSITIONEN BEETHOVENS.   Louis Köhler.   (F)
   General.   79 [1883] 417,425

THE MISSA SOLEMNIS IN D MAJOR BY LUDWIG VAN BEETHOVEN.   (G)
   Analytical program notes.   79 [1883] 553

LUDWIG VAN BEETHOVENS BEZIEHUNGEN ZU SCHWEDEN.   Heinrich Martens.   (H)
   On December 22nd 1822 Beethoven was elected a foreign member of the Royal Musical Academy of Stockholm.
   King Oscar II of Sweden, while still Crown Prince, was President of this Academy in 1870.   His address at the cen-
   tenary of Beethoven's birth is given.   Beethoven's letters of March 1st 1823 to the Royal Academy and to the King of
   Sweden (KS II 230, 231), written by Beethoven in French, are here published (in German translation) for the first time.
   The then King of Sweden, Charles XIV, had, as General Bernadotte, been French Minister in Vienna twenty-five years
   before.   Beethoven had known him then, and it is to him that the idea of the Eroica Symphony has been attributed
   (but see TK I 213).   Beethoven's letter to him at this time may have been to further his project of subscription sales
   of the Missa Solemnis to European rulers.   82 [1886] 137,147

CARL MARIA VON WEBER IN SEINEN REISEBRIEFEN.   Paul Simon.   (I)
   In a review of a published volume of Weber's letters, an account is given of his meeting with Beethoven on October
   5th 1823.   82 [1886] 329

ORCHESTERPHRASIERUNG ANALYSE DER C-MOLL-SYMPHONIE BEETHOVENS.   Hugo Riemann.   (J)
   The first movement of the Fifth Symphony is analyzed in great detail from the standpoint of the conductor, with
   guidance to him in thinking the necessary accents, phrasing, etc.   83 [1887] 105,115,134,182,202

L. VAN BEETHOVEN IM LICHTE ROB. SCHUMANNS.   Alfr. Chr. Kalischer.   (K)
   With the thesis that Schumann was the true heir and apostle of Beethoven, the author discusses Schumann's writings
   on Beethoven's individuality as man and artist, his comments on the various categories of compositions by Beethoven
   (p. 385) and on individual works (p. 406), on Beethoven's technical and aesthetic principles (p. 561), and on Beethoven's relationship to his successors (p. 19).   This lengthy study is very rich in brief biographical sketches of musicians and other contemporaries of Beethoven or Schumann.   83 [1887] 221,247,311,361,385,393,
                                                    406,439,450,459,483,561; 84 [1888]
                                                    3,19,63

NOCH EINMAL BEETHOVENS KÖNIGLICHE ABSTAMMUNG.   Alfr. Chr. Kalischer.   (L)
   This article deals primarily with a plagiarism of a paper by the author (here reprinted) in which he repeats Schindler's

NOCH EINMAL BEETHOVENS KÖNIGLICHE ABSTAMMUNG (Continued)
   statement of the falsity of the story that Beethoven was the natural son of King Friedrich Wilhelm II of Prussia, and
   explains the genesis of this story only by the tendency of popular myth to build up around any notable character.
                                        83 [1887] 417,427

NEUE MUSIK VON LUDWIG VAN BEETHOVEN. Ferruccio B. Busoni.   (A)
   Comments on the recently issued Supplement (Series 25) to the Gesamtausgabe.
                                        84 [1888] 331

EIN BRIEF BEETHOVENS. Josef Böck.   (B)
   Transcription (with facsimile of one page) of the letter of May 4th 1819 to the Philharmonic Society of Laibach.
   (KS II 135)   84 [1888] 367,379

NEUE BEETHOVENSTUDIEN. Theodor von Frimmel.   (C)
   First publication of nineteen letters (all but one to Zmeskall):

      KS II 25 (No. 593) Probable date early August 1816.
        I 303 (No. 360) From the watermark of the paper here attributed to 1802? although the tabulation
                            in B-Jahrbuch 2 says 1813, as does KS.
        I 303 (No. 361) By same reasoning, also 1802?
        I 339   By same reasoning, here also 1802?; in KS 1814; in Kalischer-Frimmel B-Briefe
                            (No. 241) 1811.
        I 301 (No. 356)
        I 237 (No. 263)
        I 162 (No. 184)
       II 24 (No. 592) Here attributed to 1815-26.
        I 288   Here, based on handwriting, attributed to about 1810.
        I 236 (No. 262) Here dated merely before 1825, and said to be possibly associated with the next letter.
        I 331
        I 319 (No. 387)
        I 319 (No. 386) The sense of these two noted would seem to reverse the order in which KS gives them.
       II 89   With no guess as to date or significance.
        I 301 (No. 357) Dating between 1804 and 1825; from handwriting probably between 1810 and 1820.
        I 302
        I 237 (No. 265)
                          Note without date or name of addressee: "Your excellency may find me in the second
                            room on the ground floor at the stated address. Ludwig van Beethoven," saying that
                            this note is not certainly to Zmeskall, and that if it is, it must be from the earliest
                            time.

   Miscellaneous documents (p. 535).

   Inscription by Beethoven (May 22nd 1793) in the memory book of a Herr Vocke.

   The memory book inscription to Lenz von Breuning which appears in WRK p. 224.

   Extract from a conversation book in which Beethoven refers to "a marble stone with gold letters as a memorial" to the brother of the person to whom he was talking or (more probably) as a memorandum for himself
   made within a year or two of the death of his brother Kaspar in 1815. In this case the book from which this
   excerpt was taken would be the earliest conversation book extant (presumably winter 1816-17).

   Letter without date, presumably shortly before May 7th 1824 to Gläser (KS II 298).

   Letter without date or name of addressee, extending an invitation to a meal with Beethoven and nephew Karl
   perhaps dating from shortly after the operation which Karl underwent in September 1816 (TK II 341). This
   letter does not appear in the tabulation in B-Jahrbuch.

   A transcript is given of the letter of rejection dated October 23rd 1815 which Brother Karl received in reply
   to his request for leave, on which Beethoven commented so bitterly (TK II 322).

   Letter without date from Brother Karl to a M. Rizzi, requesting that he make payment of 150 florins to

Beethoven because of the latters expenses in Baden and Döbling. Except for the statement that Beethoven spent summers in these towns in 1804, 1815, 1821 and 1822, the author makes no attempt either to date this letter or to explain it.

Letter of February 11th 1823 from Brother Johann to Artaria regarding two unidentified compositions.

Beethoven's personal acquaintance with Goethe (p. 559). Both artists were in Töplitz in 1812 from the 15th of July to August 5th or 6th, and presumably met several times. Further meetings in Karlsbad later in the summer seem "in the highest degree improbable."   85 [1889] 511,523,535,547,559

BEETHOVENIANA.   (A)
First publication of KBr 1181.   86 JG 57 [1890] 66 [?]

BEETHOVEN AS A CONDUCTOR. H. Kling.   (B)
Anecdotes to point the statement that "among conductors our Master would by no means serve as a model."
                    86 [1890] 471,481

GRILLPARZER: SEIN VERHÄLTNIS ZUR MUSIK UND ZU BEETHOVEN.   (C)
Biographical sketch, stressing Grillparzer's knowledge of and feeling for music and his acquaintance with Beethoven.
                    86 [1890] 493

BEETHOVEN'S COMPOSITIONS, ESPECIALLY THE CHAMBER MUSIC, IN RELATION TO THE DEVELOPMENT OF   (D)
    MUSICAL STYLE, FORM AND CONTENT. Richard Pohl.
                    86 [1890] 529

DER KNABE FRANZ LISZT UND BEETHOVEN.   Alfr. Chr. Kalischer.   (E)
The entire question of Beethoven's attitude in the spring of 1823 to the 11-year-old Liszt is shrouded in contradictions: the 1860 edition of Schindler's biography directly contradicts the 1842 edition on virtually all pertinent points. A passage in a conversation book indicates that Beethoven was (or intended to be) present at Liszt's farewell concert on April 13th 1823. The fact that the reviews of the concert did not mention him is strong evidence that actually he did not attend. The story that after the concert Beethoven went onto the stage and embraced and kissed the lad seems most improbable. (See also 'Monthly Musical Record' 66 [1936] 176)
                    87 [1891] 441,453

ARCHDUKE RUDOLPH'S REPLY TO BEETHOVEN'S NEW YEAR'S GREETING OF 1 JANUARY 1820.   (F)
First few measures of the greeting given in full in ZfMw 4 [1921] 98.
                    88 [1892] 525

LUDWIG VAN BEETHOVEN UND KARL MARIA VON WEBER, DIE DIOSKUREN DER DEUTSCHEN TONKUNST.   (G)
    Karl Plato.
An attempt to explain the eminence of Beethoven in the symphony and of Weber in romantic opera.
                    89 [1893] 205,217

BEETHOVENS "BEICHVATER." Alfr. Chr. Kalischer.   (H)
"For a full decade, Beethoven's 'Father Confessor' was the Countess Maria von Erdödy (nee Countess von Niczky)." His letter to her from the spring of 1809 (KS 1 157) is only one indication of this fact; his letters of 1815 confirm the close, almost dependent relationship, and the two sets of compositions dedicated to her (the Trios Op. 70 and the Cello Sonatas Op. 102) seem characterized by a notable depth of passion. Their relationship was terminated in 1820 by the banishment of the Countess from Austria (TK II 83).   89 [1893] 365,373,381,389,397,405

DIE GESCHÖPFE DES PROMETHEUS. Oskar Möricke.   (I)
Outline of the plot.   92 [1896] 351

MOZARTS, BEETHOVENS UND SCHUBERTS TÄNZE FÜR DAS CLAVIER. Dr. Haase.   (J)
The lesser importance of Mozart's and Beethoven's dance music as compared with Schubert's may be explained in part by the fact that neither of the former was a native Viennese, and, furthermore, that it was after the youthful creative period of each of the older musicians that the formalized ceremonial dances (Minuet, Allemande, etc.) began to give way to the folk dance. Beethoven's contredanses and Deutsche Tänze are in general of small importance; with few exceptions, his only important minutes are those which form parts of works in sonata form.
                    92 [1896] 481,493

NICHT DIE TOTENMASKE, SONDERN DIE GESICHTSMASKE BEETHOVENS AUS DEM LEBEN (1812).   E. Kuhlig.   (A)
   Beethoven's death mask should not be confused with a life mask made in 1812 by Franz Klein, which may be taken
   as a faithful likeness of the composer.   97 [1901] 424

AUTOGRAPHIANA.   Max Rikoff.   (B)
   First publication of a facsimile of an album leaf from Beethoven with ten measures of music and an inscription in
   French: "Written on April 29th 1822 when M. Boucher, the great violinist, did me the honor to pay me a visit. Louis
   van Beethoven."   97 [1901] 483

DAS ORIGINAL-MANUSKRIPT DES BEETHOVENBRIEFES AN ANNA MILDER-HAUPTMANN.   Alfr. Chr. Kalischer.   (C)
   The transcription of the letter written in January 1816 by Beethoven to Frau Anna Milder-Hauptmann (KS I 390) is
   incorrectly given by Nohn and by TV (but see TD III 537).   101 [1905] 335

                As of October 1st 1906 (following Volume 102 No. 39) the 'Neue Zeitschrift
                für Musik' was absorbed by the 'Musikalisches Wochenblatt.' From January
                1st 1911 the consolidated journal again appeared as the 'Neue Zeitschrift
                für Musik,' but Jahrgang numbers instead of volume numbers were used.

VERSUCH EINER RHYTHMISCHEN ANALYSE DES ERSTEN SATZES DER C-MOLL-SINFONIE VON L. VAN BEETHOVEN.   (D)
      Heinrich Hammer.
   A discussion of points of disagreement with Schroeder ('Musikalisches Wochenblatt' 39[1908] 136, 196) regarding the rhythmic
   analysis of the first and third movements of the Fifth Symphony.   JG 78 [1911] 4

BEETHOVEN BEIM PRINZEN LOUIS FERDINAND VON PREUSSEN.   Erwin von Oertzen.   (E)
   A circumstantial account of the concert of October 10th 1796 at which Beethoven complimented the Prince on his
   playing (TK I 196).   JG 78 [1911] 17

HARMONISCHE GRUNDWERTE BEI BACH UND BEETHOVEN.   Robert Handke.   (F)
   An analysis of the tonalities of the various sections of several Bach fugues and of the four movements of the Ninth
   Symphony.   JG 78 [1911] 303

ALBRECHTSBERGER ALS BINDEGLIED ZWISCHEN BACH UND BEETHOVEN.   Reinhard Oppel.   (G)
   Numerous quotations from Albrechtsberger's compositions indicate that from several standpoints he is stylistically a
   connecting link between the two great geniuses.   JG 78 [1911] 316

DIE BEETHOVENHÄUSER IN MÖDLING.   Hermann Hoffmann.   (H)
   Description of the two houses in Mödling in which Beethoven lived during his summer holidays in 1818-20.
                                                                              JG 78 [1911] 375

DIE BEETHOVENHÄUSER IN MÖDLING.   Theodor von Frimmel.   (I)
   In the summers of 1818 and 1819 Beethoven lived in the 'Hafnerhaus'; in 1820 only in the Christhof, contrary to the
   statement of Hoffmann (p. 375).   JG 78 [1911] 408

GUILLIETTA GUICCIARDI -- DIE 'UNSTERBLICHE GELIEBTE' BEETHOVENS?   Max Unger.   (J)
   A comparison of various statements in the letters with post-coach schedules and weather reports of the Bohemian spa
   area indicates that the year 1812 corresponds excellently with the known facts as other years do not.   The Immortal
   Beloved could not have been Guillietta.   JG 78 [1911] 501

BEETHOVENS NEUER LIEBESBRIEF -- EINE FÄLSCHUNG?   Max Unger.   (K)
   The writer is not impressed with the doubts that Bekker throws on the authenticity of the recently-discovered Immortal
   Beloved letter (but see 'Die Musik' 11_2 [1912] 40).   JG 78 [1911] 513

BEETHOVENS VERGESSLICHKEIT.   M. Kaufmann.   (L)
   When Beethoven went from Teplitz to Karlsbad in the summer of 1812 he forgot his identity card. (See also 'Der
   Merker' 7 [1916] 231)   JG 79 [1912] 85

ZU BEETHOVENS PLAN EINER AUSGABE SEINER SÄMTLICHEN WERKE.   Max Unger.   (M)
   Beethoven's long letter of October 15th 1810 to Breitkopf & Härtel, which contains a single sentence (KS I 207) indicating that he had thought about a collected edition, was written after these publishers had brought out Gesamtausgaben

of Mozart, Haydn and Clementi. The next reference to this project was in a letter of February 15th 1817 to Nicholas (or perhaps Peter Josef Simrock (Kalischer 'Briefe' 2nd edition 1911 III 162) with the words: "As soon as you can, let me have your ideas regarding the publication of a complete edition of my works, starting with the pianoforte music. In many respects this would be quite a task, since so many faulty editions of my works are floating around the world." No action resulted, nor did any later from Artaria. A couple of references to the idea appear in the conversation books of 1820, as connected with the publishers Steiner and Eckstein. Beethoven makes a definite proposal in the letter of June 5th 1822 to Peters (KS II 195). In a letter of July 3 (27?) 1822 to Brother Johann Beethoven says that Steiner & Co. "want to have in writing that I will give them all my works." Tobias Haslinger (a partner of Steiner) published the first of the three youthful (1783) Pf sonatas in 1822-23 with an authentication by Beethoven (dated November 17th 1822) that these sonatas formed part of a collected edition being brought out with Beethoven's approval. It is interesting to note that in this edition these are marked "Geschrieben im 10ten Lebensjahr," compared with the inscription on the first edition that they were by LvB "alt eilf Jahr." Nothing further of such an edition is known. Later (1824-26) Beethoven suggested the project to Schott and to Schlesinger; perhaps it was to the Haslinger project that Beethoven referred in his letter of October 13th 1826 to Schott (KS II 455).   JG 80 [1913] 449

BEETHOVEN ALS SPRACHREINIGER.   (A)
Instructions regarding tempi and interpretations were given in German as well as in Italian in Opp. 81a, 90, 101 and 109. During 1825 Beethoven and Holz coined German words to replace various familiar musical words of Italian derivation (KS II 398; see comments in Kalischer 'Beethoven Briefe' V 180).
                                         JG 80 [1913] 520

ÜBER EINIGE UNBEKANNTE VERERBTE STICHFEHLER IN BEETHOVENSCHEN SINFONIEN.   Max Unger.   (B)
Copy of a letter from Czerny regarding errors in the scores of the 3rd, 4th, 5th and 6th Symphonies with comments.
                                         JG 81 [1914] 34

NEUE BRIEFE AN BEETHOVEN.   Max Unger.   (C)
Letters from Hoffmeister & Kuhnel and its successor firm C. F. Peters & Co., including a long reply to Beethoven's letter of February 15-18, 1823 (KS II 226).   JG 81 [1914] 409

PORTRAITS OF BEETHOVEN'S PARENTS.   Max Unger.   (D)
The portraits by Kaspar Benedikt Beckenkamp that probably represent Beethoven's father and mother are reproduced and discussed.   JG 81 [1914] 414

GELEGENHEITSKOMPOSITIONEN VON BEETHOVEN.   Max Unger.   (E)
Discussions and corrected transcription of: Canon of September 21st 1819 for Schlesinger (KS II 142); album sheet of January 20th 1823 for Countess Marie Wimpffler (KS II 220); canon (said by Schindler to have been written on February 20th 1823) for Count Moritz Lichnowsky (KS II 228); first publication of canon dated June 4th (1825?) for Dr. Braunhofer, "Ich war hier"; canon of December 16th 1825 for Theodor Molt of Quebec, Canada (KS II 412).
                                         JG 81 [1914] 501

BEETHOVEN "DER BELGIER."   Max Unger.   (F)
Polemic against reference to Beethoven in a French journal as the "purest form of French genius."
                                         JG 81 [1914] 557

BEETHOVENS STELLUNG ZU BACH UND HANDEL.   Konrad Huschke.   (G)
The number of works by Bach which were known to Beethoven was "pitifully small." Handel's works, on the other hand, were available in substantially complete form, but his admiration for this composer was more for his "independent, valiant, austere, self-confident personality than for his music."
                                         JG 82 [1915] 185

BEETHOVEN.   Romain Rolland.   (H)
Translation of the author's 'Vie de Beethoven' (serial publication 1903; book form 1909).
                                         JG 84 [1917] 253, 265, 277, 289,
                                                         301, 309

DER LETZTE VOM STAMME BEETHOVENS.   (I)
Karl Julius Maria van Beethoven, grandson of Nephew Karl, went to Belgium in his youth with his adopted brother and there became a writer for Belgian, French and English journals. Returning to Vienna at the outbreak of World War I, the brother and Karl's mother died in the spring of 1917; Karl, after some time in the military service, was at the time of this writing (summer of 1917) hospitalized by a heart ailment and general physical deterioration.
                                         JG 84 [1917] 274

DER SCHLUSSSATZ DER HELDENSINFONIE UND BEETHOVENS DARSTELLUNG DES REIN MENSCHLICHEN.   (A)
    Arthur Prüfer.
    Citation of various authorities in agreement with the contention of Riemann that the theme of the Eroica Finale and
    the Prometheus Variations was to Beethoven of the most fundamental significance.
                          JG 86 [1919] 195,205

EIN SKIZZENBLATT BEETHOVENS. Max Kalbeck.   (B)
    A page from a sketch book by Beethoven which contains sketches for the 'Scene at the Brook' is probably one of the
    28 or 29 pages torn from the 1808 sketch book (see NB II 252). The author comments on Schindler's story of the quo-
    tation of the song of the goldammer in this movement, and points out that the songs of the blackbird and the oriole
    might have inspired the opening theme of the first movement. JG 86 [1919] 309,325

              'Neue Zeitschrift für Musik' was changed to 'Zeitschrift für Musik' in the spring of
              1920, when the journal became a semi-monthly publication instead of a weekly

BEETHOVENS INSTRUMENTALMUSIK. E. T. A. Hoffmann.   (C)
    Apparently a festival address.   JG 87 [1920] 185

BEETHOVENS SONATA QUASI FANTASIA OPUS 27 No. 1. Heinrich Schwartz.   (D)
    Suggestions for the student. C natural instead of B natural as the fifth note in the triplets in the twelfth measure of
    the first movement is recommended.   JG 87 [1920] 240

WELCHER TAG IST BEETHOVENS GEBURTSTAG? Adolf Sandberger.   (E)
    The weight of evidence favors the statement of Wegeler (WRK p. 5) that December 17th was the date of Beethoven's
    birth as well as of his baptism.   JG 87 [1920] 449

BEETHOVENS JUGENDSONATEN UND SONATINEN. Edwin Janetschek.   (F)
    For fullest understanding of the 32 sonatas of the accepted canon, familiarity is necessary with the six early sonatas
    and sonatinas without Op. number; the three of 1783 dedicated to Maximilian Friedrich, the 'Leichte Sonata' frag-
    ment in C major, and the two posthumous sonatas in G major and F major (NV pp. 147-48).
                          JG 87 [1920] 451

ZUR TEXTGESCHICHTE VON BEETHOVENS FIDELIO. Wilhelm Zentner.   (G)
    A discussion of the changes made by Sonnleithner in Bouilly's original, and of those made by Treitschke in the libretto
    as prepared by Sonnleithner (see also JG 88 [1921] 60).   JG 87 [1920] 452

BEETHOVEN AND BERLIN. P. Martell.   (H)
    A summary of the few known facts regarding Beethoven's visit to Berlin in June 1796.
                          JG 87 [1920] 456

BEETHOVENS ANDANTE FAVORI. Martin Frey.   (I)
    Transcription of many of the sketches for the 'Andante favori.'   JG 87 [1920] 459

BEETHOVEN IM GESPRÄCH. [Johann Wenzel] Tomaschek.   (J)
    Extract from Tomaschek's autobiography, giving his account of his two visits to Beethoven on October 10th and
    November 24th 1814. This same material appears virtually complete in Frimmel's 'Beethoven Handbuch' II pp. 325ff,
    and, somewhat abbreviated, in 'Musical Times' December 15th 1892 p. 20 and in TK II 297.
                          JG 87 [1920] 463

GOETHES BEZIEHUNGEN ZU MUSIKALISCHEN PERSONEN WÄHREND SEINER KURAUFENTHALTE IN KARLSBAD   (K)
    1785-1823. M. Kaufmann.
    During the twelve visits which Goethe made to Karlsbad, he met a number of prominent musicians besides Beethoven.
                          JG 88 [1921] 8

DIE BEETHOVEN-AUSSTELLUNG DER PREUSSISCHEN STAATS-BIBLIOTHEK IN BERLIN. Wilhelm Altmann.   (L)
                          JG 88 [1921] 26

LUDWIG VAN BEETHOVENS 'LEONORA.' Adolf Brockmann, Jr.   (M)
    An account of the incident in the French Revolution on which Bouilly founded his story of Leonore. The original
    'Florestan' and 'Leonore' were Count von Semblancay and his wife Blanche.
                          JG 88 [1921] 60

BEETHOVEN UND DER HARMONISCHE DUALISMUS. Karl Pottgiesser.   (A)
JG 88 [1921] 212

BEETHOVENS "NEUNTE" UND IHRE ANGEBLICHE FORMLOSIGKEIT. Emil Liepe.   (B)
The last movement of the Ninth is of the form: Introduction, theme with 11 variations, coda.
JG 88 [1921] 229

SPOHRS VERHÄLTNIS ZU BEETHOVEN. Johann Lewalter.   (C)
Excerpts from Spohr's autobiography, telling of his first meeting and subsequent association with Beethoven, and of
the obviousness of Beethoven's deafness at the time of the first performance of the Seventh Symphony (December 8th
1813).   JG 88 [1921] 257

ZUR FRAGE DES HARMONISCHEN DUALISMUS. Jos. Achtélik.   (D)
Polemic against Pottgiesser (p. 212).   JG 88 [1921] 386

ZUR FRAGE DES HARMONISCHEN DUALISMUS. Karl Pottgiesser.   (E)
Reply to Achtélik (p. 386).   JG 88 [1921] 451

EINE PROPAGANDA FÜR BEETHOVENS SINFONIEN IN A- UND F-DUR IM JAHRE 1816. M. Kaufmann.   (F)
An arrangement of the 'Battle of Vittoria' Op. 91 for string quintet, issued by Steiner in February 1816, contained a
laudatory advance notice of the forthcoming Symphonies in A and in F. (The score and parts of these two works were
issued by Steiner in the autumn of 1816 -- 'Philobiblon' 9 [1936] 339)
JG 89 [1922] 36

DER BELGIER BEETHOVEN. Georg Göhler.   (G)
"Antwerp attained its glory under German kings; at the time in question (the departure of the older Beethovens to
Bonn) it had since 1714 been Austrian. Within its borders lived representatives of many nationalities, and the name
'Beethoven' itself shows clearly enough that its bearer was of Germanic stock, at that time called low German or
Netherlandish or Flemish, but in no case Belgian."   JG 89 [1922] 339

HUNDERT JAHRE BEETHOVENS FIDELIO IN DRESDEN. Otto Schmid.   (H)
Contemporary review, and summary of the history of Paer's 'Leonora.'
JG 90 [1923] 139

'Zeitschrift für Musik' became a monthly publication in 1924 with Jahrgang 91

DIE FÜHRUNG DER MELODISCHEN LINIE IN BEETHOVENS C-MOLL-SINFONIE. Georg Göhler.   (I)
Imaginative interpretation of the philosophy underlying the music, with fancied tie-ins as regards the contour of the
melodic line.   JG 91 [1924] 60

DIE URAUFFÜHRUNG DER MISSA SOLEMNIS VOR 100 JAHREN.   (J)
The first performance of the Missa Solemnis was in St. Petersburg on March 24th 1824. The next known complete
performance was in the little Bohemian city of Warnsdorf in 1830. The first truly German complete performance
was in Dresden on March 13th 1839.   JG 91 [1924] 85

DIE HUMANITÄTSMELODIEN IM "FIDELIO." Alfred Heuss.   (K)
The author traces the development of the melody of 'O Gott! Welch ein Augenblick!' (GA 20/206 p. 258) from the
Trauerkantate of 1790 (GA 25/264 p. 26) through 'Leonore' (Pf. score 1907 p. 246). A passage sung by Don Fernando
(GA 20/206 p. 249) shows a spiritual kinship (text as well as music) to 'In diesen heil'gen Hallen' from 'The Magic
Flute.' A phrase used at two quite different times by Leonora seems to have some motival significance.
JG 91 [1924] 545

BEETHOVENS BEZIEHUNGEN ZUR POLITIK. Karl Nef.   (L)
Beethoven's acquaintances have said that politics was a never-ending topic of his conversation. His youth in Bonn
was in surroundings in which he saw the advance of the spirit of progress. The third 'Bettina' letter (KS I 263), genuine or spurious, gives a faithful picture of one aspect of Beethoven's attitude towards political rulers. In Vienna his
genius enabled him to maintain himself on a plane of complete equality with the high nobles with whom he associated. His close association with Bernadotte, French ambassador to Vienna, was indicative of his tastes and thinking. He withdrew the dedication of the Eroica from Napoleon when he could no longer look upon him as the apostle
of freedom. In his later years he followed English politics closely. As compositions based on political subjects may

BEETHOVENS BEZIEHUNGEN ZUR POLITIK (Continued)
be included the Eroica, the two Kriegslieder, the 'Battle of Vittoria,' the 'Abschiedsgesang,' and (to an extent) the two early Bonn cantatas. The indirect influence of political events and thought on his music was even more profound, notably the influence of post-Revolutionary French composers, showing itself not only in his instrumental compositions, but most strikingly in Fidelio.   JG 92 [1925] 269,343

ÜBER DAS BEETHOVENSCHE FINALE UND ÜBER DEN SCHLUSSSATZ DER ZWEITER SINFONIE.   F. X. Pauer.   (A)
Beethoven was the first composer to make the finale of a cyclic work the emotional climax rather than merely a tapering off. This is notably the case with the finale of the Second Symphony, which is here analyzed.
JG 92 [1925] 276

JOHANN VINCENZ RICHTER, EIN VORKÄMPFER FÜR BEETHOVEN.   Edmund Richter.   (B)
Biographical sketch of J. V. Richter, the first conductor of the Missa Solemnis in Vienna (May 1824) and other cities.
JG 92 [1925] 280

EIN ÜBERZÄHLIGER TAKT IN DER PASTORAL SINFONIE.   Alfred Heuss.   (C)
Otto Singer contends that m. 24 of the first movement is a repetition of the previous measure which was added in error, as shown by the symmetry of the melody and the dynamics (but see JG 94 [1927] 203).
JG 92 [1925] 288,460

GEGEN DIE ROMANTISIERUNG KLASSISCHER MUSIK.   Jón Leifs.   (D)
A detailed study of dynamics in the first movement of the Eroica. JG 92 [1925] 633

ANSCHAUUNGEN UND VORSTELLUNGEN DES JUNGEN BEETHOVEN.   Karl Gerhartz.   (E)
The influence (other than musical) of Neefe, of the Breunings, and of the university circles in Bonn had a lasting effect on the intellectual development of Beethoven.   JG 92 [1925] 715

WIE EINIGE GROSSE EINGEBUNGEN IN BERÜHMTEN LIEDMELODIEN ZUSTANDE GEKOMMEN SIND.   (F)
Alfred Heuss.
A detailed consideration of the way in which Beethoven set music to words in his 'Die Ehre Gottes in der Natur' Op. 48 No. 4.   JG 93 [1926] 68

NEUE MITTEILUNGEN ÜBER BEETHOVENS LETZTE LEBENSTAGE.   Elsa Bienenfeld.   (G)
Extracts from two letters written by Johann Baptist Streicher (son of Andreas Streicher) to Johann Andreas Stumpff.
JG 93 [1926] 96

DICHTERISCHE FREIHEITEN IN ROLLANDS "BEETHOVEN."   Otto Erich Deutsch.   (H)
JG 93 [1926] 489

BEETHOVEN -- EINE ÄSTHETISCHE BETRACHTUNG.   Erich Klocke.   (I)
JG 93 [1926] 665

BEETHOVEN IN DER GEGENWART.   Alfred Heuss.   (J)
Centenary essay.   JG 94 [1927] 130

VON RHYTHMUS DER "FREUDE"-MELODIE BEETHOVENS.   Rudolf Steglich.   (K)
A detailed study of various leading phrases of the choral finale of the Ninth Symphony from the standpoint of interpretation and conducting technique.   JG 94 [1927] 137

WIE BEETHOVEN VON NEEFE UNTERRICHTET WURDE.   Felix Huch.   (L)
Fiction.   JG 94 [1927] 144

AUS BEETHOVENS SKIZZENBÜCHERN.   Paul Mies.   (M)
A detailed study of the working out in successive sketches of certain passages of Fidelio and of the A minor Quartet Op. 132.   JG 94 [1927] 149

DIE DREI BEETHOVENBRIEFE BETTINAS.   R. Gottschalk.   (N)
The history is given of the three letters, first published in 1839. The second of the letters, February 10th 1811 (KS I 208), may without hesitation be accepted as genuine. The first, August 11th 1810 (KS I 195), and the third, August 15th 1812 (KS I 263), however, contain much internal evidence of Bettina's authorship rather than Beethoven's:

the use of phraseology which had appeared in earlier letters between Bettina and other correspondents than Beethoven, faulty chronology in reference to various compositions, and passages which seem incompatible with Beethoven's psychology. No one except Bettina makes definite claim to have seen the originals of the first and the third letters, though the autograph of the second is extant; Bettina's contemporary correspondence apparently refers to only one letter. Her statements about her relations with Goethe are known to be untrustworthy.

JG 94 [1927] 154

BETRACHTUNGEN ZUR HEUTIGEN BEETHOVEN-"PFLEGE." Edmund Schmid.   (A)
Diatribe against editors and interpreters (Bülow in particular) who see fit to oppose their judgment and taste by deviating from the unmistakable notation of Beethoven's autographs. Examples are given from Opp. 53, 73, 106, 109, and 111.   JG 94 [1927] 197

FIDELIO-AUFFÜHRUNGEN UND GROSSE LEONOREN-OUVERTÜRE. Rudolf Hartmann.   (B)
It must be assumed that Beethoven knew what he was doing when he replaced the great Leonora Overture by the E major Fidelio Overture for the performance of the opera in the version in which it now lives. There is no place in the opera itself (e. g., as an introduction to Act II) where the Leonora Overture can be inserted with artistic verity. It may safely be concluded that the conductor who performs the Leonora Overture as part of a production of Fidelio does so only for the satisfaction of his own ego.   JG 94 [1927] 200

DER ÜBERZÄHLIGE TAKT IN DER PASTORALSINFONIE. Eugen Tetzel.   (C)
It is probable that certain passages in Beethoven autographs (e. g., the apparently redundant measure near the end of the first movement of the Fourth Symphony -- NZfM 15 [1841] 149) are in fact errors, but the author does not feel that the claim against the disputed measure early in the first movement of the Pastoral Symphony (JG 92 [1925] 288, 460) has been proved.   JG 94 [1927] 203

UND UM DIE DOMINANTE-TONICA-STELLE DER EROICA HERUM. Alfred Heuss.   (D)
A comprehensive study of the development of the famous transition to the recapitulation section of the first movement of the Eroica as indicated by the sketch books, with further discussion of various other passages of the movement in their roles as supporters for the dissonant passage -- "perhaps the most crucial few measures in the nineteenth-century music." The final installment of this paper touches on the influence which Beethoven's attitude towards Napoleon had on this work.   JG 94 [1927] 545, 609; JG 95 [1928] 7, 73

BEETHOVENS SCHÄDEL. F. A. Schmidt.   (E)
When Beethoven's body was exhumed in October 1863 for reburial, nine fragments of his skull (all that then remained) were given to Dr. Gerhard von Breuning, who reassembled the skull, replacing the missing bone fragments by plaster of Paris. It is from this reconstruction that all casts and photographs of Beethoven's skull have been made. The inevitable inaccuracies of this reconstruction make any present-day study of the skull useless for diagnostic purposes, specifically as regards the presence of bony overgrowths for thickenings as indications of syphilis.

JG 94 [1927] 688

DER HERKUNFT DER FAMILIE VAN BEETHOVEN. Otto Redlich.   (F)
A summary of the discoveries of Pols and Van Aerde (as given in 'Les ancêtres flamandes de Beethoven' by the latter scholar) that grandfather Ludwig was the son of Michael the baker and grandson of Cornelius the cabinetmaker, and that these ancestors were from Malines, not from Antwerp. Michael was made a freeman of the city of Cleves on April 10th 1739, shortly before he joined his sons Cornelius and Ludwig in Bonn.

JG 95 [1928] 327

DIE BEIDEN GROSSEN BDUR-TRIOS DER DEUTSCHEN MUSIK. Konrad Huschke.   (G)
Thoughts on Schubert's Trio Op. 99 and Beethoven's 'Archduke' Trio Op. 97.
JG 95 [1928] 682

EIN VERGESSENES BEETHOVENHAUS. August Pohl.   (H)
Beethoven spent parts of one or perhaps several summers during the years 1784-92 with the von Breunings in their country house at Kerpen (between Cologne and Aachen).   JG 95 [1928] 692

EIN BRIEF CARL GOLDMARKS ÜBER BEETHOVEN.   (I)
Letter to an unknown colleague written immediately after the centenary celebration of December 1870 in Vienna.
JG 97 [1930] 454

DER SINN DES CHORFINALES IN BEETHOVENS NEUNTE SYMPHONIE.   Otto Baensch.   (A)
    The rearrangement which Beethoven made in Schiller's poem was not to fit the words to a predetermined musical
    setting but rather to adapt the poem itself to Beethoven's thinking.
                                        JG   97 [1930] 1007

AUFFINDUNG DER GRABSTELLE DER MUTTER BEETHOVENS.   JG   99 [1932] 428   (B)

DIE ENTSCHLEIERUNG DES BEETHOVEN-GEHEIMNISSES.   "Deutobold Fürchterlich."   (C
    A satire on analytic interpretation.   JG 102 [1935] 130

STICHFEHLER UND FRAGLICHE STELLEN BEI BEETHOVEN.   Max Unger.   (D
    After exhaustive research in an attempt to prepare completely accurate versions of various compositions by Beethoven,
    the author estimates that in the GA there must be more than a thousand errors in notes, dynamics, etc.: in one brief
    composition ('Neue Liebe, neues Leben' Opus 75 No. 2) more than a dozen errors were found (see JG 103 [1936] 1049).
    The situation is no better in the field of Beethoven's letters: in the version of the Heiligenstadt will given by Kalischer
    ("the greatest source of confusion in Beethoven scholarship") there are no fewer than 115 errors, and much of the work
    by Frimmel is little better.   Mistakes and questionable readings are pointed out in the four overtures to Leonora and
    Fidelio (Opp. 72a, 72b, 138), the Overture to the Dedication of the House (Opus 124), and many errors in the Violon-
    cello Sonata Opus 69, including (unbelievable as it may seem) nearly half of those pointed out by Beethoven in his
    letter of July 26th 1809 to Breitkopf & Härtel (KS I 172; the list presumably that given in KS I 354; see also KS I 174).
                                        JG 102 [1935] 635,744

VON UNGEDRUCKTE MUSIK BEETHOVENS.   Max Unger.   (E)
    The following works were found in a private collection of manuscripts in Switzerland: Cadenza to the first move-
    ment of the G major Concerto Op. 58 (H-52), presumably from the spring of 1809. Transition to the rondo of the
    G major Concerto Op. 58 (H-53), presumably from the spring of 1809. Short cadenza to the rondo of the G major
    Concerto Op. 58 (H-54), presumably from the spring of 1809. Transition to the rondo of the Pianoforte Concerto
    Op. 61 (H-55), presumably from the spring of 1809. Two canons on 'Te solo adoro' (H-230,231), probably from
    the spring of 1824. Unaccompanied vocal ensemble on 'Geschlagen ist der Feind' (H-232) from 1814. Unaccom-
    panied vocal ensemble on 'To - bi - as' (H-233) written some years later than 1814. Canon for four male voices
    and string bass on 'Bester Magistrat, ihr friert' (H-229), probably referring to the Vienna magistrate who heard the
    guardianship case, and written about 1819. Pianoforte arrangement of the song 'Freudvoll und leidvoll' Op. 84 No.
    4 (H-67) published herewith. It is conjectured that this arrangement was made for Toni Adamberger, who created
    the role of Clärchen, and that the arrangement dates from the spring of 1810. Two settings of 'Que le temps me
    dure' (H-90) (see 'Die Musik' 1_2 [1902] 1078) published herewith. Attributed to the beginning of 1793.

                                        JG 102 [1935] 1193

BEETHOVEN AND E. T. A. HOFFMANN.   Max Unger.   (F
    "A critical consideration of the traces of Hoffmann's influence in Beethoven's works." The Hoffmann Canon (GA
    23/256 No. 8; KS II 171) is discussed at length. The letter of March 23rd 1820 to Hoffmann (see 'Die Musik'
    13_1 [1913] 147; KS II 170) is reproduced in facsimile and transcribed with an attempt at complete accuracy. (See
    also p. 1340)   JG 102 [1935] 1204

DIE BEETHOVENBILDER VON NEUGASS.   Max Unger.   (G
    Two portraits of Beethoven by Isidor Neugass are in existence, one quite certainly a copy of the other.
                                        JG 102 [1935] 1211

BEETHOVENS MUTTER.   Hermann Unger.   (H
    A brief account of Beethoven's mother and of Beethoven's boyhood, based on the Fischer MS. Photographs are given
    of several of the houses in Bonn in which Beethoven lived.   JG 102 [1935] 1216

DIE AUFFINDUNG DES GRABES DER MUTTER BEETHOVENS.   (I

    GESCHICHTLICHE VORAUSSETZUNGEN DER AUFFINDUNG.   F. Knickenberg.   (J
        Through information given by Heinrich Baum (great-grandson of Gertrude Baum, Beethoven's godmother) the
        grave of Beethoven's mother in the 'Alten Friedhof' in Bonn was located with certainty and her remains exhumed.
                                        JG 102 [1935] 1219

UNTERSUCHUNG UND IDENTIFIZIERUNG DES SKELETTS.   (A)
 A detailed description is given of the skeleton assumed to be that of Frau Beethoven, leading to the conclusion
 that none of the anthropometric, medical, or dental data are incompatible with the assumed identification.
 Anthropological Study, F. Wagenseil; Pathological-anatomical Study, W. Ceelan; Aurist's Study, K. Grünberg;
 Dental Study, G. Korkhaus.   JG 102 [1935] 1219, 1223, 1228

BEETHOVENS ERSTE LEONORE.   August Pohl.   (B)
 Biographical sketch of Pauline Anna Milder-Hauptmann, on the occasion of the 150th anniversary of her birth on
 December 13th 1785.   JG 102 [1935] 1232

EIN BRIEF BEETHOVENS AN GRILLPARZER.   Georg Kinsky.   (C)
 The letter "to an unknown poet" supposed to date from 1808-10 (KS I 176) was actually written to Grillparzer in the
 spring of 1823. The "opera poem" referred to is a projected libretto on the subject of Melusine.
                                                   JG 102 [1935] 1234

BEETHOVEN AND E. T. A. HOFFMANN.   Hans Kuznitzky.   (D)
 Defense against criticisms by Unger (p. 1204).   JG 102 [1935] 1340

BEETHOVEN'S ANCESTORS.   Ph. van Boxmeer.   (E)
 From 'De Brabantsche Folklore' August/October 1935 through the Essen 'National-Zeitung' for November 17th 1935.
 Records of the transfer of land show that a stated parcel in Nederockerzeel came to the ownership of Cornelius van
 Beethoven and his wife Catherina (Leempoels) van Beethoven on February 16th 1637 by inheritance from the wife of
 Marcus van Beethoven, and that this parcel was sold on March 14th 1676. This can be taken as almost conclusive
 proof that Cornelius was the son of Marcus. Cornelius lived in Malines from 1677 to 1684, then returned to Neder-
 ockerzeel, where his last child was born. The name Beethoven (in various spellings) was borne by branches of the
 family in these towns and in Bergh and Compenhout; a document dated September 14th 1460 refers to Walter van
 Beethoven. (This article was also summarized in 'Musik-Woche' 4 [1936] No. 5 p. 14)
                                                   JG 103 [1936] 7

EIN UNBEKANNTES FRANZÖSISCHER BRIEF LUDWIG VAN BEETHOVENS.   Max Unger.   (F)
 On December 27th 1822 Johann van Beethoven wrote to Pacini, the publisher in Paris, saying that he represented his
 brother Ludwig in matters of business, offering a new Trio for two Violins and Viola (possibly a revision of Op. 87)
 and a new overture (probably the 'Dedication of the House' Op. 124), and suggesting that the composer could be
 prevailed upon to compose various quartets and quintets if terms could be agreed upon. On April 5th 1823 Beethoven himself wrote to the publisher, saying that all he could then offer were 33 Variations on a Waltz (Op. 120),
 six Bagatelles for Pianoforte (Op. 119), and two songs to words by Goethe and Matthison with accompaniment for
 pianoforte solo or ensemble. This is one of the few letters in French written it its entirety by Beethoven: most
 other letters in French were written by an amanuensis and merely signed by the composer. Johann's letter contains
 the first reference to Beethoven's project of issuing the Missa Solemnis in manuscript copies to the royal courts of
 Europe, and refers to a letter of June 22nd 1822 from the publisher in which request is made for quartets and quintets.
 Note that this request antedates that of Galitsin by more than five months. The author refers to a letter dated February 11th 1823 from the publisher (as yet unpublished) in reply to Johann's letter, offering 500 francs for the Trio
 and Overture. In 1822-23 Beethoven did not live in the house of Brother Johann's brother-in-law Obermayer at 61
 Kothgasse, where Johann stayed during the winter, but in No. 60, immediately adjacent. Of considerable number
 of letters in French by Beethoven, only 4 are holographic: Kal 1149, M-70, M-72, and one to an "Altesse."
 (Regarding this statement, see M-70 Note 1)   JG 103 [1936] 414

"DER UNBEKANNTE BEETHOVEN."   Ferdinand Pfohl.   (G)
 Review of a piano arrangement of the 'Folksong Variations' Opp. 105 and 107.
                                                   JG 103 [1936] 419

BEETHOVEN AND E. T. A. HOFFMANN.   Max Unger.   (H)
 Polemic against Kuznitzky (JG 102 [1935] 1340).   JG 103 [1936] 473

BEETHOVEN.   Peter Raabe.   (I)
 Festival address.   JG 103 [1936] 816

ZUM LETZTEN MALE: BEETHOVEN UND E. T. A. HOFFMANN.   Hans Kuznitzky.   (A)
JG 103 [1936] 854

ZU BEETHOVENS VIOLINSONATEN.   Arnold Schering.   (B)
The poetic associations of the Sonatas Opp. 23, 24, 30 No. 3, and 12 No. 3 are analyzed in exhaustive detail.
JG 103 [1936] 1041, 1307;
JG 104 [1937] 374; JG 105 [1938] 121

NEUE LIEBE, NEUES LEBEN: DIE URSCHRIFT UND DIE GESCHICHTE EINES GOETHE-BEETHOVEN-LIEDES.   (C)
Max Unger.

The little-known first version of this song ('Die Musik' 23_1 [1930] 19) was composed about 1798. The publication
of this version by Simrock may be fixed with considerable accuracy in early 1808, and quite possibly was carried
out without Beethoven's approval or cooperation.   The generally-known version (based on the earlier one but differing radically from it) was dated 1809 on the manuscript, and probably dates from the end of the year. Op. 75
(of which this song is No. 2) was probably published in the first days of November 1810, together with Opp. 72, 74,
76, 77, 78, and 79.   Hasty publication resulted in a considerable number of errors in the first edition.   Many other
songs date from about this same period; Beethoven's sudden urge to the composition of songs may well have been due
to his thoughts of marriage about this time.   The relationship of Bettina Brentano with Beethoven and Goethe is discussed at some length.   The manuscript of the 1809 version was most carefully compared with the song as it appears
in the GA (23/219).   No less than twelve errors were found, and a corrected version is given herewith.
JG 103 [1936] 1049

KLINGER AND BEETHOVEN.   Konrad Huschke.   (D)
A discussion of Klinger's statue of Beethoven.   JG 103 [1936] 1077

BEETHOVENS "OBERHOFMEISTER": NANETTE STREICHER.   Max Herre.   (E)
Biographical sketch of Maria Anna Stein (1769-1833), who in 1794 or 1793 married Johann Andreas Streicher.
Beethoven had known her since her girlhood, and from about 1813 to the time of his death she was his constant
confidante in domestic and personal matters.   JG 103 [1936] 1079

DIE NEUEINRICHTUNG DES BONNEN BEETHOVEN-HAUSES.   Joseph Schmidt-Görg.   (F)
A report on the changes instituted by the recently appointed Director, Dr. Ludwig Schiedermair.
JG 103 [1936] 1085

WAGNER AND BEETHOVEN.   Peter Raabe.   (G
Festival address.   JG 104 [1937] 865

JOHANN VAN BEETHOVEN.   August Pohl.   (H
Biographical sketch.   On the death of Brother Johann, Nephew Karl was his sole heir, receiving an estate of 42,564.53
florins.   "Thus was fulfilled a wish close to the heart of our Beethoven."
JG 105 [1938] 67

ZUR ENTSTEHUNGS-UND AUFFÜHRUNGSGESCHICHTE VON BEETHOVENS OPER "LEONORE."   Max Unger.   (I)

The first reference to Beethoven's plan to write an opera is found in a letter dated February 12th 1803 from Brother
Johann to Breitkopf & Härtel: "You have probably heard that my brother has been engaged by the Wiedener Theatre
to write an opera." Further mention of this project was made in the newspapers in April 1803 and following months.
The opera in question was to be based on the book "Vestas Feuer" by Schikaneder (see 'Die Musik' 22_1 [1930] 409).
The composer apparently received the libretto about the beginning of November 1803, but by the end of the year
the project seems to have been abandoned.

Three letters to Sonnleithner are given which have been published before (e. g., 'Beethoven-Forschung' 1 [1911] 3),
but which do not appear in Beethoven biographies or collections of Beethoven letters.   About the end of 1803
Sonnleithner replaced Schikaneder in a controlling position in the Vienna opera; this development may have led

Beethoven to return 'Vestas Feuer' to its author and to request a libretto from Sonnleithner. A letter from Beethoven to Sonnleithner without date (probably from March or at the earliest February 1804) requests Sonnleithner to provide him with a completed book as soon as possible, so that he can work right through and have the opera completed by June (1804) at the latest. It also refers to a change of dwelling on the part of Beethoven, quite possibly to make more convenient his cooperation with Sonnleithner, and mentions a projected departure from Vienna. The author postulates that this might be a concert tour to Paris, which Beethoven considered for some years but never carried out. Various of Nottebohm's conjectures of dates in connection with Leonora and other works of this time (see in particular 'Ein Skizzenbuch aus dem Jahre 1803' [1880]) are a year too early. Specifically, the date "Am 2ten Juni" on the manuscript of the Second Act Finale is almost certainly 1805 not 1804. The same doubt applies to dates for Opp. 85, 56, 55, 53, 48 No. 3, etc.

The second of the Sonnleithner notes, probably from the late spring or early summer of 1805, requests "the last four verses" and states that he will write the overture during the rehearsal period. A fact not generally known is that the first performance was originally scheduled for October 15th 1805 (the name day of the Empress Marie Theresia) but that about the end of September, while rehearsals were in full swing, the censor decreed that the opera was "not fit for public performance." A letter dated October 2nd 1805 is given from Sonnleithner to the Chief of Police, in which he points out reasons why the censor should reverse his findings. A few days later this was done. It should be noted that the postponement of the first performance from October 15th to November 20th was not because of this mischance, but because of the difficulties of the music which required additional rehearsal time. The decision to shorten the opera, and the actual work of revision (during December 1805) were apparently carried out without Sonnleithner's assistance. The third letter from Beethoven to him (probably from early March 1806) refers to this fact, and indicates that the revised libretto (still bearing the name 'Leonore' rather than 'Fidelio') was being published at Beethoven's expense. Extracts are given from a letter from Stephan von Breuning regarding the performance of the revised version, and from a letter from Röckel describing the quarrel between Beethoven and Baron Braun which culminated in Beethoven's request that the score be returned and the opera withdrawn.

JG 105 [1938] 130

ZU DEN ERSTDRUCKE EINIGER WERKE BEETHOVENS. Max Unger.   (A)

The first edition of the four versions of the song 'Nur wer die Sehnsucht kennt' was not that of the Kunst und Industrie Comptoir in September 1810 (NV p. 181), but was one issued by Simrock early in 1809 (not later than May). Simultaneously with the first publication of the Pianoforte Sonata Op. 81a as listed in NV, with title page in French, there was also an edition with title page in German and with the music from the same plates as the French titled version. A copy of this German first edition is in the Vienna Stadtbibliothek. It was this edition which was referred to by Beethoven in his letter of October 9th 1811 to Breitkopf & Härtel (KS I 230): "I have just received Das Lebewohl etc., I see that you really have other copies with French title." No edition has been found with both French and German text on the title page. The author refers to the observation in NV (p. 78) that the sonata was originally issued in two parts, remarking that this statement was doubtless due to the appearance of two different plate numbers (1588 for the first movement and 1589 for the second and third movements). An alternative conjecture is that the different numbers were used by an engraver who thought from the superscription on the manuscript that two different compositions were involved: Das Lebewohl (first movement) and Die Ankunft (second and third movements). A letter of January 1st 1877 from Theodor Steingräber to A. W. Thayer (referred to in TK IV 122) states that the earliest edition of the Pianoforte Sonata Op. 106 was with title page in French: "Grande Sonata pour le Piano-Forte" (in contradiction of the statement of NV). It is probable that the edition with the French title page was issued for sale outside Germany simultaneously with the usually accepted version, so that both may properly be considered first editions.

The compositions appearing as GA 25/303-05 are dated in the autographs in Beethoven's own hand. Details are given of the collections of dances, issued by C. F. Müller, in which each of these little compositions first appeared. It is not known what led Beethoven to lay his pen down even momentarily from his work on the last quartets to write these three dances. No. 303 "Waltzer (Es-dur) von L. v. Beethoven. Vien am 21ten Novemb. 1824." No. 304 "Waltzer (D-dur) Geschrieb. am 14ten Novemb. 1825 von L. v. Beethoven." No. 305 "Ecossais Geschrieb. am 14ten Novemb. 1825 von L. v. Beethoven." The following dates of publication have been definitely fixed from publisher's records. Op. 121b Opferlied 23 July 1825, Op. 122 Bundeslied 23 July 1825, Op. 124 Dedication of the House Ov. 7 Dec 1825, Op. 125 Ninth Symphony (score) 28 Aug 1826.

JG 105 [1938] 139

ZU BEETHOVENS ITALIENISCHER GESANGSMUSIK.   Max Unger.   (A)

Thayer (TV-264), Nottebohm ('Beethoven's Studien' pp. 207ff.) and Hess ('Schweizerische Musik-pädagogische Blätter' 1936 pp. 181ff. and 'Neues Beethoven-Jahrbuch' 7 [1937] pp. 122ff.) have given the basic listing of Beethoven's Italian a capella songs, which were written for the most part as exercises during his studies with Salieri (1793-1802). He also wrote the following Italian songs with accompaniment.

GA 25/279	"O care selve" (1794).
Op. 65	"Ah! perfido" for soprano and orchestra. Written in the first half of 1796; published 1805 with Pf accompaniment.
NV p. 178	"La Partenza" for voice and Pf. Written 1798 or earlier; published 1803.
Op. 116	"Tremate, empj, tremate" for STB and orchestra. Written in 1801-02; probably took its present form for its first public performance on February 27th 1814; published 1826.
GA 25/271	"Primo amore piacer del ciel" for soprano and orchestra. Written "very early"; first published in GA.
H-80	"No, non turbati" for soprano and string orchestra. Written in 1801-02; not published.
H-81	"Nei giorni tuoi felici" for soprano, tenor and orchestra. "First Vienna years"; unpublished.
NV p. 180	"In questa tomba oscura" -- text set by 63 composers, including Beethoven, and published in 1808.
Op. 82	"Vier Arietten und ein Duett." Composed 1809-early 1810; published March 1811.
H-97	"Un lieto brindisi" for STTB and Pf. Composed in 1814; unpublished.

The months at the end of 1809 and in early 1810 form Beethoven's love song period: in this time he wrote or completed Opp. 75, 82, 83, the two Clärchenlieder, Op. 84 Nos. 1 and 4, and others. This activity may be associated with his intention to marry Therese Malfatti. The nationality of his intended bride may explain the number of Italian songs (5) from this period, although none of the songs were dedicated to her. Two autograph copies of 'Hoffnung' (Op. 82 No. 1) are extant. Of these, one corresponds very closely to the published version; the other is full of corrections and changes, apparently made by the composer at some undetermined time after the publication of the generally known version. The revised version is published herewith.

JG 105 [1938] 150

BEETHOVEN-COLLIN-SHAKESPEARE.   Paul Mies.   (B)

Beethoven's overture to 'Coriolanus' was written for Collin's drama, which differs materially from the far better known one of Shakespeare. The form of this overture is discussed, with special reference to its differences from Beethoven's other overtures and sonata movements, and the conclusion is drawn that "the differences resulted from the association of the overture with the drama."   JG 105 [1938] 156

BEETHOVENS MERGENTHEIMER REISE.   August Pohl.   (C)

A general account of the journey (TK I 111-16), with quotations from the account of the Abbé Junker.

JG 105 [1938] 161

WO WOHNTE BEETHOVEN IN WIEN?   Hermann Güttler.   (D)

A list of the various houses in Vienna which Beethoven occupied, as "a guidebook for those making a musical tour of Austria."   JG 105 [1938] 770

ZU JOH. NEP. MÄLZELS 100. TODESTAG, DEM 21. JULI 1838.   Fritz Müller.   (E)

A brief biographical sketch, in which the statement is made that practicable metronomes had been made as early as 1700.   JG 105 [1938] 771

ZUFALL ODER ABSICHT?   P. Neubert.   (F)

In mm. 63-64 of the slow movement of the E minor Quartet Op. 59 No. 2 the principal theme of the movement is modified in the Vcl to the notes B A C H.   JG 105 [1938] 1374

DIE ENTHÜLLUNG DES BREUERSCHE BEETHOVEN-DENKMAL IN BONN.   August Pohl.   (G)

JG 106 [1939] 187

CARL CZERNYS ERINNERUNGEN AN BEETHOVEN.   Max Unger.   (A)
A summary of some of the important points brought out in Schünemann's article of the same title in NBJ 9 [1939] 47.

JG 107 [1940] 606

DER VERDIENSTE VON BEETHOVENS VATER UM DIE GRÜNDUNG EINES DEUTSCHEN NATIONAL THEATERS IN BONN.   (B)
Max Unger.
Summary of material given by Pfeffer in DM 28_1 [1935] 13 and later included in his book 'The Theater in Bonn.'

JG 108 [1941] 251

BEETHOVENS FLÄMISCHE VORFAHREN.   Joseph Schmidt-Görg.   (C)
The same ancestral line is given here as appears in 'Beethoven und die Gegenwart' [1937] 134.

JG 108 [1941] 299

BEETHOVEN-BRIEFE.   Max Unger.   (D)
The most recent collection of Beethoven letters (Kastner-Kapp) includes 1474 items, of which about 20 are marginal
notes and the like which do not belong in a collection of letters. In addition, about 210 letters (including some receipts, contracts, powers of attorney, etc.) are known, including about 20 which KK lists without text or with abbreviated text. Thus a total of some 1650 letters are now known, and in a few centuries the number will doubtless exceed 2000. The following letters, not appearing in any collection, but previously published in newspapers or obscure
journals, are given: MM 16, MM 18, MM 147, MM 148, MM 319, MM 420.

JG 109 [1942] 197

ANNA CATHERINA BETHOFFEN.   Stephan Ley.   (E)
A register of baptisms in Bonn shows the names of Hermann Pfeiffer and Anna Catherina Bethoffen as parents of a
child baptized in 1702. The author suggests the possibility (purely as a conjecture) that Anna Catherina was from
Flanders and that years later she suggested to her relatives (?) Michael and Cornelius that they move to Bonn.

JG 112 [1951] 304

EIN BEETHOVENWORT.   Kurt Huber.   (F)
Metaphysical discussion.   113 [1952] 130

BEETHOVENS WIDMUNGEN.   Stephan Ley.   (G)
Of Beethoven's numbered works, 52 (more than one-third) are without dedication. Of the others, a few were apparently dedicated without Beethoven's approval, others strictly for favors received or hoped for, and some in true
friendship or affection. Quite a number of people to whom Beethoven was very close (e. g. , Neefe, Schenck, Marie
Bigot, Marie Pachler, Nannette Streicher) were not honored by a dedication. Others received a large number: the
Lichnowsky family, 11; the Archduke Rudolph, 9; Prince Lobkowitz, 7; Count Browne and his wife, 7; Count Fries,
5; Prince Kinsky and his wife, and Babette Keglevich, each 4. Of the sixty persons receiving dedications, only
seven were commoners.   113 [1952] 135

BEETHOVENS ZUKUNFTSPLÄNE.   Konrad Huschke.   (H)
At the time of his death, Beethoven was actively considering his Tenth Symphony, Music for Faust, an oratorio, a
mass, a requiem, an overture on B A C H, chamber music for strings and wind instruments, perhaps a second opera,
and more works for piano. Facsimiles are given of sketches for the B A C H Overture and for the Tenth Symphony.

113 [1952] 138

AUS BEETHOVENS SKIZZENBUCH (ZUM STREICHQUINTETT OPUS 29).   Wilhelm Virneisel.   (I)
Six known pages of sketches for Op. 29 are discussed in detail, of which two are given in facsimile.

113 [1952] 142

DAS BEETHOVENBILD ROMAIN ROLLANDS.   Hermann Fähnrich.   (J)
The course of Rolland's thinking and writing about Beethoven is summarized.

113 [1952] 147

CAROLINE VAN BEETHOVEN.   Hedwig M. v. Asow.   (K)
In 1873 and again in 1878 the Philharmonische Concerte in Vienna made donations for the relief of Nephew Karl's
widow.   113 [1952] 150

WO SIND BEETHOVENS SKIZZEN ZUR ZEHNTEN SYMPHONIE? L u d w i g M i s c h .   (A)
  Evidence is cited to show that the Tenth Symphony had been sketched far more extensively than is represented in the
  only known sketches, those given by Schindler in 'Musikalisch-kritische Repertorium' 1 [1844] 425, 467, 511. These
  sketches may be together in the hands of some unknown collector, or they may have been on loose sheets which have
  been dispersed.   116 [1955] 132

BEETHOVENS "NEUNTE" IN ORIGINALFASSUNG.   (B)
  "Every score of the Ninth shows how it was originally planned to sound, but no orchestra plays it that way. Prepos-
  terous but true: for three generations no one has heard the Ninth in its original version. " The changes invariably
  made are in doublings, in scorings, and in the writing-in of notes unplayable on natural horns and trumpets.
                                                                     116 [1955] 141

EIN UNBEKANNTES "IMPROMPTU" VON BEETHOVEN. L u d w i g M i s c h .   (C
  Facsimile, transcription, and brief discussion of KHV-WoO 61a (MM 427).
                                                                     117 [1956] 195

SIND AENDERUNGEN IN BEETHOVENS INSTRUMENTATION ZULÄSSIG? L u d w i g M i s c h .   (D
  Except for a single note (d above middle C), Beethoven's horn parts at one place or another include every note of the
  chromatic scale from the 4th harmonic (middle C) to the 16th harmonic two octaves higher. This was practicable
  because of the capability of hand and lips to alter a note with still acceptable quality. Thus, to rewrite horn parts
  to correspond to the freedom typical of the romantic period is to do what Beethoven could have done if he wished
  but did not see fit to do. Modification of trumpet parts falls within the same reasoning. There is no necessity for
  transposing violin or flute parts to the higher octave to exceed Beethoven's self-imposed limitation of a'''. Appar-
  ent lack of balance supposedly due to Beethoven's deafness is the fault of the conductor, not of the music. "Beethoven knew what he was doing. Would that his interpreters could say the same. "
                                                                     117 [1956] 618

ZU BEETHOVENS "IMPROMPTU." L u d w i g M i s c h .   (E
  The translation in Schindler's Beethoven-Biographie (1844) of the article in 'Harmonicon'3 [1825] 222 (see MM 427)
  is in part incorrect. It is doubtful that Dietrichstein was the librarian to whom the English visitor applied.
                                                                     117 [1956] 709

BEETHOVENS CHORLIEDER MIT KLAVIERBEGLEITUNG. W i l l y H e s s .   (F
  Beethoven's songs with unison choral refrain include Op. 52 No. 1 and WoO 109, 111, 117, 119, and 122, all from
  1797 or earlier. His mature works include the little cantatas WoO 103, 105, and 106. The autograph of the
  'Hochzeitlied für Nanni Giannatasio' WoO 105, in C major, for solo and unison chorus, was published in 'Der Bär'
  [1927] 157. M&L 17 [1936] 238 describes the autograph of a version in A major for solo and 4-part chorus, which
  was published in England in 1858. A facsimile of this English edition is given.
                                                                     118 [1957] 152

DER ERSTE SATZ DER "EROICA." H e l m u t D e g e n .   (G
  Analysis.   118 [1957] 156

BEETHOVENS LETZTE STUNDEN. S t e p h a n L e y .   (H
  Section 31 of the author's 'Wahrheit, Zweifel und Irrtum. '   118 [1957] 194

DER "KORRIGIERTE" BEETHOVEN. K u r t J a n i t z k y .   (I
  Changes in Beethoven's orchestration may be justified by the change in instrumental construction, orchestra composition, and concert hall size of today.   118 [1957] 304

FUGE UND FUGATO IN BEETHOVENS VARIATIONENFORM. L u d w i g M i s c h .   (J
                                                                     119 [1958] 75

WIEWEIT SIND BEETHOVENS PARTITUREN FEHLERFREI? G o t t h . E . L e s s i n g .   (K
  The author points out what appears to be an error in the score of Leonore Overture III, mm. 154-160, and proposes
  a correction.   119 [1958] 509

KORRIGIERTER BEETHOVEN? W o l f g a n g H i l t l .   (
  The author proposes a course that is an alternative to that suggested by Janitzky (118 [1957] 304).
                                                                     119 [1958] 648

DIE HAMMERKLAVIER-SONATE. Hermann Keller.   (A)
    The author questions certain of Beethoven's metronome markings, discusses the disputed transition to the recapitulation
of the first movement (A natural or A sharp?), and mentions the desirability of performing the first three movements as
a single work, with the closing fugue separated as Op. 133 was from Op. 130.
119 [1958] 706

BEETHOVEN-FÄLSCHUNGEN. Willy Hess.   (B)
    A description is given of two collections that contain compositions attributed to Beethoven.
119 [1958] 715

AUTOGRAPHS UND ORIGINALAUSGABEN BEETHOVENS. Edmund Schmid.   (C)
    Comments on Schenker's discussion of disputed passages.   119 [1958] 746

AUS BEETHOVENS NOTIZKALENDER. Stephan Ley.   (D)
    Superficial description of kitchen calendar that Beethoven used in 1819, 1820, and 1823. A few typical entries re-
garding the hiring and firing of kitchen maids are given. The fact is mentioned that the canon Fettlumerl was written
on the last page of the 1823 calendar.   120 [1959] 504

BEETHOVENS GROSSNEFFE IN AMERIKA. Paul Nettl.   (E)
    Substantially the same material as M&L 38 [1957] 260.   120 [1959] 506

BEETHOVEN-PATHOGRAPHIE. Dieter Kerner.   (F)
    The author states his reasons for believing that Beethoven suffered from congenital syphilis.
120 [1959] 510

WIE VIELE FASSUNGEN DER MARZELLINEN-ARIE GIBT ES? Willy Hess.   (G)
    Six versions in all are known.   120 [1959] 514

SCHWEIZER VERMÄCHTNIS FÜR DAS BEETHOVEN-HAUS. Dagmar Weise.   (H)
    A general account of the bequest from Dr. Bodmer to the Beethovenhaus that includes more than 400 Beethoven letters.
121 [1960] 410

DIE IKONOGRAPHIE IN DER BEETHOVENFORSCHUNG. Stephan Ley.   (I)
    A discussion of the classes of items that should be included in an iconography.
121 [1960] 413

BUSONIS KRITIK AN BEETHOVENS LETZTEN QUARTETTEN. Hans Moldenhauer.   (J)
    Busoni does not include these quartets among Beethoven's finest works.
121 [1960] 416

DIE VOLLENDUNG DER KLASSISCHEN KUNST" -- EIN UNGESCHRIEBENER BAND DER BEETHOVENFORSCHUNG   (K)
    ROMAIN ROLLANDS. Hermann Fähnich.
Rolland had planned a Beethoven study in five parts. Of these, the first (up to 1800) was postponed until the end
and never started. The period 1806-15 is represented only by 'Goethe et Beethoven,' but a treatment of this period
in three sections was outlined. For the portions that were never written, 'Jean-Christophe' must serve as a substitute.
121 [1960] 418

BEETHOVENS SKIZZENBUCH ZUR CHORFANTASIE OPUS 80. Dagmar Weise.   (L)
    A detailed discussion of the sketch book published in 1957 by the Beethovenhaus.
122 [1961] 226

IENI AMORE. Hermann Keller.   (M)
    A detailed discussion of WoO 65.   122 [1961] 230

BEETHOVENS VERHÄLTNIS ZUM MESSETEXT. Gunther Baum.   (N)
    Comments on Beethoven's settings of certain phrases in Opp. 86 and 123.
122 [1961] 444

NEUE NEEFEIANA.   Irmgard Leux.   (A)
   Recently discovered biographical material is given. Neefe's correspondence shows that the statement (TK I 36) "he
   seems not to have left Bonn at all" is not well founded: actually he appears to have made a number of short trips;
   e. g. , in 1784-86 separate visits to Frankfurt, Cologne and the Spanish Netherlands. The "two symphonies" (TK I 36)
   are in reality the overtures to two of his operas; for "Sechs Sonaten am Clavier zu singen" read "Sechs Serenaten. . ."
   In addition to the dedication to the Countess von Hatzfeld of a set of variations by Beethoven (TK I 37N), Neefe also
   dedicated to her his Variations on the March from 'Zauberflöte.' The compositions by Neefe which are known (mostly
   unpublished) are discussed in great detail.   1 [1924] 86

AUS BRIEFEN JOHANNS VAN BEETHOVEN.   Heinrich Rietsch.   (B)
   After a brief listing of the descendants of Nephew Karl, the author lists and summarizes the known letters of Brother
   Johann. (See also 3 [1927] 42)   1 [1924] 115

BEETHOVEN ALS GASTHAUSBESUCHER IN WIEN.   Theodor von Frimmel.   (C)
   The author lists a considerable number of the inns in and near Vienna the names of which come up in accounts of
   Beethoven's life.   1 [1924] 128

ZUR DRAMATURGIE DES FIDELIO.   Hermann W. v. Waltershausen.   (D)
   "It is the function of operatic work to spontaneous life." From this standpoint the author discusses each character,
   the action and its significance, and the staging. As for the choice of Overture, the author says that the Leonore
   Overture No. 3 is dramatically and musically most suitable (the Second Overture being ruled out because of the change
   in the trumpet fanfare) but that the interpolation of this overture before the last scene is musically and dramatically
   unforgivable.   1 [1924] 142

WORAUF BERUHT DIE BEKANNTE WIRKUNG DER DURCHFÜHRUNG IM I. EROICASATZE.   Alfred Lorenz.   (E)
   The first movement of the Eroica is an exception to the generalization that in the first movements of Beethoven
   symphonies the development section is slightly shorter than the exposition section:

	E	D			E	D
I	97:	68		VI	138:	140
II	100:	84		VII	114:	97
IV	154:	152		VIII	103:	86
V	124:	123		IX	159:	141

In the Eroica the ratio is 147:250

   The author bases his analysis of the development section on the division made by Leichtentritt in his 'Musikalischen
   Formenlehre' (the measure numbers used here are for convenience those given in Wier's 'The Nine Symphonies of
   Beethoven in Score'):

Leichtentritt		Lorenz
I	152 - 165	Transition
II	166 - 177	Transition Theme followed by
III	178 - 219	Principal Theme
IV	220 - 235	Transition Theme followed by
V	236 - 283	Fugato (closely akin to a motif from the Principal Theme)
VI	284 - 299	Episode (closely akin to a motif from the Principal Theme)
VII	300 - 321	Principal Theme
VIII	322 - 337	Episode
	338 - 365	Canonic development of the Principal Theme
IX	366 - 397	Transition to the Recapitulation Section

   By this analysis the development section assumes close resemblance to an AABA form.
                                                      1 [1924] 159

LA CULTURA DI BEETHOVEN IN ITALIA.   Guido Pannain.   (F

1833	Seventh and Third Symphonies (Florence)
1833-38	First and Second Symphonies
1838	Müller performed Beethoven piano works in his Italian concert
1839	Piano transcriptions of the Symphonies by German arrangers (2 hands, 4 hands) issued by Italian publishers

1842	Italian editions of the Sonata in C sharp minor Op. 27 No. 2 and the C minor Trio Op. 1; Egmont Overture performed
1843	Fifth Symphony performed
1844	Journal article regarding the discordant passage in the Eroica
1846	Three Beethoven concerts (Milan)
1851	Pastoral Symphony performed
1854-55	Performances of Beethoven chamber music
1862	Popular concerts in Naples include Beethoven symphonies and overtures
1864	G major Trio selected as trial piece in piano competition
1866	Società del Quartetto (Florence) organized
1869	Fidelio performed (Milan?)
1870	Beethoven centenary brings many performances, including Emperor Concerto and Op. 97

Thereafter performances of Beethoven works became increasingly regular matters in Italian musical life. Publication of books and articles on Beethoven became more frequent; the most important ones are listed.

1 [1924] 184

DIE VOGELSTIMMENMOTIVE IN BEETHOVENS WERKE.   Robert Lach.   (A)
  After a discussion of Beethoven's love of nature, and of the use which his predecessors had made of bird songs as motival or stylistic material (from the sixteenth century), the author discusses several passages in the Pastoral Symphony: the nightingale-quail-cuckoo at the end of the second movement; the passage in this movement referred to by Beethoven as being based on the song of the yellow-hammer (cited by Schindler as being the arpeggios in mm. 59ff, but more likely the repeated notes in mm. 19-20); the opening theme of the Scene at the Brook with its similarity to the song of the robin; the trills early in this movement as reminding one of the lark; and a motif in the scherzo resembling the song of the titmouse.   Moreover, the "bebung" in Op. 110 may be a version of the nightingale song, and mm. 75-78 and 81-84 in the first movement of Op. 106 is not unlike the song of the chaffinch. (See also 8 [1938] 73)   2 [1925] 7

METRISCHE STUDIEN ZU BEETHOVENS LIEDERN.   Arnold Schering.   (B)
  A very detailed study is made of the metrical structure of the following songs: Mignon (Op. 75 No. 1). Busslied (Op. 48 No. 6). Adelaide (Op. 46). Nur wer die Sehnsucht kennt (NV p. 180 -- four versions). Ich liebe dich (NV p. 178). Sehnsucht (NV p. 182). An die Hoffnung (Op. 32). The analysis indicates that the thought of a four or eight measure period as the fundamental rhythmic unit is completely without foundation.

2 [1925] 23

DIE LIEDER BEETHOVENS.   Ernst Bücken.   (C)
  While Beethoven's early songs are characterized by a vocal line which gives more regard to the melody than to the prosody of the text, the first sketches of a number of the songs are definitely of a declamatory nature, later smoothed out melodically.   It should be noted that in a song as early as 'Die Klage' (1789-90) the romanticism of Schubert was foreshadowed to an amazing extent. In 'Neue Liebe, neues Leben' the sonata form with coda is chosen as most suitable for the text of the song. In the Gellaert Songs Op. 48 (pub. 1803) Beethoven at length achieved his own distinctive style; a most pronounced use of declamation within the framework of classic melody-writing.   Beethoven's early songs were written at a period when imitative following of the text by the music (e.g., Haydn's 'Creation') was being replaced by subjective interpretation of the text.   Beethoven's advance in this direction, melodically and harmonically, makes him "the first composer to advance along the path which led through the songs of Schubert to the music dramas of Wagner and the songs of Wolf."

2 [1925] 33

KLEINE BEITRÄGE ZU BEETHOVENS LIEDERN UND BÜHNENWERKE.   Hans Moser.   (D)

WER WAR HERROSEE?   (E)
  The poet of Beethoven's 'Zärtliche Liebe' (NV p. 178) was Carl Friedrich Wilhelm Herrosee (1754-1821), a reformed church clergyman.   The poem consists of five stanzas, and the song in its original form (presumably the

WER WAR HERROSEE? (Continued)

first edition, issued by Praeg in 1803 (NV p. 179), and certainly the version included in Haslinger's manuscript collection) was a strophic setting of all five stanzas ("Beglückt durch mich") (see 'Die Musik' 6$_2$ [1907] Beilage following p. 136). This version may date from about 1796, with the final version (based on the second stanza and part of the third) from about 1800, though possibly as late as 1803.

2 [1925] 43

DIE STROPHENWIEDERHOLUNGEN IN DEN GELLERTLIEDERN.   (A)

Of the six songs of Op. 48, two (the second and the third) include dal segno markings as indication that perhaps Beethoven contemplated a strophic use of some of the many other stanzas of the poems; the fourth and fifth of the songs set only the first of many such stanzas. Attempts are described to extend the duration of this song cycle in performance by the use of some of the other stanzas. In spite of great care, this attempt was of only limited success.   2 [1925] 51

ZEILENTAUSCH ALS BAUGESETZ.   (B)

A parallelism is found between the structure of old French ballads and the songs of the German Minnesingers on the one hand and Beethoven's song 'Maiïed' (Op. 52 No. 4) on the other, to the extent that in both cases the interchange or substitution of entire measures establishes a division of the composition into Stollen and Abgesang.

2 [1925] 54

SCHLUSSDEVISEN.   (C)

Examples are given of song in which Beethoven closed with an echo of the motif with which the song opened.

2 [1925] 55

IST "LEONORE" FÜR "FIDELIO" NUTZBAR ZU MACHEN?   (D)

An outline is given of a proposed fourth version of the opera to be made up by selection of the strongest portions from each of the three present versions. This would save from oblivion certain parts of 'Leonore' which are omitted from 'Fidelio' or which in the revision were weakened.

2 [1925] 56

EINE NEUARBEITUNG DER "RUINE VON ATHEN" UND "GESCHÖPFE DES PROMETHEUS."   (E)

A new text is proposed for the 'Ruins of Athens' music, in praise of music and of Beethoven as its greatest exemplar, with 'Prometheus' being presented as an indication of Beethoven's greatness.

2 [1925] 60

BEETHOVENS KOMPOSITIONEN VON GOETHES "NUR WER DIE SEHNSUCHT KENNT." Th. W. Werner.   (F)

A consideration of Beethoven's fourfold setting as a study of his approach to the Lied and of the effect of this particular poem upon him.   2 [1925] 66

BEETHOVEN UND DAS WIENER HOFTHEATER IM JAHRE 1807. Max Unger.   (G)

The author contends that passages in Beethoven's letters of May 11th 1807 (certainly not 1806) to Franz von Brunsvik (KS I 102): "I can't get on with the princely theater rabble" Lobkowitz, Schwartzenberg, Esterhazy and the others who took over the Royal Imperial Court Theater from Baron Braun at the end of 1806 (TK II 98) and of July 26th 1807 to Prince Esterhazy (KS I 130): "I had the misfortune to be disappointed of my benefit day at the theater" show conclusively that Beethoven's request for a permanent engagement at the Theater (KS I 110) could have been made not earlier than the fall of 1807, and probably in November or at the beginning of December. As further evidence in favor of this dating: Beethoven's request for a benefit concert, in the last paragraph of his petition, may be paraphrased: "If I receive the assignment which I ask, I shall be so busy that March 25th is about as soon as I could be ready for a concert, but if I do not receive it the few weeks from now until Christmas will be enough for my necessary preparation." The statement ('Allgemeine Musikalische Zeitung' 10 [1808] 239) dated December 26th 1807 that Beethoven was to be engaged at the theater would hardly have been many months after the petition had been submitted. This chronology does not conflict with two undated letters to Heinrich von Collin mentioning Beethoven's hope for a benefit concert: one which by internal evidence may confidently be assigned to March 1808 (KS I 133 No. 145) and one (KS I 121) probably written later. The latter of these refers to a promise by Court Councillor Joseph v. Hartl that if Beethoven would collaborate in a concert for theater charities (which he did on November 15th 1808) he would have a benefit for himself (this being the concert of December 22nd 1808 at which the Fifth and Sixth Symphonies received their first performances).   2 [1925] 76

ZUR WIENER BALLETTPANTOMIME UM DEN PROMETHEUS. Robert Haas.   (H)

A list is given, with detailed annotations and references, of ballets which received their first performances at the

Hoftheater in Vienna between 1791 and 1807 (as regards ballet, this list amplifies that given in TD II 575ff).
Brief biographical sketches are given of Anton Muzzarelli, Salvator Vigano and others in the history of the ballet
in Vienna, and the general regulations posted in 1795 for the members of the ballet company at the Hoftheater
are given. Beethoven's 'Prometheus' was first performed on March 28th 1801, and thereafter thirteen other times
in 1801 and nine times in 1802. Vigano (who had moved to Milan in 1804) gave in that city on May 22nd 1813
the so-called 'Greater Prometheus,' with music taken from Beethoven's Prometheus music and from compositions
by Haydn, Weigl and others. Another similar indiscriminate selection of music was used in the 'Prometheus' produced in Vienna on November 18th 1843 by August Hus, based on Vigano's 'Greater Prometheus' scenario, which
is given herewith. (See also 'Zeitschrift für Musikwissenschaft' 3 [1921] 223)

2 [1925] 84

CHERUBINIS EINFLUSS AUF BEETHOVENS OUVERTÜREN. Arnold Schmitz.   (A)

Beethoven's great admiration of Cherubini's music is well known. The author cites similarities in details between
various Beethoven overtures (chiefly Fidelio and the Leonora Overtures) and overtures by Cherubini and (to a lesser
extent) Méhul. In matters of structure there are both similarity and differences. Like Cherubini (and like Mozart),
Beethoven laid little stress on the development sections of his overtures except in the Leonore Overture No. 2,
where development takes place at the expense of recapitulation. He did not go as far in his overtures as Cherubini
did in thematic development within the exposition and recapitulation sections and the coda. The nature of the
thematic material itself which Beethoven used seems to have been influenced more by Méhul than by Cherubini.
All things considered, though, there can be no doubt that in his overtures Beethoven was much influenced by
Cherubini.   2 [1925] 104

BEETHOVENS C-DUR-MESSE OPUS 86 ALS KIRCHLICHES WERK. B. A. Wallner.   (B)

Though written as an occasional composition (for the Name-Day of Princess Marie Esterhazy, September 13th
1807) and thrown in the shade by the Missa Solemnis, the C major Mass is "one of the master's most intimate
works . . . the starting point of a new type of religious music." In support of these contentions, the Mass is
analyzed in considerable detail, with comparisons with masses by Mozart and the two Haydns. In the opinion
of the author, the use of various instruments banned by the encyclical "Annus quo" of Pope Benedict XIV
(February 19th 1749) does not invalidate this mass (or many others) for liturgical use.

2 [1925] 119

ZUR NEUNTEN SYMPHONIE. Otto Baensch.   (C)

WANN ERSCHIEN DIE PARTITUR?   (D)

The score was advertised in 'Caecilia' in the spring of 1826, but it is probable that copies were not available
for subscribers (or for Beethoven himself) until well into the fall -- very likely only after the first Berlin performance on November 27th 1826.   2 [1925] 137

ÜBERLIEFERUNG.   (E)

The following manuscripts and editions must be considered in any question regarding the authentic text of
the Ninth Symphony: autograph, now (1925) in the Staatsbibliothek in Berlin, of which a facsimile reproduction has been published; manuscript sent to Schott in 1825 (still in possession of the firm) as copy for
the engraved score which appeared in 1826; first edition of the engraved score (all evidence indicates
that this edition was not proofread by Beethoven); manuscript copy of the score which Beethoven sent to
the Philharmonic Society of London (now in possession of the Society); copy of the score of the first three
movements and the parts of the Finale sent to Ries for the performance at Aachen on May 23rd 1825 (present location not known); note that in the letter referring to this score (KS II 362) the numbering of the
measures of the first movement excludes the sixteen measures of introduction preceding the unison statement of the principal subject; text of the baritone recitative introducing the choral portion of the Finale
that differed from the accepted version (TD V 168); manuscript copy sent by Beethoven to the King of
Prussia in the fall of 1826 (now in the Staatsbibliothek); and scores (if they can be found) used in the
performances at Frankfurt on April 1st 1825 and at Leipzig on March 6th 1826, on the chance that they

ÜBERLIEFERUNG (Continued)

might contain changes or corrections by Beethoven himself. In any attempt to work out a definitive version of the Symphony, due weight must be given to pertinent material in Beethoven's letters, as well as to such points as that mentioned in TD V 89 regarding a change contemplated in the baritone recitative.

2 [1925] 139

METRONOM.   (A)

Although Beethoven's own interpretations were very free, he strongly favored metronomization of his works, as shown in NB I 126, II 519, KS II 458, and other letters. Schindler ('Biographie' [1860] II 247) says: "When a composition by Beethoven was performed, his first question was always, 'How were the tempi?' Everything else seemed of secondary interest to him." Beethoven's metronomic indications for the Ninth Symphony are found in various places: In the autograph the notation appears: "108 oder 120 Mälzel" for the first movement; though no note value is given, only a quarter note could have been meant. The Italian tempo designation is "Allegro non troppo e (sic) un poco maestoso"; the latter phrase appears to have been added later. The copy for King Friedrich Wilhelm III is metronomized throughout. Letter of October 13th 1826 to Schott & Sons (KS II 454). This letter was in Karl's hand, but was signed by Beethoven. In the letter and in both places in the score sent to the King of Prussia the 'molto vivace' of the second movement was shown as 116 = half note, not 116 = dotted half note. Since the letter of October 13th was not received in time for the metronome marks to be incorporated in the engraved score, Schott published the 'Metronomische Bezeichnung der Tempi, mitgeteilt von Componisten' in 'Caecilia' 6 [1827] 158. As in the letter, the molto vivace did not include the dot after the half note. A deviation from the letter which has been definitely proved by comparison with the manuscript letter itself to have been a typographical error is that the finale presto is shown as MM = 96 instead of the correct value 66. (Even to the present day this error has been retained in published scores, though it was corrected in the Edwards 1949 reprint of the GA.)

Beethoven's letter of March 18th 1827 to Moscheles is given in the book by Mme. Moscheles: 'Aus Moscheles Leben' [1872] I 150; this letter is copied faithfully (except for the postscripts) in TD V 471 and very incorrectly in KS II 472. The letter was in Schindler's hand but was signed by Beethoven. Except for the omission of dots after notes, the metronome markings are those of the 'Caecilia' publication, including the MM = 96 for the finale presto. Of the two alternative explanations: (a) that Beethoven had revised his metronome markings since his letter of October 13th 1826, or (b) that Schindler copied the metronome markings as they appeared in 'Caecilia,' the latter seems far more probable. Schott's second edition of the score included the metronome markings (with notes dotted correctly), but gave the faulty tempo MM = 96 for the presto of the finale. In the presto of the scherzo the correct designation half note = 116 was given, but the stem of the half note was stamped so lightly that the incorrect reading whole note = 116 came into use (e.g., GA 1/9 p. 102).

To summarize, the metronome markings which appear in the GA are those assigned by Beethoven except for two errors: (p. 102) the presto of the scherzo should be half note = 116, not whole note = 116, and (p. 174) the presto of the finale should be dotted half note = 66, not dotted half note = 96.

2 [1925] 142

TEXT.   (B)

A number of questioned readings (notes, dynamics, bowing methods (KS II 355), words for the chorus, etc.) are discussed at length.   2 [1925] 156

DER ANGEBLICH BEETHOVENSCHE KLAVIERKONZERTSATZ. Hans Engel.   (C)

In 1888 Adler announced the discovery of a movement of a hitherto unknown movement of a piano concerto by Beethoven ('Vierteljahrsschrift für Musikwissenschaft' 4 [1888] 451); this movement was later included in the GA 25/311. From stylistic considerations, various writers have expressed doubt of the authenticity of this work, but now the author confirms these doubts with the discovery of a Piano Concerto Op. 15 by Johann Josef Rösler (1771-1813), composed in 1802 and published by André in 1826, the first movement of which is the 'Concerto Movement' attributed to Beethoven. A biographical sketch of Rösler is given, the three movements of the Concerto are discussed in detail, certain general characteristics of the piano concerto as accepted in Vienna at the turn of the century are considered, and a catalog of Rösler's compositions is given.

2 [1925] 167

BEETHOVEN'S PIANO PLAYING.   C. L. Jünker.   (A)

Jünker is quoted from the "musik. Korrespondenz der teutschen filharmonischen Ges." (1791, p. 380f): "His playing differs so completely from the usual manner in which the piano is used that it seems as though he was trying to establish a completely new path for himself."   2 [1925] 168

AUSGEWÄHLTE DICHTUNGEN ZU EHREN BEETHOVENS 1827-1927.   (B)

Poems by Zedlitz (1827), Mayerhofer (1827), Hiller (1850), Bodenstedt (1870), Cornelius (1870), and Schmidbonn (1927).   3 [1927] 5

DAS ERBE BEETHOVENS UND UNSERE ZEIT. Adolf Sandberger.   (C)
Centennial essay.   3 [1927] 18

ZUR BIOGRAPHIE JOHANN VAN BEETHOVENS (VATER). Ludwig Schiedermair.   (D)

The author points out that Father Johann was far from being as black as he has been painted (indeed, he hardly could have been).   Until death removed the stabilizing influence of his wife (in 1787) he was a competent chorister and teacher and a well accepted member of the community.   A transcription is given of a document dating from the second half of 1785 or the first weeks of 1786, signed in the name of an attorney for Johann, which recounts the fact that Johann had made gifts of value totaling 431 reichsthalers to Belderbusch (d. January 1784), former minister to the Elector Max Friedrich, in consideration of Belderbusch's implied assurance that he would arrange for Johann's appointment as Kapellmeister.   Since the appointment was not made, the petition requests that the value of the gifts be paid back to Johann.   With the petition was submitted an itemized list of the gifts, signed by Johann and thereby providing one of his few known signatures.   The author remarks that in the signature the name was spelled correctly ("Jean van Beethoven"), so that the many perversions of the name in the documents of the Electoral Court may be attributed to the carelessness of clerks rather than to Johann's ignorance.   The supposed attorney, mayor of the town of Honnef (some ten miles up the river from Bonn) shortly thereafter disclaimed all knowledge of the affair. The true story proved to be that the whole business was a project of one Johannes Steinmüller, who a year or so earlier had attempted similar extortion, that time directly from the heirs of Belderbusch ('Der junge Beethoven' p. 48). Johann's participation in the unsavory affair (as accomplice rather than as instigator) may well be taken as evidence of weakness rather than of active fraud.   3 [1927] 32

NOCHMALS JOHANN VAN BEETHOVEN UND ANDERES. Heinrich Rietsch.   (E)

In the indenture by which Johann leased his Gneixendorf property to one Franz Alexander in August 1820, the property is described as including a house of 24 rooms, "143 yoke acres (about 203 English acres) of grounds, 4 1/2 days' work of meadows, 22 quarters of vineyards."   The climate in which Beethoven spent his last autumn is discribed as characterized by "early and late frosts, very dry, so that in the late summer and autumn droughts are usual; winds of considerable strength the year round, mostly from the west."   The dispute between Johann and Amalie (daughter and heir of Therese, Johann's wife) and later with Amalie's widower over the estate which Therese left is discussed.   A letter from Nephew Karl's family defending his good name is reprinted from the 'Neue Wiener Tagblatt' of March 17th 1903.   Brief comment is made regarding the name "Hoven" in musical history. (See also 1 [1924] 115)   3 [1927] 42

MITTEILUNGEN EINES ZEITGENOSSEN ÜBER BEETHOVEN. Ludwig Schmidt.   (F)

Brief excerpts from letters written in 1824 and 1827 by Georg August von Griesinger (1769-1845) to the archaeologist Karl August Böttiger, mentioning the memorial sent to Beethoven in 1824 (TK III 153) and the ceremonies following Beethoven's death. (See also 'Der Bär'(B&H) 1927, p. 23)   3 [1927] 49

ZU BEETHOVENS BRIEFWECHSEL MIT B. SCHOTTS SÖHNEN IN MAINZ.   Max Unger.   (A)

    Corrections and amplifications are given to the letters which Kalischer numbers 1029, 1053, 1134, 1135 and 1198. The author mentions that the score of the Ninth Symphony sent to Schott shows the handiwork of at least five different copyists.   3 [1927] 51

INTERPRETATIONSSTUDIEN.   Jón Leifs.   (B)

    A very detailed discussion of the Funeral March and the finale of the Eroica from the conductor's standpoint.
3 [1927] 62

GEDANKEN ÜBER EINE STILGERECHTE AUFFÜHRUNG DES "FIDELIO."   Fritz Cortolezis.   (C)

    For the reason that the difference between an inspired and a pedestrian performance of a composition lies primarily in what we call "style," which in turn involves the most complete understanding of every detail of a work, 'Fidelio' is discussed almost measure by measure as regards tempo, dynamics, nuances, etc.
3 [1927] 91

ZWEI ZUR URSCHRIFT DER NEUNTEN SYMPHONIE GEHÖRIGE VERIRRTE BLÄTTER.   Otto Baensch.   (D)

    Comments on a letter from Edward Speyer to the Editor of the London 'Times' (November 28th 1907): Speyer's defense of Schindler is quoted from another writing, referring to him as "a thoroughly honorable, cultured and witty man," though one easily capable of making enemies. It is to this latter characteristic that Heinrich Heine's "malicious invention" regarding Schindler's visiting-card may be attributed (TK III 93). In a review of "The (Paris) Musical Season of 1841" reprinted in 'Musical Quarterly' 8 [1922] 437, Heine is quoted: "Less ghastly than Beethoven's music did I find Beethoven's friend l'ami de Beethoven, as he everywhere produced himself here, I believe even on his visiting-cards." Regarding this, Sandberger, Editor of the 'Neues Beethoven-Jahrbuch,' adds: "I am not sure that this defense by Sir Speyer (sic) and the eminent author holds good; on the other hand, I seem to remember having seen one of these visiting-cards." Schindler's birth date has been established as June 13th 1795. Schindler's statement that Beethoven had given him the autograph of the Ninth Symphony appears on p. 140 of the first (1840) edition of 'Beethovens Leben' and the same page of the second (1845) edition, but was entirely omitted from the third (1860) edition. Though the note in question appears in the discussion of the occurrences of the year 1824, the gift was not made during that year. The transaction whereby Schindler turned over his collection of Beethoveniana to the Royal Library in Berlin (now the Staats-Bibliothek) in exchange for a life annuity was initiated in August 1845, but the actual delivery of the material to the representative of King Friedrich Wilhelm IV took place only on January 21st 1846. Schindler held out some of the material, which was sold to the library after his death on January 16th 1864.

    Schindler's intimate association with the composer covered in all only between six and seven years: from April 1819 (TK II 378) to the time of Beethoven's death, with the exception of the period March 1825 - August 1826 (TK III 196). To explain Beethoven's gift to him of the autograph of the Ninth Symphony, Schindler stated that in 1821 a servant had used the only existing manuscript of the Kyrie of the Missa Solemnis as wrapping paper (this story regarding the Missa Solemnis appears on p. 119 of the 1840 and 1845 editions of 'Beethovens Leben' but was omitted from the 1860 edition). To avoid the possible loss of the Ninth Symphony (said Schindler) the manuscript was placed in his care. The gift in question actually took place only on February 21st 1827 after the Symphony had been published, so that Schindler's intimation that the gift was made to preserve an unpublished work from possible careless loss is wholly without foundation.

    To summarize, Schindler received the autograph of the Ninth Symphony on February 21st 1827 as a gift from Beethoven. On or before September 14th 1827 he removed the coda of the scherzo from the score and presented it to Moscheles. Moscheles in turn gave it to the singer Henry Phillips (1801-1876) on June 14th 1846. In the summer of 1907 the pages appeared at an auction in London and were bought by Edward Speyer. In the alla marcia of the finale, the autograph of the Symphony now in the Staats-Bibliothek in Berlin jumps from the 12th measure (last measure on p. 211 of GA 1/9) to the entry of the tenor at the 45th measure. The missing measures, which Beethoven quite obviously inserted after he had completed the finished draft of the Symphony, are on six pages formerly in the collection of Charles Théodore Malherbe and now in the Library of the Paris Conservatoire. (See also 4 [1930] 137) Beethoven's letter of March 18th 1827 to Moscheles (KS II 472) was in Schindler's handwriting, but metronomic indications (including the erroneous "96" for the presto of the finale) were in another hand.

This fact, stated for the sake of complete accuracy, does not change any conclusions previously arrived at regarding the correct speed for this passage in the Symphony: whether copied by Schindler or by some unidentified third person, the figures were almost certainly taken from the erroneous 'Caecilia' listing.

3 [1927] 103

BEETHOVEN-PROGRAMME. Friedrich Munter.   (A)
On the principle that a well-designed concert or cycle of concerts requires (generally speaking) a consciously planned "emotional crescendo," a considerable number of programs are suggested for concerts or cycles of Beethoven's music alone or of the music of Beethoven together with other composers.

3 [1927] 114

E. T. A. HOFFMANN AND BEETHOVEN. Erwin Kroll.   (B)
Hoffmann's first artistic recognition of Beethoven seems to have been only in 1805 when, as conductor of the 'Musikalische Gesellschaft' in Warsaw he performed Beethoven's First and Second Symphonies. The years 1808-13 saw his transition from practicing musician through musical journalist to poet; it was during this period that his association with Rochlitz of the 'Allgemeine Musikalische Zeitung' led to his preparation of (unsigned) reviews of five of Beethoven's works: Opp. 67 (not 68), 62, 70, 86 and 84. Aside from these, many references (direct or indirect) to Beethoven as the embodiment of Hoffmann's "romantic ideal of music" appeared in his writings over the years. That Beethoven was aware of this support is shown by his letter of March 23rd 1820 to Hoffmann (KS II 170) and by references to the poet in conversation books of the same period. In 1826 Brühl advised Beethoven against going ahead with an opera on Grillparzer's 'Melusine' because of the similarity of the basic idea (a water-fairy) to that of Hoffmann's 'Undine,' already on the Berlin stage. Hoffmann's compositions, romantic music in classical form, show appreciable influence of Beethoven's style; Beethoven, in turn, showed more than traces of the same spirit of the era which Hoffmann embodied.

As a writer on musical subjects, not until Schumann did anyone approach Hoffmann in importance. Combining the knowledge of the musician with the feeling of the poet, he was able in his writings to embody to the full the spirit of romanticism which he saw all around him and which he saw as the distinctive characteristic of Beethoven. "Haydn and Mozart (Hoffmann believed) were indeed romantics, but Beethoven was the first sovereign of the realm, the 'true romantic composer, more than any other.'" To Hoffmann may be attributed the recognition of Beethoven's musical dualism: the classic in form, the romantic in expression. Not every detail of Hoffmann's analyses of various Beethoven works may now be accepted, but "Hoffmann the unsuccessful musician became a poet and, thus transformed, served as the first worthy herald of the greatest musician of his time."

3 [1927] 125

BEETHOVEN UND DIE ROMANTIK. Karl Hasse.   (C)
"Stylistically, Beethoven stands at the threshold of romanticism, especially in many of the works of his middle period, but he has not passed across this threshold." Notable among ways in which Beethoven foreshadows romanticism are the importance which he gives to tone color (in compositions for piano as well as for orchestra) and the introduction of the short simple composition under the name of Bagatelles.

3 [1927] 143

BEETHOVEN. Ludwig Schiedermair.   (D)
Centenary address.   4 [1930] 5

ZU BEETHOVENS HUNDERTSTEN TODESTAG. Hans Joachim Moser.   (E)
Centenary address.   4 [1930] 21

BEETHOVEN IM KURORT BADEN BEI WIEN. Theodor von Frimmel.   (F)
An extensive amplification of material first published in the 'Neue Freie Presse' of November 3rd 1902 and later in the 'Neue Musik Zeitung' 43 [1922] 97, as well as in the article 'Baden' in the 'Beethoven-Handbuch.'

BEETHOVEN IM KURORT , etc. , (Continued)

Beethoven's partiality for Baden and Wiener Neudorf was due in part to the baths and to the ready accessibility of these towns from Vienna, either by post-wagon or on foot. It is probable that Beethoven first visited Baden not long after his arrival in Vienna in 1792. The renovation of the great organ of the parish church of Baden in 1795 may have drawn Beethoven thence because of his organ playing in the Bonn days. Beethoven's association with Count Johann Georg Browne, dating from 1797 or earlier, undoubtedly took him to the Count's place in Baden, though the first concrete evidence of this is Ries's statement (WRK p. 108, TK I 350) presumably from 1802. Beethoven is known to have been in Baden in at least seventeen different years. These visits are discussed chronologically, with commentaries on his associates there, discussion of his musical activities and his letters while in Baden, etc.   4 [1930] 39

ANDREAS STREICHER IN VIENNA. Otto Clemen.   (A)

Dr. Karl von Bursy of Kurland, the friend of Amenda who had several meetings with Beethoven in the summer of 1816 (TD III 556) also met with others of the Beethoven circle during his stay in Vienna. Extensive excerpts from his diary give accounts of his meetings with Dorothea von Erdmann and with Andreas and Nannette Streicher. He mentions that a seven octave piano with a walnut case cost 250 fl. CM. A letter from Streicher to Bursy, dated May 29th 1818, is given in which Streicher advises that he has shipped to Bursy the piano that he had ordered, and also lists currently available music of Beethoven and others.   4 [1930] 107

PAER'S 'LEONORA' AND BEETHOVEN'S 'FIDELIO.' Richard Engländer.   (B)

Many citations are given from Paer's opera (situations, text, music) to bear out the author's contention that Beethoven must have been familiar with Paer's work as well as with the Bouilly-Gaveaux version when he wrote 'Fidelio.'

4 [1930] 118

ZUR NEUNTEN SYMPHONIE (NACHTRÄGLICHE FESTSTELLUNGEN). Otto Baensch.   (C)

Extensive details are added to the author's comments on the copy of the Ninth Symphony which Beethoven sent to the Philharmonic Society of London (2 [1925] 141). The title page with dedication, the headings of the four movements, and the tempo indications are in Beethoven's hand, indicating that Beethoven had himself checked this score. The metronome markings were entered in pencil and copied over in ink, very possibly by Sir George Smart. The incorrect dotted half note = 96 for the presto of the finale is followed by a question mark in pencil (note that Sir George had discussed the tempo of the recitative with Beethoven in 1825, TD V 45). The notation "non ligato" which Beethoven requested in his letter of January 26th 1825 to Schott (KS II 355) and which is omitted from the Schott manuscript and from the copy sent to the King of Prussia (and from the GA 1/9 pp. 18, 52) is given in the Philharmonic Society copy. In the passage (GA 1/9 p. 260 mm. 2ff.) where the Schott manuscript has the questioned variant "frech" the Philharmonic Society manuscript, like the copy sent to the Kind of Prussia, has Schiller's "streng" (see also 'Die Musik' 19$_2$ [1927] 486). Various other details are cited in which the Philharmonic Society manuscript differs from the others. According to William Wallace, thirteen performances of the Ninth Symphony were given in London between its premiere on March 21st 1825 under Sir George Smart and the end of 1900. Minor amplifications are also given to the article which appeared in 3 [1927] 103. (See also 'Allgemeine Musik Zeitung' 59 [1932] 134)   4 [1930] 133

ZUM BILDNIS DER AMALIE SEBALD. Arnold Schering.   (D)

In addition to the generally known portrait by Dora Stock, another has come to light: a miniature on ivory, presumably by Johann Hensinger, dating from 1815.   5 [1933] 5

DIE AACHENER ABSCHRIFT DER NEUNTEN SYMPHONIE. Otto Baensch.   (E)

On May 23rd 1825 an incomplete performance of the Ninth Symphony was given under Ries as a part of the Niederrheinische Musikfest in Aachen, previous performances of this work having been in Vienna (May 7th and 23rd 1824 -- Beethoven), London (March 21st 1825 -- Smart), and Frankfurt a. M. (April 1st 1825 -- Guhr). No score was available from Schott, but on March 19th Beethoven wrote to Ries that a week or so previously he had sent him the score of the first three movements and the parts of the finale (TD V 166; Pr #862). The score of the finale was made up from these parts by Uhlig, a local copyist. Because of the difficulty of the music and the pressure of other necessary preparations, the scherzo and portions of the adagio were omitted in the performance. The full score of the first three movements and the chorus-master's score of the finale (sent by Beethoven to Ries) and the full score of the finale (prepared in Aachen) have recently been discovered. Careful collation of the score of the purely instrumental movements with the autograph discloses few differences other than in dynamic markings. The chorus-master's score of the finale shows many corrections of details in Beethoven's hand (capitalization of first words in lines, division of syllables for better singability). While the book of words issued to the audience at the festival shows a change of text in the opening solo (TD V 168), the score conforms to the accepted version. The questioned variant "frech" does not appear (see 4 [1930] 135). Several other minor textual points are mentioned.

The score of the finale made by Uhlig from the parts which Beethoven sent is similarly discussed, with special reference to the bassoon part in the first and second instrumental variations. In Beethoven's letter of March 19th 1825 to Ries he mentioned that the contrabassoon part had been omitted from the set of parts sent the previous week, but said that it had been sent separately. No part for the contrabassoon appears in the locally copied score, indicating that the missing part had not been sent after all.   5 [1933] 7

DAS DOPPELAUTOGRAPH BEETHOVEN-SCHUBERT. Otto Erich Deutsch.   (A)

In the collection of the Gesellschaft der Musikfreunde is a pair of sheets on which appear: (1) A fair copy in Beethoven's hand of the song 'Zärtliche Liebe' (GA 23/249), composed about 1800, published 1803. (2) An incomplete 'Andantino' for piano in Schubert's hand, dating probably from June 1817. (3) An exercise on the study of the clefs by an unidentified music teacher and his pupil. (4) An unsigned notation: "Des unsterblichen Beethovens Handschrift. Erhalten den 14ten August 1817(sic)." (5) "Johs. Brahms, im April 1872." (6) "Von Brahms dem Archiv der Gesellschaft der Musikfreunde geschenkt am 25. October 1893." The author identifies (3) as in the hand of Schubert and an unknown pupil, and (4) as by Anselm Hüttenbrenner, to whom Schubert apparently gave one of the pair of sheets. This sheet went from Hüttenbrenner to the collector Johann Nepomuk Kanka and from him to Brahms. The other sheet became the property of Eduard Schneider (as noted in NV p. 178), from whom Brahms obtained it. (6) was written by Eusebius Mandyczewski, Archivist of the GdMf. No satisfactory reproduction of this manuscript is available.   5 [1933] 21

EINE SCHWEIZER BEETHOVEN-SAMMLUNG. Max Unger.   (B)

A partial catalog is given of a Beethoven collection in the hands of an unnamed Swiss collector. A tabulation is given (date, addressee, first words) of 25 letters claimed to be unpublished (though in fact at least four of them had been published when this article appeared and thirteen others which do not appear in KBr, Prel, KK, or other published collection of Beethoven letters.   5 [1933] 28

DIE BEETHOVEN-HANDSCHRIFTEN DER SAMMLUNG LOUIS KOCH. Georg Kinsky.   (C)

A detailed catalog is given of the Beethoven items in "the finest and most valuable collection of musical autographs privately owned in Germany" -- that of the estate of Louis Koch in Frankfurt a. M. Twenty Beethoven musical manuscripts and 55 autograph letters are described in detail. One of these letters is not in Kastner: a letter of April 1st 1817 to Johann Baptist Rupprecht: "Ich ersuche Sie recht sehr, doch . . ." first published in the 'Neue Zürcher Zeitung' in December 1920.   5 [1933] 48

BEETHOVENS BACHKENNTNIS. Ernst Fritz Schmid.   (D)

Contradicting the belief that the general study of Bach dates only from Mendelssohn's revival of the Matthew Passion in 1829, the author contends that in Vienna at the time of Haydn, Mozart and Beethoven an intensive knowledge (though limited in scope) of Bach's works was sought. Schindler's Nachlass included copies of the following compositions, with many notations in Beethoven's hand: the first part of the Well Tempered Clavier, the 2 and 3-part Inventions, the D minor Toccata, and three Partitas (Nos. 2, 4, and 5). Seyfried ('Beethovens Studien' (1832) Anh. pp. 44-45 lists the 'Kunst der Fuge' as being in Beethoven's Nachlass. Entry No. 114 in this listing: "Fuge" is amplified by Thayer ('Chronologisches Verzeichniss' [1865] 177) to read: "Fuge von Sebastian Bach im Quartett, geschrieben von Beethoven." This manuscript, now in the archives of the Gesellschaft der Musikfreunde, was a setting for string quartet of the first 19 measures of the B minor Fugue, No. 24 of the WTC. Among the items privately sold before the auction, Thayer (p. 174) shows: "1 Band geschriebener Inventionen und Praeludien von Bach" as having been bought by Prince Lichnowsky. The author gives reasons for his belief that Beethoven was

BEETHOVENS BACHKENNTNIS (Continued)

also acquainted with the second volume of the WTC. Schindler ('Beethoven's Leben' [1860] I 45) indicates that in Beethoven's association with Baron von Swieten during his first years in Vienna he came to know some of the Bach motets. At that time the motets were available only in manuscript copies, but in 1802 and 1803 Breitkopf & Härtel issued two volumes of the motets, and it is presumably to these that Beethoven referred in his letter of April 8th 1803 (KS I 72). Swieten owned the six English and French Suites and probably the Italian Concerto and the A minor Violin Sonata, all of which Beethoven presumably came to know.

In 1809 Beethoven requested of Breitkopf & Härtel any available scores of the masters, including "Bach, Johann Sebastian Bach, Emanuel, etc." (KS I 173). Additional Bach scores were available to Beethoven in the library of the Archduke Rudolph (KS II 139 No. 772) and from Raphael Georg Kiesewetter. Beethoven's publishers Traeg and Hoffmeister brought out editions of Bach which Beethoven undoubtedly came to see (KS I 39, 42). NB II 286 points out Beethoven's familiarity with the Chromatic fantasy and Fugue. In a letter of October 15th 1810 to Breitkopf & Härtel Beethoven quotes from the B minor Mass (KS I 207); he apparently did not receive from them the copy which he requested, for on September 9th 1824 he asked Nägeli to send him a copy (KS II 332). Nothing is known of Beethoven's acquaintance with Bach's organ works, though Beethoven's praise of Bach to the organist Freudenberg (TK III 203) indicates such knowledge. Throughout this article the author depreciates the impression given by Schindler that Beethoven's knowledge of Bach was slight and sketchy.

5 [1933] 64

ERFAHRUNGEN BEIM STUDIUM VON BEETHOVENS KLAVIERSONATEN. Walter Petzet.   (A)

The first writer to give assistance in the performance of Beethoven piano sonatas was Karl Czerny in his 'Die Kunst des Vortrags der älteren und neueren Klavierkompositionen' (1846). His division of the works into three periods ante-dated the "three styles" of von Lenz (1852), though Schlosser (1828) had used the same concept, and Schindler (1840) said that Beethoven himself had had the same idea. Czerny's close association with Beethoven lent great weight to his recommendations, and in 1878 Brahms (in a letter to Clara Schumann) praised Czerny's work highly. Karl Reinicke's 'Briefe an eine Freundin über die Beethovenschen Klaviersonaten' (1899), though frequently wrong in details, is "wholeheartedly to be recommended." Schenker for Opp. 101, 109, 110 and 111, and Busoni for the Fugue of Op. 106 left little for successors to do. Of formal analyses of the sonatas in book form, those of Nagel and Reimann are the most comprehensive, though the latter complicates the problem unduly by his obscure and arbitrary analyses of the harmony and the phrasing. On a less elaborate scale, the book by Peters, 'Beethovens Klaviermusik' (1925) is undoubtedly more useful than Volbach's book. The biographical works of Thayer, Marx and Bekker have much valuable information.

The standard edition of the sonatas in the nineteenth century was that of Köhler; Pauer in 1927 carefully differentiated between Beethoven's material and his own. The influence of Bülow appears in the editions of Klindworth, Lamond, d'Albert and Buonamici. The edition by Epstein (1926) is to be highly recommended; Bussmeyer is careful not to intrude his editorial ideas. The major differences in opinion between editors on specific passages are discussed, including: Should the repeats in the first movements of the Bonn Sonata in F minor and the Pathétique include the slow introduction? Beethoven does not indicate; the author says yes. In the first movement of Op. 26, should the several variations be played at the same tempo and without pauses? The various editors are in complete disagreement on both questions. How should the damper pedal be used in the trio of the Funeral March of Op. 26, in the Recitative in Op. 31 No. 2, in the first movement of Op. 57 (before the final Piu allegro) and in certain other passages? In m. 11 of Op. 27 No. 2 should the fifth quaver in the accompaniment progress in octaves with the bass, as shown in the autograph, or remain stationery? The author says that autograph or no, such progression is unthinkable. What phrasing should be used at various points in Op. 28 and in Op. 57? In m. 171 in the first movement of Op. 106, should the reading be F or E? In mm. 223-25, A flat, A sharp or A natural? In m. 305 of the Fugue, should the first note in the left hand be E natural or F? In m. 132 of Op. 111 should the next-to-the last note in each hand be A flat or G? All editions give the former, but the recently-published facsimile of the autograph clearly shows the latter. The author observes that nowhere in the sonatas did Beethoven himself use the indication mf.

5 [1933] 84

BEETHOVEN UND DIE VARIATION.   Joseph Müller-Blattau.   (A)

An analysis in considerable detail of the more important sets of variations for piano.

5 [1933] 101

BEETHOVENS OPFERLIEDKOMPOSITIONEN.   Kurt Herbst.   (B)

The author recognizes four settings of Matthisson's poem, in the order: I, Voice and Piano (unpublished).
II, Voice and Piano (GA 23/233). III, 3 solo Voices, Chorus, Small orchestra (2 clarinets, horn, viola, violoncello) (GA 25/268). IV, Soprano solo, Chorus, Orchestra (2 clarinets, 2 bassoons, 2 horns, strings) Op. 121b
(GA 22/212). I is found in a sketch book in Berlin; the sketch discussed in NB I 50 (referred by him to Op. 121b)
is clearly for this version. Adequate evidence for assigning a date for this version is not available, though the
author mentions that the poem had been published in 1790 and that Matthisson's personal association with Bonn
dates back to his visit to that city in September 1786. It is possible, then, that version I may have been made
in Bonn. The first 14 measures (differing only slightly from NB I 50) are given, and the differences between I
and II are discussed in some detail. Sketches which are extant for II may be assigned to 1798-99 (certainly not
earlier than 1798). The sketches given in N65 p. 10, dating from 1802, are clearly for an instrumental version,
which ultimately was completed as III. This version as Beethoven wrote it has not been published: GA 25/268
is "a combination of the orchestral accompaniment of III and IV, made in the mid-nineteenth century by Julius
Rietz 'in accordance with Beethoven's instructions.'" In the autograph of this version in Vienna, contrabasses
are not used, which corresponds with Beethoven's description of the first of the songs referred to in his letter of
February 1823 to Peters (KS II 226). Excerpts are given from a letter of March 4th 1823 from Peters to Beethoven with which the songs sent the previous month were returned. III was probably one of the songs offered
by Beethoven to Simrock in his letter of March 10th 1823 (Schmidt, p. 57), and to Lissner on May 7th (KS II
251). It was this version "für Solostimmen und Chor mit Begleitung einiger Instrumente" that was performed
at the Gesellschaftskonzert on April 4th 1824.

Beethoven's letter of November 1824 to Schott (KS II 343) says: "To my brother . . . I have, in place of paying a sum I owe him, handed over . . . three songs of which two with choruses . . . have accompaniments for
full orchestra or for piano alone." The letter of May 7th 1825 to Schott (KS II 365) also refers to IV (note that
the change which Beethoven requested is not correctly shown in GA 22/212 p. 8 m. 1). Letters to Ries of
March 19th 1825 (Prel. No. 862; TD V 166) and April 9th 1825 (KS II 362) indicate that Beethoven proposed this
work for performance at the Niederrheinische Musikfest of 22-23 May. IV was published by Schott in 1825 (NV
p. 116) as "Opus 121" (presumably the designation "Opus 121b" was made by NV to differentiate this work from
the 'Kakadu Variations' published by Steiner in May 1824 as "Opus 121"). Note that NV is clearly wrong in
stating that it was this version which was performed in Vienna on April 4th 1824, though the mistake is a very
natural one, since at the time when Nottebohm was writing, the existance of III was not known. The significance is not clear of Beethoven's statement in his letter of August 1st 1826 to Ehlers (KS II 432): "The original
and rough draft (of the Opferlied) was only found later." (NOTE by DWM. It must be noted that the organiza-
tion of this paper, which contains a mass of information, does not lend itself to easy or effective summarization.)

5 [1933] 137

DAS ETHOS DES KLANGES IN BEETHOVENS VIOLINKONZERT.   Otto Schilling-Trygophorus.   (C)

In a piano concerto the solo instrument contrasts with the orchestra, while in a violin concerto the solo instrument
is really 'Violono principale,' to amplify and intensify the symphonic character of the music given to the orchestra.
This characteristic displays itself with notable fidelity in Beethoven's Violin Concerto. As Jonas ('Zeitschrift für
Musikwissenschaft' 13 [1931] 443) has shown, studies for this concerto include many alternative versions of passages
for the solo instrument, some of them possibly made at the suggestion of Franz Clement, who gave the first performance of the work. In the transcription as a concerto for piano, Beethoven sometimes used alternative readings
which he had discarded in his writing for the violin.

5 [1933] 154

DIE EROICA, EINE HOMER-SYMPHONIE BEETHOVENS? Arnold Schering.   (A)
   The author matches up the music of the Eroica with various passages and situations in the Iliad.

                                    5 [1933] 159

DIE ORGANISCHE EINHEIT IN BEETHOVENS 8. SINFONIE. Oskar Kaul.   (B)
   A very detailed analysis.   5 [1933] 178

KLEINE BEETHOVENIANA. Stephan Ley.   (C)
   John Georg Reichsgraf von Browne-Camus (1768-1827), to whom Beethoven referred as his "first Maecenas" in the
   dedication of the string trios Op. 9, was the son of the Russian Field Marshal George von Browne, of Irish descent.
   It is not known why Beethoven dedicated to the Count or his wife no fewer than seven works (Opp. 9, 10, 22, 48 and
   three sets of variations) between the years 1798 and 1803. Beethoven's first meeting with the Count was no later than
   1797; there is no record of contact between the two men after 1805. Johannes Büel, tutor in Count Browne's household, was on most intimate terms with Beethoven, but his name has not appeared in biographical accounts of the
   composer. References which probably are to him (e. g., Nohl's 'Konversationshefte' [1924] 421) as Bühl have been
   taken to mean Johannes Bihler (Frimmel 'Handbuch' I 41). An entry in Büel's Stammbuch by Beethoven: "Freundschaft ist Schatten gegen den Sonnenstrahl . . ." is dated June 29th 1806. From Therese von Brunsvik's diary a
   description is given of her ancestral castle at Martonvásár, with its 'Beethoven-tree' which was still standing in
   1927. Countess Erdödy's summer place at Jedlersee, though partly destroyed by fire in 1863, is for the most part
   still standing. There is an impressive Beethoven collection at Schloss Raudnitz (near Prague), which was the seat
   of Prince Lobkowitz. (See also 'Atlantis' 9 [1937] 59) A portrait, supposedly of Beethoven ('Velhagen und Klasings
   Monatschrift' 41$_2$ [1927] 39), shows such puffy lips and a right eye so definitely deformed that its authenticity must
   be questioned.

   Following notes are given for consideration in a much needed complete and adequately annotated edition of Beethoven letters (the author uses Kastner-Kapp as his basis of reference; references here are as far as possible to Kalischer
   'Briefe'):

          KBr 301 and 302 certainly should follow KBr 308.
          KK 535 (Prel 377) is certainly later than KK 540 (KBr 474).
          The similarity of the opening words of KBr 572 ("To?, 1816?"), which KK 880 gives as "To F.
             Tschischka, 1818," and KBr 763 (= KK 883) "To the Vienna Magistrate, February 1st 1819"
             indicate that the two letters were written only a short time apart.
          KK 1196, 1197 and 1200 belong together. (This is done in KBr 988, 989, and 990)
          KK 1201 does not go with KK 1200 (and the others just mentioned). (In KBr, as No. 1008, it is
             separated from them)
          KBr 1160 should be dated July 30th 1826. (Though this was the date of the event therein referred
             to (Nephew Karl's attempt at suicide), it is probable rather than certain that the letter was
             written on the same day)
          The date "March 17th 1827" for KBr 1217 is in Schindler's handwriting, not Beethoven's, and is
             open to much suspicion. ("1828" in KS II 471 is of course a misprint)
          KK 1249 (not in KBr, though assigned to "1824," certainly was written after KK 1328 (= KBr 1104),
             dated "August 13th 1825."
          KBr 48 is certainly no more than a summary (from a catalog or some such source) of KBr 49. The
             same is true of KK 941 with reference to KK 911.
          KBr 159 is only the postscript of KBr 262, not a separate letter. (Note that KBr dates these two
             letters three years apart; KK (Nos. 166, 154) dates both "1808")
          KK 942 is no more than a couple of sentences taken bodily from KK 905 (neither letter in KBr).
          KK 1042 is not a letter. (NOTE by DWM. That is of course true of many items included in
             each of the principal collections of letters: receipts, newspaper notices, Stammblattbuch
             writing, etc.)
          "Herbstmonat" is explained as "September" in KK 257 and as "October" in KK 260 (and KK
             259). (NOTE by DWM. From information given in KBr 225, 224 and 226, KK is presumably
             right and the mistake presumably by Beethoven. Notations on the autographs of these letters,
             probably made in the office of Breitkopf & Härtel, state that KK 259, and 260, though dated
             "Herbstmonath" by Beethoven, were actually written in October "Weinmonath")
          Similar uncertainties exist in KBr 110 (KK 123), where Beethoven dated a letter "Heu-Monath"
             (August) but B&H says "September"; KBr 201 (KK 208) where Beethoven dated his letter "am

19ten Wein-Monath" (October 19th) but where the reply to the letter was sent on October 2nd; and in KBr 430 (KK 488) where Beethoven says "March" and Breitkopf & Härtel say "May." It is of course possible that the mistakes were made by the clerk in the publishing house. In weighing this possibility, though, two points should be considered: correct handling of correspondence was a matter of routine in a business office as it certainly was not with Beethoven; and letters like KBr 160, dated November 1st 1088, KBr 202, dated Wednesday December 2nd 1809 (December 2nd 1809 was a Saturday), KBr 409 dated September 21st 1841, and KBr 428 dated February 29th 1815 show that Beethoven and the calendar did not always see things eye to eye.

KBr 219 (next-to-the-last line of the postscript) should read "votre pays." KK 1362 (= Pr 1296 should read: "que vous manquez." In KBr 221 (paragraph referring to the Song of the Flea) nachsuchen should read nachstechen.

Great need exists for a critical edition of source material regarding Beethoven's life, in which the countless errors and unfounded statements now current might be brought to light and corrected. Such a study should scrutinize the writings of contemporaries like Wegeler & Ries, Gerhard von Breuning and Schindler, as well as those quoted in works like Leitzmann and Kerst. As an example of the contradictory statements from authoritative sources which must as far as possible be reconciled, comments on Beethoven's knowledge of Latin, French and Italian are cited to prove simultaneously that he had fluent command of each of the three languages and that his knowledge of them was little more than zero. Reference is made to an article in the 'Vossische Zeitung' for January 30th 1934 regarding the unpublished canon 'Fettlümerl, Bankert haben triumphiert' (H-216) referred to in KS II 288.

6 [1935] 26

NEUES ZU BEETHOVENS LEHRJAHR BEI HAYDN.   Fritz von Reinöhl.   (A)

The known history of Beethoven's studies with Haydn is recounted. Three pertinent letters have recently been found: (1) Letter of November 23rd 1793 from Beethoven to the Elector Maximilian Franz: "Der höchsten Gnade Euer Churfürstlichen Durchlaucht mich ganz würdig . . ." in which he expresses his gratitude for the year of study already completed and his hopes for further support from the Elector. (2) Letter of November 23rd 1793 from Haydn to the Elector, transmitting five compositions to indicate Beethoven's progress: "Quintet" (presumably lost; both of the youthful quintets (Opp. 4, 16) were probably written not much before 1797); "8-voice Parthie" (undoubtedly the Octet Op. 103); "Oboe Concerto" (lost); "Variations for Piano" ('Se vuol ballare'? Op. 44? Waldstein Variations?); "A Fugue" (none from this period is known). Giving a most flattering estimate of Beethoven's ability: "From an impartial consideration of these pieces, expert and amateur alike must contend that in time Beethoven will become one of the foremost musicians of Europe. I shall be proud to be known as his teacher." Requesting for the coming year an increase in Beethoven's allowance from 500 fl. to 1000 fl., explaining that he (Haydn) had been compelled to lend Beethoven 500 fl. during the year just past to keep him out of the hands of the userers. The repayment of this loan by the Elector was also requested. (3) Reply of December 23rd from the Elector to Haydn: "Since all of the compositions which you sent, excepting only the fugue, had been already completed and performed here in Bonn before (Beethoven) went to Vienna this second time, they can give me no measure of the progress which he has made in Vienna." In addition to Beethoven's allowance of 500 fl. he had his regular salary of 400 fl. (though the records of the Elector's treasurer do not show this salary payment). The Elector could not see why this total of 900 fl. should not have been sufficient. Would it not be advisable for Beethoven to return to Bonn to resume his work there, with prospect of a further sojourn in Vienna at some future time? (See also 8 [1938] 80)

6 [1935] 36

BEETHOVEN IN REGENSBURG, 1795.   Eduard Panzerbieter.   (B)

In the 'Regensburgisches Diarium' of December 1795 the following entries appear under 'Arrivals and Departures':

"13 December . . . (arrived) 2 Herren Gebrüder Breuning, Kaufleute von Bonn . . ."
"14 December . . . (arrived) Herr Bathofen, Mediziner aus Göttingen . . ."
"15 December . . . (departed for Vienna) Hr. Bathofen, . . . Hrn. Gebrüder Breuning . . ."

This is the journey referred to in the Nachtrag to the Wegeler-Ries 'Notizen' (WRK p. 215), and in Stephan von Breuning's letter of January 21st 1796 to his mother (Ley 'Beethoven als Freund' [1927] 249, but it will be noted that the travelers joined forces not in Nuremberg but in Regensburg. The author discusses various possibilities regarding the place of this trip in Beethoven's activities of that period. (But see 'Allgemeine Musik Zeitung' 63 [1936] 260; 'Neues Beethoven-Jahrbuch' 8 [1938] 81)   6 [1935] 48

SÉJOURS DE BEETHOVEN EN HONGRIE.   M a r i a n n e   d e   C z e k e .   (A)

The only definitely authenticated visits of Beethoven to Hungary are the following: To Pressburg (Pozsony, now Bratislava, Czechoslovakia). Beethoven's letter of November 19th 1796 to Streicher (Sonneck p. 182) proves that he spent at least a week in Pressburg at that time. It is possible that he made many other visits to or through this city, but no other are documented. To Buda and to Martonvásár. Newspaper reviews prove that Beethoven played the Horn Sonata Op. 17 in Buda with Punto on May 7th 1800. A letter of September 6th from Zmeskall to Franz von Brunsvik refers to the enjoyable stay which Beethoven had in Martonvásár (after and perhaps before the concert in Buda). Schindler says that Op. 57 was composed at Korompa (near Pressburg) and Martonvásár in the summer of 1806, but corroborative evidence of this fact is not at hand. To Kismarton (Eisenstadt). Beethoven conducted the first performance of the C major Mass Op. 86 at Kismarton (seat of Prince Eszterházy) on September 13th 1807. Schindler's account of the falling-out between Beethoven and the Prince (TK II 108) is not correct: the coolness which certainly existed (shown by the fact that the published edition was dedicated to Prince Kinsky instead of to Prince Esterházy), and by the fact that the manuscript of the mass was not given to him) was due to the fact that Beethoven had been given quarters in one of the administration buildings rather than in the castle. In any event, the quarrel could not have been serious: Beethoven did not leave Kismarton until three days later (September 16th), and the next year the Prince sent Beethoven 100 fl. for a box for his concert on December 22nd 1808.

It is generally known that three works of Beethoven had their first performances in Hungary: the Mass in C major Op. 86 (September 13th 1807, as discussed above) and the overtures 'Ruins of Athens' Op. 113 and 'King Stephen' Op. 117, composed specially for the opening of the Theatre Royal in Pesth and first performed on February 9th 1812. In addition, a concert given at Pressburg on December 22nd 1822 by the tenor Wilhelm Ehlers included: "Beethoven's two newest compositions, Menuette concertante for full orchestra, composed on November 4th for Herr Hensler (the 'Gratulations-Minuet' GA 2/13), and Matthisson's 'Opferlied' for three solo voices and chorus (GA 25/268) composed for this concert out of friendship for the concert giver." Thus the performance of this version of the 'Opferlied' in Vienna on April 4th 1824 was not its first performance.

Lists are given of Beethoven relics in Hungary, of Beethoven's Hungarian friends, and of the eleven works (Opp. 7, 15, 34, 45, 57, 70, 77, 78, 102, 'Ich denke dein' Variations, 'La stessa' Variations) dedicated to Hungarians.

6 [1935] 52

DER LIEDERDICHTER REISSIG.   O t t o   E r i c h   D e u t s c h .   (B)

Christian Ludwig Reissig, mentioned most uncomplimentarily in three of Beethoven's letters to Breitkopf & Härtel (February 4th 1810 (KS I 186), October (or September) 11th 1810 (KS I 205), and October 15th 1810 (KS I 207); see also KS I 175) was the author of seven poems which Beethoven set (Op. 75 Nos. 5 and 6, and five songs listed in NV pp. 181-82). He was born in Kassel in 1783 and came to Vienna in 1809. He voluntarily enlisted as a Second Lieutenant in an Austrian Infantry regiment in March of that year, but after only two months was invalided out of the service because of wounds of the head and legs. The next year he was given the honorary rank of Captain of Cavalry for his meritorious service, but this appointment was withdrawn when he left for Constantinople some months later. There are indications that in 1814 and 1815 he fought with the Spanish forces against Napoleon. After 1823 (when he was referred to as a Colonel of the English army living in Vienna) no record of him has been found. His collected poems "Blümchen der Einsamkeit" were published in 1809 and reissued in 1815. Of these poems, 52 were set by one or more composers; in all, more than 100 settings by more than 40 composers are known, including many of the best-known musicians of the period.   6 [1935] 59

ZUR VERSTEIGERUNG VON BEETHOVENS MUSIKALISCHEM NACHLASS.   G e o r g   K i n s k y .   (C)

The sale of the books and manuscripts on November 5th 1827 was very poorly planned, unless the facts were that a few of those concerned were anxious to stifle competition at the sale. Only a single advertisement of the auction was published (in the 'Wiener Zeitung' of September 7th 1827 -- see Seyfried's 'Studien' Anhang), so that many musicians and publishers (e.g., Breitkopf & Härtel, Peters, Schlesinger, Simrock, Schott) living outside Vienna who might have wished to be present knew nothing about the auction until it was all over. Furthermore, the listing of the several lots (as given in TV and other sources was most unenlightening. Of the first 188 lots, comprising the Beethoven autographs (sketches, sketch books and original manuscripts) almost two-thirds were bought by two publishers (81 by Artaria, 39 by Haslinger); the names of the purchasers of each lot are given. About 60 of the 131 items constituting sales groups II, III and IV (sketches and manuscripts) are identified, and their present whereabouts (if known) stated.   6 [1935] 66

DIE BEETHOVENHANDSCHRIFTEN DER PARISER KONSERVATORIUMSBIBLIOTHEK.   M a x   U n g e r .   (D

A detailed list is given of the Beethoven manuscripts and letters in this library, which ranks with the collections in Berlin, Vienna, and Bonn (and a private collection in Switzerland) as "one of the richest and most important collections of Beethoven manuscripts in foreign lands," surpassing that of the British Museum in manuscripts, though not in letters. This list amplifies and corrects that published by Tiersot ('Revue de musicologie' 8 [1927] 65). Among the letters in the collection is one of April 5th 1823 to Pacini (a publisher in Paris): "C'est mon frere, qui me disait, que vous . . ." (first published, subsequent to this article, in 'Zeitschrift für Musik' JG 103 [1936] 416). A letter dated December 22nd 1822 to Pacini from Brother Johann asks his aid in selling a manuscript copy of the Missa Solemnis to the French court. It will be noted that this is earlier than the date indicated in TK III 92 (first week of 1823, as shown in letter of January 7th 1823 to Griesinger, KS II 219) as the inception of Beethoven's idea of the sale to royal courts of manuscript copies of the Missa Solemnis.   6 [1935] 87

CARL MARIA VON WEBER AND BEETHOVEN.   Erwin Kroll.   (A)
During Weber's first visit to Vienna in 1803 his interest was in Vogler, not in Beethoven. In the next years there is no indication that Weber had any very close contact with Beethoven's music, though Weber as well as Beethoven was a contributor to the collection of settings of 'In questa tomba' in 1808. In December 1809 Weber published a satirical sketch aimed at Beethoven's Fourth Symphony (TD III 15). As conductor in Prague, Weber produced Fidelio in November 1814; the work impressed him, but was not a success with the public. In the next years he spoke with favor about several of Beethoven's works: the overtures to Prometheus and Egmont, the First Symphony and the Choral Fantasia. The success of 'Der Freischütz' in 1821 led to the composition of 'Euryanthe,' which Weber conducted in Vienna in its first performance early in 1822. Beethoven had expressed enthusiasm for Freischütz and for its composer, but again the two men did not meet. Letters were exchanged in the spring of 1823, but except for a draft of one of Weber's letters (KS II 271) all are lost. Thereafter Weber's name appears often in the conversation books, and the two men finally met on October 5th 1823.   6 [1935] 124

DER ERSTDRUCK VON BEETHOVENS FLÖTENSONATE.   Willy Hess.   (B)
This work as first published in 1906 in an edition by Ary van Leeuwen includes so many changes from the manuscript that "the style of the original is fundamentally changed . . . (Leeuwen) went at his revision with unparalled unscrupulousness and arbitrariness. His edition must necessarily be designated as a falsification." The deviations of the Leeuwen edition from the original manuscript are stated in great detail.
                                      6 [1935] 141

BEETHOVENS BEARBEITUNGEN EIGENER WERKE.   Friedrich Munter.   (C)
Transcriptions must be differentiated from revisions (e. g. , the two versions of Op. 18 No. 1, the successive versions of Fidelio and its Overtures) and from arrangements which include substantial modifications (e. g. , the various settings of the Opferlied, the Quintet Op. 4 based upon the Octet Op. 103). The following are listed as (presumably the only) transcriptions by Beethoven of his own compositions (the years given are the dates of the transcriptions).

    Piano Quartet Op. 16 from Quintet for Piano and Wind Op. 16 (1797)
    String Quartet in F from Piano Sonata in E Op. 14 No. 1 (1802)
    Piano Trio Op. 38 from Septet Op. 20 (1803)
    Piano Trio from the Second Symphony Op. 36 (1806)
    Piano Concerto from Violin Concerto Op. 61 (1807)
    Funeral March for Orchestra (Incidental Music to 'Leonore Prohaska') from the second movement
        of the Piano Sonata Op. 26 (1814)
    String Quintet Op. 104 from Piano Trio Op. 1 No. 3 (1817)
    Arrangement for Piano 4-hands (Op. 134) of the Grosse Fuge for String Quartet Op. 133 (1826)

Each of these works (as well as Op. 4) is discussed at considerable length, with special reference to the changes in figuration and voice distribution which Beethoven made. The Trio Op. 38 is referred to as being perhaps a better piece of chamber music even than the Septet Op. 20 on which it was based; the next one of the transcriptions, however (that of the Second Symphony Op. 36) is characterized as little more than a transcription for piano with added violin and 'cello. The importance which Beethoven assigned to the arrangement of Op. 61 as a piano concerto is shown by the cadenzas which he wrote for this version: GA 9/70a Nos. 9 and 10, H-55 and H-264. In addition to the transcriptions discussed here, mention is made of Altmann's paper ('Zeitschrift für Musikwissenschaft' 3 [1920] 129) on an unfinished arrangement for piano trio of the string trio Op. 3 which presumably is by Beethoven. Various opus numbers (41, 42, 60, 61, 63, 64, 75) were pre-empted during Beethoven's lifetime for transcriptions which certainly were not by him.   6 [1935] 159

BEETHOVENS FLÄMISCHE ABSTAMMUNG.   André M. Pols.   (A)

The belief that the great-grandfather of the composer was Henry Adelard dates back to Leo de Burbure, whose statements were given authority by acceptance by Fétis in his 'Biographie universelle des musiciens' (1860).   On at least
two occasions doubt was thrown on this genealogy: In 1885, when an anonymous writer in 'L 'Escaut' of Antwerp said
that de Burbure's assumption was deceptive, and in 1899 when Deiters pointed out that a branch of the Beethoven
family in Bonn had come from Malines.   Only in 1927 was the Malines descent of the composer definitely established.   The earliest assumption for the origin of the name -- from Beet (the vegetable) and Hof (garden) -- was ultimately discarded, as was the later postulated derivation from the town of Bettenhofen.   According to the author
(based on the work of Auguste Vincent), the name comes from the name of a manor Betho, near Tongern, the
etymology of which is beter (improved) and ouwe (land).   The first record of the name is Betue (1267) then successively Betuwe, Betouwe and Bethove (1582).   (See also Closson 'The Fleming in Beethoven' [1936] 162)   About this
time a certain Jan Smeets of this village was referred to as Jan van Bethoven (John from the village of Bethoven).
Enough of the history of Henry Adelard is given to show that his son Ludwig could not have been the Kapellmeister
at Bonn.   The forebears of great-grandfather Michael are traced, and the life story of Michael and of his son Ludwig
(the grandfather) up to the time of Ludwig's marriage is given in detail.   A contemporary account is given of the appearance of Ludwig in Amsterdam as a bass soloist in 1747.   The temperamental characteristics of Beethoven which
most clearly indicate his Flemish descent are enumerated.   7 [1937] 17

ZU BEETHOVENS GEBURTSTAG.   Stephan Ley.   (B)

A note from Albrechtsberger to Beethoven, dated December 15th (probably 1795) starts: "All good wishes to you to-
morrow on your name-day" (certainly a confusion for birthday).   Even though Beethoven may not have known the year
of his birth, there can be no doubt that within the family circle the birthday itself was observed.   The knowledge
which led to Albrechtsberger's letter could have come to him only from Beethoven himself or possibly from one of
Beethoven's brothers, and therefore can be taken as representing the tradition of the composer's own household.   The
author believes that this evidence far outweights the remark by Nephew Karl in a conversation book of 1823 (TK I
53), referring to December 15th or 17th as the composer's birthday, especially since Karl based his statement on the
baptismal certificate, which makes no reference to the date of birth.   The author accordingly concludes that December 16th may with confidence be assumed to be the actual day of the composer's birth.
                                           7 [1937] 29

EIN UNBEKANNTE OPERNENTWURF FÜR BEETHOVEN.   Ludwig Schiedermair.   (C)

TD III 486 mentions an opera book which was sent to Beethoven by a certain Dr. Hellmuth Winter.   The letter of
transmittal has recently been published, in which the writer points out that the composition of music for his text
will offer to the composer "the most brilliant path to immortality."   The third act of Winter's 'Theodor und Emilie'
is in the archives of the Beethovenhaus.   Excerpts are given, including Winter's instructions as to the nature and
amount of music that he wants.   The date of this libretto is 1810, not 1815 as postulated by TD.   The author suggests that Beethoven might have had this text in mind when in his letter of May 20th 1811 to Breitkopf & Härtel
(KS I 215) he refers to the "poverty of intellect" of the poets who write opera librettos.
                                           7 [1937] 32

DIE DURCHFÜHRUNGSGESTALTUNG IN BEETHOVENS SONATENSÄTZEN.   Wilhelm Broel.   (D)

An exhaustive study of the procedures which Beethoven habitually uses in the development sections of movements
in sonata form.   7 [1937] 37

STILKUNDLICHE BEMERKUNGEN ZU BEETHOVENSCHEN WERKEN.   Paul Mies.   (E)

TAKT UND MELODIEWEIT.   (F)

As a minor Beethoven mannerism, the fact is pointed out that not infrequently in passing from sketch to
finished work he lengthened the breath of his melodic line either by throwing two measures into one by
change of time signature or by halving the note values.   The reverse procedure (doubling the note values)
is rare, and has been discussed by the author elsewhere ('Beethoven's Sketches', trans Mackinnon, [1929]
182).   7 [1937] 91

(A)

AUSDRUCKSSTUDIEN.
  A brief commentary on the fragmentary notes and remarks in sketch books, on manuscripts and elsewhere, as
further material for the study of Beethoven's mental processes. Special mention is made of the fact that the two
songs Op. 82 Nos. 3 and 4, though in contrasting moods, are written to the same Italian lyric, though the translator of these texts into German (Chr. Schreiber) provided two quite different sets of words for the two songs.
                                                7 [1937] 95

(B)

DIE 32 VARIATIONEN IN C-MOLL; EINE FORMUNTERSUCHUNG.
  Instead of Leichtentritt's division of this work into four sections, with variations 12, 23 and 30 serving as points
of rest, the author considers it as a "spiral variation," with the several variations grouping themselves: 1-11,
12-16, 17-22, 23-29, and 30-32. (NOTE by DWM. Might the dramatic character of the first group, the lyr-
ical character of the second group, the agitation and conflict of the third, and the figurational similarity which
the fourth shows to the first serve as an (admittedly far-fetched) basis for terming the form "sonata variations":
Exposition (first group) 1-11, Exposition (second group) 12-16, Development 17-22, Recapitulation 23-29, Coda
30 to end.)   7 [1937] 100

WELCHE WERKE BEETHOVENS FEHLEN IN DER BREITKOPF UND HÄRTELSCHEN GESAMTAUSGABE? Willy Hess.   (C)
  A listing, with brief bibliographical comments, of 265 authentic compositions by Beethoven which do not appear in
the Gesamtausgabe (see also 9 [1939] 75).   7 [1937] 104

(D)

HANS VON BÜLOW AND BEETHOVEN. Friedrich Munter.
  A discussion of the service which Bülow (1830-94) rendered to the music of Beethoven, as conductor, pianist, editor
and teacher. At the disputed enharmonic passage just before the recapitulation in the first movement of the Piano
Sonata Op. 106, Bülow was convinced that a small but unmistakeable natural appeared before the critical A in the
autograph. The noteworthy characteristics of Bülow's editions of Beethoven piano works (the sonatas from Op. 53 to
Op. 111, together with four earlier sonatas and some 25 other piano works) are discussed at length. The several sets
of titles which he applied at one time or another to the variations of Op. 120 are given.
                                                7 [1937] 131

(E)

DIE BEETHOVEN-HANDSCHRIFTEN DER FAMILIE W. IN WIEN. Max Unger.
  The author mentions that about one-fifth of the Beethoven letters listed in auction and antiquarian catalogs are still
unpublished, and that the present location of more than one-third of the published letters are not known. Among
other manuscripts, the collection described contains the autographs of the Romanze in F for Violin and Orchestra
Op. 50 and of the Piano Sonata in E major Op. 109. A hitherto unknown sketch book from early 1819 to about 1820
contains sketches for Op. 120, followed by the first sketches for the Kyrie of the Missa Solemnis. Hitherto it has been
believed that the Diabelli Variations were not contemplated before 1820 (see NB II 568). The letter to Artaria given
in Prel 1235 is assigned to a date not earlier than 1819 and not much later. The letter to Steiner given in KK 1010
is written on paper watermarked "1826" and is assigned to the spring of that year.
                                                7 [1937] 155

(F)

KÖLNER AHNEN BEETHOVENS. Joseph Schmidt-Görg.
  An amplification (five or six generations back) of the line of descent of Beethoven's mother.
                                                8 [1938] 53

NEUE SCHRIFTSTÜCKE ZU BEETHOVENS VORMUNDSCHAFT ÜBER SEINEN NEFFE. Ludwig Schiedermair.   (G)
  The refusal (dated October 23rd 1815) of Brother Karl's request of October 13th for a leave of absence (referred to in
TK II 322) which angered Beethoven so much is given in full, and may be paraphrased: Neither Brother Karl's dossier
nor the report of an examination made of him by the Chief Surgeon of the General Hospital indicate any incurable
disease, but lead rather to the belief that his frequent absences in the past three years were due to "a singular and
discreditable unwillingness to work, resulting from habitual laziness." Brother Karl is therefore directed to carry out
the duties of his position with diligence and regularity in order not to set a bad example to other employees. His duties are believed to be light and his working conditions healthful and pleasant, but if nevertheless he should wish to
transfer to some other post, every effort will be made to arrange it. In view of the medical report on which the decision was based, which denied Karl's claim of illness, the first part of this reply does not seem unduly harsh, and
the second part really considerate of Karl's desires. Beethoven's bitter comment (published in part in TK II 322;
here given in full) might well have been directed against an incompetent examining physician, but hardly against

NEUE SCHRIFTSTÜCKE, etc., (Continued)

Karl's supervisor. A hitherto unpublished draft of a part of Beethoven's memorandum of February 18th (KK 954) is given. It is known (TK II 331) that in December 1815 Beethoven applied to the court to bar Brother Karl's widow from the joint guardianship, that on December 21st the Vienna magistrate reported pertinent facts regarding Johanna van Beethoven to the Landrecht, and that on January 9th 1816 a finding in Beethoven's favor was announced. A letter of December 20th 1815 from Beethoven to the Landrecht: "So ungern der Unterzeichnete einer seiner Familie . . ." is here published for the first time; the decision of January 9th is also given in full.

8 [1938] 59

KLEINE BEETHOVEN-STUDIEN.   Max Unger.   (A)

BEETHOVENS WOHNUNGEN WÄHREND DER BESETZUNG WIENS IM JAHRE 1809.   (B)

Although Beethoven's letter of April 27th 1809 to Zmeskall (KS I 163) speaks of rooms which he had found in the Klepperstall, it is most probable that about the beginning of May 1809 Beethoven moved from the Countess Erdödy's house at Krugerstrasse 1074 to Walfischgasse 1087 (authority: letter to Gleichenstein containing the statement: "I am now living at Walfischgasse 1087, on the second floor." Thayer III[1] 77 agrees that Beethoven did not go direct from the Countess' house to the Klepperstall, but TD III[2] 138 is noncommittal as to whether or not he occupied the Klepperstall quarters for a short time). During the bombardment of Vienna, Beethoven spent one night (or perhaps a longer time) with Brother Karl, and probably returned immediately thereafter to the Walfischgasse, remaining there almost certainly until the beginning of August. With the political situation that existed in the summer of 1809, a holiday at a resort seems most improbable. His abode during the winter of 1809-10 is not known with certainty, but very probably it was in the Teinfaltstrasse, returning in April 1810 to the Pasqualati house where he had lived at intervals since 1804.

The letter (or letters) to Zmeskall given in KS I 236 (No. 262) and KS I 145 (No. 159) (TD III 137) are puzzles which may be explained in either of two ways: (a) They are (as generally accepted) two parts of the same letter, dating however from 1813, the first year that the flier Degen made out-of-door flights in Baden (see KS I 297 No. 346), and the first year that Beethoven was at Sauerbad (correct name Sauerhof). (b) More probably, they are not parts of the same letter. This is apparently the opinion of KS and of KK Nos. 154 and 166, though not of TD III 137 (note that nothing in the letter itself bears any relationship to the subject matter of the postscript). In this event, the letter proper (KS I 236 No. 262; KK No. 154) was written in Vienna in the summer of 1809; the postscript (KS I 145 No. 159; KK No. 166) belongs to some other letter from September 1813.

8 [1938] 65

EIN UNBEKANNTER AUS BEETHOVENS KREISEN.   (C)

The letter in KK No. 254 ('Zeitschrift für Musikwissenschaft' 2 [1920] 423) was to a correspondent whose name was Wildfeger (or possibly) Wildheger or Schildfeger). TV p. 172 refers to an autograph of a trio in the hands of "Herr Wilhelm Wildfeyr in Muglitz" but NV p. 144, spelling the name "Wildfer," says that this was only a copy. The copy might have come to Herr W. from Beethoven or from the Brentanos, for whom the trio was written. In Nohl's 'Konversationshefte' (1924) both Hofrat Karl Peters (p. 308) and Joseph Czerny (p. 394) refer to one "Wildfeuer," who apparently was in the service of a Count (?) Kallowrath. Of the variants of spelling, the author favors "Wildfeger," but solicits the help of other researchers in finding out more about this member of Beethoven's circle of acquaintances.   8 [1938] 69

ERGÄNZUNGEN UND BERICHTIGUNGEN ZU FRÜHEREN BÄNDEN DES NEUEN BEETHOVEN-JAHRBUCH.   (D)

To 'The "Bird-Call" motif in Beethoven's works' (2 [1925] 7) may be added the appearance of such motifs in many of Beethoven's songs: Adelaide Op. 46, Der Wachtelschlag GA 23/234 (which foreshadows the rhythmic figure of the Pastoral Symphony), various sections of An die ferne Geliebte Op. 98, Mailied Op. 52 No. 3, Sehnsucht Op. 83 No. 3, and especially Der Gesang der Nachtigall GA 25/277. In connection with 'Beethoven and the Vienna Court Theater in 1807' (2 [1925] 76), the fourth word from the end of Beethoven's petition should read "Weihnachtsfeyertagen" (see KBr I 180). The petition may more accurately be dated "about the middle of December 1807."

'The Ninth Symphony' (2 [1925] 137). (a) As already disclosed in 'Zeitschrift für Musik' JG 105 [1938] 149, the first copies of the first edition of the Ninth Symphony were issued on August 28th 1826, though very likely copies for all subscribers were not available until later. (b) The statement (2 [1925] 139) that the engraver's copy of the score of the Ninth Symphony went forward in two sections between January 22nd and February 5th 1825 is contradicted by the first lines of Beethoven's letter to Schott of January 22nd 1825 (KS II 353), beginning:

"On the 16th of January both works (Opp. 123 and 125) were delivered to Friess . . ." A new transcription of this letter is given, with minor corrections, decipherment of the material stricken out in the assignment (which is much like the opening sentence of Beethoven's letter of February 5th 1825 to Schott (KS II 358), correction of Kalischer's reading "Brockhausen" to (Franz) "Stockhausen," and various commentaries on the content of the letter, all of which might appropriately be joined to the article in 3 [1927] 51. (c) The corrector of the proofs of the Ninth Symphony, not named by Baensch (2 [1925] 139), was stated by Schindler ('Leben'[1860] II 151) to be Ferdinand Kessler, a violinist, composer and teacher of Frankfurt. As stated in p. 68 supra, Beethoven's references to the flyer Degen, mentioned in 'Beethoven's association with Baden (near Vienna)' (4 [1930] 57, 61) can refer only to the year 1813. Polemic against Sandberger regarding comments in the review by the latter of Unger's monograph 'Beethovens Handschrift' (4 [1930] 143). A misprint is corrected in the article 'A Swiss Beethoven collection' (5 [1933] 28), and recent accessions to the collection are mentioned.

'New information on Beethoven's year as a student with Haydn' (6 [1935] 39). (a) Op. 4 was published without dedication (see NV p. 197). (b) The lost Oboe Concerto was at one time in the possession of Diabelli & Co. (TV p. 168), so it is possible that it may reappear. (c) The fact that the works which Beethoven sent to the Elector as the fruits of his first year's study were (with one exception) compositions which he had written in Bonn (though very likely revised in Vienna), indicates the fact (important if true) that in his first year of study Beethoven concerned himself almost solely with theory, thereby laying the foundation of his future technique as a composer, but producing no works of importance during that year.

The "Herr Bathofen, Mediziner," mentioned in 'Beethoven in Regensburg, 1795' (6 [1935] 48), whom the Breunings met in Regensburg was certainly Johann, not Ludwig. Wegeler's reference to this meeting (WRK p. 215) is an error, deriving from the reference in Stephan von Breuning's letter of January 21st 1796 to his mother (Ley: 'Beethoven als Freund' p. 249) to "Beethoven, who we unexpectedly met in Nürnberg (sic) and who journeyed from there in company with us." (See also 'Allgemeine Musik Zeitung' 63 [1936] 260) Supplementing Beethoven's visits to Hungary (6 [1935] 52), at the head of any list of Beethoven's Hungarian friends should be placed the name of Zmeskall. While his family was originally Czech, the branch from which the 'Music Count' came had for many years been resident in Hungary. Thus the number of works dedicated to Hungarians should be increased by Op. 95 and by one or two canons. 'The auction of Beethoven's musical Nachlass' (6 [1935] 66). Incidental comment is made on two of the works included in the sale. 'The Beethoven manuscripts in the Library of the Paris Conservatory' (6 [1935] 87). Minor corrections.

                                                     8 [1938] 73, 74, 78, 79, 80-83

GRUNDSÄTZLICHES ZUR BEETHOVEN-IKONOGRAPHIE. S t e p h a n L e y .   (A)
In the iconography of Beethoven (the assembling of pictures of everything pertinent to his life and works) the following principles should be observed: The collection should be limited to persons, places and things that Beethoven had himself seen: e.g., Schiller, Prince Galitsin, and the Schotts were of the first importance in Beethoven's life, but since he never met any one of them, their pictures should not be included in a Beethoven iconography. Pictures of the town of Bonn in 1732 (when Grandfather Ludwig settled there) and of the Beethoven monument in the Zentralfriedhof should be omitted. A 'View of Vienna from Nussdorf' would be appropriate, since Beethoven was often in Nussdorf, but indiscriminately chosen pictures of Vienna streets of Beethoven's time are hardly pertinent; while the Congress of Vienna led to the composition of 'Der Glorreiche Augenblick' Op. 136, Beethoven did not see the Congress in session, so a picture of the Congress would not be germane. Within these limits, the ultimate in completeness should be sought: portraits of the master himself and of all persons with whom he had contact, of places and buildings that he knew, of details of his daily life, of writings from his pen and from contemporary journals regarding his works and his affairs.

The mass of his writings is so great that selectivity should be exercised in the direction of including material of some significance in Beethoven's history: e.g., a letter like that to the Immortal Beloved or the Heiligenstadt will rather than just any letter; the Flute Duet of August 1792 or the opening pages of the Kyrie of the Missa Solemnis with the words: "Von Herzen, möge es wieder zu Herzen gehen" rather than just any page of musical manuscript. Even the most casual contact with Beethoven should warrant inclusion: e.g., a portrait of Count Wielhorsky, the Russian music-lover, would be in order because of Hiller's account of the meeting of the Count with Beethoven (see also Nohl: 'Beethoven, Liszt, Wagner' [1874] 95ff). Too much stress cannot be laid on the requirement that all material included must be of unchallengeable authenticity. The pictures must show the subject as Beethoven saw it: e.g., a scene of Vienna in 1900 or a portrait of Sonntag or Schröder-Devrient in the 1840's would be next to valueless. Title pages of first editions should be carefully authenticated (old reprints might easily fool

GRUNDSÄTZLICHES ZUR BEETHOVEN-IKONOGRAPHIE (Continued)
the unwary).   Portraits should be reproduced from the originals, not from contemporary copies which suffer from
the limitations imposed by even the best methods of reproduction in Beethoven's day.   As far as is practicable,
the arrangement should be chronological.   8 [1938] 84

DIE BEDEUTUNG VON SKIZZEN, BRIEFEN, UND ERINNERUNGEN FÜR DIE STILKUNDLICHE FORSCHUNG.   (A)
     Paul Mies.
The mental and physical habits (e. g. , the considerable importance to many composers of improvising at the piano
as an aid to the act of composition) of many composers, from Bach to Reger, are considered in extensive and anecdotal detail as they may be illuminated by sketch books or by accounts given by the composers themselves.   Among
the points made which are specifically applicable to Beethoven are: Of the three reasons which Nottebohm (NB II
Einleitung) gave for the study of Beethoven sketch books, the determination of date of composition, the disclosure
of works which were started but never finished, and their value as "a glimpse into Beethoven's workshop," the third
is considered today as being by far the most valuable.   The work of Braunstein on the first Leonora Overture Op. 138
('Beethovens Leonore-Ouverture' (1927) show that: In general, the sketch books do not serve as an absolutely depend-
able basis for the determination of chronology; and the intermingling of sketches of various works is not a safe indication that the works were completed at the same time.   The study of first editions, engravers' proofs, autographs,
and sketches may be of value in resolving uncertainties in the texts of compositions as they are currently available.

The characteristics of Beethoven's literary style include: Most of the time a diction without attempt at literary
grace, though in moments of emotional stress (e. g. , the letter to the Immortal Beloved (KS I 47, TK I 327), the
Heiligenstadt will (KS I 59, TK I 352), the letter of consolation to Countess Erdödy (KS I 408), letters and journal
entries regarding Nephew Karl) his writing takes on real distinction.   (NOTE by DWM. The last lines and the post-
cript of the letter of August 19th 1826 to Schott (Son p. 144) are to one reader the most moving of Beethoven's
written words).   His complete lack of descriptive writing, his love of puns and of fantastic diction, his use of pet
phrase-forms in many variations, almost as a musician makes many modifications of a single theme, and the addition of humor in music to humor in words which resulted in his many canons, a form which rarely appears in his
serious work.   8 [1938] 104

BEETHOVENS STUDIEN ZUR INSTRUMENTATION.   Georg Schünemann.   (B)
Loose sheets of manuscript now in the Berlin State Library (erroneously described in the Artaria Catalog as having
arisen from Beethoven's studies with Albrechtsberger) include fifteen pages (probably dating from Beethoven's
instruction of the Archduke Rudolph in 1817-19) which constitute the only known studies by Beethoven of the capabilities of individual instruments.   A large part of the material deals with the horn, with special consideration
for those notes outside the harmonic series which are usable and those which are not.   The capabilities and limitations of the clarinet, the various sizes of trombones, and the usable triple- and quadruple-stopping of the 'cello
are also set forth.   The author cites passages from Beethoven's own works which show how closely he followed his
own stated rules of instrumentation.   8 [1938] 146

BEETHOVENS "ERSTE" -- EINE B-A-C-H SYMPHONIE.   Erich Schenk.   (C)
The author cites the following reasons for considering Op. 21 as a "B-A-C-H" symphony: Beethoven worked
(though many years after the First Symphony) on at least two other B-A-C-H compositions: a projected overture
referred to in sketch books of 1822-25 (NB II 12, 167, 474, 542, 577ff) and the 'Kuhlau' canon (KS II 400).
Certain passages of the symphony (e. g. , the frequent progressions by half steps, the opening measures of the
andante cantabile) are stylistically similar to works of the baroque period.   The symphony was dedicated to a
noted proponent of Bach, Baron Gottfied von Swieten.   The notes B-A-C-H or their transpositions appear in
several places in the symphony: First Movement mm. 1, 3-4 (2nd Fl, 2nd Ob, 1st Cl); mm. 81, 85-86 (Vcl);
mm. 83-86 (Vln I, then Vln II); mm. 189-92 (Cl I); mm. 196-99 (Fl II, Ob II, Cl I); Second Movement
mm. 49-51 (Cl I, Bsn II, Vln II), paralleled in mm. 149-51.
                                          8 [1938] 162

EINE ZWEIFELHAFTE STELLE IN BEETHOVENS 7. SYMPHONIE.   Friedrich Munter.   (D)
In mm. 285 of the first movement (GA 1/7 22-1-2) the strings retain tonic harmony throughout the measure,
whereas the wind instruments in the second half of the measure change to subdominant harmony.   In the corresponding measure of the exposition (m. 96 - 10-1-6) the harmony in all instruments changes to subdominant
in the second half of the measure.

In favor of the accepted reading of m. 285 is the fact that it follows the unambiguous reading of the autograph. Reasons for believing that the passage in a slip of Beethoven's pen are: In actual performance the clash of harmonies is not heard, the subdominant chord of the wind instruments drowning out the tonic harmony in the low strings. It seems most improbable that Beethoven would 'throw away' so revolutionary a harmonic innovation. Though Beethoven has several times written a clash of tonic and dominant harmonies, there is no other case of tonic against subdominant.

Commentaries by Joachim (that the passage is in error) and by Weingartner (that the passage "is a true piece of Beethoven daring, and must not be interfered with or explained away") are quoted, and a simple change in the string writing is suggested to give unalloyed subdominant harmony.

8 [1938] 173

ZU FELIX VON WEINGARTNERS BEETHOVEN-BEARBEITUNGEN. Friedrich Munter.   (A)
   Modifications are suggested in certain of the points commented on by Weingartner in his 'On the Performance of Beethoven's Symphonies. '   8 [1938] 178

DIE FORM DES BEETHOVENSCHEN VIOLINKONZERT. Hans Joachim Moser.   (B)
   The following analysis is given (references are to GA 4/29 page, system, measure):

First Movement

   Tutti Exposition 1-88 (6-2-10): at least eight distinct thematic ideas, the section as a whole lying in or around the tonic. While there are relationships between various of the themes, the opening rhythmic motif is the most important.

   Solo Introduction mm. 89-100 (7-1-1 to 7-3-2): passage work on the dominant seventh.

   Solo Exposition mm. 101-89 (7-3-3 to 13-1-4): substantially identical with the Tutti Exposition except for the important fact that mm. 118-43 (8-3-2 to 10-2-3) form a modulation to the dominant, so that the last half of the Solo Exposition is in the dominant. Thus mm. 1-88 and 101-89 represent the usual repeated exposition of the normal sonata form, except that while the repetition has the normal tonic-dominant key relationship, the first statement (as regards tonality) is comparable to the restatement of a recapitulation section.

   mm. 186-223 (13-1-1 to 15-2-1) correspond in content to the violin solo mm. 89-100 which separates the two appearances of the exposition. This time, however, the passage ends in a deceptive cadence (dominant seventh of E major to F major) like mm. 26-27; each case continues with the same motif in the minor.

   The author points out that mm. 178-284 (12-2-3 to 20-1-6) correspond very closely to mm. 452 (31-1-3) to the end of the movement, and refers to this section as an "abbreviated recapitulation. " (NOTE by DWM. The measure-by-measure correspondence seems to run only in mm. 178-235 (12-2-3 to 16-2-2) vs. mm. 452-510 (31-1-3); after the latter section and the cadenza the return to the second theme leads at once to the short coda.)

   Repetition of the solo introduction passage work mm. 285-299 (20-1-7 to 21-1-4) leads to the actual development section. mm. 309-29 (21-3-1 to 22-3-6) are based on the turn in the first theme, and mm. 330-64 (23-1-1 to 25-1-5) on the five-note rhythm of mm. 1-2, to which a new melodic idea appears as a descant.

   The recapitulation mm. 365 (25-2-1) to the end of the movement is quite normal, though the thematic material after the second theme (immediately following the cadenza) is mostly omitted, the coda starting at m. 518 (35-2-2). (NOTE by DWM. In numbering measures in this movement, the author apparently picked up an extra measure or made a corresponding error in his counting at some point shortly after m. 406. It might also be noted that m. 217 of the rondo (54-2-4) is omitted from the score in the Eulenberg edition.)

DIE FORM DES BEETHOVENSCHEN VIOLINKONZERT (Continued)

Summary (slightly modified by DWM)

Tutti statement	1 - 88
Solo introduction	89 - 100
Solo restatement	101 - 185
Abbreviated recapitulation	178 - 284
Development	285 - 299
	300 - 308
	309 - 329
	330 - 364
Recapitulation	365 - 535

Second Movement

Theme	1 - 10
Variation I	11 - 20
Variation II	21 - 30
Variation III	31 - 40
Transition	41 - 44
Contrast A	45 - 55
Theme Variation IV	56 - 65
Contrast B	66 - 70
Contrast A	71 - 79
Contrast B	80 - 86
Theme	87 - 88
Bridge to rondo	89 - 91

Third Movement -- Rondo

(key)		
D	Subject (three-fold statement	1 - 45
D→ A	Contrast A	46 - 92
D	Subject	93 - 122
g	Contrast B	123 - 173
D	Subject	174 - 218
D→G	Contrast A	219-

The remainder of the movement, to its close at m. 360, is based on the subject.

9 [1939] 16

DIE URAUFFÜHRUNG EINES BEETHOVENSCHEN MEISTERWERKES IM JAHRE 1939.   Willy Hess.

'Nei giorni tuoi felici,' duet for soprano and tenor with small orchestra (TV 264 No. 25; H-81) was sketched about the end of 1802 and completed in score shortly thereafter. TD III 619 lists this duet among the works which Beethoven offered to Steiner in 1817 (the author says more probably in 1815). Steiner did not accept it, and the 23-page score passed via the Artaria Collection (No. 168) to the Imperial Library in Berlin. After incidental editing by the author, the duet received its first performance in Winterthur on February 10th 1939. Orchestral and vocal scores have been published by Eulenberg.   9 [1939] 26

WEITERE ZWEIFELHAFTE STELLEN IN DEN NEUN SYMPHONIEN BEETHOVENS.   Siegmund von Hausegger.

Mention is made of a large number of questioned readings, mostly dynamics but including note values, notes them-selves, the instruments used (especially as regards doubling), and in the finale of the Ninth details of the text. The author points out that we are far from a definitive version of the nine symphonies.

9 [1939] 31

CZERNYS ERINNERUNGEN AN BEETHOVEN.   Georg Schünemann.

Carl Czerny's association with Beethoven, first as pupil and then as friend and companion, extended over some thirty years (from 1797 he lived in an atmosphere of Beethoven (TK I 236), and he first met and played for the master about 1800, Frimmel: Beethoven-Handbuch I 102). His writings, which include commentaries on Beethoven "not always

consistent nor reliable as to details," are as follows: (a) An autobiographical note from 1830, barely a page long.
(b) 'Erinnerungen aus meinem Leben' (1842, MS). Apparently available to Thayer; excerpted in 'Signale' 28 [1870]
929; otherwise apparently unpublished. Most of the material which appeared in 'Signale,' together with additional
excerpts, are given here. (c) Notes for Otto Jahn (Autumn 1852, MS with commentaries by Schindler). Apparently
available to Thayer; otherwise presumably unpublished. (d) Article on Beethoven in Cocks' 'Musical Miscellany'
(London) August 2nd 1852 (see TK I 196). (e) Statements given in NB I 136, II 75, 182, 243, 356, 503.

The 'Anecdotes and Notes on Beethoven' written for Jahn are presumably given here in full. The following matters
mentioned therein may be noted as being novel or of especial interest: It is in this writing that Czerny's statement
regarding the Variations Theme of the Septet Op. 20 (TK I 278) is found. The author cites evidence that the theme
was taken from the folksong 'Ach Schiffer,' not the reverse. Czerny says that Kuffner wrote the text for the Choral
Fantasie Op. 80 (TK II 129), but NB II 503 disagrees. The author sides with Czerny, not with Nottebohm. Czerny
states that Beethoven himself made the piano arrangement of the Prometheus music (presumably that published in
June 1801 as Op. 24) Regarding the progress of Beethoven's deafness, Czerny says that though ear trouble had been
noted in 1800, Beethoven heard speech and music well as late as 1812, but that by 1817 the deafness was so marked
that he no longer could hear music. To this observation Czerny appends a list of works: (a) Written after deafness was
complete. (b) Started at an earlier time and completed after 1817 (including Opp. 109, 110, 111, 124 and 125).
Czerny says that these three piano sonatas were written for a 5 1/2 octave piano rather than for the 6 octave instrument
for which the last piano works were written. Schindler assigns Opp. 110 and 111 to 1820-21. (c) Completed before his
deafness but published after 1817.

Czerny says that until deafness intervened, Beethoven was accustomed to compose with the help of the piano, and to
try over bothersome passages countless times. The contention that a certain passage in Op. 57 is played incorrectly
(and given incorrectly in the GA) is not borne out by the clear evidence of the autograph. He says that he has been
assured that the closing theme of the first movement of the Kreutzer Sonata Op. 47 was taken from an already published composition by Kreutzer -- "this may explain the dedication" -- but gives no reference. Czerny describes
Beethoven's playing and improvising at some length, and says that Opp. 77 and 80 and the choral finale of the Ninth
Symphony give a true picture of his style. He states (but Schindler denies) that in the years 1818-20 Beethoven often
improvised at private gatherings in Czerny's studio.   9 [1939] 47

ELCHE WERKE BEETHOVENS FEHLEN IN DER BREITKOPF UND HÄRTELSCHEN GESAMTAUSGABE? (ERSTER NACHTRAG). (A)
     Willy Hess.
Corrections and additions to the list given in 7 [1937] 104.   9 [1939] 75

ETHOVEN ALS WEGWEISER FÜR SPÄTERE DEUTSCHE SINFONIKER. Walter Petzet.   (B)
A consideration of the influence of Beethoven on Schubert, Schumann, Brahms and Bruckner.
                                                   10 [1942] 15

RKUNDLICHES ÜBER BEETHOVENS BEERDIGUNG UND ERSTE GRABSTÄTTE. Stephan Ley.   (C)
Transcriptions of an on-the-spot account of Beethoven's funeral and of various receipts and other documents in connection with it.   10 [1942] 25

E FRÜHESTEN BEETHOVEN-AUFFÜHRUNGEN IN DER SCHWEIZ. Edgar Refardt.   (D)
A statistical study. Among many other dates given are: First performance in Switzerland of a Beethoven orchestral
work: Coriolanus Overture, December 6th 1808 (Zurich). First performance in Switzerland of a Beethoven symphony,
First Symphony, 1811 (Zurich). First performance in Switzerland of a Beethoven choral work, Christus, 1813 (Bern).
First performance in Switzerland of a Beethoven concerto, unidentified piano concerto, 1820 (Bern). First performance
in Switzerland of the Missa Solemnis, portions 1834 (Geneva), complete 1871 (Zurich).
                                                   10 [1942] 36

ETHOVEN AM KLAVIER. August Schmid-Lindner.   (E)
An extended discussion of Beethoven as a pianist and of the interrelationship of his pianism, the development of the
piano as an instrument, and his compositions for piano.   10 [1942] 40

E DYNAMIK IM FORMALEN RHYTHMUS MEHRSÄTZIGER WERKE, INSBESONDERE VON BEETHOVENS TANZ-ZYKLEN. (F)
     Willy Hess.
A general consideration of symmetry in single movements and in sonatas of the Bach-Handel period as regards tempo,
tonality and content, and (the reverse) of the underlying progressive force typified in the C minor Symphony, in which
the key of C major appears: In the first movement, only in the return of the second theme in the recapitulation; in the

DIE DYNAMIK IM FORMALEN RHYTHMUS MEHRSÄTZIGER WERK , etc. , (Continued)
second movement, each of three appearances of the fanfare; in the third movement, the entire trio; In the fourth movement, the movement as a whole except for the reminiscences of the scherzo.   The principles thus developed are applied to the analysis of all of Beethoven's known dance cycles (many of which do not appear in the GA) especially as regards tonality.   (See also 'Schweizerische Musik Zeitung' 79 [1939] 476; 'Die Musik' 32_1 [1940] 191).
10 [1942] 59

FIDELIO IN GOTIK UND BAROCK.   Bertha Antonia Wallner.   (A
The 'conjugal love' motif of the Fidelio story may be traced back to a fifteenth century folksong which became the basis of a seventeenth century drama under the title 'Acroama' by the Jesuit Jakob Bidermann.   Performances of this drama or its modifications by other writers (some with incidental music) took place in many cities of Germany and Austria during the century following 1650.   The story was assigned sometimes to the period of the Crusades and sometimes to the Thirty Years War.   Detailed synopses of several versions are given.
10 [1942] 78

NEUES MUSIKBLATT *

DAS HEUTIGE BEETHOVEN-BILD.   Karl Joachim Krüger.   (B
The trend of Beethoven biography since the composer's death is summarized in the statement: "Beethoven as he is portrayed today comes more from the spirit of our times than from the personality of the composer. "
16 [1937] No. 31, p. 1

EIN NEUENTDECKTES WERK VON BEETHOVEN.   Georg Schünemann.   (C
In addition to the generally known 'March' written for Christoph Kuffner's drama 'Tarpeja' (GA 2/14), Beethoven also wrote an overture for the drama, presumably used at the first performance on March 26th 1813 but not heretofore published.   The story of the drama is summarized, and the relations between Beethoven and Kuffner over a period of nearly twenty years are discussed.
18 [1939] No. 44, p. 1

DAS BEETHOVEN-ARCHIV IN BONN.   O. Kaul.   (D
General.
18 [1939] No. 44, p. 7

GESETZ UND FREIHEIT IN DER BEETHOVEN-INTERPRETATION.   Georg Kuhlmann.   (E
Freedom is permissible in sforzati and in rubato.   No categorical rule can be laid down regarding repeats.
20 [1941] No. 64, p. 1

NEW MUSIC REVIEW AND CHURCH MUSIC REVIEW

BEETHOVEN'S CHORAL SYMPHONY AND CHORAL FANTASIA.   H. E. Krehbiel.   (
General discussion of the Symphony (especially the last movement) with quotations from the sketch books, and citation of passages from the Symphony and the Fantasia to indicate a parallelism of melody and harmony as well as of concept and method.   (See also AmZ Ser. 3: 7 [1872] 123)   4 [1905] 184,231

SOME BEETHOVEN SKETCHES.   H. E. Krehbiel.   (
Detailed description of eight pages from a sketch book (possibly that described in NB II 283) attributed to the period September 1810 - March 1811 and devoted almost exclusively to Op. 97.
4 [1905] 376,428

BEETHOVEN'S MASS IN D.   Daniel Gregory Mason.   (
Nontechnical analysis.   5 [1905] 574

* Became Neues Musikblatt in 1934.   In 1946 resumed publication as Melos.

STUDY OF BEETHOVEN'S FIFTH SYMPHONY.   Thomas Whitney Surette.   (A)
An analysis suitable for "Appreciation of Music" classes in schools.
5 [1906] 1224,1290

"BEETHOVEN" SOCIETY IN 1819.   (B)
A Beethoven Society in Portland, Maine formed in 1819, had 55 members in 1821.
7 [1908] 353

HERESE VON BRUNSWICK AS THE IMMORTAL BELOVED.   (C)
F. de Gerando, grandnephew of Therese von Brunswick, states reasons why he believes that Therese was not the
Immortal Beloved. The anonymous author of this article, (identified as Philip Hale in TK I 346) and also Jean
Chantavoine, are not impressed by de Gerando's arguments.   8 [1909] 423,512

EETHOVEN AND GEORGE THOMSON. J. Cuthbert Hadden.   (D)
A very readable summary of the relationship and correspondence between the two men.
9 [1910] 482

EETHOVEN AS A MARTYR. Hermann Kretzschmar.   (E)
"Beethoven, next to Wagner, is the most pitied composer." The development of the custom of Beethoven pity is
examined, with the conclusion: "Only if one side of the story is as largely exaggerated as the other is minimized,
can it be maintained that Beethoven was not appreciated by his time." (See also 26 [1927] 87)
10 [1911] 185

EETHOVEN AS LOVER. J. Cuthbert Hadden.   (F)
An account of Beethoven's interest in the opposite sex.   · 10 [1911] 587

EETHOVEN'S DEAFNESS IN RELATION TO HIS WORKS.   (G)
An article by a "well-known composer" who "has for many years been completely deaf." The handicaps of deafness
for a composer are manifold and heavy: loss of the never ending flow of natural sounds (a heavy burden for a nature
lover like Beethoven); "the 'fatigue of deafness,' a condition which calls for the necessary service of three faculties:
the hearing, to distinguish as much as possible; the sight, to watch the lips in conversation; and the mind, to piece
together and reason out words and sentences imperfectly understood"; head noises; necessary dependence on tonal
vision without the possibility of aural verification of effects. The author feels, however, that with Beethoven the
forced benefit of intense concentration more than offset these handicaps.
21 [1922] 219

USICAL COMPOSITIONS OF DOUBTFUL AUTHORSHIP. Orlando A. Mansfield.   (H)
Some works credited to Beethoven are listed: (a) In the "Easy Sonata in C" dedicated to Eleanor von Breuning (NV
p. 148) the third movement which is sometimes given was written by Ferdinand Ries. (b),(c) As stated in NV p.148,
the authenticity of the posthumous sonatas in G and in F is open to question. (d) "Beethoven's Adieu to the Piano"
is a "flagrant forgery." (e) In the mid-19th century a song "The Dream of St. Jerome, by Ludwig van Beethoven"
was hashed up from Op. 48 No. 2 plus a contrasting section which was "merely a couple of meagre themes repeated
several times with most commonplace harmonies."   23 [1924] 374

ETHOVEN'S HAPPINESS. Cecil Forsyth.   (I)
"One is forced to agree . . . that Beethoven was not in the main unhappy. We do not believe that love troubled him
seriously. The fact that after his death the celebrated love letters were found in his desk -- not in hers, whoever she
may have been -- clinches the matter." He had constant access to the countryside. He was surrounded with many
friends, "chosen of his own will from any and every class of society." For years on end he was able to devote himself
exclusively to composition. He secured widespread recognition during his lifetime from publishers and music lovers
alike. (See also 10 [1911] 185)   26 [1927] 87

FEW PUNCTILIOS IN BEETHOVEN'S NINTH SYMPHONY.   J. G. Prod'homme.   (J)
Digest of portions of the article by Baensch in 'Neues Beethoven-Jahrbuch' 2 [1923] 137.
27 [1928] 49

DWIG VAN BEETHOVEN.   Alexander Brent-Smith.   (K)
Popular essay.   30 [1931] 281

ÜBER DIE VERBINDUNG DER BEETHOVEN'SCHEN MUSIK ZU GOETHES EGMONT MIT DER AUFFÜHRUNG DIESES   (A
    TRAUERSPIEL.   Ludwig Bischoff.
    Suggested cueing and abridgement of the music to fit within the framework and the audience habits of a stage presen-
    tation of the drama.   1 [1853] 41

STOPPELLESE.   (B
    Reprint of a "Musical letter from a blockhead" (originally appearing in the 'Allgemeine Zeitung' No. 217) which
    commented adversely on the introduction of voices into the Ninth Symphony.
                                                             1 [1853] 77

ZU BEETHOVENS MISSA IN D.   A. Schindler.   (C
    The tempo of the Benedictus (not given in the score) should be as stated in Beethoven's letter of January 26th 1825
    to Schott (KS II 356).   1 [1853] 113

W. VON LENZ ÜBER BEETHOVEN.   (I
    Review of 'Beethoven et ses trois styles.'   1 [1853] 121,137,145

EIN URTHEIL C. M. VON WEBERS ÜBER BEETHOVEN.   August Hitzschold.   (
    A letter dated May 21st 1810 from Weber to Hans Georg Nägeli refers to Beethoven's more recent works as "confused
    chaos."   1 [1853] 153

WIE EIN CAPELLMEISTER UNFREIWILLIGER MITARBEITER DER NIEDERRHEINISCHE MUSIK-ZEITUNG WIRD.   (
    Heinrich Dorn.
    Polemic against Schindler regarding the tempo indication of the Benedictus of the Missa Solemnis.
                                                             1 [1853] 168

NOCH EINMAL: C. M. V. WEBER ÜBER BEETHOVEN.   Ludwig Bischoff.   (
    A musical fable written by Weber in 1809 foreshadows his opinion of four years later that a man who could write the
    Seventh Symphony was fit for the madhouse.   1 [1853] 171

FÜR STUDIERENDE VON BEETHOVENS CLAVIER-MUSIK.   A. Schindler.   (
    A discursive account of the influence of Clementi and Cramer on Beethoven's concept of piano playing and on the
    pianism of the mid-nineteenth century. (See also p. 168)   2 [1854] 155

OFFENER BRIEF AN HERRN A. SCHINDLER IN FRANKFURT AM MAIN.   Ferdinand Hiller.   (
    Attack on Schindler in connection with the article on p. 155.   2 [1854] 168

BEETHOVEN'S DEAFNESS.   (
    Inquiry as to the date of complete deafness and as to the first works written after deafness, mentioning that in 1813
    Beethoven conducted a performance of Op. 91 in such a way as to indicate that his hearing was still adequate.
                                                             2 [1854] 192

DIE OUVERTURE (Nr. 2) ZU BEETHOVENS LEONORE (Fidelio).   A. Schindler.   (
    Otto Jahn recently found a score of this overture which contained various passages omitted from the (Schindler) version
    published in 1840 by Breitkopf & Härtel. The author is convinced that the new passages are genuine. He also says
    that the shortened version of the overture (published in 1840) was used at the first performance of the 1814 revison of
    the opera, the new overture not being ready. (As to the overture used at this performance, see TK II 278)
                                                             2 [1854] 212

ÜBER BEETHOVENS TAUBHEIT.
    While Beethoven was aware of oncoming deafness in 1801, ear trumpets and the like became necessary only several
    years after 1808. The author played under Beethoven's direction in 1813, at which time "there was no doubt that the
    condition of his hearing was very critical. He recognized this fact."
                                                             2 [1854] 213

ZU BEANTWORTUNG DER FRAGEN ÜBER BEETHOVENS TAUBHEIT, IN Nr. 24 DIESES BLÄTTER.   A. Schindler.
    Beethoven's last public appearance (as a pianist) was in two performances of Op. 97 on April 11th 1814. On February
    21st 1816 the 'Allgemeine Musikalische Zeitung' (18 [1816] 121) made its first reference to Beethoven's deafness,
    "which made him incapable of conducting his own works." By 1818 his hearing had become too weak to make spoken
    conversation practicable, even with an ear trumpet, the only exception being that for several years after this he was
    able to converse with the Archduke Rudolph with the use of the smallest of his ear trumpets. "It can be stated that in

1819 our Master was still in a condition to correct the piano playing of others." Beethoven's performances at the piano for groups of friends in 1822 were referred to in the 'Allgemeine Musikalische Zeitung' 24 [May 8th 1822] 310. In April 1824 he coached the two female soloists for the first performances of the Missa Solemnis and the Ninth Symphony. "There can be no doubt that at that time Beethoven could hear individual voices or a few voices, at least with his left ear, though he could not hear masses of sounds." In August 1825 he coached rehearsals of Op. 132.

2 [1854] 223

TRADITIONELLES. DAS ALLEGRETTO SCHERZANDO IN BEETHOVENS ACHTER SINFONIE BETRACHTET.   (A)
A. Schindler.
The proper speed for the allegretto scherzando is that of Beethoven's own metronome marking for the Maelzel Canon: eighth note = 72. The conductors who take the movement much faster completely lose its spirit. (For reconciliation of this statement with Beethoven's own marking of eighth note = 88 for this movement ('Allgemeine Musikalische Zeitung' 19 [1817] 874). (See 4 [1856] 57)   2 [1854] 385

POLEMIC AGAINST WAGNER REGARDING THE FINALE OF THE EROICA. A. Schindler.   (B)

3 [1855] 55

BEMERKUNGEN ÜBER DEN VORTRAG EINIGER BEETHOVEN'SCHEN SONATEN.   (C)
Suggestions of tempi and dynamics for Opp. 13, 26, 27 No. 1, 31 No. 2, and 57.

3 [1855] 321, 340

BEETHOVEN UND SEINE AUSLEGER. A. Schindler.   (D)
During the second and third decades of the nineteenth century a private group in Bremen was active in the performance of Beethoven's music.   4 [1856] 13

MÄLZELS METRONOM ERSTER UND ZWEITER CONSTRUCTION. A. Schindler.   (E)
The first model of the metronome to be put on the market (in 1815) was so expensive that few were sold. A smaller model was brought out a few years later at a lower price by (Leonhard) Maelzel, younger brother of Johann Nepomuk, but the rates of the two machines were so different that metronome marks were meaningless without a statement as to which model was referred to. It may be assumed that the indications given by Beethoven in 'Allgemeine Musikalische Zeitung' 19 [1817] 873 were based on the earlier (large) machine; Czerny's tempi for the piano works referred to the smaller (Vienna) model. Beethoven's failure to assign metronome marks for his last works with the exception of the Ninth Symphony -- thus abandoning his championship of the metronome as expressed in his letter to Ignaz von Mosel (KS II 69) -- may well have been due to the confusion introduced by the undesirable conflicts in the readings of the two models of metronome. In the last analysis, the tempo of works by Beethoven must be guided largely by the judgment of the greatest artists. (Note that Nottebohm (NB I 126) and Frimmel (Beethoven Handbuch I 407) completely disagree with Schindler's statements of facts as well as with his conclusions.)

4 [1856] 57

BEETHOVEN AND CHERUBINI. A. Schindler.   (F)
In spite of his letter of 1823 to Cherubini (KS II 234), Beethoven was unfamiliar with Cherubini's sacred works.

4 [1856] 168

EIN FREIMÜTHIGES WORT ÜBER DIE NEUNTE SINFONIE VON BEETHOVEN. Karl Overweg.   (G)
The author explains why he does not care for the last movement of the symphony.

4 [1856] 185

EIN BRIEF BEETHOVENS AN JOHN ELLA.   (H)
Imaginary letter "Mein guter Ella -- mein klarköpfige Freund! Ich hatte mir vorgenommen, an Sie zu schreiben."

4 [1856] 217

BEETHOVENS MUSIK ZU DEM BALLET: DIE GESCHÖPFE DES PROMETHEUS.   (I)
Copy of an article by Leopold Sonnleithner regarding performances of various versions of this ballet.

4 [1856] 378

HISTORISCHE NOTEN ZUR "LEONORE" VON BEETHOVEN. L. Sonnleithner.   (J)
In its first version ('Leonore') the opera received a single performance (November 20th 1805), and in its second version there were performances between March 29th and April 10th 1806. The first performance of 'Fidelio' was on May 23rd 1814. In all of these performances the role of Leonora was taken by Frau Anna Milder; in later years Frau Antonia Campi often sang this role. Wilhelmine Schröder (born October 6th 1805) appeared as Leonora for the

HISTORISCHE NOTEN ZUR "LEONORE" VON BEETHOVEN (Continued)
  first time on November 22nd 1822. The first appearance of the Leonora story in opera was in Paris in 1798 (book by
  J. N. Bouilly, music by Gaveaux). This book was translated into German for Beethoven by Joseph Sonnleithner, and
  into Italian for Paer by an unknown translator. Paer's opera was given in Dresden in 1805 and in Vienna in German
  translation on February 9th 1809 and several times in 1810.   5 [1857] 6

DREI BRIEFE, ZWISCHEN BEETHOVEN UND ZELTER GEWECHSELT.   (A
  Letter of February 8th 1823 from Beethoven (KS II 223), Zelter's reply of February 22nd 1823, and letter of March 25th
  1823 from Beethoven.   5 [1857] 22

'BEETHOVEN, SES CRITIQUES ET SES GLOSSATEURS,' PAR ALEXANDRE OULIBICHEFF. L. Bischoff.   (B
  Extended review.   5 [1857] 97,105,113,137

SALE OF A BEETHOVEN LETTER.   (C
  Letter without date to Mlle. de Gerardi offered for sale as described in KS I 24.
                                              5 [1857] 312

THE PLENI SUNT COELI AND OSANNA OF THE MISSA SOLEMNIS. A. Schindler.   (D
  While Beethoven was at work on the Missa Solemnis, Schindler suggested the use of a chorus rather than soloists for
  these two passages, but Beethoven said unequivocally, "They must be solo voices." These parts of the Missa were not
  performed at the concert in 1824 when the other movements received their first performance. The author is sure that,
  had they been performed then, the soloists would have prevailed upon Beethoven to change his mind, since at best the
  version as written can be effective only with superbly gifted soloists with accompaniment of a reduced orchestra. The
  author believes that the 'Pleni sunt coeli' should be taken at a simple allegro rather than at Beethoven's allegro pesante.
                                              5 [1857] 326

BEMERKUNGEN ÜBER DEN VORTRAG BEETHOVEN'SCHEN SINFONIEN.   (
  Detailed suggestions on tempi, phrasing, etc., of the Fifth Symphony.
                                              5 [1857] 337

EINE ANEKDOTE AUS L. VAN BEETHOVENS LEBEN.   (
  The letter and anecdote given in KS II 414 (No. 1127).   6 [1858] 246

BEETHOVENS FIDELIO.
  A very detailed and critical review of C. E. R. Alberti's 'Ludwig van Beethoven als dramatischer Tondichter."
                                              7 [1859] 201

DIE FÜNF LETZTEN VIOLIN-QUARTETTE BEETHOVENS.
  Statement of the order of composition.   7 [1859] 390

BEETHOVEN AND PAER. Ferd. Hiller.
  Hiller says that Paer himself told him the well-known story (see TK II 37) that when Beethoven and Paer were together
  at a performance of Paer's 'Leonora,' Beethoven remarked, "Oh que c'est beau, que c'est intéressant! Il faut que je
  compose cela." The Editor quotes Berlioz's version of the same story: "Votre opéra me plaît; j'ai envie de le mettre
  en musique!" but raises the question as to whether the incident could have taken place, since apparently Paer left
  Vienna forever early in 1803, and there is no record of a performance of his Leonora in Vienna up to that time. (See
  also p. 273)   8 [1860] 190

BEETHOVEN AND WILHELMINE SCHRÖDER-DEVRIENT.
  A dramatic account of the famous soprano's first appearance as Leonora in November 1822.
                                              8 [1860] 246

BEETHOVEN AND PAER. L. Sonnleithner.
  Paer's opera was undoubtedly composed during 1805 and 1806, so that neither Beethoven nor his librettist could have
  been influenced by Paer's work. The only possible foundation for the story is that Paer was in Vienna during March
  and April 1803, and might have mentioned to Beethoven his project of composing an opera on the Leonora story. It
  may be noted that although the 1806 libretto of Beethoven's opera was entitled 'Leonora, oder der Triumph der
  ehelichen Liebe,' all performances of the opera -- 1805, 1806, 1814ff -- were under the same 'Fidelio.'
                                              8 [1860] 273

SPOHR AND BEETHOVEN.   (A)
  Extracts from Spohr's 'Autobiography' and other sources to indicate that he had great regard for Beethoven's music
  and for Beethoven personally. (See also 14 [1866] 92)   8 [1860] 361

BEETHOVENS MISSA SOLEMNIS.   (B)
  Circumstantial account of the events leading to the composition of the Missa Solemnis, and suggestions for a usable
  German translation of the Latin text. (See also 'Rheinische Musik-Zeitung'1 [1850] 169)
                                                          8 [1860] 383,385,393,417

BEETHOVENS MUSIK ZUM PROMETHEUS-BALLET.   (C)
  List of the 16 numbers constituting the complete incidental music, with brief program notes to indicate the significance
  of each number in the stage presentation.   9 [1861] 85,94

EINE STIMME AUS BELGIEN ÜBER BEETHOVENS MESSE IN D-DUR.   (D)
  Polemic against an unfavorable review of the Missa Solemnis, presumably by Fétis the Younger. (See also p. 235)
                                                          9 [1861] 201

DIE ORGEL IN BEETHOVENS MISSA SOLEMNIS.   A. Schindler.   (E)
  The author believes that the organ is definitely not an integral part of the Missa Solemnis as Beethoven conceived the
  work, but that it was added to the score for some or all of three reasons: To reinforce the small number of orchestral
  players which could be accommodated in the cathedral at Olmütz (where the Archduke Rudolph was to be enthroned;
  To assist in holding the performers together under extreme difficulties of placement in this cathedral; To give color
  to Beethoven's statement in his advance announcement of the work that it could be performed as an oratorio as well
  as for liturgical purposes. (Note the statement in NV (Introduction, Note 4) that the organ part was added after the
  work was otherwise complete and in score.)

  Regarding the vocal range required for the chorus sopranos, the author points out: that the usual orchestral pitch of
  the 1820's was almost a half-tone lower than at present, and that the work was certainly written for boy sopranos and
  altos (not for women), for whom the repeated high B flats would have no terrors. He suggests that for present-day performance either the tuning pitch of the orchestra be lowered by a significant amount or that the credo be transposed
  from B flat to A.   9 [1861] 233

FÉTIS DER AELTERE ÜBER BEETHOVENS MISSA SOLEMNIS.   (F)
  A distinctly unfavorable review of the Missa Solemnis by "the greatest musical scholar and critic of France and
  Belgium." (See also p. 201)   9 [1861] 235

DER BEETHOVEN'SCHE NACHLASS IN DER KÖNIGLICHEN BIBLIOTHEK ZU BERLIN.   A. Schindler.   (G)
  A circumstantial account of the negotiations by which Schindler's collection of Beethoveniana passed to the Imperial
  Library.   9 [1861] 313,321

DER GERMAN TEXT OF THE C MAJOR MASS OPUS 86.   (H)
  The German translation by Rochlitz used in some versions of the first three sections of the C major Mass is heartily
  condemned. (See also 8 [1860] 394)   10 [1862] 42

BEETHOVEN IN GNEIXENDORF.   (I)
  Anecdotes from Michael Krenn, Beethoven's servant in Gneixendorf in the fall of 1826.
                                                          10 [1862] 94

EIN BRIEF VON BEETHOVEN.   (J)
  Letter without date to Joseph von Warena (sic) (KS I 282). The 'Overture of Hungary's Benefactor' was of course the
  'King Stephan' Overture Op. 117. (See also p. 167. In the comments on this letter in KS, note that the issue of the
  journal in which publication took place is No. 16, dated April 19th.)
                                                          10 [1862] 121

BEETHOVENS NACHLASS.   (K)
  Certain Beethoven documents in the Imperial Library are withheld from use for ten years.
                                                          10 [1862] 160

BEETHOVENS BRIEF IN Nr. 16.   (L)
  The letter to Varena dates from the spring or summer of 1813.   10 [1862] 167

BEMERKUNGEN ÜBER DEN VORTRAG DER SINFONIA EROICA.   (A
    A detailed analysis with particular regard to the problems of accentuation and dynamics in the first movement.
                                            10 [1862] 257,265,273,281

BEETHOVENS PATRIOTISCHE COMPOSITIONEN.   (B
    A general account of the history of 'The Battle of Vittoria' Op. 91 and of 'Der glorreiche Augenblick' Op. 136, with
    suggested alternative text for the latter work as more suitable for contemporary performance.
                                            11 [1863] 81

BEETHOVEN UND DIE AUSGABEN SEINE WERKE.   (C
    A critical review of the Gesamtausgabe and of an article by Otto Jahn on the various complete editions of Beethoven's
    works ('Grenzbote' 1864).   12 [1864] 97

DER HORNEINSATZ IM ERSTEN ALLEGRO DER SINFONIA EROICA.   (D
    The horn entry is not on the tonic triad of E flat, but is an anticipatory appoggiatura for the dominant seventh in the
    following measures of the orchestral tutti.   12 [1864] 144

A BEETHOVEN LETTER.   (E
    Letter of March 1825 to the Schuppanzigh Quartet (KS II 361). (This publication almost certainly anticipates the
    appearance of this letter in Nohl's 'Briefe' (No. 322), listed in BJ 2 as its first publication.)
                                            13 [1865] 15

THE UNPLEASANTNESS BETWEEN WEBER AND BEETHOVEN.   (F
    Weber's early attacks on the Eroica were completely forgotten in his enthusiasm for Fidelio and in Beethoven's
    approbation of Freischütz and Euryanthe. The meeting between the two composers on October 5th 1823 is described
    in detail. The two men never met or corresponded again: a part of the reason for this may be that associates of Beet-
    hoven brought to his attention Weber's early attacks on the Eroica, which up to that time Beethoven had not known of.
                                            13 [1865] 17

EIN SKIZZENBUCH VON BEETHOVEN.   (G
    Detailed review of Nottebohm's publication (1865) of this title.   13 [1865] 97

BEETHOVEN'SCHES.   (
    Excerpts from Thayer's 'Chronologische Verzeichniss.'   13 [1865] 107,118

CURIOSA.   (
    Comments by Johann Nikolaus Forkel (1749-1828) on Beethoven, a composer far too modern for this critic's taste
    or understanding.   13 [1865] 231

BEETHOVENS BRIEFE.   (
    Detailed review of Nohl's first volume of Beethoven letters.   13 [1865] 241

EINIGE BRIEFE VON BEETHOVEN.   (
    Ten letters from Nohl's volume, with brief comments.   13 [1865] 268,299

ZWEI BISHER UNGEDRUCKTE BRIEFE VON LUDWIG VAN BEETHOVEN. W. Speyer.   (
    EDr of Kal 804, 875   13 [1865] 300

FÜNFTACTIGE RHYTHMUS BEI BEETHOVEN. Rud. Westphal.   (
    Five-measure groupings within the melody of the first movement of Op. 27 No. 2 are considered from the standpoint
    of classical prosody.   13 [1865] 297

THE MUSIC TO 'KING STEPHAN.'   (
    Program notes.   13 [1865] 343

THE MASS IN C MAJOR OPUS 86.   (
    History of the work, and scathing comments on the German text of Rochlitz whereby the first three sections became
    'Three Hymns.'   13 [1865] 357

DIE ERSTE AUFFÜHRUNG VON BEETHOVENS NEUNTER SINFONIE.   (A)
   A refutation of the anecdote (recently published by J. B. Allfeld) that at the final rehearsal for the first performance
   of the Ninth Symphony one of the soloists, Caroline Unger, stamped on the score and tearfully told Beethoven that
   the music could not be sung.   14 [1866] 2

BEETHOVENS 33 VARIATIONEN (OPUS 120) ÜBER EINEN WALTZER VON DIABELLI.   (B)
   The titles which von Bülow assigned to each of the variations are listed.
                                                    14 [1866] 86

PERSÖNLICHE VERHÄLTNISSE GROSSER MEISTER ZU EINANDER: SPOHR UND BEETHOVEN.   A. Schindler. (C)
   The author has grave doubts of Spohr's familiarity with Beethoven's works or admiration for his music.
                                                    14 [1866] 92

EINIGE BEMERKUNGEN ZU DEN PARTITUREN DER 3., 5. UND 6. SINFONIE VON BEETHOVEN IN DER NEUEN LEIPZIGER   (D)
      AUSGABE.
   The author finds no justification for dropping the ties in the three measures of horn notes on the dominant seventh in
   the first ending of the trio of the scherzo of the Eroica Symphony. He is convinced that the empty measure (m. 389)
   in the coda of the first movement of the Fifth Symphony, appearing in the Gesamtausgabe (p. 18 m. 2) as in former
   editions, is merely a perpetuation of a copyist's error. The insertion of three measures of triplets for the first violin
   at m. 301-03 of the first movement of the Sixth Symphony (GA p. 16, last three measures), as recommended by
   Schumann ('Neue Zeitschrift für Musik' 15 [1841] 149) is a correction which is long overdue. The author approves of
   the omission of the alternative concert ending for certain of the Egmont numbers. An excerpt is given from Jahn's
   'Gesammelte Aufsätze' [1866] 288-89 regarding the consideration which Beethoven gave to revising his early Pf
   works to take advantage of the increased scope of the keyboard.   14 [1866] 313

DIE PASTORAL-SINFONIEEN VON JUSTIN HEINRICH KNECHT (1784) UND LUDWIG VAN BEETHOVEN (1808).   (E)
   Knecht's symphony 'Le portrait musical de la Nature' was published by Bossler in 1784, about the time that this same
   publisher brought out several of Beethoven's youthful works, so that it is possible that Beethoven became familiar with
   Knecht's symphony. Its program bears a notable similarity to Beethoven's Sixth Symphony.
                                                    14 [1866] 379

MOZART AND BEETHOVEN: RAPHAEL AND MICHEL ANGELO.   Franz Lorenz.   (F)
   The differences between the two composers are comparable to those between the two painters.
                                                    15 [1867] 51

DIE GESCHÖPFE DES PROMETHEUS.   (G)
   A detailed synopsis of the ballet in its original version has been found and is given herewith.
                                                    15 [1867] 142

                                        NOTES

THE AUTOGRAPH OF OPUS 96.   Oswald Jonas.   (H)
   Corrections in the autograph show that "certain features -- among them, one of the most effective passages in the
   entire work -- came to Beethoven's mind only as he wrote."   3 [1946] 143

THE NUMBERING OF BEETHOVEN'S MINOR WORKS.   Otto Erich Deutsch.   (I)
   A list is given of the 23 works bearing numbers between 1 and 38 which are not opus numbers.
                                                    4 [1946] 36

FACSIMILE, TRANSCRIPTION, AND TRANSLATION OF KAL 130.   Hans Nathan.   (J)
                                                    5 [1948] 470,574 (sic) 474

FALLING LEAVES.   Barbara Duncan.   (K)
   Facsimile of pp. 46-47 of sketch book from 1819 (otherwise lost) with sketch of Quoniam of Missa Solemnis.
                                                    6 [1948] 118

THE MUSIC COLLECTION OF THE HEINEMANN FOUNDATION.   Edward N. Waters.   (A)
   This collection includes sketches for Op. 73, an unknown musical souvenir to the text 'Ars longa,' autograph of
   Kal 512, and household account sheet (facsimile facing p. 198).   7 [1950] 186

THE LETTERS OF BEETHOVEN.   Emily Anderson.   (B)
   Corrections or amplifications are given of the following Kal letters: 62, 104 (with facsimile), 186, 277, 316, 525,
   639, and 1154; transcriptions and translations are given of MM 175 (with facsimile), MM 178, and MM 408 (with
   facsimile).   9 [1952] 544

SCENA AUS VESTAS FEUER.   Donald W. MacArdle.   (C
   A brief history of this unfinished opera is given.   12 [1954] 133

THE FIRST EDITIONS OF OPUS 13 AND THE 'TANDELN UND SCHERZEN' VARIATIONS WoO 76.   Richard S. Hill. (D
   Proof is offered that Franz Anton Hoffmeister, not Joseph Eder, issued the original edition of these two works.
                                          15 [1958] 396

ÖSTERREICHISCHE MUSIKZEITSCHRIFT

BEETHOVEN UND WIEN.   Karl Kobald.   (E
   Brief and general.   1 [1946] 15

EIN SELTSAME ENTLEHNUNGSFALL -- BEETHOVEN - HÄNDEL.   Zolton Fakete.   (F
   A passage in Händel's 'Deborah' is almost identical with a passage in the C minor Symphony.
                                      2 [1947] 289

BEETHOVEN UND SEINE ENGLISCHEN FREUNDE UND VERLEGER.   Hermann Ullmann.   (
   Beethoven's early fame in Britain is shown by Thomson's approach to him as early as 1803. His 'God Save the King'
   variations and 'Rule Britannia' variations, published in 1804, and the 'Wellington's Victory' of ten years later stemmed
   from his antipathy to Napoleon but enhanced his acceptance in England and might have led to a journey to that country.
   Ries went to London in 1813, and thereafter Beethoven corresponded with him, Robert Birchall, J. B. Cramer, Sir George
   Smart (who had performed 'Christus' as early as 1814), Cipriani Potter, and Neate.

   The Philharmonic Society secured the performing rights to the first four symphonies, and in 1815 commissioned several
   new works for a fee of 75 guineas, but received instead the overtures Opp. 113, 115, and 117. In November 1822 the
   Society paid Beethoven £50 for 18 months exclusive rights to the Ninth Symphony. Beethoven accepted the fee, but
   the first performance was in Vienna and the work was dedicated to the King of Prussia. The first performance in England of the Ninth Symphony was on 24 December 1832 (! !). In 1817 and again in 1824, plans for a visit to England
   by Beethoven were proposed by the Philharmonic Society. On his deathbed, Beethoven welcomed a loan of £100 from
   the Society, made at the instigation of Moscheles, Neate, and Stumpff.
                                        3 [1948] 43

BEETHOVENS OPERNPLÄNE.   Wilhelm Fischer.
   The many opera books that Beethoven considered are listed, and the characteristics of Leonore-Fidelio are discussed.
                                        3 [1948] 197

EIN LIED AUS BEETHOVENS FRÜHZEIT.   Adolf Erler.
   On a sketch sheet dating from early Vienna or Bonn is a preliminary setting of a little six line lyric by an unknown
   poet: 'Traute Henriette,' together with studies for the revision of certain passages. A transcription of the song is
   given in a Beilage.   4 [1949] 23

BEETHOVENS KONVERSATIONSHEFTE: EINIGE KORREKTUREN ZU SCHÜNEMANNS KOMMENTAR.
     Otto Erich Deutsch.
   28 corrections or amplifications are given to Schünemann's three volumes.
                                        4 [1949] 336

EIN NEUER BEETHOVEN-FUND.   (A)
    Discovery at the Peabody Museum in Baltimore of the autograph of the canon 'Da ist das Werk.'
4 [1949] 346

UNSTERN ÜBER BEETHOVENS FIDELIO.   Anton Bauer.   (B)
    The obstacles that preceded the opera as we know it included (1) the taking over of the Theater an der Wien in
February 1804 from Schikaneder by his enemy Baron Braun, which led to the suspension of Beethoven's work on the
opera for some months until Schikaneder and Braun patched up their difficulties; (2) the objection of the censor,
whom Sonnleithner persuaded to give his approval only with difficulty; (3) the occupation of Vienna by the French,
with the consequent departure of most of the music loving public; and (4) the almost uniformly unfavorable reviews
that the new opera received.   5 [1950] 130

GOETHES "FAUST" UND BEETHOVEN.   Max Unger.   (C)
    A general discussion of the relationship of Beethoven to Goethe and his writings.
5 [1950] 182

DIE "BAGATELLEN" OPUS 126 VON BEETHOVEN.   Erwin Ratz.   (D)
    A detailed analysis to show that in these works of Beethoven's last period there is the identity of form and content
that distinguished a true work of art.   6 [1951] 52

BEETHOVEN, WORT UND TON.   Wilhelm Waldstein.   (E)
    Although Beethoven's music is at its greatest when conveying dramatic emotions, the composer in general turned
away from writhing of music to words. The author contends that this was because Beethoven was unwilling to sub-
ordinate the flow of his musical thought to the limitations imposed by an assigned text.
7 [1952] 75

GEGENWARTSAUFGABE DER BEETHOVENWISSENSCHAFT.   Max Unger.   (F)
    The need is set forth for new or revised editions of various fundamental works of Beethoveniana.
7 [1952] 78

DIE ORIGINALFASSUNG DES STREICHQUARTETTES OPUS 130 VON BEETHOVEN.   Erwin Ratz.   (G)
    A plea that the B flat quartet always be performed with the closing fugue ("That Beethoven allowed himself to be
persuaded to write a new finale was an act of resignation"), a scrutiny of the six movements of this version to disclose the unity of the earlier movements with the fugue, and a pointing out that the new finale, written after Op.
135 and after the fatal shock of Nephew Karl's attempt at suicide, could not be a unified part of the quartet written more than a year earlier.   7 [1952] 81

DIE KLAVIERTRIO-FASSUNG DES SEPTETTS UND DER ZWEITE SYMPHONIE.   Wilhelm Fischer.   (H)
    At the end of the eighteenth century the Pf-Vln-Vcl trio occupied the same place in transcriptions for home use
that, thanks to Czerny's labors, the arrangements for piano four-hands did for most of the nineteenth century.
The problems of arranging a work of orchestral or quasi-orchestral scope for three instruments are discussed.
7 [1952] 88

ET HOMO FACTUS EST.   Romain Rolland.   (I)
    Excerpts from his book 'Beethovens Meisterjahre' (1930).   7 [1952] 92

STRAVINSKY ÜBER BEETHOVEN.   Igor Stravinsky.   (J)
    Stravinsky's reactions as he was in his maturity led to a restudy of Beethoven's piano music.
7 [1952] 156

BEETHOVEN-HANDSCHRIFTEN IN AMERIKA.   Artur Holde.   (K)
    The scope, especially as regards Beethoven items, of various large collections in the United States is indicated.
7 [1952] 301

DREI NEUE BEETHOVEN-BRIEFE.   Otto Deutsch.   (L)
    First publication of MM 165, MM 169, and MM 180.   8 [1953] 79

ZUM VORTRAG VON BEETHOVENS KLAVIER-SONATEN.   Friedrich Gulda.   (M)
    Discussion of matters of program composition, tempi, pedalling, and the like that must be weighed by the concert
artist.   8 [1953] 287

DIE OUVERTÜREN DES "FIDELIO. " Wilhelm Furtwängler.   (A)
  The performance of the great Leonora Overture after the dungeon scene has an artistic justification comparable to the
  summing up of Siegfried's life in the Funeral March.   9 [1954] 371

BEETHOVENS "FIDELIO" UND DIE ÖSTERREICHISCHEN MILITÄRSIGNALE. Leopold Nowak.   (B)
  Various trumpet signals of the Austrian army are given for comparison with the climactic trumpet call in Fidelio.
                                                               10 [1955] 373

VOM GESELLIGEN BEETHOVEN. Max Unger.   (C
  A conjectural reconstruction in much detail of the festive meal given by Hensler to his associates on 4 November
  1822 (see TK III 82; SchKH II 290).   12 [1957] 91

ZUM "GESELLIGEN BEETHOVEN. " Otto Deutsch.   (D
  Supplemental notes on the article by Unger. The restauranteur was Wolfgang Reischl (not Reichl). Frau Hensler
  had died in 1821. Hensler's daughter Josepha married Johann Siegmund von Scheidlin (not Scheidl) and after
  Hensler's death managed the theater until 1826.   12 [1957] 163

EINE WICHTIGE QUELLE ZU BEETHOVENS 4. KLAVIERKONZERT. Paul Badura Skoda.   (E
  A copy of the first and third movements of Op. 58, probably intended for the use of the engraver, with extensive
  corrections and changes in Beethoven's hand, is in the library of the GdMf. The added material is given.
                                                               13 [1958] 418

BEETHOVENS ABSCHRIFT EINER HÄNDEL-FUGE. Willy Hess.   (F
  Facsimile of a transcription for string quartet by Beethoven of the fugue from the overture to Handel's 'Solomon. '
                                                               14 [1959] 511

                                   OVERTONES

BOURDELLE'S "BEETHOVEN. "   (
  Photograph and brief description of the sculptured head by Emile Antoine Bourdelle (1861 - 1929).
                                                                1 [1930] 215

A NOTE ON BEETHOVEN'S SONATAS FOR PIANO AND VIOLIN. Boris Goldowsky.   (
  Brief popular commentary, chiefly on the Kreutzer Sonata Op. 47.
                                                                2 [1931] 134

                                   PHILOBIBLON

BEETHOVEN-ERSTDRUCKE BIS ZUM JAHRE 1800. Georg Kinsky.   (
  A scholarly discussion of the first editions of compositions by Beethoven which were published not later than 1800,
  with brief discussions of the publishers who during this period and later were most active in bringing out Beethoven's
  works.   3 [1930] 329

EIN UNBEKANNTES BILDNIS BEETHOVENS VON GUSTAVE DORÉ. Arthur Rümann.   (
  A caricature of Beethoven with a bear's body appeared among the illustrations which Doré made for a book for Saintine.
                                                                4 [1931] 141

EINE VERGESSENE GOETHE-KOMPOSITION BEETHOVENS. Otto Erich Deutsch.   (
  In addition to the generally known settings by Beethoven of Goethe's 'Das Göttliche' -- the one from his early twenties,
  the three-voice canon 'Edel sey der Mensch, heilfreich und gut!' (1821), and a six-voice canon on the same words for
  Louis Schlösser (May 6th 1823) -- Beethoven made a setting of these words (11 measures for voice and Pf) on January
  20th 1823 for the album of Baroness Marie von Eskeles.   5 [1932] 173

BEETHOVEN'S EARLIEST PUBLICATIONS.   Georg Kinsky.   (A)

7 [1934] 355

DIE HANDSCHRIFTEN VON BEETHOVENS EGMONT-MUSIK.   Georg Kinsky.   (B)
   Information is given as to the present location of sketches, autographs and holographic copies, and copies corrected
   by the composer.   7 [1934] Supp. to No. 3

DIE ERSTAUSGABE UND HANDSCHRIFTEN DER SYMPHONIEN BEETHOVENS.   Georg Kinsky.   (C)
   "At the beginning of the nineteenth century, engraved scores of orchestral works were virtually unknown." This
   article discusses in considerable detail Beethoven's relations with his various publishers as these facts bear upon the
   publication of the symphonies, and also discusses the known autographs and corrected scores, mentioning the fact
   that the manuscripts of the first three symphonies apparently disappeared during Beethoven's lifetime. The earliest
   recorded editions of the symphonies are as follows:

Symphony	Parts		Score	
No.	Date	Publisher	Date	Publisher
1	End of 1801	Hoffmeister & Co.	Spring 1822	Simrock
2	March 1804	Kunst & Ind Komp	Spring 1822	Simrock
3	October 1806	Kunst & Ind Komp	Middle or late 1822	Simrock
4	March 1808	Kunst & Ind Komp	1823	Simrock
5	April 1809	B & H	January 1826	B & H
6	April 1809	B & H	May 1826	B & H
7	Autumn 1816	Steiner	Autumn 1816	Steiner
8	December 1816	Steiner	December 1816	Steiner
9	June 1826	Schott	June 1826	Schott

9 [1936] 339

REVUE DE MUSICOLOGIE *

NE LETTRE INÉDITE DE BEETHOVEN (1825).   J. G. Prod'homme.   (D)
   French version of the paper which originally appeared in the 'Musical Quarterly' 3 [1917] 620. (See also 'Die Musik'
   16₁ [1923] 11)   1 [1919] 233

NE LETTRE INÉDITE DE BEETHOVEN À L'ÉDITEUR H. A. PROBST.   Charles Bouvet.   (E)
   Facsimile and French translation of a letter dated February 25th 1824 to H. A. Probst, offering songs (probably Opp.
   121b, 122 and 128), bagatelles (Op. 126), and the 'Dedication of the House' Overture Op. 124 for publication. This
   is presumably Beethoven's first letter to Probst, whose reply is not extant. (For the further course of this correspondence
   see TK III 178 and TD V 103.) (See also 'Die Musik' 16₁ [1923] 11)
                                                          3 [1922] 13

ETHOVEN ET LA COLLECTION ARTARIA.   Georges Saint-Foix.   (F)
   In effect, a condensation (without the analytical material) of the paper in 'Rivista musicale italiana' 30 [1923] 177.
                                                          8 [1927] 1

NE LETTRE INÉDITE DE BEETHOVEN À L'ÉDITEUR SCHOTT, DE MAYENCE.   J. G. Prod'homme.   (G)
   A letter without date (presumably from 1826 is given in facsimile, transcription and translation. It refers to Beethoven's humorous biography of Haslinger (see KS II 396) and refers to errors in an unnamed composition (presumably
   the Missa Solemnis). The author discusses the 'Paternostergässler.'
                                                          8 [1927] 6

ANUSCRITS DE BEETHOVEN.   Julien Tiersot.   (H)
   An annotated catalog of the Beethoven manuscripts in the Library of the Conservatoire in Paris.
                                                          8 [1927] 65

---

* First two volumes of this journal (1917-21) published under the title Bulletin de la Société Francaise de Musicologie.

UN LIED ET UNE SONATE DE BEETHOVEN: LE WACHTELSCHLAG ET LA SONATE OPUS 31 No. 3.   (A)
    J. G. Prod'homme.
    The author finds some kinship, thematically and rhythmically, between the sonata and the song (NV p. 179) which
    was written a few years earlier. Both may be looked upon as manifestations of the composer's intense love of nature
    which found its climactic manifestation in the Pastoral Symphony.
                                                    11 [1930] 36

DE QUELQUES DOCUMENTS BEETHOVENIENS. Jean Boyer.   (B)
    A list is given of a substantial number of Beethoven autographs and other documents in the library of the University
    of Tübingen and at Schloss Banz in Marburg.   34 [1952] 131

SUR LES RELATIONS DE BEETHOVEN AVEC CHERUBINI. Jean Boyer.   (C)
    Cherubini was brought to Vienna by Baron Braun of the Hoftheater, arriving on 27 July 1805 and staying until 9 March
    1806. He undoubtedly attended the premiere of Leonore on 20 November 1805 and met Beethoven. In early May
    1823 Beethoven gave to the violinist Louis Schlösser a letter of introduction to Cherubini, as a result of which Schlösser
    was admitted to the Conservatoire. A draft is known of a letter from Beethoven to Cherubini in November 1825 intro-
    ducing the flutist Sedlaczek (MM 433). A facsimile and a careful transcription are given of the draft of a letter to
    Cherubini dating from the first quarter of 1823 (Kal 881), including a memorandum to Schindler that Kalischer does
    not give. Facsimiles are also given of two proposed title pages for the Missa Solemnis, with corrections in Beethoven's
    hand. For comparison, a facsimile of the first edition title page is also given.
                                                    36 [1954] 134

                              REVUE INTERNATIONALE DE MUSIQUE

AUTOGRAPHIANA. Charles Malherbe.   (D
    Discussion of musical autographs in general, with mention of a considerable number of Beethoven autographs, and
    a facsimile of Beethoven's memory book page to Alexandre Jean Boucher.
                                    No. 1 [1898] 15; No. 15 [1898] 897

ADÉLAIDE DE MATTHISON, MUSIQUE DE BEETHOVEN. H. Kling.   (E
    An analysis of the poem and the music.   No. 11 [1898] 668

UNE VISITE À BEETHOVEN. Richard Wagner.   No. 17 [1898] 1025   (F

FIDELIO. F. de Ménil.   (G
    General and historical.   No. 19 [1899] 1171

DU MOUVEMENT DANS QUELQUES OEUVRES DE BEETHOVEN. Jean Louis de Casembroot.   (H
    The validity and applicability of Beethoven's tempo indications, by word or by metronome mark, is open to grave
    doubt.   No. 22 [1899] 1364

                              REVUE MUSICALE 1901-1912

LE VANDALISME MUSICAL: BEETHOVEN MIS AU POINT PAR CASTIL-BLAZE. Jean Chantavoine.   (I
    The opera published under the title: "Léonore, mélodrame en trois actes suivis d'un épilogue, d'après J. N. Bouilly,
    paroles de Castil-Blaze, musique de Beethoven" bears a vague resemblance to 'Fidelio' as far as the story goes, but
    the music is a pastiche of numbers from the opera (with many improvements over Beethoven) and from various of the
    Beethoven symphonies. Castil-Blaze was the nom de plume of Francois Henri, Joseph Blaze (1784-1857).
                                                    1 [1901] 463

LA JOIE DANS LA MUSIQUE DE BEETHOVEN. Albert Bazaillas.   (J
    The 'Ode to Joy' is the crowning work of a composer whose music throughout reflected the sublimation of joy.
                                                    2 [1902] 1

BEETHOVENIANA. Jean Chantavoine.   (A)
 A lengthy sketch is extant of a setting of Goethe's 'Rastlose Liebe,' apparently dating from 1792-96.
                                  2 [1902] 409

BEETHOVEN COMPOSITEUR POUR "BOÎTE À MUSIQUE." Jean Chantavoine   (B)
 The manuscript which contained the adagio for a mechanical instrument published by Kopfermann ('Die Musik'
 1_2 [1902] 1059; 1_3 [1902] 1193; H-70) also includes an allegro in G (H-72?) which is given herewith.
                                  3 [1903] 66

LA VE SYMPHONIE DE BEETHOVEN (ANALYSE RHYTHMIQUE). Jules Combarieu.   (C)
 Transcription of a university lecture.   6 [1906] 298

LES SONATES DE PIANO DE BEETHOVEN. Henri Quittard.   (D)
 Analyses after the style of a class in music appreciation. In the discussion of Op. 53, exhibits are given in musical
 type to show a resemblance between Beethoven's 'Andante Favori' (originally intended for this sonata) and a theme
 from a sonata by Rust.

     La Sonate Pathétique, La Sonate Pastorale, 12e Sonate (Op. 26).   (E)
                                  9 [1909] 396, 415, 453

     Sonate en "ut" majeur (Op. 53).   10 [1910] 326   (F)

PAER ET BEETHOVEN: À PROPOS DE LA MARCHE FUNÈBRE DE LA 12e SONATE. Henri Quittard.   (G)
 A study of the Funeral March from Paer's opera 'Achilles' (transcribed herewith) gives full substantiation to Ries's
 story (TK I 290) that Beethoven was spurred by this march to the writing of the march in the Pf Sonata Op. 26.
                                  9 [1909] 534

'ANALYSE RHYTHMIQUE DES SYMPHONIES DE BEETHOVEN' BY DORSAN VAN REYSSCHOOT. Jules Combarieu. (H)
 Preface to this book and analysis of the First Symphony, the principal attention being paid to the use of the terms
 of classical prosody (e. g. , the opening measures of the Minuet are made up of "tétrapodies trochaiques anapestiques").
                                  11 [1911] 161

'LÉONORE OU L'AMOUR CONJUGAL' BY BOUILLY AND GAVEAUX. J. G. Prod'homme.   (I)
 Reprint of article previously published in 'Sammelbände der Internationalen Musikgesellschaft' 7 [1906] 636.
                                  11 [1911] 257

L'IMMORTELLE BIENAIMÉE DE BEETHOVEN. J. G. Prod'homme.   (J)
 Discussion of the newly found letter of July 8th ('Die Musik' 10_4 [1911] 131) (later (Ibid. 11_2 [1912] 40) shown to be
 spurious). The author uses the letter as evidence that it and the well known threefold letter must have been written
 in 1801 to Giulietta Guicciardi.   11 [1911] 354

ENCORE L'IMMORTELLE BIENAIMÉE DE BEETHOVEN. J. G. Prod'homme.   (K)
 The letter in question is almost certainly a forgery.   11 [1911] 379

                          REVUE MUSICALE 1920-

SUR LA SENSIBILITÉ ET L'INTELLIGENCE BEETHOVÉNIENNES. André Coeuroy.   (L)
 The sensitiveness which found its outlet in a flood of compositions also manifested itself in Beethoven's relationship
 with his friends, with nature, with the divinity. His intelligence, deprived of early formal training but avid for
 sharing the great thoughts of literature, focussed itself completely on musical expression.
                                  2 No. 3 [1921] 1

LES DÉBUTS DE BEETHOVEN À PARIS. J. G. Prod'homme.   (M)
 The first acquaintance with Beethoven's music in Paris was probably brought about by Heinrich Simrock, brother of
 Nicholas the horn-player and publisher in Bonn. Heinrich lived in Paris from 1792 to his death in 1839 at the age of
 85 years. During his first ten years there he was active as a horn-player and teacher, and in 1803 established a
 branch of his brother's publishing business, importing editions of Beethoven's compositions from Germany and Austria.
 As late as 1817 Beethoven was known in Paris almost exclusively by his trios. Beethoven's first apostle in Paris was

LES DÉBUTS DE BEETHOVEN À PARIS (Continued)
Francois Antoine Habeneck, who in the first decade of the century performed his early quartets and his first two symphonies. In 1815 the first two movements of the Eroica were drowned out by laughter. As late as 1828 the only symphonies which had been heard were the first two and parts of the third and the seventh. The first complete performance of the Seventh Symphony was in April 1828 in an arrangement for Pf 8 hands (Liszt was one of the players). The first performance of the Eroica in its entirety was at the first concert of the Société du Conservatoire (March 9th 1828); by March 27th 1831 all nine had been heard. (See also 'Die Musik'19 [1927] 400)
2 No. 3 [1921] 13

L'ÉTERNELLE CONTROVERSE. André Coeuroy.   (A)
Summary of an exchange of letters appearing in 'Cäcilia' of 1828 (with editoral comment) in which the charge is made and rejected that Beethoven's last-period works might well have emanated from an insane asylum.
2 No. 3 [January 1st 1921] 93

DEUX VISITES À BEETHOVEN EN 1823 ET 1825. J. G. Prod'homme.   (B)
Translation of letters published in 'Harmonicon' 2 [1824] 10 and 3 [1825] 222.
2 No. 3 [January 1st 1921] 89

LES INSTRUMENTS DU TEMPS DE BEETHOVEN. J. G. Prod'homme.   (C
Comment on the three principal piano manufacturers of Beethoven's early Vienna days (Walter, Schanz, Streicher) and on the rudimentary state of wind instruments of that period.   2 No. 6 [April 1st 1921] 95

VUES SUR BEETHOVEN. André Suarès.   (D
Brief essays on many aspects of Beethoven's life, works and influence: his personal appearance; his indomitable nature; Beethoven and Romanticism; The Man and the Artist; The Symphony After Beethoven; The Last Works for the Pianoforte; "Beethoven never smiled"; Improvisation; Beethoven and Victor Hugo; Beethoven and Tonality; The Adagio of Op. 106; The Universality of Beethoven; Music and Literature; the Twilight of Classicism.
2 No. 8 [1921] 193; 3 No. 1 [1921] 1;
3 No. 5 [1922] 193; 4 No. 9 [1923] 193

UN MAÎTRE DE BERLIOZ: ANTON REICHA. Daniel Lazarus.   (E
As professor of counterpoint and fugue at the Conservatoire from 1817, Reicha was an instructor of Berlioz (in 1826) and of Franck (in 1835). Excerpts are given from his 'Cours de haute composition musicale,' a work of great novelty which undoubtedly had much effect on the young Berlioz. (See also 7 No. 1 [1925] 37)
3 No. 8 [1922] 255

UN AMOUR DE BEETHOVEN: ADELAIDE. Martial Douel.   (F
It seems probable that 'Adelaide' (Op. 46) was created under the influence of Beethoven's passion for Magdalena Willman, and that its influence extended over into other works: the first and third Pf concertos, the first and fourth Pf sonatas, the seventh Vln sonata, and even the seventh string quartet, the Vln concerto and the 'Ode to Joy' of the Ninth Symphony. (This paper, with a few omissions, appears in translation in 'Musical Quarterly'13 [1927] 208)
6 No. 9 [1925] 45

NOTES SUR ANTON REICHA. Lucien de Flagny.   (G
A biographical sketch of Reicha and copies of letters from distinguished contemporaries (Meyerbeer, Cherubini, and others) to indicate that during his lifetime Reicha stood in the forefront of living musicians. (See also 3 No. 5 [1922] 255)   7 No. 1 [1925] 37

ACTION DE GRÂCES A BEETHOVEN. Romain Rolland.   (H
Centenary address.   8 No. 6 [1927] 3

NOTRE BEETHOVEN. André Suarès.   (I
Centenary essay.   8 No. 6 [1927] 17

UNE NOUVELLE RÉVÉLATION DE LA JEUNESSE DE BEETHOVEN. Georges de Saint-Foix.   (J
A study of the two unpublished string quartets at the Berlin Library which, with four already discussed ('Rivista musicale italiana' 30 [1923] 177; 'Revue de musicologie' 8 [1927] 1) form a series of six from the Artaria Collection, until recently were attributed to Mozart (K. Anh 291a). The author is even more convinced than before that they are early works of Beethoven (1787-91). The form of each movement of the last two quartets is discussed, though with few quotations in musical notation.   8 No. 6 [1927] 28

LA FIN DE BEETHOVEN.   J. G. Prod'homme.   (A)
 A popular account of the master's last year, with particular respect to his fatal illness.
8 No. 6 [1927] 38

UN PROPAGATEUR DE BEETHOVEN: HECTOR BERLIOZ.   Adolphe Boschot.   (B)
 Berlioz's 'Notice biographique sur Beethoven' (1829), written with ardent enthusiasm but sound fact, created a forceful impression in a musical center where, even five years later, the principal musical library (the Conservatorie) did not so much as possess the scores of Beethoven's string quartets. The brilliance of Berlioz's critical articles of the next few years (collected in 1862 under the title 'A travers Chants') kept the wonders and powers of Beethoven constantly before the musical public. 8 No. 6 [1927] 60

LE CONCERTO DE VIOLON DE BEETHOVEN.   Marc Pincherle.   (C)
 Though now forgotten, Franz Clément (1780-1842), for whom the concerto was written, was a brilliant musician and executant in many fields. In the years following 1814 Baillot had made Paris familiar with the earlier chamber music of Beethoven. On March 23rd 1828 he gave the first performance in Paris of the violin concerto, and repeated it on May 11th 1828; thereafter it was not heard again there until 1847. The first performance in London was on April 9th 1832; the first performance in Vienna after its premiere on December 23rd 1806 was by Vieuxtemps (age 14) on March 16th 1834. The true position of the concerto in music was recognized only when on May 27th 1844 it was performed in London by Joachim (age 13) with Mendelssohn conducting. 8 No. 6 [1927] 77

BEETHOVEN ET VIGANO (LE BALLET DE PROMÉTHÉE).   André Levinson.   (D)
 Beethoven's interest in the dance (as shown by the composition of more than a hundred contredanses, minuets and other works in dance forms) brought him in contact with "the greatest choreographer of his day," Salvatore Vigano, in the composition of Die Geschöpfe des Prometheus, Op. 43. An attempt is made to outline the action of the ballet from the music and the incomplete notes which are available. The ballet received about thirty performances in 1802 and 1803; in a revival in 1813 a part of Beethoven's music was replaced by numbers from Haydn's 'Creation.' 8 No. 6 [1927] 87

LES PREMIERES EXÉCUTIONS D'OEUVRES DE BEETHOVEN À BRUXELLES.   Ch. Van den Borren.   (E)
 Beethoven's name first appeared in programs of concerts in Brussels on March 1st 1817, in the performance of an "Ouverture à grand orchestre," otherwise unidentified. The septet Op. 20 was performed on May 21st 1820, and on December 1st 1822 a "Symphonie de Beethoven" (probably No. 1, 2, or 4, and probably incomplete). Christus am Oelberge Op. 85 was performed on November 1st 1825, and thereafter the name of Beethoven became increasingly common in Brussels concert halls. 8 No. 6 [1927] 98

LES CAHIERS DE CONVERSATION DE BEETHOVEN.   Jean Chantavoine.   (F)
 The many problems involved in editing the conversation books and the fact that they represent only one side of a conversation render them of less value for specific details than as a means of recreating the atmosphere of Beethoven's circle when rapidly read in considerable volume. 8 No. 6 [1927] 105

NOTE SUR BEETHOVEN ET HOFFMANN.   André Coeuroy.   (G)
 It is surprising that not until 1820 (KS II 170) did Beethoven write to Hoffmann in recognition of the brilliant and enthusiastic criticisms which had appeared for several years after 1810.
8 No. 6 [1927] 110

LE DÉCLIN DE BEETHOVEN.   Lionel Landry.   (H)
 "It is the <u>death</u> of Beethoven of which we are observing the centenary."
8 No. 6 [1927] 114

LE "RETOUR À BEETHOVEN."   Charles Koechlin.   (I)
 It is to be wished that it might be possible to break through a century's accretion of tradition and truly "return to Beethoven." 8 No. 6 [1927] 125

LA LETTRE DE BEETHOVEN À L'IMMORTELLE AIMÉE.   Romain Rolland.   (J)
 The author stresses two deductions from the text of the letter: (1) "However ardent the man may be, it is evident that it is the woman who loved the more deeply"; and (2) "The writer of the letter was a man of mature years, marked not only by brilliant success as a concert virtuoso, but by a modesty which characterizes the consecrated master." Of the four years in which July 6th fell on a Monday, only 1812 checks with the historical and psychological facts as a possible year of writing. As for the identity of the Immortal Beloved, the most that can be done is to rule out various candidates. "Finally, Thérèse von Brunsvik remains as the most probable, but her chances are highly doubtful."

LA LETTRE DE BEETHOVEN À L'IMMORTELLE AIMÉE (Continued)
"To sum up, it is certain that the letter dates from July 1812, and that it marks, not the first explosion but rather the last outburst of that period of ten or twelve years (1801-12) from which flowed so incredible a torrent of passion and creation."   8 No. 11 [1927] 193

LES ASCENDANTS FLAMANDS DE BEETHOVEN.   Ch. Van den Borren.   (A)
The researches of André Pols show convincingly that the grandfather of the composer was not the son of Henri Adélard van Beethoven, the only family of that name in Antwerp. Van Aerde has just shown that the grandfather was the Ludwig van Beethoven who was in the choir of the cathedral of St. Rombaut in Malines.
                    8 No. 11 [1927] 210

UN BRUXELLOIS, AMI OUBLIÉ DE BEETHOVEN: VICTOR COREMANS.   Ernest Closson.   (B)
Extracts from the memoirs of Victor Amédée Jacques Marie Coremans (1802-72), who knew Beethoven during 1815-21.
                    9 No. 1 [1927] 22

LA JEUNESSE DE BEETHOVEN.   Edouard Herriot.   (C)
Draft of material later appearing in the author's 'La Vie de Beethoven' [1929] 53-75.
                    9 No. [?] [1928] 193

LÉONORE.   Romain Rolland.   (D)
Chapter IV from the book 'From the Eroica to the Appassionata.'   9 No. 9 [1928] 225

LES SOEURS BRUNSVIK ET LEUR COUSINE DU "CLAIR DE LUNE."   Romain Rolland.   (E)
Appendix III from the book 'From the Eroica to the Appassionata.'
                    9 No. 11 [1928] 417

SOUVENIRS DE FAMILLE SUR BEETHOVEN.   Magda von Hattingberg.   (F)
Account books of the great-grandfather of the author, Wilhelm von Böcking, councillor and physician in ordinary to the Emperor Francis I, show that Beethoven had been engaged as teacher for his wife Christine. The monthly payment was 9 fl. plus 4 kröner carfare. An anecdote regarding young Gustav Adolf Schuster of Heiligenstadt is given, and an account of a visit to Beethoven's lodgings the day after his death. The author says that in a hospital in Vienna in 1916 her father spoke with the last remaining Beethoven, a descendant of nephew Karl who had been an unknown journalist in Paris before he was recalled to Austria for his military service, and whose death and burial a few weeks later went quite unnoticed.   10 No. 4 [1929] 93

LES COMPOSITIONS INCONNUES DE XAVIER FRANCOIS KLEINHEINZ.   Émile Haraszti.   (G
Biographical sketch of F. X. Kleinheinz, an acquaintance of Beethoven (born 1772, died 1832), and discussion of his compositions.   11 No. 102 [1930] 229

LE XVe QUATUOR DE BEETHOVEN.   Yves Lacroix-Navaro.   (H
Beethoven's medical history is given in detail as a basis for explaining the Dankegesang, and the music of the quartet is discussed movement by movement.   15 No. 143 [1934] 104,197

AMICUS BEETHOVEN SED MAGIS AMICA MUSICA.   André Saurès.   (I
"The man who always wished to go from heart to heart instead reached only the intellect."
                    16 No. 160 [1935] 266

QUELQUES ERREURS DANS DES PARTITIONS CÉLÈBRES CORIGÉES PAR TOSCANINI.   Vincenzo Tommasini.   (J
Corrections of passages in the Seventh and Ninth Symphonies, the Leonore No. 3 Overture, Tristan and Meistersinger.
                    17 No. 162 [1936] 1

VUES SUR BEETHOVEN.   Emmanuel Buenzod.   (K
Chapter IV from the book 'Pouvoirs de Beethoven.'   17 No. 162 [1936] 7

SUR BEETHOVEN, SCHUBERT, WEBER.   Raymond Petit.   (L
Impressions.   17 No. 164 [1936] 171

LA BEAUTÉ CONTRE LA IXe SYMPHONIE.   André Suarès.   (M
"Beethoven was deaf, and he forces us never to forget it."   17 No. 169 [1936] 336

BEETHOVEN ET L'ORGUE.   Cecil Austin.   (A)
    Beethoven's contact with the organ was almost exclusively during his youth at Bonn. It is suggested that his practice
of playing the organ developed a legato style of piano playing that at that time was most unusual. (A translation of
this paper, slightly condensed, appeared in 'Musical Times' 80 [1939] 525.
18 No. 174 [1937] 233

RICHARD WAGNER AND BEETHOVEN.   Jean Louis Cremiéux.   (B)
    Quotations from Wagner's writings as indicating the influence which Beethoven had on him.
18 No. 174 [1937] 240

BEETHOVEN -- LE CHANT DE LA RÉSURRECTION.   Romain Rolland.   (C)
    Extract from the book of the same title.   18 No. 179 [1937] 377

MÉDITATION SUR LE MASQUE DE BEETHOVEN.   Alain de Vrécourt.   (D)
19 No. 186 [1938] 95

LE LORIOT (?) DE LA SYMPHONIE PASTORALE.   Ernest Closson.   (E)
    The author postulates that in Schindler's story ('Beethoven-Biographie' (ed. Kalischer, 1909) p. 198) that the arpeggio
passages in the 'Scene am Bach' (mm. 58ff) were an idealization of the song of the gold-hammer (Ger.: Goldammer),
the name of the bird was misunderstood or remembered incorrectly by Schindler, since the song of the gold-hammer
has not the least resemblance to this arpeggio, and that the bird which Beethoven actually named was the blackbird
(Ger.: Amsel). (See also 'Musical Times' 33 [December 15th 1892] 14)
19 No. 186 [1938] 95

MOZART AND BEETHOVEN.   Jacques Duron.   (F)
    General.   No. 231 [1956] 163

REVUE PLEYEL

LE CENTENAIRE DE LA 9e SYMPHONIE.   Walter Damrosch.   (G)
    Centenary tribute.   No.   1 [October 1923] 11

LES DERNIERS MOMENTS DE BEETHOVEN.   (H)
    French translations of Beethoven's letter of March 18th 1827 to Moscheles (KS II 472); letters of March 24th and
April 4th 1827 from Schindler to Moscheles; letter of March 28th 1827 from F. B. Streicher to A. M. Stumpff.
No.   5 [February 1924] 5

BEETHOVEN ET LA FRANCE.   Jean Chantavoine.   (I)
    The influence of France and of French ideas (especially of Napoleon) on Beethoven is discussed, and the gradual
spread of Beethoven's music through France is summarized.   No.   8 [May 1924] 5;
No.   9 [June 1924] 5

SUR LA MORT DE BEETHOVEN.   (J)
    French translation of the two letters from Schindler to Moscheles (see No. 5 supra).
No. 42 [March 1927] 180

L'HÉRÉDITÉ FLAMANDE DE BEETHOVEN.   Ernest Closson.   (K)
    Summary of the article by Pols ('De Gulden Passer' 9 [1927] 51) showing that Grandfather Ludwig could not have been
the son of Henry Adelard, and of the discoveries of van Aerde proving that Ludwig was the son of Muchael.
No. 48 [September 1927] 376

RHEINISCHE MUSIK- UND THEATER-ZEITUNG *

ALS BEETHOVEN EIGENE WIRTSCHAFT FÜHRTE.   Wolfgang A. Thomas-San Galli.   (L)
    Beethoven's domestic problems as referred to in letters to Nannette Streicher and to Zmeskall.
12 [1911] 83

---

* Journal merged with Deutsche Musiker Zeitung after 1930.

BEETHOVENS WETTKÄMPFE MIT DEM KLAVIERSPIELER WÖLFL.   Theodor von Frimmel.   (A)
   Study of those of Wölfl's compositions that are still extant indicates that Wölfl was very much a follower of Mozart.
                                                           12 [1911] 87

ERRINERUNGEN AN BEETHOVEN -- 1844-45.   Grillparzer.   (B)
   Quotations from unidentified writings of the poet.   13 [1912] 508,524

DIE PERSÖNLICHEN BEZIEHUNGEN ZWISCHEN BEETHOVEN UND SCHUBERT.   W. A. Thomas-San Galli.   (C)
   The common interests and activities of the two composers and their large number of mutual friends make it almost
   certain that they were personally acquainted.   14 [1913] 264,288

PRINZ LOUIS FERDINAND.   (D)
   Excerpts from a biography by E. Wintzer, including discussion of his relations with Beethoven.
                                                           17 [1916] 96

DIE LEONOREN-OUVERTÜREN UND DAS THEATER.   Eugen Kilian.   (E)
   Performances of the opera should be introduced by the Fidelio overture or occasionally by the Leonora No. 1. The
   "Great" Leonara Overture should be reserved for the concert hall.   20 [1919] 419

BEETHOVEN UND DAS SCHUPPANZIGH-QUARTETT.   G. Kinsky.   (F)
   "Schuppanzigh was no inspired virtuoso, no heaven storming bearer of immortal fire, but was without question an excellent Konzertmeister and above all a masterful chamber music player. He was rightly looked upon as the foremost
   quartet player of his time." Beethoven probably met Schuppanzigh (b. 1776) and his associates Sina, Weiss and N.
   Kraft, as well as Zmeskall, in the mid-1790's at the palace of Prince Lichnowsky. Schuppanzigh conducted the
   Augarten concerts from about 1795 to about 1805, and began public performance of quartet music in the winter of
   1804-05. In 1808 he, with Sina, Weiss and Linke, formed a quartet for Prince Rasumovsky, and remained in the
   Prince's service until the castle burned on 31 December 1814. From the spring of 1816 until 1823, Schuppanzigh
   was on a virtuoso tour through North Germany, Poland and Russia. The 'Falstafferel' canon (Kal 903) was Beethoven's
   greeting when Schuppanzigh returned to Vienna in April 1823. The quartet appearences were resumed on 14 June
   1823 with Holz (instead of Sina), Weiss and Linke. In 1828 Schuppanzigh became Director of the Court Opera. He
   died on 2 March 1830.   21 [1920] 235

VON BEETHOVENS HANDSCHRIFT UND MANUSKRIPTEN.   G. Kinsky.   (G)
   The locations (as of the date of the article) of many Beethoven autographs are given.
                                                           21 [1920] 238

ZUR EGMONT MUSIK -- EIN VADEMECUM FÜR DAS THEATER. Eugen Kilian.   (H)
   Beethoven's music can be used with its full effect only with the original Goethe version of the drama, not with
   Schiller's revision. The music of the entr'actes must start immediately upon the fall of the curtain and continue
   into the resumption of the stage action. In practice there must be at least one break in the evening's performance,
   and this can come best by using the E flat larghetto as introduction to the third act rather than as a bridge, though
   even this interruption weakens the effect of the musico-poetic unity.
                                                           21 [1920] 428

EINE BEETHOVEN-PHANTASIE. Wolfgang A. Thomas-San Galli.   (I)
   Random thoughts inspired by Op. 77.   22 [1921] 274,286

ZUR NEUESTEN BEETHOVENLITERATUR.   Adolf Sandberger.   (J)
   Reprint from NBJ 5 [1925].   27 [1926] 142,242,275

ZUR ERFASSUNG DER BEETHOVENLITERATUR.   Nelsbach.   (K)
   A real need exists for a complete catalog of the Beethoven literature.
                                                           28 [1927] 24

BEETHOVENS LEIDEN UND STERBEN.   Max Grünewald.   (L)
   Résumé of familiar facts.   28 [1927] 96

BEETHOVEN AND THE HAMMERCLAVIER.   Georg Kinsky.   (A)
    The development of the piano and of Beethoven's use of it and demands upon it are summarized. The first edition
    of Op. 106 appeared in 1819 with the title page in French: "Grande Sonate pour le Piano-Forte . . ." and only in
    1823 did a reprint appear with a German title page: "Grosse Sonate für das Hammer-Klavier . . ."
28 [1927] 97

BEETHOVEN ALS BRIEFDICHTER.   Richard Elchinger.   (B)
    Comment on the various literary styles appearing in Beethoven's correspondence, from the letter to the Immortal
    Beloved through the Zmeskall correspondence to the letter to Wolanek.
28 [1927] 285

RHEINISCHE MUSIK-ZEITUNG FÜR KUNST-FREUNDE UND KÜNSTLER

DEUTSCHE TEXT DER MESSE.   (C)
    The German text used by Rochlitz in a version ('Three Hymns') of the first three movements of the C major Mass
    Op. 86 is completely unsuited to the music. A translation of the Latin of the mass is given which conforms to the
    spirit of the ceremonial as well as to the metrical demands of the musical setting.
1 [1850] 169

ZWEITE SINFONIE VON L. VAN BEETHOVEN.   (D)
    Poem.   1 [1850] 189

BEMERKUNGEN ÜBER DEN VORTRAG BEETHOVENSCHER SINFONIEN.   (E)
    Intensive study of Beethoven's dynamics, with examples drawn from the symphonies and the two masses.
1 [1851] 217,233,257,265

A FRENCH TRANSLATION OF THE 'ODE TO JOY.'   (F)
    A translation of Schiller's text in a French edition of the score is most unsatisfactory.
1 [1851] 315

TONKUNST FÜR ALLE.   (G)
    A discussion of Beethoven's practices in rhythm, harmony, melody, and the building up of climaxes, either dynamic
    or emotional.   1 [1851] 329,337,353

. VAN BEETHOVENS WERKE.   (H)
    Review of the first edition of Breitkopf & Härtel's 'Thematisches Verzeichnis.' The reviewer indicates that this work
    for the first time assigned the opus numbers now accepted for Opp. 81a, 81b, 121a, 129 and 136. He deplores the lack
    of any attempt to indicate dates of composition (pointing out that the opus numbers are most deceptive in this respect),
    and gives a preliminary tabulation of this kind. He notes that the melody of the second part ('Gegenliebe') of the song
    'Seufzen eines Ungeliebte' (GA 23/253) is identical with the theme of the principal section of the Choral Fantasia
    Op. 80.   2 [1851] 521,529

BEETHOVENS STUDIEN,' EIN ERWIESEN UNTERGESCHOBENES WERK.   F. Derckum.   (I)
    The book of this title by Seyfried is found to be made up in considerable measure of passages from accepted text books
    by Fux, Albrechtsberger and other 18th century pedagogues. (Since Seyfried in 1826 edited Albrechtsberger's 'Sämt-
    liche Schriften,' in which many of the examples appear, it is difficult to understand how he could have included them
    in 'Beethovens Studien' as original work.) Schindler (pp. 559, 583) states that Beethoven made no claim that the
    sheets of exercises from which the book was compiled were his own work, but rather that they were exercises which
    Albrechtsberger had worked out for his pupils.   2 [1851] 572

BEETHOVENS MUSIK ZU DEN RUINEN VON ATHEN.   (J)
    The history of this work, and the content of the Festspiel by Kotzebue and of the music, are given in some detail.
2 [1851] 661

DIE ZWEI UNBERECHTIGEN TAKTE IM SCHERZO DER V. SINFONIE VON BEETHOVEN, NEBST EINIGEN ANDERN   (K)
       RHYTHMISCHEN BEDENKEN.
    The two extra measures appearing in the scherzo of the Fifth Symphony (see Kal 222) are still generally used in per-
    formance, but the autograph shows that these measures were the prima volte of a repetition of scherzo and trio before

DIE ZWEI UNBERECHTIGEN TAKTE IM SCHERZO DER V. SINFONIE, etc. , (Continued)
the coda (as in the Fourth and Seventh Symphonies) which through oversight were not stricken out when the repetition
was abandoned. The rhythm of the bridge to the finale, in which there seems to be one measure too many, can be
clarified by accenting the eighth measure from the end (entry of the eighth notes in the basses). The open measure
at m. 389 of the first movement appears in the autograph, but on no one of the systems in this measure is a rest written.
2 [1852] 777

COMMENTS ON KAL 663.   A. Schindler.   3 [1853] 1051   (A

SUGGESTIONS REGARDING THE PERFORMING OF THE FOURTH SYMPHONY.   L. Bischoff.   (B
3 [1853] 1077

RIVISTA MUSICALE ITALIANA

L'INTERPRÉTATION ARTISTIQUE DE L'ORAGE.   Maurice Griveau.   (C
Chiefly a detailed description of the fourth movement of the Pastoral Symphony.
3 [1896] 684

RITRATTI E CARICATURI DI BEETHOVEN.   Theodor von Frimmel.   (L
Beethoven's personal appearance as described by contemporaries and delineated by painters and sketchers.
4 [1897] 17

UN RIVAL DE BEETHOVEN: JOSEPH WOELFL.   R. Duval-Den'lex.   (F
Biographical sketch.   5 [1898] 490

IL FINALE DELL' "EROICA."   Dino Sincero.   (F
Popular analysis.   7 [1900] 493

LA SONATA A KREUTZER.   Dino Sincero.   ((
Popular analysis of the first movement.   8 [1901] 603

GRILLPARZER AND BEETHOVEN.   H. Kling.   ((
Translation (into French) of those parts of Grillparzer's 'Memoirs' which deal with Beethoven. An introduction points
out that the poet was musically no more than a dilettante, but that he had a broad acquaintance among musicians.
10 [1903] 485

UN QUADERNO DI AUTOGRAFI DI BEETHOVEN DEL 1825.   Cecilio de Roda.   ((
A very detailed study (in 1907 issued as a pamphlet of 112 pages under the same title) of a sketch book which
apparently was used for the principal working out of the last three movements of Op. 132 and for all of Opp. 130 and
133. In addition, there are a considerable number of thematic fragments which never appeared in a completed work,
and various verbal notes, including what is apparently a draft of a letter to Diabelli (KK 1115) regarding the French
edition of the Piano Sonata Op. 111 and the Variations Op. 120. (NOTE by DWM. A sketch book presumably used at
the same time as this one is described at great length by M. Iwanow-Boretzky in 'Musikalische Bildung' (Moscow) 1927
and summarized in 'Melos' ('Neues Musikblatt') 7 [1928] 407)   12 [1905] 63,592,734

BEETHOVEN AND BARON DE TRÉMONT.   H. Kling.   (
An excerpt from the 'Memoirs' of the Baron dealing with Beethoven, with brief comments.
15 [1908] 275

BEETHOVEN ET SES RELATIONS AVEC LE COMPOSITEUR ET ÉDITEUR DE MUSIQUE SUISSE: HANS GEORGES NAEGELI,   (
DE ZÜRICH.   H. Kling.
Nägeli's publishing house was founded in 1791; in June of that year the first issue of 'Répertoire des Clavecinists'
appeared. Some of Beethoven's variations were reprinted in the 'Répertoire' in 1794-95, and in 1803 and 1804
the three piano sonatas Op. 31 appeared in the same publication. Correspondence from 1824 and 1825 is given regarding the publication by Nägeli of a volume of his own poems (see KS II 327, 331, 342) which appeared in 1825;
a volume of critical essays for amateurs ('Vorlesung über Musik') was published in 1826 with dedication to the Archduke Rudolph.   19 [1912] 566

LE IMPERFEZIONI D'UN' OPERA DI BEETHOVEN (IL CORO FINALE DELLA IX SINFONIA).   Andrea Della Corte.   (A)
   The choral finale of the Ninth Symphony is an adaptation of words to music by which both the music and the words
   suffer.   26 [1919] 545

MOZART ET LE JEUNE BEETHOVEN.   Georges de Saint-Foix.   (B)
   The influence of Mozart shows itself first and very markedly in the resemblance of the first of the piano quartets
   (1785) to the violin sonata K. 379; compositions prior to these quartets are quite free from Mozartian characteristics.
   The resemblance continues in the trio for flute, bassoon and piano GA 25/294, in the various concerted pieces for
   wind instruments of the Bonn period -- Opp. 103, 81b, 71 and the rondino -- and in the early works for strings --
   Opp. 3, 4, 8, 9. (Also in 'Musical Quarterly' 6 [1920] 276) The author strongly suspects that the variations for piano
   on 'Venni amore' as we now know them are in revision dating from about 1801 of the first version published in 1791
   (by Goetz and reissued in 1794 by Schott -- see 'Philobiblon' 3 [1930] 332) and now lost. The posthumous trio in E
   flat (NV p. 143) is attributed by Schindler to Beethoven's fifteenth year, but the independence of the form and the
   maturity of the style indicates that Thayer's postulation of 1791 as its date of composition (TK I 137) is much closer
   to the truth.

   The concerto movement in D major GA 25/311 is "one of the most complete and most perfect imitations of the style
   and spirit of Mozart which Beethoven ever made." (Note, however, that in 'Neues Beethoven-Jahrbuch' 2 [1925] 167
   this work was proved to be a composition of J. Rösler and not of Beethoven.) Faithful following of the example of
   Mozart is found in Opp. 16, 44, 87, 'Se vuol ballare' variations for piano and violin, 'La ci darem' variations for two
   oboes and English horn, and in various variations for piano. Certain manuscripts in the British Museum, attributed to
   Mozart, are undoubtedly by Beethoven. These include the trio in D major Anh. 52a, the rondo in B flat for piano K.
   511a, three pieces for piano four hands Anh. 41a, and a minuet in C major for orchestra Anh. 25a. (Note that all
   but the last of these were published in 1926 as 'Oeuvres inédites de Beethoven,' edited by Saint Foix.) These works
   are discussed in detail, with facsimiles of the manuscripts. (But see 'Music & Letters' 26 [1945] 47; 27 [1946] 24)
                                                    27 [1920] 85

NOUVELLE CONTRIBUTION À L'ÉTUDE DES OEUVRES INCONNUES DE LA JEUNESSE DE BEETHOVEN.   (C)
      Georges de Saint-Foix.
   The author contends that four quartets in the manuscript collection of the British Museum and two in the Imperial
   Library in Berlin, hitherto attributed to Mozart (Anh. 291a), are actually an early venture by Beethoven in the field
   of the string quartet. The possibility that they were written by Pleyel is discussed and rejected. The first four of
   these quartets -- in E flat, F minor, C major and G major -- are discussed in detail, with thematic excerpts, and
   brief mention is made of the last two -- in D major and B flat. The reasons for attributing these works to Beethoven
   (postulated period of composition 1786-91) are given in extenso.   30 [1923] 177

BEETHOVEN E LE SUE CINQUE SONATE PER VIOLONCELLO.   Eugenio Albini.   (D)
   A popular analytical discussion.   30 [1923] 203

UNE VISITE AU BEETHOVENHAUS À BONN.   E. Adraiewsky.   (E)
   Popular. A facsimile is given of Verdi's letter of acceptance of honorary membership in the Society of the
   Beethovenhaus.   31 [1924] 581

QUADERNI DI CONVERSAZIONE DI BEETHOVEN.   A. Albertini.   (F)
   A general discussion in connection with the publication of Nohl's transcription.
                                                    33 [1926] 28

MAESTRI, ALLIEVI E CRITICI DI BEETHOVEN.   Edoardo Roggeri.   (G)
   A popular discussion and in some cases a picture is given of each of Beethoven's teachers -- his father, Tobias
   Pfeiffer, Franz Ries, Rovantini, Brother Willibald, Neefe, Mozart, Haydn, Albrechtsberger, and Salieri -- and of his
   most important pupils -- the Archduke Rudolph, Carl Czerny, Ferdinand Ries. Mention is also made of others in his
   circle of friends and acquaintances -- Kreutzer, Weber, Schindler, Liszt, Schubert. A few of the most frequently
   quoted criticisms of his works are given.   34 [1927] 210

BEETHOVEN.   Ermino Tocilj.   (H)
   An extended discussion of Beethoven's artistic evolution, with special regard to the revolutionary spirit of his time.
                                                    36 [1929] 478

LE RETOUR "IMPREVU."   Maurice Griveau.   (A)
   A detailed analysis of the sonata in E flat Op. 31 No. 3. Fanciful names are given to each of the motival fragments,
   and much emphasis is laid on the contour of the melodic line.   37 [1930] 572; 38 [1931] 37,226

IL FINALE DELL' "EROICA" E LE SUE INTERPRETAZIONI.   Feri de Pauer Peretti.   (B)
   This is a continuation of the study inaugurated by the author in 'Zeitschrift für Musik' JG 92 [1925] 276 and continued
   in 'Neue Musik Zeitung' 48 [1927] 393. After quoting the comments of other authors, the movement is analyzed and
   commented upon section by section. The sixth variation (mm. 211ff) is referred to as the first instance in Beethoven
   of the influence of Hungarian folk music, which was introduced into symphonic music by Haydn and which also appeared in Beethoven's Sixth and Seventh Symphonies and his Overture to King Stephan Op. 117.
                                                           39 [1932] 531

L'ARCHER DIVIN.   Maurice Griveau.   (C)
   A detailed and fanciful analysis of the first movement of the sonata in G major Op. 31 No. 1, the author having in
   mind the statue of Hercules the Archer.   42 [1938] 636

LA RIVOLUZIONE FRANCESE NEL "FIDELIO."   Jean Boyer.   (D)
   A few phrases in Fidelio have obvious similarity to phrases from the Marseillaise.
                                                           44 [1940] 243

'DON GIOVANNI' AND 'FIDELIO.'   Antonio Capri.   (E)
   An account of the composition and early history of each opera.   47 [1943] 188

SI FA O NON SI FA LA CADENZA NEI CONCERTI DI BEETHOVEN.   Ludwig Misch.   (F)
   Excerpt from 'Beethoven Studies' [1953] 171.   54 [1952] 152

UN ORATORIO DI BEETHOVEN PER L'AMERICA.   P. Nettl.   (G
   Condensed from 'Musica' 6 [1952] 297.   54 [1952] 348

PROLEGOMENI A BEETHOVEN.   Luigi Magnani.   (H
   General.   57 [1955] 3

ROYAL MUSICAL ASSOCIATION PROCEEDINGS

THE MANNERISMS OF BEETHOVEN. J. S. Shedlock.   (I
   Many examples are given of Beethoven's marked fondness for certain procedures: The type of diminution known as
   "ribattuta" (as in the Song of the Nightingale in the Pastoral Symphony); the use of a fragment of a theme subject
   to make it the germ of a new thought: "separating where there was no joint; dividing where there was no natural
   division"; the use of motival units in several movements of a work (e.g., the falling fourth at the beginning of the
   chief subjects of each of the first three movements of the Ninth Symphony); repetition almost an insanitum of notes
   or figures (e.g., trio of the scherzo of Op. 135); use of the chord and of the key of the minor second (e.g., opening
   of Op. 95); simultaneous use of tonic and dominant harmony; "hammer strokes" followed by a pause; completely individual use of pedal points. (See also 23 [1897] 67)   12 [1886] 43

THE RONDO FORM AS IT IS FOUND IN THE WORKS OF MOZART AND BEETHOVEN.   C. F. Abdy Williams.   (J
   The various component parts of the rondo are discussed in detail, with examples of varying procedure from the works
   of Mozart and Beethoven.   17 [1891] 95

A FEW WORDS ON THE SUCCESSIVE EDITIONS OF BEETHOVEN'S NINTH SYMPHONY.   George Grove.   (K
   Variations are pointed out between the first edition of this symphony and later editions.
                                                           21 [1895] 65

THE TRIUNE ELEMENT IN BEETHOVEN AS SPECIALLY EXEMPLIFIED IN THE PIANOFORTE SONATAS.   (
      George Langley.
   Beethoven makes far more frequent use than other composers studied of the threefold repetition of an idea, and the
   manner in which he uses this repetition is quite distinctive.   23 [1897] 67

SOME ASPECTS OF BEETHOVEN'S INSTRUMENTAL FORMS. Gustav Ernest.   (A)
  A general discussion of the use and development which Beethoven made of the various important forms, and a study
  of the application to his sonata-allegro movements of Zeising's Law: "If the division of an object into two unequal
  parts is to appear well proportioned, the smaller must stand in the same proportion to the larger as the latter to the
  whole" (e.g., the most pleasing division of 130 is 50 + 80, since 50/80 = 80/130). Using the measure as a unit,
  42 out of 55 sonata-allegro movements in the trios and the Pf, the Vln, and the Vcl sonatas conform to this law within 2 percent; of the other 13 movements, 11 conform to some other simple law of symmetry.
                                           29 [1903] 73

LUDWIG VAN BEETHOVEN. Alexander Brent-Smith.   (B)
  Centenary address: an attempt "to reconstruct his position in 1827; to explain his position in 1927; and to forecast his
  probable position in 2027."   53 [1927] 85

                    S.I.M.; REVUE MUSICALE

LETTRES DE BEETHOVEN À LA FAMILLE BRENTANO. J. G. Prod'homme.   (C)
  French translation of about a dozen letters.   1 [1905] 514

UNE VISITE À BEETHOVEN. Jean Chantavoine.   (D)
  Excerpt from the memoirs of Baron de Trémont. 2_1 [1906] 393

JEAN SÉBASTIEN BACH ET BEETHOVEN. E. Marchand.   (E)
  An attempt to show that Beethoven was prone to use motival formulas which are also found in Bach.
                                           2_1 [1906] 537; 2_2 [1906] 64

GIOVANNI PUNTO. H. Kling.   (F)
  Biographical article on the horn virtuoso for whom Beethoven wrote Op. 17. The author questions Ries' statement
  (TK I 267) that Beethoven played only from sketches at the time of the first performance of the sonata.
                                           4 [1908] 1066

QUELQUES NOTES DE BIBLIOGRAPHIE BEETHOVÉNIENNE. Jean Chantavoine.   (G)
  An extensive and stimulating review of the collections of letters by Prelinger and by Kalischer, the fifth volume of
  TDR, and other recent publications. Two letters (presumably hitherto unpublished) are given: Draft of a letter (not
  later than May 1824) written in French to Duport, appearing in a conversation book and referred to in TD V 81:
  "J'apprend votre amitié en m'accordant . . ." Letter (assigned to 1809) in French to Baron de Trémont: "Côme il
  me falloit aujourd'hui aller . . ."   5 [1909] 559

UN THÈME DE HAENDEL DANS LA NEUVIÈME SYMPHONIE DE BEETHOVEN. Julien Tiersot.   (H)
  The subject of a passacaglia in an organ concerto by Handel ('Handelgesellschaft' XXVIII p. 129) is almost identical
  with the passage: "Seid umschlungen" in the Ninth Symphony.
                                           6 [1910] 359

CHAMBER MUSIC IN FRANCE. Paul Landormy.   (I)
  Excerpts are given from a review of a concert in February 1849. Op. 59 No. 2: "Merely a work of erudition"; Op. 132
  (or perhaps Op. 127): "This quartet is one of the last works of Beethoven, when he was deaf, somewhat brutal, mis-
  anthropic, and taking refuge in a vague religious mysticism. His thoughts are vague, and lose themselves in endless
  development."   [?] [August-September 1911] 42

DE L'EXÉCUTION DES OEUVRES DE BEETHOVEN. Roger Cousinet.   (J)
  A plea for greater rhythmic freedom. 7_2 No. 8-9 [August-September 1911] 86

UNE OEUVRE INCONNUE DE BEETHOVEN POUR MANDOLINE ET PIANO. Arthur Chitz.   (K)
  In the library of Count Clam-Gallas in Prague the author found five autographs of works for Mandoline and Clavier:
  the two appearing in GA 25/295, 296 (the autograph of the latter, bearing the dedication: "Pour la belle J. (Josephine,
  Countess Clary) par L. V. B." showing that the version in the GA was from a preliminary and fragmentary manuscript),
  and three unknown compositions, the score of one of which, a sonatine in C major, is given herewith. No further
  mention is made of the other two new works. The history of Beethoven's sojourn in Prague in 1796 is briefly recounted.
                                           8_2 No. 12 [December 1912] 24

LES MANUSCRIPTS DE LA BIBLIOTHÈQUE DE BERLIN.   C. Saint Saens.   (A)
    Remarks on details of notation observed in a study of the score of the Ninth Symphony, and two corrections in the
accepted version of the piano concerto in E flat Op. 73. 9_2 No. 11 [November 1913] 2

SACKBUT

NOTES ON RICHARD STRAUSS AND BEETHOVEN.   Arthur Symons.   (B)
    A brief paragraph of aesthetic comment on each symphony and on some of the chamber works.
                                       1 [1921] 397

THE INFLUENCE OF MUSIC ON CHARACTER AND MORALS: III. BEETHOVEN, SYMPATHY AND PSYCHO-ANALYSIS.   (C)
    Cyril Scott.
    Material later published in 'The influence of music on character and morals' 1928, pp. 30 - 41.   (NOTE by DWM.
The author is almost certainly wrong in saying that the composer's elder sibling Ludwig Maria was a female child,
and in his correction of Beethoven to the effect that this child was born three years (not two) before the composer.
The dates are respectively April 2nd 1769 and December 17th (?) 1770, 'Beethoven und die Gegenwart' [1936] 136)
                                      5 [1924] 131

SOME NOTES ON FIDELIO.   W. G. Whittaker.   (D)
    The staging, lighting and costuming of this opera can be very bad, but offer a fruitful challenge to the director who
is not bound by convention.   The dramatic possibilities in the story, which the actual libretto misses in large measure,
are discussed.   The author believes that Beethoven approached the writing of this opera "with uneasiness and hesitation,"
but "by sheer force of genius and tremendous power arrived at his results by his own methods, methods not common to
opera."   "A second opera would probably have been as great an advance as was the mass in D upon that in C."   Consideration is invited, "which may seem sacrilege," to eliminating the last scene of the opera, and possible methods
are suggested.   8 [1927] 65

TOLSTOY ON THE SONATA PATHÈTIQUE.   (E)
    Excerpt from an unpublished autobiographical writing.   8 [1927] 109

BEETHOVEN FOR STORM.   Mrs. Cyril Scott.   (F)
    Fiction.   13 [1933] 153

SCHWEIZERISCHE MUSIK-ZEITUNG UND SÄNGERBLATT

ROMANTISCHE DEUTUNGEN DER IX. SINFONIE BEETHOVENS.   Karl Nef.   (G)
    A detailed account of the predominantly unfavorable opinion of the Ninth Symphony held for many years in many
quarters.   55 [1915] 257,271,287; 56 [1916] 1

BEETHOVENS LITERARISCHE BILDUNG.   (H)
    Review and extended summary of article by Albert Leitzmann in the 'Deutsche Rundschau' 154 [1913] 271.
                                       56 [1916] 3

BEETHOVENS WELTANSCHAUUNG.   Viktor Louys Le Kisch.   (I)
    Rhapsodic.   56 [1916] 50

AUS BEETHOVENS GEISTIGER WERKSTÄTTE.   Robert Lach.   (J)
    The difference in appearance between the manuscripts of Haydn and Mozart and those of Beethoven is very great:
the former clear and neat, the latter scratched out and almost illegible.   The Beethoven manuscripts, and above all
the Beethoven sketch books (considered in conjunction with his diaries and conversation books) are invaluable in the
study of his creative process.   A striking fact, by these means proved past doubt, is that Beethoven almost never wrote
a composition straight through, but instead had at all times a number of compositions in process simultaneously.   His
mind was constantly pouring forth musical ideas of the most widely varied kinds, which were at all times being churned

around in his mind and shaping themselves for their ultimate use. This relentless process of modification continued
in many cases after the composition had reached the stage of fair copy (e. g. , 'Adelaide') or even publication (e. g. ,
the successive 'Leonora' overtures and the many changes in engraved proof sheets).

60 [1920] 353

ZUR GESCHICHTE DER BEETHOVENFORSCHUNG. Adolph Sandberger.   (A)
  The critical dates in the history of Beethoven scholarship in its classical period must include: 1810 E. T. A. Hoffmann's
  recognition of the necessity of uniting the study of form with that of content; 1840 Richard Wagner's first appearance as
  a champion of Beethoven, with his novel 'Eine Pilgerfahrt zu Beethoven'; 1851 Otto Jahn's application of the philologi-
  cal method in his study of Leonora; 1858 Alexander Wheelock Thayer's first published contribution to Beethoveniana,
  his article on Beethoven's youth in 'The Atlantic Monthly' 1 [1858] 847; 1864 Martin Gustav Nottebohm's Verzeichnis,
  followed the next year by the first of his publications on the sketch books, which laid the foundation for the true chronological study of Beethoven's creative work. Aside from these peaks, the work of many other important contributors
  to Beethoven scholarship is discussed: Seyfried (in the Appendix to the 'Studien' rather than in the 'Studien' itself),
  Wegeler, Ries, Anders ('Détails biographiques' 1839), Schindler, Deiters and Riemann, Marx, Lenz and Séroff vs.
  Oulibischeff, Wasielewski, and many others.   62 [1922] 216,227,241

ZUR 150. WIEDERKEHR DES GEBURTSTAGES (27. MAI) VON HANS GEORG NÄGELI.   Max Unger.   (B)
  Biographical sketch with special emphasis on Nägeli's association with Beethoven. Transcription of Kal 1039 is given.

63 [1923] 193,209,225

DIE SCHICKSALE DER FESTMESSE BEETHOVENS. Grunsky.   (C)
  An account of the incredibly slow growth into acceptance of the Missa Solemnis. The first performance was in St.
  Petersburg on March 26th 1824, and two sections had been performed in Paris on April 12th and 16th before the first
  partial Viennese performance on May 7th 1824. The first complete performance in Germany was in Cologne on May
  27th 1844, with other performances in Leipzig the next year. There is no record of any performance anywhere between
  1845 and 1855. Berlin first heard the entire Missa Solemnis in 1856 (and not again until 1886), Vienna only in 1861.

63 [1923] 361

PARALLELEN ZU DEN LEONOREN-OUVERTÜREN. Eduard Fueter.   (D)
  The overture as an introduction to the opera as a whole rather than merely to the first scene dates only from Gluck and
  Mozart; the use in the overture of melodic material from the opera is first encountered in Gluck's 'Paride ed Elena'
  (1770). Cherubini's overture to 'Lodoiska' (1791) and Paer's overture to 'Leonora' (1804) have certain notable resemblances to the Great Leonora overture. The development of the overture after Beethoven is briefly discussed.

64 [1924] 368

BEETHOVEN ALS "KAPITALIST." Max Unger.   (E)
  The dunning letter of December 29th 1820 from Steiner to Beethoven indicates that some years previously the composer had advanced money at interest to the publisher. An unpublished letter of July 16th 1816 from Beethoven to
  Steiner (here given in part) indicates that during the four years from the death of Brother Karl in November 1815 to
  the time of Beethoven's purchase of the bank shares in 1819, Beethoven's capital of approximately 10,000 fl. WW
  was invested through Steiner, either in the latter's publishing business or with a third party.

65 [1925] 57

VERSUCH EINES NEUEN TEXTES ZUM LETZTEN SATZE DER 9. SYMPHONIE VON BEETHOVEN.   Hansi.   (F)
  Facetious.   66 [1926] 90

BEETHOVEN. Konrad Falke.   (G)
  Centenary essay.   67 [1927] 137

BEETHOVEN ALS KLAVIERSPIELER UND IMPROVISATOR.   (H)
  A summary of familiar facts.   67 [1927] 139

BEETHOVEN ALS IMPROVISATOR. Eduard Fueter.   (I)
  An anecdote (not generally known) told by Camille Pleyel states that Beethoven was scheduled to improvise at a
  public concert in Vienna, but that after a few minutes of tentative preluding rose from the piano and excused himself, explaining to Pleyel the next day that since inspiration did not come there was nothing for him to do but to
  take his hat and leave. The author quotes this anecdote as interesting and as possible, whether or not authentic.

67 [1927] 140

BEETHOVEN ALS DIRIGENT. August Richard. (A)

In Bonn Beethoven became routined as an organist and as an orchestra cembalist, but had no opportunity to serve a similar apprenticeship as a conductor. By the time he attained the position where he was called upon to conduct his own works, his deafness had become an insuperable obstacle, and he was further handicapped, almost without exception, by inadequately prepared performances. Familiar comments by contemporaries on Beethoven as a conductor are quoted.   67 [1927] 141

EIN BESUCH BEI BEETHOVEN. Max Unger. (B)

Republication of a forgotten account (dating from 1826) of a visit to Beethoven, probably by Gottlieb Wiedebein.
67 [1927] 145

EINE ZEITGENÖSSISCHE HUMORISTISCHE KRITIK ÜBER BEETHOVEN. (C)

An account in dialect of a performance of "Wellington's Victory" in 1814.
68 [1928] 23

BEETHOVEN AND WEIGL. Eduard Fueter. (D)

The finale of the clarinet trio Op. 11 is a set of variations on a theme generally accepted as having been taken from Weigl's opera 'Amor marinaro.' The author points out that not only does the style of this theme not seem typical of Weigl, but that a contemporary piano transcription of the opera does not contain the melody in question. He concedes, however, that piano transcriptions of operas published at that time, being intended principally for home use, not infrequently omitted some of the ensemble numbers.   68 [1928] 217

NOCH EINMAL BEETHOVEN UND WEIGL. Eduard Fueter. (E)

Examination of the manuscript score of Weigl's opera shows that, as generally believed, the theme which Beethoven used was taken from the opera, but that Beethoven made slight modifications in the melody to fit it better to his purpose.   68 [1928] 326

BEETHOVENS TANZKOMPOSITIONEN. Willy Hess. (F)

For Orchestra:

12 Deutsche (1795)	GA 2/16
12 Menuetten (1795)	GA 2/17
12 Deutsche (1796-97) (The score of these dances is lost, but a Pf transcription is extant	H - 5, H - 48, H - 265
12 Ecossaises (formerly in the Artaria Collection, then owned by Prieger. If identical with TV-136, comp. 1806, pub. 1807. Not in GA)	H - 4
12 Menuetten (1799) Ed. Chantavoine, pub. 1906	H - 3
12 Contredanses (1802)	GA 2/17a
Ecossaise for Military Band (1810)	GA 25/289
Gratulationsmenuette (1822)	GA 2/13

For smaller groups: 2 Vln and Bass:

6 Menuetten mit Trios (TV-293)	H - 15
6 Ländlische Tänze (1800) Pf arrangement by Beethoven	GA 25/291, GA 18/197
7 Ländlische Tänze, probably for 2 Vln & Bass. Score lost; Pf arrangement extant	GA 18/198

String Quartet or Piano:

Menuette in A flat (about 1795) (See TD I xiv)	H - 21, H - 58

Violin and Piano:

6 Deutsche Tänze (1795)	GA 25/308

Piano:

Menuette in E flat (1795; the earliest known dance composition by Beethoven)	GA 18/193
6 Menuetten (before 1800)	GA 18/194
Allemande in A major (about 1800)	GA 25/307
2 Walzer in E flat, D major (1824, 1825)	GA 25/303, 304
2 Ecossaises in E flat, G major (1825?)	GA 25/305, 306
6 Ecossaises in E flat (Unlike the above, this is a composition of some substance)	GA 25/302

7 or 8 instrument 'tavern band'
    11 Wiener Tänze ('Mödlinger Tänze' (1819)
        Published by Breitkopf & Härtel in 1908 --
        "the crown of Beethoven's compositions in
        dance form."   H - 31

(Note that H - 50, 51 are unpublished sketches and fragments of dance compositions. See also NBJ 9 [1939] 76)
                                  70 [1930] 866

FORM UND GESTALTUNG EINES BEETHOVENSCHEN SINFONIETHEMAS. R. Eidenbenz.   (A)
    Study of the principal theme of the allegro of the first movement of the First Symphony according to the methods
    of Riemann's metrical analysis.   71 [1931] 241

ERINNERUNGEN AN BEETHOVEN. Franz Grillparzer.   73 [1933] 256   (B)

BEETHOVEN AND FRIEDRICH ROCHLITZ. Hans Ehinger.   (C)
    A general discussion of the importance of Rochlitz's writings as editor-in-chief of the Leipziger 'Allgemeine
    Musikalische Zeitung' on the growth of Beethoven's recognition.   73 [1933] 380

BEETHOVENS HUMOR IN SEINER NOTENHANDSCHRIFTEN. Georg Kinsky.   (D)
    Various instances are cited from anecdotes, conversation books, manuscripts and letters of the composer's sense of
    humor and his fondness for puns.   73 [1933] 513

DIE SONATENFORM UND DIE WIEDERHOLUNG DER EXPOSITION. Willy Hess.   (E)
    In many sonatas by Haydn and Mozart there is a 'second repetition' (of the development and the recapitulation).
    This repeat is to be observed only when the development is so unimportant that the movement is in effect not a
    sonata at all but a work in binary form. The 'second repeat' occurs in Beethoven only in a few youthful works
    which in the truest sense are not sonatas at all.   73 [1933] 749

ZU BEETHOVENS HEILIGENSTÄDTER TESTAMENT. Georg Kinsky.   (F)
    The history of this document after Beethoven's death as given by Thayer (TK I 351) is not accurate. Upon Beethoven's
    death his papers were taken by Schindler and Stephan von Breuning for use by Rochlitz (at Beethoven's request) in the
    preparation of an official biography. In September 1827 Schindler sent a transcript of the will to Rochlitz, who pub-
    lished it on October 17th 1827 in the 'Allgemeine Musikalische Zeitung' 29 [1827] 705. Presumably Artaria withdrew
    the document, because of its intimate character, at the time Beethoven's papers were being appraised before the
    public sale of November 5th, and on November 21st gave it to Jakob Hotschevar, guardian of Nephew Karl, who
    (according to the indorsement) gave it to Brother Johann. There is no convincing evidence that the document passed
    to Gräffer or to Fuchs, as stated by Schindler and Thayer respectively, but in 1840 Liszt offered it for sale in London
    for 50 guineas, presumably on behalf of Amalie Waldmann-Stölzle, the illegitimate daughter of Brother Johann's
    wife. (NOTE by DWM. Amalie died on March 10th 1831, leaving a 4-month old son.) In 1843 the will was ac-
    quired by the violinist Ernst, who presented it in 1855 to Jenny Lind and her husband Otto Goldschmidt. In 1890
    Goldschmidt donated the will to the library of his native city of Hamburg.
                               74 [1934] 519

ZU BEETHOVENS FIDELIO. Willy Hess.   (G)
    Only one number appearing in both the 1805 and the 1814 versions of Fidelio was omitted from the 1806 version as
    actually performed: Rocco's "Gold" aria (No. 4 in the final version). Though not performed, a revised version of
    this number appears in the draft score of the 1806 revision of the opera, the aria in this form differing somewhat in
    text and in music from both the 1805 and the 1814 version.   74 [1934] 743

ZURÜCK ZU BEETHOVEN? Erhart Ermatinger.   (H)
    An attempt to explain the renascence of Beethoven's popularity after a loss of interest following World War I.
                          75 [1935] 371

52 UNGEDRUCKTE VOLKSLIEDERBEARBEITUNGEN BEETHOVENS. Willy Hess.   (I)
    A list is given of 52 unpublished folk song settings or unpublished variants of published settings.
                    76 [1936] 236

ZUR VIELDEUTIGKEIT VON BEETHOVENS INSTRUMENTALMUSIK. Max Unger.   (J)
    Commentaries by various eminent musicians show that even such a relatively direct work as the Overture to Coriolanus
    is susceptible to widely varying programmatic interpretations.   77 [1937] 434

NEUES ZU BEETHOVENS UNGEDRUCKTEN ZAPFENSTREICHEN.   Willy Hess.   (A
   NOTE by DWM. This is the first version of an article which in revised form appeared in 'Die Musik-Woche'
   7 [1939] 292. The only important difference is that in this earlier version no mention is made of H-263.
77 [1937] 525

WARUM SCHRIEB BEETHOVEN DIE VIERTE OUVERTÜRE ZU "FIDELIO"?   Ludwig Misch.   (B
   The question of which overture to use with the opera limits itself to two -- the Leonora No. 3 and the Fidelio
Overture -- since Beethoven never approved the Leonora No. 1 as an introduction to the opera, and since for the
1806 revision he superseded No. 2 by No. 3. Pertinent to the entire question is the fact that while the first revision
(resulting in the Leonora No. 3 Overture) was carried out under the pressure of the urgings of friends and the failure
of the 1805 performances, the revision and refining of Op. 72a to Op. 72b (the presently accepted version) was primarily due to the prompting of the composer's artistic judgment. There was no external incentive to abandon the
Leonore Overture No. 3 in favor of something different, though the reversal of the order of the first two numbers in
the opera -- with the curtain rising on a number in A major instead of one in C minor -- demanded some adjustment
of tonality. Beethoven made some attempts to transpose and rework the Leonore Overture No. 1 (NB I 74), but did not
carry these efforts very far. The possible revision of either of the other two overtures was similarly not the answer.
Aside from the musical impracticability of the necessary transposition, Beethoven might well have hesitated to supersede two overtures which had already gained favorable reception in the concert hall.

   Beethoven's insistence that artistic unity be secured is indicated by his dissatisfaction at the first 1814 performance
with the use of the 'Ruins of Athens' Overture Op. 113 instead of the Fidelio Overture (TK II 278). It is noteworthy
that he preferred to use for this performance an overture completely foreign to the opera rather than to avail himself
of either of the overtures which had been written for earlier versions of the opera. The author intimates that by this
time the two Leonora Overtures had become independent entities which were quite apart from the opera, doubly so
because of the contrast between the grandeur of the overtures and the lightness of the opening scene on the stage. All
this points to the conclusion that the composer's final decision was that the only suitable overture to be used in performance was the Fidelio Overture in E major.   78 [1938] 112

GEDANKEN ÜBER BEETHOVENS V. SINFONIE.   Hermann Scherchen.   (C
   Among Beethoven's sketches for the scherzo of the C minor Symphony are copied the theme and other portions of the
finale of Mozart's G minor Symphony. The author discusses the relationship of this theme of Mozart to Beethoven's
scherzo, of the andante cantabile of the Jupiter Symphony to Beethoven's finale, and also comments on the structural
use which Beethoven made in the finale of the Mozart themes and of motifs from earlier movements of the Fifth
Symphony.   78 [1938] 341

EINEM BEETHOVEN-ZYKLUS.   Anna Roner.   (
   A popular commentary on the piano sonatas (the last five being mentioned only very briefly). The marked difference
between Op. 2 No. 1 and the first two movements of Op. 10 No. 1 as compared with the other sonatas of these two sets
leads the author to surmise that they may have been written or largely developed in Bonn.
78 [1938] 517; 79 [1939] 53

EIN BEETHOVEN-URAUFFÜHRUNG.   Willy Hess.   (
   The duet 'Nei giorni tuoi felici' (H-81), composed about 1800, received its first performance on February 18th
1939. The score, of which the autograph was received by the Staatsbibliothek from the Artaria collection, was subjected to the minimum amount of editing by the author to prepare it for performance. The author says that Beethoven's regard for the work is shown by his vain attempt seventeen years after its composition to find a publisher.
79 [1939] 41

BEETHOVENS "APPASSIONATA."   Edmund Schmid.   (
   Careful comparison with the autograph shows that Op. 57 as it appears in Krebs' 'Urtext' contains scores of minor
deviations from the original.   79 [1939] 161

DIE URGESTALT DES "FIDELIO."   Willy Hess.   (
   A detailed but popular discussion of the differences between the 1805 version of Fidelio as restored by Prieger and the
generally known 1814 version.   79 [1939] 222

DIE DYNAMIK VON BEETHOVENS GROSSFORMEN.   Willy Hess.   (
   The twelve German dances GA 2/17 and the last movement of Op. 2 No. 2 are analyzed from the standpoint of formal
unity. (See also Neues Beethoven-Jahrbuch 10 [1942] 59)   79 [1939] 476

DIE GRENZEN DES KLAVIERS.   Max Schneider.   (A)

"The piano of today resembles the piano of Mozart's time almost as little as it does the cembalo or the clavichord. The first practicable pianos, dating from the mid-eighteenth century, hardly exceed the clavichord in volume of tone. The tone quality of these instruments is bell-like, not comparable with modern pianos, and the extraordinarily shallow fall of the keys requires an exceptionally accurate touch which present-day pianists find very difficult. In general, the piano of Beethoven's day differs but slightly from that of Mozart: the great advances in mechanical design start with Erard's repeat mechanism (1823) and Babcock's cast-iron framing (1825)." There is no foundation for the belief that Beethoven wrote for some "piano of the future." (According to NV, of the first 15 piano sonatas (Op. 31 and earlier) only 4 (Opp. 14, 22, and 28 were designated "for pianoforte" rather than "for clavecin or pianoforte.") Beethoven made specified use of the shifting pedal with separate positions for 3 strings, 2 strings and 1 string (e. g., the adagio of Op. 106). He wrote presto and prestissimo octave glissandi (e. g., finale of Op. 53) which were quite practicable on the piano of his day with its very shallow key fall. The development of piano writing through the romantic and modern eras is followed in some detail.   80 [1940] 1

DEUTSCHE TÄNZE FÜR KLAVIER ZU VIER HÄNDEN (PETERS).   Willy Hess.   (B)

Nine German dances for 4 hands, now published in an edition by Carl Bittner, were taken from an autograph album of about 1815 (now in the Staatsbibliothek in Berlin) which belonged to an unidentified amateur. Without further facts, the question of authenticity must be left open. If genuine, they certainly date from a period earlier than 1815, and they are probably arrangements of dances originally for orchestra.
80 [1940] 104

ZUM KAPITEL "BEETHOVEN UND DIE KRITIK."   Max Unger.   (C)

A letter (late July or August 1810) to Zmeskall (previously published but omitted from the collections): "Es wird wohl in Ihrem Bureau Abschreiber geben . . ." refers to an obituary poem published in the Leipzig 'Zeitschrift für die elegante Welt' in honor of Countess Pauline von Schwartzenberg, who died heroically in a fire in Paris on July 1st 1810. From the same journal is quoted a rhapsodic interpretation of the Pastoral Symphony by Friedrich Mosengeil-Meiningen on which Beethoven made favorable comment.   80 [1940] 138

BEETHOVEN UND DIE SPIELUHR.   Willy Hess.   (D)

Works by Beethoven for the Spieluhr, recently edited by Schünemann for piano 4 hands (Schott) include the following: (a) Allegro and minuet in C (Artaria 186, TV 29; Part II of Schünemann's publication). This was not certainly for the Spieluhr, and is not to be confused as Schiedermair did ('Der junge Beethoven' p. 172) with the sonata for violin and piano Artaria 131. (b) Adagio in F, scherzo in G, allegro (Schünemann Part I). These were probably composed in 1792 for Count Deym. The adagio in its original version is far richer in detail than in Schünemann's arrangement; the arrangement for Pf and Vcl made by J. van Lier (Steingräber, 1902) is much closer to the original. The original was published by Kopfermann in DM 1$_2$ [1902] 1059; 1$_3$ [1902] 1193. (See also Zeitschrift für Instrumentenbau 23 [1902] 88, Almanach der deutschen Musikbücherei [1927] 320, ZfMw 14 [1932] 215) (c) Grenadiersmarsch (not included in the Schünemann edition). See Almanach der deutschen Musikbücherei [1927] 320 ZfMw 14 [1932] 215.
80 [1940] 237

DIE KADENZEN IN DEN KLAVIER-KONZERTEN VON MOZART UND BEETHOVEN.   Max Albert.   (E)

The Emperor Concerto was the first concerto in musical history in which all material of the nature of a cadenza was written out by the composer, with specific instructions at the traditional 6/4 chord of the first movement (GA 9/69 p. 45) that no cadenza of the performer's choosing is to be used. This was a logical result of the growth of the concerto form from being merely a display piece, combined with the fact that since Beethoven had returned from the concert platform he could gain desired artistic continuity for his concertos only by writing out the cadenzas. The fact that the cadenzas which Beethoven wrote for all his piano concertos were not published until the appearance of the GA (1866-68) gives explanation to the still encountered use of these concertos of cadenzas by others, but it does not justify such use.   82 [1942] 37

VERGLEICHENDE CHARACTERISTIK VON C- UND D-MOLL WERKEN BACHS UND BEETHOVENS.   Ernst Isler.   (F)

An extended summary is given of the aesthetic characteristics of the several tonalities as stated by writers from Plato to Berlioz. The more important compositions of Bach, Beethoven and other composers in the keys of C minor and D minor are named. The author concludes that any effect of tonality on the characteristics of a composition is completely in the mind of the composer who may select a given key to express a characteristic which he feels is associated with that key. (See also p. 124)   83 [1943] 1, 40

ZUR TONARTSCHARAKTERISTIK.   K. v. Fischer.   (G)

Agreeing in general with the conclusions of Isler, the author points out that "listening to music is primarily a psychological process rather than merely an acoustic and physiological one."
83 [1943] 124

ALTE STREITFRAGEN UM "FIDELIO."   Kurt Rothenbühler.   (A
   Arguments are given for the performance of Fidelio without pauses, and for the use in such a performance of the
   Leonora Overture No. 3 as entr'acte music. The author postulates that in the first performance in 1814 of the present
   version of the opera the 'Ruins of Athens' Overture Op. 113 was used at the beginning of the performance so that the
   famous overture might be available for entr'acte use.   83 [1943] 400

IST BEETHOVEN DER AUTOR EINER FLÖTENSONATE?   Paul Vosseler.   (B
   The flute sonata (in the hand of an unknown copyist) found in Beethoven's Nachlass (TK I 138) bore the inscription "1
   Sonata fecit (?) di Bethoe . . ." The author knows of no evidence disproving the authenticity of this work (though it
   is definitely an unperfected draft rather than a finished composition), and detailed stylistic analysis shows many features consonant with Beethoven's authorship. The work was much more probably planned for the same group for whom
   the trio for clavier, flute and bassoon GA 25/294 (1787-90) and the romanza for clavier, flute, bassoon and small orchestra (H-13) of 1788-90 were written (the Westerhold family (TK I 121) ?) than for J. M. Degenhard, for whom Beethoven wrote the flute duet (H-14): the latter work calls only for a very elementary performing technique, whereas the
   sonata (like the trio and the romanza) makes substantial demands on the virtuosity of each performer. In the edition
   Flute Sonata by Leeuwen published in 1906 (see 'Neues Beethoven-Jahrbuch' 6 [1935] 141) the editor made changes so
   extensive that the result must be considered a composition by Leeuwen based on Beethoven rather than a performing
   version of Beethoven's Sonata. (See also p. 293)   84 [1944] 190

ZUR BEETHOVENS FLÖTENSONATE.   Willy Hess.   (C
   Remarks supplemental to the paper by Vosseler.   84 [1944] 293

BEETHOVENS THEATERPLÄNE.   Otto Erich Deutsch.   (D
   Aside from many works indirectly connected with the stage -- ballets, overtures, interpolated songs, incidental music,
   variations on opera arias, etc. -- Beethoven was actively interested in operatic ventures for most of his creative life.

1803	Studies for 'Vestas Feuer' (Schikaneder) -- abandoned, with some material carried over into Fidelio.
1804-06	Fidelio (first and second versions).
1807	Application for the post of Hoftheater-Kompositeur, with obligation to write a grand opera and a singspiel each year.
1807	Text for a comic opera (author and title unknown) considered.
1808	Discussions with Collin on possible operas: 'Armida,' 'Macbeth,' and 'Bradamante.' Idea of 'Macbeth' toyed with until 1822; the 'Bradamante' libretto taken over by Reichardt.
1808	Text submitted by Joseph Ludwig Stoll (?).
1808	From this year or earlier until his death, Beethoven considered an opera on the 'Faust' story.
1809	A singspiel on an Indian subject discussed with Joseph von Hammer-Purgstall.
1811	Talks with Treitschke on a text based on 'Les ruines de Babylon.'
1811	Beethoven purchased a dozen printed opera books without finding any suitable for him.
1812	Several texts by Theodor Körner considered.
1812	'Attila' suggested by August von Kotzebue.
1813-14	Revision of 'Fidelio.'
1814	Text 'Mathilde' proffered by Karoline Pilcher.
1816	Treitschke asked for a text on 'Romulus and Remus.'
1816	Text of 'Bacchus' by Berge considered.
1818	Kanne asked to prepare a libretto on 'Claudine von Villa Bella.'
1820	Schreyvogel expressed regret that he had given the sketch of a Spanish opera to Weigl instead of to Beethoven.
1821-22	An opera on 'Bacchus' discussed with Ignaz Jeitteles (cousin of the poet of Op. 98).
1823	Opera on Schiller's 'Bürgschaft' suggested by Ferdinand Leopold von Biedenfeld.
1823	Attempts to get together with Grillparzer, first on a mythological cantata and then on operas 'Drahomira' or 'Melusine.'
1825	Johann Sporschil suggested that the 'Ruins of Athens' music be adapted to the opera text 'Die Apotheose im Tempel des Jupiter Ammon.'

                                                      85 [1945] 76

EINE ERLÄUTERUNG CARL LOEWES ZU BEETHOVENS NEUNTER SINFONIE.   Georg Kinsky.   (E
   Analysis prepared by Loewe for a performance of the symphony in Stettin in 1830.
                                                      85 [1945] 191

ARIANTEN ZUM SOLOPART VON BEETHOVENS G-DUR-KONZERT.   Willy Hess.   (A)
   Beethoven's own revisions as given in NB II 74 are presented in somewhat more complete form. A plea is made for
   a Gesamtausgabe which will include variant material such as is available for this concerto, the violin concert, the
   rondo in B flat for piano and orchestra, and other relatively familiar works, as well as including the more than 200
   authentic compositions not in the Breitkopf & Härtel GA.   85 [1945] 348

INE UNBEKANNTE ROMANZE BEETHOVENS.   Willy Hess.   (B)
   Brief discussion of the unpublished 'Romanza for clavier, flute, bassoon and small orchestra' (NB II 70; Schiedermair
   JB p. 219 No. 45; H-11), from the autograph in the British museum. The manuscript is apparently part of the slow
   movement of a work in several movements, probably written for the Westerholt family in Bonn.
                                                     86 [1946] 413

ACH, MOZART, BEETHOVEN.   Erwin Ratz.   (C)
   A contribution to the "countless attempts to determine what, in the last analysis, are the fundamental differences
   between the three great masters of classical music."   87 [1947] 145

IE TEILWIEDERHOLUNG IN BEETHOVENS SINFONIESÄTZE.   Willy Hess.   (D)
   On the thesis that Beethoven adapted his form to the content of his music, the author contends that it is to him
   "obvious that the repetition constitutes an integral part of the work, and that the repeat marks have the same binding
   effect on the performer as any other directions in the score." Various movements are discussed in which Beethoven
   included repeats, omitted repeats, changed his mind on the matter (e. g. , first movement of the Eroica; scherzo of
   the Fifth), and in one case (finale of Op. 135) specifically left the decision to the discretion of the executants.
                                                     88 [1948] 8

ARIE BIGOT (née Kuéné) À NEUCHÂTEL.   Edouard M. Fallet.   (E)
   Biographical sketch.   88 [1948] 419

ETHOVEN UND DIE MANDOLINE.   Willy Hess.   (F)
   A brief and general discussion of the works for mandolin with the statement that a hitherto unknown theme and
   variations in D major and a final version of the adagio in E flat (GA 25/296) were published in 1940 as Nos. 1 and 2
   of the 'Sudetendeutsches Musikarchiv' by Karl Michael Gamma.   88 [1948] 421

ETHOVENS NEFFE KARL.   Walter Abegg.   (G)
   Superficial.   89 [1949] 93

OICA-VARIATIONEN OPUS 35 UND EROICA-FINALE.   Kurt von Fischer.   (H)
   The two works are analyzed in some detail, and the following formal schemes are suggested:

                              Eroica Variations
         Intro   1st Mvt   2nd Mvt   Finale
       ThB + 3V // MelTh + V 1-3: V 4-7: V 8-13 // V 14-15 // Fugue, 2 Mel V

                           Finale of Eroica Symphony
         Intro   Expos   Devt   Recap   Coda
       Intro, ThB + 2 V // MelTh // 1F   1V   2V   2F   3V // 4V // Coda
         g   E flat   E flat   c   D   g E flat E flat E flat   Ab-g-E flat

   The two works are in no sense piano and orchestral versions of the same idea, nor is Op. 35 a study for the symphony,
   but rather a forerunner.   89 [1949] 282

R URSPRUNGLICHE SCHLUSS DES 1. SATZES IN BEETHOVENS VIII. SINFONIE.   Alfred Orel.   (I)
   NB I 25 describes an old timpani part that indicates that the coda of the first movement of the Eighth Symphony was
   originally much shorter than in its final version; a violin part of this shorter version is also known. This shorter version
   is listed by Hess as H-2. A loose page has been found which gives the discarded 10-measure coda in score, which is
   given herewith.   90 [1950] 50

ETHOVENS CHORFANTASIE UND DIE IX. SINFONIE.   Roland Tenschert.   (J)
   Op. 80 may be looked upon as a bridge between the 'Seufzer' songs of 1794 and the finale of Op. 125.
                                                     91 [1951] 97

EIN ÜBERSEHENES GESPRÄCH MIT BEETHOVEN.   (A
    The account by Johann Peter Pixis of a concert of 15 November 1817 at which the Choral Fantasy was played (Anton
    Halm) and of his conversation with Beethoven afterwards has never been published in its entirety.
                                                    91 [1951] 170

EINE MERKWÜRDIGE NOTEHANDSCHRIFT.   Otto Erich Deutsch.   (B
    General discussion of the four Mozart-Kozeluch-Beethoven manuscripts in the British museum.
                                                    92 [1952] 14

EINE BACH-BEARBEITUNG BEETHOVENS.   Willy Hess.   (C
    Facsimile and discussion of a 5-page autograph arrangement by Beethoven of the fugue in B flat minor from the Well-
    Tempered Clavier for string quintet.   The autograph apparently dates from about 1801.
                                                    93 [1953] 401

EINE MERKWÜRDIGE TRIO SONATE VON B.   Willy Hess.   (D
    A general discussion of the 'Sonata a tre' arranged by Pochon (Fischer).
                                                    93 [1953] 502

EINE BACH- UND HÄNDEL-BEARBEITUNG BEETHOVENS.   Willy Hess.   (E
    A general discussion of Beethoven's hasty and unfinished arrangement for string quartet of the B minor fugue from the
    Well-Tempered Clavier.   The arrangement of Handel's overture to Solomon for string quartet is not an arrangement
    in the true sense, since Beethoven did little more than copy Handel's string parts, presumably for study purposes.
                                                    94 [1954] 142

BEETHOVEN IN HISTORISCHER UND KÜNSTLERISCHER SICHT.   Erich Herzmann.   (F
    "One does Beethoven an ill service by bringing before the public immature or less successful works as mighty
    revelations."   94 [1954] 319

ZWEIFELHAFTE UND UNTERGESCHOBENE WERKE BEETHOVENS.   Willy Hess.   (G
    Each of the considerable number of works of this category is discussed in detail.
                                                    94 [1954] 452

ZU DEN BEETHOVEN-FÄLSCHUNGEN.   Marta Walter.   (
    A list of waltzes falsely attributed to Beethoven is given.   95 [1955] 55

EIN UNGEDRUCKTER STREICHQUINTETTSATZ BEETHOVENS.   Willy Hess.   (
    First publication of a prelude and the first measures of a fugue (H-29; see also NB II 158) intended for the Haslinger
    Gesamtausgabe but laid aside because of the possibilities latent in the fugue subject that became realized in the
    scherzo of Op. 125.   The prelude may be used with Op. 137, which is the fugue actually delivered to Haslinger.
                                                    95 [1955] 424

MOZART AND BEETHOVEN.   Henri-Frédéric Amiel.   (
    Comment from 1835 on the differences of style and emotional content of two quartets by the two composers.
                                                    96 [1956] 210

BEETHOVEN UND DIE SPIELUHR.   Willy Hess.   (
    Beethoven's works for mechanical organ and their transcriptions are discussed.   The author suggests that the most
    practicable way of performing such compositions now is in arrangements for wind instruments.
                                                    97 [1957] 295

EIN BRIEFWECHSEL ZUR BEETHOVEN-FORSCHUNG (ROMAIN ROLLAND -- ANTON KIPPENBERG).   Hermann Fähnrich. (
    Correspondence during the years 1923-1937 between Rolland and Kippenberg, proprietor of the Inselverlag and president
    of the Goethe-Gesellschaft, that discusses the German translations of some of Rolland's books on Beethoven.
                                                    97 [1957] 384

ANTIKE METREN BEI BEETHOVEN.   Werner Bauer.   (
    The rhythmic structure of the allegretto of Op. 92 is analyzed in detail from the standpoint of classical prosody.
                                                    98 [1958] 249

JACK WERNERS NEUESTER BEETHOVEN-"FUND."   Willy Hess.   (A)
     Various publications of unfamiliar Beethoven works by Werner are briefly discussed.
               98 [1958] 298

SUR LES TRACES DE L'"IMMORTELLE BIEN-AIMÉE" DE BEETHOVEN.   Willy Tappolet.   (B)
     Kaznelson's conclusions are summarized. It is improbable that the famous letter was ever delivered.
               98 [1958] 422

LA "VERSION D'ORCHESTRE" DE LA GRANDE FUGUE, OPUS 133, DE BEETHOVEN -- UN DÉSAVEU DE WEINGARTNER.   (C)
       Ivan Mahaim.
     The author discusses the tonal and motival interrelationships between the last five quartets. It seems to be his belief that a demand for an orchestral version of Op. 133 could come only from one who did not know the work in its original form. The transcription by Weingartner is analyzed in detail with reference to Weingartner's interpretive markings. A tabulation is given of the performances of Op. 133 during the period 1826-1913, which convincingly documents the neglect of this work in concert programs.   99 [1959] 126

DE QUELQUES SOURCES BEETHOVÉNIENNES DE CÉSAR FRANCK.   Jean Matter.   (D)
               99 [1959] 231

NOUVELLE VERSION D'UNE LETTRE APOCRYPHE DE BEETHOVEN À L'ÉDITEUR MAURICE SCHLESINGER DE PARIS.   (E)
       Ivan Mahaim.
     In 1867 M. Schlesinger wrote an article for the Badeblatt of Baden in which he claimed for himself the credit for having turned Beethoven's mind to the writing of what we know as the last five quartets -- a claim that is supported by the letter given as No. 122 in BusV -- and gives a different version of the letter (MM 458) that accompanied the manuscript of Op. 135 in October-November 1826 (given as And. 1538a).
               99 [1959] 316

SCHWEIZERISCHES JAHRBUCH FÜR MUSIKWISSENSCHAFT

BEETHOVENS WERKE UND IHRE GESAMTAUSGABE.   Willy Hess.   (F)
     Beethoven's efforts to arrange for a complete edition of his works is outlined, the scope and limitations of the Breitkopf & Härtel Gesamtausgabe are discussed, and a list is given of 204 works the authenticity of which is subject to little or no doubt (plus an additional 18 works which are lost or of doubtful authenticity) which are not in the GA. (For extension of this list see 'Neues Beethoven-Jahrbuch' 7 [1937] 104; 9 [1939] 75.)
               5 [1931] 163

SCORE

A NOTE ON BEETHOVEN'S PEDAL MARKS.   William Glock.   (G)
     The importance is stressed of strict observance of those pedal markings which Beethoven himself gave. Passages from Opp. 31, 32, 37, 53, 58, and 110 are cited as examples.   No. 3 [January 1950] 24

BEETHOVEN: THE MORALITY OF POWER AND THE CONQUEST OF SERENITY.   Wilfred Mellers.   (H)
               No. 16 [June 1956] 36

CONFUSION AND ERROR.   Norman Del Mar.   (I)
     Disputed readings in various editions of scores and parts of Leonore Overture No. 3 and Op. 61.
               No. 22 [February 1958] 28;
               No. 23 [July 1958] 38

THE FIRST VERSION OF BEETHOVEN'S C MINOR SYMPHONY.   Robert Simpson.   (J)
     Arguments are given for restoring the repeat in the scherzo that gave rise to the "superfluous" two measures referred to in And. 272, and for observing the repeat in the finale.   No. 26 [January 1960] 30

NEW MUSIC: BEETHOVEN'S CHORAL FANTASY. H a n s K e l l e r .   (A)
    An analysis by which the variations "fall into three, disclosing a ternary scheme that encompasses exposition,
    development, and recapitulation. "   No. 28 [January 1961] 38

SIGNALE FÜR DIE MUSIKALISCHE WELT

BISHER UNGEDRUCKTE BRIEFE VON L. VAN BEETHOVEN, Nos. 1, 2.   (B)
    Letters appearing as KS I 27 (Nos. 34, 35).

                10 [1852] 33

SCHICKSALE DER 9. SYMPHONIE VON BEETHOVEN ZU FRANKFURT AM MAYN.   (C)
    At the time of writing, no complete performance of the Ninth Symphony had been given in Frankfurt, and the Missa
    Solemnis was still unheard there.   10 [1852] 91

BISHER UNGEDRUCKTE BRIEFE VON L. VAN BEETHOVEN, No. 3.   (D)
    Letter appearing as KS II 331.   11 [1853] 137

BISHER UNGEDRUCKTE BRIEFE VON L. VAN BEETHOVEN, Nos. 4-10.   (E)
    Letters appearing as KS II 219 (No. 866), II 322 (No. 1015), II 365 (No. 1065), II 26 (No. 595), II 297 (No. 968),
    II 434 (No. 1162), and letter without date to Holz, starting: "Werther! Kommen sie also morgen einige Stunden vor
    dem Speisen" (not in KS or K 'Briefe'; not listed in B-J II). Note that letter No. 1065 is given as "An seinen Bruder
    Carl van Beethoven" -- probably an error for Brother Johann rather than for Nephew Karl.
                14 [1856] 281

BISHER UNGEDRUCKTE BRIEFE VON L. VAN BEETHOVEN, Nos. 11, 12.   (F)
    Letters appearing as KS II 454 (No. 1192) and I 314.   14 [1856] 396

BISHER UNGEDRUCKTE BRIEFE VON L. VAN BEETHOVEN, Nos. 13-17.   (G)
    Letters appearing as KS I 365, I 369, II 434 (No. 1161), II 217 (No. 861), and letter without date to Linke, starting:
    "Lieber Linke -- erzeigen sie mir die Gefälligkeit" (not in KS or K 'Briefe'; not listed in B-J II). Note that in letter
    1161 the time is given as "3 Uhr," not "5 o'clock. "   14 [1856] 591

BEETHOVENS LETZTE WERKE.   (H)
                16 [1858] 73, 129

EIN VERBINDENDER TEXT ZU BEETHOVENS "RUINEN VON ATHENS" VON ROBERT HELLER.   (I)
    Verses by Heller are reported to be much more suitable for performance with Beethoven's music than the original
    text by Kotzebue (see also 18 [1860] 88).   17 [1859] 89

BEETHOVEN'S FIDELIO IN PARIS.   (J)
    Review of a performance in which the libretto (and the music?) was fundamentally changed.
                18 [1860] 313

BEETHOVENS GEBURTSHAUS UND SEIN GRAB. B. S c h o l z .   (K)
    Dedicatory address.   19 [1861] 21

LUDWIG VAN BEETHOVENS WERKE. W a s i e l e w s k i .   (L)
    Review of the first few signatures of the GA.   20 [1862] 241

NOCH EIN PORTRAIT BEETHOVENS. C. F. H e c k e l , Jr.   (M)
    Through the intercession of the Streicher family, Beethoven was prevailed upon during the period 1814-18 to sit for
    an oil painting by Christoph Heckel, a young friend of the Streichers.
                22 [1864] 176

BAILLOT IN WIEN BEI HAYDN UND BEETHOVEN.   (N)
    In 1805 Baillot, escorted by Reicha, met Haydn and Beethoven in Vienna.
                24 [1866] 557

SIR GEORGE SMART.   (A)
   Obituary (died February 23rd 1867).   25 [1867] 409

Dr of M-351 TO CLEMENT.   26 [1868] 1092   (B)

BEETHOVEN ALS WIENER FREIWILLIGER.   (C)
   Fictionalized account of Beethoven's acceptance into the Vienna militia as a volunteer in 1796.
                                                28 [1870] 593

BEETHOVEN UND DER MALER DANHAUSER.   (D)
   Fictionalized account of the efforts of Danhauser to prevail upon Beethoven to allow him to make a life mask.
   (See p. 897)   28 [1870] 833

DIE MASKE BEETHOVENS. Eugen von Miller.   (E)
   The author possesses a life mask which on good authority is said to have been made by Danhauser (but see 29 [1871] 100).
                                          28 [1870] 897

CZERNY ÜBER BEETHOVEN.   (F)
   Extracts from Czerny's autobiography.   28 [1870] 929

BEETHOVENS MASKE BETREFFEND. C. F. Pohl.   (G)
   The only life mask of Beethoven was made in 1812 by Johann Adam Klein. At this time Danhauser was only seven
   years old. Klein was a close friend of Danhauser's father, and gave him the mold of the life mask, which afterwards
   was preserved with that of Danhauser's death mask. The sculptor Anton Dietrich made a bust of Beethoven in 1821.
                                        29 [1871] 100

DIE NOCH LEBENDEN NACHKOMMEN BEETHOVENS.   (H)
   Brief account of Nephew Karl and of his five children.   31 [1873] 129

FRIEDRICH WIECK BEI BEETHOVEN.   (I)
   Brief account by Wieck of a meeting with Beethoven in 1826.   31 [1873] 897

EIN BRIEF BEETHOVENS.   (J)
   Letter appearing as KS 1 10.   32 [1874] 913

BEETHOVENS WOHNUNG IM SCHWARZSPANIERHAUSE IN WIEN.   (K)
   Description of Beethoven's lodgings as given by Gerhard von Breuning.
                                        33 [1875] 705

BEETHOVENS ERARD-FLÜGEL. Ed. Hanslick.   (L)
Records of the firm of Erard show that on the 18 Thermidor of the year XI of the republic (August 7th 1803)
Sebastian Erard presented Beethoven with a piano, which now (1875) is in the State Museum in Linz.
                                        33 [1875] 929

EIN BRIEF UND EINE QUITTUNG VON BEETHOVEN.   (M)
   Receipt dated February 3rd 1807 for 500 florins paid by Count Oppersdorf "for a symphony which I have written for
   him" (see Sonneck p. 104), and letter to the Count without date (Sonneck p. 105 says "Early spring 1808") saying
   that the symphony which he had written for the Count was ready, that it had 3 Trb and piccolo in the last movement,
   and that Beethoven had recently had trouble with his finger.   38 [1880] 723

BEETHOVEN'S MISSA SOLEMNIS IN D.   (N)
   The first known liturgical performance of the Missa Solemnis took place in Warnsdorf (Bohemia) on June 29th 1830.
   The participants, all from that locality, totalled only about 90.   42 [1884] 369

CLARE." Elise Polko.   (O)
   Description of a household account sheet; EDr of MM 311 and MM 337.
                                        45 [1887] 449

AUCH ETWAS VON BEETHOVEN.   (P)
   Extracts from the memoirs of Baron de Trémont.   50 [1892] 465

WIE BEETHOVEN VON DER BEDEUTUNG DER KUNST DACHTE. (A)
The third and most doubtful of the Bettina letters (KS I 263).　52 [1894] 929

ÜBER BEETHOVENS MÄRSCHE. (B)
A preliminary attempt to list Beethoven's marches for military band (see also 'Die Musik-Woche' 7 [1939] 292).
Referring to the marches ultimately appearing in GA 25/287, the author says: "The first of these marches appeared
during Beethoven's lifetime in a 'Collection of Quicksteps for the Prussian Army' issued by Schlesinger, under the
title 'York'schen Corps 1813' in an arrangement for full military orchestra."
54 [1896] 995

ÜBER DAS NEUE BEETHOVEN-BILDNISS.　Rosalie Gräfin von (geb. Sphor) Sanerma. (C)
The etching by Arendt of the portrait of Beethoven made by Stieler in 1819 is a most unsatisfactory piece of work.
55 [1897] 306

BEETHOVENS MISSA SOLEMNIS AND NINTH SYMPHONY.　Alfred Heuss. (D)
An introduction to the two works in which points of aesthetic similarity are compared. The Ninth Symphony represents
the fulfillment of the promise for the world which the Missa Solemnis held out.
62 [1904] 5,36

DER HUNDERTJÄHRIGE FIDELIO.　Friedrich Brandes. (E)
Brief historical account of the successive versions of the opera.　63 [1905] 1199

LISZT, BEETHOVEN, WAGNER. (F)
Arthur Smolian has pointed out resemblances between passages in Liszt's 'Dante' Symphony, Beethoven's Op. 106, and
Wagner's 'Tristan und Isolde.'　66 [1908] 657

EIN BEETHOVEN-FUND.　Friedrich Spiro. (G)
A 'Sonatina in C major' for mandoline is dedicated to Josephine Clary (later the Countess Clam-Gallas), for whom
Beethoven wrote the aria 'Ah, perfido' (TK I 194).　71 [1913] 274

NEUE METRISCHE AUSLEGUNG IN BEETHOVENS SIEBENTER.　A. Siloti. (H)
71 [1913] 1349

ZU SILOTIS METRISCHE AUSLEGUNG DES SCHERZOS IN BEETHOVENS SIEBENTER.　Max Steinitzer. (I)
71 [1913] 1416

NOCHMALS: DER RHYTHMUS IM SCHERZO DER SIEBENTER.　Friedrich Spiro. (J)
These three papers give arguments for and against beating the scherzo of the Seventh Symphony (or at least thinking
it) in 6/4 rhythm rather than in 3/4.　71 [1913] 1564

"BEETHOVEN-KULTUS."　Ferdinand Scherber. (K)
Defense of a predominance of Beethoven's music on wartime programs.
72 [1914] 1405

BEETHOVEN UND SEINE ANKLÄGER.　Walter Hirschberg. (L)
Gustav Ernest has come to the defense of Beethoven's honor, especially in connection with his strife with his sister-in-
law, his plea to the London Philharmonic Society towards the end of his life that he was destitute, his promise of the
Missa Solemnis to no less than six publishers and its actual sale to a seventh, the charges that in many cases he had
been paid for works which he never delivered, and Beethoven's charges of faithlessness against the Kinsky estate in
the matter of his annuity. Ernest feels that he was able to justify Beethoven's statement: "Next to God, my honor is
the one thing most important to me."　73 [1915] 185

EINE NEUE BEETHOVENBÜSTE.　Hans Schorn. (M)
Comments on a new bust by Hermann Volz.　74 [1916] 515

ABERMALS EINE NEUE BEETHOVEN-STATUE.　August Spanuth. (N)
Comments on a new statue by Breuer.　74 [1916] 650

GLOSSEN ZUM "LETZTEN BEETHOVEN."　Ferdinand Scherber. (O)
Anecdotes and general observations.　78 [1920] 1115

ÜBER BEETHOVENS KLAVIER-SONATEN. Walter Petzet.   (A)
A general discussion, stressing the variety and the formal freedom of the sonatas.
78 [1920] 1117

BEETHOVENS LETZTE QUARTETTE. James Simon.   (B)
General.   78 [1920] 1120

BEETHOVENS ORCHESTER. Paul Ertel.   (C)
A brief discussion of the increase in scope of the orchestra as Beethoven wrote for it. The author recommends rewriting passages to take advantage of the melodic capabilities of valve horns and trumpets (e. g. , use of horn instead
of bassoon in the recapitulation of the first movement of the Fifth Symphony).
78 [1920] 1123

BEETHOVEN ALS MENSCH. Max Chop.   (D)
A general discussion of Beethoven's appearance and habits.   78 [1920] 1125

BEETHOVEN DER SYMPHONIKER. Hans Tessmer.   (E)
General.   78 [1920] 1163

WIE FEIERN WIR BEETHOVEN? Ludwig Misch.   (F)
A plea that festival programs in important centers include a substantial proportion of seldom heard works.
78 [1920] 1183

BEETHOVEN ALS OPERNKOMPONIST. Ernst Edgar Reimerdes.   (G)
A general account of the history of Fidelio during the composer's lifetime, and brief mention of other unfulfilled
opera projects.   78 [1920] 1207

NEUE BEETHOVENIANA. Felix von Lepel.   (H)
Anecdotes.   81 [1923] 950

IRRUNGEN DES ÖFFENTLICHEN URTEILS. Max Chop.   (I)
Extended quotations are given from unfavorable reviews of works from all of Beethoven's period of composition.
82 [1924] 551

THE VIOLA WHICH BEETHOVEN PLAYED IN BONN.   (J)
When Beethoven left Bonn in 1792 he gave Franz Ries the viola which he had used as Ries's pupil and in the court
orchestra. This instrument remained in the Ries family until it was recently presented to the Beethovenhaus. (Reprinted from the 'Kölnische Zeitung' of March 25th 1924.)   82 [1924] 721

BEETHOVENS KONVERSATIONSHEFTE. Hanns Gensecke.   (K)
Beethoven used the conversation books from about 1818 for the replies of those with whom he was conversing, for his
own side of the conversation when conditions were such that he could not talk loud, and for personal notes, calcula-
tions, and the like. Of about 400 books which originally existed, only 138 have been preserved. They are most
difficult for the researcher to use, because of the uncertainty of the order of the books and of the pages within a single book, the fragmentary nature of the entries, and the illegibility of the writing. Three thoughts run through the
entire series: Beethoven's deep concern for Karl's welfare, his never ending strife with servants, and the burden of the
master's deafness and illness. The books are throughout a mosaic of the intimate and the banal, but are an inescap-
able must for the person who would attempt to understand the human Beethoven.
83 [1925] 1557

"FIDELIO"-AUFFÜHRUNGEN UND DRITTE "LEONOREN"-OUVERTÜRE. Rudolph Hartmann.   (L)
There is no place for a performance of the Leonora Overture in a performance of the opera Fidelio.
83 [1925] 1641

BEETHOVENS VERHÄLTNIS ZUM GEISTELEBEN SEINER ZEIT. Karl Westermeyer.   (M)
Beethoven's personal library was relatively small, and he did not have access to many books in the libraries of his
friends. From his early days he was much influenced by Rousseau, but he was in no sense a democrat of the Rousseau
school. His ideas coincided in many ways with those of Kant, but there is no reason to believe that this was as a result of any study which he had made of Kant's teachings (e. g. , at the University of Bonn, where Beethoven matriculated on May 14th 1789). He loved Homer (the Odyssey more than the Iliad) and Shakespeare. His admiration for
Klopstock, Schiller and Herder had little direct influence on his music. Between him and Goethe, the other great
German genius of the era, there was great mutual respect but complete lack of understanding.
85 [1927] 496

BEETHOVENS ETHIK.   Paul Reisenfeld.   85 [1927] 499   (A

ÜBER DAS FORTSCHRITTLICHE IN BEETHOVENS SYMPHONIEN.   Ernst Schliepe.   (B
    Only in the case of Wagner does any other composer show as tremendous a growth as does Beethoven between his first
and last symphonies.   The importance of Beethoven's use of the scherzo may be exaggerated: in the last symphonies
of Haydn and Mozart a ländler-like movement has begun to take the place of the socially outmoded minuet, and in
the last dozen of Beethoven's works in sonata form, the scherzo is found only in Op. 106.   It is in the musical content
that the great advance is shown.   For the first time, symphonies were written for concert performance before intelligent amateurs who gave the music their full attention during its performance by players of the highest technical skill.
In the Pastoral Symphony and Wellington's Siege he laid the groundwork for the program symphony and the symphonic
poem of his successors.   His freedom of form and his introduction of orchestral polyphony represented sharp breaks from
the methods of his great predecessors.   Beethoven was at once the great classicist, the great innovator, and the great
herald of romanticism.   85 [1927] 503

BEETHOVENS OPUS 86 UND DIE FLUCHT AUS EISENSTADT.   G. Birnbaum-Lux.   (C
    An account is given, substantially as by Schindler (TK II 108), of Beethoven's anger at a supposed slighting reference
to this work (the Mass in C major) by Prince Esterhazy.   A letter of January 16th 1811 to Breitkopf & Härtel is published (perhaps for the first time) in which Beethoven asks them to issue the score of the Mass without waiting for the missing organ part or for the correction of many errors in the engraved plates.   (The letter of February 19th 1811 to the
publishers is obviously a continuation of this discussion.)   85 [1927] 507

GRILLPARZERS 'ERRINERUNGEN AN BEETHOVEN.'   (D
    Memoirs of several summers at the time Beethoven hoped for an opera libretto from Grillparzer; Grillparzer's oration
at Beethoven's grave; his address at the unveiling of the monument at Beethoven's grave in the autumn of 1827.
                                        85 [1927] 508

BEETHOVENS LEIDEN UND STERBEN.   Max Grünewald.   (E
    There is no record of a family history of deafness.   Failure of hearing apparently began in Beethoven's 28th year, the
left ear before the right, with an ever present rushing and roaring.   The diarrhea and indigestion which followed him
all his life began about the same time.   In 1821 Beethoven experienced an attack of jaundice; after that time he drank
heavily in company with Karl Holz, and cirrhosis of the liver resulted.   Beethoven's temperament was such that he made
no attempt to modify his customs or habits to favor his health -- the journey from Gneixendorf in December 1826 which
brought on his fatal illness is a case in point.   From the report of the autopsy (which the author quotes) the conclusion is
drawn that the deafness resulted from a congenital weakness of the auditory nerves, perhaps induced by the intemperance
of his forebears.   85 [1927] 514

BEETHOVEN AND BRAUNSCHWEIG.   Karl Bloetz.   (E
    The acceptance of Beethoven's music in Braunschweig was due largely to the influence of Gottlieb Wiedebein (1779-
1854).   His first contact with Beethoven is explained by Beethoven's letter of July 6th 1804 (KS I 85); he met Beethoven while he was in Vienna, and kept in communication with him for the next ten years.   The association apparently stopped suddenly at that time: Wiedebein's name does not appear in the conversation books.   It was probably
through Wiedebein's influence that the first performance of a Beethoven symphony took place in Braunschweig (January
15th 1815).   In 1823 Wiedebein became Kapellmeister to the Count, and works by Beethoven appeared promptly on his
concert programs.   Curiously enough, no notice of Beethoven's death was taken in Braunschweig, either in the journals
or by concert programs.   A Beethoven quartet was heard in Braunschweig for the first time in 1830; in 1831 and 1832
there were performances of five Beethoven symphonies, ten quartets, and a number of overtures.
                                        85 [1927] 517

BEETHOVENS KLANGORAKEL AN DIE NACHWELT.   Willi Hille.   (C
    Centenary address.   85 [1927] 609

'DIE GESCHÖPFE DES PROMETHEUS.'   Friederike von Krosigk.   (D
    Review of a performance of the ballet with choreography by Albrecht Knust, who followed as well as he was able the
sketchy outlines of the plot and action that have come down from the performance under Vigano in 1801.
                                        85 [1927] 708

EIN BEETHOVEN AUTOGRAM IN DANZIG.   Waldemar Kloss.   (J
    In Kurland in 1915 a military messenger found the wreckage of a framed portrait of Beethoven, on the back of which
was an autograph letter to Amenda.   The author says that the genuineness of the letter has been verified, but gives no
other information regarding it.   85 [1927] 864

BEETHOVEN IM BILDE SEINER ZEITGENOSSEN.   Waldemar Kloss.   (A)
   In addition to the highly idealized oil painting by Stieler, Beethoven sat in 1817 for a crayon portrait by August Karl
   Friedrich von Koeber (1793-1864). Kloeber's account of his meeting with Beethoven is given.
                                                85 [1927] 959

FÜRST BISMARCK UND BEETHOVENS KREUTZERSONATE.   Waldemar Meyer.   (B)
   Anecdote of a request performance before the Prince.   87 [1929] 328

DER BÜHNENHELD BEETHOVEN.   Gerhard Krause.   (C)
   Mention of several recent dramatic works (stage play, motion picture, operetta) with Beethoven as the hero.
                                                88 [1930] 1461

MINNIE VAN BEETHOVEN.   Maria Komorn.   (D)
   A portion of the material appearing in 'Musical Quarterly' 18 [1932] 628, giving the author's personal recollections
   of one of the three daughters of Nephew Karl.   89 [1931] 439

BEETHOVENS VII SYMPHONIE.   Emil Petschnig.   (E)
   An investigation of the events and conditions of Beethoven's life during the period of composition of this symphony
   (1808-12) in an attempt to reason out the programmatic ideas in Beethoven's mind on which the work was based.
                                                89 [1931] 721

GRILLPARZERS MUSIKÄSTHETIK.   S. Brichta.   (F)
                                                89 [1931] 724

BEETHOVENS STEGREIFSPIEL.   Konrad Huschke.   (G)
   Beethoven was one of the great pianists of history, but was completely unique as an improviser. Many anecdotes from
   contemporaries are given which bear upon his power in this regard.
                                                89 [1931] 930

DER EWIGE BEETHOVEN.   Paul Reisenfeld.   (H)
   A review of two books: unfavorable to an unnamed volume of detailed harmonic analyses by August Halm, and
   favorable to Richard Specht's 'Bildnis Beethovens.'   89 [1931] 983

GRILLPARZER AND BEETHOVEN.   S. Brichta.   (I)
   Grillparzer, "perhaps the most musical of all poets," was more affected by beauty than by power. While his contact
   with Beethoven was an intimate one, he looked upon Beethoven as "a path along which only he himself might travel,"
   while Mozart was "a highway for all."   91 [1933] 649

FRANZ GRILLPARZER ALS KOMPONIST.   Ernst Mannheimer.   (J)
   A group of songs by Grillparzer are in every way amateurish.   91 [1933] 697

EIN BESUCH C. M. VON WEBERS BEI L. v. BEETHOVEN.   Gustav Bock.   (K)
   Account of a very friendly visit between Weber and Beethoven on October 5th 1823.
                                                92 [1934] 145

GIBT ES EINE MONDSCHEIN-SONATE?   Hans Söhner.   (L)
   Rellstab's act in fastening the popular name on this work does a great disservice to a noble and virile composition.
                                                92 [1934] 443

SPOHR AND BEETHOVEN.   Konrad Huschke.   (M)
   Spohr saw much of Beethoven during the period 1812-16, but in his comprehension of his music never got beyond the
   Op. 18 quartets.   92 [1934] 681

BEETHOVEN IM SPIEGELBILD SEINER MUSIK.   Hans Söhmer.   93 [1935] 338   (N)

BEETHOVENS MENSCHLICHES LEIDEN.   Max Grünewald.   (O)
   A rehash and condensation of 85 [1927] 514.   93 [1935] 806

ZWEI UNBEKANNTE BEETHOVEN-BRIEFE.   Felix v. Lepel.   (P)
   Note without date, presumably to Haslinger, requesting his presence. Letter without date (presumably 1815-17) to
   Zmeskall, agreeing to sit for a portrait. (Was this the crayon drawing by Kloeber in 1817 mentioned in 85 [1927] 959?)
                                                94 [1936] 311

"FIDELIO" OUVERTÜRE.   (A
    Beethoven's decision to compose a completely new overture for the first performance of the revised 'Fidelio' in 1814
    should be taken as irrefutable proof that the composer dissociated the several 'Leonora' overtures from the opera as a
    stage presentation. These overtures belong only in the concert hall; any insertion of them in a performance of the
    opera is false alike to Beethoven's expressed wishes and to the artistic unity of the opera.
                                                94 [1936] 325

EINE ANLEIHE BEETHOVENS BEI WILLIAM BYRD.   B. Heid.   (B
    The theme of Byrd's variations on "The Carman's Whistle" is virtually identical with a passage in the finale of the
    Ninth Symphony: "Seid umschlungen, Millionen."   94 [1936] 649

EINE UNBEKANNTE BEETHOVEN-OPER.   Felix v. Lepel.   (C
    81 pages of sketches are extant for the first scene of the projected opera 'Vestas Feuer' on a book by Schikaneder,
    which was abandoned in favor of 'Leonora.'   94 [1936] 681

BEETHOVEN ZUM GEDÄCHTNIS.   Edith Skopik.   (D
    Memorial essay.   95 [1937] 186

RICHARD WAGNER UND BEETHOVENS "NEUNTE."   Edith Skopik.   (E
    Popular acceptance of the Ninth Symphony was greatly furthered by Wagner's unremitting championship.
                                                95 [1937] 317

ZWEI UNVERÖFFENTLICHTE KOMPOSITIONEN BEETHOVENS.   Felix v. Lepel.   (F
    The 'Punschlied' and the fragment of a violin concerto in C are published for the first time in Schiedermair's 'Der
    junge Beethoven.'   96 [1938] 643

                                        SIMROCK JAHRBUCH

ZUR GESCHICHTE DES HAUSES SIMROCK.   Erich H. Müller.   (G
    Several letters are given from Beethoven and his brother Karl.   1 [1928] 3

BEETHOVEN AND SIMROCK.   Erich H. Müller.   (H
    A complete list is given of Simrock issues of Beethoven's works during his lifetime, arranged in order of plate number.
    Copies are given of many if not all of the letters which passed between Simrock, Beethoven, Ries, Karl and others over
    a period of thirty years, including most of the 16 letters listed as "unpublished" in BJ 2 [1909] 303. An interesting char-
    acter sketch is given in a letter of May 6th 1803 from Ferdinand Ries to Simrock: "Karl Beethoven is the greatest skin-
    flint in the world. For a ducat he will go back on his pledged word fifty times over: in this way he makes no end of
    enemies for his worthy brother." In a letter of 22 October 1803, Ferdinand Ries says regarding the Sonata Op. 47, "You
    will probably dedicate it to Louis Adam and Kreutzer as the first violinist and pianist in Paris."
                                                2 [1929] 10

                                            TONWILLE

[Compositions of Beethoven are discussed according to Schenker's special technique of   (
    formal and harmonic analysis. In many cases, pertinent quotations are given from
    the writings of other students of the works discussed:]

        Fifth Symphony.
            The author lists a considerable number of discrepancies between the autograph and the GA in 2 No. 5 [1923] 12,
            39 and 2 No. 6 [1923] 19, 30.   1 No. 1 [1922] 27; 2 No. 5 [1923] 10;
                                                                 2 No. 6 [1923] 9

        Pf Sonata in F minor Opus 2 No. 1.   1 No. 2 [1922] 25

        Pf Sonata in G major Opus 49 No. 2.   2 No. 4 [1923] 20

        Pf Sonata in F minor Opus 57.   3 No. 1 [No. 7?] [1924] 3

EINE VERWAHRUNG. Heinrich Schenker.   (A)

In the autograph of the Pf Sonata in C minor Op. 81a, the titles of the three sections were given in German (as stated in NV). The translation of these titles into French ('Les Adieux, l'Absence et le Retour') in the first edition was an act of the publishers (Breitkopf & Härtel) in opposition to the expressed wish of the composer and the spirit of the music which here is made the occasion of a chauvinistic diatribe against all things French.

1 No. 1 [1922] 50

BACH-BEETHOVEN. Heinrich Schenker.   (B)

Beethoven's genius enabled him not only to learn from Bach but to learn to adapt the older composer's means to new uses.   2 No. 5 [1923] 43

BEETHOVENS METRONOMISCHE BEZEICHNUNGEN. Heinrich Schenker.   (C)

The excessive rigidity of the metronome as a guide for performance was recognized by Beethoven (see NB I 126). The author suggests that from the metronome marking and the number of measures in a movement or an extended passage the time for performance be computed, and that this time be used as a guide in attempting to set an average tempo in accord with the composer's expressed wishes. As regards the cases in which Beethoven's own metronome markings seem definitely too fast for today's taste, two thoughts must be borne in mind: (1) the process of composition has many of the characteristics of improvisation, so that the composer himself might be expected to tend towards a faster tempo then seems suitable to the recreator or the listener; and (2) based on this first consideration, Beethoven's interpretation and technique of performance would have been adapted to the more rapid tempo.

2 No. 5 [1923] 52

BEETHOVEN-WOLANEK. Heinrich Schenker.   (D)

To the well-known letter from the copyist Wolanek, with Beethoven's irate comments (KS II 357) the author adds the comment: "Since that time the copyist Wolanek has spawned millions of Wolaneks, but Beethoven remains the unique. Millions of Wolaneks continue to come, and under all names are performing, conducting, criticizing, explaining and teaching -- there is still but one Beethoven. Would that we could drive home to all Wolaneks Beethoven's words: 'Pray do Mozart and Haydn the honor of keeping their names from your lips. '"

2 No. 6 [1923] 43

BEETHOVEN ZU SEINER OPUS 127. Heinrich Schenker.   (E)

The passage referred to in Beethoven's letter written during the summer of 1825 to Prince Galitsin (KS II 386) is not in the C sharp minor quartet (as suggested by Kalischer) or at the close of the E flat quartet Op. 127 (Shedlock's suggestion), but in m. 48 of the second movement of the latter quartet (the 11th full measure of the andante con moto). (See also 3 No. 2/3 [No. 8/9?] 55)   3 No. 1 [No. 7?] [1924] 39

BEETHOVEN AS A WRITER OF EPIGRAMS. Heinrich Schenker.   (F)

Comments on the letters appearing in KS II 323, 353, 358, 382 (No. 1088).

3 No. 1 [No. 7 ?] [1924] 42

HUNDERT JAHRE IX. SINFONIE. Gottfried Keller.   (G)

Festival address.   3 No. 2/3 [No. 8/9 ?] [1924] 53

VERÖFFENTLICHUNGEN

BEETHOVEN ÜBER EINE GESAMTAUSGABE SEINER WERKE. Max Unger.   (H)

Facsimile and transcription of KK 1051, and summary of Beethoven's efforts to secure a publisher for a collected edition. (See also 'Neue Zeitschrift für Musik' JG 80 [1913] 449)   [1920]

BEETHOVENS STREICHQUARTETT OPUS 18 Nr. 1 UND SEINE ERSTE FASSUNG. Hans Josef Wedig.   (I)

The position of the string quartet in Vienna in the 1780's and 1890's is reviewed, with commentaries on the quartets of Fränzl, Kozeluch, Pleyel, and especially Förster, who is considered of importance in his influence on Beethoven and as a composer in his own right. The history of the composition of Op. 18 No. 1, especially in its relationship to other Beethoven works of the period, is discussed. The copy of the first version of this quartet presented to Amenda with Beethoven's inscription on the title page (KS I 26) is in the library of the Beethovenhaus. The deviations of this version from the one generally known are discussed in great detail, and the early version is printed complete.

[1922]

BEETHOVEN: UNBEKANNTE SKIZZEN UND ENTWÜRFE.   Arnold Schmitz.   (A)
    A general discussion is given of the importance of the sketches to all aspects of Beethoven scholarship.   Four pages
    of sketches in the Beethovenhaus Museum are transcribed and commented upon in detail.   The first sheet (written
    on both sides) gives a hitherto unknown second trio to the scherzo of Op. 9 No. 1, dating probably between mid-
    1798 and the end of 1800.   Beethoven's notation on the sketch indicates definitely that he wished this new trio to
    be inserted in the score.   The second sheet includes sketches for the allemande in A major GA 25/307 and for the
    song 'Es war einmal' Op. 75 No. 3 GA 23/219, as well as numerous other sketches which were not used in completed
    works.   Facsimiles and complete transcriptions of the four pages are appended.
                                                    [1924]

BEETHOVENS HANDSCHRIFT.   Max Unger.   (B)
    Beethoven's method of forming his characters (capital and lower case, German and Latin), his figures, orthography,
    punctuation, and abbreviations are discussed in exhaustive detail, with plates giving facsimiles of each individual
    character.   The letters to Zmeskall (KS I 21 No. 23), Treitschke (KS II 25) and Nephew Karl (KS II 328), extending
    over a period of about thirty years, are given in facsimile and in meticulously faithful transcription, with commen-
    taries.   Beethoven's musical script is considered in similar detail: notes and rests, clefs, accidentals, etc.   Facsim-
    iles from various periods are given and discussed: Rondino (end of Bonn period), 'Für Elise' (attributed to April 1810),
    Op. 111 (January 1822).   The well-known diatribe against the copyist Wolanek (KS II 357) is in no sense a Beethoven
    letter: it was not sent nor intended to be sent to anyone, but was merely Beethoven's way of relieving himself in an
    outburst of anger.   [1926]

UNBEKANNTE MANUSKRIPTE ZU BEETHOVENS WELTLICHER UND GEISTLICHER GESANGSMUSIK.   Joseph Schmidt. (C)
                                                    [1928]

    EINE BEETHOVEN ZUGESCHRIEBENE CHORALBEARBEITUNG.   (D)
        A Beethoven autograph containing a four part setting of a chorale by Graun and a canon for four voices is shown
        to be merely a copy by Beethoven of this material from a textbook by Kirnberger.
                                                    [1928] 5

    DIE ORIGINALHANDSCHRIFT DES SCHWEDISCHEN WIEGENLIEDES.   (E)
        In 'Der Bär' (B&H) for [1927] 159 Lütge reported the discovery of a collection of songs of various nations which
        Beethoven had arranged for Thomson.   The autograph of the Swedish Lullaby (listed by Lütge as No. 21 in this
        collection) has recently come to light and is carefully transcribed.
                                                    [1928] 10

    DIE DEUTSCHER TEXTE ZU BEETHOVENS C-DUR MESSE.   (F)
        The Mass in C major Op. 86 was originally published in 1812 with the liturgical Latin text and also with German
        text of a completely different nature to make the work suitable for performance in Protestant churches and in the
        concert hall.   The 'Three Hymns' were musically (Kyrie + Gloria), (Credo), (Sanctus + Benedictus + Agnus Dei).
        The review of the mass ('Allgemeine Musikalische Zeitung' 15 [1813] 413) commented unfavorably on the Ger-
        man text.   Beethoven's letter of February 19th 1811 to Breitkopf & Härtel (KS I 210) referred to a Dr. Schreiber
        as the author ("translator").   This was probably not Dr. Aloys Schreiber, who had nothing to do either with re-
        ligious music nor with Breitkopf & Härtel, but rather Dr. Christian Schreiber (1781-1857), member of the staff
        of the 'Allgemeine Musikalische Zeitung' and translator of the text of the four ariettas and a duet Op. 82 (from
        Italian, not (as Kalischer says) from French).   In April 1823 a new set of German words by Benedict Scholtz
        (1760-1824) was presented to Beethoven, who found it much better than Schreiber's version.   It was the Scholtz
        setting which Beethoven commended to Schott in May 1825 (KS II 366) in connection with a possible new edition
        of the C major mass.   The three versions of the text (Latin, Schreiber, Scholtz) are given complete.   In the opin-
        ion of the author the text by Scholtz, from an artistic standpoint, is inferior to that of Schreiber.   Neither is to-
        day of more than historical importance.   [1928] 13

BEETHOVEN: BEITRÄGE ZUM LEBEN UND SCHAFFEN NACH DOKUMENTEN DES BEETHOVENHAUSES.   (G
    Ludwig Schiedermair.   [1930]

    NOTIZEN ÜBER EINE KAFFEEMASCHINE.   (H
        Beethoven's fondness for coffee, mentioned by Schindler and others, is further shown by an autograph copy
        (dated September 23rd 1825) of what was presumably an advertising claim for a new type of coffee machine.
                                                    [1930] 5

BLÄTTER AUS DEM HAUSHALTUNGSBUCHE.   (A)
    Recently discovered pages from Beethoven's household account book for July and August 1825 are transcribed.
[1930] 6

EIN HULDIGUNGSBLATT AN DIE BARONESSE VON WESTERHOLT.   (B)
    Facsimile is given of a greeting card which Beethoven sent in the late 1780's to a young lady whom Wegeler
referred to as having been one of Beethoven's "Werther-Loves."
[1930] 11

EIN BRIEF AN DR. ANTON BRAUNHOFER.   (C)
    Letter probably from mid-April 1825; "Wir danken ihnen für den wohl gegebnen und . . ."
[1930] 11

EIN KONVERSATIONSHEFT.   (D)
    A conversation book, apparently dating from March 1818, is transcribed in full (as far as it is legible).
[1930] 12

BOLERO-ENTWÜRFE.   (E)
    A sheet has been found containing sketches for the 'Bolero a solo No. 1' (TV 177 No. 14; 'Die Musik'
2_1 [1902] 431; Ibid 30_2 [1938] 820) and for the 'Bolero a due' (TV 177 No. 13) referred to as Nos. 5 and 6 in
'Der Bär'(B&H) for [1927] 161. These sketches and the boleros resulting from them were a part of Beethoven's
work on folk song arrangements.   [1930] 17

EIN AN IGNAZ SCHUPPANZIGH GERICHTETER SCHERZGESANG.   (F)
    Description of the autograph of the 'Lob auf den Dicken' given in Grove (ed. 4, 1940) IV 687).
[1930] 20

SYSTEMATISCHE ORDNUNG BEETHOVENSCHER MELODIEN.   Wilhelm Haas.   (G)
    Some 5700 melodies and melodic fragments are arranged in a finding list according to their rhythmic and melodic
characteristics, and keyed back to the GA.   [1932]

DER GRAF VON WALDSTEIN UND SEIN VERHÄLTNIS ZU BEETHOVEN.   Josef Heer.   (H)
    Ferdinand Ernst Joseph Gabriel, Count von Waldstein and Wartenberg zu Dux was born in Vienna (not in Dux) on
March 24th 1762. His life history and his characteristics as a composer are traced in great detail, and the three
works of Beethoven which are most directly connected with Waldstein -- the Piano Sonata Op. 53, the Variations
for piano four hands on a theme by Waldstein GA 15/122, and the Ritterballett GA 25/286 -- are discussed from the
standpoint of their indication of the relations between Beethoven and Waldstein.
[1933]

DIE GESTALTUNG WELTANSCHAULICHER IDEEN IN DER VOKALMUSIK BEETHOVENS.   (I)
    Ludwig Ferdinand Schiedermair.
An extensive discussion of the three primary concepts of humanity, hope and religion as they appear in Beethoven's
texts and as they are treated in his musical settings.   [1934]

VIERTELJAHRSSCHRIFT FÜR MUSIKWISSENSCHAFT

BRIEFE BEETHOVENS AN FERDINAND RIES.   Hermann Deiters.   (J)
    Ferdinand Ries (1784-1838), son of Franz Anton and grandson of Johann, came from Bonn to Vienna in 1801, where
he became a pupil and close friend of Beethoven. In 1805 he left Vienna for his military service; turned down, he
spent a few years in Paris. In 1808-09 he was again in Vienna; then, after further travels, he settled in London from
1813 to 1824. Returning to Germany, he lived in Godesberg bei Bonn and then in Frankfurt a M until his death. Of
the 34 letters which Ries includes in the 'Notizen,' the originals of 17 were made available to the author and are
published here in a corrected version; two letters previously unpublished are also given. The corrections to the letters
from the 'Notizen' have apparently been made in KS, but the other two letters do not seem to have been included.
(1) Letter without date (probably from 1824) in which Beethoven says that he will send metronome markings for 'Christus am Oelberge,' and suggestion of several benefit concerts to include the Ninth Symphony, the Missa Solemnis, etc.

BRIEFE BEETHOVENS AN FERDINAND RIES (Continued)
  (2) Letter dated March 19th 1825, stating that the previous week he had sent the scores of the symphony (the Ninth),
  the Opferlied, and an overture. This article gives first publication (here marked **) and first complete publication
  (here marked *) of the following letters (KBr numbering): 48**, 49*, 50**, 58*, 68, 84, 69, 83, 90**, 100, 203, 476,
  494**, 502*, 509*, 869*, 901*, KK 1274**, KK 1279**.   4 [1888] 83

EIN SATZ EINES UNBEKANNTER KLAVIERKONZERTES VON BEETHOVEN. Guido Adler.   (A)
  Orchestra and solo parts were discovered in Prague of the first movement of a composition described on the title page
  as 'Concerto in D-dur für Pf mit Orchester von L. von Beethoven.' Careful study of this movement has convinced the
  author that it is actually a composition of Beethoven, dating from the period 1788-93. (It is included in the GA Ser.
  25 No. 311, but see Neues B-Jahrbuch 2 [1925] 167.)   4 [1888] 451

DIE ENSTEHUNGSZEIT DER OUVERTURE ZU LEONORE No. 1 OPUS 138, MIT ANSCHLIESSENDEN KRITISCHEN   (B)
    BEMERKUNGEN ZU NOTTEBOHMS BEETHOVENIANA. Albert Levinsohn.
  The author believes that Nottebohm exercised too little caution in his use of the sketch books to settle questions of
  chronology (both in assigning dates of composition and in determining the order in which several successive versions
  of a given passage had been evolved). The fallacy in the procedure used by Nottbohm and followed by other scholars
  is that Beethoven might use a sketch book of years before if it happened to be convenient at hand and had blank pages
  or even a few blank staves. An example of this practice is unwittingly cited by Nottebohm in NB II 463, where sketches for the Battle of Vittoria are directly followed by sketches for the A flat Pf Sonata Op. 110 and the Missa Solemnis
  which were composed at least six years later. This flaw in Nottebohm's basis of establishing chronology throws doubt
  on the accepted dating of many works: the opera Leonora and its several overtures, and also Opp. 12, 14, 15, 19, 26,
  53, 54, 56, 57, 58, 67, 69, 73, 80, 91, 93, 96, and 101.   9 [1893] 128

ZEITSCHRIFT FÜR BÜCHERFREUNDE

BEETHOVEN AUTOGRAPH LETTERS SOLD.   (C)
  Reference to sale at auction of two letters (neither appearing in 'Beethoven Jahrbuch' 2). (1) Signed "L. v. B." in
  which Beethoven said, "In meinem alten Tagen schreibe ich an Sie, um ihnen Glück zu wünschen." (2) Another,
  beginning: "Gestern war ich nicht Ludwig sondern der Teufel." No further information given.
                                            3 [1899] 123

A SONG SETTING BY BEETHOVEN. Anton Schlossar.   (D)
  "In the issue (of 'Selam, Ein Almanach für Freunde des Mannigfaltigen von J. F. Castelli') for 1816, Rupprecht's
  poem 'Merkenstein' is so set to music by Beethoven (GA 25/276) that 'this little volume would form a particularly
  desirable musical gift.'"   3 [1899] 302

SETTINGS BY BEETHOVEN OF POEMS BY GOTTFRIED AUGUST BÜRGERS. Erich Ebstein.   (E)
  Beethoven set three of Bürger's poems: 'Mollys Abschied' (Op. 52 No. 3), 'Das Blümchen Wunderhold' (Op. 52 No. 8),
  and 'Seufzer eines Ungeliebter und Gegenliebe (GA 23/253). Although Op. 52 was published in 1805, it is most probable that the songs which make it up had been written in Bonn and discarded, and that they were in 1805 turned over
  to Breitkopf & Härtel by Brother Johann without the knowledge or consent of the composer (TK I 140). It may be
  noted that in 1780 Neefe (at that time Beethoven's teacher and guide) published seven songs to texts by Bürgers.
  Note that 'Das Liedchen von der Ruhe' (Op. 52 No. 3) is by H. W. F. Ueltzen, not by Bürgers.
                                            7 [1903] 187

DOUBTFUL PASSAGES IN BEETHOVEN AUTOGRAPHS.   (F)
  Referring to the manuscript of the Waldstein Sonata Op. 53, the statement is made: "In various passages which otherwise are not clear, Beethoven has marked the notes with letters, or written out the obscure passage clearly on a separate staff."   10 [1906] Beiblatt Heft 6 p. 7

VON DICHTERN, DIE IN SCHWACHEN STUNDEN KOMPONIERTEN -- UND UMGEKEHRT. Leopold Hirschberg.   (G)
  After listing and briefly discussing a number of creative artists each of whom is known for substantial accomplishments
  in several fields (the written word, painting, music), the author presents what he believes to be a complete collection
  of the original writings which were set to music by Mozart, Beethoven, Weber, Schubert and Schumann. Beethoven is

represented by 38 examples, all brief and of negligible literary value, ranging from the invocation to Zmeskall in 1796 (KS I 14) to the motto words of the closing movement of Op. 135. Half of the texts were set as canons; most of the others are examples of his fantastic whimsy.   NF 8 [1916] 1

BEETHOVEN AND HOMER.   Albert Leitzmann.   (A)
"Beethoven is the last of the series of geniuses who were solitary autodidacts." The small library which he left on his death included copies of contemporary and classical literary works, well thumbed and copiously marked and annotated. His copy of the Iliad has been lost, but his copy of the Odyssey (in Voss' translation) indicates, as Schindler recounted, that towards the end of his life, he spent more and more time with "his oldest friends and teachers from Greece: Homer, Plato, Aristotle, Plutarch and their companions." A list is given of more than fifty passages in Beethoven's copy of the Odyssey which he had underscored or marked with marginal comments.
                                         NF 8 [1917] 322

ZEITSCHRIFT FÜR DEUTSCHLANDS MUSIKVEREINE UND DILETTANTEN

EINE ORIGINAL-ANECDOTE VON BEETHOVEN.   (B)
Anecdote of request by D . . . for permission to play Op. 130 in which Beethoven demands 50 fl., and facsimile of 'Es muss sein' Canon H-208.   3 [1844] 133

EIN BRIEF BEETHOVENS.   Carl Holz.   (C)
EDr Kal 1131.   4 [1845] 353

EIN BRIEF VON VAN BEETHOVEN.   (D)
EDr of Kal 79.   5 [1845] 10

VERZEICHNISS ALLER BISHER ERSCHIENENEN ABBILDUNGEN LUDWIG VAN BEETHOVENS.   Aloys Fuchs.   (E)
List of 37 copper engravings and lithographs, 5 miscellaneous pictures (not of Beethoven), 4 medals, and 8 busts or statuettes.   5 [1845] 11

DIE ENTHÜLLUNGSFEIER DES BEETHOVEN-MONUMENTS ZU BONN IM AUGUST 1845.   (F)
Detailed account.   5 [1845] 49

BLICKE IN BEETHOVENS CONVERSATIONBÜCHER UND IN SEIN LEBEN.   A. Schindler.   (G)
                                         5 [1845] 129

NOCH EINMAL SCHINDLER.   (H)
Criticism of Schindler for publishing excerpts from the conversation books. Karl Holz joins in the invective, quoting from the last paragraph of Kal 953.   5 [1845] 145

ZEITSCHRIFT FÜR MUSIKWISSENSCHAFT

BEETHOVEN STUDIES: I. GOETHES 'WEST-ÖSTLICHER DIWAN.'   Albert Leitzmann.   (I)
The author gives the passages which Beethoven marked in his copy of the collection of poems.
                                         1 [1918] 156

THE PARENTS OF BEETHOVEN'S MOTHER.   (J)
Digest of a newspaper article. Beethoven's maternal grandfather was Heinrich Keverich, born in Ehrenbreitstein in 1701 and chief cook at the electoral court. His wife was Maria Klara Westorff of Coblentz, daughter of the Senator Johann Bernard Westorff. Of the four sons and two daughters of this family, Beethoven's mother, Maria Magdelena (born December 19th 1746), was the youngest. Before she was seventeen years old she married Johann Leym, chamberlain at the court at Ehrenbreitstein. One son died in infancy, and Leym himself died in 1765. The young widow became acquainted with Johann van Beethoven while he was a guest at an inn where Mme. Keverich and her daughter lived. Within a few years Johann had relieved his mother-in-law of her property, and she died destitute in 1768.   1 [1919] 263

DIE EINHEIT DER BEETHOVENSCHEN KLAVIERSONATE IN AS DUR OPUS 110.   A r m i n   K n a b .   (A)
   In general the Beethoven piano sonatas attain unity of the several movements by content rather than by line, though
   there are a number in which some motival fragment occurs in several movements: e. g. , Op. 2 No. 3 with m r m f
   (r) or its equivalent in the principal themes of each of the four movements, and germinal motifs in the last two movements of Opp. 3, 10, 13, 106, 111. Perhaps the most intensive use of this technique of composition is in Op. 110,
   based almost completely on two germinal motifs: (1) d f r s, and (2) l s f m or its inversion. The sonata is analyzed
   in detail from this standpoint.   1 [1919] 388

"HÖREN" UND "ANALYSIEREN."   G u s t.   B e c k i n g .   (B)
   An extended discussion of Hugo Riemann's technique of analysis as exemplified in his book on the Beethoven sonatas.
                                                                      1 [1919] 587

UNGEDRUCKTE BRIEFE BEETHOVENS.   G e o r g   K i n s k y .   (C)
   (1) Note without date (probably autumn of 1804) to Ries, asking him to correct the concerto (probably Op. 37) and
   saying that his illness was no better. (2) Note without date (probably about 1810) to a Herr Wildfeger regarding plans
   for an outing at Baden. (3) Letter of August 19th 1819 to Karl Bernard, as published in KK No. 904. (4) Letter without
   date (probably 1819) to Karl Bernard, of which a few lines are given in KK No. 942. (5) Letter without date (probably
   1819-20) to Karl Bernard, of which a few lines are given in KK No. 941. (6) Letter without date (but established to
   have been written at Mödling on June 20th 1822) to Georg August von Griesinger, saying that when he returned to the
   city he would look him up, and that he had been ill for five months. (7) Letter of September 13th 1822 to Franz
   Brentano regarding the honorarium from Simrock for the Missa Solemnis.
                                                                      2 [1920] 422

ÜBER TEXTCRITIK, ANALYSE UND BEARBEITUNG VON MUSIKWERKEN.   H e r m a n n   W e t z e l .   (D)
   A discussion of Riemann's book on the piano sonatas and of Schenker's analyses of four of the last five piano sonatas,
   with the recitative introduction to the Arioso dolente of Op. 110 taken as an example for specific comparison and
   comment.   2 [1920] 429

DAS "AIR AUTRICHIEN" IN BEETHOVENS OPUS 105.   A l f r e d   O r e l .   (E)
   In a letter to Steiner & Co. to which KS II 1 assigns the date 'December 1st 1816' and which TD III 628 dates "about
   December 1816," Beethoven requests a copy of a song 'A (or Ein or An) Schüsserl und a Reindl. " The author has
   found a song with words in a collection of songs with guitar accompaniment by C. L. Costenoble, and has also found
   indications that it was used as the subject of variations in the first decade of the nineteenth century (vide last paragraph of Beethoven's letter). The melody quoted in K 'Briefe' (Ed. 2) III 85 as being the song in question is almost
   certainly one of the instrumental variations. It is this melody that Beethoven uses as 'Air autrichien' in Op. 105 No.
   3, so that it may be concluded that the composition of Op. 105 was under way by early 1817. The known dates of
   composition of the song settings for Thomson on which four of the other five parts of Op. 105 are based does not conflict with this dating.   2 [1920] 638

BEETHOVENS UMARBEITUNG SEINES STREICHTRIOS OPUS 3 ZU EINEM KLAVIERTRIO.   W i l h e l m   A l t m a n n .   (F)
   A manuscript arrangement of the first movement and the first 43 measures of the second movement of the string trio
   Op. 3, certainly in Beethoven's autograph, may be an attempt to arrange this work as a trio for Vln, Vcl and Pf.
   In passing from the original to the arrangement, the Vln part is unchanged and the Vla part (with only minor changes)
   becomes the Pf right hand; for the other two parts (Vcl, Pf left hand) either the Vcl is unchanged and a simple Pf left
   hand is added or the original Vcl part becomes the Pf left hand and a new free Vcl part is added. The date of this
   manuscript is uncertain: resemblances are found to similar manuscripts both of 1801 and of 1817. The Pf trio arrangement, as far as it was carried, is given in engraved score.   3 [1920] 129

BEETHOVENS OKTETT OPUS 103 UND SEINE BEARBEITUNG ALS QUINTETT OPUS 4.   A l f r e d   O r e l .   (G)
   The differences between the two works are discussed in great detail. The date of composition of the quintet is fixed
   only as "between 1792 and 1796. "   3 [1920] 159

ZUR GESCHICHTE DER BEETHOVENSCHEN "PROMETHEUS"-BALLETMUSIK.   R o b e r t   L a c h .   (H)
   In 1813, a dozen years after the original production of the two-act ballet to music by Beethoven, Vigano adapted
   the same story to a six-act ballet, using music by Beethoven and other composers (the so-called "greater Prometheus"
   ballet). Another version of the "greater Prometheus," to music by Beethoven and Mozart, and apparently based
   closely on Vigano's work, was staged in 1843 at the Vienna Court Opera by its ballet master A. Hus. The book of
   this last version, with much detail, is given herewith.   3 [1921] 223

BEETHOVEN IN DER JÜNGSTEN GEGENWART. Alfred Heuss.   (A)
Polemic against Pfitzner (see also 7 [1925] 409).   3 [1921] 237

[Itemized the material sold by Schindler to the Preussische Staatsbibliothek in 1843.]   (B)
Wilhelm Altmann.
An incomplete autograph of Op. 125, a fair copy of the 1814 version of Fidelio with Beethoven's corrections, the
autograph of Op. 59 No. 2, various sketches, 31 letters, 136 conversation books. In 1861 he offered further material
that was not accepted, but this finally went to the library by purchase from Nowotny in 1880.
3 [1921] 429,432

DER GROSSE TAKT. Eugen Tetzel.   (C)
By "super-measure" is meant "the joining together of two to twelve measures to form a single group." The number
of measures within a super-measure may vary freely within a single movement. The super-measure is used frequently
by Beethoven; in some works (e. g. , the scherzo of the Ninth Symphony) the composer acknowledges the fact by such
indications as "ritmo di tre battute." The specific application of the concept of the super-measure to the first movement of the C minor Symphony, grasped in part by Weingartner, is elaborated in much detail, and the difference between Weingartner's analysis and that of the author is analyzed.   3 [1921] 605

ERINNERUNGEN AN ERZHERZOG RUDOLPH, DEN FREUND UND SCHÜLER BEETHOVENS. Paul Nettl.   (D)
In some recently discovered manuscripts were found several unpublished compositions of the Archduke Rudolph: two
sets of variations (undoubtedly those referred to in Beethoven's letters of June (or July) 1st 1823 (KS II 263), July 15th
1823 (KS II 268) and August (?) 1823 (KS II 284), and a sketch of some sixty measures to words starting, "Lieber
Beethoven, ich danke für Ihre Wünsche zum neuen Jahre."   4 [1921] 95

BEETHOVENSTUDIEN: II. NINA D'AUBIGNY'S "BRIEFE ÜBER DEN GESANG." Albert Leitzmann.   (E)
Schindler (1860 II 181) mentions a book entitled 'Briefe an Natalie über Gesang' by Nina d'Aubigny-Engelbrunner
(published in 1803) as an item in Beethoven's library "much esteemed and recommended." After a brief biographical
sketch of the sisters d'Aubigny (Susanna and Nina) the author gives excerpts from the book, with which he is not
impressed.   4 [1922] 358

AN UNKNOWN BEETHOVEN LETTER. Max Friedländer.   (F)
Publication of MM 327.   4 [1922] 365

DER GROSSE TAKT. Theodor Wiehmayer.   (G)
The author claims precedence over Tetzel 3 [1921] 605 for whatever is novel or useful in his concept of the "Grosse
Takt," and discusses certain passages of the first movement of the C minor Symphony in which he differs as to
rhythmic analysis. A reply by Tetzel defends his position.   4 [1922] 417

ÜBER BEZIEHUNGEN BEETHOVENS ZU MOZART UND ZU PH. EM. BACH. Reinhard Oppel.   (H)
The author points out the similarity of the variations theme of Mozart's Wind Serenade in C minor K. 388 (later
arranged as a string quintet K. 406) and the finale of Beethoven's quartet Op. 18 No. 4. He also stresses the basic
similarity between the first movement of Op. 2 No. 1 and certain compositions of K.P.E. Bach and J. S. Bach. A
passage in Dvorak's quintet Op. 97 resembles the variations theme of Beethoven's Sonata Op. 26, and an allusion to
a motif of the Pastoral Symphony appears in Dvorak's Violin Sonata Op. 57.
5 [1922] 30

EIN BRIEF BEETHOVENS. Wilhelm Hitzig.   (I)
Letter of February 6th 1823 to Friedrich Duncker, Cabinet Secretary to the King of Prussia and apparently an old
friend, in which Beethoven refers to his ill health of the two or three years previous and to the burdens which the
care of Nephew Karl has thrown upon him, and solicits Duncker's assistance in securing a subscription to the Missa
Solemnis from the King of Prussia.   6 [1924] 266

BEETHOVEN'S USE OF THE SONG 'MARLBOROUGH.' Max Friedlaender.   (J)
Among many other composers, Beethoven used this folksong (in the 'Battle of Victoria' Op. 91).
6 [1924] 318

A BEETHOVEN LETTER.   (K)
An undated letter (probably from 1813) to Zmeskall, saying that he would dine that day with Maelzel.
6 [1924] 350

EINE SKIZZE ZUM ZWEITEN SATZ VON BEETHOVENS STREICHQUARTETT OPUS 132?   Arnold Schmitz.   (A)
  A passage in the trio of the scherzo of Op. 132 which Deiters (TD V 265) pointed out as a borrowing from one of the
  dances for the Redoutensaal is also found in the allemande in A for Pf (GA 25/307), and even more fully in an early
  version of this same allemande.   6 [1924] 659

DAS HOCHZEITSLIED FÜR GIANNATASIO DEL RIO VON BEETHOVEN.   Wilhelm Hitzig.   (B)
  The autograph of the Marriage Cantata for Fanny del Rio (TK III 13), lost for many years, has been found.   An adaptation, published by Ewer & Co. in England in 1858 under the title 'The Wedding Song' is quite inaccurate.
                    7 [1924] 164

ZWEI BISHER UNBEKANNTE BRIEFE BEETHOVENS.   G. Kinsky.   (C)
  (1) Letter without date (from content probably July 18th 1812) to Breitkopf & Härtel, apparently transmitting letter to
  Emilie M. (KS I 259), and referring to disputed honorarium mentioned in the letter of the previous day (KS I 258).
  (2) Letter without date (probably December 1814 or January 1815) to Philipp Pribyll referring to Johann Evang. Fuss.
                    7 [1924] 191

BETRACHTUNGEN ÜBER BEETHOVENS EROICA-SKIZZEN.   Alfred Lorenz.   (D)
  A study of the sketches in Nottebohm's 'Ein Skizzenbuch aus dem Jahre 1803' and of the growth of other works as
  manifested in their sketches to confute the contention of Pfitzner that everything worth while in musical composition
  comes in its perfect form by a flash of inspiration.   7 [1925] 409

BEETHOVEN IN OFEN IM JAHRE 1800.   Ervin Major.   (E)
  Beethoven and Punto (the horn player) were in Ofen (Buda) during the first week of May 1800.
                    8 [1926] 482

ZU BEETHOVENS LEONOREN-OUVERTÜRE Nr. 2.   Wilhelm Lütge.   (F)
  As discussed in 'Der Bär' [1927] 146 by the present author, a copy of the Leonora Overture No. 2 with many corrections
  in Beethoven's hand undoubtedly represents his final intentions.   Several of the transitional passages are abbreviated,
  the repetition of the trumpet call is omitted, and a considerable number of other changes are made.   (See also pp.
  349, 368)   9 [1927] 235

DIE BRIEFE GOTTLIEB CHRISTOPH HÄRTELS AN BEETHOVEN.   Wilhelm Hitzig.   (G)
  Copies of eighteen letters to Beethoven written in the years 1801-05 and 1810, and three letters (1802-03) to Brother
  Karl.   9 [1927] 321

FORMPROBLEME DES SPÄTEN BEETHOVEN.   Moritz Bauer.   (H)
  Primarily a discussion of Beethoven's development in fugal composition, with incidental mention of his modifications
  of classical sonata form and of his use in his mature period of the variations form.   A list of all his compositions in
  fugal form is given.   9 [1927] 341

GIBT ES ZWEI FASSUNGEN VON DER OUVERTÜRE LEONORE Nr. 2?   Josef Braunstein.   (I)
  Polemic against the importance of the version claimed by Lütge (p. 235) to be Beethoven's revision of the familiar
  version.   The difference between the two versions is discussed in detail.   (See also p. 368)
                    9 [1927] 349

DAS ORCHESTER-CRESCENDO BEI BEETHOVEN.   Alfred Heuss.   (J)
                    9 [1927] 361

REVIEW OF A BOOK BY BRAUNSTEIN: 'BEETHOVENS LEONOREN-OUVERTÜREN'.   Wilhelm Lütge.   (K
  Continuation of the dispute between these two authors (see p. 349) regarding the Leonora Overtures.
                    9 [1927] 368

BEETHOVEN. SONATA APPASSIONATA.   (L
  Facsimiledruck.   Statement of certain of the differences between Beethoven's autograph and the accepted version of
  this sonata.   10 [1927] 61

BEETHOVENS ERSTE REISE NACH WIEN IM JAHRE 1787.   Eduard Panzerbieter.   (N
  A contemporary newspaper notice proves that Beethoven spent nights in Munich on April 1st and April 25th 1787.
  From this and other data his journey may be reconstructed as follows: He left Bonn not later than March 20th.   The
  route by way of Munich was not the shortest, quickest or cheapest, but was probably decided upon so that he could

meet Dr. von Schaden and his wife at Wallerstein, to whom Reicha had commended him. He journeyed from Wallerstein to Munich with them, but there is reason to believe that the relations were not as cordial as his later letter (KS
I 2) would indicate. The objective of the journey to Vienna was study of the piano (not of composition) with Mozart.
He had originally planned a considerable sojourn: he took with him from Bonn only enough money for his journey,
and in Vienna would depend on his quarterly stipend as an employee of the Elector in Bonn. His relatively brief stay
in Vienna (two weeks or less) was due in part to Mozart's preoccupation with the illness of his father. Beethoven started his return journey about April 20th, spent the night of April 25th in Munich, briefly revisited Von Schaden, and arrived in Bonn in mid-May.   10 [1927] 153

BEETHOVENS GESAMMELTE WERKE. Otto Erich Deutsch.   (A)
    In mid-1803 Breitkopf & Härtel suggested to Beethoven the preparation of a collected edition of his works (see letter
of June 2nd 1803 from Härtel 9 [1927] 326). There is reason to believe that the projected edition was planned to include the Pf works only. Later that year Zulehner of Mayence announced a collected edition of Beethoven's works
for Pf and strings, against which Beethoven issued a public warning (KS I 79). With his letter of August 21st 1810
to Breitkopf & Härtel (KS I 197) Beethoven sent a letter from one of his friends, suggesting the project of a Gesamtausgabe. The author says that during 1816 Beethoven discussed the project of a collected edition with Friedrich Hofmeister of Leipzig (no reference given), but that these talks were countered by a tempting offer from Steiner & Co.,
which however came to nothing. From 1817 to the end of 1820 Beethoven's letters to Peter Josef Simrock refer often
to the project; in 1820 Artaria and Steiner showed interest.

    During the few years following 1818 Tobias Haslinger had prepared a manuscript collection of Beethoven's works
running to 62 volumes, dedicated to and ultimately purchased by the Archduke Rudolph. While this collection contains some corrections which may be attributed to Beethoven, its value is probably "more calligraphic than auto-
graphic." The project of publishing a complete edition met insuperable difficulties because of the ownership of
various individual compositions by publishers who in many cases were quite unwilling to release their rights. However, between 1828 and 1837 (with a supplementary volume in 1845) Haslinger brought out some 74 compositions in
a "Collected Edition" dedicated to the Archduke Rudolph. The series was very incomplete, including only works for
Pf, Pf and Vln, Pf and Vcl (Op. 17 only), Pf trio, string quartet, and concertos arranged for Pf solo; even in these
categories many works were omitted, including a considerable number of which publication rights were owned by
Haslinger. The author also lists a few early collections in single categories, starting with Schlesinger's collection
of string trios, quartets and quintets (1827) and Probst's collection of symphonies arranged for four hands (1828).
                                                            13 [1930] 60

NEUES ZU BEETHOVENS VOLKSLIEDER-BEARBEITUNGEN. Willy Hess.   (B)
    Collation of the contents of certain manuscripts in the Prussian State Library with TV and other material discloses that
at least 46 songs by Beethoven are extant which have not been published.
                                                            13 [1931] 317

DAS AUTOGRAPH VON BEETHOVENS VIOLINKONZERT. Oswald Jonas.   (C)
    The autograph of the violin concerto contains many alternative readings, some of which appeared in the published
versions of the concerto (either for violin or in the Pf concerto version), others being stricken out or merely not used.
The author discusses these variants at length.   13 [1931] 443

EINE UNBEKANNTE CANZONETTA BEETHOVENS. J. H. Blaxland.   (D)
    A canzonetta "La Tiranna" by Beethoven to words by William Wennington was published in London some time during
the period 1799-1808, and is given herewith. There is reason to believe that about 1799 Beethoven became acquainted with Wennington, of whom a brief biographical sketch is given.
                                                            14 [1931] 29

ZUR CHRONOLOGIE VON BEETHOVENS "OPFERLIED." Oswald Jonas.   (E)
    Beethoven made at least four settings of this poem: (1) Solo Song (GA 23/233), composed not earlier than 1798
(NB II 478, though NV p. 178 says "1795" at the latest) and first published in 1808 (but regarding an edition of this
song earlier than the first one listed in NV see 'Die Musik' 23_1 [1930] 19 and 'Zeitschrift für Musik' 103 [1936] 1048).
(2) Setting for three solo voices, chorus and orchestra (GA 25/268), presumably the first of the songs referred to in
Beethoven's letter of February 15th-18th 1823 to Peters (KS II 226). As Mandyczewski says in the Revisionsbericht to
Ser. 25, it was this version, not Op. 121b as stated in NV, that was performed on April 4th 1824. (3) Setting for solo
voice, chorus and orchestra Op. 121b (GA 22/212), certainly a revision of GA 25/268 rather than the other way round
(see TD IV 469). It is doubtless to this version that Beethoven refers in letters to Reis of March 19th 1825 (KK p. 753)
and April 9th 1825 (KS II 363). Probably written in the summer or fall of 1824 (NB II 542), sent to Schott in November
1824 (KS II 343), published in 1825. (4) Setting for solo voice, unpublished and otherwise unreferred to here.
                                                            14 [1931] 103

ZUR SINNDEUTUNG DER 4. UND 5. SYMPHONIE VON BEETHOVEN.   Arnold Schering.   (A)
    The first three movements of the Fourth Symphony have as a background three poems by Schiller; the finale is
a "Stroll by a Brook." The C minor Symphony is another example of "esoteric program music": a "symphony
of national exaltation" which does not follow any specific poem.

16 [1934] 65

BEETHOVENS SKIZZEN UND IHRE GESTALTUNG ZUM WERK.   Oswald Jonas.   (B)
    The importance of Beethoven's sketches in developing the form as well as the content of a finished composition
is discussed, with examples drawn from Opp. 10, 24, 93 and 96.   16 [1934] 449

EIN SKIZZENBLATT BEETHOVENS AUS DEN JAHREN 1796-97.   Benedikt Szabolcsi.   (C)
    A leaf from a sketch book contains an extended study for the third movement of the Pf Concerto Op. 15, a
passage from the Quintet Op. 4 (or possibly from the Octet Op. 103), and an unidentified rondo theme in E flat.

17 [1935] 545

HOMMAGE À L. VAN BEETHOVEN. J. Jongen.   (A)
 Centenary address.   9 [1927] 29

LES ORIGINES BELGES DE BEETHOVEN. P. Bergmans.   (B)
 Brief and popular biographical sketch of Grandfather Ludwig (described as the son of Henry Adelard) and of Father
 Johann.   9 [1927] 33

LE GRAND-PÈRE DE BEETHOVEN. Paul Bergmans.   (C)
 On the strength of Bake-master Fischer's statement that Grandfather Ludwig had said that he was born in Ghent, the
 author searched the parish records of that city without finding a trace of any van Beethoven. Otherwise, this article
 is merely a correction of the author's earlier paper (9 [1927] 33) in accordance with the genealogy worked out by
 Pols ('De Gulden Passer' 9 [1927] 51).   10 [1928] 37

ACTA MUSICOLOGIA

AN EARLY EDITION OF SCORES OF SYMPHONIES BY HAYDN, MOZART AND BEETHOVEN. Georg Kinsky.   (D)
 The firm of Cianchettini & Sperati in London published scores of 18 symphonies of Haydn, six of Mozart, and the
 first three of Beethoven in subscription series in 1807-09. The Beethoven Second Symphony formed the issue of
 November-December 1808, the First that of January-February 1809, and the Eroica that of March-April 1809.
 This was much earlier than the first German publication of the scores (Simrock, 1822-23).
              13 [1941] 78

ZWEI B-DUR-THEMEN (EINE BEETHOVEN-SCHUBERT STUDIE). Ludwig Misch.   (E)
 A similarity is noted between the principal theme of the last movement of Beethoven's quartet in B flat Op. 130
 and the theme of the finale of Schubert's posthumous piano sonata in B flat. The author analyzes the harmonic
 structure of the Beethoven theme, coming to the conclusion that the movement in which it occurs, though written
 after the rest of the quartet, was in its creation made an integral part of the quartet.
              13 [1941] 85

ALLGEMEINE DEUTSCHE LEHRERZEITUNG

BEETHOVEN AND PESTALOZZI. Ernst Linde.   (F)
 While it is very possible that Beethoven never even heard the name of Pestalozzi, a link between the two men was
 the close and lasting friendship between each of them and Therese von Brunswick, who from 1808 to her death in
 1861 was an ardent disciple of Pestalozzi's pedagogical ideals.   60 [1908] 181

ALLGEMEINE HOMÖOPATHISCHE ZEITUNG

BEETHOVEN UND DIE HOMÖOPATHIE. Max Unger.   (G)
 In July 1823 an unidentified visitor from Leipzig (SchKH III 359) told Beethoven that Dr. Hahnemann (founder of
 the science of homeopathy) and an associate Dr. Müller in Leipzig had cured cases of deafness worse than his.
 There is no indication that Beethoven followed up this possibility. In Kal 1022 the author's reading of an almost
 illegible word ("homeopathic doctor" where Kalischer-Shedlock has "consulting doctor") indicates that Beethoven
 was being attended in August 1825 by a homeopathic physician for his stomach ailments.
              [1951] 55

ALLGEMEINE ZEITUNG DES JUDENTUMS

BEETHOVEN UND DIE RUSSISCH-JUDISCHE VOLKSMUSIK. James Rothstein.   (H)
 Folk songs and liturgical melodies current in Russian Jewry duplicate note for note (though at much slower tempi)
 important themes from Opp. 13 and 57. In these cases (and also in the case of a song similar to Papageno's aria
 "Ein Mädchen oder Weibchen" which Beethoven used as the subject for Vcl variations) it is probable that the borrowing was from Beethoven (or Mozart), not by them.   70 [1906] 200

LUDWIG VAN BEETHOVENS ERSTE LIEBE.   A. Lewinsky.   (A)
  From originals in the Bibliotheque Nationale in Paris, Alfred Prins has published an exchange of letters from the
  spring of 1792 between Beethoven and a 17-year-old Jewish girl Rahel Löwenstein: May 8th 1792 -- an eight line
  love poem from Beethoven: "Wie lange sucht vergebens/Dich doch..." May 11th 1792 -- reply in similar form.
  May 19th 1792 -- letter from Beethoven: "Ich nenne Dich Du! Du verzeihst mir..." in which Beethoven urges
  Rahel to embrace Christianity so that he can marry her.   May 28th 1792 -- reply from Rahel maintaining her fidelity to her faith and her people.   June 3rd 1792 -- letter from Beethoven: "Rahel, Dr Holde! Ich und Du -- wir K
  inder!..." as a letter of farewell. (NOTE. This correspondence is stated to have taken place in the spring of
  1792 while Beethoven was in Vienna. Note that in fact he was in Bonn at this time, not having been in Vienna
  between his visit to Mozart in the summer of 1788 and his final departure from Bonn in 1792. Are these letters
  actually from the spring of 1793?)   85 [1921] 10

ALLGEMEINER MUSIKALISCHER ANZEIGER

VERZEICHNIS DER SÄMMTLICHEN PORTRÄTS VON LUDWIG VAN BEETHOVEN WELCHE IN DEM ZEITRAUME VOM   (B)
        1801 BIS 1839 ERSCHIENEN SIND.   Aloys Fuchs.
  Twenty published portraits are listed.   11 [1839] 206

ALSACE FRANCAISE

CONFIDENCES DE BEETHOVEN.   Adolphe Boschot.   (C)
  Popular account of a meeting with Stumpff in September 1824. 11_1 [1931] 152

AMERICAN-GERMAN REVIEW

BEETHOVEN'S SIGNATURE IN THE "TENTH SYMPHONY."   Bayard Quincy Morgan.   (D)
  In his first symphony, Brahms intentionally plagiarized Beethoven.
                                                     5 No. 3 [February 1939] 9

AMERICAN JOURNAL OF PSYCHOLOGY

BEETHOVEN'S CONCEPT OF THE "WHOLE."   Paul C. Squires.   (E)
  Newman's concept of Beethoven's creative process as being similar to that of a sculptor who visualizes his statue
  in a block of marble and merely cuts away what he does not want is a "tempting but superficial analogy; to us it
  appears as a most misleading, downright dangerous device. We are convinced that all lines of evidence justify
  us in concluding that Beethoven's themes are properly to be regarded as so many primordial cell-constellations,
  bearing within them the potentialities of colossal configurations that finally come to fruition as growth phenomena
  ... not something laid bare little by little under a scalpel."   48 [1936] 684

AMERICAN MERCURY

BEETHOVEN.   O. G. Sonneck.   (F)
  Centennial essay.   10 [1927] 316

THE "HAMMERKLAVIER" SONATA FOR ORCHESTRA.   Ernest Newman.   (G)
  Detailed and favorable review of Weingartner's orchestration of Op. 106.
                                                     22 [1931] 241

THE PLAYING OF BEETHOVEN'S VIOLIN MUSIC. William Kozlenko.   (A)
General.   1 [1935] 39

BEETHOVEN'S OPUS 18 QUARTETS. Peter Hugh Reed.   (B)
"A summary of estimates and recordings."   3 [1937] 123

BEETHOVEN'S OPUS 59 QUARTETS. Peter Hugh Reed.   (C)
Popular.   4 [1938] 4

ANNALES POLITIQUES ET LITTÉRAIRES

LE CENTENAIRE DE BEETHOVEN. Camille Mauclair.   (D)
Centenary essay.   88 [1927] 303

LA VIE AMOUREUSE DE BEETHOVEN. Henry Bordeaux.   (E)
Superficial and misleading.   88 [1927] 304

LES DÉBUTS DE BEETHOVEN A PARIS. Georges Huisman.   (F)
Brief and popular account of performances under Habeneck, for the most part during Beethoven's lifetime.
                                              88 [1927] 306

ANNALS OF OTOLOGY, RHINOLOGY, AND LARYNGOLOGY

THE DEAFNESS OF BEETHOVEN. Ira Frank.   (G)
Popular.   44 [1935] 327

DISEASE -- OR DEFAMATION? Charles K. Carpenter.   (H)
The only statements by Thayer that can be taken as even indirect reference to possible luetic infection are in TK I
253, II 87, and II 294. "Thayer asserts that Beethoven did not always escape the common penalties of transgression,
that a reference to the absolute purity of his morals is not well-founded, and that a physician had destroyed his correspondence lest some of it fall into careless hands. That is a slim foundation, but it covers all that Thayer committed
to print. All the rest of the so-called evidence cited by later biographers is at second or third hand, and refers to documents which are not produced and which cannot be published." The rumor about two significant prescriptions was
started by Grove in his Dictionary article of 1879. Frimmel and Leo Jacobsohn built elaborately on documents which
are referred to but not identified or quoted. Newman's contention that Beethoven's syphilitic infection may be taken
as an established fact is examined in great detail and found to be wholly unsupported by evidence. Non-medical
writers since 1927, however, in general follow Newman. The author joins with many other medical men whose opinions he cites in the conclusion that no evidence, clinical or documentary, worth a second glance has been adduced to
give basis for the widespread popular opinion that Beethoven was luetic.
                                              45 [1936] 1069

ANTHROPOLOGISCHE GESELLSCHAFT IN WIEN: MITTEILUNGEN

DIE CRANIEN DREIER MUSIKALISCHER KORYPHÄEN. C. Langer von Edenberg.   (I)
Anthropometric measurements, with discussion, of the skulls of Haydn, Beethoven, and Schubert.
                                              17 [1887] 33

BERICHT AN DEN GEBEINEN LUDWIG VAN BEETHOVENS. A. Weisbach.   (J)
Report of a detailed examination of Beethoven's skull.   18 [1888] 73

APOLLO; A JOURNAL OF THE ARTS (London)

AN APPROACH TO BEETHOVEN'S FINAL STRING QUARTETS. Martin Johnson.   (K)
Non-scholarly discussion for the intelligent amateur.   33 [1941] 88

---

* Volumes 1-10 published as American Music Lover.

BEETHOVEN AND BOURDELLE.   Emmanuel Bondeville.   (A)
  From 1888 or before to the year of his death (1929) the sculptor was almost obsessed by the idea of Beethoven as a
  subject, and made repeated studies of the composer as well as several completed sculptures.
                                              NS 32 [1936] 263

                                              ART ET MÉDECINE

UN SOURD DE GÉNIE.   Paul Voivenel.   (B)
  Rhapsodic commentary on a thesis submitted by René Apperce at Lyon.
                                              [June 1931] 40

                  ATHENAEUM; A JOURNAL OF LITERATURE, SCIENCE, THE FINE ARTS,
                              MUSIC AND THE DRAMA (London)

REVIEW OF SCHINDLER-MOSCHELES 'LIFE OF BEETHOVEN.'   (C)
  The review includes Kal 36, Kal 300, and a part of the Heiligenstadt will.
                                              [1841] 123,150

BEETHOVEN AND CLEMENTI.   J. S. Shedlock.   (D)
  Facsimile of parts of the letter from Clementi to his partner Collard (TK II 102), with first statement of the fact
  that two and a half years after the date of Beethoven's contract he had received no payment.
                                              120 [1902] 134

                                              ATLANTIC MONTHLY

BEETHOVEN: HIS CHILDHOOD AND YOUTH.   (E)
  An account of Beethoven's Bonn years, rather flowery but notably in advance of other Beethoven biographical
  material up to that time. (NOTE by DWM. A letter from the Associate Editor of 'The Atlantic Monthly' dated
  October 6th 1948 reads: "Our records indicate that you are correct in attributing the article on Beethoven to
  Alexander Wheelock Thayer.")   1 [1858] 847

A CENTURY OF BEETHOVEN.   Harvey Wickham.   (F)
  Long but readable centenary essay.   139 [1927] 355

GOETHE AND BEETHOVEN.   Romain Rolland.   (G)
  An abridged translation of the author's book of the same title.   143 [1929] 187

                     ATLANTIS; LÄNDER, VÖLKER, REISEN (Berlin)

EIN BILD VON BEETHOVENS UNSTERBLICHER GELIEBTEN?   Stephan Ley.   (H)
  Of two miniatures found in Beethoven's Nachlass, one has been definietely identified as a portrait of Giulietta
  Guicciardi (identified by Count Gallenberg, her son). The other has been assumed to represent Countess Marie
  Erdödy, but comparison with an authenticated portrait of the Countess shows that this identification is almost
  certainly incorrect. Does the unidentified miniature represent the unidentified addressee of the famous letter?
                                              5 [1933] 766

SCHLOSS GRÄTZ BEI TROPPAU: BEETHOVEN UND DIE FÜRSTLICHE FAMILIE LICHNOWSKY.   Stephan Ley.   (I)
  Popular and general account of Beethoven's friendship with the Lichnowsky family, and pictures of the estate at
  which Beethoven visited in 1806 and 1811, still (in 1937) owned by the family.
                                              9 [1937] 59

BEETHOVEN UND FÜRST LOBKOWITZ.   Stephan Ley.   (J)
  A popular but detailed account of Beethoven's relationship with Prince Joseph Franz Max Lobkowitz (1772-1816).
                                              9 [1937] 748

BEETHOVEN UND DIE GRÄFLICHE FAMILIE BRUNSVIK. Stephan Ley.   (A)
   In his relationship with various members of the Habsburg nobility, Beethoven was formal with the Esterhazys (to whom
   he dedicated the Mass in C major Op. 86 and the Three Marches for Piano Four Hands), friendly with Lobkowitz,
   even closer to Lichnowsky, and most intimate of all with the Brunsviks. His friendship with the daughters Therese
   and Josephine (Deym) is described with quotations from the letters and journals of the two girls. The author rules
   out Therese and Giulietta Guicciardi (a relative of Count Joseph Brunsvik, uncle of Therese and Josephine) as being
   possibly the Immortal Beloved, but in this connection mentions the well-recognized affection between Beethoven
   and Josephine. A bust of Beethoven by Janos Pasztor in the grounds of the Brunsvik estate in Martonvasar (south-
   west of Budapest) is portrayed.   12 [1940] 101

VON UNGEDRUCKTE MUSIK BEETHOVENS. Willy Hess.   (B)
   Discussion in some detail of many of the unpublished works; facsimile of p. 1 of Zapfenstreich No. 1 (H-7) and of
   p. 1 of the trio of Zapfenstreich No. 3 (H-9).   EDr of two settings of vocal quartet Nei campi e nelle selve (H-179,
   H-182).   25 [1953] 209

                              AUSLESE

BEETHOVENS TESTAMENT.   (C)
   Transcription (without comments) of the Heiligenstadt will.   10 [1936] 561

                          BACH-JAHRBUCH

WORKS OF BACH THAT WERE AVAILABLE TO BEETHOVEN.   (D)
   As late as 1792, the only works of Bach that had been printed were the four parts of the Clavierübung, the 2- and
   3-part Inventions, the Kunst der Fuge, the Musikalisches Opfer, various chorale preludes for organ, and a few minor
   works. The two parts of the Well-Tempered Clavier, some of the organ music, four clavier concertos, the St. Luke
   Passion, parts of the Christmas Oratorio, 25-30 cantatas, and a few miscellaneous works were available in manuscript
   copies from commercial sources. Even by the year of Beethoven's death, this list had not been sensibly increased except by the chromatic fantasy and fugue, the sonatas for violin and clavier, the Magnificat, the D major suite for orchestra, and commercial manuscript copies of the sonatas for violin solo and the suites for 'cello solo. Beethoven's
   familiarity with the works of Bach (e.g., the B minor Mass, Kal 226) must have come largely from privately circulated manuscript copies.   3 [1906] 84

BEZIEHUNGEN BACHS ZU VORGÄNGERN UND NACHFOLGERN. Reinhard Oppel.   (E)
   A parallelism is drawn between the fugue in A flat of the second book of the WTC and the fugue of Beethoven's
   Op. 110.   22 [1925] 11

                              BÄR

DIE ERSTEN FIDELIO-AUFFÜHRUNGEN IN BERLIN. Alfred Chr. Kalischer.   (F)
   Material later published (with minor changes) in 'Beethoven und seine Zeitgenossen' I 137-62.
                                           12 [1886] 342,354

LUDWIG RELLSTAB IN SEINEM PERSÖNLICHEN VERKEHRE MIT LUDWIG VAN BEETHOVEN.   (G)
   Alfred Chr. Kalischer.
   Material later published (with minor changes) in 'Beethoven und seine Zeitgenossen' I 269-86.
                                           12 [1886] 536,546

BEETHOVEN AND ZELTER. Alfred Chr. Kalischer.   (H)
   Material later published (with minor changes) in 'Beethoven und seine Zeitgenossen' I 213-38.
                                           13 [1886] 7,24,35

BEETHOVEN UND DER VARNHAGEN-RAHEL'SCHE KREIS. Alfred Chr. Kalischer.   (I)
   Material later published (with minor changes) in 'Beethoven und seine Zeitgenossen' I 97-117.
                                           14 [1887] 8,22,35,48

ZUR VORGESCHICHTE VON BEETHOVENS NEUNTER SINFONIE. M. Frey.   (J)
   Fiction.   24 [1898] 31

DIE WELTANSCHAUUNG IN BEETHOVENS TONKUNST.   V. Grüner.   (A)
   Centenary address.   58 [1927] 156

BERICHTE DER WISSENSCHAFTLICHEN GESELLSCHAFT PHILOMATHIE IN NEISSE

DIE POETISCHE IDEE IN BEETHOVENS WERKEN.   Blaschke.   (B)
   Summary of a paper which apparently contended that in each composition Beethoven had some specific picture
   before his eyes.   39 [1928] 142

BERLINISCHE MUSIKALISCHE ZEITUNG

MUSIKAL. NACHRICHTEN AUS BONN.   Christian Gottlob Neefe.   (C)
   Mention that Beethoven had gone to Vienna the previous November to study with Haydn, and quotation of letter
   from him as given in Kast 12 (M-503).   [26 October 1793] 153

BIBLIOFILIA

DÉCOUVERTE DU MANUSCRIT AUTOGRAPHE DE LA DIXIÈME SONATE DE L. VAN BEETHOVEN.   Leo S. Olschki. (D)
   The history of the sonata is summarized, with the conclusion that it was completed at the end of December 1812.
   The first three movements were probably completed in February 1812 and were obviously written fluently. The last
   movement contains many corrections and deleted passages. Translation is given of a note from the journal 'Marzocco'
   telling of this discovery and of a performance of the sonata from this manuscript. Facsimiles of the first pages of the
   first and second movements are included. (NOTE by DWM. This manuscript is now in the Morgan Library in New
   York City.)   9 [1907] 1

BIBLIOTHÈQUE UNIVERSELLE ET REVUE SUISSE

LES AVATARS DE "FIDELIO."   Anna Déborah d'Alsheim.   (E)
   An account of the history of the opera.   70 [1913] 293

BLACKWOOD'S EDINBURGH MAGAZINE

A MEETING WITH BEETHOVEN.   Edward Blackwood.   (F)
   Note starting: "We were in Germany for a month last spring, and took the opportunity of spending part of a day with
   our friend Beethoven." Article from the 'Wiener Zeitschrift für Kunst' regarding the recent acquisition by Beethoven
   of a Broadwood piano is quoted in full.   5 [1819] 697

PIANISTS OF THE PAST.   Charles Salaman.   (G)
   Anecdote given on TK I 263 told by Neate at age 92 was direct from Beethoven himself.
                                                    170 [1901] 312

BLÄTTER DER STAATSOPER

DER LEIDENSWEG DES "FIDELIO."   Julius Kapp.   (H)
   A recounting of known facts.   1 No. 2 [17 December 1920] 2

BEETHOVENS LETZTE TAGE (UNBEKANNTE BRIEFE UND DOKUMENTE).   (I)
   Excerpts from letters written by Schindler in February and March 1827, and an account of the funeral published in the
   'Wiener Presse' and still extant in the hand of the Archduke Rudolph.
                                                    1 No. 2 [17 December 1920] 9

BEETHOVEN IN EIGENEN WORT.   (J)
   Article which includes two letters claimed to be published for the first time: "Ich glaubte nicht vorgestern, dass Sie
   so früh kommen würden..." (To Schindler "Donnerstag 4 Mai" 1815? 1820? 1826?) "Folge deinem Führer und Vater;
   fliehe alles, was deine..." (To Nephew Karl; no date.)   1 No. 2 [17 December 1920] 13

STIMMEN ÜBER BEETHOVEN.   (A)
   Quotations from articles by E. T. A. Hoffmann, Spohr (Beethoven als Dirigent, 1815), Berlioz (Das Quartett Cis moll
   Op. 131 -- first publication of comments by Berlioz on one of the Habeneck concerts), Wagner (revised ending of his
   'Beethoven').   1 No. 2 [20 December 1920] 14

ZUR "MISSA SOLEMNIS." Bruno Walter.   (B)
   Essay.   1 No. 2 [17 December 1920] 20

BEETHOVEN UND DIE MODERNE. Hans Pfitzner.   1 No. 2 [17 December 1920] 23   (C)

BOOKMAN

BEETHOVEN: A STUDY IN PERSONALITY. Max Byron.   (D)
   Centenary essay.   71 [1927] 334

Boston Public Library
MORE BOOKS

LUDWIG VAN BEETHOVEN. Edward Ballantine.   (E)
   Centenary essay.   2 [1927] 41

A BEETHOVEN LETTER.   (F)
   Facsimile, transcription and translation of letter to Amalie Sebald (KS I 268 No. 306).
                                                     2 [1927] 46,84

BEETHOVEN IN BOSTON: FIRST AMERICAN PERFORMANCES OF HIS WORKS. Richard G. Appel.   (G)
   Compositions by Beethoven began to appear on Boston programs shortly after 1820. The nine symphonies received
   their premieres between 1841 and 1853; the first performance of the Missa Solemnis was on March 12th 1897. Much
   miscellaneous information on early Beethoven performances in Boston and in the United States is given.
                                                     2 [1927] 47

BOSTON SYMPHONY ORCHESTRA PROGRAMS

THE 'GROSSE FUGE' OPUS 133. Philip Hale.   (H)
   Program notes.   [1916-17] 154

BEETHOVEN'S LAST QUARTETS. Theodore Helm.   (I)
   A translation by F. H. Martens of pp. 169-73 of the author's 'Beethovens Streichquartette' (1910).
                                                     [1916-17] 160

ROMANCE (CANTABILE). John N. Burk.   (J)
   Program notes on H-11.   74 [1955] 729

BÜCHERWURM

BEETHOVEN ALS MASS UNSERER ZEIT. Richard Benz.   (K)
   Centennial essay.   12 [1927] 161

THE PHILHARMONIC SOCIETY'S BUST OF BEETHOVEN.   Edward Speyer.   (A)
    The bust by Johann Schaller (1777-1842), presented to the Philharmonic Society of London with great pomp in 1870,
    was not made from life, and is of no especial historic or artistic importance.
                                                        24 [1913] 164

CHRONIQUE MÉDICALE

LA SURDITÉ DE BEETHOVEN.   Klotz-Forest.   (B)
    Popular, with quotations from letters, memoirs of associates, etc.   The author diagnoses the deafness as being due
    to otitis media.   12 [1905] 321

LA DERNIÈRE MALADIE ET LA MORT DE BEETHOVEN.   Klotz-Forest.   (C)
    The author quotes some thirty letters from the period 1812-25 in which Beethoven comments on ill health of one
    kind or another.   The course of his last illness is traced with many quotations from the conversation books.   The
    author agrees with Drs. Malfatti and Wawruch that "Beethoven's fatal illness was the result of excessive drinking."
                                                        13 [1906] 209,241

CICERONE

BEETHOVEN-DENKMAL IN BERLIN.   Kuhn.   (D)
    Studies submitted by Edwin Scharff and by Rudolf Belling in the competition for a Beethoven memorial in Berlin
    are portrayed.   18 [1926] 711,721

CONTEMPORARY REVIEW

BEETHOVEN.   Daniel F. Wiseman.   (E)
    Centenary essay.   131 [1927] 352

THE NINTH SYMPHONY OF BEETHOVEN.   Ashley Sampson.   (F)
    Fanciful interpretation.   153 [1938] 734

DAHEIM

BEETHOVENS JUGENDLIEBE.   Ludwig Nohl.   (G
    Popular account of Beethoven's acceptance into the family of the von Breunings, and statement that Beethoven's
    interest in Eleonore's friend Jeannette d'Honrath of Cologne was the cause of the coolness referred to in Beethoven's
    letter of 2 November 1793 to Eleonore (KS I 7 No. 6).   1 [1865] 390

BEETHOVENS LETZTE TAGE.   Ludwig Nohl.   (H
    Popular account based on Schindler.   .   2 [1866] 480

LUDWIG VAN BEETHOVEN.   Ferdinand Hiller.   (I
    Popular biographical sketch.   7 [1871] 246,262

DAS BEETHOVENHAUS IN BONN.   Ferdinand Pfohl.   (J
    Popular description.   27 [1890] 204

DAS SOGENANNTE BEETHOVENBILDNIS VON G. v. KÜGELGEN.   Theodor von Frimmel.   (K
    The miniature which is generally accepted as a portrait by Gerhardt von Kügelgen of Beethoven at the age of about
    16 years is actually a copy by Count Egloffstein of a known portrait of the poet Max von Schenkendorff.   (This article
    also appeared verbatim (or substantially so) in 'Velhagen und Klasings Monatshefte' 5 [1891] 207.)
                                                        27 [1891] 395,642

BEETHOVEN IN TEPLITZ. Wolfgang A. Thomas.   (A)
An account of Beethoven's holiday in August 1811 with Varnhagen von Ense, Baroness Elise von der Recke and
Amalie Sebald, and of his holiday in the summer of 1812 with Goethe and with Amalie. (See also 'Neue Musik-
Zeitung' 7 [1886] 62)   46 No. 49 [3 September 1910] 19

DIE NEUNTE SINFONIE VON BEETHOVEN IN BERLIN. Martin Jacobi.   (B)
Popular account of the first Berlin performance on November 27th 1826.
                                                                    49 No. 1 [5 October 1912] 25

BEETHOVEN ALS GOETHEKENNER. W. A. Thomas-San Galli.   (C)
Popular   51 No. 32 [8 May 1915] 24

LENAU AND BEETHOVEN. Konrad Huschke.   (D)
There is no evidence that Lenau knew Beethoven personally, though undoubtedly he saw the composer often in the
Vienna taverns. For all his life Lenau was much influenced by Beethoven's music.
                                                                    53 No. 14 [6 January 1917] 10

BEETHOVEN AND GOETHE. Konrad Huschke.   (E)
Popular summary.   54 No. 50 [14 September 1918] 8

BEETHOVENS "UNSTERBLICHE GELIEBTE." Wilhelm Meyer.   (F)
Popular biographical sketches of Giulietta Guicciardi and Therese von Brunsvik as possible Immortal Beloveds.
                                                                    55 No. 11 [14 December 1918] 9

BEETHOVEN UND DIE WELT. W. J. Kleefeld.   (G)
Emotional commentary on the principal compositions.   62 No. 49 [4 September 1926] 17

ZUR HUNDERTSTEN WIEDERKEHR VON BEETHOVENS TODESTAG. Paul Oskar Höcker.   (H)
Centenary essay.   63 No. 26 [26 March 1927] 1

DIE SINFONIE DER FREUDE. Wilhelm Kleefeld.   (I)
Popular account of the conception and composition of the Ninth Symphony.
                                                                    63 No. 26 [26 March 1927] 9

BEETHOVEN UND DIE TANZKUNST. Christiane Rautter.   (J)
Beethoven's memorandum book shows that while he was living with Prince Lichnowsky he took dancing lessons from
a certain Andreas Linder. Beethoven's works for the dance, or influenced by the dance, are many: the 12 Minuette
and Deutsche Tänze for the Redoutensaal (22 November 1795) and the Ecossaises written shortly before his death.
The dances written for two violins and bass were certainly written to be danced to: that was the standard instrumental
combination for dancing. Had Vigano been able to comprehend Beethoven's greatness, 'Prometheus' would doubtless
have been the first of a series of works which changed the ballet as much as Beethoven changed the symphony.
                                                                    68 No. 6 [5 November 1931] 13

DER TITAN LUDWIG VAN BEETHOVEN. Friedrich Herzfeld.   (K)
Popular biographical sketch.   77 No. 11 [11 December 1940] 7

DEUTSCH-AMERIKANISCHE GESCHICHTSBLÄTTER

THE DATE OF COMPOSITION OF THE RONDO A CAPRICCIO OPUS 129. Bernhard Ziehn.   (L)
After stating: "This rondo embraces a compass of but five octaves, and must have been written before 1803," the
author sarcastically reviews the "proofs" offered by Hans von Bülow in his edition of this composition to show that
it should be included in Beethoven's "last period."   26-27 [1927] 83

WIE SICH BEETHOVEN ZU DER AKADEMISCHEN FRAGEN VON DER ENGLISCHEN GRÖSSE DER HALBTÖNE VERHEILT.   (M)
       Bernhard Ziehn.
Citations are given, mostly from the quartets, to show that Beethoven thought and wrote entirely in the tempered
scale. Examples are given of almost every interval concerned, from a doubly augmented unison to represent a
major second to a doubly diminished ninth as a true octave.   26-27 [1927] 228

BEETHOVENS PRAGER AUFENTHALT IM JAHRE 1796.   Arthur Chitz.   (A)
   In his letter of February 19th 1796 from Prague to Brother Johann (KS I 12) Beethoven referred to friends whom he
   had acquired there.   Marginal notations on sketches made during the stay in Prague indicate that these friends included the piano teacher Franz Duschek and his wife (a singer), another outstanding singer of the city Agathe Ulrich,
   and the amateur and patron Anton von Schindelar.   While in Prague Beethoven wrote two pieces for mandoline and
   clavier (GA 25/295-96) and also a third one, a sonata movement in C major, published herewith (and also in 'S.I.M.
   Revue Musicale' 8 [1912] No. 12 p. 24).   From the sketches it can be stated with assurance that all three of these
   numbers were written for the Countess Josephine Clary (later the Countess Clam-Gallas), to whom the concert aria
   'Ah perfido!', Op. 65, was dedicated.   13 [1913] 28

DEUTSCHE BÜHNE

BEETHOVEN AND BERLIN.   Wilhelm Widmann.   (B)
   Records do not show when the first performance of a Beethoven work in Berlin took place.   On February 26th 1813
   the overture to Egmont was performed, and a lukewarm commentary on it is quoted from a letter from Zelter to
   Goethe.   (It is noted that from 1801 to 1819 the music used for stage performances of the tragedy was that of
   Reichardt, not of Beethoven.)   An announcement of the first Berlin performance of Fidelio (October 11th 1815)
   shows that the Leonora was Frau Josephine Schulze (née Killitschgy); Milder-Hauptmann sang the role in its second
   performance three days later, and thereafter for a total of eleven performances out of her 21 guest appearances (see
   Beethoven's letter of January 6th 1816 to her (KS I 390), in which "Kappelmeister B" is probably Bernhard Anselm
   Weber, the conductor of the Berlin performances.)   The members of the Berlin cast are discussed.   'Christus am
   Oelberge' and 'The Battle of Vittoria' were performed on May 8th 1816; other first performances are listed, and
   many later productions of Fidelio are discussed.   13 [1921] 2,24

DEUTSCHE EINHEIT

BEETHOVEN UND DIE BÜRGERLICHE FREIHEIT.   Stubmann.   (C)
   Centenary address.
                                                      9 [1927] 263

DEUTSCHE GESANGSKUNST

DRAMATURGISCHE ERLÄUTERUNG EINZELNER BÜHNENGESTALTEN: FIDELIO.   H. von der Pfordten.   (D)
   A detailed consideration of the problems which face the singer, the conductor and the stage manager at many
   specific points in the opera.   1 [1901] 184

DEUTSCHE KUNST UND DEKORATION

EIN WORT VON BEETHOVEN.   (E)
   An inspirational essay on the remark attributed to Beethoven: "Künstler weinen nicht; Künstler sind feurig."
                                                      34 [1931] 269

(A)

NEUE BEETHOVENSTUDIEN. Theodor von Frimmel.
  EDr MM 309 From the writing, the letter would seem to have come from about 1820. Ignaz Arlet, with two
partners, took over the tavern 'Zum schwarzen Kameel' on 21 June 1818 and retired from the business in 1832.
The letter cannot be dated closer than 1818-26. A hitherto unpublished sketch is given of the andante of the
Piano Sonata in D major Op. 28 in what approaches its final form, except that the section in D major is omitted.
EDr MM 202, which the author dates certainly between 1814 and 1824 and probably between 1814 and 1817.
                                    18 [1891] 2

(B)

NEUE BEETHOVENSTUDIEN. Theodor von Frimmel.
  EDr (?) Kal 1033: Frimmel recounts incidents connected with Beethoven's residence in the apartment on the
fourth floor of Johannesgasse Nr. 1. EDr MM 45: "The name 'Baumann' is written in roman characters. In the
lower loop of the 'B' a small roman 's' appears, to indicate 'saumann' (dirty fellow) instead of Baumann. Beethoven could not pass up such a joke." No date is assigned for the letter; the addressee may have been the court
actor Friedrich Baumann or his brother Anton. The only other reference to Baumann in the correspondence (Kal
355) does not help. The one-act singspiel 'Adrian von Ostade' (book by Treitschke, music by Weigl) was first
performed in Vienna on 3 October 1807, and was heard 125 times in the next fifteen years. Frimmel places this
letter not long after the premiere of the singspiel. EDr MM 229: From content and style, almost certainly to
Nanette Streicher, 1817 or 1818. Note the reference to the Küchenbuch in another letter from early January 1818
(Kal 574, there incorrectly dated -- see NBJ 197).   20 [1893] 25

(C)

NEUE BEETHOVENSTUDIEN. Theodor von Frimmel.
  With reference to the fantastic military titles in Beethoven's correspondence with his friends at Steiner's, a letter
from Piringer to Beethoven is cited in which Piringer signs himself "Illustrissimi Generalissimi humillimus servus."
A Stammbuch formerly owned by Piringer is described which contains an Allegretto in B minor (WoO 61) inscribed
by Beethoven, "Allegretto von ludwig van Beethoven am 18ten Februar 1821." This is given in full (see also
Frimmel 'Beethoven'(6th ed.) pp. 64, 66, facsimile of first page).
                                    20 [1893] 65

(D)

NEUE BEETHOVENSTUDIEN. Theodor von Frimmel.
  A letter dated 9 April 1818 from Johann Wolfmayer offers Beethoven 100 ducats for the Requiem Mass that he said
he planned to compose (see NB II 504). Beethoven's address is given as "Auf der Landstrasse, Gärtnergasse Nr. 26
'zum grünen Baum' 2. Stock." Probably at Wolfmayer's instigation, Beethoven was on 1 October 1819 elected an
honorary member of the Guild of Merchants of Vienna, of which Joseph Ritter von Henickstein was one of the
directors. The letter of transmission of Beethoven's diploma of membership in the Royal Swedish Academy of
Music (see Kal 877) is described. The letter is dated "Stockholm, 31 January 1823." A silver plate engraved
with the well-known sketch by Joseph Daniel Boehm (BStud I 128) is described. EDr MM 100: Frimmel assigns
the date "about 4 July 1811," saying, "The last dated letter before the journey bears the date 4 July and was
written from Vienna" (Kal 244). (Note however that Kal 246 of 20 July was also written from Vienna.) EDr MM
258, MM 264.   22 [1895] 17,29,45,61

DEUTSCHE MEDIZINISCHE WOCHENSCHRIFT

(E)

LUDWIG VAN BEETHOVENS GEHÖRLEIDEN. Leo Jacobsohn.
  Popular account, favoring Beethoven's youthful attack of typhoid fever as the cause of the ultimate deafness.
                                    36 [1910] 1282

(F)

BEETHOVENS GEHÖRLEIDEN UND LETZTE KRANKHEIT. Leo Jacobsohn.
  In a letter dated October 29th 1880, Alexander Wheelock Thayer refers to Beethoven's affliction with venereal
disease as "well known to many" and states that "his ill health and his deafness perhaps come from the same common
cause." Rolland doubted that Beethoven believed himself afflicted with syphilis, saying: "How could he have had so
little regard for his own reputation as to have authorized an autopsy if he knew the source of his ills?" The generally
known facts of Beethoven's deafness and of the progressive failure of his health in his last months indicate to the author that both conditions were probably venereal in origin, presumably from congenital syphilis. In the absence of
serological proof, the question must remain in doubt.   53 [1927] 1610

NOCH EINMAL: "BEETHOVENS GEHÖRLEIDEN UND LETZTE KRANKHEIT." F. A. Schmidt.   (A)
     The contention of Jacobsohn (Ibid. 53 [1927] 1610) that Beethoven's skull showed malformations that might have
     been attributable to syphilis is not borne out by the evidence.   54 [1928] 284

ENTGEGNUNG AUF VORSTEHENDEN AUFSATZ. Leo Jacobsohn.   (B)
     The fact that no malformation showed in the death mask, as pointed out by Schmidt, may have resulted from a
     "pious retouching" of the mask.   54 [1928] 284

DEUTSCHE MITTE *

BÜHNENENTWURF ZU FIDELIO. L. E. Redslob.   (C)
     Sketches, lighting plans, etc. by five eminent stage directors.   2 [1932] 144

DEUTSCHE REPUBLIK

BEETHOVEN UND UNSER ZEIT.   (D)
     Centennial essay.   1 No. 22 [1927] 1

DEUTSCHE REVUE

UNGEDRUCKTE BRIEFE BEETHOVENS. Alf. Chr. Kalischer.   (E)
     First publication (with comments) of twenty letters to Zmeskall and twenty letters to Nannette Streicher, from
     the collection of Otto Jahn. 23_1 [1898] 73

NEUE FOLGE UNGEDRUCKTER BRIEFE BEETHOVENS. Alf. Chr. Kalischer.   (F)
     First publication (with comments) of fifty letters to seventeen different addressees, from the collection of Otto
     Jahn. Of the letters published in 23 [1898], none of those to Zmeskall are EDr, all but No. 12 and No. 14 to
     Nannette Streicher are EDr; all to miscellaneous addressees except Nos. 2, 9, 11, 26, 27, 37, 39, 42, and 43
     are EDr. 23_2 [1898] 100,212,346

VOM BONNER BEETHOVENHAUS. Ludwig Schiedermair.   (G)
     General description. 38_1 [1913] 121

BEETHOVEN AND BETTINA. Albert Leitzmann.   (H)
     A letter from Bettina dated July 9th, originally published in 'Die Gartenlaube' [1870] 314 is reprinted in part
     with comments. Proof is given that this letter was written to Alois (or Anton) Bihler, and the year is doubtless
     1810. The description of Beethoven which Bettina gives in this letter "bears the stamp of truth in whole and in
     detail." Bihler's account of his acquaintance with Bettina is also quoted from 'Die Gartenlaube,' and his reply
     to the letter of July 9th is given. 43_1 [1918] 109

---

* Published 1930-32 as Kreis von Halle.

KARL MARIA V. WEBERS BEZIEHUNGEN ZU LUDWIG V. BEETHOVEN UND FRANZ SCHUBERT. Konrad Huschke. (A)
It is noteworthy that upon Weber's first visit to Vienna in 1803, his journal and letters mention most of the city's
great and near-great in music but make no reference to Beethoven. Weber's comments on the Eroica, for the
Stuttgart 'Morgenblatt' of 1809, are also given, as well as a letter to Nageli (March 26th 1810) containing uncomplimentary references to Beethoven. During his second sojourn in Vienna, in 1813, Weber also made no mention of
Beethoven. Acquaintance with 'Fidelio,' which Weber conducted in Prague in 1814, and later with 'Christus am
Oelberg' and other works, finally made Weber fully aware of Beethoven's greatness. In 1823, after further performances of 'Fidelio' in Dresden under Weber's direction, quite a number of letters (now unfortunately lost) were
exchanged between the two composers. They finally met at Baden on October 5th 1823 in company with Haslinger
and one of Weber's pupils. The personal relations between the two men were most cordial, but basic differences in
artistic objective prevented any complete understanding. 44_2 [1919] 184, 274

DEUTSCHE RUNDSCHAU

THE BETTINA LETTERS. Louis Ehlert. (B)
In a review of the third volume of Thayer-Dieters, the author casts doubt on the championship by Moriz Carrière
of the genuineness of the Bettina letters.   21 [1879] 162

BEETHOVENS BRIEFE AN BETTINA. Moriz Carrière. (C)
The author renews his contention that the Bettina letters are authentic, and undertakes to publish in the near future
a revised reading of the one of the letters which is still available to him.
22 [1880] 317

"BEETHOVENIANA." Philipp Spitta. (D)
Essay on Beethoven's method of composition, inspired by the publication of Nottebohm's "Zweite Beethoveniana."
54 [1888] 58

KLINGERS BEETHOVEN. Karl Koetschau. (E)
Appreciation.   111 [1902] 461

AUS DEN JUGENDJAHREN DES DRESDNER MUSIKDIREKTORS AUGUST RÖCKEL. Hubert Ermisch. (F)
This article on Karl August Röckel (1814-1876) includes a brief biographical sketch of his father Joseph August
Röckel (1783-1870), the Florestan of the 1806 Fidelio performances. (See also 'Signale' 28 [1870] 759; 'Die
Musik' 27 [1905-06] 303)   130 [1907] 229

STUDIEN ZU BEETHOVENS BRIEFE. Albert Leitzmann. (G)
A very detailed and uncomplimentary review of Kalischer's 'Beethovens Briefe,' commenting unfavorably on
Kalischer's faulty readings of the text, his improvements on Beethoven's orthography, his truculent and sneering
references to Theodor von Frimmel and other eminent and able scholars, his questionable chronology, the inaccuracy and non-scholarly nature of his commentaries, and especially (in connection with the Immortal Beloved
letters) his presentation as established facts of what actually are very controversial opinions.
135 [1908] 76

BEETHOVEN AND THERESE MALFATTI. Albert Leitzmann. (H)
The author contends (in opposition to Riemann) that Beethoven's relationship with Therese was a flirtation rather
than a serious love affair. A careful and (for the first time) complete transcription is given of the letter (KS I 126)
which the author refers to as Beethoven's only certainly authentic letter to Therese, and remarks on the vast difference between the tone of this letter and of those to the Immortal Beloved. The author gives reasons for attributing
this (undated) letter to the last week of April or the first week of May 1810, in which case it must have been written
from Vienna, and discusses the content of the letter in great detail. The material sent with it was undoubtedly a
transcription of 'Freudvoll und leidvoll' from the Egmont music. Passages from Beethoven's letters to Gleichenstein
are cited to bear out the contention that Beethoven's feeling towards Therese was only superficial. The utter unreliability of tradition and anecdote as a basis for studying the love affairs of great men is made clear. Evidence

BEETHOVEN AND THERESE MALFATTI (Continued)
of this kind for and against the hypothesis of a serious consideration of marriage on the part of Beethoven and Therese is presented. Beethoven's request to Wegeler in 1810 for a baptismal certificate may well have been in connection with his intentions towards the Immortal Beloved.   149 [1911] 276

BEETHOVENS LITERARISCHE BILDUNG.   Albert Leitzmann.   (A)
The sources of Beethoven's literary scope may be envisioned from the books which made up his personal library and from the poems which (as song texts) moved him to composition. Beethoven was influenced greatly by Homer and by Shakespeare, even though (since he had no literary knowledge of foreign languages) he was dependent upon translations. His song texts indicate his regard for Schiller and for various of the contemporary Viennese poets. Goethe was more important to him as a man and a force than as a poet.
                                                154 [1913] 271

BEETHOVENS PROZESSE.   Max Reinitz.   (B)
Among the attorneys who served Beethoven in his many legal tussles were Drs. Kanka, Adlersburg, Wolf, Seb. Bach, Schönauer, Reger (Beyer?) and Varena. Review of the various court cases in which Beethoven was engaged from 1814 on show him in a most unfavorable light. The history of the following suits, with extracts from court records, is given: (1) The suit against Johanna van Beethoven (wife of Brother Karl) in October 1814 on her note for 1500 gulden to cover advances to and withholdings by Karl (this suit was conducted by S. A. Steiner on Beethoven's behalf). (2) The assignment and publishing agreement with S. A. Steiner & Co. (3) The annuity suit against Prince Franz Josef Lichnowsky. (4) The annuity suit against the heirs of Prince Kinsky. (5) The legal battle with Maelzel over the 'Battle of Vittoria' Op. 91. (6) Other suits and controversies. (See also pp. 27, 450)
                                                162 [1915] 248

THE ASSISTANCE RENDERED BY MAELZEL IN THE COMPOSITION OF THE 'BATTLE OF VITTORIA.'   Max Reinitz. (C)
                                    162 [1915] 274,451

BEETHOVEN UND SEINE ANKLÄGE.   Gustav Ernest.   (D)
A defense of Beethoven in the various cases discussed by Reinitz (p. 248) and in his charge of double-dealing in the sale of the Missa Solemnis. Various statements made by Reinitz are questioned.
                                                162 [1915] 27,450

WAS BEDEUTET UNS BEETHOVEN.   Anton Mayer.   (E)
Centenary essay.   210 [1927] 235

DEUTSCHE SHAKESPEARE-GESELLSCHAFT JAHRBUCH

COLLIN UND SHAKESPEARE.   Wilhelm Münch.   (F)
A comparison of the two dramas on Coriolanus.   41 [1905] 22

DEUTSCHE THALIA

DAS EHEPAAR HAIZINGER IN PARIS UND DIE PARISER ERSTAUFFÜHRUNG DES "FIDELIO" IM JAHRE 1829.   (G)
    Alfons Fritz.
The first performance of Fidelio in Paris (May 30th 1829) was as part of a brief season given by the company of the Stadttheater of Aachen. Beatrice Fischer sang Leonora and Haizinger, Florestan. The three performances were received with enthusiasm, though performances of other operas during this season were very coolly received.
                                                1 [1902] 36

BEETHOVEN UND DIE DICHTER. Richard Benz. (A)
　　Though he worked with tones rather than with words, Beethoven was a great poet.
　　　　　　　　　　　　　　　　　3 No. 12 [March 25th 1927] 1

DIE NICHTGESCHRIEBENE BEETHOVEN-AUFSATZ. Heinrich Eduard Jacob. (B)
　　Facetious.　　　　　　　　　　　　3 No. 12 [March 25th 1927] 1

EINE UNVERÖFFENTLICHE "KONVERSATION" BEETHOVENS. Walther Nohl. (C)
　　Excerpt from Conversation Book No. 28 (April 5-13th 1823) in which Beethoven comments on Brother Johann and
　　discusses deafness with a deaf fellow-countryman named Sandra.　　3 No. 12 [March 25th 1927] 3

BEETHOVENS HUMANITÄT. Karl Tschuppik. (D)
　　Centenary essay.　　　　　　　　　　3 No. 12 [March 25th 1927] 2

BEETHOVEN IN DER MEINUNG DER JUNGEN MUSIKER: EINE RUNDFRAGE. Felix Joachimson. (E)
　　Comments by Krenek, Weill, Ravel, Janacek, Auric and others. A reproduction is given of "an unknown Beethoven
　　portrait by J. P. Lyser," showing Beethoven reclining in a wooded dell by a brook with music paper at hand.
　　　　　　　　　　　　　　　　　3 No. 12 [March 25th 1927] 3

DEUTSCHE ZEITSCHRIFT **

SCHUBERT AND BEETHOVEN. Paul Marsop. (F)
　　Reprint (slightly abridged) of a part of the article originally appearing in 'Die Gegenwart' 34_2 [1888] 325.
　　　　　　　　　　　　　　　2 [1888] 85

BEETHOVEN. Karl Lamprecht. (G)
　　Beethoven's life and works from the standpoint of the overall history of German cultural growth (an excerpt from
　　the author's extensive 'Deutsche Geschichte.'　　　20_2 [1907] 189,243

WARUM ICH DEN "FIDELIO" LIEBE. Karl Söhle. (H)
　　"A letter from an enthusiast."　　　　　20 [1907] 603

MISSA SOLEMNIS UND NEUNTE SYMPHONIE. Georg Göhler. (I)
　　A philosophic analysis of the two works to justify the author's reference to them as Beethoven's "supreme achieve-
　　ment, belonging together like the Old and New Testaments or the two parts of Faust."
　　　　　　　　　　　　　　　　21_3 [1908] 68

BEETHOVENS "SZENE AM BACH." A. Halm. (J)
　　An analysis which contends that there are various basic flaws of construction in the movement, and an even greater
　　mistake of artistic judgment in introducing the realism of the birdcalls.
　　　　　　　　　　　　　　　　27_3 [1914] 15

BEETHOVEN.　　　　　　　　　　　34_1 [1920] 135 (K)

BEETHOVEN. Alexander Berrsche. (L)
　　A polemic against various contemporaries in the guise of a centenary essay.
　　　　　　　　　　　　　　　　40_1 [1927] 353

---

*　Volumes 1-10 were published as Literarische Welt.
** Volumes 1-25 were published as Kunstwart.

DER MISSBRAUCHTE BEETHOVEN. L. Thurneister.   (A)
    Not only was Beethoven plagued by fate and by disappointments during his life, but a hundred years after his
    death his shade is subjected to the ordeal of festivals guided by those with their own ends to attain.
                                4 [1927] 565

DEUTSCHES MUSEUM

BEETHOVENS LIEDER. H. M. Schletterer.   (B)
    Extended but non-critical review of GA 23. 16_1 [1866] 321,358

DEUTSCHLAND

BEETHOVEN. Paul Bekker.   (C)
    Centennial essay.   [1927] 218

DEUTSCHLANDS ERNEUERUNG

BEETHOVEN. Reinhold Zimmermann.   (D)
    Chauvinistic sesquicentennial essay.   4 [1920] 767

DIETSCHE WARANDE EN BELFORT

A NEW BEETHOVEN. M. E. Belpaire.   (E)
    The writer of a set of sea-poems who uses the pseudonym Zeemeeuwe shows himself to be a Beethoven of word-
    painting. $[1912_1]$ 225

DE LANGZAME TEMPO'S IN 'T BEETHOVEN-WERK. M. E. Belpaire.   (F)
    Excerpts from the author's book 'Beethoven, een kunst- en levensbeeld,' discussing nonanalytically the slow move-
    ments of many of the piano sonatas as well as of some of the quartets, duo-sonatas and symphonies.
                          $[1913_1]$ 27,155

BEETHOVENS SONATEN VOOR KLAVIER. M. E. Belpaire.   (G)
    Program notes for a series of concerts traversing the 32 piano sonatas.
                    24 [1924] 324

BEETHOVENS LEEFKRACHT. M. E. Belpaire.   (H)
    Centenary essay.   27 [1927] 257

DE TRAGISCHE SYMPHONIE. Hendrik Andriessen.   (I)
    The Ninth Symphony is Beethoven's 'Tragic Symphony,' in which Schiller's text falsifies the disillusionment of
    the music.   27 [1927] 262

BEETHOVEN ALS VLAMING.   Ernest Closson.   (A)
   While "it is a matter of unimportance what the nationality of a great man may be, . . . nevertheless the Flemish
   influence in Beethoven's genius is so clearly evident that many foreign musicologists have taken note of it. "
27 [1927] 266

KRITISCHE BESCHOUWING DER PIANOWERKEN VAN BEETHOVEN.   Jan Chiapusso.   (B)
   Passages are cited from various piano sonatas to bear out the author's contention that with relatively few exceptions
   Beethoven's writing for the piano is that of a man to whom thoughts of the orchestra came most naturally.
27 [1927] 269

DE STIL VON BEETHOVENS KLAVIERSONATEN.   Lodewijk Ontrop.   (C)
   A detailed but nonanalytical discussion.   27 [1927] 274

BIBLIOGRAPHIE OVER BEETHOVEN IN DE HOOFDBIBLIOTHEEK DER STAD AMSTERDAM.   Emm. de Bom.   (D)
   An extensive bibliography, classified generally by subject, covering journal articles (for the most part included in
   these abstracts) and books.   27 [1927] 311

NAKLANK OP DE BEETHOVENFEESTEN.   M. E. Belpaire.   (E)
   The universal recognition of the Beethoven centenary is compared with the recent celebration in honor of St.
   Francis of Assisi (died 1226). An account of Beethoven's death as given in 'Aus dem Schwarzspanierhaus' is
   reviewed.   27 [1927] 683

HET THEISME IN HET LEVEN EN DE KUNST VAN BEETHOVEN.   Th. Absil.   (F)
   Extensive quotations from Beethoven's letters and sayings, and from the writings by which he was influenced, to
   show that he was a theist, though not a deist and definitely not (as Haydn stated) an agnostic. Especial stress is
   laid on the inscription from the Temple of Isis which Beethoven had on his desk: "I am what I am," etc. Certain
   of his works (especially Opp. 123 and 125) are discussed in considerable detail to show that the composer must have
   been a man of deep and abiding spirituality. The question remains open as to whether or not Beethoven (like Haydn
   and Mozart) was a Freemason.   33 [1933] 16,100

PROEVE VAN STYLISTISCHE VERGELIJKING: BACH - MOZART - BEETHOVEN.   Jan L. Broeckx.   (G)
   A general survey summarized in a tabulation which shows how basically the three composers differ in their thematic
   material, harmony, dynamics, and adaptation of their music to instrumental performance.
[1941] 396,452

DISQUES

THE STRING QUARTETS OF BEETHOVEN.   Joseph Cottler.   (H)
   Popular.   2 [1931] 198,250

DONAULAND

DAS LEID DES VAN BEETHOVEN.   Josef Friedrich Perkonig.   (I)
   Fiction.   2 [1918] 1017

BEETHOVEN. J. Lambkin.   (A)
  Centenary essay.   180 [1927] 242

BEETHOVEN IN UNIFORM. Elsie Codd.   (B)
  A discussion of Beethoven's service in the Electoral court in Bonn.
                                                       201 [1937] 144

                              Edinburgh Bibliographical Society
                                  TRANSACTIONS

THOMSON'S COLLECTIONS OF NATIONAL SONG, WITH SPECIAL REFERENCE TO THE CONTRIBUTIONS OF HAYDN   (C)
     AND BEETHOVEN. Cecil Hopkinson and C. B. Oldman.
  A detailed bibliographical study of the various editions of the song collections which Thomson issued. The dates of
  publication of the Haydn and Beethoven settings are given (four Beethoven settings were first published only in 1841),
  and a thematic index is given of the settings by the two composers (187 songs by Haydn, 126 songs by Beethoven).
  Data on first publication include the following editions: (A) 'Original Irish Airs' 1st ed. Vol. I (Preface dated 1814,
  colophon 1814); (B) 'Original Irish Airs' 1st ed. Vol. II (Preface dated May 1816, colophon 1816); (C) 'Welsh Airs'
  1st ed. Vol. III (colophon 1817); (D) 'Scottish Airs' Vol. V (Preface dated June 1818, colophon 1818); (E) 'Scottish
  Airs' 1st octavo ed. Vol. II (colophon 1822); (F) 'Scottish Airs' 2nd octavo ed. Vol. VI (which is the first edition of
  this volume) (colophon 1824, Preface dated May 2nd 1825, presumable publication date spring-summer, 1825); (G)
  'Scottish Airs' Appendix to 8th (1838) edition; (H) 'Melodies of Scotland' 1st ed. (Coventry & Hollier) Vol. VI (1841).
  First publications by Thomson: 25 Scottish Songs Op. 108: all in D (NV says Nos. 1, 15, 16 not in this edition), 25
  Irish Songs (NV p. 163): all in A, 20 Irish Songs (NV p. 166): Nos. 1-4 in A; Nos. 5-20 in B, 12 Irish Songs (NV p.
  169): all except Nos. 2 and 7 in B; Nos. 2 and 7 not published by Thomson, 26 Welsh Songs (NV p. 170): all in C,
  12 Scottish Songs (NV p. 173): No. 1 in E; Nos. 2, 3, 4, 8, 9 and 12 in F; Nos. 5 and 6 in G; Nos. 7, 10 and 11 in H,
  12 Various Folksongs (NV p. 175): No. 3 in E; No. 5 in F; No. 1 in G; Nos. 2, 6, 8, 11 in B; Nos. 4, 7, 9, 10 and 12
  not published by Thomson, 'As I was awand'ring' (not in VN, TV): E. NOTE. In a few cases the original edition
  differs from the GA in minor points: key, different words, solo instead of duet, etc.
                                        2_1 [1938-39] 1

THOMSON'S COLLECTIONS OF NATIONAL SONG . . . ADDENDA ET CORRIGENDA.   (D)
     Cecil Hopkinson and C. B. Oldman.   3 [1954] 121

                              EDINBURGH REVIEW

NEW LIGHT ON BEETHOVEN. H. Heathcote Statham.   (E)
  Essay in the form of a review of books by d'Indy, Rolland, Walker, and Kalischer.
                                                       217 [1913] 118

BEETHOVEN'S SONATAS. George Sampson.   (F)
  A popular but stimulating discussion of the piano sonatas, one by one.
                                                       245 [1927] 258

                              EIDGENÖSSISCHES SÄNGERBLATT

UNBEKANNTE A-CAPPELLA GESÄNGE BEETHOVENS. Willy Hess.   (G)
  In the GA, the instrumental works are in general fairly complete, except for compositions for the Spieluhr (none

given) and for mandolin (fewer than 50 percent given).   Of vocal works, more than 50 canons and musical jokes
are missing; to the 132 arrangements of folksongs, 53 must be added, of which 30 are still unpublished; of the Italian
a cappela songs none are given.   A careful bibliographical study is presented of these songs H-170 to 190 and H-193,
with EDr of the Terzet 'Ma tu tremis' H-174.   17 [1953] 143

ELSEVIER'S GEÏLLUSTREERD MAANDSCHRIFT

BEETHOVEN GEZIEN DOOR BOURDELLE.   S. P. Abas.   (A)
   A favorable commentary on Bourdelle's statues of Beethoven.   92 [1936] 25

EUGENIK *

DIE BEETHOVEN-LEGENDE.   von Behr-Pinnow.   (B)
   The supposed dipsomania of Beethoven's paternal grandmother is entirely without foundation in fact; the father's
addiction to drink appeared only after the death of Beethoven's mother, and was probably due to bad companions
rather than to any constitutional tendency.   Thus it is completely false to say that Beethoven had a hereditary
tendency towards alcoholism.   3 [1928] 60

EUPHORION

CLEMENS BRENTANOS BEZIEHUNGEN ZU BEETHOVEN.   Alfred Christlieb Kalischer.   (C)
   Much of the information regarding this relationship is nebulous, but it appears probable that Brentano first met
Beethoven in Vienna in 1804.   His wife, the poetess Sophie Mereau, had provided the lyric for Beethoven's song
of 1792, 'Feuerfarb' Op. 52 No. 2.   The author believes that Brentano's poem 'Symphonie' was inspired by hearing
a performance of the Eroica at a private gathering at the home of Prince Lobkowitz.   In commemoration of the death
of Princess Luise of Prussia, Brentano wrote the text of a cantata which was submitted to Beethoven and which he
planned to set but never completed.   This cantata is referred to in the second of the Bettina letters (KS I 209 No.
228); very possibly in Teplitz that summer Beethoven explained to Brentano the reasons for his abandonment of the
project.   Incidentally, the author gives reasons for believing that Beethoven first met Tieck in Vienna in 1808, not
in Prague in 1813.   The brilliant success of the Seventh Symphony and Wellington's Victory in the first months of
1814 (Brentano was in Vienna from July 1813 to July 1814) led Brentano to indite four poems to Beethoven which are
found in the Nachlass.   In 1815 he published a review of the first Berlin performance of Fidelio ('Music & Letters'
27 [1946] 248).   2 [1895] 36 Ergänzungsheft

CHRISTOPH KUFFNERS GESPRÄCHE MIT BEETHOVEN.   Alfred Christlieb Kalischer.   (D)
   The author does not agree with the doubts which Nottebohm (NB II 503) and Thayer (TK III 59) throw on Kuffner's
authorship of the text of the Choral Fantasy Op. 80.   The Choral Fantasy was written in 1808, and five years later
Beethoven wrote the March for Kuffner's 'Tarpeja.'   There is no indication of further association between the two
men until the summer of 1825, when Holz refers to Kuffner (presumably to a projected oratorio text), though Beethoven's failure to go through with his project of setting Bernard's 'Sieg des Kreuzes,' (referred to in his letter of
September 23rd 1824 to Hauschka (KS II 336) is attributed by the author to the influence on Beethoven of Kuffner's
writings.   A conversation book for April 1826 records a long conversation (here transcribed) between Beethoven and
Kuffner, bearing chiefly on the proposed oratorio 'Saul and David.'   Conversation books of a few months later include references to this oratorio, and Dr. Wawruch's account of Beethoven's last days mentions that the thought of
it was in Beethoven's mind to the end.   3 [1897] 169 Ergänzungsheft

---

* Volumes 3-5 were published as Volksaufartung, Erbkunde, Eheberatung.

BEETHOVEN AND GRILLPARZER. Alfred Orel. (A)

Grillparzer was not in complete sympathy with Beethoven: his ideal composer was Mozart, and he went along with the swing of Viennese operatic taste in the 1820's from German to Italian. At the same time, he had the highest regard for Beethoven as a creative artist. These facts must be taken as a background for the request made by Dietrichstein in the fall of 1822 that Grillparzer prepare an opera book for Beethoven. In the conversation book of May 1823 Grillparzer indicated as a possible subject for an opera the Bohemian legend of Drahomira, with its conflict between the heathen ruler and his Christian son Wenzel. A third subject which he considered (in addition to the libretto 'Melusine' which was finally agreed on) was 'Traum ein Leben.' Grillparzer's inherent romanticism as well as Beethoven's tendency for absolute rather than illustrative music resulted in an unbridgeable aesthetic gap between the two artists. It was for this reason that Beethoven found it impossible to be moved to composition by 'Melusine.' 28 [1927] 273

BEETHOVENS GESCHICHTLICHE STELLUNG. Karl Nef. (B)

Until his last years, when his renewed study of Bach showed its effects, Beethoven was above all the master of homophony. The Ninth Symphony must be considered as the foreshadowing of a Tenth Symphony in which the union of orchestra and voices would be perfected and complete. An important contribution by Beethoven to German music was the introduction of various characteristics of French music, notably pathos. He was a foreshadower of romanticism, but the author writes at length to prove that Beethoven himself was assuredly no romantic. Especially in the field of instrumental music the romantic composers could not have written as they did without Beethoven. His influence on the history of musicians is fully as great as on the history of music. He was the first great musician to gain international repute as a completely German master (unlike Handel, Haydn and Mozart, who were international in their music, Bach would have merited the same classification except that his music did not become generally known until well into the 19th century). 28 [1927] 286

BEETHOVEN AND THE ORGAN. Karl Nef. (C)

"It is impossible to play a melody on the organ with shading and dynamic expressiveness, but expressiveness in the setting forth of a melody is a sine qua non of Beethoven's music." This fact and the homophonic nature of his musical thoughts adequately explain Beethoven's failure to write for the organ.
28 [1927] 289

EUROPÄISCHE REVUE

BEETHOVEN'S LEONORA. Romain Rolland. (D)

Translation by Erwin Rieger of the material appearing in pp. 218-60 of Ernest Newman's version of 'Beethoven the Creator: From the Eroica to the Appassionata' (1929). 4_1 [1928] 177,248

EUROPE

BEETHOVEN. Romain Rolland. (E)

Centenary essay. 13 [1927] 289

BEETHOVEN AND GOETHE. Romain Rolland. (F)

Material later appearing on pp. 21-113 of the author's book of the same title (1930).
14 [1927] 5,184

BEETHOVEN.   (A)
  "Whenever Beethoven nods like Homer or errs against his own knowledge, we look upon him as amenable to the
  canons of sound criticism. "   1 [1820] 94

THE EFFECT OF ASSOCIATION ON MUSICAL TASTE: A SKETCH OF A TRANSLATION OF BEETHOVEN'S TRIO pa. (sic) (B)
     70 No. 1.
  Fanciful interpretation, notable only for its early date and the country of its publication.
                                                                 2 [1821] 139

FAMILIENGESCHICHTLICHE BLÄTTER

BEETHOVENS MUTTER. Fritz Winzenburg.   (C)
  Discussion (with minor changes and amplifications) of article by Wagner in 'Trierische Chronik' NF 16 [1920] 162.
                                                                 19 [1921] 49

ZU BEETHOVENS AHNENTAFEL. Heinrich Milz.   (D)
  Similar to preceding paper.   23 [1925] 18

FEUER

BEETHOVEN -- VERSUCH EINER SYNTHESE. Hans Mersmann.   (E)
  The growth and development of Beethoven's musical art is traced, leading to the conclusion that he can be compared
  only with Goethe. 2_1 [1921] 215

FOREIGN QUARTERLY REVIEW

"LUDWIG VAN BEETHOVEN--EINE BIOGRAPHIE DESSELBEN . . ." BY JOH. ALOYS SCHLOSSER.   (F)
  An extended essay, with Schlosser's book as a pretext, which gives a vigorous and illuminating picture of the
  attitude towards Beethoven of the musical Englishman of 1831.   8 [1831] 439

FORSCHUNGEN UND FORTSCHRITTE

ZUR FRAGE DER BEETHOVENDEUTUNG. Arnold Schering.   (G)
  A summary of the author's reasons for associating many of Beethoven's compositions with specific works of
  literature or poetry.   11 [1935] 207

FORTNIGHTLY *

BEETHOVEN'S LETTERS. Esther Meynell.   (H)
  Popular and conventional.   NS 121 [1927] 356

---
* Published 1865-1934 as Fortnightly Review.

THE VIOLIN MUSIC OF BEETHOVEN.   Edith Lynwood Winn.   (A)
    Banal comment for amateurs.   2 No. 6 [March 1915] 9

FRAU

BEETHOVEN AND BETTINA.   Berta Witt.   (B)
    A popular summary, with extensive quotation from Bettina's correspondence with Goethe and with Beethoven.
                                                    34 [1927] 395

FRETTED INSTRUMENT NEWS

UNKNOWN COMPOSITION BY BEETHOVEN FOR MANDOLIN AND PIANO.   Alfred E. Johns.   (C)
    Translation of the article by Chitz (SIM 8 No. 12 [December 1912] 24); publication of the mandolin part (re-edited)
    but no piano part; polemic.   9 No. 6 [November-December 1941];
                                                    10 No. 1 [January-February 1942];
                                                    10 No. 2 [March-April 1942];
                                                    10 No. 3 [May-June 1942]

GARTENLAUBE

EIN NEUES KÜNSTLER-DENKMAL.   J. C. Lobe.   (D)
    Popular account of Beethoven's life and artistic style.   [1862] 457

DAS "DONAUWEIBCHEN" IN PRAG.   (E)
    A popular account of the life of Wenzel Müller and his daughter Therese, which includes the following story,
    referred to by Kalischer ('Beethoven und seine Zeitgenossen' I 155) as "more poetical than historical, and to be
    taken cum grano salis." Müller was so much irked by the acclaim of Beethoven, who had written only one opera
    while Müller had written a hundred, that he swore never to attend a performance of Fidelio. When his daughter
    Therese Müller-Grünberg, famous in the role of Marzelline, took part he relented, and was so moved by Milder-
    Hauptmann in the title role that he admitted to Therese that he would gladly give up everything he had written had
    only he composed "that thing."   [1867] 776

FIDELIO.   Rudolph Bunge.   (F)
    Popular account of the history of the opera in its first and second versions, based on the memoirs of Joseph Röckel.
                                                    [1868] 601

EIN MUSIKABEND BEIM PRINZEN LOUIS FERDINAND.   (G)
    A fictionalized account of the Prince and his love for music, in which he is supposed to have requested that
    Beethoven come to Berlin from Leipzig to play for him on a date specifically given as 10 October 1796 (apparently
    exactly ten days before the death of the Prince). Kalischer ('Beethoven und seine Zeitgenossen' I 26) points out
    that Beethoven was neither in Berlin on 10 October 1796 nor in Leipzig shortly before that date.
                                                    [1868] 724

DAS BILD DES MEISTERS.   J. C. Lobe.   (H)
    Discussion of the Stieler portrait as the only true representation of the composer which we have.
                                                    [1869] 646

BEETHOVEN UND "DAS KIND. "   (A)
   Recollections of Bettina Brentano by an unidentified lawyer from his university days, and letter dated "Vienna,
   July 9th" (without year) from Bettina to him giving her impressions of Beethoven. (See also 'Deutsche Revue'
   43₁ [1918] 109)   [1870] 314

ZUM GEDÄCHTNISS DES MEISTERS. Ludwig Nohl.   (B)
   Centenary essay based on biographical fragments and anecdotes.   [1870] 860

AUS DEN LETZTEN LEBENSTAGEN BEETHOVENS. La Mara, pseud. (Marie Lipsius)   (C)
   Biographical sketch of Beethoven's last dozen years.   [1877] 197

DIE BEETHOVENS IN BONN. Ludwig Nohl.   (D)
   Biographical sketches of the composer's grandfather, father and mother, based largely on the Fischer MS.
                    [1879] 612

BEETHOVENS "SCHAFFNERIN EURYKLEIA. " Ludwig Nohl.   (E)
   Popular account of Beethoven's friendship with and dependence on Nannette Streicher.
                    [1880] 388

BEETHOVEN IN DER KLEMME. Ernst Pasqué.   (F)
   Fictionalized account of Beethoven's struggles with a passage in the finale of Fidelio (GA 20/206 pp. 255-56).
                    [1888] 864

ERINNERUNGEN AN BEETHOVEN. Johannes Schmal.   (G)
   Account of an interview in 1900 with an old man who, as a boy of 12, had known Beethoven in Gneixendorf in
   1826, and a description of the room in which Beethoven had lived during his last visit to Gneixendorf.
                    [1901] 32

WIENER BEETHOVENHÄUSER. Joseph Aug. Lux.   (H)
   Popular article with 8 photographs.   [1908] 65

BEETHOVEN. Franz Wugk.   (I)
   Sesquicentennial essay.   [1920] 819

WALDMÜLLERS BEETHOVENBILDNISS. Wilhelm Lietge.   (J)
   Popular account.   [1927] 210

ERINNERUNGEN EINES HAMMERKLAVIERS. Heinrich Reiffenscheid.   (K)
   Photograph and brief account of the piano given by Beethoven to Ries, who in turn gave it to Nikolaus Simrock,
   great-grandfather of the author.   [1927] 210

BEETHOVEN IN BADEN. Alfred von Ehrmann.   (L)
   Popular account of Baden in Beethoven's time.   [1927] 212

FAMILIE BEETHOVEN. Grete Masse.   (M)
   Popular and uncritical account of Grandfather Ludwig (stating his descent as from Heinrich Adelard), the two
   brothers, and Nephew Karl.   [1927] 214

GEGENWART

EIN ÄSTHETISCHER MINOTAURUS. W. Mohr.   (N)
   A performance at the Dusseldorf Künstler-Liedertafel of 'Beethoven's Pastoral Symphony with Living Pictures'
   is described and deplored.   5 [1874] 250

REVISED READING OF A BETTINA LETTER.   (A)
   Moriz Carrière's revised reading of Beethoven's letter of February 10th 1811 to Bettina (KS I 208).
                                           17 [1880] 127

BEETHOVEN AND AMALIE SEBALD-KRAUSE.   Alfr. Chr. Kalischer.   (B)
   Biographical sketch of Amalie and first publication of seven letters to her from the fall of 1812.
                                         26 [1884] 323

A COMPARISON OF SCHUBERT AND BEETHOVEN.   Paul Marsop.   (C)
   "Beethoven must be classed among the liberators of mankind; Schubert among the benefactors."
                                32_2 [1888] 325

BEETHOVEN UND SEINE BIOGRAPHEN.   S. Bagge.   (D)
   General comments on the status of Beethoven biography as introduction to a review of Wasielewski's 'Ludwig
   van Beethoven.'   36 [1889] 198

GEISTESKULTUR *

EINE UNSTERBLICHE INSCHRIFT.   R. Salinger.   (E)
   A manuscript copy of an inscription from the Temple of Isis ("Ich bin, was da ist" etc.) which Beethoven is known
   to have had on his desk recently appeared in an auction catalogue.   The importance to Beethoven and to certain
   other great creators of the mythological significance of Isis as the Mother of Mothers is discussed.
                                         29 [1920] 281

BEETHOVEN.   Hans David.   (F)
   A consideration of various aspects of Beethoven the composer from the metaphysical standpoint.
                                         36 [1927] 223

GERMANOSLAVICA

BEETHOVEN IN DER RUSSISCHEN SCHÖNEN LITERATUR DES 19. JAHRHUNDERTS.   Michael P. Alekseev.   (G)
   Starting in the 1830's, the interest in Beethoven's music in Russia reflected itself in a steady and sizeable output
   of writings on Beethoven by Russian poets and novelists, many of which are not listed in Kastner's 'Bibliotheca
   Beethoveniana.'   2 [1932] 163,301

GEWERKSCHAFT

ZU BEETHOVENS 100. TODESTAG.   Felix Günther.   (H
   Centennial essay.   31 [1927] 253

GIDS

BEETHOVEN.   Matthijs Vermeulen.   (I
   Centenary essay.   91 [1927] 422

---

* Volumes 29-32 were published as Geisteskultur und Volksbildung.

LA SORDITÁ DI BEETHOVEN. Guglielmo Bilancioni. (A)
General.   69 [1921] 531

Goethe-Gesellschaft
SCHRIFTEN

GEDICHTE VON GOETHE IN COMPOSITIONEN SEINER ZEITGENOSSEN. Max Friedlaender. (B)
This collection of 78 songs (with popular commentaries) includes five by Beethoven, as well as his sketch of a
setting of 'Erlkönig.'   11 [1896] 143

GOETHE-JAHRBUCH

BEETHOVEN UND FRAU RATH AN BETTINA. L. Geiger. (C)
Transcription from 'Allgemeine conservativ Monatsschrift' 3 [1880] 79 of Moriz Carrière's revised reading of
Beethoven's letter of February 10th 1811 to Bettina (KS I 208).   1 [1880] 373

GRANDE RÉVUE

WAGNER ET LA HANTISE DE BEETHOVEN. W. Berteval. (D)
An extended survey of Wagner's compositions from the standpoint that they represent various aspects of his
apostleship of Beethoven.   142 [1933] 597

GREGORIANISCHE RUNDSCHAU

BEETHOVENS ERSTE MESSE. (E)
Brief and popular.   8 [1909] 168

GREGORIUS-BLATT FÜR KATHOLISCHE KIRCHENMUSIK

KIRCHENMUSIKALISCHES AUS BEETHOVENS BRIEFEN. (F)
Beethoven letters which contain references to church music (composed or projected) include the following:
KS I 130, 139, 141, 142, 184, 257 KS II 200, 212, 236, 238, 262, 306, 333; Letter of March 10th 1823 to Simrock
(see 'Simrock Jahrbuch' 2 [1929] 10); Letter of March 10th 1824 to Schott (see 'Die Musik' 34 [1942] 285).
                                                41 [1916] 90

DIE EROBERUNG VON BEETHOVENS MISSA SOLEMNIS FÜR DIE LITURGIE. Alfred Schnerich. (G)
Dates of considerable number of liturgical performances of the Missa Solemnis are given, including three in 1927.
In Linz on May 1927 Cardinal Piffl was celebrant.   51 [1927] 187

ET INCARNATUS EST UND WANDLUNGSMUSIK IN BEETHOVENS MISSA SOLEMNIS. Wilh. Kurthen. (H)
A discussion of several sections of the Missa Solemnis from the standpoint of the religious understanding which
the music displays.   52 [1928] 65

AUS BEETHOVENS SPÄTERN LEBENSJAHREN: 1. MITTHEILUNGEN AUS EINEM TAGEBUCH.   L u d w i g   N o h l .   (A)
   Material which, in much modified form, appeared in Nohl's 'Eine stille Liebe zu Beethoven, nach dem Tagebuch
   einer jungen Dame' (1875). 16_1 II [1857] 23

AUS BEETHOVENS SPÄTERN LEBENSJAHREN: 2. UNGEDRUCKTE BRIEF BEETHOVENS.   L u d w i g   N o h l .   (B)
   28 letters from the period 1816-18, almost all bearing on one aspect or another of the guardianship over Nephew
   Karl.   This article includes first publication of the following 28 letters to Giannatasio del Rio (numbers from
   Kalischer 'Briefe,' 1st ed.):   495, 563, 566, 570, 562, 565, 517, 567, 569, 522, 568, 530, 571, 578, 579, 580, 490,
   668, 669, 670, 564, 671, 675, 647, 660, 681, 728, 729. 16_1 II [1857] 50

BRIEFE VON BEETHOVEN.   (C)
   Letters from the summer of 1812 to Franz von Brunswick (2) and Amalie Sebald (8).
                                                             18_1 II [1859] 236

BEETHOVEN UND DIE AUSGABEN SEINE WERKE.   O t t o   J a h n .   (D)
   Material later published in the author's 'Gesammelte Aufsätze über Musik' [1866] 271ff.
                                                             23_1 I [1864] 271, 296, 341

EIN BRIEF BEETHOVENS.   (E)
   The author mentions Beethoven's relationship with Dorothea Ertmann, the Brentanos and Elizabeth Hummel (née
   Röckel) as indication of the part which women played in the composer's life. Regarding the Bigots, he quotes ex-
   tensively from Reichert's letters of December 1808-January 1809 ('Vertraute Briefe') and publishes for the first time
   Beethoven's letter without date to Marie Bigot and her husband. (NOTE by DWM: From Reichert's letters it would
   seem that the several Bigot letters (KS I 136-38, 171) were much more probably from the spring and summer of 1809
   than from the year 1808 to which Kalischer assigns them.) Beethoven's letter of the first week of December 1813 to
   Hummel (KS I 299) is also published for the first time. 26_1 II [1867] 100

ZUR C-DUR-MESSE VON BEETHOVEN.   C. F. P o h l .   (F)
   The title page of the score of the C major Mass in the library of the church at Eisenstadt (with Beethoven's corrections)
   bears the title in Beethoven's own hand as given in KS I 131 and differing in slight detail from that given in TV-137
   and NV. Evidence is presented to show that the first performance was on September 13th 1807, the Sunday after the
   name-day of Princess Marie Esterhazy (September 8th). Later performances are briefly mentioned. Beethoven's
   letter of July 26th 1807 to Prince Esterhazy (KS I 130) is published for the first time, together with a draft of
   Esterhazy's reply of August 9th 1807 to this letter and a letter of July 22nd 1807 to Beethoven from Dr. Schmidt
   (TD III 33). 27_2 II [1868] 245

ZUM BEETHOVENTAGE.   (G)
   Centenary essay. 29_2 II [1870] 441

EIN GEBET BEETHOVENS.   L u d w i g   N o h l .   (H)
   Preliminary version of the author's 'Beethovens Leben' [1877] Part 1 Chapter 4.
                                                             32_1 II [1873] 41

AUS BEETHOVENS SPÄTEREM LEBEN -- ENTSTEHUNG UND ART DER GROSSEN MESSE.   L u d w i g   N o h l .   (I)
   Preliminary version of the author's 'Beethovens Leben' [1877] Vol II pp. 185-220.
                                                             33 II [1874] 201, 253

ZWEI UNGEDRUCKTE SCHRIFTSTÜCKE BEETHOVENS.   L u d w i g   N o h l .   (J)
   First publication of the communications of September 25th 1818 and December 15th 1818 to the Lower Austrian
   Court (KS II 159, 161), with commentaries. (NOTE by DWM. BJ 2 erroneously attributes the first publication of
   these letters to Nohl's 'Mosaik für Musikalische-Gebildete' [1882].)
                                                             34_2 I [1875] 20

AUS BEETHOVENS LETZTER SCHAFFENZEIT (DAS ERSTE DER LETZTEN QUARTETTEN).   L u d w i g   N o h l .   (A)
Preliminary version of the author's 'Beethovens Leben' [1877] Part II Chapter 12.
$$34_2 \text{ II [1875] 201,251}$$

BEETHOVEN ALS MÄRTYRER.   H e r m a n n   K r e t z s c h m a r .   (B)
   A translation of this article, slightly condensed, appears in 'The New Music Review' 10 [1911] 185. The contention
(brought to general acceptance by Nohl's biography) that Beethoven was treated harshly by the world in which he lived
is still widely accepted in spite of the many facts in contradiction which were given publicity by Thayer and others.
The bases of Nohl's contention were three: Beethoven's own complaints and accusations, unfavorable comments by
contemporary musicians, and the slow acceptance of certain of his greatest works. Beethoven's irascibility is well
known, but neither accounts of him by his acquaintances, his own letters, nor the prevailing mood of his compositions give ground for belief that Beethoven thought of himself as being at odds with the world, or that his grumbles
were more than superficial. Rochlitz, in a letter to Härtel, wrote that through all Beethoven's oddities there "glows a
truly child-like good humor, carelessness and trustfulness." His tirades "are only explosions of fancy and momentary
excitement. They are blustered out without any arrogance, without any bitterness or ugliness of mood -- with a light
mind, good spirit, a humorously bizarre capriciousness; and then it is all over." Schindler was able to see hostility towards Beethoven by other musicians wherever he looked. To the limited extent to which this was true, the hostility during Beethoven's years of maturity was in most cases towards his personality rather than towards his music, and even this
was apt to be exaggerated by Beethoven's admirers. From the time of the Second Symphony, the support of Rochlitz in
the columns of the 'Allgemeine Musikalische Zeitung' far more than offset the carpings of lesser critics, and long before Beethoven's death his towering genius was acknowledged by critics and reviewers wherever his music was known.

   It may be granted that the last sonatas and quartets, Fidelio and the Missa Solemnis were slow in gaining acceptance.
For the sonatas and quartets this may be explained simply by the fact that they were far ahead of their time in form
and content, so that years had to pass to let the world grow to understand and admire them. The slowness with which
Fidelio was accepted was due primarily to the fact that it was a "horror-opera" of a type popular at the turn of the
century, under the influence of the French Revolution, but that by the time the work had assumed its final form it
was out of date by much more than fifteen years through the political events of the interim period and their effect
upon culture and thought. As for the Missa Solemnis, it is liturgically quite impracticable, but it was written at a
time when concert performances of such music were almost completely out of custom and when most of the choruses
in existence were wholly unqualified to attempt the technical demands of the music. There are many evidences that
instead of martyrdom Beethoven attained an eminent degree of worldly success: (1) his acceptance as an equal by the
outstanding men of his day, in intellectual pursuits and society alike; (2) his ability to demand and receive prices for
his works far in excess of those paid to any of his contemporaries or predecessors; (3) the fact that no less than six publishers vied for the first rights to the Missa Solemnis, and that nearly as many sought the privilege of bringing out a
collected edition of his works; (4) the fact that he was the first composer whose symphonies were published in score;
and (5) perhaps most conclusive, the fact that even during his lifetime his music had become the standard by which
all other composers were measured. "Only by giving far too much weight to some considerations and far too little
to others can the contention be maintained that Beethoven was underrated by his contemporaries. "
$$61_1 \text{ [1902] 79}$$

BEETHOVEN'S EROICA.   K a r l   N e f .   (C)
   According to Kreutzer, the idea of a Heroic Symphony dates back to Beethoven's acquaintance with Count Bernadotte
in the spring of 1798; Dr. Bertolini associates the plan with Napoleon's flight from Egypt in May 1798. Sketches
cited by Lenz as the first for the Eroica appear in a sketch book of 1801. It is possible that the idea of a Funeral
March may have arisen from the death of Gen. Abercrombie at Alexandria (March 21st 1801), and that the earliest
of the sketches (which were apparently for the finale) may instead have been for the Variations Op. 35 which certainly preceded the symphony. Sketching of the symphony was actively pursued during 1802, and the work of composition
proper seems to have been undertaken only in the summer of 1803 in Oberdöbling. The symphony was probably completed shortly after Beethoven's return to Vienna in the fall. Ries's story (WRK p. 93) that Beethoven struck Napoleon's
name from the title-page is substantiated by Prince Lichnowsky (TK II 24). It was without doubt Beethoven's interest
in everything which had to do with the spirit of liberty, as focussed in the French Revolution, which led him to dedicate a symphony to Napoleon. The development of the symphony in the sketch book, as presented by Nottebohm, is
discussed at length. It is probable that the first performance of the symphony was a private one for Prince Louis
Ferdinand by Prince Lobkowitz in the summer of 1804. A semi-public performance early in 1805 at the home of
Würth, the banker of Vienna, brought the first reviews of the work; the first public performance was on April 7th 1805
with Beethoven as conductor. The parts were published in October 1806 and the score in 1823.
$$64_1 \text{ [1905] 539,611}$$

BEETHOVENS WELTANSCHAUUNG. Hermann Seeliger.   (A)
  A study of Beethoven's adjustment to his world and to himself.   72₃ [1913] 109

GRILLPARZER-GESELLSCHAFT JAHRBUCH

GRILLPARZER ON BEETHOVEN.   (B)
  A letter of 10 July 1826 from Grillparzer to Katharina Frölich contains the passage: "They tell me that Beethoven
  has accepted the commission to set my opera book for Berlin.   That means more grief for me (Das wird wieder
  neue Hudeleien geben)."   1 [1890] 103

ANSELM HÜTTENBRENNERS ERINNERUNGEN AN SCHUBERT.   Otto Erich Deutsch.   (C)
  This article contains various incidental references to Beethoven. (a) A requiem for double chorus which Hüttenbrenner
  wrote in 1825 was sung at the memorial service for Beethoven in Graz.   An account is given of Hüttenbrenner's letter
  to Thayer regarding Beethoven. (b) The memoirs include the statement: "For Beethoven, to whom Schubert had un-
  hindered access, he had the highest regard." (c) In a letter of 21 February 1858 to Ferdinand Luib, Hüttenbrenner
  quotes Beethoven as having said about Schubert: "He had a divine spark." ("Der hat den götteschen Funken," or perhaps, "Wahrlich, in dem Schubert wohnt ein göttlicher Funke!") In a rather rambling letter dated two days later,
  Hüttenbrenner told of various incidents which led him to conclude that Schubert was acquainted with Beethoven.
                                                            16 [1906] 99,104,122,138

ZUR GESCHICHTE DER THEATER WIENS.   Karl Glossy.   (D)
  An extraordinary collection (more than 300 pages) of excerpts from the records of the Imperial Censor's Office and
  the Imperial Theater Management for the period 1801 to 1820.   The names of several hundred individuals connected
  with Beethoven are mentioned.   On pp. 83-84 the author gives such details as are known of the attempt by the censor
  to prohibit the performance of Leonore in October 1805.   The volume is well indexed.
                                                            25 [1915] 1

GULDEN PASSER

IS LODEWIJK VAN BEETHOVEN VAN ANTWERPSE OORSPRONG? André M. Pols.   (E)
  A study of the van Beethovens of Antwerp in the seventeenth century, especially of the line which includes Henry
  Adelard, leading to the conclusion "that it is impossible that the third child of Henry Adelard, who was baptized
  on December 23rd 1712, could have been the grandfather of Ludwig van Beethoven, for the simple reason that in
  1753 he was no longer alive."   9 [1927] 51

HAAGSCH MAANDBLAD

LUDWIG VAN BEETHOVEN. Willem Pijper.   (F)
  Centenary essay.   7 [1927] 227

BEETHOVEN ALS TANZKOMPONIST. Ludwig Gerheuser. (A)
A review of Kinsky's edition (H-15) of the 'Gesellschaftsmenuette' for 2 violins and bass (T-293) of about 1795, in
which the author makes the point that the lightness of spirit which all Beethoven's burdens could not quell led to
an interest in dance music which manifested itself in one way or another all his life.
4 [1935] 52

HEFTE FÜR BÜCHEREIWESEN

BEETHOVEN-LITERATUR IN DER VOLKSTÜMLICHEN BÜCHEREI. Konrad Ameln. (B)
Some 45 books then in print in German on various aspects of Beethoveniana are listed and commented upon from the
standpoint of the librarian or the general reader. Several lists of books on Beethoven to meet various budgets are
given. 11 [1927] 92

HILFE

BEETHOVEN IM GESPRÄCHE. Albrecht Schaeffer. (C)
Review of book of the same title by Felix Braun. [1916] 425

HIMMELSWELT

BEETHOVEN UND DIE MUSIK DER SPHÄREN. Karl Kostersitz. (D)
An astronomer who is also an enthusiastic amateur quartet player states that for years before he knew of the
inspiration which Czerny attributed to Beethoven for the adagio of the quartet in E minor Op. 59 No. 2 (TK II 75)
he had thought of that movement as the 'astronomical adagio' from the feeling that it gave him of being on a high
mountain under the stars. 37 [1927] 176

HOCHLAND

ZUR BEETHOVENFORSCHUNG. Eugen Schmitz. (E)
Quotation from 'Die Musik' 10_4 [1911] 131 of text and part of discussion of supposed newly-discovered letter to the
Immortal Beloved (see p. 266). 9_1 [1911] 142

ZUR MUSIKALISCHEN BEHANDLUNG DES MESSENTEXTES. Eugen Schmitz. (F)
A comparison of the general approach and the setting of specific passages in Palestrina's Missa Papae Marcellus,
Bach's B minor Mass, Beethoven's Missa Solemnis, and Liszt's Graner Mass.
9_1 [1911] 236

NOCHMAL BEETHOVENS UNSTERBLICHE GELIEBTE. Eugen Schmitz. (G)
Statement that the letter referred to on p. 142 is probably spurious.
9_1 [1911] 266

---

* Published 1933-43 as Zeitschrift für Hausmusik.

GOETHE AND BEETHOVEN. Eugen Schmitz.   (A)
    Quoting a passage from Wilhelm Meister, the author believes that Goethe found an interest only in that music
(vocal or programmatic) which had a direct connection with words. Accordingly, his interest in Beethoven could
be only as with a famous and gifted man, not with a musician per se. Goethe's first hearing of any of Beethoven's
music was probably in October 1807 when an alto singer, Henriette Hässler, sang an aria in his presence (probably
'Ah perfido'). Bettina's enthusiasm for Beethoven and the incidental music to Egmont stimulated his interest before
the meeting of the two men in the summer of 1812. Neither seemed to find the other personally very congenial. In
subsequent years Regierungsrat Friedrich Schmidt, an excellent amateur pianist who played much music by Beethoven,
and Marianne von Willemer kept Beethoven in Goethe's mind, and after 1819 Zelter, Boucher and Rochlitz were
friends of both men. The basic reason for Goethe's lack of interest in Beethoven was that as regards music the poet
was definitely of the 18th century in his tastes, and could neither understand nor sympathize with Beethoven's music.
9_1 [1912] 482

EINE UNBEKANNTE JUGENDSINFONIE BEETHOVENS. Eugen Schmitz.   (B)
    The author doubts the authenticity of the recently discovered Jena Symphony.
9_1 [1912] 655

ZUM VERSTÄNDNIS VON BEETHOVENS "EROIKA." Eugen Schmitz.   (C)
    The Eroica has suffered because of a tendency to make it into a "military" symphony, and to write military programs
for each movement. This is a completely false understanding of Beethoven's motivation: his hero was a hero of life,
not merely a hero of warfare. The struggle in the first movement is a spiritual struggle, not a clashing of weapons.
The form of the Funeral March (patterned after Rameau and Gretry) may be taken as a tribute to Bernadotte in the
same way that the introduction of Russian themes into Op. 59 was a tribute to Rasumovsky; the March itself is infinite-
ly more than music to accompany a corpse to its grave. With struggle and sorrows past, the third movement typifies
humor and lightness of heart, and the finale represents the hero's labors.
9_1 [1912] 747

EINE KRIEGSERINNERUNG IN BEETHOVENS MISSA SOLEMNIS. Eugen Schmitz.   (D)
    The introduction of warlike music in appropriate passages of the Mass ('et in terra pax'; 'dona nobis pacem') was an
accepted practice among Beethoven's contemporaries -- vide Haydn's 'Nelson Mass' of August 1798 and his
'Paukenmesse' of two years later. Beethoven's Agnus Dei is analyzed to show the appropriateness of the two martial
episodes, with the suggestion that their emotional content corresponds to a challenge to the "inner and outer peace"
which Beethoven prayed for. The choice of a fugato subject so obviously resembling 'And He shall reign' for Handel's
Hallelujah Chorus is at once a tribute to a much admired composer and an affirmation for the peace which Beethoven
sought. 13_2 [1916] 218

BEETHOVENS BILD IM SPIEGEL DER GEGENWART. Richard von Alpenburg.   (E)
    Centenary essay. 24_2 [1927] 246

ILLUSTRATED LONDON NEWS

FIDELIO AT HER MAJESTY'S THEATER, 20 MAY 1851.   (F)
    At this performance (Leonora, Cruvelli; Florestan, Sims Reeves; cond. Balfe) several male principals of the company
paid honor to the opera and its composer by singing in the Prisoners' Chorus.
18 [1851] 448

ILLUSTRIRTE ZEITUNG

ZU BEETHOVENS 100JÄHRIGEM GEBURTSTAG. A. Tottmann.   (G)
    Centenary essay.   55 [1870] 422

DAS BEETHOVEN-DENKMAL IN WIEN.   (A)
    Description with detailed illustrations.   74 [1880] 296

NEUE BEETHOVEN-BILDNISSE. Theodor von Frimmel.   (B)
    "About half of the portraits of the great composer which we have are by amateurs; among the others the work of only
    two famous artists appears: Stieler and Waldmüller." A life-mask made by Franz Klein in 1812 is the best source of
    information of the composer's actual appearance. As stated in 'Neue Zeitschrift für Musik' 76 [1880] 361, one of
    Beethoven's contemporaries referred to the medallion by Jos. Dan. Böhm as a very faithful likeness.
                                                               85 [1885] 647

EIN BEETHOVEN-BILDNISS. Theodor von Frimmel.   (C)
    An oil painting made by Mähler in 1814-15 is of importance in the series of Beethoven portraits.
                                                               96 [1891] 442

BEETHOVENS "UNSTERBLICHE GELIEBTE." Lina Schneider.   (D)
    Popular article identifying Therese von Brunswick as the Immortal Beloved.
                                                               96 [1891] 602

GRÄFIN GIULIETTA GUICCIARDI UND BEETHOVEN. La Mara, pseud. (Marie Lipsius)   (E)
    Popular biographical sketch.   97 [1891] 118

NEUE AUFGEFUNDENE BEETHOVEN-BILDNISSE. Theodor von Frimmel.   (F)
    Two pencil sketches (full length, from left side and from rear) by an unknown artist, though they look more like
    Beethoven of the 1820's than of the 1800's, may nevertheless be the sketches referred to in Beethoven's letter of
    1803 (?) to Frau Gerardi-Frank (KS I 24 No. 30, dated "1798?").
                                                               99 [1892] 76

GOETHE, MOZART AND BEETHOVEN. A. v. Winterfeld.   (G)
    There is no indication that Mozart returned the interest and admiration which Goethe showed for him. Goethe saw
    Mozart once (in 1763) but there is no record that they ever met. The known facts about Goethe's association with
    Beethoven are summarized.   113 [1899] 249

DAS BEETHOVEN-STANDBILD IN BONN. Sofie Frank.   (H)
    Photograph and description of the statue by Gottfried Welter.   123 [1904] 540

BERÜHMTE DARSTELLERINNEN DES FIDELIO. Carlos Droste.   (I)
    Brief comments on the chief Leonoras of the early and mid-19th century, with photographs and comments on
    twelve of the best-known contemporary portrayers of this role.   126 [1906] 370

BEETHOVEN. James Simon.   (J)
    Sesquicentennial essay.   155 [1920] 607

MANY ILLUSTRATIONS IN WIDE VARIETY BEARING ON BEETHOVEN.   (K)
                                                               168 [1927] 390-408

BEETHOVEN. Josef Stollreiter.   (L)
    Centenary essay.   168 [1927] 390

BEETHOVENS LEBENSWEG. Horst Sigwart.   (M)
    Popular biographical sketch.   168 [1927] 392

WIE SAH BEETHOVEN AUS? Wilhelm Lütge.   (N)
    Word picture from contemporary portraits and descriptions.   168 [1927] 396

BEETHOVENS FREUNDESKREIS. Karl Geiringer. (A)
  Popular account with many portraits.   168 [1927] 397

BEETHOVEN AND GOETHE. Valerian Tornius. (B)
  Brief popular account.   168 [1927] 403

BEETHOVENS LETZTE ERDENTAGE. Stephan Ley. (C)
  Popular account of the last year of Beethoven's life, and of his funeral ceremonies.
      168 [1927] 404

BEETHOVEN UND DIE NACHWELT. Max Unger. (D)
  Popular account of the growth of the acceptance of Beethoven's works and of the literature about him.
      168 [1927] 407

BEETHOVEN UND DER DICHTER. Hans Steguweit. (E)
  Fiction.   168 [1927] 409

BEETHOVEN IN DER ERZÄHLENDEN DICHTUNG DER GEGENWART. Paul Bulow. (F)
      168 [1927] 418

BESASS BEETHOVEN WIRTSCHAFTLICHES VERSTÄNDNIS? Otto Conrad. (G)
  The author quotes Max Reinitz in the contention that Beethoven's proclivity for lawsuits and his handling of financial
  matters proved him a practical man of affairs.   168 [1927] 419

INSELSCHIFF

BEETHOVEN. Hugo von Hofmannsthal. (H)
  Sesquicentennial essay reprinted from the Vienna 'Neue Freie Presse' of 12 December 1920, p. 1.
      2 [1921] 97

ERINNERUNGEN AN BEETHOVEN. Franz Grillparzer. (I)
      3 [1922] 123

BEETHOVENS TAUBHEIT. Romain Rolland. (J)
  Excerpt from his book 'Beethovens Meisterjahre.'   11 [1929] 38

Institut de France
COMPTES RENDUS DE L'ACADÉMIE DES SCIENCES
(Paris)

NATURE DE LA SURDITÉ DE BEETHOVEN. Marage. (K)
  From a reconstructed curve of Beethoven's auditory acuity at various ages and from other information, the author
  gives a diagnosis of otitis of the inner ear.   186 [1928] 110

SURDITÉ ET COMPOSITION MUSICALE. Marage. (L)
  The type of deafness from which Beethoven suffered, while blocking out external sounds (and thereby minimizing
  the effect upon him of the work of his contemporaries and of the actual sounds of his own compositions), stimulated
  the auditory centers to Beethoven's inestimable advantage as a composer.
      186 [1928] 266

CAUSES ET CONSÉQUENCES DE LA SURDITÉ DE BEETHOVEN. Marage. (M
  Working closely with Romain Rolland, the author has become convinced that Beethoven's deafness resulted not from
  otiosclerosis but from an otitis of the inner ear attributable to a congestion resulting from the tremendous mental

concentration to which Beethoven subjected himself (see Rolland's 'Beethoven: Les grandes époques créatrices' pp. 297-313, esp. pp. 304, 309).   189 [1929] 1036

INTERNATIONAL JOURNAL OF PSYCHO-ANALYSIS

BEETHOVEN AND HIS NEPHEW. Richard and Editha Sterba.   (A)
Excerpts from the book (1954) of the same title.   33 [1952] 470

INTERNATIONAL MUSICIAN

SCORING FOR THE HORN FROM HAYDN TO STRAUSS. Joseph Braunstein.   (B)
Except in the Eroica Symphony, Beethoven sedulously avoided stopped tones (except to correct the pitch of partials 7, 11, 13 and 14) through the period of the first four piano concertos and the first six symphonies. The well-known passage for three horns in Fidelio (GA 20/206 p. 124) is a marked deviation from his usual practice in its requirement for the indiscriminate use of natural and stopped notes without change in musical texture. The valve horn was announced in the 'Allgemeine Musikalische Zeitung' 17 [1815] 309, and Eduard Constantin Lewy, first horn of the Vienna Court Opera from 1822, was an enthusiastic proponent of the new instrument. He brought to Vienna his younger brother, Joseph Rudolf (who later adopted the name Lewy-Hoffmann), and it was Joseph the valve horn player who was fourth horn in the premiere of the Ninth Symphony.
47 No. 10 [April 1949] 22

INTERNATIONAL RECORD OF MEDICINE *

BEETHOVEN'S PHYSICIANS. Waldemar Schweisheimer.   (C)
The dozen or more physicians who attended Beethoven at one time or another are briefly commented upon. Regarding Dr. Wawruch the author says: "He was a careful and sympathetic physician who made no mistake either in the diagnosis or the treatment of Beethoven's disease."   149 [1939] 235

INTERNATIONALE MONATSSCHRIFT FÜR WISSENSCHAFT, KUNST UND TECHNIK **

LUDWIG VAN BEETHOVEN. Hermann Kretzschmar.   (D)
Beethoven scholarship has concerned itself too much with the accumulation of facts and too little with the understanding of the man and the content of his music. Beethoven's heredity had little influence: he was not a typical Netherlander nor Rhinelander, and only in his father and his grandfather is there any trace of musical talent. Neefe would have had a place in musical history as a pioneer of German lieder even had he not been Beethoven's teacher, and this tendency of the teacher, transmitted to the pupil shows itself in the typical Beethoven adagio. The acquaintance with Bach which Neefe gave to Beethoven was of importance, but as a child of his time Beethoven's tendency was away from the contrapuntal, except as he returned to this mode of musical thought in his last years. The musical atmosphere of the Electoral Court was of the first importance in Beethoven's development: it fostered his virtuosity in sight-reading, it taught him the workings of the orchestra, it stimulated his creative imagination and encouraged his early essays in composition. His first important composition -- the 'Trauerkantate' -- is of very uneven merit, but its best sections are most remarkable for a 20-year old lad. Some of the other Bonn compositions show an amazing maturity: Opp. 1, 3, 4, 52 No. 2. His formal education was conspicuously slight, but in his maturity he became a broadly-read man. The world owed a tremendous debt to the long-suffering patrons in Vienna who made possible Beethoven's development as we know it. At the beginning of the 19th century composition was not in itself a field of musical specialization: the composer had to be a virtuoso or (for the composer of operas) a traveling impresario. Thus Beethoven's

---

* Published 1934-50 as Medical Record.
** Volumes 1-5 were published as Internationale Wochenschrift für Wissenschaft, Kunst und Technik.

LUDWIG VAN BEETHOVEN (Continued)

virtuosity as pianist and improviser was of great importance in the first part of his career in Vienna, and in his visits to Prague, Berlin and other centers. After 1798 his travels as a virtuoso were in large measure abandoned, but his innate tendency to roam expressed itself in his habitual walks through the meadows and forests outside Vienna. "Forests and flowers were the best friends of his imagination, which flourished most richly in God's out-of-doors." Beethoven's relatively small output (as compared with Bach's 300 church cantatas or Haydn's 104 symphonies) was a further indication of the transition of the composer from the status of a productive artisan for current needs to that of a creative artist. This trend in the history of music was especially important to Beethoven because of his relentless self-criticism. Pointing out that Beethoven wrote imperishable works in all fields except those of organ music and a capella song, the author discusses his accomplishments in the several categories, and the evidence of the sketch books as to the course of his mind in the long process of composition.

3 [1909] 635,669

Internationale Musikgesellschaft
REPORT OF THE FOURTH CONGRESS

ÜBER EINE REVISION DER BEETHOVEN-GESAMTAUSGABE.   Friedrich Spiro.   (A)

A plea is made for an entirely new Gesamtausgabe, to supersede the present one in completeness and correctness and in the inclusion of a Revisionsbericht. Numerous examples are given of specific points at which the present edition is faulty.   [1911] 72,372

A YOUTHFUL SYMPHONY BY BEETHOVEN DISCOVERED AT JENA.   Fritz Stein.   (B)

Abstract of paper appearing in 'Sammelbände der Internationalen Musikgesellschaft' 13 [1911] 127.

[1911] 73

International Society for Musical Research
REPORT OF THE FIRST CONGRESS

RAMEAU AND BEETHOVEN.   Paul Marie Masson.   (C)

Passages from Rameau's operatic works are cited or quoted which the author believes are in the style of Beethoven.

[1930] 174

Iowa University
STUDIES IN THE PSYCHOLOGY OF MUSIC

A MUSICAL PATTERN SCORE OF THE LAST MOVEMENT OF THE BEETHOVEN SONATA OPUS 27 No. 2.   (D

C. E. Seashore and Laila Skinner.

A visual recording of the time and intensity relations in a specific performance of the composition named.

4 [1936] 263

JAHRBUCH DER LITERARISCHEN VEREINIGUNG WINTERTHUR

BEETHOVENS VOKALE UND INSTRUMENTALE VOLKSLIEDERBEARBEITUNGEN.   Willy Hess.   (E

An admirable summary is given of Thomson's song project, of Beethoven's contribution to this project, and of his independent interest in this type of music, which led to his setting some 55 songs that did not appear in the Thomson collection. Since the texts for which Beethoven's settings were intended were not made available to him, and since in any event a harmonization which will retain the essence of an unaccompanied folksong (if indeed it is possible under any circumstances) requires of the composer deep understanding of the national characteristics of the race that produced the song, Beethoven's settings took on the nature of independent compositions based on the melodies given.

This is especially the case with Opp. 105 and 107, in which the variations form is used and which for this reason are musically the most rewarding of all of Beethoven's folksong writing.
[1943] 162

KANTATE VON LUDWIG VAN BEETHOVEN. Willy Hess.   (A)
EDr of the cantata 'Un lieto brindisi' H-97 for STTB and piano, composed for the Name-day of Dr. Johannes Malfatti, with careful Revisionsbericht. A German text is used: Johannisfeier begehn wir heute!
[1945] 247

VERZEICHNIS DER BEETHOVEN BETREFFENDEN VERÖFFENTLICHUNGEN VON WILLY HESS. Willy Hess.   (B)
List of 67 papers on Beethoven published by the author during 1925-45, mostly in newspapers and Swiss musical journals of limited circulation and availability.   [1945]

JAHRBUCH DES DEUTSCHTUMS IN LETTLAND

BEETHOVENS BALTISCHE BEZIEHUNGEN. V. Grüner.   (C)
The name of Karl Ferdinand Amenda (a Courlander) first appears in a note to Zmeskall (KS I 14) in which Beethoven asks him to bring with him a guitar-player -- probably Gottfried Heinrich Mylich, another Courlander. A detailed biographical sketch of Amenda is given, extended excerpts are quoted from a manuscript in the possession of the Amenda family recounting Amenda's first meeting and association with Beethoven in 1798-99, and the friendship of the two men is discussed at great length. Amenda's letter of March 20th 1815, to which Beethoven replied on April 12th (KS I 360), is given. What apparently was Beethoven's last contact with Amenda was through a letter of introduction which Amenda gave to Karl von Bursy, brother-in-law of Mylich, on the occasion of a trip to Vienna in the spring of 1816. An extended account of his meeting with Beethoven is given from Bursy's diary. Johann Georg Count Browne (described by Beethoven in the dedication of the Trios Op. 9 as his "first Maecenas") was a native of Livonia, though his ancestor Thomas Browne emigrated from Ireland in the time of Henry VIII. A history of the family and of Beethoven's association with the Count and Countess is given in elaborate detail. Beethoven's close friendship with the von Brunswicks bears upon the Baltic countries to the extent that Josephine von Brunswick, to whom Beethoven was much attached, was for four years the wife of Count Deym, a Balt, and later the wife of Baron Christoph von Stackelberg, an Esthonian.   [1925] 68

JENAISCHE ALLGEMEINE LITERATUR-ZEITUNG

WELLINGTONS SIEG. Gottfried Weber.   (D)
Original version of the review which appeared nine years later in 'Cäcilia' 3 [1825] 155 changed only in unimportant matters of phraseology. The review analyzed Op. 91 in detail, with quotations in musical notation, and stressed the reviewer's belief that the work was wholly unworthy of Beethoven's genius.
JG 13 III [August 1816 Nos. 145,146]
217,225

JOURNAL OF ABNORMAL AND SOCIAL PSYCHOLOGY

THE PROBLEM OF BEETHOVEN'S DEAFNESS. Paul C. Squires.   (E)
A very detailed study of the subject, with extensive quotations from many writers and a bibliography of 88 references. "In fine, we hold that all of Beethoven's symptoms and the entire course of his disease -- in so far as we are able to separate fact from fiction -- are not only absolutely consistent with the diagnosis of acquired syphilis, but overwhelmingly demand this pronouncement . . . . All the medical data being perfectly consistent with the acquired syphilis theory in Beethoven's case, we find that the circumstantial evidence is irresistably convincing when added thereto. Our verdict can be nothing else than this: Beethoven suffered from acquired syphilis 'beyond a reasonable doubt. '"
32 [1937] 11

BEETHOVEN'S DEAFNESS. Maurice Sorsby.   (A)
　　"It is not at all unlikely that Beethoven's deafness was of that indeterminate type so commonly seen in practice,
a type that does not lend itself to any definite diagnosis, being a composite lesion of all possible affections leading
to deafness. " "The circumstantial evidence (that Beethoven was luetic) is hardly deserving of any serious attention,
and even if it were proved that Beethoven had syphilis, there is nothing to prove that this was the cause of his deafness
or of his cirrhosis. "   45 [1930] 529

KANTSTUDIEN

KANT AND BEETHOVEN. Karl Vorländer.   (B)
　　Passages are quoted from Schiedermair's 'Der junge Beethoven' to show that in Bonn Beethoven must have been in a
social group conversant with and sympathetic to the ideals of Kant.
                                                         31 [1926] 126

KATHOLIK

AUS BEETHOVENS BRIEFEN.   (C)
　　Popular biographical sketch, analysis of the composer's character and personality, discussion of his relations with his
friends (regarding Zmeskall, Ries and Schindler, "he used them more like lackeys"), and affirmation of his sincere
adherence to Catholic doctrine, all interlarded with copious extracts from his letters.
                                                         NF 25 [1871] 181

KREIS

"BEETHOVEN-DÄMMERUNG?" Rudolf Maack.   (D)
　　A discursive essay on Beethoven and various writings about him, in contention that his works and his influence on
music are not fading into twilight.   8 [1931] 495,545

AUS "BEETHOVEN." Romain Rolland.   (E)
　　Excerpt from the German version of 'Ludwig van Beethoven' (Rotapfel-Verlag, 1926) pp. 68-88, giving material
which appears in Eaglefield-Hull's English translation pp. 42-54.
                                                         9 [1932] 455

KULTUR UND SCHALLPLATTE

VARIATION. Hans Mersmann.   (F)
　　A popular discussion of the Andante of Op. 18 No. 5 as an example of Beethoven's early variations technique.
                                                         1 [1929] 3

BEETHOVENS STREICHQUARTETTE. Hermann Unger.   (G)
　　Very brief popular discussion of each quartet.   1 [1930] 57

BEETHOVEN-SCHÄTZE DER STAATSBIBLIOTHEK. Johannes Wolf.   (H)
　　Brief discussion, with especial reference to sketches, drafts and autographs of the string quartets.
                                                         1 [1930] 61

BEETHOVEN'S DISEASES.
Abstract of article by Schweisheimer in 'Münchener medizinische Wochenschrift' 67 [1920] 1473.
200 [1921] 41

LEHRERIN *

BEETHOVENS BEZIEHUNGEN ZUR FRAUENWELT. C. Haass.   (B)
A popular article on Frau van Beethoven, Jeanette d'Honrath, Eleonore von Breuning, the Immortal Beloved (who
may have been either Giulietta Guicciardi or Therese von Brunsvik), and Nanette Streicher.
24 [1908] 717

LEIPZIG

BEETHOVEN AND LEIPZIG. Wilhelm Hitzig.   (C)
There is no definite proof that Beethoven was ever in Leipzig, but letters given in Schiedermair's 'Der junge Beethoven'
show that he intended to go to Leipzig as a part of the tour that took him to Dresden in 1796. Beethoven's real con-
tact with the city, aside from the many musicians from Leipzig whom he knew, was with the two publishing houses
Breitkopf & Härtel and Hoffmeister, and with the influential 'Allgemeine Musikalische Zeitung' published there from
Beethoven's twenty-eighth year.   3 [1927] 165

LIBRO ITALIANO

BEETHOVEN, CATTOLICO, CLASSICO E ITALIANIZZANTE. Mario Baratelli.   (D)
Review of Antonio Bruers' 'Beethoven: catologo storico-critico di tutte le opere' (1940).
4 [1940] 689

LISTEN

BEETHOVEN'S STRING QUARTETS -- THEIR PERFORMANCE. Boris Kroyt.   (E)
Popular.   [May 1945] 3

BEETHOVEN'S STRING QUARTETS -- THEIR MUSICAL MEANING. Kurt List.   (F)
Popular.   [May 1945] 5

LITERATUR **

GOETHE, BEETHOVEN, KLEIST. Philipp Witkop.   (G)
Introduction to a monograph on Heinrich von Kleist, comparing the three contemporaries and discussing their attitudes
towards one another.   22 [1920] 513

GEDANKEN AM 6. APRIL.   (H)
A performance of the Ninth Symphony brings the thought that a world at war accords ill with the 'Ode to Joy.'
43 [1941] 377

---

*   Volumes 1-26 were published as Lehrerin in Schule und Haus.
** Volumes 1-25 were published as Literarische Echo.

ÜBER EINIGE UNBEKANNTE VERERBTE STICHFEHLER IN BEETHOVENSCHEN SYMPHONIEN. Max Unger.　　　(A)
Music is far more subject to errors in reproduction than is literature or painting, both because of the inconspicuousness of mistakes on the printed page and because of the lack of absolute standards of right and wrong. Accordingly, the transmission of errors in music from edition to edition is an ever-present danger which throws a grave responsibility on all editors. An article by Czerny ('Neue Wiener Musik-Zeitung' 2 [1853] 59) giving corrections to five passages in the Third, Fourth, Fifth and Sixth Symphonies is reprinted, as is the mention by Schumann ('Neue Zeitschrift für Musik' 13 [1840] 144; 15 [1841] 150) of the error which Czerny cited in the Fourth Symphony. The history of each of the errors which Czerny listed (its genesis and its correction) is discussed.
[1914] 138

MECKLENBURGISCHE MONATSHEFTE

BEETHOVEN UND BRUCKNER IN DIESER ZEIT. Erich Reipschläger.　　　(B)
Rhapsodic praise of the two composers.　　　9 [1933] 603

MÉDECINE INTERNATIONALE

LA SURDITÉ DE BEETHOVEN. Georges Canuyt.　　　(C)
Popular account of the progress of Beethoven's deafness, the treatments and facilities that he used, an account of the autopsy, and a discussion of various possible causes, leading to the conclusion that there is inadequate evidence to declare that Beethoven had acquired syphilis but that the course of the deafness was consonant with a conjecture of hereditary syphilis.　　　41 [1933] 373; 42 [1934] 21,53,85,
117

MEDIZINISCHE WELT

DER KRANKE BEETHOVEN. Gustav Ernest.　　　(D)
Biographical sketch.　　　1 [1927] 491

VON BEETHOVENS ÄRZTEN. Stephan Ley.　　　(E)
A lengthy and semi-popular discussion of the various physicians who at one time or another attended Beethoven.
8 [1934] 747

AN BEETHOVENS LETZTEN KRANKENLAGER. Stephan Ley.　　　(F)
Extensive quotations from the conversation books on the course of Beethoven's illness and treatment.
10 [1936] 1058,1094

MENSCHHEIT

BEETHOVENS POLITISCHE GESINNUNG. Immanuel S. Franz.　　　(G)
Familiar facts are assembled to show Beethoven's innate championship of freedom.
14 No. 11 [March 18th 1927] 74

LA DIXIÈME SYMPHONIE.   Henry Bourgerel.   (A)
   "We know that he planned out a symphony to compare with the Ninth as the Ninth did with the Eroica . . . The
   Tenth Symphony was Beethoven's own spirit."   22 [1897] 447
                                                           Série Moderne

L'IMMORTELLE BIEN-AIMÉE DE BEETHOVEN.   F. de Gerando.   (B)
   The author, great-grand-nephew of Therese von Brunsvik, pays his respects to the logical aligning of arguments with
   which La Mara believes she has proven Therese to have been the Immortal Beloved, but states his own reasons for being
   equally convinced that Therese was not the addressee of the famous letters.
                                                           79 [1909] 92

UN MEMOIRE DE BEETHOVEN SUR SA FAMILLE.   J. G. Prod'homme.   (C)
   Apparently a translation of the memorandum referred to in Beethoven's letter of March 6th 1820 to Winter (KS II 166).
   Beethoven's side in the dispute with Nephew Karl's mother is stated at great length.
                                                           102 [1913] 738

LES ORIGINES FLAMANDES DE BEETHOVEN.   J. G. Prod'homme.   (D)
   Non-critical biographical sketch of Grandfather Ludwig and Father Johann.
                                                           129 [1918] 454

BEETHOVEN EN FRANCE.   J. G. Prod'homme.   (E)
   A lengthy and scholarly study.   194 [1927] 589

BEETHOVEN.   Jean Marnold.   (F)
   Centenary essay.   195 [1927] 5

LE PROBLEME MUSICAL: BACH ET BEETHOVEN.   Marcel Bitsch.   (G)
                                                           226 [1931] 310

MIDLAND MUSICIAN *

SEPTET OPUS 20.   (H)
   Superficial program notes.   2 [1926] 59

WELLINGTON'S VICTORY OPUS 91.   (I)
   Program notes.   3 [1927] 123

THE STRING QUARTETS.   (J)
   Popular discussion.   3 [1927] 84,121,217

MÖDLINGER DEUTSCHEN WOCHENBLATT

BEETHOVEN IM STREICHER'SCHEN KLAVIERSALON.   Theodor von Frimmel.   (K)
   General remarks on the concerts and performers associated with the Streicher salon.
                                                           [6 August 1916]

DIE MITARBEITERSCHAFT BEETHOVENS ZU DER WIENER PIANOFORTESCHULE VON STARKE.   (L)
      Theodor von Frimmel.
   See 'Merker' 8 [1917] 24. As No. 34 of Part III of the Pianoforteschule, Starke included the theme and some of the
   variations of the Archduke Rudolph's set of variations on Beethoven's 'O Hoffnung' WoO 200.
                                                           [13 August 1916]

---

* After November 1926 became British Musician and Musical News.

DESTRUCTION OF VIENNA POLICE ARCHIVES. A. Hajdecki. (A)
    In the early 1870's the bulk of the old police records in Vienna were discarded for reasons of space, so that further running down in that quarter of information regarding Beethoven (the dispute with Artaria regarding Op. 29 is cited) cannot be expected to attain any great degree of success. 2 [1902] 66

MONATSSCHRIFT FÜR DAS DEUTSCHE GEISTESLEBEN **

BEETHOVEN'S FIDELIO. Ferdinand Pfohl. (B)
    Popular historical account. 15 [1905] 89

BEETHOVENS "UNSTERBLICHE GELIEBTE." Theodor von Frimmel. (C)
    To the extent that Mariam Tenger's identification of Therese von Brunsvik as the Immortal Beloved rests on the testimony of Spaun, it can be disregarded, since Spaun's nephew quotes his uncle as having said that he was often in the same tavern as Beethoven but that he never met him personally. With Hevesy's support of Therese von Brunsvik in mind, the author secured considerable information regarding the circle of young ladies around Therese, from contemporary members of the von Brunsvik family. Regarding Unger's contention that the letters were written in 1812 and that Bettina was the Immortal Beloved, as set forth in 'Musikalisches Magazin' 37 [1911], the author states that the sonnet which Beethoven was supposed to have written to Bettina is definitely not authentic. Unger's analysis is summarized, and the author feels that Unger's positiveness is beyond the soundness of his argument. The supposed "fourth letter" reported by Bekker ('Die Musik' 10_4 [1911] 131) is discussed from the standpoint of handwriting and declared unquestionably false. 14_1 [1912] 393

LUDWIG VAN BEETHOVENS HUNDERTJÄHRIGER TODESTAG. Karl Söhle. (D
    Centennial essay. 1 [1927] 177

DAS WAHRE UND DAS ROMANTISCHE BEETHOVEN-BILD. Herman Unger. (E)
    A review of Arnold Schmitz's 'Das romantische Beethovenbild.' The Beethoven portrayed by Bettina von Arnim -- the simple peasant and the first of the Romantics -- never existed in the flesh, but this picture has influenced biographers from that day to this. 14 [1932] 103

ARMER BEETHOVEN! Walter Abendroth. (F
    The author sharply disagrees with the thoughts on which Schering's 'Beethoven und die Dichtung' is based. 18 [1936] 846

MÜNCHENER MEDIZINISCHE WOCHENSCHRIFT

BEETHOVENS KRANKHEITEN. W. Schweisheimer. (G
    A circumstantial account of the development of Beethoven's deafness and of his last illness and autopsy. The author concludes that Beethoven should in general be considered a "good patient" as far as following prescribed courses of treatment is concerned, and that there is little to indicate that even with present-day medical knowledge the results of his ear ailment (presumably an ailment of the inner ear of unknown etiology) or of his last illness (cirrhosis of the liver, presumably non-malignant) could have been avoided. 67 [1920] 1473

DIE KRANKHEITEN BEETHOVENS. Friedr. Schultze. (H
    The author considers it very probable that Beethoven's various maladies -- deafness, digestive complaints, and fatal liver ailment -- were of luetic origin. 75 [1928] 1040

---

  * Published 1900-02 as Monatsberichte über Kunstwissenschaft und Kunsthandel.
 ** Published 1898-1916 as Bühne und Welt; from 1917-1939 as Deutsches Volkstum.

HOW TO DEVELOP CHAMBER MUSIC.   Marion M. Scott.   (A)
   Suggestions for amateurs.   7 [1925] 299

THE BEETHOVEN CENTENARY.   Basil Maine.   (B)
   Referring to the superiority of the middle period works to the last period works, especially as regards the quartets:
   "Let our tributes go to him, then, for the might and the eloquence of his works when he was in full possession of his
   powers, not for his incoherence after the mists had descended upon his mind."
                               9 [1927] 75

MUSIKALIENHANDLUNG BREITKOPF & HÄRTEL MITTEILUNGEN

BEETHOVENS UNSTERBLICHE GELIEBTE.   La Mara, pseud. (Marie Lipsius).   (C)
   On February 2nd 1811 Therese von Brunswick wrote to her sister Josephine that she had received through her brother
   Franz a note from Beethoven which she copied in full (TD III 270; KK 264). The portrait of Therese referred to in
   the note is doubtless the one now in the Beethovenhaus Museum.
                          [March 1910] 4102

BEETHOVEN AND BREITKOPF & HÄRTEL.   (D)
   Brief summary of the relationship between the composer and the publishing house.
                    No. 126 [November 1920] 5162

ZUM BEETHOVENJAHR.   (E)
   Announcement of works to be published in the centennial year.   No. 138 [January 1927] 1

UNVERÖFFENTLICHE BEETHOVEN-LIEDER.   (F)
   Announcement of first publication of 24 folk-songs of various nationalities, in arrangements similar to those made
   for Thomson.   No. 139 [March 1927] 1

MUSICA SACRA

WOLLFREI GEDANKEN ÜBER BEETHOVENS "MISSA SOLEMNIS."   (G)
   The Missa is "a drama, the hero of which is Jesus Christ."   23 [1900] 41

MOZART, HAYDN UND BEETHOVEN ALS KIRCHENKOMPONISTEN.   Fr. X. Gruber.   (H)
   Contention that the liturgical works of the three greatest Viennese composers should not be banned under the
   Motu proprio.   55 [1925] 15

BEETHOVEN'S MISSA SOLEMNIS.   (I)
   A discussion of the writing of the Mass, of Beethoven's relations with the Archduke Rudolph, of Beethoven's attitude
   towards religion (with the conclusion, hardly substantiated by the evidence which is presented, that Beethoven was a
   believer in doctrinal religion), of the publication and early performances of the Mass, and briefly of the structure of
   the work as a piece of liturgical music. These commentaries are followed by a popular analytic discussion of the
   music, with many examples in musical notation.   56 [1926] 15,45,69,101; 57 [1927]
                               312,352,372

THE MISSA SOLEMNIS.   Hugo Wolf.   (J)
   Brief commentary.   56 [1926] 108

BEETHOVEN.   Josef Lechthaler.   (K)
   Centennial essay.   57 [1927] 136

BEETHOVENS VERHÄLTNIS ZUR RELIGION.   K. Weinmann.   57 [1927] 142   (L)

BEETHOVEN UND DIE KIRCHENMUSIK.   Fidelis P. Boeser.   (A
    An article apparently motivated by the ban on Beethoven's two Masses imposed by the <u>Motu proprio.</u>
                                                57 [1927] 148

BEETHOVENS CHARAKTER.   Guido Adler.   (B)
    Reprint from the 'Almanach der deutschen Musikbücherei' [1927] 75.
                                                57 [1927] 153

                                MUSICAL AMERICA

WAS GOETHE JEALOUS OF BEETHOVEN?   Romain Rolland.   (C
    Many of Goethe's friends were strong adherents of Beethoven, notably Johann Heinrich Friedrich Schütz, Regierungsrat
    Friedrich Schmidt, and J. N. Hummel, as well as Zelter Tomaschek, Rellstab and Rochlitz. Goethe was also emotion-
    ally involved with two Beethoven performers: Anna Milder-Hauptmann and (especially in 1823) the Polish pianist Marie
    Szymanowska. "Goethe admitted, recognized, even admired his greatness, but did not like it."
                                            [10 February 1931] 6;
                                            [25 February 1931] 7

BEETHOVEN'S 'LOST' PIANO CONCERTO.   Herbert F. Payser.   (D
    The E flat concerto of 1784 (as orchestrated by Willy Hess) is discussed in detail on the basis of analyses and information
    provided by Dr. Joseph Braunstein. It is contended that Hess' version is in many ways not in the style or the technical
    capabilities of Beethoven or of the orchestras of 1784: e.g., "Hess' manner of horn setting conforms rather to that of
    Fidelio or later romantic scores"; in Hess' cadenza a piano of six octave range is required, while Beethoven limits him-
    self to 4 1/2 octaves. Certain parallelisms are found between this work and concertos by Neefe and by Dittersdorf.
    (NOTE by DWM. Private communication from Dr. Braunstein states that Peyser is in error in saying that Beethoven
    "later transplanted one striking chromatic phrase from this Concerto to the C minor Trio Op. 1 No. 3." The phrase in
    question came from one of the piano quartets of 1785.)   69 No. 4 [March 1949] 35

BEETHOVEN SCORE UNEARTHED.   Ludwig Misch.   (E
    Summary of Hess' work on unfamiliar Beethoven compositions, and review of 'Scena' from 'Vestas Feuer.'
                                            [August 1954] 8

TO REPEAT OR NOT TO REPEAT.   Ludwig Misch.   (F
    Translated reprint of 'Musica' 8 [1954] 185.   [August 1955] 12

                    MUSICAL COURIER AND REVIEW OF RECORDED MUSIC *

BEETHOVEN, HIS LIFE AND WORKS.   Waldemar Rieck.   (G
    Popular biographical sketch.   [16 December 1920] 6

BEETHOVEN'S CHARACTER AND HABITS REVEALED BY CONVERSATION BOOKS SOON TO BE PUBLISHED.   (H
        Richard Sonehall.
    Excerpts from the conversation books. Regarding Beethoven's claim to aristocratic lineage, he himself wrote in one
    of the books: "'Van' signifies nobility only when it stands between two proper names: e.g., Bentinx van Diezerheim,
    Haft van Streelen, etc., etc. Hollanders could give the best information about this insignificant signification."
                                            [16 December 1920] 8

BEETHOVEN AND OUR OWN TIME.   Oscar Bie.   (
    Centennial essay.   [16 December 1920] 8

_____

    * Volumes 5-163 were published as Musical Courier.

WHY BEETHOVEN'S SYMPHONIES WILL NEVER BE EQUALLED. Felix Weingartner.   (A)
  General.   [16 December 1920] 9

BEETHOVEN ON THE VALUE OF INTELLECTUAL WORK. Max Unger.   (B)
  Translation and discussion of letter given in KK 1051 (see also 'Veröffentlichungen des Beethovenhauses' No. 1).
                                                              [20 December 1920] 9

BEETHOVEN -- THE HUMAN SIDE.   (C)
  Popular.   [20 December 1920] 22

BEETHOVEN'S VIOLIN COMPOSITIONS. Theodore Spiering.   (D)
  Completely unimportant.   [20 December 1920] 26

A FRENCH MUSICAN'S TRIBUTE TO BEETHOVEN. Albert Wolff.   (E)
  Brief centennial essay.   [20 December 1920] 38

THE HAUNTS OF THE MASTERS. Adeline O'Connor Thomason.   (F)
  Popular biographical sketch and travelogue of a visit to Beethoven spots in Bonn and Vienna.
                                                              [24 March 1927] 6

SOME PORTRAITS OF BEETHOVEN AND HIS FRIENDS. André de Hevesy.   (G)
  Sixteen "portraits that tell the story of Beethoven's life," with commentary of Sunday supplement standards.
                                                              [24 March 1927] 8

A PICTORIAL BIOGRAPHY OF LUDWIG VAN BEETHOVEN.   (H)
  About 40 pictures of people and places.   [24 March 1927] 10

BEETHOVEN. O. G. Sonneck.   (I)
  Centennial essay reprinted from 'American Mercury.'   [24 March 1927] 14

BEETHOVEN'S MUSIC IN FRANCE. Clarence Lucas.   (J)
  Popular but sound discussion of the first days of Beethoven's music in France.
                                                              [24 March 1927] 15

BEETHOVEN CENTENARY OBSERVANCE OF 57 YEARS AGO. Elly Ney.   (K)
  Festivals in the United States and in Bonn in 1870.   [24 March 1927] 16

A HITHERTO UNPUBLISHED LETTER BY BEETHOVEN ADDRESSED TO ZMESKALL.   (L)
  Facsimile, transcription and translation of M-174.   [n. d.]

BEETHOVEN AS A LINGUIST. Karl Eugen Schmidt.   (M)
  Beethoven's recognition of his own weakness in languages other than German is acknowledged in various of his letters·
  e.g., the opening sentence of his letter of 15 May 1816 to Neate (KS I 409) apologizing for "fauts contre la langue
  francaisses"; letter of 1807 (?) to Troxler (KS I 115): "I better understand how to make myself intelligible to the
  foreigner by playing rather than by speaking." According to the author, however, the remarkable letter to Birchall
  given in (KS I 376) is a translation by some unknown German living in London of a letter written in German by
  Beethoven. Aside from the patter of musical terms it seems probable that his acquaintance with Italian was even
  less than with French. As evidence of this, his letter of 9 February 1821 to the Italian Carlo Soliva of Milan (M-
  328), here published for the first time, was written in French instead of in the addressee's mother tongue. The author concludes that most of Beethoven's letters in English, French and Italian were written for him by someone reasonably at home in the language, and that the few letters in these languages by Beethoven himself, with other evidence,
  indicate that Beethoven "really did not understand or speak any of the three languages whose knowledge is so gener-
  ously assigned to him on the strength of his correspondence."   [3 February 1927] 14

FACSIMILE OF LETTER M328 TO SOLIVA.   [24 February 1927] 6   (N)

BEETHOVEN -- THE CONQUEROR. Ruth E. French.   (O)
  Superficial, distorted and inaccurate biographical sketch.   105 No. 9 [27 August 1932] 6

GOETHE AND THE WORLD OF MUSIC. R. M. Kerr.   (A
   Facsimile of the first page of 'Freudvoll und leidvoll'; pencil drawing of Beethoven by August Semmler.
[1 April 1949] 6

MUSICAL DIGEST

MORE ABOUT BEETHOVEN. Maurice Dubois.   (B
   A lengthy quotation is given from 'L'Indépendance Belge' summarizing the discoveries of Pols and van Aerde regarding the parentage of Grandfather Ludwig.   12 No. 12 [November 1927] 22

MUSICAL MIRROR AND FANFARE

GREAT SONG WRITERS: LUDWIG VAN BEETHOVEN. Ernest Haywood.   (C
   Beethoven's laborious process of working over his material to fit it most perfectly for the composition in hand is
completely inappropriate for song composition. A few of his songs are of high merit: Opps. 83 No. 1, 88, 46, 98.
The ingenuity which he displayed in the Thomson arrangements should not be completely neglected.
11 [1931] 119

THE "GROSSE FUGE" OF BEETHOVEN. Sidney Grew.   (D
   For many years this work was condemned but almost never heard. The author suggests that its lack of favor was
perhaps due to a fugal style so completely different from the much more familiar fugal style of Bach. He quotes
Harold Bauer in the opinion that possibly a number of the harmonic clashes may be due to a corrupt text. Suggestions for the study of the Fugue are given.   11 [1931] 152

THE KREUTZER SONATA. Alexander Brent-Smith.   (E
   Popular analysis.   11 [1931] 274

MUSICAL NEWS AND HERALD *

BEETHOVEN'S PIANOFORTE.   (F
   Brief description of the piano presented to Beethoven by Broadwood. Ferrari is identified as "a well-known musician
who accompanied Mr. Broadwood to Vienna when he made Beethoven's acquaintance."
3 [1892] 197

MUSICAL OBSERVER

BEETHOVEN'S STRING QUARTETS. Theodor Helm.   (G
   Translation of the book of the same title by Alice Mattullath.   12 [1915] to 15 [1917]

MUSICAL OPINION AND MUSIC TRADE REVIEW

BEETHOVEN'S THIRD STYLE. A. Eaglefield Hull.   (H
   The author postulates that in three years of comparative silence (1815-18) Beethoven was steeping himself in the works
of Bach (which were only gradually becoming available), and thereby learning at once the technique and the importance

_____

* Published 1891-1920 as Musical News

of polyphony. His piano sonatas written thereafter were essays in this new concept, culminating in Op. 111, "a coalesced sonata-fugal form, followed by a constellation of variations."

47 [1923] 276

BEETHOVEN AND HIS POETS. A. Eaglefield Hull.   (A)

Regarding the quality of Beethoven's literary taste, "we cannot argue much from the fact that Goethe was his prime favorite. Beethoven could no more ignore Goethe than an English composer could ignore Shakespeare."

48 [1925] 823

BEETHOVEN AND ENGLAND. "Schaunard"   (B)

Summary of Beethoven's dealings with the Philharmonic Society and of his attitude towards England.

50 [1927] 571

BEETHOVEN -- THE MIND AND THE MUSIC. A. J. Sheldon.   (C)

A discussion of Beethoven's intellectual growth as mirrored in his music. "Beethoven's contribution to the structural development of music was his emancipation of the art from form as a limiting consideration."

50 [1927] 587

BEETHOVEN -- A LIFE SKETCH. H. Orsmond Anderton.   (D)

Popular biographical sketch. (NOTE by DWM: In speaking of Beethoven's choral works, the author refers to "the practically negligible work known as 'Engedi.'" The Preface to 'Engedi, or, David in the Wilderness,' issued in vocal score by Novello about 1860, reads in part as follows: "The author of the words of the sacred drama now submitted to the British public under the title of 'Engedi,' had long regretted that the music of Beethoven's noble oratorio 'Christus am Oelberge,' appeared to be forever excluded (as a whole) from public performance, by the objectionable nature of the German libretto, and, having seen that every attempt hitherto made to modify the original subject had failed to produce the desired effect, he has been induced by considerations of the analogies of the sacred history, to make the following attempt to adapt the musical ideas of the immortal Beethoven, to the facts of Saul's persecution of David." The new libretto was based on passages from I Sam xxiii, xxiv. Grove (art.: Mount of Olives) says: "The strong feeling prevailing in England against the appearance of our Saviour as a personage . . . led to a version by Dr. Hudson of Dublin in 1842, in which the story was changed to that of David and the title to 'Engedi.' This compromise was adopted as lately as 1905, at the Bristol Festival." 'Engedi' has apparently served its purpose: the publishers report that the oratorio under this name has been allowed to go out of print.)   50 [1927] 592

BEETHOVEN AT BONN AND VIENNA. A. Eaglefield Hull.   (E)

Superficial discussion of "the part played throughout by his circle of friends, first those of Bonn and then those at Vienna."   50 [1927] 595

BEETHOVEN AND THE ORGAN. Stanley Lucas.   (F)

A popular account of Beethoven's organ playing in Bonn.   50 [1927] 704

BEETHOVEN'S LESSER KNOWN PIANO WORKS. A. Eaglefield Hull.   (G)

Rambling article with extended discussion of the Phantasy Op. 77: "undoubtedly the only written record of Beethoven's style of extemporization."   50 [1927] 791,889

GREAT LOVE" -- THE BEETHOVEN VIOLIN CONCERTO. Robert Elkin.   (H)

50 [1927] 1077

BAGATELLES OR VARIATIONS? Philip T. Barford.   (I)

Contention that Op. 119 Nos. 7 and 8 "were influenced by the orientation of Beethoven's musical thought when he was working on the Diabelli Variations.   76 [1953] 277

BEETHOVEN AND THE MEANING OF MUSIC. Henry Rayner.   (J)

General.   78 [1955] 593

A BEETHOVEN FALLACY. Leonard Duck.   (K)

The fallacy is that because of the development of music since 1827, Beethoven's compositions are now easier to understand.   78 [1955] 663

BEETHOVEN AS A READER.   A. M. Henderson.   (A
  The books owned by Beethoven at the time of his death are listed, and the six volumes known to have belonged to
  him are described. These are characterized by much marking in pencil, and by the droppings of wax resulting
  from Beethoven's habit of reading in bed.   79 [1956] 407

BEETHOVEN AND VARIATION FORM.   Philip Barford.   (B)
  A rambling discussion of the variations that Beethoven wrote in his last years.
                                                  84 [1960] 15

'FIDELIO' AND ITS OVERTURES.   R. W. S. Mendl.   (C
  Following the plan used by Sir Henry Wood, "Why not play the overtures 'Leonore No. 1,' 'No. 2,' and 'No. 3'
  as a group, in the opera house, followed by an interval, and then the opera 'Fidelio' in its final version, beginning
  with its own E major overture?"   84 [1961] 673

THE BEETHOVEN HOUSE AT BONN.   Gerard Bourke.   (D
  Popular.   84 [1961] 741

MUSICAL STANDARD

BEETHOVEN'S GREAT E MINOR QUARTET.   Harold E. Knapp.   (E)
  Popular analysis.   7 No. 9 [April 1907] 8

"A TRAVERS CHANTS."   Hector Berlioz.   (F)
  Eleven installments between p. 51 and p. 267. Translation by Edwin Evans, Sr. of Berlioz's commentaries on the
  symphonies, the trios and 'Fidelio,' published in 1862.   NS 1 [1913]

SIR GEORGE GROVE AND BEETHOVEN.   (G
  Epigrammatic excerpts from Sir George's article in the 'Dictionary.'
                                              NS 3 [1914] 362

BEETHOVEN'S AUTOGRAPH SCORES.   (H
  A plea for the extensive publication of facsimiles.   NS 3 [1914] 363

MUSICAL WORLD

DISCOVERY OF BEETHOVEN DOCUMENTS -- BEETHOVEN AND ARTARIA.   J. A. Shedlock.   (I)
  Translation and discussion of erratically selected portions of the official records in the lawsuit regarding the Artaria
  edition of the String Quintet Op. 29, given in TD II 587-609. (See also 'Musical Quarterly' 34 [1948] 567)
                                              69 [1889] 487,509,526

MUSICIAN

THE INFLUENCE OF BEETHOVEN'S MALADY UPON HIS SPIRITUAL NATURE.   J. Ermoloff.   (J)
  Popular.   12 [1907] 373

MUSIK IM UNTERRICHT

BEETHOVEN INTERPRETATION.   Edith Picht-Axenfeld.   (K
  To attain a true understanding of a work as Beethoven conceived it, it is not enough to turn to the Urtext so that the
  interpretations of editors may be avoided. Changes in technical methods and in the significance of such conventions

as the indications of slurs require that the performer integrate into his interpretation methods and concepts that are completely different from those involved in the performance of romantic or modern music.

43 [1952] 65

FACSIMILE OF KAL 1053.   43 [1952] 67   (A)

BEETHOVEN ALS LEHRER. Paul Mies.   (B)
    Accounts from many pupils indicate that Beethoven as a teacher was energetic and brusque, that he was a perfection-
    ist, and that he laid great stress on proper fingering. The course of study that he laid out for the Archduke Rudolph is
    outlined, and some of his comments on the statements of earlier authorities are given.

43 [1952] 68

WAS FEHLT IN DER GESAMTAUSGABE DER WERKE BEETHOVENS? Willy Hess.   (C)
    A considerable number of compositions omitted from the GA but published elsewhere or that are still unpublished are
    discussed briefly, and nine articles by the author, giving extensive treatment of missing compositions in various cate-
    gories, are cited.   43 [1952] 71

ANTONIO SALIERI -- EIN LEHRER BEETHOVENS. Fritz Schröder.   (D)
    A popular but detailed biographical sketch.   43 [1952] 78

DIE ERSTE FASSUNG VON BEETHOVENS LIED "FEUERFARB." OPUS 52 No. 2. Willy Hess.   (E)
    A version of the song, earlier than the one generally known but carefully worked out by the composer and complete
    in every detail, exists in manuscript and is here published for the first time.

[November 1955]

ZWEI BEETHOVEN-ERSTVERÖFFENTLICHUNGEN.   (F)
    The early version of 'Feuerfarb' is an actual first publication; the C major fugue for piano, edited by Dickinson, was
    published in 'Musical Times' 96 [1955] 76.   [November 1955]

MUSIK UND VOLK

SCHERING'S BEETHOVEN-DEUTUNG. Guido Waldmann.   (G)
    An extensive summary.   4 [1937] 125

MUSIKALISCHE CHRONIK

ZUR BEETHOVEN-LITERATUR DER LETZTEN JAHRE (1880 bis 1886). Theodor von Frimmel.   (H)
    A review and summary of a considerable number of journal and newspaper articles dealing with Beethoven. Regard-
    ing mention of 'Zum Romisch Kaiser' in 'Neue Zeitschrift für Musik' 76 [1880] 361, the author says that Beethoven
    taught at this address but did not live there. In connection with the concert of the Siegfried Ochs Gesangverein on
    March 24th 1886, reference is made to "a communication from the Yearbook of the Bonn Lesegesellschaft from which
    it is learned that a poet in Bonn (name unknown) wrote the text of a Trauerkantate auf den Tod Josef's II; a young mu-
    sician, member of the Gesellschaft, composed the music. The ceremony took place on March 19th 1790, but for var-
    ious reasons the cantata was not performed. It seems possible that this was Beethoven's Trauerkantate. " "From a
    notation on the autograph of 'Tremate, empi' Op. 116, it seems eminently probable that the poet of the text was
    Bettoni. "   1 [1886] 49,65

MUSIKALISCHE RUNDSCHAU

BEETHOVENS LEBENSVORBILD. Ludwig Nohl.   (I)
    As far as is known, this article is not in any library in the United States, but Frimmel ('Musikalische Chronik' 1 [1886]
    72) says, "detailed, but without any trace of independent research, merely put together from Thayer's material. "

1 [1886] 137,147

DIE WIEDERBESTATUNG DER STERBLICHEN ÜBERRESTE LUDWIG VAN BEETHOVENS.   (A)
    In June 1888 Beethoven's body was exhumed from its grave in the Währinger Ortsfriedhof (where it had lain since
    1863) and reinterred with much ceremony in the Centralfriedhof. The skull was carefully examined (many mea-
    surements are given) and it was concluded that the cast made in 1863 corresponded to the actual skull "with all
    the accuracy attainable in such cases. "   3 [1888] 259

KARL CZERNYS BEZIEHUNGEN ZU BEETHOVEN.   F. A. von Winterfeld.   (B)
    A summary based on Czerny's 'Autobiography. '   6 [1891] 48

HEILIGENSTADT.   (C)
    Testament.   6 [1891] 126

NEUE ERRINERUNGEN AN BEETHOVEN.   (D)
    Excerpts from the 'Memoirs' of Baron Tremont as published in the 'Guide musicale. '
                               7 [1892] 108

MUSIKPÄDAGOGISCHE BLÄTTER *

DAS FREUDEMOTIV ALS GRUNDMOTIF DER NEUNTEN SINFONIE.   Karl Steinfried.   (E)
    Certain germ-motifs appear in all four movements, as well as in other works by Beethoven and by other composers.
                             15 [1892] 321

ÜBER DEN CHARAKTER BEETHOVENSCHER MUSIK.   Eugen Tetzel.   (F)
    A total of 251 movements of Beethoven compositions (mostly works in sonata form, omitting the string quartets and
    trios) were classified into nine groups according to their mood, and these groups in turn tabulated under four classes
    of the general nature: Serious, Sublime, Charming, Exuberant. The relative percents for these four groups were
    twenty-two percent, seventeen percent, forty-one percent and twenty percent. This analysis was taken as proof
    that the concept of Beethoven as a composer of music predominantly earnest or tragic is unfounded.
                             36 [1913] 97

MUSIKWELT

BEETHOVENS BÜHNENMUSIKALISCHE ABSICHTEN.   Rudolf Hartmann.   (G)
    A summary of the many starts which Beethoven made on works for the stage, from the 'Ritterballet' of 1791 to the
    six uncomposed libretti found in the Nachlass.   7 [1927] 81

MUTTERSPRACHE

BEETHOVENS DEUTSCHE KUNSTAUSDRÜCKE.   Richard Gottschalk.   (H)
    Explanatory notations in German appear in Opp. 81a, 68, 115, 123, 132, 135. Statements of tempo or expression in
    German in addition to or instead of in Italian are found in Opp. 48, 90, 98, 101, 109, 110, 123 and 130. Beethoven
    used the word Hammerklavier instead of Pianoforte in Opp. 101 and 106, and the word Veränderungen in place of
    Variationen in Op. 120 and in the 4-hands Variations on a Song by Goethe. With Holz, Beethoven worked out a
    considerable number of Germanic substitutes for words of non-Germanic origin (e. g. , Arie = Luftgesang; Konzert =
    Tonstreitwerkversammlung), and discussed the general idea in his letter to Holz of August 24th 1825 (KS II 397; KBr
    V 181). In thinking that Beethoven was less than completely serious in this project, the author agrees with Schindler
    and disagrees with Kalischer.   42 [1927] 65

---

* Published 1878-1910 as Klavier-Lehrer.

BEETHOVENS DEUTSCHE KUNSTAUSDRÜCKE.   (A)

Beethoven's invention of words of purely Germanic derivation to substitute for loan-words in current use was all of a part with the spirit of invention which he showed in coining new German words from old ones: e. g. , "wenn Du . . . briefwechselest" (letter to Wegeler in 1800, KBr I 48).   42 [1927] 233

MUZICA

O SCRISOARE INEDITA A LUI BEETHOVEN. Viorel Kosma.   (B)

Facsimile and transcription of MM 364.   Heft 5 [1951]

NASSAU (COUNTY) MEDICAL NEWS

THE DEAFNESS OF BEETHOVEN -- TRAGEDY OR TRIUMPH? Eugene H. Coon.   (C)

Popular.   24 [1951] No. 11 p. 1

NATION

WHY A BEETHOVEN SOCIETY? Henrietta Strauss.   (D)

Carping.   110 [1920] 377

BEETHOVEN: 1770-1920. Hugo von Hofmannsthal.   (E)

Sesquicentennial essay; a translation of most of the material appearing in the Vienna 'Neue Freie Presse' December 12th 1920 p. 1 and also in 'Das Inselschiff' 2 [1921] 97.   111 [1920] 776

NATION; WOCHENSCHRIFT FÜR POLITIK, VOLKSWIRTHSCHAFT UND LITERATUR (Berlin)

BOUILLY'S "LEONORE" UND DER TEXT ZU BEETHOVENS "FIDELIO." J. V. Widmann.   (F)

Examples are given of many passages in Fidelio that are direct translations of Bouilly's text. Other passages are cited in which the version that Beethoven used (1805? 1806? 1814?) was changed in sense as well as in wording. The author points out that in three passages in Shakespeare's 'Cymbeline' the heroine , in male attire and in search of her husband , identifies herself as "Fidelio. "

Cymbeline	III vi	60- 61	Belarius:	What's your name?
			Imogen:	Fidele , sir.
	IV ii	379	Lucius:	Thy name?
			Imogen:	Fidele , sir.
	V v	117-118	Cymbeline:	What's thy name?
			Imogen:	Fidele , sir.

12 [1895] 710

NEUE ILLUSTRIERTE

"BEETHOVEN: ABORT REINIGEN!   (G)

Brief popular but accurate account of the history of Nephew Karl and his descendants according to recently discovered material.   [15 September 1956]

BEETHOVEN. Wolfgang Lindner.   (A)
    Lengthy sesquicentennial address.   48 [1921] 25

NEUE RUNDSCHAU

GRÄFIN THERESE BRUNSVIK, DIE UNSTERBLICHE GELIEBTE BEETHOVENS. La Mara, pseud. (Marie Lipsius).   (B)
                                      19 [1908] 77

NEUE RUSSLAND

BEETHOVEN IN SOWJETRUSSLAND. Alexander Rimskij-Korssakow.   (C)
    From the socio-psychological and aesthetic standpoint, Beethoven stands very high with the Kommissars, and his
effect on the cultural level of the country continues to be great. His direct influence on contemporary composers,
however, is negligible compared with that of Schumann, Berlioz, Liszt, Wagner and the Impressionists. (Quoted
from the 'Frankfurter Zeitung')   4 Nos. 3-4 [May 1927] 50

NEW FRIENDS OF MUSIC, NEW YORK PROGRAM BOOK

No Title.   (D)
    Popular essays and program notes on most of the principal chamber works. Gerth-Wolfgang Baruch (1938-39); Irving
Kolodin (1939-40); Konrad, Mark and Wolff Brunswick (1943-44); Curt Sachs (1944-45).
                                    [c. 1938-39]

NEUE SCHWEIZER RUNDSCHAU *

BEETHOVEN. Hans Jelmoli.   (E)
    Sesquicentennial essay.   23 [1920] 217

BEETHOVENS VOLKSLIEDER. Fritz Gysi.   (F)
    In discussing Beethoven's arrangements for Thomson the author contends that this project was assumed by Beethoven
not merely for the money involved (which was not great) but for the interest which he found in the characteristics of
the various national temperaments as illustrated in their folksongs.
                                    20 [1927] 817

NEW OUTLOOK **

BEETHOVEN: A BIOGRAPHY. Robert Haven Schauffler.   (G)
    First draft of biography later appearing as 'Beethoven -- the man who freed music' (1929).
                    151 [1929] 603,648; 152 [1929] 7-424

---

*   Published 1908-18 as Wissen und Leben.

** Volumes 150-160 were published as Outlook and Independent.

BEETHOVEN IN THE MODERN WORLD. J. W. N. Sullivan. (A)
  Centenary essay.   51 [1927] 221

NEW STATESMAN

"FIDELIO" IN 1881 AND 1889. W. J. Turner. (B)
  Summary of essay by Theodor de Wyzewa in which he comments on the complete reversal of his opinion of 'Fidelio'
  between a hearing in 1881 (when Wyzewa was 19 years old) and one in 1889.
                                                    28 [1927] 475

BEETHOVEN AND THE FUTURE. Edward Sackville West. (C)
                                              NS 21 [1941] 322,363

New York. Metropolitan Museum of Art
BULLETIN

BEETHOVEN BY BOURDELLE. Preston Remington. (D)
  Brief but emotional comment on the head by Emile Antoine Bourdelle (1861-1929) which the Museum had recently
  acquired.   22 [1927] 4

New York Academy of Medicine
BULLETIN

BEETHOVEN FROM AN OTOLOGIST'S POINT OF VIEW. Irving Wilson Voorhees. (E)
  Popular biographical sketch.   Series 2, 12 [1936] 105

NORD UND SÜD

LUDWIG VAN BEETHOVEN IN BERLIN. Alf. Chr. Kalischer. (F)
  Material later appearing as Chapter 1 of 'Beethoven in Berlin,' Volume I of the author's 'Beethoven und seine
  Zeitgenossen.'   39 [1886] 214

BEETHOVEN UND DER PREUSSISCHE KÖNIGSHOF UNTER FRIEDRICH WILHELM III. Alf. Chr. Kalischer. (G)
  Material later appearing in 'Beethoven und seine Zeitgenossen' [1908-10] I 329-85.
                                                    49 [1889] 197,362

GRILLPARZER AND BEETHOVEN. Alf. Chr. Kalischer. (H)
  Material later appearing in 'Beethoven und seine Zeitgenossen' [1908-10] IV 157-209 with minor omissions.
                                                    56 [1891] 63

ANTONIE UND MAXIMILIANE BRENTANO ALS VEREHRERINNEN BEETHOVENS. Alf. Chr. Kalischer. (I)
  Material later appearing (with minor changes and omissions) in 'Beethoven und seine Zeitgenossen' [1908-10] III 167-98.
                                                    85 [1898] 54

IN NEUER BEETHOVENSCHATZ. Alexander Hajdecki. (J)
  First publication of 14 letters to Josef Karl Bernard and one to Nephew Karl.
                                      124 [1908] 345,524; 125 [1908] 146

LE COEUR DE BEETHOVEN.   Paul Valayer.   (A)
  A popular essay on Beethoven and his feminine friends.   142 [1936] 105

NOUVELLES LITTÉRAIRES ARTISTIQUES ET SCIENTIFIQUES

AUTOUR DE BEETHOVEN.   André de Hevesy.   (B)
  A rather unorganized commentary on various writings on Beethoven, with the statement that Zmeskall at his death
  had bequeathed a very detailed diary to Joseph de Zmeskall, doyen of the family.   Joseph lent this diary to Joseph
  von Sonnleithner, who presummably made a copy of it, but neither copy nor original is now known.   A study of
  the correspondence and diaries left by Therese von Brunsvik indicates that as late as 1814 she was exchanging letters
  with Beethoven.   This fact would seem to rule her out as the Immortal Beloved; for this distinction the author names
  Giulietta Guicciardi as "almost certain. "   60 No. 232 [26 March 1927] 1

NUOVA ANTOLOGIA

INTERPRETAZIONE DELL' "EROICA."   Fernando Liuzzi.   (C)
  Popular analysis.   330 [1927] 190

IL MONDO SPIRITUALE DI BEETHOVEN.   Arturo Farinelli.   (D)
                                                          333 [1927] 273

GLI AMICI DI BEETHOVEN.   Edoardo Roggeri.   (E)
  Brief and popular comments on Beethoven's relationship with a score or more of his friends.
                                                          335 [1928] 195

OBERSCHLESISCHE MITTEILUNGEN

BEETHOVEN UND DIE FAMILIE LICHNOWSKY.   Ludwig Jüngst.   (F)
  A summary of known facts.   3 [1937] 395

OPEN COURT

BEETHOVENIANA.   Philipp Spitta.   (G)
  A study of Beethoven's creative process, based on the studies of the sketch books by Nottebohm.
                                                          3 [1889] 1871,1897

A PILGRIMAGE TO BEETHOVEN.   Richard Wagner.   (H)
  Fiction.   10 [1896] 5031,5043,5048

THE MISSA SOLEMNIS.   Baron von der Pfordten.   (I)
  An extended discussion of the Missa Solemnis as "a powerful dramatic fantasy to which Beethoven was inspired by
  the text of the Mass. "   24 [1910] 523

THE EROICA SYMPHONY OF BEETHOVEN.   Baron von der Pfordten.   (J)
  A popular analysis.   25 [1911] 501

BEETHOVEN'S CHARACTER AND DESTINY.   Baron von der Pfordten.   (K)
  Popular biographical essay.   25 [1911] 641

LUDWIG VAN BEETHOVEN.   "The Editor."   (A)
  Popular biographical sketch.   25 [1911] 685

BEETHOVEN'S NINTH SYMPHONY.   Baron von der Pfordten.   (B)
  Essay, with discussion of Wagner's commentary.   32 [1918] 332

ORPHEUS*

FIDELIO.   F. Treitschke.   (C)
  EDr of Kal 375 and Kal 381.   The author gives an account of his part in the final revision of the opera.   (NOTE. Most
  of this article is transcribed, with comments, in Kufferath, 'Fidelio' [1913] 114ff.)
                                       2 [1841] 258

OST UND WEST

DAS NEU BEETHOVEN-DENKMAL IN BONN.   Julius Levin.   (D)
  Favorable comment on a bust of Beethoven by Naum Aronson.   6 [1906] 79

OSTDEUTSCHE MONATSHEFTE

BEETHOVENS BALTISCHE FREUNDE UND VEREHRER.   Oswald Zienau.   (E)
  Popular discussion of Beethoven's relationship with Amenda, Baron Brown, and Karl von Buroy (friend of Amenda.
  Mention is made of the fact that Baron Christoph von Stackelberg, who married Josephine Deym (thought by some
  to have been the Immortal Beloved) was an Esthonian.   10 [1929] 628

ÖSTERREICHISCHE GITARRE-ZEITSCHRIFT

BEETHOVEN UND DIE WIENER VOLKSMUSIK.   Karl Kobald.   (F)
  Beethoven's interest in Austrian folk-music is shown by the 'Air Autrichien' of Op. 105, the 'Air Tirolien' of Op. 107,
  the melodies of the third and fifth movements of the Pastoral Symphony, the 'Mödlinger Tänze,' and other writings.
  In his letter of March 18th 1820 to Simrock (KS II 168) he includes his own transcription of two folk-songs, and
  Schindler mentions this interest several times.   Beethoven is known to have been in contact with the guitar virtuoso
  Mauro Giuliani.   1 [1927] 50

BEETHOVEN UND DIE GITARRE.   Theodor von Frimmel.   (G)
  The little that is known about the guitarists Mylich and Mauro Giuliani and the mandolinist Wenzel Krumpholz is
  summarized in the form of biographical sketches.   1 [1927] 53

BEETHOVEN AND GIULIANI.   Johann Friedrich Reichardt.   (H)
  Review of a concert in the last months of 1808 which included Beethoven's Overture to Coriolanus and solos by Giuliani.
                                       1 [1927] 54

HANS VON BÜLOWS EROIKA-WIDMUNG.   Robert Haas.   (I)
  As a part of his protest against the dismissal of Bismarck as Chancellor in 1892, Bülow contended that the Eroica should
  have been dedicated, not to Napoleon, but to the "Bruder Beethovens, den Beethoven der deutschen Politik, den
  Fürsten Bismarck."   1 [1927] 56

---

  * Volumes 1-2 were published as Orpheus, musikalisches Taschenbuch.

BEETHOVEN ALS THEATERHELD.   Victor Junk.   (A)
   Brief comment on a dozen or so dramas in which Beethoven is the hero.
                                                   1 [1927] 58

                              ÖSTERREICHISCHE RUNDSCHAU

EIN GEMEINSAMES WERK ÖSTERREICHISCHER KOMPONISTEN.   Heinrich Rietsch.   (B)
   An account of Diabelli's project of securing variations on his waltz theme from the leading composers of Austria,
   and biographical notes on most of the fifty who responded.   3 [1905] 438

EIN GEDENKBLATT.   Karl Glossy.   (C)
   The first performance of Fidelio was planned for October 15th 1805, the name-day of the Empress. On September
   30th Sonnleithner was advised by the Censor that the book of the opera was not acceptable. In a letter of October
   3rd (given herewith) Sonnleithner requested reconsideration, and after a few changes the book was approved on
   October 5th. This incident and the military situation together delayed the first performance until November 20th,
   at which time the departure of royalty and nobility from the city and the disturbed state of mind of those who remained resulted in lack of success of the opera and withdrawl after three performances. (Reprinted in 'Karl Glossys
   kleinere Schriften' [1918] 337)   5 [1905] 131

AUS BEETHOVENS LETZTEN TAGE.   Otto Erich Deutsch.   (D)
   Detailed biography of Marie Pachler-Koschak (1794-1855), and extended quotations from letters received by her from
   Johann Baptist Jenger, who was apparently a member of the inner Beethoven circle during the few months before and
   after the composer's death. The author is very definite in his statement that the idea of a love affair between Beethoven and Marie is pure invention, though without doubt the composer had real affection for her and high esteem for
   her artistry. (See also 'Neue Berliner Musik-Zeitung' 19 [1865] 381, 389, 397, 405, 413; 20 [1866] 1)
                                                   10 [1907] 189

BEETHOVEN UND GOETHE AUF DER GRENZSCHEIDE VON KLASSIZISMUS UND ROMANTIK.   Karl Lamprecht.   (E)
   Excerpt from the author's 'Deutsche Geschichte.'   13 [1907] 88

BEETHOVEN UND ERZHERZOG RUDOLPH.   Richard Wallaschek.   (F)
   First publication of letter of October 15th 1819 to the Archduke Rudolph: "Wegen der Weinlese war kein Wagen hier
   zu haben," with detailed commentary.   29 [1911] 199

NEUES ZU BEETHOVEN.   Theodor von Frimmel.   (G)
   One of the first performances of the Archduke Trio Op. 97 in Germany was by Baroness von Ertmann, Wilhelm Speyer
   and an unidentified 'cellist at a private gathering in Offenbach in 1812-13. The naturalist Hermann Schlegel, who
   was in Vienna in 1825, said that at that time Beethoven had been pushed quite into the background by the public acclaim for such figures as Rubini, Tamburini and Sonntag, and that only after his death was his importance fully real-
   ized. A letter written some time between 1815 and the fall of 1826 to the tailor Joseph Lind is published for the first
   time: "Ich bitte erzeigen sie mir die Gefälligkeit," and mention is made of another letter to Lind published in
   Kalischer 'Briefe' (2nd ed.) III 67. (Still another letter to Lind is given in KS II 297, and he is referred to in a letter
   to Gleichenstein in KS I 114.) Alternative versions of various anecdotes regarding Beethoven are discussed: of the
   occasion when he was held in jail as a vagabond; of the time when he smashed his teacup so that no one would be
   forced to use it after him; of the time when after sitting in a tavern reading music but not eating he asked the waiter
   what he owed; and of his vain attempts to engage in conversation a man who proved to be deaf.
                                                   34 [1913] 460

VEREITELTE PLÄNE BEETHOVENS.   Max Reinitz.   (H)
   The effect on the course of Beethoven's life of the Napoleonic Wars and the occupation of Vienna has not been given
   adequate study by Beethoven scholars. It broke off his intercourse with Breitkopf & Härtel, whom he had expressed a
   wish (letter of June 8th 1808, KS I 139) to have as his sole publisher. The death of Prince Kinsky and the depreciation
   of the currency resulted in financial embarrassment to Beethoven as well as unpleasant wrangles with the three noble
   patrons whose promised annuity had led him to forego plans to leave Vienna. A letter from Breitkopf & Härtel dated
   September 24th 1810 points out that Beethoven's request for a royalty of 10,000 gulden for a collected edition made
   the project quite impracticable commercially -- this quite aside from insuperable problems of copyright. On his
   deathbed Beethoven charged his friends Breuning and Schindler with the responsibility of preserving his Nachlass and
   of preparing it for publication with the assistance of Rochlitz. Rochlitz refused to undertake the work, and Breuning,

Schindler and Dr. Bach did nothing. As a result, the Nachlass was auctioned off for a pittance and the papers strewn far and wide. In 1859 an obscure publisher named August Martens bought from the estate of Nephew Karl all rights to unpublished or illegally published compositions, these rights having eight years still to run under the law, but this purchase proved to be of little value to Karl's heirs or to Beethoven scholarship.

59 [1919] 28

GRILLPARZERS REDE ZU BEETHOVENS BEGRÄBNIS. August Sauer.   (A)

The account which Grillparzer gives in his 'Memoirs' of the circumstances which led to the writing of the oration which Heinrich Anschütz read at Beethoven's grave is certainly incorrect in various details. Several differing versions of the address are extant, each with considerable claim to authenticity. These versions may be reconciled only by the technique of textual criticism, a task which should be undertaken.

62 [1920] 118

BEETHOVENS BRIEFE. Max Mayr.   (B)

A general survey of the letters according to content, mood and addressee. A passage is quoted from a letter of 1792 (otherwise unidentified) to Rahel Löwenstein: "Ich kann Dich nicht lassen, wenngleich Du eine Jüdin bist."

65 [1920] 218

BEETHOVEN UND UNSERE ZEIT. Guido Adler.   (C)

Sesquicentennial essay.   65 [1920] 260

OSTEUROPA

BEETHOVEN UND RUSSLAND. Robert Engel.   (D)

Many of Beethoven's patrons and friends were Russians or Western Europeans who had come under strong Russian influences. Note that the name of the Empress with whom Beethoven had corresponded was properly Elisabeth (surnamed Alexejewna), not Alexiewna as given in Frimmel's 'Handbuch.' The first performance of the Missa Solemnis took place on March 26th 1824 Old Style, which is April 7th New Style. The relationship of Beethoven with his various Russian friends, especially Prince Galitsin, is discussed in detail. Ulybyscheff and Lenz were only the best-known of many Russian writers on Beethoven -- a bibliography of no less than 335 titles of Russian books and journal articles on Beethoven has been prepared. The dates of the first performances in Russia of some 40 major works of Beethoven are given. The various aspects of Russia's acceptance of Beethoven and its influence on him are discussed in the greatest detail.

3 [1928] 256

PHONOGRAPH MONTHLY REVIEW

BEETHOVEN'S DEBUTS IN AMERICA. Richard G. Appel.   (E)

A popular but scholarly and inclusive account of the early interest in Beethoven in America as shown by Beethoven societies, writings about Beethoven, and performances of his music.

1 No. 1 [October 1926] 2

BEETHOVEN'S SYMPHONIES: ONE HUNDRED YEARS AFTER. Richard G. Appel.   (F)

General discussion of Beethoven's life and works (not limited to the symphonies) and of the literature about him, popular but probably completely sound.   1 [1927] 194, 242, 290

REFLECTIONS ON BEETHOVEN ON THE OCCASION OF HIS CENTENNIAL. Walter R. Spalding.   (G)

Centennial essay.   1 [1927] 292

PIANOFORTE

INSEGNAMENTO DO BEETHOVEN. Ferruccio Busoni.   (H)

"We may say, 'the divine Rossini' or 'the divine Mozart,' but must say, 'the human Beethoven.'"

4 [1923] 117

THE PHYSICAL BEETHOVEN. James Frederick Rogers.   (A)
  Popular discussion of the composer's appearance and habits, and of the fluctuations of his health.
                                84 [1914] 265

                          PRESSE MÉDICALE

LA SURDITÉ ET LA MALADIE DE BEETHOVEN. Paul Bodros.   (B)
  Beethoven's heredity was very poor: his mother died of tuberculosis in 1787, his brother Karl of the same ailment in
  1815, and his father was an alcoholic. Beethoven's attack of "typhoid fever" in 1787 may well have been an early
  manifestation of tuberculosis. It might be noted that although deafness may result from typhoid fever, it is most improbable that typhoid fever in 1787 would bring deafness starting only in 1796. Beethoven's digestive ailments, his
  asthma, his bronchitis, his rheumatism in 1820-21, and his deafness are all consonant with the basic diagnosis of
  tuberculosis: the journal of Mlle. del Rio indicates that Beethoven was constantly in fear of bloody sputum. The
  cirrhosis of the liver which caused his death, while undoubtedly favored by Beethoven's known intemperance, could
  very possibly have been of tubercular origin.   46 [1938] 949

                        PREUSSISCHE JAHRBÜCHER

ZUR JUGENDGESCHICHTE BEETHOVENS. Otto Gumprecht.   (C)
  A summary of the information contained in the newly-issued 'Ludwig van Beethovens Leben' by Thayer, a work in
  which "aesthetic considerations and enjoyment by the reader are alike given no weight."
                                19 [1867] 324

LUDWIG VAN BEETHOVEN: ETHOS UND RELIGIOSITÄT. Otto Schilling Trygophorus.   (D
  In all his works Beethoven wrote as one who was and who knew himself to be one with God.
                                207 [1927] 340

                          PROGRÈS MÉDICAL

PEUT-ON PARLER DE FOLIE CHEZ BEETHOVEN? Raymond Fontain.   (E
  Popular (the answer is apparently no).   [1911] 486

                          QUARTERLY REVIEW

THE DEAFNESS OF BEETHOVEN. Raoul Blondel.   (F
  Popular.   155 [1931] 52

                            QUERSCHNITT

BEETHOVEN-BILANZ. L. Thurneiser.   (G
  A reviewer looks down his nose at the activities of the centennial year.
                                7 [1927] 377

BEETHOVENS GEBURTSHAUS. E. Büchner.   (A)
  Detailed but popular description of the Beethovenhaus.   15 [1899] 1707

DER LEIDENSWEG DES FIDELIO. Julius Kapp.   (B)
  An account of Beethoven's difficulties with Fidelio and of his vain search for another suitable libretto.
        [1927] 699

BEETHOVEN IM SPIEGEL SEINER HANDSCHRIFT. Fritz Hocke.   (C)
  A popular personality study with occasional references to the hypotheses of graphology.
        [1927] 703

DER SCHÄDEL LUDWIG VAN BEETHOVENS. Leo Jacobsohn.   (D)
  Popular and superficial account of the funeral and reinterment.   45 [1929] 392

BEETHOVEN NACH JAPANISCHER ART. Alma Stefanie Frischauer.   (E)
  A troupe of Japanese dancers has included the Sonata Appassionata in its repertoire. A photograph shows a page of
  the music in Japanese notation.   48 [1932] 1011

BEETHOVEN DER WOHLTÄTER. Stephan Ley.   (F)
  A popular account of Beethoven as a benefactor: his various concerts for charity, the assistance of various kinds
  which he rendered to his friends, his solicitude for his brother's son (even before Nephew Karl became so important
  a part of his emotional life), etc.   52 [1936] 1250

REPERTORIUM FÜR MUSIK **

AUS BEETHOVENS SKIZZENBÜCHERN. Heinrich Hirschbach.   (G)
  Sketches for the Tenth Symphony, the Bach Overture, the Finale of Op. 131, and a march for Duport are given.
      1 [1844] 1

NOTIZ ZU BEETHOVENS ACHTER SINFONIE.   (H)
  EDr of WoO 162.   1 [1844] 55

BEETHOVEN'SCHEN MEMORABILIEN. A. Schindler.   (I)
  Beethoven had planned to dedicate the Sonata in A flat Op. 110 to Ries; then he changed his mind and instructed
  Schindler that the dedications of Opp. 110 and 111 would be to "Frau Brentano gebohren Edle von Birkenstock"
  (M-614 to that effect here receives its EDr; see also Kal 873). When finally published, Op. 111 was dedicated to
  the Archduke Rudolph, and Op. 110 was without dedication. Schindler defends his criticism of the Seyfried 'Studien. '
  A facsimile is given of the canon 'Bester Herr Graf' that differs appreciably from the version in Kal 874 and in TD
  IV 389. (The transcription in 'Musikforschung' 3 [1950]264 is correct except that the last note in the alto should read
  C instead of A.) Facsimile and transcription are given of Kal 937, for which the author gives the date "2 May 1823. "
  The "Muss es sein" canon is discussed.   1 [1844] 425,467,511

REPORT OF THE LIBRARIAN OF CONGRESS

BEETHOVEN LETTERS ACQUIRED BY THE LIBRARY. Harold L. Spivacke.   (J)
  Six letters to Zmeskall, with transcriptions by Alexander Wheelock Thayer, have been acquired by the Library:
  Kal 56, Kal 214, MM 22, MM 23, MM 73, MM 88.   [1938] 165

---

* Volumes 1-13 were published as Universum.
** Volume 1 was published as Musikalisch-kritisches Repertorium.

A LA RECHERCHE DES ASCENDANTS DE BEETHOVEN.   R a y m o n d   v a n   A e r d e .   (A)
   The author postulates that the grandfather of Cornelius was one Marcus van Beethoven, husband of Adrienne Proost,
who died on October 31st 1635 at Nederockerzeel. The basis for this statement is not made clear.   The father of
Cornelius was either Marcus, husband of Sara Haesaerts, or Arnold, husband of Catherine Verstrecke.   Abstracts are
then given of various recent researches in this field:

   (1)   van Doorslaer: 'Les van Beethovens de Malines' ('Mechlinia' 7 [1928] No. 5 p. 77).   Land records
         prove that Cornelius (father of Michael) was the son of Marcus.   Since the godfather of Marcus's
         children was Arnold, it is probable that Marcus was the son of Arnold.   For reasons not clearly
         stated it is assumed that Arnold was the son of Marcus and the grandson of Johann and Anne (Smets).
         van Aerde points out minor discrepancies between the statements of van Doorslaer and of other
         students in this field.

   (2)   Constantin le Paide: 'L'origine liégeoise des van Beethovens' ('Chronique archéologique du pays
         de Liége' 20 [1929] No. 3 p. 56).   A note on the armorial bearings of the van Beethovens in the
         fifteenth century.

   (3)   J. Brassine: 'A propos de l'origine liégeoise des van Beethovens' ('Chronique archéologique du
         pays de Liége' 20 [1929] No. 4 p. 74).   Appeal for genealogical research on the van Beethovens
         in the Liége-Limbourg area.   In connection with the abstract of this paper, van Aerde postulates
         that the van Beethovens were a noble family in the vicinity of Liége in the thirteenth and four-
         teenth centuries, and that, "gradually impoverished by wars, they came to earn their bread by
         rude labor in the fields and by the raising of cattle."

   (4)   P. van Boxmeer: 'L'atavisme musical du Grand van Beethoven et son ascendance Brabanconne'
         ('Le Folklore Brabanconne' 15 [1935] No. 85-86 p. 34).   This author is convinced that the land
         records prove that Marcus (husband of Sara Haesaerts), born about 1610, was father of Cornelius.
         Beyond this generation he places Arnold and his wife Josine van Vlesselaer, then Marcus and his
         wife Anna Smets, and finally Jean van Beethoven, born about 1500.   (This is the same chain of
         ancestry as arrived at by van Doorslaer in (1) above, and by Schmidt-Görg.) He also discusses
         early appearances of the name van Beethoven.   Van Aerde maintains that a generation intervened
         between Marcus (husband of Sara Haesaerts) and Arnold.

   (5)   A. Vincent: 'Le nom de Beethoven' ('Isidoor Teirlinck Album' [1931] 133).   This author derives
         the name Beethoven from the place-name Betho in Limbourg, plus the suffix ouwen, meaning a
         marshy area cut up by streams.

   (6)   Octave le Maire: 'Les origines Brabanconnes de Beethoven' ('Le Parchemim' 2 [1937] No. 10
         p. 135).   This author cites land records to prove that the father of Marcus (husband of Sara
         Haesaerts) was one Henry van Beethoven, husband of Catherine van Boevenkercke.   He gives
         no ancestry for this Henry except to say that he was not descended from Arnold and Josine van
         Vlesselaer.

   (7)   J. Nauwelaers: 'Les Beethovens en Brabant' ('Le Folklore Brabanconne' No. 107 [1939] 366).
         A detailed account of the trial and burning of Josine van Vlesselaer (wife of Arnold van Beet-
         hoven) for witchcraft in 1595.   At that time Arnold was sixty years old and paralyzed in one
         hand.   On July 19th 1601 he had a son Johann by his second wife Pieryne Gheerts.

   From these studies, van Aerde concludes that the family had been in Brabant from the sixteenth (probably from the
fifteenth) century, having originated in the Limbourg-Liége area.   Before 1500, and thereafter for more than 200
years, there were van Beethovens in the village of Campenhout.   Beethoven's ancestry is traced with complete certainty to his grandfather's grandfather Cornelius, the carpenter of Malines.   Cornelius's baptismal record names his
parents as Bartholomew van Beethoven and Sara Haesaerts, though in the baptismal records of the other children of
this marriage the father's name was given as Marcus.   No explanation is given for this difference in names.   Legal
documents show that Arnold (born about 1535) was married twice.   By his first wife he had four children (Marcus,
Henry, Lambert, Anna).   Anna's first child was born about 1592, making the date of her birth about 1570 and that
of her eldest brother Marcus about 1563.   It is most improbable that this was the Marcus who married Sara Haesaerts
in 1635 and was father to Cornelius in 1641 and to a daughter in 1644, since at that time he would have been 81
years old.   There are two possible explanations of the position of Marcus (husband of Sara) in the ancestral chain:
(1) that he was from a branch of the van Beethovens quite distinct from that of Arnold, or (2) that he was the grandson of Arnold through Marcus or Henry.   Data for resolving this uncertainty have not come to light.

The author concludes that the line of descent is:

Johann
|
Marcus (m. Anna Smets)
|
Arnold (m. Josine van Vlesselaer)
|
Marcus or Henry
|
? |
|
Marcus (m. Sara Haesaerts)
|
Cornelius (grandfather or Grandfather Ludwig)

(NOTE by DWM. In view of the birth dates fairly well established of 1535 for Arnold and 1600 for Marcus (husband of Sara) it does not seem necessary or logical to postulate two generations between the two men. Note that Closson ('L'element flamand dans Beethoven' (2nd ed. 1946, p. 35) states with reasonable confidence that young Marcus was the third son of Henry, son of Arnold.) The author gives disconnected data on various van Beethovens of the village of Boortmeerbeek, on the chance that future research may tie them into the composer's line of descent. The records of this parish earlier than the end of the eighteenth century were apparently destroyed in World War I. Cornelius, baptized in Berthem on October 20th 1641, was living in Malines in 1671. A facsimile and transcription are given of the contract dated October 12th 1725 between Michael van Beethoven and Antoine Colfs whereby, for a fee of 100 florins, the latter would instruct Michael's son Ludwig in organ and clavier playing. Other fragments of information are given regarding Cornelius, Michael and Grandfather Ludwig.

9 [1939] 121

REVUE BÉNÉDICTINE

BEETHOVEN PEINT PAR LUI-MÊME.   (A)
    Popular character sketch, with many excerpts from letters, conversation books, etc.
8 [1891] 558

REVUE BLEUE, POLITIQUE ET LITTÉRAIRE

LES GRANDS MUSICIENS: BEETHOVEN. Léo Quesnel.   (B)
    Biographical sketch in the guise of a review of the second volume of Thayer.
Ser. 2: 3_2 [1874] 753

LA MUSIQUE ET LE SENTIMENT RELIGIEUX. René de Récy.   (C)
    Diffuse essay following the first performance of the Missa Solemnis in Paris.
Ser. 3: [1888] 111

BEETHOVEN AND WAGNER. Raymond Bouyer.   (D)
    Review of a book by Wyzewa of the same title.   Ser. 4: 11 [1899] 786

"L'IMMORTELLE BIEN AIMÉE" DE BEETHOVEN. A. Bossert.   (E)
    Biographical sketch of Therese von Brunsvick, with generous quotations from her memoirs as given by La Mara in
    'Beethovens unsterbliche Geliebte' (1909).   47 [1909] 21

LE SECRET DE BEETHOVEN. Raymond Bouyer.   (F)
    Rhapsodic: "Beethoven's secret was . . . to transmute sadness into joy."
47_1 [1909] 443

POUR QU'ON JOUE BEETHOVEN.   (G)
    An appreciation of Beethoven as a prophet of liberty, and a plea against wartime chauvinism.
53 [1915] 490

BEETHOVEN ET RICHARD WAGNER ZU CAMP DES ALLIÉS.   Raymond Bouyer.   (A)
   Fantasy.   53 [1915] 568

SOUVENIRS DE CONTEMPORAIRES SUR BEETHOVEN.   (B)
   Extensive extracts from the writings of Rochlitz, Gerhard von Breuning, Schindler and Anselm Hüttenbrenner.
                                     65 [1927] 196,236

REVUE CATHOLIQUE DES IDÉES ET DES FAITES

LE CENTENAIRE DE BEETHOVEN.   Joseph Ryelandt.   (C)
   Centennial essay.   6 No. 47 [February 11th 1927] 9

REVUE CHRÉTIENNE

BEETHOVEN ET SON GÉNIE.   D. Landal.   (D)
   "Based on the writings of Ludwig Nohl."   36 [1889] 510

REVUE DE BELGIQUE

LES PRÉCURSEURS DE LA IXe SYMPHONIE.   Dwelshauvers-Dery.   (E)
   Beethoven's first thought of making a setting of the Ode to Joy was in 1793, eight years after Schiller's poem appeared.
About this time he wrote (reference not given): "Schiller's poems present the greatest difficulties for the musician, who
must always rise above the poet. Who can do this for Schiller?" He gave up the project for the time being without
making any sketches that have been preserved and identified as such. The second of the two Bürger songs of 1795
(Gegenliebe) contains the germ of the idea later developed in the Choral Fantasy, which in turn served as a study for
the choral finale of Op. 125. The text of the Choral Fantasy (perhaps by Kuffner, more likely by Treitschke) is a
kind of abbreviated digest of the Ode to Joy. The author sees close resemblance, in general plan and in details, between the choral portions of Opp. 80 and 125. At various times from 1809 (a year after the first performance of Op.
80) notations in sketch books or journals indicate that a musical setting of the Ode to Joy was active in Beethoven's
mind.   33 Vol. 32 [1901] 66

REVUE DE GENÈVE

BEETHOVEN.   Hugo von Hofmannsthal.   (F)
   Sesquicentennial essay.   2 [1921] 836

REVUE DE PARIS

BEETHOVEN.   J. Aloys Schlosser.   (G)
   Portions of the review of Schlosser's biography in the 'Foreign Quarterly Review' 8 [1831] 439 are here given as being
extracts from the biography itself.   33 [1831] 201

BEETHOVEN D'APRÈS SA CORRESPONDANCE.   Jean Chantavoine.   (H)
   Material later appearing as preface to the author's 'Correspondance de Beethoven.'
                                  11_1 [1904] 379

BEETHOVEN -- MUSICIEN DE LA RÉVOLUTION FRANCAISE. Julien Tiersot.   (A)

    The first effect of the French Revolution on Beethoven was that in 1794, when Bonn fell to the French, his allowance from the Elector was broken off. Beethoven's attitude at this time towards freedom was mirrored in the lyrics of his song 'Der freie Mann': the free man is one who need give no thought to the caprice of tyrants, and who is ready to lay down his life for liberty. In Vienna, his writing, his conversation, his contacts with the nobility, and his two patriotic songs (the 'Abschiedsgesang' and the 'Kriegslied' GA 23/230-31) alike take this trend. Beethoven's contact with Bernadotte for several months in the summer of 1798 stimulated his interest in Napoleon and in what Beethoven conceived to be Napoleon's ideals. Regarding the story of Beethoven striking Napoleon's name off the title page of the Eroica (completed in the summer of 1804), note that while Napoleon was crowned only in December 1804, he had announced himself as Emperor in May of that year. To the extent that the Eroica was conceived in honor of Napoleon, it was not for the victor of Austerlitz and Jena, but for "the young officer who, stepping from the ranks of the Army of the Republic, was chosen by destiny to lead that Army to victory." The music of the Eroica is discussed in detail to show that it cannot be taken as a portrait of any man. The selection of Fidelio, "a work of emancipation," as the subject of an opera is a further indication of Beethoven's innate love of freedom. It is interesting to note the slight merit and transitory nature of Beethoven's anti-French compositions of 1814-15: Wellington's Victory Op. 91, Germanias Wiedergeburt (GA 20/207d), Der glorreiche Augenblick Op. 136, and Es ist vollbracht (GA 20/207c). The Missa Solemnis is referred to as a work inspired not by religion or the liturgy but by Beethoven's love of humanity, and the choral finale to the Ninth Symphony as Beethoven's crowning plea for the unity of mankind. 17_1 [1910] 733

PETITES AMIES DE BEETHOVEN. Andre de Hevesy.   (B)

    Biographical sketches in some detail of Therese and Josephine von Brunsvik and their cousin Giullietta Guicciardi, with special reference to their relations with Beethoven, based on the private papers which Therese left at the time of her death. Many letters exchanged within the family are quoted. Without attempting to identify any one of the three girls as the Immortal Beloved, the author postulates that the initial "K" in the famous letter may refer to Korompa (near Pressburg), the seat of the Brunsvik estate. 17_2 [1910] 177,369

BEETHOVEN INTERROMPU. Constantin Photiadès.   (C)

    A discursive account of sundry of Beethoven's abandoned projects: another opera, the Mass in C sharp minor, the Tenth Symphony, the four-hand Sonata for Diabelli, the Quintet for Diabelli. 34_2 [1927] 379

APRÈS "FIDELIO." Constantin Photiadès.   (D)

    Beethoven's one opera shows that he was a born writer for the stage. 35_4 [1928] 915

REVUE DES DEUX MONDE

BEETHOVEN, SES CRITIQUES ET SES GLOSSATEURS. P. Scudo.   (E)

    Extended review of Oulibichef's book.   Ser. 2: 9 [1857] 920

LE POÈTE GRILLPARZER ET BEETHOVEN. Henri Blaze de Bury.   (F)

    In this review of the collected works of Grillparzer, especially on pp. 353-361, the reviewer quotes Grillparzer's account of his meeting with Beethoven in 1804 and his subsequent dealings with the composer.   74 [1886] 337

LA JEUNESSE DE BEETHOVEN. T. de Wyzewa.   (G)

    A full and readable account of Beethoven's Bonn years, intended to supplement the coverage of this period in the biography by J. von Wasielewski. The author stresses the resemblance between Beethoven and his grandfather and the difference from his father: "In Ludwig we find none of the defects of his father: not the inability to study or the unwillingness to work, not the love of drink or of easy money. Johann was only the intermediary through which his song received something of the physical and the moral nature of the old Flemish kapellmeister."   95 [1889] 418

LES MAITRES DE SYMPHONIE: BEETHOVEN. Emile Michel.   (A)
   Popular.   138 [1896] 168

L'"IMMORTELLE BIEN-AIMEE" DE BEETHOVEN. Th. de Wyzewa.   (B)
   However unsuitable Thayer's biographical method may have been for writing the life of an artist (and the author
   believes that this unsuitability was extreme), his methodical analysis must have destroyed forever any belief that
   the Immortal Beloved could have been Giulietta Guicciardi. The author agrees with Thayer, Tenger, La Mara
   and others that the Immortal Beloved was doubtless Therese von Brunsvick. He postulates that the famous letter
   (presumably with many others) had been sent to the Immortal Beloved, and at the end of the romance returned
   by her to Beethoven, who destroyed the others but kept this one as too sacred to destroy.
                                                      Ser. 5: 50 [1909] 456

REVUE ET GAZETTE MUSICALE DE PARIS *

BEETHOVEN ET SES DERNIERS QUATUORS. Francois Stoepsal.   (C)
   An article notably ahead of its time which contends that "the last quartets of Beethoven are composed with the same
   regularity and in a form as carefully planned as all his other works of whatever period." In proof of this the exposition section of the Quartet in A minor Op. 132 is shown to have the same constituent parts -- first theme, transition,
   second theme, codetta -- as does the corresponding section of the Quintet Op. 4.
                                                      2 [1835] 205

BEETHOVEN AND CHERUBINI. G. Kastner.   (D)
   Cherubini has assured Schindler that he never received Kal 881.   8 [1841] 134

DEUX SYMPHONIES PASTORALES. Fétis père.   (E)
   After a brief commentary on Knecht's 'Portrait musical de la Nature' the author says, "Notwithstanding its faults,
   which admittedly are considerable, I consider Knecht's symphony too interesting for the history of music not to
   preserve it."   33 [1866] 337

THE PIANOFORTE THAT BEETHOVEN RECEIVED FROM SEBASTIEN ERARD. Ch. Bannelier.   (F)
   Records of the House of Erard show that on 8 August 1803 Sebastien Erard presented a pianoforte to Beethoven, which
   is now the property of the museum at Linz.   42 [1875] 284

REVUE HEBDOMADAIRE

GOETHE AND BEETHOVEN. Stephanie Chandler.   (G
   Mention is made of the fact that Beethoven thought of Goethe only as a great poet, with no consideration of his very
   substantial worldly attainments. Goethe based his opinion of Beethoven too much on the judgments of Zelter, whose
   own musicianship was scanty and who demonstrated complete inability to comprehend Beethoven. The relationship
   between Goethe, Beethoven and Bettina is summarized.   41 [April 2nd 1932] 35

GOETHE AND BEETHOVEN. Alexandre Hérenger.   (H
   When he met Beethoven, Goethe had no awareness of the latter's greatness as a musician. The author is critical of
   Beethoven in his subsequent attitude towards Goethe, and has little good to say about Bettina's part in the matter.
                                                      41 [April 2nd 1932] 42

REVUE INTERNATIONALE DE MUSIQUE

Y A-T-IL UNE ERREUR DANS LA VIIe SYMPHONIE DE BEETHOVEN? Romain Rolland and Edgar Turel.   (I
   Arguments pro and con as to whether in a passage not clearly identified the dominant triad progresses to the tonic

---

* Volumes 1-2 were published as Gazette musicale de Paris.

triad in root position (simple cadence) or to a $\frac{6}{4}$ chord as usually shown.

1 [1938] 105

A PROPOS DE L'"'ALLEGRETTO" DE LA "SEPTIEME." Alfredo Casella.   (A)
In the passage discussed by Tufel and Rolland (p. 105) the autograph shows clearly and unequivocally a $\frac{6}{4}$ chord. (See also 'Die Musik' 33_1 [1940] 57)   1 [1938] 299

REVUE MONDIALE *

LE NEVEU DE BEETHOVEN. Jean Chantavoine.   (B)
Perhaps the most detailed study of Nephew Karl's life and character which had been made up to the time of writing, with copious pertinent quotations from the conversation books. "The traits of character which these documents (the conversation books) show to be most fundamental in Karl are an excessive keenness in argument and a habit of persiflage." While the author very loyally takes Beethoven's side in the many disputes, the quotations from the conversation books and the other points brought out show Karl in a most favorable light (and show, incidentally, that Karl had no use for Brother Johann. Two letters are published for the first time which Karl translated into French and prepared for Beethoven's signature: (1) Letter of introduction, without date, to Cherubini: "Le porteur de la présente lettre, M. Sedlatzek . . ." (2) Letter of introduction, without date, to Kreutzer: "C'est dans l'espérance que vous souveniez . . ." also for Sedlatzek.   60 [1906] 226,389

LA MALADIE DE BEETHOVEN.   (C)
Inconsequential.   177 [1927] 298

REVUE MUSICALE

LES DERNIERS QUATUORS DE BEETHOVEN. M. Fétis.   (D)
Analysis of Op. 131, pointing out Beethoven's mistakes and weaknesses.

Ser. II: 1 [1830] 279,345

REVUE PHILOSOPHIQUE ET RELIGIEUSE

LES DERNIERS QUATUORS DE BEETHOVEN. J. B. Sabattier.   (E)
General suggestions on the technique of the individual players and of the quartet as a group for the better playing of the Beethoven quartets and on the interpretation of all the quartets, especially the last five, an article showing real understanding of the works and familiarity with their content.   5 [1856] 74

RHEINISCHE BEOBACHTER

BEETHOVEN, DER RHEINLÄNDER. Wilhelm Schäfer.   (F)
Beethoven retained his Rhenish accent, his Rhenish friends, and his Rhenish traits of character in his personality and his music.   1 [1922] 623

BEETHOVEN. Heinrich Lemacher.   (G)
Prose poem.   1 [1922] 363

---

* Published 1901-1919 as Revue (Ancienne Revue des Revues).

BEETHOVEN AND THE BRENTANOS.   Heinz Amelung.   (A)
   The meeting of Beethoven and Bettina is briefly recounted, and their mutual admiration commented upon.
   Beethoven's first contact with Clemens was probably in connection with the poem which the latter wrote on the
   death of the Empress Luise. He sent this poem to his sister-in-law Toni with a letter of January 10th 1811 (given
   herewith), requesting her to pass it along to Beethoven for a suitable setting which, however, Beethoven did not
   undertake. The first meeting of the two men may have been in Teplitz or Prague in 1811, but more probably
   was in Vienna in the summer of 1813. A letter from Brentano to Beethoven, apparently written shortly after their
   first meeting, is given, as well as Brentano's enthusiastic review of the first Berlin performance of Fidelio, but
   apparently the two men never met again, nor did Beethoven set any of Brentano's poems to music.
                                                  2 [1923] 501

REDE GRILLPARZERS BEI DER ERSTEN GEDÄCHTNISFEIER FÜR BEETHOVEN.   Grillparzer.   (B)
   Oration given in the autumn of 1827 on the dedication of a monument at Beethoven's grave.
                                                  2 [1923] 503

DIE BONNER JUGENDZEIT BEETHOVENS.   Kaufmann.   (C)
   Review and summary of Schiedermair's 'Der junge Beethoven.'   5 [1926]
                                                               Der schöne Rhein - Beilage p. 1

AUS DER BONNER GESELLSCHAFT IN BEETHOVENS JUGENDZEIT.   Paul Kaufmann.   (D)
   Anecdotes and chat from the traditions and records of the author's ancestors in Bonn. The home of Hofkammerrat
   von Mastiaux was a center of musical activity for the town. Various other names connected with Beethoven's youth
   are mentioned.   6 [1927] 107

                                        RHEINISCHE BLÄTTER

LUDWIG VAN BEETHOVEN -- EIN LEBEN DES KAMPFES UND DES SIEGES.   Wilhelm Heintz.   (E)
                                       14 [January 1937] 32

BEETHOVEN UND DAS RHEINLAND.   Ludwig Schiedermair.   (F)
   Throughout his life Beethoven remained a Rhinelander.   14 [May 1937] 2

RICHARD WAGNER ÜBER BEETHOVENS CIS-MOLL-QUARTETT.   Ludwig Schiedermair.   (G)
   Facsimiles and transcription of a commentary on this quartet written in 1854, showing that the quartet was then
   neither known nor understood.   15 [1938] 318

EIN SKIZZENBLATT AUS DER "MISSA SOLEMNIS."   Ludwig Schiedermair.   (H)
   Very clear facsimile of a page from a sketchbook of the credo.   15 [1938] 388

                                        RICORDIANA

BEETHOVEN E LO SPIELUHR.   Willy Hess.   (I)
   First publication of WoO 33/3 (Allegro für die Spieluhr) in its original form.
                                                  3 [1957] No. 5

                            Rome. R. Accademia di Santa Cecilia
                                        ANNUARIO

LE OPERE DI BEETHOVEN E LA LORO EDIZIONE COMPLETA.   Willy Hess.   (J)
   Revision and augmentation by at least 25 items of the list of compositions missing from the GA, first published in
   NB J 7 [1937], with reprint of H-47 (see also 'Merker' 8 [1917] 24), EDr of two pages from H-75 (Op. 91 as arranged
   for the Panharmonicon), and EDr of the a cappella quartet 'Gia la notte' H-184.
                                                  8 [1917] 24

UNA PRIMA REDAZIONE INEDITA DELL'ARIA DI MARCELLINA NEL "FIDELIO."   W i l l y   H e s s .   (A)
  First publication of the score of H-84, with Revisionsbericht.   [1 9 5 6]

SANG UND KLANG ALMANACH

WARUM DÜRFEN WIR DIE NEUNTE SYMPHONIE AUCH HEUTE SPIELEN? F e l i x W e i n g a r t n e r .   (B)
  Prose poem.   [1 9 2 0] 2 6

SATURDAY REVIEW (London) *

BEETHOVEN'S TENTH SYMPHONY.   J o h n F. R u n c i m a n .   (C)
  In Bach's B Minor Mass "old German religious music culminates; surely in the Mass in D ('Beethoven's Tenth
  Symphony') we have the Viennese type of mass at its highest and best."
                                                      111 [1911] 206

THE JENA SYMPHONY.   J o h n F. R u n c i m a n .   (D)
  A sarcastic denial of the authenticity of the Jena Symphony.   113 [1912] 456

BEETHOVEN: THE LAST PHASE.   (E)
  A review of several concerts of the last works: "works where the reach of the composer exceeds his grasp."
                                                      129 [1920] 450

BEETHOVEN'S SONGS.   (F)
  "Beethoven was the first great composer to write true lieder," even though the type of his genius and his method of
  working were alike "not of the kind to produce perfect lyrics." Among the relatively small proportion of his songs
  that are really worthy of him should be numbered the Gellaert Songs Op. 48, the song cycle , An die ferne Geliebte
  Op. 98, and some settings of Goethe's poems, including Wonne der Wehmuth Op. 83 No. 1. In some others (e. g. ,
  Der Kuss Op. 128 and one of Klärchen's songs from Egmont Op. 84) "he fails as completely as a great man can be
  said to fail in anything to which he sets his mind. "   143 [1927] 351

BEETHOVEN.   (G)
  Centenary essay.   143 [1927] 468

THE MOTHER OF BEETHOVEN.   (H)
  Popular account of the discovery of the grave of Beethoven's mother.
                                                      153 [1932] 488

SATURDAY REVIEW (New York)

TOSCANINI AND BEETHOVEN.   E r n e s t N e w m a n .   (I)
  An enthusiastic review of the recently issued album of the nine symphonies. "Even when (Beethoven) was doing
  something apparently miscalculated and self-frustrating he knew perfectly well what he was about." Passages from
  Opp. 111, 125, and 127 are cited as examples.   [25 April 1953]

FIVE BY BEETHOVEN.   A b r a m C h a s i n s .   (J)
  Brief discussion of Beethoven's approach to the concerto form, and appraisal of available recordings of the five
  piano concertos.   [28 May 1955] 36

---

* Published 1855-1931 as Saturday Review of Politics, Literature, Science and Art.

THE TRUTH ABOUT BEETHOVEN.   Donald W. MacArdle.   (A)
    There is no sound evidence to support the contention that Beethoven was luetic.
                                        [27 August 1955] 51

NEW LIGHT ON BEETHOVEN'S 'BELOVEDS.' Paul Nettl.   (B)
    A summary of the contentions of Kaznelson that Josephine, sister of Therese von Brunsvik, and Rahel Levin were the
    Unsterbliche Geliebte and the Ferne Geliebte, that the Unsterbliche Geliebte letters almost certainly date from July
    1812, and that like the Heiligenstadt will, with which they were found after Beethoven's death were intended only
    as a cacoethes scribenei for Beethoven.   [27 April 1957] 35

                                        S C E N E

ZUR GESCHICHTE DES "FIDELIO." Georg Richard Kruse.   (C)
    A discussion of the subject which might well be taken as a model by other writers.
                                        9 [1919] 69

ÜBER BEETHOVENS BÜHNEN-DRAMATISCHE ABSICHTEN. Bruno Boelcker.   (D)
    In spite of the troubles which the first two versions of 'Fidelio' brought him, Beethoven's interest in opera remained
    high. In 1807 at Beethoven's request, Collin gave him the book of 'Bradamante,' but although Beethoven expressed
    the intention of going ahead with the music, nothing came of it. An opera to this text by Johann Friedrich Reichardt
    has long since been forgotten. Letters from 1809 (KS I 173, 178) show that Beethoven then considered writing music
    for Johann August Apel's 'Kalirrhoe,' but this plan was dropped. In June 1810 the music to Goethe's 'Egmont' was
    sent to Breitkopf & Härtel; the first performance had already taken place on May 24th 1810. On May 20th 1811
    Beethoven wrote to Breitkopf & Härtel (KS I 215): "I have written to Paris for books, for successful melodramas,
    comedies, etc. (for I cannot trust a poet here to write an original opera), to serve as a libretto." The choice fell
    on a French melodrama 'Les ruines de Babylon,' which Treitschke promptly translated. For a time Beethoven was
    most enthusiastic about this project -- he prevailed upon the authorities at the Theater an der Wien to cancel a
    performance of the melodrama, and he asked assistance of an eminent classicist on matters pertaining to the pro-
    posed opera -- but again the idea was abandoned, possibly because Beethoven's energies in the direction of dramatic
    music were turned at this time to the overture and incidental music to the Ruins of Athens (Opp. 113 and 114) and
    King Stephan (Op. 117). Beethoven's association with Kotzebue in his work on the Ruins of Athens music resulted
    in a request to the poet on January 28th 1812 (KS I 239) for an opera book which, however, was not forthcoming.
    During the next two years Beethoven's urge for dramatic writing expended itself in the revision of 'Fidelio,' but in
    1815 Treitschke's 'Romulus und Remus' occupied Beethoven's mind for a time -- the last of Beethoven's operatic
    projects.   9 [1919] 75

"FIDELIO"-BETRACHTUNGEN. Georg Hartmann.   (E)
    Suggestions regarding stage settings and tempi.   9 [1919] 78

"FIDELIO" AN DER WIENER HOFOPER. Oscar Bie.   (F)
    The staging under Mahler is described in detail. Mahler opened the performance with the Fidelio Overture, and
    performed the Leonore Overture No. 3 as an interlude in the second act between the Dungeon Scene and the Finale.
    The author agrees that all reason points against such a procedure, but in fantasy brings Beethoven to admit to Mahler
    that the liberties which the conductor had taken had brought the opera to life as otherwise was never done.
                                        9 [1919] 79

GLOSSEN ZU "FIDELIO." Eugen Kilian.   (G
    The author favors the innovation of playing the first part of the first act (through No. 5) in a room in Rocco's lodgings,
    outlines the procedure for the change in scene, and discusses other aspects of the staging. The dramatic problem re-
    sulting from Marzelline's infatuation with Leonora and disregard of Jaquino is recognized, and detailed suggestions
    for application throughout the opera are given to minimize the distracting effect which this three-cornered relation-
    ship too often brings about. No solution of the overture problem will please everybody, but the author recommends
    that the opera be opened with the Fidelio Overture or the Leonore Overture No. 1, and that the great Leonore Over-
    ture No. 3 be left to the concert hall.   9 [1919] 80

DAS KOSTÜM IM "FIDELIO." Willy Aron.   (A)
   The opera loses nothing and gains appreciably in dramatic power by being costumed as a story of the time of the
French Revolution rather than in the customary way as being of the period ca. 1600.
9 [1919] 84

ZWEI DRAMATURGISCHE FRAGEN ZU BEETHOVENS "FIDELIO." Arthur Seidl.   (B)
   The author favors the use of the title 'Fidelio' for the opera as now performed in its 1814 version, but agrees that
the 1805 version as reconstructed by Prager should be known by Beethoven's original title of 'Leonora.' He does
not, however, favor the suggestion that at the end of the opera Leonora should appear in female clothing.
9 [1919] 85

VON DER DARSTELLUNG DER "FIDELIO"-ROLLE. Paul Alfred Merbach.   (C)
   The difficulty of the role is doubly great for the reason that Leonora is the only character in the opera who is more
than a conventional lay figure. It is noteworthy that the two famous Leonoras of Beethoven's day (Anna Milder-
Hauptmann, who created the role in 1805, and Wilhelmina Schröder-Devrient, who first brought it to true greatness) were both girls still in their teens. Other famous Leonoras are briefly discussed.
9 [1919] 89

A MINOR CHANGE IN THE SECOND ACT OF FIDELIO. Erich Roether.   (D)
   It is suggested that the few spoken words appearing in the score at the time of Leonora's disclosure of herself to
Florestan be omitted.   9 [1919] 90

COSTUMING AND STAGING FOR 'FIDELIO.'   (E)
   The suggestion commented upon above (p. 85) that Leonora appear in female clothing at the end of the opera may
in large measure be met by suitable choice of costume and coiffure from the beginning. Reference is made to
several pages of costume and scenery sketches appearing as a supplement.
9 [1919] 90

BEETHOVENS EGMONT-MUSIK. Eugen Kilian.   (F)
   Beethoven's music was apparently written with Goethe's original drama in mind, even though Schiller's adaptation
was at that time most commonly used. Little interest was shown in the music at first, but as time progressed and
as Goethe's original version returned to favor, Beethoven's music became more and more an integral part of the
stage presentation. Nevertheless, a great disparity exists between Goethe's Egmont and Beethoven's. The Egmont
of the music is exclusively the Egmont of Goethe's last act, not the changing, growing character or the drama as a
whole. Beethoven's score clearly states that the Entr'actes must begin at the last word of the actor, and that at the
last chord of the music the curtain must rise. If for practical reasons there must be a break during the performance
(which in fact there must) it comes best after the second act. Various other problems of the producer are discussed.
11 [1921] 7

FIDELIO-REGIE. Ludwig Wagner.   (G)
   The author's solution to the inevitable overture problem is to play the Leonore Overture No. 3 as a prologue,
followed by a brief interval and then by the first act without further musical introduction. The costuming should
not be 16th-17th century Spanish, but rather Empire, appropriate to Revolutionary France though not specifying any
country. Scenery, lighting and staging are discussed in detail.   14 [1924] 166

BEETHOVEN UND DIE SÄNGERINNEN. Wilhelm Röntz.   (H)
   Beethoven's relations with Anna Milder-Hauptmann, Karoline Unger-Sabatier, Henriette Sontag-Rossi, and
Wilhelmine Schröder-Devrient.   17 [1927] 101

SCHAU-IN'S-LAND

EIN BEETHOVENBILD IN FREIBURG I. BR. R. Blume.   (I)
   A little known life-size head and shoulders portrait of Beethoven, painted in oils by Mähler in 1815 for Gleichenstein, is now in the possession of the widow of his grandson in Freiburg.
44 [1917] 18

DIE SYMPHONIEN BEETHOVENS IM LICHTE DER PHILOSOPHIE SCHOPENHAUERS.   A. von Gottschalck.   (A
2 [1913] 66

SCHWEIZ

ZU HERMANN HUBACHERS BEETHOVENBÜSTE [?].   11 [1907] 112   (B

SCHWEIZERISCHE BLASMUSIKZEITUNG

BEETHOVENS "MARSCH IN GESCHWINDEM TEMPO. " Willy Hess.   (C
Piano transcription of this composition of doubtful authenticity for wind band (H-263).
43 [1954] 270

BEETHOVENS KAMMERMUSIK FÜR BLASINSTRUMENTE. Willy Hess.   (D
Brief descriptions are given of each of the 17 chamber works (plus 2 arrangements) with wind instruments that have
hitherto been known, and a brief (10-measure) adagio for 3 horns is given its first publication.
47 [1958] 274

SCHWEIZERISCHE INSTRUMENTALMUSIK

NEUE VOLKSLIEDERBEARBEITUNG BEETHOVENS. Willy Hess.   (E
Beethoven's settings of continental folksongs are discussed in a review of Schünemann's 'Neues Volksliederheft,' which
contains EDr of 23 of the settings.   [15 January 1942]

SCHWEIZERISCHE MUSIKPÄDAGOGISCHE BLÄTTER

UNBEKANNTE ITALIENISCHE GESANGSMUSIK BEETHOVENS. Willy Hess.   (F
A bibliographical study of the songs listed in TV 264 and of certain allied compositions, with EDr of the a cappella
quartet 'Quella cetra' (key of G) H-175.   [1936] Nos. 14-15

BEETHOVEN'S BAGATELLE OPUS 119 No. 12. Willy Hess.   (G
This bagatelle in G major (H-245) first appeared with the others of Op. 119 in an edition by Diabelli shortly after
Beethoven's death. NB I 45 shows that it is based on a sketch of a song dating from 1800 or earlier. Kinsy (Heyer
Catalog IV) showed in 1916 that the song was 'An Laura' (H-89), probably written in 1791-92. It is not impossible
that the arrangement of this song to give the bagatelle was made by Beethoven, but this cannot be proved.   A
facsimile of the bagatelle from its first edition is given.   [July 1953] 37

BEETHOVENS ITALIENISCHE A-CAPPELLA GESÄNGE. Willy Hess.   (H
The list in TV-264 includes 13 songs not by Beethoven; several others have since been discovered. A list of 25
authentic settings is given, with full bibliographical data. EDr of quartet 'Giura il nocchier' (H-183) is given,
with an earlier version. See also 44 [1956] 80.   42 [1954] 179

BEETHOVENS ITALIENISCHE A-CAPPELLA GESÄNGE. Willy Hess.   (I
Corrections and additions to the article of the same title in 42 [1954] 179.
44 [1956] 80

LUDWIG VAN BEETHOVEN. Otto Ursprung.   (A)
   A biographical and character sketch as a centennial essay.   27 [1927] 63

DIE MISSA UND BEETHOVEN. Peter Wagner.   (B)
   The development of the mass as a musical form is stated in detail. The reason that Beethoven composed only two
   masses, in spite of his expressed interest in religious music was partly that he was by no means an ardent Catholic
   and partly that in Vienna at this time the mass as a musical form had gone out of fashion (note that the C major
   Mass was commanded by Prince Esterhazy and that the Missa Solemnis was written for a very special occasion).
   The masses with which Beethoven was most familiar were those of the Mannheim composers (performed at Bonn
   during his youth) and of Albrechtsberger. This background and the fact that his first essay in this form came at
   the time of his musical maturity (1807) explain why his mass differed so greatly from those of Mozart and Haydn,
   and also explain the coolness with which it was received. The difficulties of the Missa Solemnis, for performers
   and audience alike, result from the imperfectly solved problems of a deaf composer working in an unfamiliar medium. "There is only one single liturgical occasion which would not be overpowered by the Missa Solemñis: A
   Papal High Mass with all its attending ceremonials in St. Peter's Cathedral in Rome."
                                                        28 [1928] 220,325

                              SIONA

BEETHOVENS CHRISTENTUM. Wilh. Herold.   (C)
   As evidence that Beethoven, in his own way, was a Christian, the author cites the facts (1) that he was a creative
   artist who inspired his admirers; (2) that he wrote music of great spiritual beauty, and from time to time made remarks of a spiritual nature; (3) that in Opp. 48, 85, 86, and (above all) 123 he wrote music appropriate to spiritual
   or liturgical texts, and that at the end of his life he was contemplating other such works; and (4) that he devoted
   most of five years to the composition of the Missa Solemnis.   35 [1910] 26,61,81

ZUR AUFFÜHRUNG DER MISSA SOLEMNIS VON L. VAN BEETHOVEN IN DER PETERSKIRCHE ZU HEIDELBERG.   (D)
      Wolfrum.
   General discussion and program notes. Regarding Beethoven's rationalistic beliefs it is stated that the setting of
   three movements of the C major Mass Op. 86 made in 1823 (by Rochlitz?) as 'Hymns' with "very rationalistic"
   German words was made with Beethoven's approval.   42 [1917] 24

                              SKIZZEN

BEETHOVENS ZWEITE SINFONIE IN D-DUR.   Alfred Weidemann.   (E)
   Analysis.   13 [April 1939] 6

                        SOVETZKAYA MUZYKA

AN UNPUBLISHED BEETHOVEN LETTER.   Markheva.   (F)
   Translation into Russian of article by Kosma in 'Musica' (Bucharest), with facsimile.
                                                        Heft 9 [1951] 78

                     SOZIALISTISCHE MONATSHEFTE

BEETHOVEN UND DIE JUNGEN. Kurt Weill.   (G)
   The composer of today is building upon a foundation of musical art and aesthetics which could not exist had there
   been no Beethoven.   64 [1927] 193

DIE SINGSTIMME IN BEETHOVENS WERKE.   Hermann Freiherr von der Pfordten.   (A)
    A detailed analysis, from the standpoint of range and other requirements for vocal equipment, of the several roles in
    Fidelio, and of the Ninth Symphony, the two Masses and (more briefly) the other major vocal works.
                                  15 [1920] 49, 73

BEETHOVEN.   Hermann Freiherr von der Pfordten.   (B)
    Centennial essay.   21 [1927] 122

BEETHOVEN ALS ERZIEHER.   A. Stier.   (C)
    Centennial essay.   21 [1927] 125

BEETHOVENS "UNSTERBLICHE GELIEBTE."   P. Martell.   (D)
    Popular.   21 [1927] 134

BEETHOVEN IN DER SCHULE.   Adolf Prümers.   (E)
    Suggestions of a few songs and piano pieces as general instructional material.
                                  21 [1927] 139

BEETHOVEN UND DAS LIED.   Otto Pretzsch.   (F)
    General.   21 [1927] 153

BEETHOVEN UND DIE JUGEND.   Hans Fischer.   (G)
    Centennial address dealing with the manner and extent to which works by Beethoven should be used as instructional
    material for adolescents.   21 [1927] 273

NACHKLÄNGE ZU DEN BEETHOVENFEIERN.   A. Stier.   (H)
    Centennial essay.   22 [1927] 69

STRAD

SONATAS FOR 'CELLO AND PIANO.   Frederick Bye.   (I)
    A brief survey of the literature, with especial mention of the five sonatas and three sets of variations by Beethoven.
    The author points out that the Op. 5 sonatas were among the very first for this combination within the present day
    meaning of chamber music, and that they were written at a time when "the general progress of 'cello playing had
    not reached the stage of advancement which now makes it possible for this instrument to carry its full measure of
    responsibility, and consequently the piano has the lion's share of the music. "
                                   41 [1930] 204, 242

SÜDDEUTSCHE MONATSHEFTE

EIN UNBEKANNTE BEETHOVEN-BRIEF.   Alfred Lorenz.   (J)
    Facsimile, transcription and extended comments on a letter to Steiner (marked as received on 13 July 1824): "Geld
    aufzunehmen ist nicht . . . " (M-129). A history of the Steiner company and of Beethoven's financial dealings with
    it is recounted at some length. (See also 'Die Musik' 22 [1930] 398 and 'Deutsche Musiker Zeitung' 61 [1930] 64,
    84, 108, 128)   27 [1929] 47

ZUR HANDSCHRIFT BEETHOVENS.   Ludwig Klages.   (K)
    A discussion of the reading of personal characteristics from handwriting, with specific reference to the letter
    published by Lorenz (see above). (See also 'Deutsche Musiker Zeitung' 61 [1930] 64, 84, 108, 128)
                                 27 [1929] 49

AUTOGRAFER AV L. VAN BEETHOVEN I K. MUSIKALISKA AKADEMIEN. C. F. Hennerberg. (A)
    First publication of MM 148, here given as addressed to Vincenz Hauschka, and facsimile of sketch of part of the
    first movement of Op. 14 No. 1.   3 [1921] 83

SYMPHONIA

BEETHOVEN'S EGMONT OVERTURE. E. Elsenaar. (B)
    Popular historical and analytical commentary.   17 [1934] 102

TAT

DER REIGEN IM SCHLUSSSATZ DER NEUNTEN: EINE ANREGUNG. Carl Kellermann. (C)
    The Finale of the Ninth, for its fullest effect, should be danced as well as sung.
                                                               3 [1911] 236

DAS ERLEBNIS BEETHOVEN. Richard Benz. (D)
    Mystical centennial essay.   19 [1927] 81

TRIBUNE DE SAINT-GERVAIS

DE BACH A BEETHOVEN. Vincent d'Indy. (E)
    Beethoven's spiritual predecessors were definitely not the Italiante Haydn and Mozart, but instead K.P.E. Bach and
    Friedrich Wilhelm Rust.   5 [1899] 193,231

LES DIX-SEPT QUATRORS DE BEETHOVEN. Pierre Coindreau. (F)
    Although this survey (which was later published in pamphlet form) bears the subtitle: "After notes taken at the Scola
    Cantorum in 1900 in M. d'Indy's course in composition," it is difficult to believe that M. d'Indy's analyses could be
    so confusing and superficial.   5 [1909] 97,127,154

TRIERISCHE CHRONIK

BEETHOVENS MUTTER. J. Wagner. (G)
    Tabulation of the ancestry of Beethoven's mother for several generations. This same material, slightly reworded, is
    said to have appeared in the 'Coblenzer Zeitung' of December 9th 1920 and the 'Kölnische Zeitung' of December
    31st 1920.   NF 16 [1920] 162

TÜRMER

BEETHOVENS HELDENTUM: GELEITWORTE ZU SEINEN BRIEFEN. Karl Storck. (H)
    The author says that among all the sets of collected letters of great men which he knows, none gives so true a picture
    of the personality of the writer as do the letters of Beethoven. In these letters we are not reading words carefully
    thought out by the writer: we hear a man speak; "through these letters we come to know the man rather than the
    artist." The letters show that by Richard Strauss' criterion of battles and struggles, Beethoven certainly led a hero's
    life: a life in which art was supremely important but in which humanness was equally important.
                                                               7_2 [1905] 552

ERINNERUNGEN AN BEETHOVEN. Ferdinand Ries.   (A)
Excerpts from the 'Biographische Notizen.' 8_2 [1906] 809

BEETHOVENS UNSTERBLICHE GELIEBTE. Karl Storck.   (B)
Digest of article in 'Die Musik' 10_4 [1911] 131 regarding a new 'Immortal Beloved' letter later proved to be spurious.
                                                            13_2 [1911] 841

AN BEETHOVENS TODESTAG. Karl Storck.   (C)
Commemorative essay. 16_2 [1914] 124

BEETHOVEN - HERBART - SCHUMANN. Greissinger.   (D)
A discussion of the influence of Beethoven on Johann Friedrich Herbart (1776-1841), the metaphysician, and of the
influence of Herbart (and of Beethoven) on Schumann. 16_2 [1914] 412

BEETHOVENS SPÄTERE BEZIEHUNG ZU SEINER RHEINISCHE HEIMAT. Stephan Ley.   (E)
Especially during his first years in Vienna, Beethoven's letters inquire for his Bonn friends. His speech was that of a
Rheinlander, and a number of his friends in Vienna were from that part of the world. He commented on the resemblance between his homeland and the countryside around Vienna, and often expressed the wish to return to Bonn for
a visit. 23_1 [1921] 338

BEETHOVENS LETZTE QUARTETTE. Konrad Huschke.   (F)
Lengthy but general. 27_2 [1925] 70

WIE LUDWIG VAN BEETHOVEN STARB. Walther Nohl.   (G)
Popular account of Beethoven's last days.   29 [1927] 470

BEETHOVEN IN DER ERZÄHLENDEN DICHTUNG DER GEGENWART. Paul Bülow.   (H)
                                                            29 [1927] 486

BEETHOVENS BEZIEHUNGEN ZU FRANZ SCHUBERT. Konrad Huschke.   (I)
While the two composers knew each other's music and certainly had seen each other, it is most improbable that they
ever met.   29 [1927] 496

SCHUBERT UND BEETHOVEN BEIM VERARBEITEN IHRER MUSIKALISCHEN EINFÄLLE. Konrad Huschke.   (J)
There is no foundation for the concept of a Beethoven whose musical ideas were the result of hard labor rather than
inspiration, or of a Schubert whose only worthwhile melodies came fully perfected and without effort.
                                                            30_2 [1928] 380

BEETHOVENS A-VISTA-SPIEL. Konrad Huschke.   (K)
Popular article on Beethoven's playing at sight and from score.   32 [1930] 454

ÜBER LAND UND MEER

ZUM 17. DEZEMBER 1870. Elise Polko.   (L)
Rhapsodic centenary essay.   25 [1870] No. 12a p. 6

DIE ERSTE GROSSE BEETHOVENSPIELERIA. Ludwig Nohl.   (M)
Popular account of Beethoven's interest in women, and biographical sketch of Dorothea von Ertmann (née Graumann)
(1781-1849)   44 [1880] 655

BEETHOVENS GEBURTSSTÄTTE IN BONN. L. A. Schmidt.   (N)
Popular biographical sketch of Grandfather Ludwig and Father Johann, and brief description of the house on the
Bonngasse.   63 [1889] 7

GOETHE AND BEETHOVEN.   J. Gebeschus.   (A)
   Goethe's youthful training gave him an extensive knowledge of and familiarity with music in a wide field.   He
   had many acquaintances among composers, performers and music lovers. The regrettable lack of close association
   between Goethe and Beethoven, the two greatest Germans of their day, must be attributed solely to a complete
   personal incompatibility.   6 [1902] 421

DER KRANKE BEETHOVEN. W. Schweisheimer.   (B)
   A popular summary of the course of Beethoven's deafness (attributed by the author to a pathological condition of
   unknown origin in the inner ear whereby the auditory nerve was affected) and of the gastric and intestinal disorders
   experienced from his thirtieth year until his death of cirrhosis of the liver.
                                          25 [1921] 107

VELHAGEN UND KLASINGS KRIEGSALMANCH

BEETHOVENS "NEUNTE." Wilhelm Kleefeld.   (C)
   General.   [1920] 31

VELHAGEN UND KLASINGS MONATSHEFTE

DAS SOGENANNTE BEETHOVENBILDNISS VON G. V. KÜGELGEN.   Theodor von Frimmel.   (D)
   Same as 'Daheim' 27 [1891] 395.   5 [1891] 207

DAS BEETHOVENHAUS IN BONN. Ferdinand Pfohl.   (E)
   Popular essay.   5 [January 1891] 685

BEETHOVENS HEIMSTÄTTEN. Max Kalbeck.   (F)
   An article amplifying the thought: "Beethoven had places to live, but no home."
                                          7 [February 1893] 611

BEETHOVENS BEGEGNUNG MIT GOETHE. Eugen Sachsse.   (G)
   A detailed assembly of the known material on the relationship of the two men, and on the influence of Bettina
   Brentano on Zelter. The place which the music to Egmont has in the drama is also discussed.
                                          18 [May 1904] 289

BEETHOVEN IN SEINEN BRIEFEN. Wilhelm Kleefeld.   (H)
   General commentary on what the letters will tell the reader about Beethoven in his relations to his patrons, his
   publishers, his close companions, his nephew, and his women friends.
                                          24 [December 1909] 573

BEETHOVENS RIESENSONATE OPUS 106. Konrad Huschke.   (I)
   "An appreciation on the occasion of its centenary year."   32 [August 1918] 401

BEETHOVENS LETZTE SONATE. Konrad Huschke.   (J)
   A popular but detailed analysis of Op. 111. 37_1 [1923] 368

EIN JUGENDBILDNIS BEETHOVENS. Karl Koetschau.   (K)
   An oil painting marked 'Beethoven,' recently discovered in Bonn and dating from 1790-92, may be genuine.
                                          41_2 [1927] 39

BEETHOVEN UND DAS WIENER BALLETT. Robert Haas.   (L)
   Vienna's enthusiasm for the dance during the decade following Vigano's debut in 1793 led Beethoven to write a
   considerable number of works in various dance forms (see 'Schweizerische Musikzeitung' 70 [1930] 866), and brought
   to his attention various of the themes by other composers which he used for piano variations.
                                          41_2 [1927] 41

BEETHOVENS MASKE. Herbert Eulenberg.   (A)
    An account of Danhauser's efforts to sell the death mask which he had made and which finally became the property
    of the University of Bonn. Because of the ravages of disease and death, the mask may be assumed to be a very un-
    representative likeness. 41_2 [1927] 81

RECHTLICHE VERWICKLUNGEN BEETHOVENS. Rudolf Stammler.   (B)
    A very readable account of the circumstances leading to the annuity of 1809 and thereafter to Beethoven's suit
    against the Kinsky estate (though the suit itself is not discussed) and to the cares brought upon Beethoven by the
    guardianship of Nephew Karl. A very favorable military report on Nephew Karl dated November 20th 1831, as
    regards character and conduct is quoted. Legal complications which might have resulted in Nephew Karl's mother
    (the 'Queen of the Night') receiving the entire estate left by Beethoven are discussed. In no logical connection,
    various facts are given about Nephew Karl's son Ludwig and grandson Karl Julius Maria.
                                                               43_2 [1929] 153

MOZART-SILHOUETTEN.   (C)
    Included in material formerly belonging to the Brunsviks and recently sold were a number of cutout silhouettes re-
    putedly made by Mozart or by the Countess Erdödy during a concert. One of these is supposed to be a silhouette of
    Beethoven, and bears a notation in Mozart's hand: "I received this little portrait as a gift from Stephanie von Breun-
    ing." The silhouette bears little or no resemblance to other likenesses of Beethoven, and seems to represent a man
    of mature years, whereas Beethoven was only twenty-one when Mozart died. (See 'Deutscher Musiker Zeitung'
    62 [1931] 198 in which it is pointed out that there was no Stephanie von Breuning, and that facts of chronology make
    the entire account most improbable. $44_{[?]}$ [1930] 581,584

BEETHOVENS STAMMBUCH. Oskar Kaul.   (D)
    Description and general comments on the Stammbuch as a document comparable in importance to the Heiligenstadt
    will and the letter to the Immortal Beloved. 48_1 [November 1933] Beilage

BEETHOVEN ALS HAUSFREUND IN EINER WIENER FAMILIE. Stephan Ley.   (E)
    Popular and general account of Beethoven's friendship with Cajetan Gianatasio del Rio, his wife Anna and his
    daughters Fanny and Nanny. 54_1 [1940] 319

Verein für die Geschichte Berlins *
ZEITSCHRIFT

BERLIN IM LEBEN BERÜHMTER KOMPONISTEN. Herbert Biehle.   (F)
    A summary of Beethoven's relationship to Berlin: his single visit there in June 1796, the Berliners who were among
    his acquaintances, the performances of his works in that city, the importance to him of Berlin critics and of the
    Berlin publisher Schlesinger.   46 [1929] 3

Verein für Geschichte der Stadt Wien
BERICHTE UND MITTHEILUNGEN

BEETHOVENS WOHNUNGEN IN WIEN. Theodor von Frimmel.   (G)
    A list, with brief comments, of all known residences in Vienna and its environs which Beethoven occupied.
                                                               29 [1893] 62

---

* Published 1884-1933 as Mitteilungen.

LA MESSE SOLENNELLE DE LOUIS VAN BEETHOVEN. Georges Humbert.   (A)
    Popular.   6 [1912] 145

LE ROMAN D'UN PROTÉGÉ DE BEETHOVEN. Auguste Ehrhard.   (B)
    Romantic account of a fruitless love affair of Carl Friedrich Kubeck with a young countess to whom he was giving
    piano lessons in 1796 as an assistant teacher for Beethoven.   6 [1912] 190,213,237

VOLK *

BEETHOVEN UND DIE WENDE DER KULTUR. Richard Benz.   (C)
    Beethoven was the prophet of what is to come.   1 [1933] 101

VOLK UND RASSE

RASSENMERKMALE BEETHOVENS UND SEINE NÄCHSTER VERWANDTEN. Walther Rauschenberg.   (D)
    The anthropometric characteristics and personalities are studied (as far as the data are available) for Beethoven, his
    two parents and four grandparents, and his two brothers. "We must then identify the racial mixture that is evident in
    Beethoven as Falisch-Nordic-Eastern-Western, in which the artistic faculty of the Nordic and Falisch plays the thor-
    oughly dominant role. Equally forceful is the negative: the absence of Dinaric and above all the absence of Nearer
    Asiatic admixture."   9 [1934] 194

VOLK UND WELT

BEETHOVEN, DER WOHLTÄTER. Stephan Ley.   (E)
    Same as article in Reclam's 'Universum' 52 [1936] 1250.   [November 1937] 10

WAGNER AND BEETHOVEN. Peter Raabe.   (F)
    Beethoven, no composer for the stage, was nevertheless the most dramatic of symphonists; Wagner, with his superb
    sense of the theater, was the most symphonic of composers for the stage.
                                       [May 1938] 23

VOLKSBÜHNE

LUDWIG VAN BEETHOVEN. Leo Kestenberg.   (G)
    Centennial essay.   2 No. 6 [March 15th 1927]

DER DIRIGENT UND BEETHOVEN. Siegfried Ochs.   (H)
    The conductor of Beethoven's music, whether for chorus or for orchestra, has difficult problems to solve and great
    responsibility for solving them. The need of modifying Beethoven's scoring to attain balance and to let his ideas
    come through is at some points almost inescapable.   2 No. 6 [March 15th 1927]

---

* Volumes 1-4 were published as Völkische Kultur.

BEETHOVEN UND DAS DEUTSCHE VOLKSLIED. K a r l L i e b l e i t n e r.   (A)
    Festival address, referring to the Ode to Joy as the apotheosis of the German folksong.
                                        23 [1921] 5

EIN BEETHOVEN-MOTIV. A u g u s t E i g n e r.   (B)
    Beethoven used folksongs in three ways: (a) as a subject for variations (e. g. , Op. 107 Nos. 1 and 5); (b) intentional
    imitation of folk music (e. g. , the Mödlinger Dances, the third movement of the Pastoral Symphony); and (c) free
    use of folk melodies woven into larger works (e. g. , the second movement of the Fifth Symphony). The author
    points out a resemblance between a motif from the last movement of the Fifth Symphony and an "altes Soldatenlied,"
    though he admits that this soliders' song may be post-Beethoven.   29 [1927] 39

                            DER WEG

JUDEN UM BEETHOVEN. L u d w i g M i s c h.   (C)
    Among the Jews in Beethoven's circle of friends were Aloys Jeitteles and his cousin Ignaz, the banker Daniel Bernhard
    Eskeles and his daughter Marie the pianist (later Gräfin von Wimpfen), the Schlesingers father and son, the composer
    Meyerbeer, the pianist Moscheles, the Poetess Rahel Levin, the conductor and composer Ferdinand Hiller, the musical
    amateurs Joseph and Heinrich Eppinger, and the publisher Max Joseph Leidesdorf.
                                    [3, 10 October 1947]

ZUM KAPITEL "JUDEN UM BEETHOVEN." M a x U n g e r.   (D)
    The brothers Ofenheimer, chemical manufacturers and merchants, were also among Beethoven's friends, as shown
    by his letters MM 90 and MM 100.   [12 December 1947]

                            WELTBÜHNE

BEETHOVEN. H a n s H e i n z S t u c k e n s c h m i d t.   (E)
    A diatribe against the "international public prostitution" of centenary year festivals.
                                        23 [1927] 454

                    WESTERMANNS MONATSHEFTE **

FURIOSO. W o l f g a n g M ü l l e r v o n K ö n i g s w i n t e r.   (F)
    A romanticized narrative of Beethoven's youth supposed to have been based on accounts by Wegeler (English trans-
    lation in book form by Cambridge, Glover, 1865).   9 [1860] 1, 121, 235

BEETHOVENS TOD. L u d w i g N o h l.   (G)
    A very circumstantial account of the composer's last six months, completely distinct from the similar material in
    the author's 'Beethovens Leben' (1877).   18 [1865] 620

UNGEDRUCKTE BRIEFE BEETHOVENS. L u d w i g N o h l.   (H)
    First publication of 34 letters to Gleichenstein (KBr numbers): 140, 142, 171, 169, KK 182, 170, 135, 172, 133,
    125, 119, KK 353, 148, 149, 167, 121, 123, 124, 173, KK 147, 127, 143, 126, 156, 174, 116, 117, 137, 157, 139,
    120, 138, 158, 139.   19 [1865] 306

DIE BEETHOVEN'SCHE SINFONIE. O t t o G u m p r e c h t.   (I)
    A general essay touching on the many thoughts encompassed by its title, written from the standpoint of a time when
    the symphonies were far from being the common property of the musical world.
                                        45 [1878] 77

---

*   Volumes 1-47 were published as Deutsches Volkslied.
**   Volumes 51-100 were published as Westermanns illustrierte deutsche Monatshefte.

NOCH EINMAL BEETHOVENS SYMPHONIEN.   Otto Gumprecht.   (A)
Extended generalities for the lay reader.   57 [1885] 536,677

FIDELIO UND DER WASSERTRÄGER.   Ernst Pasqué.   (B)
Jean Nicolas Bouilly (1763-1842) was for several years from 1794 Public Prosecutor in Tours during the Reign of Terror,
after which he lived in Paris until his death. For a time he held a post in connection with the reorganization of the
public schools, but he soon gave this up in favor of a career as a dramatist and librettist. According to the author's
tale, Bouilly improvised the story of Leonore one evening at a dinner given by Mme. Scio, prima donna of the opera,
the plot being based (said Bouilly) on an actual case that he encountered while Public Prosecutor at Tours. The improvised libretto was reduced to writing, with the locale for safety's sake being stated as Spain, and the time the
seventeenth century. The name Leonore was chosen by Mme. Scio, the music was written by Gaveaux (being the
17th of his 38 operas), and on 19 February 1798 the work received the first of many brilliant and successful performances, the book and the popularity of the prima donna contributing far more than Gaveaux's music. A detailed
synopsis of the book is given, and the author points out the amusing fact that Beethoven's great drama of conjugal
fidelity was thus the result of two married men running around with an attractive young widow. The acclaim of
Leonore led Cherubini to request a libretto from Bouilly, and 'Der Wassertrㅏger,' produced on 15 January 1800,
was the result. The success in Germany as well as in France of Cherubini's opera brought its librettist to notice,
and this in turn interested other composers in Leonore. Paer's 'Eleonore' was produced in 1805 in Dresden, and
later the same year (20 November) Beethoven's opera received its premiere in Vienna. Finally in 1830 Bouilly's
libretto and Beethoven's music returned again to Paris, with Schröder-Devrient as Leonore. The years that followed showed an unhappy history of 'improvements' and adaptations of the Beethoven-Treitschke work. Rocco's 'Gold'
aria is given in its version by Gaveaux.   63 [1887] 363

AUS BEETHOVENS FRAUENKREISE.   Alfred Chr. Kalischer.   (C)
First draft of material later appearing in the author's 'Beethoven und seine Zeitgenossen' III 201-48.
                                       74 [1893] 822

ROBERT SCHUMANN, RICHARD WAGNER UND DIE NEUNTE SYMPHONIE.   Konrad Huschke.   (D)
Schumann's writings extolling Beethoven and excoriating Mendelsohn and others for their lack of understanding of
the Ninth Symphony are quoted. What Schumann fought for with words, Wagner as writer and conductor fought for
with words and deeds. "Thus the two great opposites stand side by side as standard-bearers for one of the supreme
works of music."   140 [1926] 207

BEETHOVENS LEBENSBEJAHUNG.   Wilhelm Kleefeld.   (E)
Centenary essay.   142 [1927] 29

UNVERÖFFENTLICHTE BILDNISSE AUS BEETHOVENS FREUNDESKREIS.   Stephan Ley.   (F)
The brief (fall of 1806 - March 1809) contact between Beethoven and Count Franz Joachim Wenzel von Oppersdorff
(1778-1818) of Oberglogau is described. Brief comment is given on Vincenz Hauschka, with quotations from some
of Beethoven's letters. One of the very few friendships which Beethoven made in his later years was that of the
family of Baron Johann Baptist von Puthon, whose wife Antonie also suffered from deafness. Portraits of these friends
are reproduced.   75 [1931] 511

                          WESTMARK

BEETHOVEN.   Albert Hensel.   (G)
Sesquicentennial essay of more than usual substance.   1 [1921] 476

               WIENER ALLGEMEINE MUSIKALISCHE ZEITUNG *

RÜCKBLICKE AUF DIE CHRONOMETER.   Fr. S. Kandler.   (H)
Beethoven's name is included in a substantial list of composers who (according to the author) have agreed to mark
their future compositions with the MM scale (see NB I 126).   1 [1817] 43

---

* Volumes 1-7 were published as Allgemeine Musikalische Zeitung.

(No Title)　　　(A)
　　Announcement of publication of Treitschke's poems with seven settings of certain of the poems, including WoO 147
　　(EDr) and WoO 94.　　　　　　　　　　　　　　　　　　1 [1817] 199

CANON 'DAS SCHWEIGEN' BY HERDER.　Ludwig van Beethoven.　　　　　　　　　　　　(B)
　　Riddle Canon as given in GA 23/256 No. 5 except that entry marks appear after the third note (C) and the eighth
　　note (B flat), over the fourth note are the accidentals ♮♮ , and the last phrase is marked pp cresc f (on 'Gold').
　　　　　　　　　　　　　　　　　　　　　　1 [1817] Beilage 3, Issue March 6th.

AUFLÖSUNG DES RÄTHSELS CANONS VON HERRN L. VAN BEETHOVEN.　Hieronimus Payer.　　　(C)
　　The solution proposed was explained by Payer in a canon of his own: "Herr von (sic) Beethovens Canon der ist / In der
　　Unterquint und in der Octav." (The solution in TD III 533 differs from Payer's chiefly in that TD introduces an E flat
　　in the signature, while Payer has E natural throughout except only the fourth note of the second voice. TD also con-
　　fuses the text of the Canon.)　　　　　　　　　1 [1817] Beilage 6, Issue June 5th.

ERKLÄRUNG.　Ludwig van Beethoven and Anton Salieri.　　　　　　　　　　　　　(D)
　　A high-pressure sales talk for the metronome, signed by Beethoven and Salieri (see NB I 126).
　　　　　　　　　　　　　　　　　　　2 [1818] 58

WIENER ALLGEMEINE MUSIK-ZEITUNG*

EIN AUTOGRAPH VON LUDWIG VAN BEETHOVEN.　August Schmidt.　　　　　　　　　(E)
　　Facsimile of Albumblatt Kal 867.　　　　　　　　3 [1843] 589

CARL CZERNY ÜBER SEIN VERHÄLTNIS ZU BEETHOVEN VOM JAHRE 1801 BIS 1826.　August Schmidt.　　(F)
　　First publication of two letters from Beethoven (KS I 404 No. 506 and KS II 73, the latter with minor variants.
　　　　　　　　　　　　　　　　　　5 [1845] 113

VERZEICHNISS ALLER BISHER ERSCHIENENER ABBILDUNGEN LUDWIG VAN BEETHOVENS.　Aloys Fuchs.　　(G)
　　List of 37 lithographs or engravings, 4 medallions, and 8 busts or statuettes.
　　　　　　　　　　　　　　　　　　5 [1845] 385

BEETHOVENIANA.　August Schmidt.　　　　　　　　　　　　　　　　　　　　(H)
　　Publication of certain material from Wegeler's Anhang to the Wegeler-Ries Notizen; account by Czerny of his
　　contacts with Beethoven; EDr of And. 610 and And. 878.　　　5 [1845] 437,449

(No Title)　　　　　　　　　　　　　　　　　　　　　　　　　　　　　　　　　　(I)
　　Statement that WoO was written in Fuch's album (but see KHV p. 567).
　　　　　　　　　　　　　　　　　　6 [1846] 153n

EINE ANSICHT ÜBER MOZART, BEETHOVEN UND BERLIOZ, UND ÜBER DEN HUMOR IN DER MUSIK.　　　(J)
　　　　　　　　　　　　　　　　　　6 [1846] 293,297

IN BETREFF DER BEETHOVEN'SCHEN INSTRUMENTE.　Alois Fuchs.　　　　　　　　　(K)
　　Description of the four stringed instruments presented to Beethoven by Prince Lichnowsky (TK I 276).
　　　　　　　　　　　　　　　　　　6 [1846] 594

BEITRAG ZUR LEBENSGESCHICHTE LUDWIG VAN BEETHOVENS.　Alois Fuchs.　　　　　　　(L)
　　First publication of the letter given in KS I 110.　　　7 [1847] 313

---

* 1841-44 published as Allgemeine Wiener Musik-Zeitung.

BEETHOVENS GEHÖRLEIDEN. Heinrich Neumann.   (A)
  Detailed consideration of all evidence leads to the conclusion: "Typical progress of a malady of the auditory nerve,
  which acting as a continuing focus of toxicity brought about deafness, or an otosclerosis which manifested itself in
  the form of a malady of the inner ear."   77 [1927] 1015

EIN NEUES BEETHOVEN-DENKMAL. Simon Krüger.   (B)
  Address at the unveiling of a Beethoven memorial in Baden.   77 [1927] 1540

WOCHE

DER ANTLITZ BEETHOVEN. A. Gläser.   (C)
  A popular description of Beethoven's facial appearance, and reproductions of a dozen paintings and statues of him.
                                    29 [1927] 326

WOCHENSCHRIFT FÜR THERAPIE UND HYGIENE DES AUGES

BEETHOVENS BRILLEN. Hermann Cohn.   (D)
  In the Museum of the Beethovenhaus are two pairs of glasses, of strength respectively -4.0 and -1.75 (diopters), and
  a monocle of strength -3.0. Beethoven is known not to have worn glasses as a matter of habit, but to have carried a
  lorgnette or a monocle on the street. From the examination of these glasses, the only statement that can be made
  with confidence is that Beethoven manifested a medium degree of myopia. (Reprinted in 18 [1915] 202)
                                    5 [1901] 5

YALE REVIEW

BEETHOVEN AFTER ONE HUNDRED YEARS. David Stanley Smith.   (E)
  Centenary essay.   NS 16 [1927] 445

ZEITSCHRIFT FÜR AESTHETIK UND ALLGEMEINE KUNSTWISSENSCHAFT

DIE WELTANSCHAUUNG BEETHOVENS UND IHRE GESTALTUNG IN DER 7. SYMPHONIE.   (F)
     Otto Schilling-Trygophorus.
  An exhaustive description of the music as it lies in the score, with the author's metaphysical explanations.
                                    25 [1931] 117

ZEITSCHRIFT FÜR ÄRZTLICHE FORTBILDUNG

BEETHOVENS GEHÖRLEIDEN UND DAS HEILIGENSTÄDTER TESTAMENT. C. Magenau.   (G)
  Beethoven's deafness was probably due to an ailment of the inner ear; various factors bearing on the diagnosis are
  discussed. A transcription of the Heiligenstadt will is appended.   34 [1937] 268

DAS BEETHOVEN-DENKMAL IN WIEN.   (A)
The activities leading up to the preparation of the memorial are outlined, and the statue by Kaspar Zumbusch is
described and portrayed.   15 [1880] 250

Z E I T S C H R I F T   F Ü R   I N S T R U M E N T E N B A U

EIN UNBEKANNTES ADAGIO VON BEETHOVEN FÜR EIN MECHANISCHES MUSIKWERK.   (B)
Digest of article in 'Die Musik' 1_2 [1902] 1059 and mention that a 'Grenadiermarsch' for mechanical organ by Beethoven is extant. (See 'Almanach der deutschen Musikbücherei' [1927] 320 and 'Zeitschrift für Musikwissenschaft'
14 [1932] 215)   23 [1902] 88

BEETHOVEN UND DAS CLAVIER. G. von Graevenitz.   (C)
Of great importance in Beethoven's association with the piano was the gift to him by Count Waldstein of a piano at
some time before his departure for Vienna in 1792.   It is probable that the instrument had been made by Johann
Andreas Stein.   Beethoven's interest in piano manufacture remained high from the time of his first meeting with
Stein in 1787, and the advances which the latter made in design may be traced by the advances which the former
shows in his compositions for piano.   In 1796 in Berlin Beethoven came to know the Broadwood instrument, much
more heavily built than the continental pianos. Beethoven's ultimate ownership (in 1818) of a Broadwood may have
been a part of the inspiration for the Hammerclavier Sonata. In about 1803 Beethoven had received an Erard piano
as a gift from Prince Lichnowsky, but this was a relatively lightly-constructed and inferior instrument which Beethoven held in low esteem and which he gave to Brother Johann in the 1820's. The third historic Beethoven piano
is a four-stringed Graf specially prepared for the deaf composer. (Quoted from the 'Tägliche Rundschau')
42 [1922] 1135

BEETHOVEN UND DAS HAMMERKLAVIER. Georg Kinsky.   (D)
With the disappearance of the school of composition based upon a continuo, the harpsichord-clavichord group of
keyed instruments was inevitably superseded by the pianoforte.   This transition showed itself most rapidly during
Beethoven's first decade (1770-80).   Beethoven's instruction under Neefe was probably on the harpsichord or the
clavichord, but there were certainly pianos in Bonn during his youth.   His acquaintance with Johann Andreas
Stein and his children Nanette and Mattaus Andreas, dating from 1787, furthered Beethoven's leanings towards the
piano rather than the older instruments. His contacts with the children and with Nanette's husband Andreas Streicher,
all of whom arrived in Vienna in the summer of 1794 after Stein's death, were intimate. There was close cooperation
(to great mutual advantage) between Beethoven, the creator of a style for which a new instrument was needed, and
Streicher, who was spurred by Beethoven's demands to the development of an instrument of constantly growing capabilities. In 1803 a piano from Erard in Paris gave Beethoven an extra half-octave (F - c^4 instead of the usual five
octaves F - f^3). This added scope shows itself in Opp. 53, 57 and 58 of 1804-05. Further extension in the following
years to a range of C - f^4 was taken advantage of: the Broadwood piano (1817) had a range of almost six octaves
(C - b^4), and the four-stringed Graf piano of 1825 had six and a half (C - f^4). (Regarding these three instruments,
see 'Die Musik' 2_3 [1903] 83.) The Streicher pianos and others of that period had two pedals for moving the action,
so that a notation (Op. 58, 2nd mct.): "una corda . . . due e poi tre corde . . . due, poi una corda" could be lit-
erally followed as it cannot on modern pianos on which the change is only from three to two strings. While Opp. 101
and 106 (and the autograph of Op. 109 and a manuscript copy of Op. 110 with composer's corrections) were the only
works by Beethoven marked "für das Hammerklavier," this was nothing more than a chauvinistic change of nomenclature: all the sonatas, from Op. 2 and Op. 111, were written for no other instrument than the piano.
56 [1936] 364

Z E I T W E N D E

ZUM HUNDERTSTEN TODESTAG LUDWIG VAN BEETHOVENS. Ernst Riemann.   (E)
Centennial essay. 3_1 [1927] 218

URRENT BEETHOVEN LITERATURE.   (A)
    Reference is made (among others) to the following articles not readily available in the United States: Frimmel:
    Ein ungedruckte Brief Beethovens ('Neue Wiener Musik Zeitung' 1 Nos. 35,36); Kohut: Grillparzer und Beethoven
    ('Neue Berliner Musik Zeitung' 44 Nos. 37-39); Frimmel: Neue Beethovenstudien ('Deutsche Kunst und Musik
    Zeitung' 18); Rust: Vigano's Scenario ('Neue Berliner Musik Zeitung' 45 Nos. 14-17).

                                        1 [1891] 116; 2 [1892] 13,168

                        ZENTRALVEREIN-ZEITUNG*

EETHOVEN AND RAHEL VARNHAGEN. Eugen Peterson.   (B)
    The infatuation of Beethoven for Rahel in Teplitz in 1811 is outlined as recounted by Rahel and by Varnhagen.
    The failure of the couple to see Beethoven when they were in Vienna in the winter of 1814-15 is attributed to
    Rahel's almost idolatrous patterning after Goethe in his likes and dislikes, and definitely not for the reason hint-
    ed at by Varnhagen that Beethoven's interest in Rahel was too personal.

                                        6 [1927] 169

ANN EIN JUDE BEETHOVEN VERSTEHEN? Leo Lewy.   (C)
    An enthusiastic letter by Moscheles on his youthful discovery of the Sonata Pathétique is given. Names from
    Moscheles and Joachim to Schnabel are cited to show that "here and there we find a Jew who is not completely
    debarred by his Judaism from the understanding of Beethoven. "

                                        13 [1934] Beilage to No. 1

                        ZUKUNFT

LINGERS BEETHOVEN. Hermann Bahr.   (D)
    Rhapsodic.   39 [1902] 389

EETHOVEN. Karl Lamprecht.   (E)
    Rhapsodic biographical sketch.   51 [1905] 11

                        _____

_____

* Published 1922-25 as C. V. Zeitung.

Newspapers

L. VAN BEETHOVENS ABENTEUER IN USA. Paul Nettl.   (A)

Documents recently brought to light in Vienna prove that grandnephew Ludwig, as hitherto conjectured, spent some
years in the United States. With his wife Marie and his little son Karl Julius Maria, he sailed for the United States
on 30 August 1871. For a time the family lived in Rochester, N.Y., where a son Heinrich was born, lived only six
months, and was buried. The family moved successively to Buffalo, Niagara Falls, Montreal, Detroit, Jackson,
Michigan (where Ludwig had a position with the Michigan Central Railroad), Sabula, Iowa, with a family named
Stiles, back to Jackson, on 1 January 1874 to Chicago, and in the fall of 1874 to New York. In Chicago and New
York (and later in Philadelphia) Ludwig, who had changed his name to Louis van Hoven, established the New York
Commissionaire Company. Detailed information is not available after 1875, but it is known that Ludwig, Marie,
Karl, and Meta (age 4) returned to Vienna in 1878. Information thereafter is much more indefinite, though it is
understood that for a time Ludwig was Director of the Pacific Railroad in New York. In 1890 he was ill and im-
poverished in Paris; it is not known when or where he died.   [28 September 1956] 15

BEETHOVEN UND DIE JUDEN. Paul Nettl.   (B)

The legal situation of the Jews in Vienna of Beethoven's day is briefly discussed. Beethoven's interest in Jewish music
and his many Jewish friends (notably Moscheles and Jeitteles) are cited to indicate that Schindler's charge of anti-
semitism is without foundation.   [4,18 December 1959]

AUGSBURG ALLGEMEINE ZEITUNG

BEETHOVENS LIEDER.   (C)

The author points out that in comparison not only with Schubert but with the many lesser writers of German lieder,
Beethoven's songs must take and have taken a very modest place. Individual comments on a considerable number
of the songs are given, including: 'Neue Liebe, neues Leben': "a sonata movement for voice"; Op. 82 "must be
sung in Italian, not in German"; 'Der Wachtelschlag' "magnificent"; 'An die ferne Geliebte' Op. 98: "No predecessor or contemporary, not even Schubert, had developed the song cycle to such scope and significance."
                                         [20 January 1870] 294

BEETHOVENS GEISTIGE ENTWICKLUNG. Ludwig Nohl.   (D)

A discussion of the effect on Beethoven's character and music of his early religious training, his fondness for certain
ancient and modern poets, the writings of certain non-Catholic authors and philosophers, and other similar formative
influences.   [4,5 June - 2,5,6 July 1870]

HEGEL, HÖLDERLIN, AND BEETHOVEN.   (E)

These three men -- philosopher, poet, musician -- embody the bursting of artistic bonds which typified German
creative thinking at the turn of the century.   [21 September 1870]

BEETHOVEN. H. M. Schletterer.   (F)

Centenary essay.   [17 December 1870]

"PSYCHIATRISCHES" ÜBER BEETHOVEN.   (G)

Excerpts from a collection of intemperate criticisms of Beethoven by contemporaries great and small.
                                         [14 December 1872] 5338

BEETHOVEN UND DER FORTSCHRITT IN DER MUSIK. August Reissmann.   (H)

Many of the individual compositions, from the earliest to the last quartets, are discussed from the standpoint that
their increasing independence of scholastic rules of form shows their composer's growing independence of teachers.
                                         [9,10 August 1884]

IN UNGEDRUCKTER BEETHOVEN-BRIEF.   (I)

Copy of the article in 'Neue Freie Presse' of 28 February 1900 giving a fragment of M-815
                                         [4 March 1900] 5

BEETHOVENS NEFFE. Max Vancsa.   (J)

A detailed biographical sketch of Nephew Karl, on which Frimmel obviously drew very freely for the article of the
same title in his 'Beethoven-Handbuch.' This article is all the more creditable for the reason that it was written before the appearance of the last two volumes of Thayer-Deiters, covering the period 1815-27.
                                         [6 February 1901] 1; [7 February 1901] 5
                                         Beilage

BEETHOVENS WERKE FÜR DIE SPIELUHR.   Willy Hess.   (A)
   A general discussion of the seven known compositions for mechanical organ or Panharmonicon.
                     [22 September 1940]

EINE UNGEDRUCKTE ROMANZE BEETHOVENS.   Willy Hess.   (B)
   Discussion of H-11.   [18 July 1946]

MUSIKALISCHE SELTENHEITEN DER UNIVERSITÄTSBIBLIOTHEK BASLE.   Marta Walter.   (C)
   The library of the University of Basle owns several volumes of the edition that Haslinger planned as the first
   Gesamtausgabe to be engraved and offered to the public. The history of this edition, as well as of the calligraphic
   edition that preceded it, is summarized.   [28 June 1953]

BERLINER TAGEBLATT

UNBEKANNTES VON BEETHOVEN.   Max Unger.   (D)
   Note without date or name of addressee, but probably to Steiner & Co. about 1826: "Es droht eine Herausgabe mehrere
   Werke..." requesting that they refrain from publishing unauthorized and unedited arrangements of some of Beethoven's
   works. Note without date or name of addressee, but probably written not earlier than 1816 to Schindler, Holz or
   Nannette Streicher: "Ich grüsse Sie! Ich bitte Sie mir ihre Auslagen zu schicken und mir zu verzeihen wenn ich mich
   in Allem als ihr Schuldner ansehen muss." "Ihr Freund Beethoven."
                     [4 September 1915] 2

BEETHOVEN.   Leopold Schmidt.   (E)
   Sesquicentennial essay.   [16 December 1920] 2

WIE BEETHOVEN GEKRÄNKT WURDE.   Ernst Weizmann.   (F)
   Hitherto unpublished anecdotes.   [25 March 1927] Beiblatt

WAS IST UNS DIE BEETHOVEN-FEIER.   Leopold Schmidt.   (G)
   Centenary essay.   [26 March 1927]

EIN BISHER UNBEKANNT GEBLIEBENER BRIEF BEETHOVENS.   Leopold Schmidt.   (H)
   Facsimile without transcription of letter listed by Kastner (BJ 2 No. 101) as first published in 1903, and which appears
   in abridged form as KK No. 906.   [26 March 1927]

ZUR BEETHOVEN-JAHRHUNDERTFEIER.   Felix Weingartner.   (I)
   Centenary essay.   [27 March 1927]

DIE HULDIGUNG DER WELT.   C. H. Becker.   (J)
   Centenary messages from many countries.   [27 March 1927]

BEETHOVENS KRANKHEIT.   Josef Berberich.   (K)
   Brief popular article concerned chiefly with Beethoven's deafness, which is described as probably a congenital
   otosclerosis, with the alternative luetic etiology possible but improbable.
                     [7 February 1928] Erster Beiblatt

DEUTSCHE ALLGEMEINE ZEITUNG

BEETHOVEN UND WIR.   Walter Schrenk.   (L)
   Sesquicentennial address.   [17 December 1920] Beilage

GEDANKEN ZUR SEELISCHEN ERKENNTNIS BEETHOVENS.   Ernst Lessauer.   (M)
   Sesquicentennial address.   [17 December 1920] Beilage

DIE FRAUEN IN BEETHOVENS LEBEN.   Alice Helmrich.   (A)
   Popular.   [17 December 1920] Beilage

FIDELIO.   Friedrich Schwabe.   (B)
   General.   [17 December 1920] Beilage

BEETHOVENS ERSTE LEONORE.   Kaufmann.   (C)
   Biographical sketch of Anna Milder-Hauptmann.   [13,16 January 1927] Beiblatt

BEKENNTNIS ZU BEETHOVEN.   Bruno Walter.   (D)
   Festival address.   [25 March 1927]

LUDWIG VAN BEETHOVEN.   Walter Schrenk.   (E)
   Popular biographical sketch.   [25 March 1927]

BEETHOVEN AND ANDREAS STREICHER.   Max Unger.   (F)
   Reprinted from 'Deutsche Musiker-Zeitung' 58 [1927] 228.   [25 March 1927]

BEETHOVENS BILDE UND MASKE.   Kurt Pfister.   (G)
   Descriptions by contemporaries, and mention of a few portraits and the two masks.
                                                   [25 March 1927]

DAS FORTSCHRITTLICHE IN BEETHOVENS SYMPHONIEN.   Ernst Schliepe.   (H)
   Beethoven's position in the development of the symphony.   [25 March 1927]

DÜSSELDORFER NACHRICHTEN

BEETHOVENS HONORAR FÜR DIE "MISSA SOLEMNIS."   (I)
   Translation back into German of the English translation of MM 320 which had appeared in the London Daily
   Telegraph the previous week.   [24 February 1939]

FRANKFURTER ZEITUNG

DIE POLITISCHEN ANSCHAUUNG DES JUNGEN BEETHOVEN.   Ludwig Schiedermair.   (J)
   Like many Rheinlanders of his day, Beethoven was moved by republican ideals, but he differentiated between good
   nobles and bad. He was greatly stirred by the movement against feudalism.
                                                   [1 December 1925] 2 Erstes Morgenblatt

EIN UNBEKANNTER LIEBESBRIEF BEETHOVENS.   Paul Bekker.   (K)
   Reprint from 'Die Musik' 104 [1911] 131 regarding the spurious fourth letter to the Immortal Beloved.
                                                   [30 July 1911] 2 Erstes Morgenblatt

BEETHOVENS DINER.   Jules Jamin.   (L)
   Translation of an account of a real or fancied meeting with Beethoven, as published in 'Figaro' in the 1840's.
                                                   [9 January 1910] Viertes Morgenblatt

BEETHOVEN UND SEIN GEIGER.   (A)
  Reprint of MM 402 from London Daily Telegraph of 10 June 1939.
                                                    [17 June 1939]

KÖLNISCHE VOLKSZEITUNG

NEUES ÜBER BEETHOVENS GROSSELTERN MÜTTERLICHER SEITE. J. Wagner.   (B)
  Beethoven's mother's mother was not Anna Klara Westorff, daughter of Jacob, but Maria Magdelena Westorff,
  daughter of the Senator Johann Bernard Westorff (d. 1759). Maria Magdelena Westorff was born on December 19th
  1746 and married Johann Leym on January 30th 1763. Her son Johann Peter Anton was born on October 25th 1764
  and died in a few months. After her husband's death Marie went back to live with her mother who, to see her
  daughter taken care of before she died, acceded to her marriage with Johann van Beethoven, whom she had met
  while he was staying at the inn in Ehrenbreitstein where the Keverich mother and daughter lived. The old lady was
  forced to keep sending money from her limited funds to her daughter and son-in-law, so that she died destitute on
  September 13th 1768. A petition to the Elector of Trier from his chancellor for assistance to the widow substantiates
  this dissipation of her funds. There are strong indications that the old lady was held in great respect in her community.
                                                    [8 December 1918] Zweites Blatt,
                                                       Sonntags-Ausgabe

KÖLNISCHE ZEITUNG

RHEINISCHE AHNEN LUDWIG VAN BEETHOVENS. Karl Lohmeyer.   (C)
  Beethoven's mother, while the wife of Johann Leym, gave birth to a son Johann Peter Anton on October 25th 1764.
  Her mother, Anna Klara Westorff (b. 1707) was the daughter of the merchant Jakob Westorff and Maria Magdalena
  Schettert. She died on September 13th 1768. Jakob's father was the Electoral Customs-Inspector Tillmann Westorff;
  Anna Klara's mother (Jakob's second wife) was daughter of Johannes Franz Schettert (died August 4th 1720), an im-
  portant ship-operator along the Rhine, and Maria Magdalena Becker (died September 19th 1720). Thus, of the four
  grandparents of Beethoven's maternal grandmother, three are known to have been of Rhineland stock.
                                                    [16 December 1917] Beilage Nr. 50
                                                       Literatur- und Unterhaltungsblatt

BEETHOVENS KRANKHEITEN.   (D)
  Review of evidence in favor of the assumption that Beethoven was luetic.
                                                    [24 September 1927] Abend Ausgabe p. 2

BEETHOVENS KRANKHEITEN.   (E)
  Polemic.   [27 September 1927] 2

BEETHOVENS UNTERRICHT BEI JOSEF HAYDN. Max Unger.   (F)
  The paper by Reinöhl (NBJ 6 [1935] 36) is summarized, and points later brought out in Unger's comments in NBJ
  8 [1938] 80 are given. Regarding Beethoven's finances, it is possible that the 400 gulden from his pay as organist was
  left by him in Bonn for the support of his two younger brothers, so that he had only the subsidy of 500 gulden for living
  expenses and also for fees to his teachers. Note that the Elector Max Franz arrived in Vienna on 16 January 1794, and
  possibly talked with Haydn before the departure of the latter for London on 19 January 1794.
                                                    [27 February 1936] No. 105-06 p. 19

BEETHOVENS GEBURTSTAG. Stephan Ley.   (G)
  In a letter to Beethoven dated December 15th 1795 Albrechtsberger refers to the following day as being Beethoven's
  birthday. The death notice issued by Simrock in 1827 gives the same day of birth. Both facts indicate that it was a
  family tradition that Beethoven was born on December 16th. The author brushes aside the fact that Wegeler, Beethoven's closest friend, did not know the date of Beethoven's birth, and that Nephew Karl in a conversation book of
  1823 refers to December 15th as the probable day. The author concludes that December 16th may be taken as the
  birth date, "if not with certainty, then with a probability approaching certainty."
                                                    [2 November 1936]

NEUE VOLKSLIEDERBEARBEITUNGEN BEETHOVENS.   Willy Hess.   (A)
  Reprint of article in'Schweizerische Instrumentalmusik,'15 January 1942.
                                                    [21 January 1942]

EINE UNBEKANNTE ROMANZE BEETHOVENS.   Willy Hess.   (B)
  Recovery of the autograph of this youthful work (H-11) raises the question as to whether an eminent composer is well
  served by revival of compositions of his immature years. For Mozart the author says no, since the growth of that
  composer is in comprehension rather than in basic style: even the earliest works are "Mozartian." Not so with Wagner, nor with Beethoven, and for that reason the fullest familiarity with all the works of each of these two men is
  necessary if the development of the composer's genius is to be seen in true perspective.
                                                    [8 June 1946]

LONDON DAILY TELEGRAPH AND MORNING POST

NEW BEETHOVEN LETTERS: THE MISSA SOLEMNIS AND ITS PRICE ON THE MARKET.   Duncan Wilson,   (C)
     Schofield and Bertram.
  Translation (EDr) but not transcription of MM 320. See also M&L 20 [1939] 236
                                                    [18 February 1939] 7

NEW BEETHOVEN LETTERS: CORRECTING THE PROOFS OF OPUS 109.   Duncan Wilson, Schofield and   (D)
     Bertram.
  Translation (EDr) but not transcription of MM 321, with facsimile of p. 3 of the autograph; translation of a portion
  of Kal 575. See also M&L 20 [1939] 238.   [4 March 1939] 19

MORE BEETHOVEN LETTERS: HIS BARGAINING WITH PUBLISHERS.   Duncan Wilson, Schofield and   (E)
     Bertram.
  Translation (EDr) but not transcription of MM 325 and MM 147. See also M&L 20 [1939] 239.
                                                    [25 March 1939] 6

BEETHOVEN: A NEW LETTER -- HIS APPRECIATION OF SCHUPPANZIGH.   Hans Holländer.   (F)
  Transcription and translation of MM 402.   [10 June 1939]

LONDON SUNDAY TIMES

BETTINA AND BEETHOVEN.   Ernest Newman.   (G)
  Whether or not the first and third Bettina letters are copies of letters actually written by Beethoven, they reflect
  his way of thinking with the greatest accuracy.   [6 September 1931]

BEETHOVEN'S CONVERSATION BOOKS.   Ernest Newman.   (H)
  Reconstruction of several incidents from material in the conversation books.
                                                    [10 January 1932]

FACT AND FICTION ABOUT BEETHOVEN.   Ernest Newman.   (I)
  Because of the incompetence of the performers and the lack of a conductor, "nowhere on the Continent, as late as
  fifteen years after the composer's death, was an adequate performance of one of the later Beethoven symphonies
  possible, except at the Paris Conservatoire." This does much to explain the slow growth of Beethoven appreciation
  and understanding.   [31 January 1932]

BEETHOVEN AND THE COBRA.   Ernest Newman.   (J)
  "The object of this article is simply. . . to plead for a little plain common sense all around where Beethoven is concerned." (Addressing Beethoven): "Your life was never half as hard as you and your biographers made out, and never
  one-quarter as hard as that of other musicians who did not whine as you were always doing!"
                                                    [27 November 1932] 5

BEETHOVEN'S BIOGRAPHERS.　Ernest Newman.　　　　　　　　　　　　　　　　　　(A)
　　Some points of difference are discussed between the real Beethoven and the Beethoven created by writers of "poetic gush."　　　　　　　　　　　　　　　　　　　　　[17 December 1933]

VERGIL, BEETHOVEN AND OTHERS.　Ernest Newman.　　　　　　　　　　　　　　(B)
　　Vergil, Beethoven and Wagner (as well as Bach in works like the Kunst der Fuge) "saw the whole, so to speak, before he was sure of some of the parts."　　　　　　　　　　[5 May 1946]

THE UNIQUENESS OF FIDELIO.　Ernest Newman.　　　　　　　　　　　　　　　(C)
　　The first scene is quite out of character with the rest of the drama; the scene in the prison yard, if effectively staged, is on the face of things a stage manager's tour-de-force; no justification can be conjured up for the playing of the Great Leonora Overture before the closing scene. Yet so great is Beethoven's magic that features which seem an absolute divergence from soundness and unity prove to be the completely right thing to do: the opera "creates the taste by which it is to be enjoyed."　　　　　　　　　　　　　　[5 October 1947]

TOWARDS THE No. 9.　Ernest Newman.　　　　　　　　　　　　　　　　　　(D)
　　"Beethoven was in deadly earnest in his attitude towards the 'message' of" Schiller's 'Ode to Joy,' and was most scrupulous in his care to make the music reflect every nuance of the German text. When the finale is sung in English translation, the changes in dynamics or melodic line which Beethoven considered so important are almost certain to lose their significance. Metronome marks for the Ninth Symphony were first published in 'Cäcilia' for December 1826, taken from Beethoven's letter of October 13th 1826 to Schott (KS II 454). The autograph of this letter (still extant) shows clearly that the first presto of the finale is MM 66, but by a printer's blunder this figure was published as 96, and even in the GA the truth has not caught up with this error. Without question Beethoven intended the fanfares and the 'cello-bass recitatives to be at the same tempo, and clearly this must be 66, not 96. Beethoven's omission of the dot from the various notes which refer to triple time is of no significance. The long chain of trills in the strings at mm. 306ff in the finale is of great importance in Beethoven's conception of the passage, yet these trills are almost always drowned out by the vocal mass. For purposes of contrast the adagio should certainly pass into the finale without break. "The entry of the smiling soloists after the adagio is an atrocious barbarism that should never under any circumstances be permitted by the conductor."　　　　　　　　　　　　　　　　　　　　　　[10,17,24 October 1948]

LONDON TIMES

A STRAY LEAF FROM THE AUTOGRAPH SCORE OF BEETHOVEN'S NINTH.　Edward Speyer.　　(E)
　　Four pages containing the last 29 measures of the scherzo of the Ninth Symphony were recently bought at auction by the writer of this "Letter to the Editor." The authenticity of these pages as a part of the autograph score is beyond question. The complete autograph had been presented by Beethoven to Schindler, who removed these pages for presentation to Moscheles in consideration of his kindness during Beethoven's last illness (see 'Life with Moscheles, by his Wife' [1873] I 179). From Moscheles the sheets went to the singer Henry Phillips, and thirty years after his death appeared at the auction at which they were acquired by the present owner. (See also 'Neues Beethoven-Jahrbuch' 3 [1927] 103.　　　　　　　　　　　　　　[28 November 1907] 6

BEETHOVEN'S NINTH SYMPHONY.　C. V. Stanford.　　　　　　　　　　　　　(F)
　　B&H has stated that they will correct the erroneous metronome marking in the trio of the scherzo (see ZiMg 7 [1906] 271). As for Bsn II in the finale (GA pp. 183-187), autographs read as follows: Berlin autograph: "2te Fag col B"; Presentation copy to the King: part written out; London Phil Soc copy: part omitted by the copyist; Beethoven added: "2te Fagott sempre coi Bessi" for 49 measures.　　　　　　　　[30 October 1911] 10

NEUE ZÜRCHER ZEITUNG

BEETHOVENS GANG ZUM GLÜCK.　Rudolf Hans Bartsch.　　　　　　　　　　　(G)
　　Fiction.　　　　　　　　　　　　　　　　　[3 July 1916] Erstes Mittagblatt p. 1

BEETHOVENS VIOLINSONATEN. Florizel von Reuter. (A)
    Superficial program notes. [10 October 1919] Zweites Morgenblatt

BEETHOVEN. Hugo v. Hofmannsthal. (B)
    Sesquicentennial address. [19 December 1920] Fünftes Blatt p. 1

BEETHOVEN UND UNSERE ZEIT. Oscar Bie. (C)
    Sesquicentennial essay. [19 December 1920] Fünftes Blatt p. 2

BEETHOVEN IN SEINEN BRIEFEN. Rudolf K. Goldschmit. (D)
    General. [19 December 1920] Fünftes Blatt p. 2

BEETHOVEN AND J. B. RUPPRECHT. Max Unger. (E)
    Brief biographical sketch of Rupprecht; EDr of MM 219 of 1 April 1817 (see also MM 285 of 30 April 1820 to
    Schlesinger, which also refers to Rupprecht). No reason is known for Beethoven's wrath at Rupprecht as expressed in
    his letter of 1823 to Bernard (perhaps M-94; see also Kal 943). [19 December 1920] Fünftes Blatt p. 3

ZUM PORTRÄT BEETHOVENS. (F)
    General, with quotation of Frimmel's low opinion of the death mask.
    [19 December 1920] Fünftes Blatt p. 3

NIETZSCHE ÜBER BEETHOVEN. Hans Hartmann. [24 December 1920] Drittes Mittag- (G)
    blatt p. 1

BEETHOVENS FIDELIO. Louis Gauchat. (H)
    General but detailed history of the opera, with some analysis of the differences in the several versions.
    [1, 3, 4, 5 January 1921]

WAGNER AND BEETHOVENS 'EGMONT.' Max Fehr. (I)
    The score of the Egmont music from which Wagner conducted in Zurich on 20 January 1852, containing some of his
    notations, is still extant. [10 March 1924] Erstes Morgenblatt p. 1

BEETHOVEN AND HANS GEORG NÄGELI. (J)
    In the 1790's Nägeli republished the 'Se vuol ballare' Variations, the 'Es war einmal' Variations, and the 'Waldstein'
    Variations in his 'Repertoire des clavicinistes' within a year of their Edr. The two men met in 1801 or 1802, and
    Beethoven sent him the Op. 31 Sonatas for publication. Nägeli's edition was very faulty; Beethoven made corrections
    and Simrock issued an 'Edition très correcte.' Op. 31 Nos. 1 and 2 appeared in the 5th number of the 'Repertoire' at
    the beginning of 1803; No. 3 in the 11th number in 1804. There is no record of further contact between the two men
    until 1824, when Nägeli wrote to him regarding a subscription (Kal 1021, 1025). (See also BStud II 123; Riv mus ital
    19 [1912] 566) [23 March 1927] Erstes Morgenblatt
    p. 1; Abendausgabe p. 1

BEETHOVENS GEISTIGE SENDUNG. Richard Benz. (K)
    Centennial essay. [27 March 1927]

BEETHOVENS BILDNIS UND MASKE. Kurt Pfister. (L)
    General. [27 March 1927]

BEETHOVENS NATURGEFÜHL. Wilhelm Zeutner. (M)
    General. [27 March 1927]

SCHUBERT AND BEETHOVEN. Ernst Isler. (N)
    Testimony is conflicting as to whether or not Schubert met Beethoven when he came to his lodging to ask the priv-
    ilege of dedicating to Beethoven the Four Hand Variations on a French Song Op. 10 (published April 19th 1822). In
    any event, Schubert's work seems to have been favorably known to Beethoven.
    [18 November 1928] Blatt 3

EINE UNGEDRUCKTE KANTATE BEETHOVENS. Willy Hess. (O)
    Brief description of 'Un lieto Brindisi.' [12 November 1936]

EIN UNVERÖFFENTLICHTER SCHERZCANON BEETHOVENS. W i l l y H e s s.   (A)
   The long lost manuscript of the 5-voice canon 'Da ist das Werk, sorgt um das Geld, 1 2 3 4 5 6 7 8 9 10 11 12
   Dukaten' has been found in the library of the Peabody Conservatory of Music in Baltimore. This canon was almost certainly Beethoven's last completed work, presumably having been written to celebrate completion of the
   new finale of the Quartet in B flat Op. 130. A facsimile of the manuscript is given, but no transcription.
                                                                  [21 May 1949]

DER UNBEKANNTE BEETHOVEN. W i l l y H e s s.   (B)
   A detailed and thoughtful discussion and appraisal by categories of the considerable number of works by Beethoven
   (many of which are in the GA) that have been largely or entirely dropped from the performing repertoire. A facsimile of H-214 is given.   [16,23,30 June, 7,14,21 July 1952]

JACK WERNERS UNBEKANNTE BAGATELLEN. W i l l y H e s s.   (C)
   Of two piano pieces edited by Werner and issued as "hitherto unpublished works of Beethoven," one is the Klavierstück GA 25/301 and the other an 'Introduction and Waltz' published in an English musical journal in January 1835
   and almost certainly spurious.   [25 January 1954]

"DER SCHÜLER BEETHOVEN WAR DA." W i l l y H e s s.   (D)
   Popular account of Beethoven's instruction under Haydn, Schenck, Albrechtsberger, and especially Salieri, with
   EDr of an a capella duet for soprano and tenor 'Sei mio ben' (see H-191).
                                                                  [16 July 1955]

NEW YORK HERALD-TRIBUNE

RARE EVENT: BEETHOVEN SONATA CYCLE. M a r t i n L. B e r n s t e i n.   (E)
   A popular but scholarly account of the Beethoven piano sonatas as music for public performance. Clara Wieck in
   the late 1830's and Liszt in the 1840's were the two artists who did most to bring these works to concert halls.
                                                                  [11 October 1953]

NEW YORK TIMES

GROSSE FUGE FOR PIANO FOUR HANDS, OPUS 134. H a r o l d B a u e r.   (F)
   Note by the author to his edition of this work, including the statement: "The quartet score fails to correspond
   exactly with the parts, and the piano version (arranged by Beethoven himself) corresponds with neither."
                                                                  [6 October 1929]

THE OVERTURES TO 'FIDELIO.' O l i n D o w n e s.   (G)
   The controversy over the order in which the four overtures were written is summarized, and a letter on the history
   of Op. 138 from Braunstein is given.   [23 February 1941]

BEETHOVEN CONCERTO. O l i n D o w n e s.   (H)
   Comments on the youthful Piano Concerto in E flat (GA 25/310), the accompaniment for which has been orches-
   trated by Willy Hess.   [23 January 1949]

'FIDELIO' REVALUED. O l i n D o w n e s.   (I)
   "Mixed with an appalling amount of old-fashioned buncombe, in book and score, it also contains in a unique
   manner an indestructible core of greatness . . . If ever a work endured in spite of multitudinous, glaring weaknesses, that work is Beethoven's 'Fidelio.'" Chapter and verse are given.
                                                                  [18 March 1951] 7 Music Section

BEETHOVENIANA. Henry E. Krehbiel.   (A)
    Extracts from Thayer's notebooks, including anecdotes, most of which are found in 'Life of Beethoven'; facsimile
    of autograph of first page of additional trombone parts (alto and tenor) for the trio of the scherzo of Op. 125 (start-
    ing at GA 1/9-110-1-6). The author postulates that this autograph indicates that parts for alto and tenor trombone
    at this point were an afterthought.   [29 January, 5,12 February 1898]

MUSICAL AUTOGRAPHS. Henry E. Krehbiel.   (B)
    Facsimilie is given of an autograph of GA 22/210-15-1-4 to 7 ('Ah, Perfido!'), below which are sketched 26
    measures which apparently extend the 'Heidenröslein' idea given in NB II 474,576, together with 14 measures of
    another unidentified sketch. The author points out a similarity between the opening phrase of the 'Heidenröslein'
    sketch and a figure in the 'Ah, Perfido!' autograph.   [27 February 1898]

A NEW BEETHOVEN SONG. Henry E. Krehbiel.   (C)
    Facsimile is given of a hitherto unknown sketch of a setting of 'Heidenröslein,' together with a performing version
    arranged from it by Henry Holden Huss.   [6 March 1898]

                            THE OBSERVER (London)

AN UNKNOWN LETTER OF BEETHOVEN. Percy A. Scholes.   (D)
    First publication of a translation of letter of October 13th 1817 to Nannette Streicher: "Gern möchte ich ihnen
    Schreiben wie ich hier einigen . . . " A facsimile is given of the first page of the letter, but it is not transcribed.
    In the letter Beethoven says he will probably lose 800 florins "through a rotten solicitor and a still worse perjured,
    pretended friend." The word "schein" (pretended) is explained as a pun on the name of the false friend (Schein).
    The letter also says that Beethoven will return the next day about noon.
                                                     [22 February 1925] 10

ANOTHER BEETHOVEN LETTER. Percy A. Scholes.   (E)
    Translation only of MM 106. Regarding MM 225, the author concedes that he has no evidence that any friend
    named Schein ever existed.   [8 March 1925] 10

                            DIE SCHWEIZ (Basel)

FÜNFZIG JAHRE "JENAER SINFONIE" -- DAS ENDE EINER LEGENDE.   (F)
    H. C. Robbins Landon has discovered in a monastery in Göttweig (Lower Austria) a set of parts of the so-called
    "Jena Symphony" bearing the name of Friedrich Witt as the actual composer.
                                                     [20 March 1957]

                            DER TAG (Berlin)

ANMERKUNGEN ZU BEETHOVENS MUSIK. Wilhelm Furtwängler.   (G)
    General.   [5 March 1918]

BEETHOVEN ALS ERZIEHER. Gustav Ernest.   (H)
    Essay on Beethoven's creative processes as shown in the sketch books, in his willingness to cease work in any form
    in which he had made his ultimate contribution (e.g., his last 21 years without a successor to the Violin Concerto,
    19 years after the Emperor Concerto, 16 years after the Archduke Trio), and in certain aspects of the Third, Fifth
    and Ninth Symphonies.   [28 June 1918]

BEETHOVENS TAUBHEIT.   Ida Boy-Ed.   (A)
   No statements of Beethoven's contemporaries regarding his deafness could be completely objective, since they knew
   that he was deaf, and would accordingly have been excessively quick to observe supposed results of that deafness.
   As a specific example, now dishonored, the belief was sincerely held for many years that the last piano sonatas,
   written while the composer was completely deaf, were for that reason wholly unplayable.
                                                              [27,28 November 1919]

BEETHOVENS GEHÖRLEIDEN.   Leo Jacobsohn.   (B)
   A summary is given of the history and symptoms of Beethoven's deafness, leading to the diagnosis: otosclerosis of
   luetic origin.   Contrary to his earlier opinion, the author does not believe now that the youthful attack of typhus
   was concerned.   Evidence is referred to which (in the opinion of the author) proves not only that Beethoven was
   luetic, but that he knew himself so to be.   [12 December 1919]

                              VOSSISCHE ZEITUNG

IGNAZ MOSCHELES' VERKEHR MIT BEETHOVEN.   Alf. Chr. Kalischer.   (C)
   A detailed account of Moscheles' association with Beethoven, from their first meeting in 1810 to Beethoven's
   death, with extensive quotations from Moscheles' 'Life of Beethoven' and from the conversation books.
                                                              [9,16 April 1893]

KATALOG XXIV. V. A. Heck.   (A)
 Item 44: 3-voice canon (C major, 7m.) "Freundschaft ist die Quelle wahrer Glückseeligkeit" dated "in der
 Brühl 1814 an 20ten September." Vide KS I 335 No. 409: "I took a beautiful walk yesterday with a friend in
 the Brühl."

KATALOG XXVI.   (B)
  Facsimile of letter in KS II 442 No. 1179.

KATALOG 42.   (C)
  Facsimile of letter in KS II 415 No. 1129.

KATALOG 47.   (D)
  Item 8: Facsimile of letter first published in NFP [20 December 1903] 35 (M-185).
                                    [n.d.]

KATALOG XXXIX. AUTOGRAPHEN-VERSTEIGERUNG. Leo Liepmannssohn.   (E)
  Discussion, with partial transcription of: Beethoven's last letters to Moscheles and Schindler's letters which accompanied them; A sketch book devoted to Opp. 120 and 123; A sketch book devoted to Op. 131; A score of
  Op. 136 with many corrections in Beethoven's hand (probably the copy from which Beethoven conducted the first
  performance on 29 November 1814); Facsimile of Beethoven's correction of word division in the Fidelio duet to
  read: "Re - tterin des Ga - tten"; Facsimile and transcription of quotation referred to by Schindler as having
  been kept by Beethoven under a glass on his worktable: "Ich bin, was da ist . . . "; Engraver's copy of Op. 132
  with many corrections by Beethoven; Programs, letters from Beethoven's associates, etc.
                                    [17,18 November 1911] 7ff,58ff

KATALOG 498. AUKTION MUSIK-AUTOGRAPHEN, STUTTGART. J. A. Stargardt.   (F)
  Holograph copy of 'Hochzeitslied' (with facsimile of first page (see ZfMw 7 [1924] 164; 'Der Bär' [1927] 157;
  Holograph of three instrumental parts (Vln, Vla, Basso) for the introduction to the Choral Fantasia Op. 80, later
  replaced by piano solo (with facsimile of the Vln part); Copy with autograph title page and corrections of 53
  National Airs for Thomson; Copy with autograph title page and corrections of 24 National Airs for Thomson (see
  'Der Bär'[1927]159); Copy of first edition of Terzett 'Tremate' Op. 118 with autograph corrections.
                                    [10 October 1951]

LIEPMANNSSOHN CATALOG 62.   (G)
  Item 8: "L'Arcadia in Brente, drama per mus. da rappresentarsi nel teatro della corte di S. A. E. di Colonia nel
  tempo del carnavale dell' a. 1771." Included in the cast: Fabrizio, il Signor van Beethoven (Maestro di Capella);
  il conte Bellezza, il Signor Giovani van Beethoven. (Cf TK I 26)
                                    [1888]

                            BEETHOVEN-FEIER

	Item 298: EDr Kal 150		Item 301: EDr (incomplete) Kal 821	(H)
	299 372		326 807	
	300 828		328 95	
	355 M-811			

                                    [1890]

                    FÜHRER DURCH DAS BEETHOVEN-HAUS ZU BONN

P. 47 EDr Kal 1187   (I)
Nachtrag p. 7 EDr (incomplete) Kal 829.   [c. 1898]

                        KATALOG DER HANDSCHRIFTEN

Item 40: Incipit: "Ich bitte Sie ja nicht, jezt auf Haussrath zu denken. . . "   (J)
Item 52: Addressed to Sir George Smart, not to the London Philharmonic Society (letter from Dr. Schmidt-Görg,
14 July 1954).   [1935]

Bibliography

Abert, Hermann. GESAMMELTE SCHRIFTEN UND VORTRÄGE VON HERMANN ABERT. Edited by Friedrich Blume. Halle, M. Niemeyer, 1929.

Andreas, Willy and Scholz, Wilhelm von, editors. DIE GROSSEN DEUTSCHEN. Berlin, Propyläen-Verlag, 1935.

Artaria & Co. VERZEICHNIS VON MUSIKALISCHEN AUTOGRAPHEN. . .VORNEHMLISCH DER REICHEN BESTÄNDE AUS DEM NACHLASSE. . .LUDWIG VAN BEETHOVENS. . .IM BESITZE VON AUGUST ARTARIA. Vienna, Artaria, 1893.

BEETHOVEN IN SEINEN BEZIEHUNGEN ZU FRANZ GERHARD WEGELER UND DESSEN EHEGATTIN ELEONORE GEB. VON BREUNING. (Brochure prepared for a festival performance of the Missa Solemnis in Coblenz on 15 December.)

BEETHOVEN-KALENDAR AUF DAS JAHR 1907. Berlin, Schuster & Löffler, 1907.

Duboc, Edouard [Robert Waldmüller]. WANDER-STUDIEN. Leipzig, T. Thomas, 1861.

Frimmel, Theodor von. BEETHOVEN STAMMBUCHBLATT. 6th edition, 1921.

Frimmel, Theodor von. BEETHOVEN-STUDIEN. 2 volumes. Munich, G. Müller, 1905-6.

Gerigk, Herbert, editor. MEISTER DER MUSIK UND IHRE WERKE. Berlin, R. Bong, 1936.

Hase, Oskar von. BREITKOPF & HÄRTEL GEDENKSCHRIFT UND ARBEITSBERICHT. 2 volumes. Leipzig, Breitkopf & Härtel, 1917-19.

Heck, V. A. L. V. BEETHOVEN ZUM 100-JÄHRIGE TODESTAGE, 26. MÄRZ 1927.

Helmolt, Hans F. DAS EHRENBUCH DES DEUTSCHEN VOLKES. Berlin, W. Undermann, 1924.

Hoffmann, Hans and Rühlmann, Franz, editors. FESTSCHRIFT FRITZ STEIN ZUM 60. GEBURTSTAG. Braunschweig, H. Litolff, 1939.

Huschke, Konrad. UNSERE TONMEISTER UNTER EINANDER. 1928

Jahn, Otto. GESAMMELTE AUFSÄTZE ÜBER MUSIK. 2nd edition. Leipzig, Breitkopf & Härtel, 1867.

Kalischer, Alfred Christlieb. BEETHOVEN UND SEINE ZEITGENOSSEN. BEITRÄGE ZUR GESCHICHTE DES KUNSTLER UND MENSCHEN. 4 volumes. Berlin, Schuster & Löffler, 1908.

Ley, Stephan. WAHRHEIT, ZWEIFEL UND IRRTUM IN DER KUNDE VON BEETHOVENS LEBEN. Wiesbaden, Breitkopf & Härtel, 1955.

Mennicke, Carl, editor. RIEMANN-FESTSCHRIFT ZUM SECHZIGSTEN GEBURTSTAG. Leipzig, M. Hesse, 1909.

Müller-Reuter, Theodor. BILDER UND KLÄNGE DES FRIEDENS. Leipzig, W. Hartnung, 1919.

Müller von Königswinter, Wolfgang. FURIOSO OR PASSAGES FROM THE LIFE OF LUDWIG VAN BEETHOVEN. Cambridge, Glover, 1865.

Naumann, Emil. ILLUSTRIERTE MUSIKGESCHICHTE. 2nd revised edition. Stuttgart, Union deutsche Verlags-gesellschaft, 1908.

Nelson, Robert Uriel. THE TECHNIQUE OF VARIATION; A STUDY OF THE INSTRUMENTAL VARIATION FROM ANTONIO DE CABEZÓN TO MAX REGER. Berkeley, University of California Press, 1948.

Nohl, Ludwig. MOSAIK. FÜR MUSIKALSICH-GEBILDETE. Leipzig, Gebrüder Senf, 1882.

Nohl, Ludwig. NEUE BRIEFE BEETHOVENS.

---

* Abstracts of above books were presented in original MacArdle manuscript but are here omitted.

Nottebohn, Gustav.   BEETHOVENIANA. AUFSÄTZE UND MITTHEILUNGEN. Leipzig, J. Rieter-Biedermann, 1872.

Nottebohn, Gustav.   ZWEITE BEETHOVENIANA. Leipzig, J. Rieter-Biedermann, 1887.

Orel, Alfred, editor.   EIN WIENER BEETHOVEN-BUCH. Wien, Gerlach & Wiedling, 1921.

Orlik, Emil.   KLEINE AUFSÄTZE. Berlin, Propyläen Verlag, 1924.

Osthoff, Helmut, editor, et al.   FESTSCHRIFT ARNOLD SCHERING ZUM SECHZIGSTEN GEBURTSTAG. Berlin, A. Glass, 1937.

Papp, Viktor.   BEETHOVEN, ÉLETE ÉS MŰVEI. Budapest, Pantheon, 1927.

Papp, Viktor.   BEETHOVEN ÉS A MAGYAROK. Budapest, Szerzo kiadasz, 1927.

Pfitzner, Hans.   DIE NEUE ÄSTHETIK DER MUSIKALISCHEN IMPOTENZ. Munich, Verlag der Süddeutschen Monatshefte, 1920.

Preussner, Eberhard.   DEUTSCHE MÄNNER. 1938

Quenouille, Rene.   LE DÉSÉQUILIBRE MENTAL DE BEETHOVEN. Thesis, Faculté de médecine de Paris, 1925.

Reimann, Heinrich.   MUSIKALISCHE RÜCKBLICKE. Berlin, Harmonie Verlagsgesellschaft für Literatur und Kunst, 1900.

Reti, Rudolph.   THE THEMATIC PROCESS IN MUSIC. New York, Macmillan, 1951.

Rogers, Joel Augustus.   SEX AND RACE. New York, J. A. Rogers Publications, 1940.

Rosenberg, Alfred.   BLUT UND EHRE; EIN KAMPF FÜR DEUTSCHE WIEDERGEBÜRT. Munich, Zentralverlag der N.S.D.A.P., 1935.

Sallès, Antoine.   LES PREMIÈRES EXÉCUTIONS À LYON DES OEUVRES DE BEETHOVEN. 1927

Sandberger, Adolf.   AUSGEWAHLTE AUFSÄTZE ZUR MUSIKGESCHICHTE. Munich, Drei Masken Verlag, 1921.

Scherchen, Hermann.   THE NATURE OF MUSIC. Chicago, H. Regnery, 1950.

Schmidt-Görg, Joseph.   SONDERAUSTELLUNG AUS DER BEETHOVEN-SAMMLUNG. H. C. Bodmer-Zurich. 1953

Schmitz, Arnold, editor.   BEETHOVEN UND DIE GEGENWART. FESTSCHRIFT DES BEETHOVENHAUS BONN. LUDWIG SCHIEDERMAIR ZUM 60. GEBURTSTAG. Berlin, Dummler, 1937.

Schöne, Alfred, editor.   BRIEFE VON BEETHOVEN AN GRÄFIN MARIE ERDÖDY. Leipzig, Breitkopf & Härtel, 1867.

Schweisheimer, Waldemar.   BEETHOVENS LEIDEN, IHR EINFLUSS AUF SEIN LEBEN UND SCHAFFEN. Munich, G. Müller, 1922.

Smart, Sir George Thomas.   LEAVES FROM THE JOURNALS OF SIR GEORGE THOMAS SMART. Edited by H. Bertram Cox and C.L.E. Cox. London, New York, Longmans and Co., 1907.

Spemann, Franz.   HARMONIEN UND DISSONANZEN. Berlin, Furche-Verlag, 1928.

Springer, Brunold.   DIE GENIALEN SYPHILITIKER. Berlin, Verlag der Neuen Generation, 1933.

Stehr, Hermann.   DAS STUNDENGLAS; REDEN, SCHRIFTEN, TAGEBÜCHER. Leipzig, P. List, 1936.

Stein, Maximilian.   VORTRÄGE UND ANSPRACHEN VON MAXIMILIAN STEIN. Frankfurt am Main, Kauffmann, 1929 (?).

Thayer, Alexander Wheelock.   EIN KRITISCHER BEITRAG ZU BEETHOVEN-LITERATUR. Berlin, W. Weber,
     1877.

Unger, Max.   EIN FAUSTOPERNPLAN BEETHOVENS UND GOETHES. Regensburg, G. Bosse, 1952.

Unger, Max   LUDWIG VAN BEETHOVEN UND SEINE VERLEGER S. A. STEINER UND TOBIAS HASLINGER IN WIEN,
     ADOLPH MARTIN SCHLESINGER IN BERLIN. Berlin, Schlesingersche Buchhandlung, 1921.

Upton, William Treat.   ANTHONY PHILIP HEINRICH, A NINETEENTH CENTURY COMPOSER IN AMERICA.
     New York, Columbia University Press, 1939.

Vincent, Auguste.   LE NOM DE BEETHOVEN, PAR AUGUSTE VINCENT. EXTRAIT DU 'ISIDOOR TEIRLINCK
     ALBUM.' Louvain, De Vlammsche drukkerijj, 1931.

Virneisel, Wilhelm.   KLEINE BEETHOVENIANA.

Volkmann, Hans.   BEETHOVEN IN SEINEN BEZIEHUNGEN ZU DRESDEN. Dresden, Literatur Verlag, 1942.

Volkmann, Hans.   NEUES ÜBER BEETHOVEN. Berlin, Hermann Seemann, 1904.

Waltershausen, Hermann Wolfgang von.   MUSIK, DRAMATURGIE, ERZIEHUNG; GESAMMELTE AUFSÄTZE.
     Munich, Drei Masken Verlag, 1926.

Weinmann, K., editor.   FESTSCHRIFT PETER WAGNER ZUM 60. GEBURTSTAG. Leipzig, Breitkopf & Härtel,
     1926.

Winternitz, Emanuel.   MUSICAL AUTOGRAPHS FROM MONTEVERDI TO HINDEMITH. Princeton, N. J.,
     Princeton University Press, 1955.

Author Index

Index to Compositions

Index of Correspondents